The British 'B' Film

The British 'B' Film

Steve Chibnall & Brian McFarlane

Foreword by Rona Anderson

A BFI book published by Palgrave Macmillan

First published in 2009 by
PALGRAVE MACMILLAN

on behalf of the

BRITISH FILM INSTITUTE
21 Stephen Street, London W1T 1LN
www.bfi.org.uk

There's more to discover about film and television through the BFI. Our world-renowned archive, cinemas, festivals,
films, publications and learning resources are here to inspire you.

Palgrave Macmillan in the UK is an imprint of Macmillan Publishers Limited, registered in England,
company number 785998, of Houndmills, Basingstoke, Hampshire RG21 6XS. Palgrave Macmillan in the US is a
division of St Martin's Press LLC, 175 Fifth Avenue, New York, NY 10010. Palgrave Macmillan is the global academic
imprint of the above companies and has companies and representatives throughout the world. Palgrave® and
Macmillan® are registered trademarks in the United States, the United Kingdom, Europe and other countries.

Cover design: couch
Cover image: (front) Rona Anderson and Dermot Walsh in *Torment* (John Guillermin, 1949, © Adelphi Films);
(back) Phyllis Calvert discovers she is in a 'B' film (*A Lady Mislaid*, David MacDonald, 1958, Welwyn Productions)
Text design: couch
Stills from the Steve Chibnall Collection; those on pp. 19, 137, 145, 147, 158 courtesy of BFI Stills, Posters and Designs

Set by Cambrian Typesetters, Camberley, Surrey
Printed in China

This book is printed on paper suitable for recycling and made from fully managed and sustained forest sources.
Logging, pulping and manufacturing processes are expected to conform to the environmental regulations of the
country of origin.

British Library Cataloguing-in-Publication Data
A catalogue record for this book is available from the British Library

ISBN 978–1–84457–319–6 (pbk)
ISBN 978–1–84457–320–2 (hbk)

Contents

Acknowledgments

Our gratitude is due to the many people who supplied us with copies of rare 'B' pictures: they include Paul Quinn, Alan Kibble, Andrew Spicer, Richard Dacre, Tony Hutchinson, Mike Taylor, Geoff Mayer, Roger Mellor, Sue Harper and Jeffrey Richards. We also thank John Oliver and Bryony Dixon of the Cataloguing Department of the British Film Institute for help in locating films, Janet Moat, the BFI's Special Collections curator, Richard Jeffs of the Harold Baim Collection, Ronald Grant of the Cinema Museum, film historian Roger Mellor, Bill Cooke, historian of Southall Studios and Kate Lees of the Adelphi Films Archive.

We are also grateful to Lloyd Michaels, editor of *Film Criticism*, for permission to use some of the material from Brian McFarlane's article, 'Pulp Fictions: the British B Film and the Field of Cultural Production'; Andrew Clay for permission to quote from interviews with Guido Cohen and Brian Clemens carried out during his PhD research at De Montfort University; and Allen Eyles for supplying data on the circuit exhibition of supporting features.

This has turned out to be a rather big book about a lot of small movies. It has been completed during difficult circumstances in both our lives and has acted as solace and distraction. Those nearest and dearest to us are no doubt as relieved as we are, however, that it has been finally put to bed. We thank them for their patience and support, and Rebecca Barden at BFI/Palgrave for her enthusiastic backing of the project. Finally, we thank Rona Anderson, Queen of the British Bs, for so readily agreeing to write the Foreword to the book.

We dedicate this work to Geraldine McFarlane and Paola Merli.

Foreword

Growing up in Edinburgh in the 1930s, I was an avid film fan. We had a veritable feast on a Saturday afternoon, with a newsreel, a cartoon and then a double feature, with a 'B' movie before the interval. When I was actually involved in 'B' features in the 1950s, no one took them seriously because they were churned out in three weeks. But the very fact that they *were* made quickly was the result of everyone concerned being so experienced. They knew what they were doing and there was no waste of time or money.

It's great to have a book about them now, and fifty years later they often look sharp and entertaining. They made their points and moved on. If, like me, you were married and had children, the idea of three weeks' work was very attractive as you weren't away from home for too long – you lived at home and certainly never went on location as that would have been far too expensive!

Once you were on the sound stages, they were all pretty much the same, cold and draughty. Merton Park, squeezed into a suburban street, was probably the smallest, but the method of working was the same in them all: arrive at 6am for hair and make-up, then a welcome break for tea and bread-and-dripping, a great favourite with the crew – and me. It set you up for the day, which finished at 6pm.

The second feature was often a training-ground for new directors, and I had the pleasure of working on some of the earliest films of Ken Hughes, John Guillermin and Wolf Rilla who all went on to bigger things. I also had some smashing leading men, like John Bentley, Guy Rolfe (a demon at cards), Dennis Price (suave and sophisticated) and those charmers, Robert Beatty and Dermot Walsh. There were as well two nice Americans, Richard Carlson and Richard Conte; a Hollywood actor gave the film added kudos.

I wish we could see more of these films today as those we do see on television so often look better than we thought at the time. I was mostly playing 'Joan' or 'Mary', forever being polite and helpful, but sometimes, as in *The Black Rider* with Jimmy Hanley, I was allowed to pull on trousers and jump on the back of a motor-bike. I loved that. Looking back, I think what a great lark it all was – and what a great life.

Rona Anderson
February 2009

Preface

American Producer (Richard Basehart): 'You know as well as I do that the little picture is finished.'
British Studio Boss (Roger Livesey): 'Perhaps I shouldn't have out-lived it.'

The Intimate Stranger (1956), scr. Howard Koch (as Peter Howard),
d. Joseph Losey (as Joseph Walton)

There is no reason at all why small pictures should not be good pictures.

The Cinema Studio[1]

Pinewood, late September 1960: a watershed moment. Something is happening here that tells us so much about the relationship between British cinema and Hollywood. Everywhere there are swords and sandals, tunics and togas, pyramids and palm trees, megaphones and mega-structures. 20th Century-Fox has taken over England's premier studios to make the lavish epic, *Cleopatra* (1963), the most expensive movie ever shot there, or anywhere else in the country. The studios' back-lot has been transformed into ancient Alexandria, but it is really the future we are witnessing: the increasing use of British facilities to make Hollywood's 'runaway' productions for international markets. But in a tiny corner of the great studios, on Stage G, the past *can* actually be seen. Space has somehow been found for a small unit under old-Etonian, Alfred Shaughnessy, to make a creepy picture about a pantomime dame who is not quite what he seems. This is a species of British film-making whose days are truly numbered. This is a 'B' film. Here there is no Technicolor, no CinemaScope and no Stereophonic Sound; just monochrome, academy ratio and monaural music. Appropriately enough, this Bryanston production is called *The Impersonator* (1961), because if *Cleopatra* is the real McCoy, then this is merely an impersonation. *Cleo* boasts the giant talents of Elizabeth Taylor, Richard Burton and Rex Harrison among its cast of thousands, while Shaughnessy's supporting feature can muster only John Crawford, Jane Griffiths, John Salew and Patricia Burke – hardly household names. A million pounds has been spent on Liz Taylor's mighty epic before the cameras even roll. *The Impersonator* has a miniscule budget of £23,000, and its sixty-four minutes will be shot in three weeks. In twice that time, *Cleopatra* will record only eleven useable minutes of film before aborting the whole Pinewood venture and de-camping to Rome.[2]

As the sun sets over Alexandria, Shaughnessy's unit moves outside and dresses the back gate of the Studios to represent the entrance to an American Air Force base in the North of England. There are barely enough lamps to illuminate the setting, but Shaughnessy and his cinematographer, John Coquillon, take advantage of the flood of ambient light created by the night shoot on the adjoining

Alexandria Harbour set. It is a situation emblematic of the relationship of dependence and subordi-
nation that exists between the humble British second feature and the sort of production – over-paid,
over-sexed and over here – that it is designed to support. 'We were very much the poor relations
during those three weeks at Pinewood,' recalled Shaughnessy, 'struggling on a low budget and shooting at great speed with much enforced economy.'[3] They were struggling, he might have added, to re-
create a little piece of the USA on that cosmopolitan back-lot, to generate enough signifiers of
American culture to make their film acceptable to the transatlantic audiences needed to ensure profitability.[4] Indeed, problematic Anglo-American relations is one of the main themes of *The
Impersonator*. The northern society it depicts is one with an American garrison whose personnel are
accused of being 'noisy', 'chasing skirt' and 'throwing their money around'. The judgment of one local
woman is that 'All Americans are gangsters', while the film's cute kid (eight-year-old John Dare)
would prefer them all to be cowboys. In the end, however, it is the American sergeant, falsely accused
of murder, who is the hero, and the British masquerader, the perverse pantomime dame, who is the
villain of the piece. In *The Impersonator*, as at Pinewood during its filming, the brash, confident and
affluent Americans are encamped on British soil, determined to be the protagonists in the drama of
its national cinema. Theirs is the economic power, and theirs will be most of the glory in the years
to come. Low-budget local dramas like *The Impersonator* will soon be as outmoded as the pantomime dame. Within a year, the actor who played the eponymous role, John Salew, will be dead,
and Alfred Shaughnessy will never direct another picture. When the curtain comes down – as it literally does – in the last frames of *The Impersonator*, it signals a wider finality. The black-and-white
British 'B' film, which has supplied thirty years of indigenous supporting-feature entertainment and

Nothing like a dame: John Salew in *The Impersonator* (1961)

just about out-lived its American counterpart, is coming to a close. By the time the *Cleopatra* road-show ends its journey round the Odeons of Great Britain, few will ask the question 'What's on with it?' If they do, the answer is likely to be 'a few advertisements and a couple of trailers'.

Four decades later, some might say that it is not worth raising the curtain again on a minor film like *The Impersonator*, but in its day it was praised by those grand dames of film criticism Dilys Powell (*Sunday Times*) and Penelope Gilliat (*Observer*). In the cineaste journal the *Monthly Film Bulletin*, the reviewer hailed it as 'a second feature which has been thought about and worked on, and which shows it'.[5] Among the trade papers, *The Daily Cinema* found it an 'Exciting and neatly contrived mystery ... another feather in Bryanston's cap'.[6] As Shaughnessy himself commented: 'I have always believed that lavish sets, huge crowds and great stars in expensive costumes are no substitute for originality, visual imagination and a good script.'[7] *The Impersonator* was certainly one of the better examples of its class, but it was by no means unique among its peers. So now, perhaps, it is time to ask the question 'What *was* on with all those big-budget movies that dominate our notions of cinema history?', and to chart the rise and fall of the British second feature. The first ten years of this story – covering the consequences of the 'Quota' Acts in the 1920s and 1930s – has already been told in Steve Chibnall's *Quota Quickies*.[8] Now, in this book, we will examine what type of 'B' pictures the combination of cultural policy, production economics and audience demand brought forth in the years of war, austerity and 'affluence' between 1940 and 1965. We will address the issues of who made these films, under what conditions, with what results. What were they like, who wrote them, who starred in them and what sort of image did they present of the society in which they were filmed? What, in short, is the big picture as far as these small pictures are concerned?

1 Big Ships and Little Ships

The Bs at War

> To my mind it is nothing short of sacrilege to see a great picture massacred in the public interest by having to associate it with tripe contained in a totally unnecessary second feature.
>
> Teddy Carr, United Artists' executive[1]

The early months of World War II, the period of the 'phoney war', created confusion and uncertainty among Britain's film producers and distributors who wondered if cinemas would be closed down, studios requisitioned and personnel conscripted. It was a difficult time for planning investments, but at least there were films on the floor, or in the pipeline awaiting release. None of these were yet commonly termed 'B films'. Lower-budget productions were generally referred to as 'programmers' or 'second features'. The latter, usually forty-five minutes to an hour in length, were unpretentious films designed to occupy a supporting position on the double bills that most cinemas favoured, changing them either weekly or, more usually, twice weekly. Cinemas would hire these supporting films at a modest flat rate, usually as part of a package offered by the distributor. Only a lucky few would be exported to overseas markets. The 'programmer' was a film lasting over an hour that offered flexibility to cinema programme-builders. It might play as a supporting feature at the picture palaces owned by the three major circuits – Odeon, Gaumont British and ABC – but it might also be strong enough to be billed as a main attraction or a 'co-feature' in the independent houses that constituted the majority of cinemas throughout the 1940s and 1950s. If so, its makers and distributors would be entitled to a percentage of box-office takings. It might also be offered for overseas distribution. This meant that a programmer could afford a budget that was higher than that of a humble second feature.

After 1927, film distribution and exhibition in Britain was regulated by protectionist legislation that imposed a 'quota' of screen time for home-produced films, often termed 'quota pictures'.[2] Exhibitors were required to devote a set minimum percentage of their programmes to British-registered product, and distributors (renters), including those owned by Hollywood studios, were expected to offer their customers a slightly higher percentage of British footage. Following widespread complaints that American renters had been discharging their quota obligations by making or commissioning inferior, deliberately loss-making pictures contemptuously called 'quota quickies', the most recent Films Act had raised the minimum cost criterion for films to qualify as 'renters' quota'. Consequently, Hollywood's British subsidiaries were more or less obliged to distribute indigenous programmers, rather than more cheaply made second features, as only these were likely to be expensive enough to count as renters' quota and thus allow the distribution of their American movies. British producers, on the other hand, were usually free to make cheap second features that would qualify for 'exhibitors' quota' only.

There might have been 'a war on, you know', but the quota regulations were still in force and, come hell or high explosive, British films would continue to be exhibited. To begin with, both British and American distributors emptied the shelves of their stockrooms. Among the releases from English renters like Associated British and British Lion were a proportion of programme pictures and second features. Associated British had Herbert Brenon's *The Flying Squad* (1940), a second adaptation of the Edgar Wallace story, in the pipeline. It featured Sebastian Shaw as a dashing copper, with strong support from Jack Hawkins and Phyllis Brooks, the sort of Hollywood import who would become a commonplace in British second features after the war. As its production base was at Elstree, one of the first studios to be requisitioned for war production, Associated British was obliged to turn to alternative sources for product. Ealing supplied a sentimental Robert Stevenson film in which Clive Brook was appropriately cast as a British actor returning incognito from Hollywood to a seaside town. Its nostalgic title, *Return to Yesterday*, must have summed up the wishful thoughts of its audience in the early months of 1940. Much grittier and more memorable was Ealing's *The Proud Valley* (1940), a superior programmer in which a rich-voiced Paul Robeson sacrificed his life for others down a Welsh mine. The film had gone into production just before the outbreak of war, and its ending had been re-tailored to the needs of wartime propaganda.[3] The director was Pen Tennyson, a promising talent who sadly would not outlast the war, and the film was judged 'Good, but somewhat depressing, entertainment' by *Film Report*, the booking guide of the Cinematograph Exhibitors' Association (CEA).[4]

British Lion distributed two old-fashioned melodramas from one of the leading quota-quickie producers, George King, who was gradually beginning to raise his aspirations. *The Chinese Bungalow* (1940) was a workmanlike adaptation of the stage play, previously filmed in 1931. A steamy tale of death and adultery on an oriental plantation, it starred Paul Lucas in oriental make-up and Kay Walsh. *Crimes at the Dark House* (1940), based on Wilkie Collins' *The Woman in White*, was another in the long line of Tod Slaughter blood-and-thunder melodramas. Slaughter gave his customary fruity portrayal of Victorian villainy as the dastardly rascal who is masquerading as the knight he has murdered. *The Cinema* trade magazine described it as 'truly an uncompromising tale of unbridled wickedness'.[5]

As for the American distributors, MGM, Columbia and United Artists confined their activities to making or handling first features. Those still in the business of distributing programmers and second features searched their vaults to find any quota pictures that had been buried there. RKO unearthed two 'quickies' made four years earlier. Alfred Goulding's *Honeymoon Merry-Go-Round* (1940), a Claude Hulbert and Monty Banks farce, was set in Switzerland. Although it did have an early minor performance by the now-popular Sally Gray, critical opinion was scathing.[6] The second film, *The Mysterious Mr Davis* (1940), starred the once-popular Henry Kendall, and had been written, produced and directed by the French film-maker Claude Autant-Lara. It also had an early performance by a rising star, in this case Alastair Sim, but its comedy was no less feeble than *Honeymoon Merry-Go-Round*'s. 20th Century-Fox also looked at what was gathering dust in its basement and discovered something rather more interesting, William Cameron Menzies' gangster film *Four Dark Hours*, a second feature which had been made in 1937. While wartime reviewers were unimpressed, this film, re-titled *The Green Cockatoo* (1940), had quite a lot going for it: a cast that included John Mills, Robert Newton and Rene Ray, photography by Mutz Greenbaum, and a script by Graham

Greene. It deserved better treatment, but when it was finally released critics were hungry for material that was more contemporary. They were a little kinder on Fox's more recent production, Harry Lachman's *They Came By Night* (1940), an off-the-shelf jewel-thieves drama, starring Will Fyffe. However, it was scripted by Frank Launder and Sidney Gilliat, and was significant for introducing Phyllis Calvert in her first starring role.

Warner Bros.'s production factory at Teddington also had a string of programmers awaiting release or in production. Roy William Neill's thrillers, *His Brother's Keeper* (with screen debutant Clifford Evans as a stage sharp-shooter and the glamorous Tamara Desni as a gold-digging blues singer) and *Murder Will Out* (which teamed the popular John Loder and Jane Baxter) had been completed before the outbreak of the war. So too had Herbert Mason's *Dr O'Dowd*, an Irish medical melodrama with a cast that boasted a bevy of future stars like Patricia Roc and Peggy Cummins. Even Warner's films entering general distribution in the traumatic summer of 1940 continued to be set in a world with no sign of the war. There was little topicality in David Macdonald's *The Midas Touch*, adapted from Margaret Kennedy's novel, and a stagey and far-fetched melodrama that largely squandered the talents of Barry K. Barnes and Judy Kelly. One indignant Welsh viewer, who praised *The Proud Valley* as a true representation of the 'British scene and temperament', complained that *The Midas Touch* was 'a flagrant copy of American stuff' and was simply 'the latest British film to drive me out of the cinema', seemingly oblivious to the fact that it had been produced by an American company.[7] Barnes was partnered by the vampish Greta Gynt in the more action-packed comedy drama *Two for Danger* (1940), directed by the tireless George King and scripted by Teddington's house writer, Brock Williams, again with scant awareness of prevailing conditions.[8]

The first Teddington production to acknowledge contemporary circumstances was Redd Davis's spy comedy, *That's the Ticket* (1940). It showcased Sid Field's first starring role, but was strictly for the easily amused, and rather too crude for the critics: 'The chief ingredients of the picture are a perpetual "drunk", comedians dressed up as women and a mud-pie battle,' commented one, while another conceded that it might help audiences 'forget the blitzkrieg for an hour'.[9] There was rather more originality and social relevance in Warner's *The Briggs Family* (1940), the story of the problems of a lower-middle-class family in wartime. However, the realistic atmosphere created by director Herbert Mason in the domestic scenes was undercut by the more fantastical final courtroom sequence in which Pa Briggs (Edward Chapman), a lawyer's clerk, successfully defends his wayward son (Peter Croft), who is charged with burglary. A planned series based on the family was shelved.

RKO also updated its output with David Macdonald's *Law and Disorder* (1940), an espionage comedy drama featuring the thoroughly over-exposed Barry K. Barnes, who had three films released in the first three months of 1940. Here, he could do little to combat weak direction, stock characterisation and pulp-fiction plotting. At Paramount British, *Spy for a Day* (1940) was a topical comedy vehicle for Duggie Wakefield, who played a shy farm hand who becomes a war hero after being abducted by German agents and foiling their plot. The film was lifted slightly above the run of second features by the feel for comedy of its director, Mario Zampi.

If anything, British distributors were even slower to adapt their supporting features to the requirements of propaganda. Grand National offered a more-lavish-than-usual programmer *Room for Two* (1940), directed by Maurice Elvey continuing his career on the margins of top-flight cinema. As a vehicle for Winston Churchill's son-in-law the 'violin-playing comic' Vic Oliver (supported by the glamour of Frances Day and Greta Gynt), it might have been expected to do well. Unfortunately, it was overtaken by events when the romance of its Venetian setting was undercut by Italy's entry into the war.[10] British Lion took a year before it did its bit with the rousing featurette *John Smith Wakes Up* (1940), depicting the nightmare of a London bookshop owner (Elliott Makeham) who imagines that the spirit of Nazism has infected English life. He dreams that his son has denounced him to the regime, which orders his books to be burned, and realises that he needs to be more determined in the defence of freedom. The CEA's *Film Report*, however, was uneasy with this sort of unadulterated propaganda in an entertainment film: 'The play is naive in conception and there seems little point in the whole business, except to ram home what we are all agreed upon, i.e. that freedom is worth fighting for. Such an ideal does not need the vapourings of a disordered brain to point the moral.'[11] The down-market distributor Equity British almost prided itself on providing entertainment divorced from the serious concerns of the moment. Its sepia-tinted Leslie Fuller and Wally Patch comedy, *Two Smart Men* (1940), made by quota-quickie veteran Widgey Newman at M. P. Studios, Boreham Wood, was announced as 'an unsophisticated comedy tuned to the demands of present-day audiences', with 'no direct or indirect reference to the war in the entire picture'.[12] Newman reluctantly acknowledged the war in his next film, *Henry Steps Out* (1940), the story of a waster (George Turner) who is ordered to join the army by his tyrannical wife (Margaret Yarde) but fortuitously lands a job as a bathroom orderly at an ATS camp. Wally Patch was in it again, just as he seemed to be in every comedy at the time.

The Government, however, could see no particular use in the war effort for this sort of independent production, which simply clogged up the supporting programme and reduced space for Ministry of Information (MoI) films and other worthy material. World War II offered the burgeoning British documentary film movement a unique opportunity not simply to cement its place in the national cinema but to achieve a position of aesthetic dominance by associating itself with the urgent hopes and desires of the country. As Dickinson and Street have commented:

> Documentary film-makers became more influential than they were ever to be again. The magazine *Documentary News Letter* provided a platform for their views on information, propaganda and film policy. They took an increasing interest in the controversies surrounding government policy towards the entertainment industry, and were for many reasons practically less isolated from their colleagues in features than they were before or after the war. Because of the increased demand for documentary films and the shortage of facilities for making features, most of the feature companies turned partly to making factual shorts for the Ministry of Information. The shortage of technicians further encouraged an exchange of labour between the studios and documentary companies.[13]

As far as supporting features, were concerned, the interests of Government and of American film producers in Britain were in accord. Hollywood companies were phasing out 'B' pictures in order to concentrate on films with maximum international appeal, while the Government were not only keen to use more of cinema supporting programmes for propaganda, but happy for Hollywood companies operating in England to make exportable films with that proportion of their earnings that they were now obliged to reinvest in British production. The Films Act was duly amended to encourage the production of bigger films that might be saleable in overseas markets.[14] Warners and 20th Century-Fox responded immediately by announcing a change in production policy in favour of larger pictures.[15] The last of the Warner's low-budget programmers was Herbert Mason's *Fingers* (1940), a very slight tale of an East End jewellery fence (Clifford Evans) who tries to follow a West End girl (Leonora Corbett) into high society before realising he has made a mistake and returning to the working-class girl (Elizabeth Scott) who loves him. Warner's billed it as the tale of 'an affair that makes Mayfair gasp and the East End rock', but the CEA's *Film Report* called it 'an artificial story, crudely told'.[16]

The primary responsibility for supplying quota supporting features passed for the first time to British distributors. By and large, it was not a responsibility that they were either prepared for or able to honour. While a handful of second features were made in the first year of the war, the supply became increasingly scarce as the hostilities continued. No British second features were trade-shown in the first half of 1941, until Pathé released the first of its wartime *Pathétone Parade* compilations at the end of June. The Gaumont circuit, desperately short of programmers, even screened the Australian comedy *Dad Rudd MP* (1941) and pressed the latest in the popular *Old Mother Riley* series into service as a support. In the absence of conventional supporting material, British distributors increasingly embraced their patriotic duty by handling the work of Ministry of Information, Crown and armed forces film units.[17] They were encouraged by enthusiastic reviews in all sections of the press. Harry Watt's 'super support', *Target for Tonight* (1941), described by *Picture Show* simply as 'the real thing', was screened on both the Odeon and Gaumont circuits.[18] *Picture Show* added that the film,

> is so thrilling that one's interest is held from start to finish so completely that one resents the slightest sound that interrupts one's thoughts. ... This is a film to make every man and woman of the British Empire proud to belong to it and proud of the men Churchill described in his never-to-be-forgotten speech as the few to whom so many owed so much.[19]

Documentarist Donald Taylor of Strand Films was in no doubt about the meaning of the success of Watt's picture:

> In 1941 the documentary came into its own. This once-despised theory of film-making has produced more films than ever before, with a wider exhibition than ever before, and the humble, one-reel instructional film has grown up until an epic like *Target for To-Night* has made certain a general acceptance of the documentary method by the public. It is proving the contention that, once documentary went before the public on a large scale, it would have an immediate and universal appeal.[20]

The following year, the documentary cemented its position on the cinema programme. British Lion handled Humphrey Jennings' legendary Crown Film Unit (CFU) short, *Listen to Britain* (1942).[21] Associated British distributed Compton Bennett's Fleet Air Arm tribute *Find, Fix and Strike*, made by Ealing, and Pat Jackson's highly acclaimed CFU featurette, *Ferry Pilot* (both 1942), billed as 'The story of the "Back Room Boys" who make *Target for Tonight* possible'. As the *Documentary News Letter* (*DNL*) commented, the film suggests 'that friendly people, with a sense of humour and a deep love of their craft, may be no less efficient than the grim automata beloved of Nazi ideologists'.[22] The reference was to the men shown in the film, but the comment might apply equally to the documentarists who made it. The *DNL* was even more enthusiastic about Renown's *The Harvest Shall Come* (1942), Max Anderson's dramatisation of four decades in the tough and poorly rewarded lives of farm labourers, filmed in Suffolk with John Slater in the leading role:

[It] marks one of documentary's most significant steps forward. It is the first genuine story film made with the documentary purpose and by documentary method ... There are no false situations and there are none of the story twists so dear to the hearts of our professional scriptwriters ... The story is fiction, but it reflects the life of every British farm labourer and is heart-tearing in its sincerity and in the power of its deliberate under-statement ... There is a lack of technical polish about the film which only adds to its quality as a rugged documentary.[23]

This now largely forgotten 'rugged documentary', which eschewed pictorial lyricism and rural romanticism in favour of stark verisimilitude, thus pointed a potential new direction for the supporting feature, a road ultimately not taken.

GFD distributed the Army Film Unit's hour-long *Desert Victory* (1943), the morale-boosting record of Rommel's defeat in Libya, as well as Humphrey Jennings' CFU Civil Defence documentary *Fires Were Started* (1943).[24] Ealing took responsibility for distributing Jack Lee's CFU documentary *Close Quarters* (1943), an unvarnished seventy-five-minute account of the submarine war in the North Sea, as well as Jennings' *The Silent Village* (1943), an imaginative recreation of the Nazi atrocity at Lidice, Czechoslovakia, transposed to a Welsh mining community. The power of the latter film was such that the London paper the *Evening Standard* used its leader column to endorse the production: 'See this film, terrible in its terror, and be filled with holy hatred against the men perpetrating similar crimes every day their foul system festers in Europe.'[25]

While most distributors were increasingly happy to settle for these sophisticated documentaries as supports for their first features, a few companies continued to turn out conventional fiction programmers. The leading story in film production in the first years of World War II was the rise of British National (BN), the obscure company that had made *Turn of the Tide* (1935). It was the company with which J. Arthur Rank had begun his venture into cinema, but Rank had departed before the outbreak of the war, leaving British National to be taken forward by his friend, the wealthy widow, Lady Yule. With other producers wondering how to react to the changed conditions of wartime, BN seized the time and raised its standard at Elstree's Rock Studios, bringing others – like Michael Powell and Emeric Pressburger – rallying round. Soon films were also being made for BN at Hammersmith's Riverside Studios, backed by distribution by Anglo-American. As well as bona fide 'A' features like *Gaslight* (1941) and *One of Our Aircraft is Missing* (1942), BN also made programmers. One of the first wartime offerings was *The Second Mr Bush* (1940), a simple-minded theatrical farce from which even a lively director like John Paddy Carstairs could squeeze little humour. An average of nine BN films were produced each year, many by independent film-makers working under the flag of BN. Rank would adopt a similar modus operandi – although on a somewhat grander scale – when he extended his exhibition and distribution empire into the production sector in the later war years. In fact, it was Rank's General Film Distributors (GFD) which released the Lady Yule-financed second feature, *The Man at the Gate* (1940, USA: *Man of the Sea*), a sort of follow-up to *Turn of the Tide*. Both films were directed by Norman Walker, were adaptations of stories by Leo Walmsley, and both featured Wilfred Lawson as the weather-beaten patriarch of a fishing family.[26] *The Man at the Gate* even recycled some of the footage from *Turn of the Tide*, but was more studio-bound and sentimental. It was clearly geared to the needs of the war effort, and dealt reassuringly with a mother's fears that her remaining son might be lost at sea. Its message, 'Put your hand in the hand of God', was one very much approved by J. Arthur Rank.

British National's head of production was John Baxter, a film-maker with a pedigree as a champion of working-class themes and everyday stories. During his time at BN, his productions increased in size and prestige, but he continued to value modest productions that were true to life. One trade advertisement during the launch of his film *The Shipbuilders* (1943) depicted his previous pictures as vessels in an Atlantic convoy with the positive and optimistic message: 'Big ships and little ships – each with a purpose – each with its cargo of entertainment – each manned by a British crew – each contributing to the experience that will enable bigger and better ships to be built in the years to come.'[27] Working in parallel with Baxter was the husband and wife partnership of Leslie and Elizabeth Hiscott, which made pictures for British National initially at Jack Buchanan's Riverside Studios. Their first venture was *Tilly of Bloomsbury*, a romantic comedy of class masquerade which went into production in January 1940. The second was the more topical *The Seventh Survivor* (1941), a spy drama (with plenty of comedy relief from Ronald Shiner and Wally Patch) set, like a number of wartime films, in a lighthouse – emblematic, one might argue, of Britain's isolated and beleaguered position as the light in the European darkness. The same formula was applied to the Hiscotts' third production, another nautical thriller, *Sabotage at Sea* (1942), made at Teddington, again with Shiner and Patch supplying comedy cameos. In spite of its preponderance of talk over action, *To-Day's Cinema* was happy to recommend the picture as a 'Very acceptable popular support'.[28] It was quickly followed by the complicated comedy thriller, *The Lady from Lisbon* (1942) with Jane Carr in the title role and similar endorsements from the trade reviewers: 'Elizabeth and Leslie Hiscott have turned out another commendable little offering here – a subject which earns praise for its ingenuity and the all-round quality of its production.'[29] By the time the Hiscotts produced the well-received comedy *The Butler's Dilemma* (1943), they had effectively moved beyond the supporting feature into co- and first-feature

Suspense beneath the revolving beam: trade advertisements for two lighthouse thrillers

territory. Critics judged this vehicle for the madcap antics of Richard Hearne funny enough to constitute an attraction in its own right.[30]

Associated British also distributed a couple of programmers in 1941–2. There was more espionage beneath a revolving beam in Lawrence Huntington's grim *Tower of Terror* (1941), filmed at Welwyn and on the island of Flatholm off the Welsh coast for the production company of John Argyle, another quota-quickie merchant with raised aspirations. As the title suggests, this film strove for an eerier atmosphere and packed more suspense than *The Seventh Survivor*, but, as *Film Report* complained, the story was 'naive and full of incredibilities', while most of the characters were 'artificial' and much of the action 'unconvincing'.[31] Its saving grace was Wilfred Lawson, perfectly cast as the half-demented lighthouse keeper. The trade reviewers were more enthusiastic about Huntington's *Suspected Person* (1942), a competently made, but ultimately dull, gangster yarn involving American mobsters on the trail of bank-robbery loot brought into Britain by an errant member of the gang. The cast was strong, with Clifford Evans as the marked man, future Gainsborough star Patricia Roc as his sister, Robert Beatty as a pursuing gangster and David Farrar as the Police Inspector, but it remains difficult to care about the fate of any of them.

The most regular producer of British programmers during the war years was Butcher's Film Service. The firm's head of production, F. W. Baker, was no stranger to wartime conditions. He had been working in the industry since the Boer War, and had produced the first British picture after the outbreak of hostilities in 1914. He repeated the feat in 1939 with Oswald Mitchell's *Jail Birds* (1940), a riotous comedy starring Albert Burdon and Charles Hawtrey escaping from prison in drag.[32] Patriotic as ever, Butcher's adapted the established comedy formats of its programmers to the wartime context. Oswald Mitchell directed *Sailors Don't Care* (1940), which chronicled the efforts of three keen but slow-witted tars on an Estuary Defence unit, who eventually succeed in catching a spy. The film was short of star appeal, but did include a young Michael Wilding. Mitchell's follow-up, *Pack Up Your Troubles* (1940), was another service comedy with character actors Reginald Purdell and Wylie Watson as a couple of accidental heroes, but the cast also included, Patricia Roc as an ATS girl. Roc also starred with Sebastian Shaw in the equally patriotic, but rather less typical for Butcher's, *Three Silent Men* (1940), a mystery concerning the death of a fifth columnist, which was directed by Daniel Birt.[33] Oswald Mitchell returned for the Albert Modley Home Guard comedy with songs, *Bob's Your Uncle* (1941), a sort of grandfather of television's *Dad's Army* (although considerably less rib-tickling) made at Welwyn Studios. There were more laughs in Maclean Rogers' *Front Line Kids* (1942), an occasion for Leslie Fuller's comic antics, which also drew attention to the problem of packs of unsupervised children running amok in towns and cities while their parents were engaged in war work. Here, however, the catapult-toting kids were mainly on the right side of the law, helping the police to round up a gang of blitz looters. The film is notable for Fuller's drag performance as 'Aida Down' during which he flirts with a vicar.[34] Rogers also directed two topical vehicles for the celebrity radio comics, Elsie and Doris Waters, but the popularity of the double-act was such that *Gert and Daisy's Weekend* (1941) and *Gert and Daisy Clean Up* (1942) played in most venues as main features.

It was back to large doses of Butcher's brand of rural sentimentality with Germain Burger's *Sheepdog of the Hills* (1941), set in Devon. Noting that this was a film for 'unsophisticated audiences', the *Film Report* commented: 'This is an old-fashioned story with a novelettish love interest and little effort has been made to brush it up to suit modern taste.'[35] Butcher's tried and tested entertainment formula was explicitly stated in their hit melodrama *Danny Boy* (1941) when impresario Jack Newton (Wilfred Lawson) advises songstress Jane Kay (Ann Todd):

> Always introduce something sentimental in the programme – that'll please any audience. It's funny how people enjoy themselves when they're crying. Look at my old Ma: unless she weeps a bucketful when she goes to the pictures, she isn't happy. As a matter of fact, I like a good cry myself sometimes. Some of the old numbers, they'll never die. For instance, 'The Tears of an old Irish Mother' … and 'Danny Boy'.

By 1942, however, Butcher's had lost their production base at Nettlefold Studios, Walton-on-Thames, to the war effort, and the production of conventional low-budget pictures was becoming almost impossible. *Kinematograph Weekly*'s Studio Survey noted:

> Productions of superior quality are now the aim of all our companies and independents, who wish to make the most of facilities and materials, to say nothing of the stars available. This is all to the good, and perhaps we have seen the end of the 'quota quickie', which reduced the whole industry and made it the laughing stock of the British public – and Hollywood.[36]

A year later, British Studios had lost 50 per cent of their floor space and 80 per cent of their technicians. Only nine studios out of twenty-two were operational, and most of those had suffered bomb damage. George King pointed to an enormous increase in production costs that meant 'it is no longer a commercial proposition to make "programme" pictures', and therefore 'practically no second-features are now being made in this country'.[37]

Production of Feature Films by Studio, 1940–2[38]

Studios	1940	1941	1942
Denham	8	15	14
Ealing	6	8	8
Gainsborough	2	–	4
Gaumont British	8	5	4
Highbury	2	1	1
Nettlefold's	8	1	–
Riverside	3	–	9
Rock	4	9	7
Warner's	3	5	6
Welwyn	3	7	7
Others	8	5	–
Total	55	56	60

Shortage of British films was clearly creating problems for independent exhibitors. In 1940–1, 25 per cent of cinemas failed to show the quota minimum of 17.5 per cent British material, although the overall figure achieved by all exhibitors was 23.4 per cent.[39] This indicated that, while the major circuits still enjoyed a surplus of British (mainly first-feature) product, the independents were struggling to find the cheaper films on which the fulfilment of their quota obligations depended. Prosecutions, however, were few and far between, and fines light.[40] In the 1941–2 period approximately 42 per cent of cinemas defaulted to some degree, but there was a recommendation for prosecution in less than 1 per cent of cases. The number of defaulters was significantly reduced the following year by a cut in the quota to 15 per cent and an increase in British film production, but very few of these films were the sort of bread-and-butter low-budget pictures that had previously been a staple of independent cinema programmes.

Exhibitors' Quota Defaults, 1939–45

Year	Defaults	Prosecutions
1939–40	316	3
1940–1	1402	3
1941–2	1721	4
1942–3	846	2
1943–4	977	6
1944–5	1014	6

In fact, only nine films of this type (exhibitors' quota only) were registered in the quota year 1941–2, and, by September 1942, *The Cinema* was predicting that production of second features would decline further, and might cease altogether.[41] However, the trickle of supporting and co-features from the dwindling number of British studios still open for business began to be extensively supplemented in the spring of 1942 by a programme of quota re-issues from companies like International Film Renters. Their catalogue ranged from genuinely popular pre-war thrillers like *The Terror* (1938) and *Black Limelight* (1938) to more dubious quickies like *Queer Cargo* (1938). Some longer films made during the war were also cut down to a more convenient supporting-feature length and re-issued.[42] At the same time, though, the Board of Trade was having discussions with renters with a view to eliminating second features from cinema programmes entirely in the interest of conserving film stock.[43] In the end, however, the Board stopped short of issuing an order to this effect, but rationing of stock imposed pressure on the length of programmes, and the trade voluntarily offered to reduce the number of prints for second features.[44] Exhibitors reported considerable opposition from their patrons to any attempt to curtail the double-bill programme. At a meeting of the Devon and Cornwall CEA, for example, several members protested that 'if two feature films were not shown at their cinemas the people would go away disgusted'.[45] The question was: how could supporting features continue to be produced in the face of rising costs and unhelpful government policy?

The 1938 Films Act had divided films, for quota purposes, into five categories:

1. Shorts (under 3,000 feet)
2. Exhibitors' quota only long films (production costs of less than £15,000)
3. Single quota long films (usually costing £15,000–36,000)
4. Double quota long films (usually costing £36,000–75,000)
5. Treble quota long films (usually costing over £75,000)

An analysis conducted by the Cinematograph Films Council of receipts from films produced in 1937–8 indicated that it was considerably easier to make a profit on pictures costing less than £15,000, even though they were booked at a flat rate only, than on those that cost more than this, especially those that cost £15,000–36,000.[46] However, the negative costs of studio film-making virtually doubled between 1939 and 1943, making it particularly difficult to recoup outlays on a flat-rate basis. For those making films that qualified for exhibitors' quota only, the most viable option was to economise by making shorter pictures with running times slightly over the thirty-three minutes that enabled a film to be classified as 'long'. These would be the 'featurettes', the new 'quota quickies'.

Actually, the production of featurettes had already been recommended by the same Devon and Cornwall CEA branch that had opposed the abolition of the double feature. *Kinematograph Weekly* had immediately lent its support to the request for more four-reel films running for around forty-five minutes. This type of film, it was argued, would not only increase flexibility in programme-building, allowing time for informational material supplied by the newsreels and the MoI, but might have a positive effect on the quality of supporting features, eliminating padding and speeding up narratives.[47] Although producers were initially slow to respond to the call for featurettes, it would echo into the early post-war years to the eventual regret of many in the trade and beyond.

Before the war, three- and four-reel films in a variety of genres had been produced at the rate of approximately one per month. By 1939, however, the format was being used primarily for religious dramas and variety films like the *Pathétone Parade* series and Andrew Buchanan's *Hello Fame*. The latter, distributed by Exclusive in 1940, was a showcase for new talent, most of whom never saw their names in lights – the exceptions being Jean Carr (Kent) and Peter Ustinov. Hardly any featurettes were produced in the period 1940–1, but they began to make a return with Renown's first foray into film production, C. Pattinson-Knight's *Escape to Justice* (1942), made at Marylebone Studios. It was hardly an auspicious return as the CEA's *Film Report* condemned the picture as 'mediocre' with 'amateurish' acting and direction that was 'behind the times'.[48] Distributor E. J. Fancey searched the shelves of Wardour Street and found two pictures produced at Worton Hall Studios by Alfred D'Eyncourt and directed by Walter Tennyson that had been mouldering since 1939. *The Body Vanishes* was a rural whodunit starring Anthony Hulme, while *Mistaken Identity* was an unsophisticated comedy about a shy conjurer (Richard Goolden).[49] Neither release in 1942 did much to improve the reputation of the featurette as low budget and low quality, but change for the better was effected by the actuality work of Humphrey Jennings and by *The Volunteer* (1943), a dramatisation of the career of an ordinary recruit to the Fleet Air Arm (Pat McGrath), with a whimsical commentary by Ralph Richardson, made for the MoI by Powell and Pressburger. Documentary featurettes could be produced very quickly without professional actors, and released while events were still topical. They became a regular part of the armoury of the Crown Film Unit, but were also made by other production units such as the RAF's, which released its study of balloon ships, *Operational Height* (1943), via Butcher's.

As the war moved into its fourth and fifth years, British second features almost disappeared from the major circuits. The Gaumont circuit offered only one between 1943 and 1945. The occasional supporting feature or featurette, however, continued to be made. At British National, these were the work of Donald Taylor's Strand Films which effectively became a 'B' film unit within the larger organisation, producing sponsored and non-sponsored actuality films. The unit's screen versions of the popular radio quiz show *The Brains Trust* (1943), with a collection of pipe-puffing intellectuals seated round a table, was hardly imaginative cinema, but 10 million radio listeners guaranteed that the first film of the series would be a 'red-hot title attraction which cannot miss anywhere'.[50] Strand's drama-doc, *Battle for Music* (1943), was rather more adventurous, telling the story of the London Philharmonic Orchestra's struggles to stay together under wartime conditions. Members of the orchestra played themselves in the reconstruction, and were joined by conductors Malcolm Sargent, Constant Lambert and Sir Adrian Boult, as well as J. B. Priestley, who had launched a famous appeal on behalf of the LPO. For the MoI, Strand produced the featurette *There's a Future in It* (1943). This romance about a girl (Ann Dvorak) in love with an RAF bomber pilot (Barry Morse) was a tribute to the courage of Britain's airmen and the women who wait anxiously for them to complete their missions safely. It was, in the opinion of *To-Day's Cinema*, 'powerful propaganda' of 'handy supporting length'.[51] The downbeat *Browned Off* (1944), billed as the 'Saga of a Searchlight' and promising 'Blitz Bravery – that does not come into the limelight', was made with the blessing of the War Office.[52]

Documentary drama: the press book for British National's *Battle for Music* (1943)

Rather riskily for a film distributed as entertainment, it attempted to capture the boredom of those whose duty is to stand and wait for something to happen.

As the end of the war came in sight after D-Day, almost every branch of the fighting and supporting services had a documentary tribute paid. Castleton Knight and Edward Jarratt offered an earnest salute to the work of the Air Training Corps in *Sons of the Air* (1944) for Rank, while Francis Searle responded very effectively to the challenge of depicting the experiences of a *Student Nurse* (1945). The Realist Film Unit's Alexander Shaw produced an hour-long tribute to DEMS (defensively equipped Merchant ships) and *Soldier, Sailor* (1945) for the MoI. Ealing's Charles Frend was given the task of stimulating sympathy for a Norwegian whaling crew in *The Return of the Vikings* (1944), an assignment that was rather easier in the 1940s than it would be today. Even so, as *The Cinema* noted, Frend seemed ill at ease with the treatment of his material and the result was one of the more forgettable examples of wartime actuality film-making.[53] On the other hand, the most distinguished and memorable of these documentary featurettes was MGM's tense Technicolor account of the twenty-fifth mission of a Flying Fortress, *The Memphis Belle* (1944).

There were also plenty of featurettes with much less evident propaganda intent: for example, Paul Barralet and Granville Squires' B. S. Productions combined its work on Government training films with the production of commercial actuality films. Early in 1943 Barralet produced and directed *The Pinnacle of Fame*, a film about Madame Tussaud's waxworks, that made full use of the notorious Chamber of Horrors. It was distributed by Paramount and well received by the trade. It was followed a few months later by a survey of the history and current activities of the Royal Academy of Dramatic Art, *I Want to be an Actress* (1943), and in 1945 by *Horse Sense*, a survey of equine activity from thoroughbreds to Army mules. Ronald Haines' British Foundation Pictures took time off from producing informational shorts to make entertainment featurettes, and eventually tried something a little longer, *The Man with the Magnetic Eyes* (1945). Unfortunately, it was a dismally out-dated depiction of the tracking down of a crudely disguised criminal mastermind, who, in violation of genre convention, turns out to be a character previously unknown to the audience.

As opportunities for making studio second features closed down, Widgey Newman reverted to animal-antics featurettes like *Pandamonium* (1942), *The Parrot Remembers* (1943), covering the evacuation of London Zoo to Whipsnade, *Mingling With Ming* (1943) with Wally Patch and Mabel Poulton, the canine comedy *The Peke Speaks* (1944) and *Parrot Goes to Sea* (1944), a compendium of pre-war zoo and Mediterranean travelogue footage, with commentary from Marquis the Macaw. Late in 1943, Newman changed direction and embarked on a lengthy photographic tour of Britain, running into all manner of restrictions imposed by a Government preparing for the invasion of Europe. The resulting series of travelogues, distributed by E. J. Fancey, began with *Charted Waters* (1944), a leisurely tour round the byways of Fenland. *To-Day's Cinema* described it as 'a restful little picture' which 'in spirit does not belong to the war', and, with its horse brasses, Cromwellian relics, weeping willows and light-hearted commentary, it was already anticipating the end of hostilities.[54] The Scilly Isles travelogue *West of the Sunset* (1944), credited to Newman's wife, Joan, was equally escapist. Film-makers, exhibitors and the MoI were all aware that audiences were tiring of war-related themes and looking for diversion. This was reflected in the approval given by *To-Day's Cinema* to the third of the Newmans' series *Road to Yesterday* (1944): 'This interesting tour deep into the heart of Wales takes us away for a time from the worries of wartime.'[55] By this time, however, Widgey Newman was beyond earthly cares, having died at only forty-three years of age, leaving a legacy of

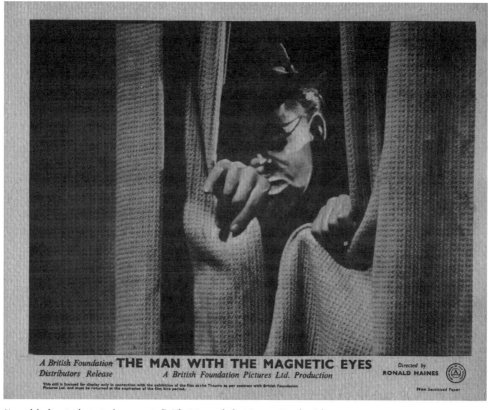

'A crudely disguised criminal mastermind': *The Man with the Magnetic Eyes* (1945)

more than fifty films. Undaunted, his widow kept the family business going, releasing their Wye Valley travelogue, *Going Wye Way*, in March 1945 and a Hertfordshire tour, *Queen of Hearts*, a few months later.

As well as travelogues and zoological novelties, the stock-in-trade of the commercial short and featurette maker was variety turns. Harold Baim's Federated Film Corporation catered for the army of factory hands with the variety revue *Playtime for Workers* (1943), which had plenty of swing numbers and a suitably propagandist finale.[56] Federated followed it up with Denis Kavanagh's *Starlight Serenade* (1944), compèred by a wise-cracking Bonar Colleano. The turns included Ike Hatch as a Kentucky minstrel and the inscrutable Wilson, Keppel and Betty in a classic performance of their sand dance. Berkeley's *Rainbow Round the Corner* (1944), directed by Victor Gover, trod much the same boards with a liberal sprinkling of ukulele melodies and a concluding homily on the need for democracy if the future of the world was to be assured.[57] A bizarre combination it might seem, but it was emblematic of the easeful coming together of banality and profundity that was so much a feature of wartime entertainment. Berkeley's next second feature was the genuinely bizarre *A Night of Magic* (1944), directed by Herbert Wynne and again featuring Billy 'Uke' Scott. This time the cabaret turns decorated the story of a man-about-town (Robert Griffith) who acquires an Egyptian princess's mummy (Marion Olive). The long-dead princess comes to life and is taken on a tour of London night spots before returning to her palace for an alcoholic orgy. The whole sorry affair turns out to be a dream. Up-and-coming actuality film-maker, Sam Lee, offered something a little more substantial with *We the People*, a featurette hosted by Bonar Colleano and Olive Wright that adopted the sort of magazine format that would become commonplace on television, but sounded a novel note in 1944.

It was no accident that travelogues and other location-shot productions, as well as variety acts filmed in theatres, dominated the supporting programme in the later months of the war, because, by the summer of 1944 there was virtually no studio space available for low-budget independent production. Butcher's were already working largely on location. Their nostalgic romance, *My Ain Folk* (1944), was shot in Scotland, where settings for its sing-songs included a factory canteen and even an open boat after a shipwreck. The Butcher's featurette *Boys of the Old Brigade* (1945), directed by A. Stanley Williamson, provided a typically nostalgic look at the lives and history of the Chelsea Pensioners, demonstrating that the residents of the Royal Hospital at Chelsea could still down a pint or two and appreciate the charms of a pretty girl. British National still had its own studios, but also joined the exodus to locations. The sheep dog epic *Loyal Heart* (1946) was filmed in Cumberland in the summer and autumn of 1944, and Oswald Mitchell had to wait until the end of May the following year to shoot interiors in the studio. The wait was blamed, however, not on a shortage of studio space but on the need for the film's star, 'Fleet the wonder dog', to fulfil his sheep-minding duties over winter and spring.[58] The picture was not worth waiting for. As *Film Report* put it: 'the film creaks uneasily all the way through', with the scenery and the dog its only redeeming features.[59] British National's high point proved to be 1942–3, after which it began to feel the competition of Rank, Korda (now returned from the USA) and the British production arms of the American studios. In 1944, BN adjusted its sights and aimed its programmers towards a lower section of the market. Star vehicles for the likes of Arthur 'Old Mother Riley' Lucan and Flanagan and Allen could still expect to garner a majority of bookings as first features, and might be co-features at worst, but for an increasing number of other pictures from the studio this was no longer the case. Films like *Meet Sexton Blake* (1944), which lost some of its juvenile audience when it was given an 'A' certificate by the BBFC, and the bucolic *Strawberry Roan* (1945) and *The Voice Within* (1946) were really co-features at best. British National worked hard to promote Maclean Rogers' gangster burlesque *Don Chicago* (1945) – billing the radio comic Jackie Hunter as 'Definitely England's New Film Star', and the film itself as 'The Funniest Story Ever Told: a laugh with every bullet, comedy with machine-gun rapidity' – but it all seemed a little desperate for a film lacking genuine star appeal.[60] *Don Chicago*, *Loyal Heart* and *Meet Sexton Blake*, with a Chinese villain named 'Slant-eyes' and David Farrar as the square-jawed hero, all played the Odeon or Gaumont circuits as supporting features.

Although the double bill had survived the war and would continue to be the preferred mode of post-war cinema programming, the position of the second feature had been challenged by a versatile film format which had proved highly adaptable to difficult conditions: the featurette. The ability of this variety of film-making to articulate national sentiments and embody educational aspirations as well as common-or-garden entertainment values was clearly evidenced in Harold Baim's *Our Mr Shakespeare* (1944). This travelogue of Stratford-on-Avon and its surrounding countryside blended patriotic and literary concerns with pictorial pleasures and, in its depiction of tourism in wartime, a strong sense of normality and continuity. 'Look here, upon this picture', wrote the Bard in *Hamlet* (Act iii Scene 4), and that is exactly what filmgoers did, allowing *Our Mr Shakespeare* to play for six months in London's West End. By the end of the war, production of featurettes was easily exceeding pre-war levels, and they accounted for most of the 'exhibitors' quota only' films that were being produced at the rate of approximately two per month in the last years of the war. Their exhibition had come to dominate the British element within the supporting programme, particularly for independent exhibitors. The question now was: would the mass production of featurettes continue as the infrastructure of film production was gradually returned to commercial usage?

2 'What's on with it?'

The Rise and Fall of the Bs

Lavishness need be no criterion of quality. I have met many cinemagoers who expressed their enjoyment of a supporting film for its originality, novelty or sincerity ... Intelligently written and handled, and having satisfactory technical qualities, there is no reason why such films should not play an important part in meeting a need.

The Cinema's Studio Correspondent[1]

With the end of the war, the battle for the British supporting programme began in earnest. Documentary-maker Jill Craigie fired the first salvo when, at a speech in Plymouth, she called for the abolition of second-feature dramas and their replacement by 'entertaining documentary films'. These, she asserted, would prove more popular with the public than the sentimental and unreal pictures it was being offered. Good documentaries would also attract new audiences and counter political apathy by cultivating a critical approach to social arrangements.[2] In truth, the traditional British second feature must have appeared to be a dead man walking. In 1945–6 only a handful of companies were producing this type of film – principally British National and, to a lesser extent, Butcher's. BN had been in its pomp only three years before, but was reduced to producing a lame comedy starring the now-forgotten Moon and Brown. The title, *What Do We Do Now?* (1946), summed up the company's dilemma. The studio would eventually shut down in April 1948, but, in the meantime, BN's former documentary wing, Strand Films, was making conventional fiction films like the follow-up to *Meet Sexton Blake*, John Harlow's *The Echo Murders* (1945), an intended co-feature in which David Farrar reprised his role as Blake. The plot, with its Nazi fifth columnists, looked back to the conflict just ended rather than forward to the gathering Cold War. For many critics, this type of film was also looking back. The future, it seemed, was in the big picture, supported possibly by an actuality short or featurette.

'Is it useful?' Documenting the Peace

While second-feature fiction films continued to sink, documentaries appeared to be riding the crest of the wave. There were increasing signs, however, that the documentary movement's ship was not an entirely happy one. In 1945, the Crown Film Unit produced Humphrey Jennings' *Diary for Timothy*, with commentary by E. M. Forster and music by Richard Addinsall. The narrative is addressed to a baby born on the fifth anniversary of the outbreak of the war and recounts the stories of a wounded fighter pilot, a farmer, a miner and an engine driver in its final days. With such talent assembled, *Documentary News Letter* might have been expected to give the film a rapturous reception, but, while marvelling at Jennings' ability to match sound with stunning images, the *DNL* remained unhappy

about the film's lack of social and ideological clarity.[3] Jennings' film met every aesthetic criterion, but
had trouble answering the perennial questions asked of any film in the documentary movement: 'Is it
useful? Does it help people?' Documentary film-making had a choice to make. It could continue to
serve the propaganda needs of the state, or it could strive for a critical voice that would encourage the
government to address the causes and solutions of problems facing the people in the peace. The *DNL*
was keen on the latter approach and, on this ground, questioned the utility of Jack Lee's *Children on
Trial* (1946), a study of the rehabilitation of two young offenders. This was another CFU production, and its distributor, Ealing, was quick to celebrate its pedigree and authenticity.[4] This was not
enough to impress the *DNL*, which attacked the complacency of Lee's message:

> *Children on Trial* gives the impression that approved schools are a complete answer to juvenile delin-
> quency. Just send the children to them and get them back as little angels in a year or two's time ... Are we
> going to keep up a policy of shining a becoming pink light on our society, blanketing off everything which
> we dislike?[5]

The *DNL* had fewer reservations about another second-feature length drama-documentary from Ealing
released around the same time: Charles Crichton's sympathetic examination of the lives and loves of
bargees, *Painted Boats* (1945). The film's neo-realist approach contrasted strongly with Maurice Elvey's
earlier treatment of a similar theme in *The Water Gipsies* (1932). Crichton's film was not only more
'realistic', but, from the perspective of the *DNL*, had its heart and politics in the right place. It was a
creditable example 'of the now accepted incursion of the documentary idea into the second-feature
world' and had experienced no trouble in holding the attention of West End audiences.[6]

Factual featurettes: trade advertisements for two early post-war examples

The lives and loves of bargees: Charles Crichton's neo-realist *Painted Boats* (1945)

There was no lack of critical edge to Paul Rotha's passionate feature documentary *Land of Promise* (1946). Even the *DNL* expressed some concern at the film's excessive demagoguery.[7] The film addressed Britain's housing problems in historical perspective, using the technique of disembodied voices to represent differing viewpoints. Rotha's *The World is Rich* (1948) was also not afraid to adopt an openly political stance in a harrowing thirty-five-minute account of the world's food problems.[8] The *Daily Herald* used its leader column to recommend the film as one everyone ought to see, and ask that readers lobby their local cinema managers to screen it in their cinemas. Even at the other end of Fleet Street's political spectrum, the *Daily Mail* described it as a work of 'merciless cinematic brilliance' and 'a picture to scald the conscience'.[9] However, the *DNL* doubted that the picture would receive the level of theatrical distribution that it so richly deserved.[10] Here was the problem for films like these: to persuade exhibitors that they would appeal to patrons. In reviewing *Land of Promise*, *To-Day's Cinema* recognised the film's qualities and acknowledged that it 'should provoke thought wherever it is shown', but felt compelled to warn its readers: 'Exhibitors, however, should realise that it has a Left Wing bias and in view of the agreement that politics are out of place in the cinema, they should view the film themselves.'[11] Such reservations caused Leslie Halliwell to complain that, in a city of almost 300,000 inhabitants, it was impossible to see a representative selection of 'reality films'.[12] A *DNL* editorial echoed his complaint, bemoaning the fact that half the cinema programme was 'taken up by bad American second features or equally noxious British "featurettes"'. The elimination of these 'low-quality' productions was seen as a necessary step in clearing the way for the more worthy and educational documentary:

During the war ... a number of films like *Target for Tonight*, *Western Approaches*, *Desert Victory* and *World of Plenty* did enjoy wide distribution in the cinemas and proved box-office successes. But with the end of the war the barriers have been raised again. Yet the success of the Rank-sponsored series, *This Modern Age*, over the post-war years proves that there is a market if the trade is willing. There is a talent and capacity in this country to produce not only shorts but longer story documentaries, to take the place of the present low-grade supporting films.[13]

This Modern Age, a series of twenty-minute films 'of vital interest to the Britisher' was Rank's response to its 'public service broadcasting' duty.[14] Produced by Moscow-born Sergei Nolbandov, who had recently been a production head at the MoI, the series was launched in September 1946, and became one of the most familiar fixtures in the supporting programme until 1950. After giving an enthusiastic reception to the series' opener, an examination of the contemporary housing crisis (*Homes for All*, 1946), the *DNL* began to criticise the series for its tendency to provide 'a soothing cup of warm cocoa', admittedly made with the very best ingredients, and it advised to start tilting at 'a windmill or two'.[15] Generally, the organ of the documentary movement was happier with the treatment given by *This Modern Age* to political issues – like the *Coal Crisis* (issue 7) – than with the way the series handled matters cultural. The provocative subject of issue 16 was *The British – Are They Artistic?*, and the *DNL* (under its new title *Documentary Film News*) quickly spotted an 'uptilted-nose atmosphere about the film' that again smacked of snobbery.[16] Undeterred, Rank produced over forty editions of what was voted by filmgoers the most popular series of shorts.[17]

Tri-partite battle lines were being clearly drawn. On one side stood the major producers, British and American, who were interested in making longer and more lavish pictures that would draw audiences as a single attraction (with only a perfunctory supporting programme). Ranged against them, and poorly equipped, was the army of small film-makers, whose interests lay in the double bill and flexible cinema programming. What power they had came not from any economic muscle, but from the stubborn resistance of cinema audiences to any attacks on a two-feature programme that they regarded as value for money. The third force, whose time had come to seize the day (or so it seemed), was composed of the documentary film movement. The movement had enjoyed enormous state patronage and retained the sympathy of the new Labour Government.[18] The penultimate year of the war had witnessed a bitter dispute between the British Short Film Makers Society, which represented non-sponsored film production, and the loftier Association of Short Film Producers containing the luminaries of the 'legitimate' documentary movement. In the autumn of 1944, the Association had sought to take advantage of the richer resources brought by official sponsorship by lobbying the Board of Trade to introduce not only a cost qualification for quota registration of shorts but also for short films to count as double and triple for quota if sufficient money had been spent on them.[19] In 1945 the movement gave birth to a further pressure group, the Federation of Documentary Film Units, which, in line with the *Documentary News Letter*, advocated that the coming Films Act should prohibit the double feature. The British Short Film Makers Society, on the other hand, called for a quota for an 'intermediate class' of pictures between 3,000 and 6,500 feet, with the aim of encouraging the production of decent second features, 'a department of film production which has been neglected and which is in fact the bread and butter of the American film industry'.[20] The documentary movement's strategy had to be to forge an alliance with the major producers – Korda was already in agreement – and try to convert small commercial film-makers to its cause. In this, the movement had considerable initial success. The British Film Producers' Association (BFPA), in its consultations on the next Films Act, recommended a separate supporting programme quota that would encourage shorts and documentaries 'in which British producers have for years been outstanding'.[21] To build on this, however, required internal unity, and that was something the brothers and sisters of the movement found hard to achieve.

In the early months of the peace, the documentary movement was able to count on the active support of Labour politicians. When Herbert Morrison addressed the annual dinner of the CEA's London and Home Counties branch, he linked a more social-realist approach to film-making with a continuing close relationship between cinema and government:

> British documentary film making took another and long step forward during the war under the Godparency of the Ministry of Information. Their fame has spread throughout the world, and we should look to it that their quality is upheld, that they are used to help us make good neighbours abroad, and perhaps friendly and willing customers ... British film studios must remember their responsibility to show the world British life, British democracy, and British ideals.[22]

As the post-war Films Bill moved through its committee stage, Labour MP Cyril Dumpleton introduced an amendment to boost the revenues of specialised and documentary film producers. He was sure that 'the ordinary person' would enjoy the output of these producers 'more than many of the second features which now disgrace our screens'. There was a high level of consensus in the parliamentary committee on the idea that once audiences were educated to appreciate the documentary short, there would be little demand for a second feature. The Conservative MP Walter Fletcher, a former independent exhibitor, declared: 'The genius of the film production of this country has been shown very largely in the production of short and documentary films.' He was backed up by the Board of Trade's Harold Wilson: 'The average cinemagoer would rather see a good English documentary film than much of the big feature stuff which he is now asked to look at.'[23]

Ultimately, however, it was exhibitors rather than politicians who would determine the fate of the documentary movement. By and large, exhibitors, whether small independents or giant combines, were not among the Labour Government's most fervent supporters and were resistant to further state involvement in the enterprise economy and attempts to influence public tastes and attitudes. As businessmen burdened with a high entertainment tax, most distrusted the state-sponsored documentary as covert left-wing propaganda, likely to pave the way for further bouts of nationalisation. Within six months of VE-Day, there was vigorous debate in CEA meetings around the country concerning the wisdom of continuing to give house-room to films sponsored by the MoI. Audiences, it was frequently said, no longer wanted 'propaganda films'.[24] The CEA rejected the idea of a 'split' quota, arguing not only that there should be no separate quota for second features but also that the 'general tendency should be either to decrease the quota for shorts or abolish it altogether'.[25] Without the support of exhibitors, the documentary movement lacked a platform from which to address the public.[26] The Government understood this well and cautioned the movement that documentary films would have to foreground entertainment values if they were to receive any kind of distribution. Even the austere and puritanical Minister for Trade and Industry, Sir Stafford Cripps, had signalled this when he addressed the Association of Specialised Film Producers in 1947.[27] He had assured the Association that: 'we must somehow or other give the public the opportunity of seeing the output of these [documentary] units, an output which I am convinced the ordinary person would enjoy more than many of the second features which now disgrace our screens'.[28] However, Cripps was careful to state the conditions necessary for such a cultural policy to be effective. First, the documentary or realist film must be 'entertainment and not education': 'You cannot and should not try to force down the throats of people who have paid to be entertained what you consider is good for them by way of education.' Second, the position of the second feature had to be challenged: 'So long as the second feature is insisted upon ... it is almost impossible to put a short into the programme.' Third, renters and exhibitors must agree to allocate a larger proportion of rental fees to the supporting programme to make the production of unsponsored quality shorts a viable economic proposition.[29] This final condition became an issue of increasing urgency as production costs soared – especially for films over 3,000 feet – following new pay rates and crewing minimums agreed with the technicians' unions.

Cripps's comments about the importance of entertainment value may have been prompted by Humphrey Jennings' most recent CFU film, *The Cumberland Story* (1947), which took a look at the modernisation of the pits and dramatised the historic dangers of mining. It was hardly Jennings at his best. Even his biographer described it as 'the most boring long film Jennings ever made, and by far the most flawed of his mature career'.[30] On the other hand, John Grierson seemed to have Cripps's remarks very much in mind when, shortly afterwards, he made *A Yank Comes Back* (1949). It starred Burgess Meredith as the returning American, as well as Paulette Goddard, and injected elements of fun and irreverence into the promotion of its message that conditions might be difficult, but the spirit of the British people is indomitable. Suddenly here was a film that was not afraid to poke fun at Stafford Cripps, employ the manic Spike Jones as its 'director of music', or show women in states of undress or complaining about coupons and shortages. It created a ripple of surprise among trade critics, but *Kinematograph Weekly* still sniffed out 'Government propaganda' in a picture that contrived to be simultaneously 'naive and pretentious'.[31]

'What use are these?' The Age of the Featurette

The attack by Cripps on second features was probably directed at American 'B' films rather than their British cousins, which, at the time, were hardly troubling the bookers because they were in such short supply. As we have seen, with studio facilities out of reach to most low-budget film-makers, the format of choice (or rather necessity) had become the featurette. These second-class entertainments, running just over the legal minimum for 'long films' (3,000 feet), varied from straight documentaries to low-budget dramas and comedies in a spectrum that took in variety shows, novelty pictures and what we would now term 'drama-docs'. In 1945–7, to the concern of CEA members trying to fulfil their quota obligations, every other British long film was one of these over-length shorts.[32] Thirty-eight were registered in 1945–6, and fifty-five the following quota year, when there were just six films running between forty-five and sixty-five minutes, the standard length of the second feature, and forty-five longer pictures.[33] 'What is the use of these 3,000 ft films?' asked the Chairman of the Edinburgh CEA rhetorically. 'The majority are of no use at all to us.'[34] His view was echoed by the Chairman of Granada cinemas, Sydney Bernstein, who hoped the next Films Act would 'prohibit the production of this type of film which is doing much to harm the good name which British films now enjoy'.[35] Although Bernstein's outburst was a little hysterical, especially in the light of the generally favourable reviews received by most featurettes in the trade press, there were a few examples of film-making at its feeblest. The *Film Report* ratings given to W. F. Elliott's comedy *The Adventures of Parker* and

Ronald Haines' story of a pools win, *The Happy Family*, both reviewed in the same week in August 1946, were among the lowest in the publication's history: six and five marks respectively.[36]

One of the leading producers of featurettes, and the man responsible for *Our Mr Shakespeare* (1944), Harold Baim, felt it necessary to defend his company's product from growing hostility, asserting that 'travel subjects' in particular had met with an enthusiastic response from audiences, and that it was 'a short-sighted policy to agitate against the smaller producer whose efforts will eventually help to make for a greater and more virile British industry'.[37] Veteran low-budgeteer, Horace Shepherd – who made *A Musical Masquerade* (1946), an ironic tale about a composer who can only get his music performed when it is believed to be by Tchaikovsky – also wrote to the trade press to warn that, in dismissing all featurettes on the basis of a few poor ones, there was a danger of throwing out the baby with the bath water. There were producers 'who are willing and eager to turn out intelligent, sincere featurettes – and are only too anxious to give the exhibitor something more ambitious as soon as he shows that he is prepared to play fair – and pay for it'.[38] Fellow featuretteer, Paul Barralet, confirmed that one Midlands' exhibitor had offered him a paltry 25 shillings to book one of his pictures for three days, but admitted that there were too many films of this type being produced.[39]

The root cause of the mushrooming of featurettes was the shortage of studio space as producers waited for facilities to be reopened after wartime requisitioning. Independent film-makers, often with documentary experience in the plethora of state information units, were obliged to stay on location, and try to broaden the commercial appeal of their actuality films with attempts at light comedy. This was most easily achieved via a witty commentary delivered by a popular radio personality like Ronnie Waldman, who combined effectively with Jack (Colonel Chinstrap) Train on the brewing and distilling documentary *What's Yours?* (1947). Waldman also supplied the narration to an accompanying film on tobacco, *Fag End* (1947), directed by future *Carry On* luminary, the camp Charles Hawtrey, and to *Birth of a Film* (1947), a documentary on feature-film production directed by Richard Gray. 'Coating the pill of instruction with entertainment is fast becoming an art in the provision of screen fare for adults,' noted *The Cinema*.[40] The combination of alcohol or tobacco and personality was always going to be a winner, but less obviously populist topics met more critical opposition. Eric Leslie's tour of Hampshire with Waldman, *Down in the Forest* (1947), for example, was criticised by the trade press for 'its tendency, like so many of its kind, to pad out the material with irrelevant sidelines' in order to push the length over 3,000 ft.[41]

Familiar aspects of British history and literature offered the chance for populist appeal without totally sacrificing documentary credibility. John George Taylor Productions delivered *After You Mr Dickens* (1945), a biographical travelogue that toured London locations associated with Charles Dickens. The distributor was E. J. Fancey (New Realm), whose Do-U-Know (DUK) Films also gave a hard sell to Cecil Williamson's Tower of London featurette, *Prisoners of the Tower* (1946). The film was marketed as if it were a horror picture:

> The horrors of the torture chamber, and the agonised shrieks of its victims as the screw twists and the rack turns. No escape! Despair of the heart that nearly drives the mind to madness – and time – an eternity of light and dark. And then – the last mile! The way to Tower Hill; a sea of eager derisive faces waiting for the performance of death. A cheer trembling on their lips that will never be heard, for it will burst forth only when the head rolls from the shoulders and the axe is dripping with blood.[42]

There were more bloody deeds in Walter West's *We Do Believe in Ghosts* (1947), a film inspired, no doubt, by post-bellum interest in the afterlife and the revival of spiritualism. It consisted of an unconvincing recitation of three chilling tales involving post-death perambulations by Charles I, Anne Boleyn, Katherine Howard and – most bizarrely of all – the jockey, Fred Archer. Richard Fisher was responsible for an even eerier featurette, *The Haunted Palace* (1949), which offered a tour of the stately ghosts of England. The ghost stories were separated by a ballerina performing excerpts from 'The Haunted Ballroom' and 'Dance Macabre'. Other featurettes also tapped into a lighter vein of British whimsy. Francis Miller's *Loco Number One* (1948) observed a retired engine driver playing with his train set while reminiscing about his favourite runs; while James Hill's *A Journey for Jeremy* (New Realm, 1949) depicted a young boy's dream of driving a steam train from Glasgow to London. Most of these offerings were, after so many traumas, understandably 'feel-good', but there was still a little room for a campaigning documentary like John Miller's *An Englishman's Home* (1946), which drew attention to delays in dealing with the housing crisis resulting from wartime bombing; or Donald Alexander's *Probation Officer* (1949), which displayed the consequences of dysfunctional family life.

The producers and directors of these films were a mixture of long-term industry professionals like Harold Baim and Horace Shepherd, those who had developed their film-making techniques on MoI documentaries, and demobbed servicemen, some of whom had enjoyed their first taste of movie-making with the film units of the services. For example, three former servicemen, L. A. Goldwater, L. E. Manuel and J. D. Toff, scraped together enough capital to make a featurette on Covent Garden market called *Early One Morning* (1947). Unfortunately, it failed to launch glittering careers in the cinema, unlike the featurette on the same subject made a few years later by Lindsay Anderson (*Every Day Except Christmas*, 1955). Among the more established film-makers was Denis Kavanagh (1906–1984), an Irishman who began his career in Hollywood in 1926 before working in the British industry as an assistant director, production manager and editor. He started making shorts in 1938 and continued after war service in the RAF and work on propaganda films. Increasingly, he turned his attention to non-sponsored subjects, making *Sportlight on Dogs* (1945) and *Hyde Park* (1946). They were followed by *Women in Sport* (1946), which was narrated by Raymond Glendenning, and paid tribute to the growing physical fitness of women. Clearly Kavanagh had not had his fill of lithe and lissom femininity, because his next picture was *Glamour Girl* (1946), a flippantly narrated look at a day in the life of a couple of showgirls (Joan Verney and Mavis Cooper).[43] It would become a staple subject for short film-makers looking for circuit bookings.[44] Working for Baim's Federated Films, he followed it up with *Plenty Questions* (1947), an innovative adaptation of the radio general knowledge quiz. Kavanagh then formed Pegasus Film Productions with Sidney Lesser and Doreen North (former continuity girl with the RAF Film Unit), making *Signed Sealed and Delivered* (1947), an account of a diplomatic bag's journey from the Foreign Office in London to the British Embassy in Paris.

The themes of the early post-war featurettes reflected the structures of feeling and preoccupations of their time: most notably pride in nation and achievement and the long-suppressed desire for leisure and recreation in the hard-won peace. *The Bulldog Breed* (1947) was actually the title of a featurette on the breeding of pedigree bloodstock, but it was also the motto of the patriotic featurettes that had been emblematic of British film-making during the war and continued in the years that followed. Public sentiment continued to support unabashed expression of what might now be thought gross sentimentality towards England's history and traditions. Emblematically, the MoI celebrated peace in Europe with the proudly titled *Our Country* (1945), an overview of wartime Britain from the point of view of a sailor on leave. *To-Day's Cinema* had no hesitation in recommending that John Eldridge's film 'should be given the widest possible showing both here and abroad'.[45]

The genre that lent itself most easily to the articulation of these sentiments was one almost as old as cinema itself: the travelogue. Before the war, it had been used primarily as a window on a more exotic world for an audience unused to foreign travel, but, with the arrival of peace, it came to be a vehicle for the patriotic promotion of the delights of the British Isles. Foremost among these were the sea and the coast. Horace Shepherd's *Cornish Holiday* and Renown's *Land of the Saints* (both 1946) featured Cornwall's rugged coastline and fishing villages. *The Skipper Puts to Sea* (1946), directed by Paul Barralet and T. A. Glover, referred back to the origins of the British documentary movement and Grierson's *Drifters* (1929). The title of Ronald Haines' *Coastline* (1947) evokes an iconic line of resistance to invasion, once so vulnerable and now so secure from threat. Donald MacDonald's *Whitstable Natives* (1948) observed the peace of the Kent fishing village, with plenty of oysters and hardy fisherfolk.

Countryside and waterways played a prominent part in the evocation of nationalist feelings, and the title of the featurette *Old Father Thames* (1946) encapsulated the way in which a sense of history flowed easily into pride in recent achievements.[46] The war had also reinforced the British self-image as an island race protected by invincible seapower. When MGM distributed the patriotic *All the King's Men* (1948), Edward Eye's survey of the training regimes and ceremonials of the Army and Air Force, *To-Day's Cinema* immediately complained that it would like to have seen coverage extended to include the Navy.[47] In fact, the Naval section had been saved for a second documentary, *The King's Navy* (1948), this time distributed by GFD.[48] The same distributors also released two equally patriotic documentaries on Britain's flagship passenger liners. MGM's *Top Liner* (1948) was Lewis G. Jonas's tour of the new *Queen Elizabeth* in her berth at Southampton docks, while GFD's *Queens of the Sea* recalled the role played by both *Elizabeth* and *Mary* as troop ships during the war. A. Digby Smith's *The Red Duster* (1951) looked at the less glamorous work of the Merchant Navy during a round-trip to Spain, while Cecil Williamson's *No Sail* celebrated the windjammers of the past and their evolution into modern racing craft.[49] There was a hearty critical reception for Basil Wright's contribution to the Festival of Britain, *Waters of Time* (1951), a portrait of the London Docks released immediately after Ealing's drama *Pool of London* (1950).[50]

Post-bellum travelogue-makers also mined sources of patriotic sentiment in the heart of Britain. After the success of *Our Mr Shakespeare*, documentary film-makers were thick on the hallowed ground of Stratford-on-Avon. C. H. Williamson's curiously titled *The Upstart Crow* (1948) took viewers on another tour of Shakespeareland in the company of narrator John Snagge,[51] while John Douglas began his theatrical survey, *The Play's the Thing* (1948), with the Shakespeare Memorial Theatre before departing for the more politically conscious Mercury and Unity companies and the more showbiz Italia Conti drama school. After years of blood, toil, sweat and tears, a vacation was top of the agenda in 1946, and appetites were whetted by *Englishman's Holiday* (1946), a reminder of the scenic beauties of Bath, Wells and Glastonbury. Moss Goodman and Victor Cochrane Hervey's featurette was not particularly memorable cinema, but it carried considerable symbolic weight as a statement of what had been fought for. This was a holiday that had been earned as never before. Equally timely was John G. Taylor's *Take it Easy* (1946), a wide-ranging survey of all kinds of entertainment and leisure activities available to the middle-class family, with a suitably light-hearted commentary. British holiday featurettes generally foregrounded history and heritage. Harold Baim's visit to the Isle of Wight, *Chip Off the Old Rock* (1946), was an early case in point, although its pride in heritage was rather distractingly overlaid by the bickering banter of its male and female narrators.

The British travelogue units were quickly joined by others. In 1946, the American producer James A. Fitzpatrick made a series of fourteen half-hour 'Traveltalks' on various British locations for international distribution in cinemas and on US television. They were very much welcomed by the British Travel Association, which attributed a significant part of the growth in tourism to the British Isles (particularly from the USA) in 1947–8 to the influence of films like these.[52] Some indigenous filmmakers had already had a similar bright idea of selling characteristic images of their country to overseas audiences. The rickety outfit British Australian Film Corporation, for example, was responsible for *A Yank in the West Country* (1945), directed in his usual simplistic style by Geoffrey Benstead. Actually there were a brace of Yanks, a pair of middle-aged hoofers, a couple of comedians and some vigorous maypole dancing in the course of this artless tour of Dorset and Wiltshire. It might conceivably have been seen in a town like Alice, but it is unlikely to have made it to Palm Springs. The same was probably true of British Lion's *Hands Across the Ocean* (1946) in which a GI and his future bride (Bill Swyre and Pearl Cameron) go on a romantic tour of Britain and Ireland. A transatlantic relationship also provided the motivation in Sam Lee's *Drake's England* (1951), Anglo-Amalgamated's breezy tour round Devon in the company of a gentleman farmer and an American girl searching for her ancestral roots.

Most of these endless travelogues were at least competently filmed, but there were inevitably some real stinkers like F. W. Attwood's *Elizabeth Takes a Holiday* (1948), described by *The Cinema* as a 'scrappy tour of various places in England with Elizabethan associations ... weak direction; indifferent photography; badly-synchronised dialogue; harsh recording'.[53] Richard Fisher's *The English Way* (1950) sounds equally embarrassing, with its 'pointless and often amateurish Norwegian-visitor commentary, made the more unacceptable by stilted acted sequences showing female friends and pantomime-style Dick Whittington, who points out places of interest'.[54] International Film Renters' *It's No Tale* (1948) lived down to its title in presenting a turgid portrait of the Isle of Man with 'indifferent editing' and 'trite commentary'.[55]

Some travelogues gave a wider geographical perspective by using footage shot before the commencement of hostilities. J. Blake Dalrymple, for example, set his yachting cruise of the Baltic, *Perchance to Sail* (1947), in 1938 and included pre-war footage of Warsaw before flashing forward to the destruction it was to suffer. However, as the post-war chaos in Europe began to subside, documentary units began to venture across the water. An irritatingly comic London waterman made it as far as Belgium in Harry May's *Skiffy Goes to Sea* (1947), while Paul Barralet was back on the briny with *Passage to Bordeaux* (1947), a record of the voyage of a cargo ship to the French wine country. It even sounded as if New Realm's romantically titled *Roman Holiday* (1947) might have travelled as far as Italy, but actually its subject was Roman remains in Britain. International's *Happy Holiday* (1947) followed a cheerfully bantering young married couple to France and Switzerland, a formula reproduced in New Realm's *Swiss Honeymoon* (1947) a few weeks later. Ronald Haines' Luxembourg travelogue, *Then There Were Two* (1948), was shot from the point of view of a couple on honeymoon, who also provided the 'determinedly informative' commentary.[56] Almost inevitably the presentation of the native culture included the making of schnapps and a wine festival, so in one way, at least, these travelogues were not as dry as they have been portrayed. Haines' *Lorelei* (1948) ditched the honey-mooners for a more direct account of a voyage through the Rhineland. It sounds thoroughly pictur-esque, but, at the time, the banks of the Rhine were still littered with bombsites. A. Digby Smith's portrait of post-war recovery, *Paris in the Spring* (Renown, 1948) was more unequivocally upbeat, but brute reality had a habit of protruding through even the most anodyne and promotional of trave-logues, as it did in the same director's *Spanish Holiday* (1950), when its carefree atmosphere was dis-rupted by the bathetic spectacle of the bull-fight, involving what *The Cinema*'s reviewer called 'scenes of revolting cruelty'.[57] Stirling's *The Way to a Man's Heart* (1948) sounded romantic, but it turned out to be a study of Danish food production. Nevertheless, it was recommended as 'very acceptable' for most cinemas.[58] British Foundation's equally misleadingly titled *A Lady Desires* (1948) moved a few miles down the road for a feast of windmills and tulip fields (and a spot of gin-making) in Holland. Conversely, there was a sad appropriateness about the title of *Last Wish* (1949), a love story grafted on to a Parisian travelogue, directed by the unfortunate Sam Lee who died while filming shortly afterwards. Adrian Reid's *Norwegian Holiday* (1951) was another romantic travelogue, doc-umenting the love affair between a British student and a Scandinavian girl, resulting in what one reviewer described as 'carefree entertainment which is definitely a delight to watch'.[59] Audiences apparently agreed, and it was the most popular featurette of the quota year.

Cinema patrons in search of footage from further afield were offered C. H. Williamson's *Bali Adventure* (1948), a journey to the picturesque island east of Java which was largely untouched by the conflicts raging elsewhere. Williamson went even further with *The Gods Can Laugh* (1948), taking a trip round the solar system to set man's struggle to harness the forces of nature in a wider context. When post-war travelogues ventured beyond Europe, however, Imperial Africa was the most favoured destination. Ambassador's *Land of the Springbok* (1945) toured South Africa with plenty of wildlife, and Frank A. Goodliffe's *Warden of the Wild* (1948) visited a Rhodesian game reserve, with human interest supplied by the warden and his family. These films regularly lent themselves to the promo-tion of ideological messages, as in Premier Distributors' *North and South of the Niger* (1949), a survey of 'what British administration is achieving and of native co-operation which is bringing higher stan-dards of living to the populace' in Nigeria.[60] Donald Swanson's *Chisoko the African* (1949) performed much the same ideological work in the context of the exploitation of copper in Rhodesia; while, in Joseph Best's *My African People* (1948), clumsily photographed and edited scenes of exotic native cus-toms were saved from accusations of racial condescension only by the commentary of the black singer, Edric Connor. In contrast, the CFU's Oscar- and BAFTA-winning *Daybreak in Udi* (Terry Bishop, 1949) placed its emphasis on Nigerians' own philosophy of 'happiness through work' and their active role in the construction of a maternity hospital.

Africa was also the spiritual home of the wild-animal featurette. Few of the 1940s offerings, how-ever, emulated the global zoological expeditions of the legendary naturalist photographer Cherry Kearton.[61] A walk on the wild side for most featurette-makers was a potter round the local zoo.[62] The idea of a new spring after the war, a time for home-building, was suggested by the whimsical New Realm featurette, *Whose Baby?* (1946), produced by Joan Widgey Newman. Lion and bear cubs took pride of place among a Noah's Ark of baby animals that warmed the hearts of the hard-headed trade reviewers. Little dignity was granted to animals in the nature featurette. Widgey Newman had begun supplying speaking voices to puppies and parrots in the 1930s, and the technique was continued in an early post-war film by Frank Chisnell, *Tom Tom Topia* (1946), in which the humorous exchanges

of Tommy Handley and the ITMA radio crowd were dubbed onto members of the animal kingdom. Colonel Chinstrap (Jack Train), for example, was a camel.

The auteur of animal documentary was F. Radcliffe-Holmes, who produced, directed and provided voice-over commentaries for his wildlife pictures. These were often films-within-films, seen projected in 16mm for the delight of his mature daughter (Honor Blake). Radcliffe-Holmes had established a reputation in the inter-war years as an intrepid African explorer, and he regularly recycled anthropological and wildlife footage shot during his expeditions, including the featurette *Jungle Scrapbook*, distributed by Renown in 1944. By this time, however, he was comfortably settled back in Britain and henceforth ventured no further than Whipsnade – not that you would have realised this from the titles of some of his featurettes. The fearless title *Denizens of the Wild* (Renown, 1945) concealed footage of animals in captivity, as did *Wild Animals at Large* (1950). Renown handled his *Winged Wonders* (1946), featuring some of the more exotic zoo birds, while Butcher's released *Springtime in Birdland* (1948), an intimate record of nest-building, filmed at Whipsnade. The more prestigious United Artists handled *Zoo Oddities* (1949), a parade of strange and lovable creatures like pandas, penguins, warthogs, ant-eaters and a 200-year-old tortoise. But it was back to the bargain basement of Equity British for the prosaically titled *Forty Minutes at the Zoo* (1949). Radcliffe-Holmes left the zoo briefly to make *Punch and Judy* (1948), a sadly under-researched account of the history of the iconic seaside puppet entertainment. 'One paragraph from the average encyclopaedia contains considerably more information on the subject than all the picture's three reels,' commented *Kinematograph Weekly* acidly.[63]

Domesticated animals were just as likely as wild ones to star in post-war featurettes. Horses paraded attractively to a facetious commentary in Ben Hart's *Once Upon a Horse* (New Realm, 1945) and Jeff Davies' *A Willing Horse* (Butcher's, 1951), smoothly narrated by Eamonn Andrews. Then they did their patriotic duty in Edward Eve's *All the King's Horses* (1947), which was given full access to the royal stables and concluded with a sentimental glimpse of an equine retirement home. Dogs were an even more popular subject. Exclusive offered Joan Widgey Newman's *The Peke's Sold a Pup* (1945), with the usual wise-cracking commentary, and Arrow distributed T. J. Roddy's *Mate O' Mine* (1948), perhaps the only film to quote Alexander the Great in its tagline: 'The more I see of men – the more I love my dog.' Butcher's handled a similar doggie epic from Harold Baim, *These Happy Breeds* (1951), which included an account of the training of police dogs, and concluded, inevitably, with 'a delightful parade of puppies'.[64]

With so much activity suspended for the duration of the war, the appetite of audiences was strong for sports on screen. Wembley was the subject of Harold Baim's *Stadium Highlights* (1946), although football was not among the bewildering variety of sports covered in thirty-six minutes. Like the following year's *Top Speed* (1947), directed by Peter Collin, and Eros's *Festival of Sport* (1951), this was a full-throttle tour of activities ranging from speedway to ping-pong. Other documentaries concentrated on a single sport. Billed by its distributors, Ambassador, as 'The Biggest Attraction since the Royal Wedding', Victor M. Gover's *It's a Great Game* (1948) was one of the more static pieces of sporting cinema. Filmed at Bushey, it consisted of an extended discussion about cricket by schoolboy idols Bill Edrich and Denis Compton, but, as the press book put it, 'All the world is interested in the private lives of Sportsmen.'[65] Its lack of movement was in stark contrast to Herbert Marshall's *Olympic Preview* (1948), which depicted athletic stars doing their day jobs as well as striving for excellence on track and field. Piccadilly Productions' study of the heavyweight boxing champion Bruce Woodcock,

The versatility of the featurette: the press book for *It's a Great Game* (1948) and trade advertisements for two movies from Monarch

Pathway to Fame (1946), attracted considerable press interest and was endorsed by influential critic Dilys Powell on the BBC.[66] Butcher's Edward G. Whiting documentary *The Fighting Spirit* (1948) and H&S's *Fifty Years of Boxing* (1950) also focused on the stars of the square ring, past and present. The thrills of dirt-track racing were presented in Sam Lee's *Speedway* (1947) and those of motor racing in Cecil H. Williamson's *Roaring Wheels* (1951), an assembly of sensational newsreel footage with an exuberant commentary. *Kings of the Turf* (1949) toured various racehorse training stables and presented some of the stars of the racecourse – equine and human. There were more stars – including some from table tennis, no less – in Jim Mellor's Associated-British production *Aqua-Show's Sports Serenade* (1949). This record of an Earl's Court event of the previous year was almost as delirious as its title: 'Little attempt at polished presentation, matter-of-fact commentary by Neal Arden, fragments of music played by Joe Loss and his orchestra.'[67] *Life's a Gambol* (1948) turned its attention to vigorous Antipodean sports to the delight of one reviewer who seemed more than happy to watch 'bronzed Australian manhood at play'.[68]

The travelogue and sporting featurette came together in Norman Hemsley's quintessentially British *Sussex Fortnight* (1950), in which a girls' cycling club toured the Downs in the company of sports commentator Raymond Glendenning, who peddled a 'penny-farthing'. Most of the stops were for horse shows, polo and race meetings. Similarly, the centrepiece of DUK Films' Isle of Man travelogue *Trophy Island* (1950) was the famous TT motorcycle race. The travelogue met the celebrity featurette in a film featuring the fading musical comedy star Jessie Matthews. In *Life is Nothing Without Music* (1947) she sang 'Sleepy Lagoon' and looked through an animated snapshot album of Devon with newsreader Alva Liddell (who unfortunately crooned 'Shenandoah'). There were other celebrity featurettes, although the genre was never a major one. The comic actor Ronald Shiner was the subject of *Rise and Shiner* (1948), Sam Lee's camera following him on a typical day. Harold Baim photographed the Bristol quadruplets on holiday in Wales for *The Good Quads of Pwllheli* (1949), which also served to advertise the Butlin's holiday camp where the babies stayed. Anglo-Amalgamated's *Shooting Stars* (1950), directed by Ray Densham, was an early attempt at the celebrity magazine, with 'intimate glimpses of popular British screen stars off duty', notably at a 'Film Garden Party'. The vivacious television presenter Sylvia Peters chatted to these familiar faces in a way that was described as 'pleasantly informal, light-hearted and discreetly revealing'.[69]

With studio space at a premium and costs rising, the magazine format provided a way of utilising short actuality clips. Enterprising film-makers quickly realised that all they needed was some inter-esting old silent footage and a moviola to compile four-reelers that, furnished with a lively commen-tary, could then be marketed as a modest supporting feature. Gilbert Church's Ambassador distribution business led the way after VE-Day with *Camera Reflections* (1945), a nostalgic compila-tion of silent cinema and newsreel clips aimed at the older viewers who had been a substantial part of the wartime audience. Pathé, however, was the company best-placed to exploit archive material, and did so in a well-received series revisiting the newsreels of the inter-war years, beginning with *Scrapbook for 1922* (1947) and *The Peaceful Years* (1948). The latter, produced by Peter Baylis and introduced by Emlyn Williams, was marketed as featuring 'the most remarkable "cast" any film has ever presented'. Pathé's Picture Library was rummaged through once more for *Scrapbook for 1933* (1950), which, with its pithy and jocular commentary, proved another critical success. Describing it as 'delightfully disrespectful', Pip Andrews in the *Sunday Pictorial* recommended it as 'A second-feature film which you should see, regardless of what the main offering is at your local'.[70] In 1952, Pathé again raided the archives to compile *Here's to the Memory*, covering the previous fifty years in fifty minutes, with the uplifting message that the British people were capable of rising above the most debilitating circumstances. Associated British's archives provided much of the material for Gilbert Gunn's *The Elstree Story*, a sixty-minute selection of extracts from the studios' output over twenty-five years, introduced by Richard Todd and interspersed with behind-the-scenes footage.

Among those exercises in film recycling that lacked Pathé's resources, one finds Fred Weiss's imag-inative *Movie-Go-Round* (1949), which used the novel idea of an argument between an old film pro-jector and a sophisticated modern version as a pretext for a compilation of old silent film clips. Gordon Myers' *Mind Your Step* (1946) assembled footage of birds and animals, dancers, mannequins, ice skaters and acrobats, as well as a visit to a stockings factory, all spuriously linked by the theme of walking by the ubiquitous narrator Ronnie Waldman. Butcher's *Information Please* (1948) offered a couple of industrial documentaries on glass-blowing and puppet-making, and a quiz asking the audi-ence to identify common objects seen from odd angles, all lashed together by Denis Kavanagh just in time for the end of the quota year. John Miller's *Destination Unknown* (1949) should perhaps have been titled 'Destination Unpredictable' as it darted wildly from St Paul's Cathedral to coal-mining in Newcastle, harvesting in Sussex to the manufacture of gas meters, and finally to the restoration of Eros in Piccadilly. At least the burlesque on smoking, *Dumb Dora Discovers Tobacco* (1946), was more thoughtfully themed, but the picture was still a hotchpotch of sketches and clips from old films that commentator Henry Kendall struggled to integrate. Film Traders' *Thrilling Emotion* (1948) focused on various hair-raising stunts and entertainment attractions at circuses, fun fairs and racetracks, as well as a man riding a bicycle down the Eiffel Tower. Mancunian Films' ever-resourceful Tom Blakeley managed to squeeze two featurettes out of a visit to Manchester's Belle Vue entertainment complex:

International Circus Review and *Showground of the North* (both 1948). The latter was confidently predicted by its publicity to be 'a picturisation which will undoubtedly be acclaimed as the foremost saga of amusement in filmland'.[71]

Many featurettes spanned the divide between documentary and narrative film-making that had been narrowed during the war years. New Realm distributed Paul Barralet's forty-four-minute *Bad Company* (1945), which, like *Children on Trial*, dramatised the issue of juvenile delinquency, but rather more sensationally. Adelphi's *Artful Dodgers* (1949) was a study of the trickery of con artists played by a cast 'which clearly places no belief in under-acting'.[72] John Dacre's *Marriage in Danger* (1948) was a drama-doc based on case files of marriage guidance counsellors.[73] Cecil Williamson's *Beyond Price* (1947) joined some spare documentary footage together with the story of the discovery of a seaman, washed up on the Welsh coast and in possession of valuable pearls. His interrogation by the police is the occasion for the revealing of his life history via suitable clips of actuality footage. Ronnie Pilgrim's *Operation Diamond* (1948), featuring Michael Medwin in an early starring role, combined dramatic re-creation of British agents' adventures in occupied Holland with conventional actuality footage of diamond-mining and -cutting. It was marketed unequivocally as a 'British Drama of Daring, Courage and Adventure' based on truth.[74] Exclusive's *Tale of a City* (1949) was another featurette that blended realism and fiction. The city was Birmingham, and the tale fell uneasily between industrial documentary and crime melodrama. 'Badly acted, crudely dialogued and indifferently directed, it's not only a poor advertisement for one of our biggest industrial centres, but shabby entertainment,' complained *Kinematograph Weekly*.[75]

The drama-doc treatment usually lent itself well to the promotion of causes. With the election of a Labour Government, the British Co-operative movement seized the moment to publicise its origins with *Men of Rochdale* (1946), a thirty-eight-minute account of the movement's Lancashire pioneers and their battle against the treachery of small shopkeepers.[76] The CEA *Film Report*, never afraid to state the bleedin' obvious, warned exhibitors that 'the film has a distinct bias towards socialism', but reassured them that it 'does give a clear outline of a remarkable story of greatness from small beginnings'.[77] In 1949, Donald Taylor resumed the pre-war experiment of using film to spread the gospels with *Which Will Ye Have?*, a dramatisation of the events leading up to the Crucifixion that was a humble harbinger for the cycle of biblical epics soon to roll from the Hollywood studios. 'Religious subjects are usually considered unsuitable for the screen,' commented *Kinematograph Weekly*, 'but sincere and artistic direction, impressive acting and appropriate stage craft make this a worthy exception to the rule. Much can be gained spiritually and nothing lost commercially by allocating it a wide playing-time,' adding: 'We risk profanity by pointing out that it is quota.'[78] In 1951, the Welsh Festival of Britain Committee commissioned *David*, the story, told in flashback, of the life of an aged school caretaker (D. R. Griffiths) who had worked in the pits before an accident forced his retirement. Praised for presenting 'a completely honest picture of the Welsh way of life', the film played at the South Bank's Telekinema before being offered for general release, where its reception varied, largely according to region.[79]

By and large, the world of the featurette was a black-and-white one. Documentary shorts in colour had begun in the mid-1930s. The Coronation of George VI was filmed in Dufay Colour and theatrically released, as was the Co-op's musical revue, *Co-operette* (1938). The first Technicolor subjects had been shot by Jack Cardiff and his operator Chris Challis in 1938 when F. W. Keller, a German aristocrat, financed a series of ethnographic travelogues under the banner *World Window*. As we have seen, *Memphis Belle* was filmed in Technicolor in 1944. Post-war, however, British colour featurettes were effectively launched by *Steel* (1945), Verity Films' detailed study of metal manufacture that was distributed by 20th Century-Fox soon after VE-Day. Colour stock, though, was generally beyond the pocket of the commercial featurette-makers. In 1948 Eric Portman provided the commentary for Dan Fish's *Say It with Flowers* (1948), but although horticulture was a popular subject the trade reviewers surprisingly struggled to raise much enthusiasm.[80] There were also reservations about British Lion's slice of Empire exoticism *Drums for a Holiday* (1950). Directed by A. R. Taylor with music by Malcolm Arnold, it contained official Technicolor footage of the 1946 Ashanti Dunbar, with scenes of 'native chiefs paying homage to HM Government', which *Kinematograph Weekly* felt struck 'a deep and resounding patriotic note'. However, these spectacular sequences were padded out with dull scenes of the harvesting of cocoa beans. 'Cocoa is obviously not the correct beverage with which to toast the Crown,' commented *Kine* indignantly.[81] More critically approved was ABFD's *Montmartre* (1950), a top-of-the-range travelogue, decorated with lightly clad artists' models and showgirls, which justified its almost sixty-minute running time with sumptuous Technicolor photography, shot by Ian Craig under the guidance of the Oscar-winning Jack Cardiff.[82] The Technicolor camera moved on from the Sacré-Coeur to Rome's San Pietro for Hans Nieler's dignified study *The Vatican* (1950). Critical approval moved with it. Chromart colour was the process used for Richard Fisher's *Dollars to Spend* (1951), a jaunt by an American couple (Jeannette Finlay and Guy Taylor) across the south of England with cross-talk accompaniment; while Baze Colour was the chosen stock for Richard Fisher's *Call of the Land* (1952), a tribute to the beauties of Northern Ireland and featuring Margaret Crawford as one of them.

By the time of Queen Elizabeth's Coronation, documentary features in colour were regularly stretching beyond the limitations of the featurette. Among the plethora of audience-grabbing films celebrating the Coronation was Pathé's fifty-minute Warner-Color *Elizabeth Is Queen* (1953), greeted by one reviewer as 'A worthy record of one of the most tremendous moments in British history.'[83] Pathé compiled Eastman Color footage of the new monarch's tour of the Commonwealth for *Welcome The Queen!* (1954), and the royal visit to Africa, in which Her Majesty visited a leper colony, was recorded in Eastman Color in *Nigeria Greets Her Queen* (1956). *Kinematograph Weekly* was suitably awestruck: 'The Queen is, of course, the centre and her radiant personality casts a warm glow on every scene.'[84]

If Elizabeth II had any serious competition as a colour travelogue star, it was from the celebrity zoologist Michaela Dennis. She and husband Armand began to expand their work beyond the confines of low-resolution black-and-white television with *Armand and Michaela Denis Under the Southern Cross* (1955). This was a sixty-seven-minute Eastman Color record of their trek through the Australian outback, highlighting the exotic flora and fauna, and providing a leavening of comedy via the antics of Michaela's endearing pets. The film was the first of a series backed by Ealing Studios, and its production values – including especially composed music by James Stevens played by the London Symphony Orchestra – far exceeded those of the average 'B' film. The press book was not afraid to claim that 'this film would be superior in any category'. The intrepid naturalists moved on to the coast for *Armand and Michaela Denis on the Barrier Reef* (1955), filmed extensively underwater, and including the courtship of the hermit crab and disturbing scenes of the massacre of baby turtles. Within a few months, Mr and Mrs Denis found themselves *Among the Headhunters* (1955) in New Guinea. As the title suggested, the emphasis here was on anthropology, and the intention was to contrast 'The Beautiful and the Savage': 'It's not every day that a woman with hair the colour of the burning sun offers such temptation to a serious hunter and collector of heads. But Michaela's was not for shrinking!'[85]

These documentaries extended the boundaries of television while trading on its nascent star-making capacity. Sir Vivian Fuchs and Sir Edmund Hillary were already stars when they trekked to the South Pole, a journey recorded in Technicolor in the 1958 documentary *Antarctic Crossing*. The length of film exposed was nearly as long as the trek: nine miles edited down to 4,000 feet.

While colour photography was largely restricted to factual films, Apex's *The Blakes Slept Here* (1954) was a rare attempt to move the Technicolor featurette in a novel direction. Co-produced by John Martin and by Richard Massingham just prior to his death, the film was stylishly directed by Jacques Brunius and presented the biography of an English bourgeois family, told in a series of flash-backs narrated by Harcourt Williams and using period film footage. *Kinematograph Weekly* thoroughly recommended it as 'delightful little gem'.[86] As far as technical innovations were concerned, the short-lived three-dimensional craze that lasted from the Festival of Britain to just after the Coronation hardly impacted on British production. One exception was the musical featurette *Melody Lane* (1953), pro-duced by Danny Angel over seven days at the Gate Studios and directed by Lewis Gilbert in the spring of 1953. Max Bygraves headlined, with support from the Beverley Sisters and the TV Toppers. The film also included an extract from *Swan Lake* featuring the Sadlers Wells Ballet.[87]

Second Features

While the actuality featurettes made hay in the post-war sunshine, what had become of the British second feature? Surprisingly, it was being kept alive partly by the attentions of its sternest critics: the documentary movement. The length of films sponsored by the MoI during the war had increased steadily.[88] Roy Boulting's unflinching *Burma Victory* was released late in 1945, and the backlog of documentary footage shot during the war was still trickling into cinemas in early 1947. For example, *School for Danger* (1947), directed by Wing Commander E. Baird for the RAF Film Unit, was a sixty-eight-minute retrospective of the Special Operations Executive's work with the French Resistance. Shot in drama-doc style with non-professional actors, it received a respectful but cool reception from trade critics who were becoming impatient to move on to more frivolous matters.[89]

In 1948, the MoI's replacement, the Central Office of Information (COI), instituted an explicit policy of producing films designed to occupy a second-feature slot on the programmes of commer-cial cinemas. The new director of the COI's Films Division, John Grierson, was given a relatively free hand by Whitehall in terms of techniques of presentation. Mindful of the fact that the agreement forged with the CEA to screen COI films in public cinemas would expire at the end of the following year, he first launched a series of innovative featurettes for commercial distribution on a percentage basis. Films like *A Yank Comes Back*, budgeted at around £15,000, were expected 'to stand or fall on their entertainment and presentation merits', and to achieve between 800 and 1,500 bookings.[90] Based at the state-leased studios at Beaconsfield, the Crown Film Unit then launched a new 'features' division to make longer drama-documentaries that could be booked as supporting features. Philip Leacock directed *Life in Her Hands* (1951), an immaculately photographed and largely unsenti-mental promotion of the nursing profession, and *Out of True* (1951), a sober essay on the treatment of mental illness. *Consider Your Verdict* (1952), intended to show overseas audiences the working of British justice, was just about finished before the unit was closed down as part of the incoming Conservative Government's curb on public spending.

Although, in 1947, Britain had fifteen studios with fifty-one sound stages, most were beyond the pocket of producers of second features. A few small studios, however, did offer affordable opportunities.

One of the smallest, Marylebone, was a converted church hall off the Edgware Road that had been a production centre for the MoI during the war. Marylebone advertised its facilities with a mini version of *Othello* (1946) directed by David MacKane with John Slater as the Moor. The compression of Shakespeare's grand tragedy into forty-four minutes was achieved by using a narrator to join up the extracts. Marylebone's calling card was successful in attracting the custom of James Carreras's Exclusive films, which was resuming production after a ten-year break. H&S Films sponsored A. Digby Smith's debut feature *Escape Dangerous* (1950, working title *The House of Doctor Belhomme*) which, during its production in the spring of 1947, was lauded as an important contribution to the renaissance of the second feature after the war, although it had a long wait for release.[91] The picture was ambitious in its French Revolutionary setting and its depiction of guillotine and tumbrel, but stolid in all other respects. Given that it was written by the film critic Oswell Blakestone and featured the acting talents of film journalist Peter Noble and his wife Marianne Stone, it might have expected the reviewers to be kind in their judgments, but they were nothing of the sort. 'Indifferent direction; stilted portrayals; dull dialogue', complained *To-Day's Cinema*, and it was spot on.[92] Digby Smith abandoned plans for further 'B' films and retreated back to the relative safety of actuality featurettes. The Marylebone Studios also negotiated an Anglo-Irish co-production deal with independent producer Patrick McCrossan. The first fruits of the deal, *My Hands are Clay*, went on the floor in August 1947, directed by Lionel (Tommy) Tomlinson. Its story of a jealous Irish sculptor was vigorously promoted by distributors Monarch with the tagline: 'A terrible mad jealousy eating into his heart turned this young genius into a fiend bent on destruction.'

The tiny Kay's Film Studios at Carlton Hill in Maida Vale, an extension of Nettlefold, were another hothouse for programmers and featurettes. It was here that fly-by-night producer/director Frank Chisnell made *Jim the Penman* (1947), a slipshod treatment of the life of James Townsend Saward (played by radio star, Mark Dignam), the nineteenth-century barrister and forger. It was conceived as the first in a series called 'Crime Never Paid', to be adapted from the radio series 'Rogues and Vagabonds' but the scheduled second film on Jack the Ripper never materialised.[93] Another occasional producer/director, Randolf J. Thompson (a.k.a. Randolph Tomson), made the equally forgettable and forgotten *Chorus Girl* (1948), appropriately, a back-stage story of the struggle for success with newcomer Jacquelyn Dunbar in the title role.[94] Carlton Hill was also used by producer Arthur Dent to make his first supporting feature, the Robert Burns biopic *Comin' Thru' the Rye* (1947), embarrassingly directed by Walter C. Mycroft. But it was also at Carlton Hill that Mario Zampi, who had been kept in enforced idleness as an internee during the war, made a modest-but-promising return to film production (in spite of the bitter winter conditions) with the well-received locked-room mystery *The Phantom Shot* (1947). The film was innovative in explicitly inviting its audience to identify clues and make deductions. Zampi then made *The Fatal Night* (1948), the picture which introduced future *Avenger*, Patrick MacNee, and which *The Cinema* singled out as 'a 55-minute film of unusual excellence':

> With a handful of comparatively unknown players and one of the smallest studios in the country it has proved that a supply of first-class second-features could be maintained by men who know their jobs. *The Fatal Night* owes its success to taut scripting of a Michael Arlen story and to clarity of purpose in handling that script on the floor. It is obvious that second thoughts or interests have not been allowed to interfere with the film's completion, and the entire unit are to be congratulated on their effort to prove that good British films need be neither expensive nor elaborate.[95]

Associated British's Welwyn Studios were also used mainly for 'B' productions when Elstree reopened after wartime requisition. Most of the films were bottom of the barrel stuff made by Frank Chisnell. *Slick Tartan* (1949) was a witless and impoverished satire of *Dick Barton*,[96] while *Rover and Me* (1949) was a sentimental rural ramble involving Mr Maggott (Edward Rigby), a kindly old tramp who helps a boy and girl with a stray dog capture some smugglers. *It Happened in Soho* (1948) was burdened by a leaden and clichéd script, and was followed by *It Happened in Leicester Square* (1949), a dull procession of variety acts occasioned by the visit of a couple of Northern lads (Harry Tate and Slim Allen) to the West End. It was directed and distributed by Geoffrey Benstead, the film-maker responsible for some of the most mind-numbing pre-war quota quickies. It struggled for any bookings and, two years later, was smuggled out again, shorn of five minutes and retitled *Hello London* (1951).[97] By that time, however, Associated British had closed down Welwyn Studios, which were judged to be no longer economically viable.

The small studios offered extraordinary opportunities to inexperienced and first-time directors. Debutants included Peter Mills, who made the Cornish smuggling drama *Journey Ahead* (1947), and Michael C. Chorlton, who shot the black-market melodrama, *Late at Night* (1946) on a shoestring for Bruton Films.[98] It was a stereotypical story of a shady night club, a plucky reporter and a villain called 'The Spider' which immediately fell foul of the critics. Chorlton quickly edited the seventy-minute film down to a more convenient length and never made another. At Carlton Hill, Alan Cullimore had been a lowly assistant cameraman before he was given the chance to write and direct a slight clairvoyant comedy called *The Clouded Crystal* (1948) for Butcher's. Even the comic creativity of the young Frank Muir, however, failed to rescue this from incipient tedium. Another first-time feature director, Richard Gray, made two crime films at Carlton Hill during the same period, *Eyes That Kill* (1947) and the hardboiled *A Gunman Has Escaped* (1948), the story of three robbers on the run after shooting a passer-by. 'As timely as today's Headlines' announced the latter film's advertisements.[99] The film's press book was confident that John Harvey, the most prominent actor in a cast of unknowns, 'will speedily rise on the ladder of film fame'.[100] The future had other ideas.

Writing in the technician's monthly *Film Industry*, Gerald Landau made a plea for a new approach to the making of second features and featurettes, calling for more experimentation:

> Made on a low budget, the films would afford an opportunity to promising young technicians and unknown artists could gain invaluable experience before the camera. Between productions, the unit could be loaned to major companies intending to try out certain effects in their films, so that the technicians need not be kept idle at the Company's expense. There is another vital argument in favour of these films. Under the Quota Act some British shorts are being widely distributed to the detriment of the industry. Ill-conceived and shoddily produced, they are, for the most part treated with scorn by cinema patrons. They are bad and their badness reflects discredit upon our films generally. Yet, deprived of enough good British features, managers are forced to show them in order to comply with the law.[101]

Landau went on to recommend the proposal to 'Mr Rank', who promptly set up a 'B' film unit at Highbury Studios under John Croydon (see next chapter). The move seemed well timed when, in the late summer of 1947, the announcement of an *ad valorem* duty on imported American films immediately resulted in Hollywood studios withholding their products from distribution in Britain. The 'B' film studios of Marylebone, Carlton Hill, Highbury, Windsor and Viking were all regularly producing second features, and American distributors had once again begun to show interest in deals with independent producers.[102] 'Onlooker' in *To-Day's Cinema*, however, immediately sounded a warning of the danger of returning to the bad old days of the 1930s:

> Ever since the *ad valorem* duty was announced, I have heard those who have the interests of our production at heart bewailing the fact that the 'quickie' merchants were already getting busy. Now, they were saying, is a chance to slip in and make a little pile while the going is good. And now, the loyalists were echoing, we are going to lose most of the good work that was put in to make British films the best in the world. The only fortunate thing I can see about it all is that major studio space is closed to these get-rich-quick people.[103]

By the end of the year, the 'get-rich-quick people' had nine second features in post-production, four in production and four planned at British studios: a total of seventeen.[104] It was hardly a quota-quickie invasion, and the numbers were small in comparison with featurette production. Renown alone had nine featurettes in its New Year programme. For *Film Industry* reporter Paul Nugat, the Hollywood export embargo was a chance for the smaller studios to stop trying to ape the output of larger production units and to 'break fresh ground by selecting stories that primarily probe the depths of British character and life in an intimate, discerning way'.[105] In response, Concord Productions, a unit recruited by director Jay Lewis when he was demobbed from the AKS and composed almost entirely of ex-servicemen, made *A Man's Affair* (1948) about a couple of miners on holiday in Ramsgate who meet Joan Dowling and glamorous Diana Decker.[106] However, the embargo also brought forth a rash of re-issues from companies like Grand National and Equity British, including some ancient quota quickies like *Death Drives Through* (1934).[107]

Quota Films Registered 1938–48[108]

Quota year	Triple	Double	Single	Exhibitor's credit 3–4,000 ft	Exhibitor's credit over 4,000 ft	Total
1938–9	10	21	47	8	17	103
1939–40	6	20	57	8	17	108
1940–1	3	19	21	7	15	65
1941–2	7	15	15	2	7	46
1942–3	8	20	17	7	10	62
1943–4	21	11	14	17	7	70
1944–5	18	11	12	19	7	67
1945–6	17	7	15	38	6	83
1946–7	26	9	9	55	8	107
1947–8	43	6	8	45	20	122
Total	159	139	215	206	114	833

An important boost to the re-issue of films had been provided in the spring of 1947 when the Hyam brothers, the owners of a chain of cinemas in inner London, had taken over Anglo-American Film Distributors and a catalogue of over a hundred pictures. Their new company was named Eros (after the famous Piccadilly statue close to the company's offices), and it would become a significant player in the British 'B' film market over the following decade. It was quickly successful in getting its quota pictures – including some from Australia – adopted by the major circuits. Eros began to establish a presence in low-budget production in 1949. Its policy was to seek out vehicles for stars and characters of proven popular appeal: Eleanor Summerfield, who had made an impact in *London Belongs to Me* (1948), starred with Terence de Marney in the boxing thriller *No Way Back*; radio's Valentine Dyall in *Vengeance is Mine*;[109] Terry-Thomas in *Melody Club*; and the famous *Daily Mirror* cartoon character, Jane, in *The Adventures of Jane* (all 1949). However, it was a cast of unknowns from Glasgow's Unity Theatre that attracted the most plaudits in *The Gorbals Story* (1950). *To-Day's Cinema* hailed this tale of struggle in tenement slums as a 'Stand-out specimen of British screencraft, worthy of wide presentation ... a picture that will be remembered when most of to-day's offerings are long forgotten.'[110] Unfortunately, it now appears to be not only forgotten but lost. Eros became the regular distributors of the Tempean films that pretty well set the standards for 'B' production in the 1950s, and later pioneered the exploitation double bill.

In June 1948, the new Films Act, for the first time, distinguished between first features and their supporting programme, establishing differential exhibitors' quota targets for each. It set the quota for first features at a challenging 45 per cent, but reduced that to 25 per cent for the supporting programme (which included shorts). One in four exhibitors was already defaulting before the increase, so the new legislation risked wholesale evasion by independent exhibitors.[111] The ACT union complained that the second-feature quota had been set too low.[112] However, 1,381 defaulting exhibitors in the first year disagreed. The vast majority of these were independents: the Odeon, Gaumont and ABC circuits managed to exceed the quota by showing an average 31 per cent of British films in their supporting programmes with only one defaulter. Overall, the average proportion of British films shown on the supporting programme was a healthy 27 per cent.[113] In line with the new General Agreement on Tariffs and Trade (GATT), the Act also abolished the renters' quota. The immediate consequence of this was significantly to reduce the flow of American capital into British production. There was no longer any necessity for the American distribution companies to make or acquire British films.

The new Association of British Film Producers announced that its dozen or so members would be able to make very little contribution to meeting the supply of films necessary for the quota while the current distribution conditions prevailed.[114] The Association quickly began to explore the possibility of securing booking guarantees from at least half the independent exhibitors to finance production. A few days later, Harold Wilson, worried by 'the grave danger' of independent production 'coming to a stop', announced the launch a new National Film Finance Corporation (NFFC) with £5 million to lend film producers via distributors.[115] The immediate intention of the scheme was to bail out the ailing British Lion, which secured a million-pound loan, but there was also help for 'B' film producer Exclusive, which received £20,000. Potentially, the NFFC was a tool to ensure that there were sufficient supporting features for exhibitors to meet the 25 per cent quota; but, unfortunately, the scheme's two most influential decision-makers – its chairman Lord Reith and his adviser, Sir Michael Balcon – had rather different priorities. While loans would continue to be made to producers of 'B' films, securing them would become increasingly dependent on meeting the expectations of

Reith and Balcon. As Sue Harper and Vincent Porter have revealed: 'By 1951, the NFFC was clearly acting as a pre-production censor. Over half the projects that it rejected were refused because it considered their scripts or their subjects to be artistically or ethically unacceptable.'[116] Consequently, despite having an immaculate record in paying back its loans, Exclusive was soon excluded from the scheme (officially on the grounds that it was now able to raise its own finance).

In spite of the NFFC initiative, independent and low-budget production activities remained in the doldrums while circuit distribution deals were so difficult to secure in advance and studio costs continued to rise. The stages of most of the studios that relied on smaller, independent productions were empty or closed.[117] Producer Horace Shepherd placed the blame firmly on government policy and the 'cock-eyed' Quota Acts:

> The new Act extends the same pernicious 'Cost Clause' to shorts and second features. Still scorning economy and efficiency, they seek to compel the producer to incur more and more cost with no means of recovering it. At the same time they have destroyed both his market and his distribution by wiping out renters' quota. Meanwhile, shorts pour in from America with no opposition, British supporting feature production programmes have to be abandoned, while first feature production from the independents has long since ceased altogether.[118]

As Shepherd correctly observed, while both the 1938 and 1948 Acts insisted on a minimum spend by film-makers, they failed to guarantee a minimum percentage return to films booked on the supporting programme. The Association of Specialised Film Producers also warned the trade of a looming production crisis unless a 'co-operative plan' for production, distribution and exhibition could be developed. Producers were handicapped by the low rates accorded to second features: 'no producer can gamble £30,000 on a second feature of quality unless he can be assured that on finding a distributor he can recover his production costs, let alone make a profit'.[119] Evidence given to the Government's Portal Committee by the ACT union confirmed the poor rate of return for second features. Although distribution on the major circuits had become the key to any chance of 'B' film profitability, even here, the rates were far from advantageous. The ABC circuit paid £25 for a weekly booking, and the Odeon only £22.10s. The union concluded that: 'It is impossible to foresee any future for good quality British second features, shorts and cartoons as long as this miserable price prevails.'[120] While returns remained derisory, studio costs for second features continued to escalate, from an average of £284 per screen minute in 1947 to £374 in 1948 following substantial increases in labour costs, materials and studio rental charges.[121] Briefly, the solution seemed to lie in an alliance between independent exhibitors and film-makers, and a consortium of exhibitors was looking to use the new studios at Paignton to produce their own films.[122]

In fact, the Labour Government, encouraged by the ACT, was seriously considering taking some of these studios into public ownership, and had set up the Gater Committee to see if this solution was needed and viable. In November 1948, it reported in the negative.[123] By the New Year, Nettlefold Studios at Walton were facing closure and appealing to the BFPA for work.[124] Happily, George Minter answered the call with a new *Old Mother Riley* film, but February saw almost three-quarters of the country's studios and more than half its total floor space idle. Only two of the studios used for second features, Viking and Merton Park, remained in use.[125] Producer Derrick de Marney (soon to start work on *No Way Back*) clearly saw the crisis as an opportunity to get rid of the irresponsible 'get-rich-quick people' and their quickies once and for all, proposing a film-making 'closed shop'. It was the sort of monopolistic proposal that would no doubt have found favour with Rank and ABPC:

> A responsible feature producer should be in a position to be able to use his own technicians or contract a good smaller producer to supply programme pictures to go with his feature ... This would soon exclude the intrusion of individuals seeking quick profits without holding any permanent stake in the industry. The distributors could help by arranging better terms for this sort of product and the exhibitors, by allocating a fairer percentage to that side of the programme.[126]

Like de Marney, the CEA was concerned about the general low quality of many British films, and published a breakdown of the ninety features released between 1 April 1948 and 25 January 1949. Of these, thirty-two were judged 'Definitely second features unacceptable to the USA market' (category B) and a further twelve were classified as merely fill-ups to complete a programme (category C). The list of 'second features' included four films with running times of over ninety minutes (*Cup-Tie Honeymoon, Holidays with Pay, Calling Paul Temple, The Story of Shirley Yorke*) and one estimated to have cost £78,000 (*Things Happen at Night*) an expenditure that no supporting feature could hope to recoup. The remainder were as follows:

CEA Classification of British Feature Films, 1 April 1948–25 January 1949[127]

Title	Producer	Length in feet	Estimated cost in £
B			
The Fool and the Princess	Merton Park	4,554	30,000
The Fatal Night	Anglofilm	4,452	15,000
A Sister to Assist 'Er	Bruton/W.L. Tritel	5,090	15,000
Penny and the Pownall Case	Production Facilities	4,229	22,000
The Last Load	Elstree Independent	5,107	13,000
Trinity House	Ace Distributors (A–B)	4,611	3–4,000
Trouble in the Air	Production Facilities	4,858	22,000
A Song for Tomorrow	Production Facilities	5,519	25,000
House of Darkness	International Motion Pictures	6,980	20,000
Secrets of the North	National Film Board of Canada	5,272	
The Clouded Crystal	A. Grossman	5,102	12,000
My Hands are Clay	Dublin Films	5,423	10,000
The Monkey's Paw	Kaye Film Printing	5,779	14,000
A Gunman Has Escaped	Condon Film Productions	5,210	11,000
The Dark Road	Marylebone Studios	6,668	12,000

Title	Producer	Length in feet	Estimated cost in £
It Happened in Soho	FC Film Productions	4715	
Loco. Number One	EFD Ltd	4,054	
Colonel Bogey	Production Facilities	4,620	24,000
Fly Away Peter	Production Facilities	5,380	21,000
Love in Waiting	Production Facilities	5,338	20,000
Date With a Dream	Tempean Films	5,000	8,500
A Piece of Cake	Production Facilities	4,144	20,000
The Peaceful Years	Pathé A–B	5,749	
Panic at Madame Tussauds	Vandyke Film Corporation	4,472	
Operation Diamond	Cine Industrial	4,870	
International Circus Review	Film Studios (Manchester)	4,000	
Badgers Green	Production Facilities	5,502	
C		All under 4,000	
To the Public Danger	Production Facilities		
Warden of the Wild	Gaumont British Instructional		
The Connors Case	National Film Board of Canada		
Escape From Broadmoor	International Motion Pictures		
Tale of a City	Baze Productions		
Say it with Flowers	Dorothy M. Fish		
It's No Tale	Sybil Leslie		
Showground of the North	Film Studios (Manchester)		
All in a Day's Work	Great Western		
Elizabeth Takes a Holiday	Instructional Entertainment		
A Million and One	Select Classic		
A Yank Comes Back	Crown Film Unit		

Effectively, the absolute upper limit for supporting-feature production was £25,000, and to spend this would require a circuit distribution deal and overseas sales. The upper limit without such a deal was probably £15,000, and this would require a product that might play in some theatres as a co-, or even a first, feature. However, this became easier to achieve with a 45 per cent first-feature quota and a relatively low level of British production. A very modestly budgeted film might well play in quota-strapped independent halls as a main attraction, providing it could display some evident elements of audience appeal. It was often an association with BBC radio that offered the opportunity for the low-budget film to improve its status. *The Twenty Questions Murder Mystery* (1950) was a classic example: made at the tiny Southall Studios, this Pendennis production starred Robert Beatty, Rona Anderson and the cast of the radio panel game *Twenty Questions*. It was Exclusive, though, that were the masters of producing this kind of product, often adapted from radio. Early in 1950, senior executive James Carreras revealed that most of the company's films played 1,500 venues, of which 600 gave the pictures top billing.[128] Most of the output of Mancunian Films was achieved on budgets (around £25,000) and with production values that most other studios would have regarded as suitable for second features, but the comedians picked to star in these films commanded such a following in the North and Midlands that the pictures were usually booked as first features (and were of standard first-feature length). For example, *Over the Garden Wall* (1950), starring Norman Evans, played the Granada circuit with additional dates on the Odeon and ABC circuits, including prestigious seaside resort venues. Total bookings were around 1,500.[129] Mancunian announced that three Frank Randall films released in the early 1950s had received 5,296 bookings in the UK, averaging 1,765 per film.[130] Even Associated British's *Take Me to Paris* (1951), with a meagre running time of sixty-six minutes, had a sporting chance of topping the bill, as it starred the popular Yorkshire comedian Albert Modley, even if he was out of his element in this screen caper.

The Committee of Inquiry set up by the Board of Trade into the diminution in production (the Plant Inquiry), which reported in November 1949, estimated the total pot of money available for second features and shorts at flat-rate rentals at only £470,000 per annum. At Viking Films, the managing director's own estimate of the budget limit for a film that would play only as a second feature was £8,000.[131] For the Plant Report, however, this was not a significant problem because any shortage of supporting feature product could be made up by the annual twenty to thirty 'failed' first features. The Association of Specialist Film Producers took particular exception to this:

> The planning and production of good British supporting films ... should not be a by-product of the first feature film industry – a kind of sump into which failures can flow and earn at least a few pounds towards their cost. Nor should it be the opportunity for reissued first features after the expiry of their first feature quota life ... So long as the two-picture programme remains, the making of long supporting films of, say, 6,000 feet in length, should be regarded as a special and important part of British film production and their place in the cinema programmes should be properly catered for and given full consideration from the creative, technical and entertainment viewpoints.[132]

The basic rules for economical production were set out by John Argyle, a veteran of the quota quickies who had since achieved considerable success at marketing budget films abroad: 'Reduce studio rental to a minimum, shooting a third of the picture on location against natural backgrounds, use one stage at a small studio only for essential interiors, keep total schedule down to 25 days, and have a polished, precise, pre-planned and sound script to work with from the first day of production.'[133] However, as studio costs rose, enterprising independent film-makers began to explore the alternative of shooting entirely outside the studio in factual settings. The trend had begun in spring 1947 when W. Howard-Borer's Unicorn Films experimented with using a Hertfordshire mansion for interiors on Oscar Burns' *Castle Sinister* (1947).[134] The experiment was successful enough for it to become a widespread strategy which influenced not only production practices, but also the type of film made by the smaller independents. Harry Reynolds's grandly titled International Motion Pictures operated a 'house-a-film' policy, using a string of rural retreats to make 'old dark house' pictures like Oswald Mitchell's *House of Darkness* (1948) and *The Man From Yesterday* (1949) which gave early starring roles to Laurence Harvey (formerly Larry Skikne).[135] For the latter film, a story of spiritualism and murder, the unit rented a large mansion near Bushey Studios for £25 per week, a considerable saving on the fees charged by even a small studio.[136] Another independent producer, Roger Proudlock of Vandyke Productions, explained the benefits to be gained:

> In the first place it undoubtedly cuts costs as much as 25 per cent. Thus it is possible to obtain much greater production value on the screen than would be the case in studio production on the same budget. An obvious example of this is that most large houses, suitable for film purposes, have enormous halls and stairways. To achieve these in the studio would demand great space and cost much money. Another advantage is that once a house has been rented, it is possible to start rehearsing artists immediately and the director can work out his set-ups, which may save a great deal of time once shooting has commenced. Finally, there is the peculiar psychological reaction among the unit which is most marked. Artists and technicians have an *esprit de corps* which I have not yet noticed in any studio. They seem to feel they are working on a worthwhile adventure, the success of which they really have to heart.[137]

Director-screenwriter John Gilling agreed that it was the only way that British low-budget film-makers could 'compete with their American counterparts in the matter of production value and the variety of settings employed', but admitted that working with factual backgrounds was 'at least half as tough again as directing a picture in a studio': 'The planning and visualisation of set-ups is too frequently accompanied by a frustrating succession of compromises between the director's ideas and the technicians' abilities to carry them out.'[138] However, this had to be set against the very real gains in verisimilitude: 'On the score of realism, the factual background method has it every time. Our job, whether we are doing it at Pinewood or a house in Battersea, is to illustrate life as it is, not to streamline it out of all recognition.'[139]

Filming away from the studio also had certain other benefits that were less often mentioned. Alfred Church, the studio manager at Bushey, pointed out that it was not unheard of for minimum union rates and crewing levels to be quietly ignored: 'By going into a big house ... and working with the minimum that a producer finds necessary, pictures can be made profitably ... and the unions don't have anything to say about it!'[140] With 25 per cent of technicians unemployed, it seems that blind eyes were turned towards irregular productions made discreetly away from studio floors. Work, after all, was work. Exclusive sought the best of both worlds by converting country mansions into semi-permanent studios with considerable success. In 1949 only fifteen second features were made at established British studios: five at Walton, five at Southall and one each at Brighton, Gate, Marylebone, Merton Park and Viking. However, a further six were completed by Exclusive/Hammer at their country house studios, while a few others were shot entirely on location.[141] The trend towards factual locations was extended to a floating studio by *The Girl is Mine* (1950), a British Lion featurette which was (unusually) produced and directed by two women: Freda Stock (producer), who had been a writer with Gaumont British, and Marjorie Deans (director), whose experience in script-editing included *Major Barbara* (1941). The cast included Patrick MacNee, Pamela

Deeming and Lionel Murton, and the small unit was largely composed of technicians with the kind of newsreel experience needed to cope with the demands of location shooting on a naval pinnace with natural exteriors at its moorings at Twickenham and along the Thames. Appropriately enough, the feel-good story by Freda's husband, Ralph Stock, was about the crew's ability to overcome the problems caused by extortionate rates charged to keep the boat afloat. These were familiar problems for any independent producer.[142] In this instance, however, help is provided by an American (Murton), which was perhaps prophetic of the coming importance to the British film industry of production finance from the USA.

In 1950, with no sign of a significant recovery in production, the Board of Trade's President, Harold Wilson, was finally forced to concede that the high first-feature quota was not working and adjusted it to 30 per cent. But he rejected the recommendation of the Cinematograph Films Council (CFC) that the supporting-programme quota should be reduced, and left it untouched at 25 per cent. The reaction in the north-west of England, traditionally a hostile zone for the output of London's 'B' film factories, was swift. In Manchester, where twice-weekly changes of programme were still the norm, three-quarters of exhibitors had already defaulted on the supporting feature quota, and now called for the CFC's 15 per cent recommendation to be honoured.[143] Other CEA branches soon rallied in support. Exhibitors defaulting on their supporting feature quota reached 2,195 in 1949–50, almost as many (2,335) as those defaulting on the much higher first-feature quota. Even the major circuits managed only 24 per cent in respect of the supporting-feature quota.[144] Prosecutions remained few and far between, and convictions difficult to secure. The New Regent of Ladywood, Birmingham, a 600-seat cinema which had applied unsuccessfully for quota relief, was initially fined £50 (with 13 guineas costs) for showing only 8.6 per cent of British supporting films. However, the cinema's basic defence – that British films were 'useless' for screening to a clientele that demanded 'Western action films, slapstick or rough stuff' – was accepted on appeal and the conviction quashed.[145]

The number of supporting-feature defaulters continued to rise to 2,340 in 1950–1. This represented half of all cinemas. Producers were particularly concerned that the increase in defaulters was in spite of a constant level of supply during this period:

Year	Second features	Shorts
1949	48	184
1950	50	232
1951	49	222

It seemed to the Association of Specialised Film Producers that the law designed to protect the livelihoods of its members was being increasingly flouted with impunity. Not surprisingly, the Association called for a Board of Trade inquiry, a move that, equally predictably, whipped up a storm of protest at the CEA summer conference.[146]

Despairing of a genuine upturn in production, and disappointed at the government's failure to nationalise elements of film production and distribution, the technicians' union eventually determined to form its own film-making co-operative. ACT Films was announced at the union's AGM in April 1950. The Board of Directors included Anthony Asquith, Sidney Cole and Ralph Bond. It was intended that the new co-op would make a series of modestly budgeted first features with support from the National Film Finance Corporation. Instead, ACT quickly became a regular producer of 'B' films.

The production crisis at last began to abate in the summer of 1950 with agreement on the Eady Levy, which would plough a small sum per cinema seat sold back into production.[147] Six months later, however, circuit bookers were still reporting a worrying shortage of second features: 'We are often at our wits' end to find proper support for our major feature. Our concern has not been just fulfilment of quota but to balance a programme at all. In the event, we have had to fall back on two-reelers and the like.'[148] Distributors Monarch turned in desperation to the worthy Australian scientific drama *Strong Is the Seed* (1950) about the life's work of William Farrer (Guy Doleman) to eradicate the dreaded rust disease in wheat. The review in *To-Day's Cinema* did not try to pretend that 'Britishers will become passionately worked up about such an issue', but at least it was food for the supporting-feature quota at a time of famine.[149] Arrow distributors could even expect bookings for *Fake's Progress* (1950), an artless piece of slapstick, amateurishly directed by Ken Fairburn, in which a clerk is initiated into the techniques of spivery. Future-Goon Harry Secombe provided a commentary, but the debacle was still dismissed by *Kinematograph Weekly* as a candidate for the worst film ever 'put out in the name of quota'.[150]

Among the renters, perhaps the company most guilty of offering a shoddy diet to exhibitors was H&S Films. During 1950, H&S maintained a steady stream of forgettable featurettes like *Father to Son* (a study of traditional craftsmanship) and *Round Rainbow Corner*, Link Neale's nostalgic look at GIs in Piccadilly during the war, padded out with a bit of dog-racing and ice hockey. 'The talent is indifferently presented and the editing and commentary are even worse,' was *Kinematograph Weekly's* caustic comment on this 'dreary Museum piece'.[151] Certainly, the output of H&S revived memories of the quota quickies of old. In fact, some of the company's reissues *were* the quota quickies of old, including John Mills' horsewhipping melodrama *The Lash* (1934). Just in case this might have over-stimulated its audiences, H&S calmed them down again with Link Neale's *Keep Moving* (1951). The title might have sounded lively enough, but it spent most of its thirty-six minutes discussing the storage and purification of water.[152]

For small exhibitors, fulfilling the supporting-feature quota was made more difficult by some renters' attempts to persuade them to take, as main attractions, films that had played on the circuits as second features. Such films were often all these exhibitors could afford as audiences started to decline, but they were left with very few products available to book for their supporting programmes. Second-feature production shortages continued in the quota year 1951–2. Only fifty-eight films were available, and twenty-three of these were 3,500 feet or below, and therefore unsuitable for independent exhibitors requiring double bills. Rank's John Davis stated categorically: 'The number of second feature British films to satisfy the market is inadequate.'[153] A year later, a report on the period from the national bookers committee of the CEA suggested that most British supporting features had little box-office appeal. The report surveyed 2,000 cinemas of all types and asked managers to place each film in one of six categories of box-office appeal.

Box-office Appeal of (Second) Feature Films Registered by the Board of Trade as British from 1 April 1951 to 31 March 1952[154]

E = excellent business; AB = above average; A = average; B = below average; P = poor; VP = very poor							
Title	**Distributor**	**Grading expressed as a percentage of total appraisals**					
Second features		E	AB	A	B	P	VP
No Resting Place	ABFD			5	30	40	25
Here's to the Memory	AB-Pathé		32	49	13	6	
Penny Points to Paradise	Adelphi			23	16	29	32
Death is a Number	Adelphi			18	32	36	14
The Kilties are Coming	Adelphi			28	8	40	24
I Was a Dancer	Adelphi				9	36	55
Assassin for Hire	Anglo-Amalgamated		4	40	24	28	4
Mystery Junction	Anglo-Amalgamated		5	45	15	30	5
Chelsea Story	Apex		11	21	26	21	21
African Jim (SA)	Apex			7	26	20	47
Cheer the Brave	Apex		9	14	18	36	23
The Armchair Detective	Apex			17	28	33	22
Blind Man's Bluff	Apex			35	20	35	10
The Kangaroo Kid (Au)	Apex			35	35	25	5
The Magic Garden (SA)	British Lion	5		10	24	18	43
Sing Along With Me	British Lion				8	27	65
There Is Another Sun	Butcher's	3	3	28	30	30	6
The Scarlet Thread	Butcher's		6	28	16	31	19
Madam Louise	Butcher's			35	19	38	8
Salute the Toff	Butcher's		4	44	20	28	4
Home to Danger	Eros			26	26	37	11
The Six Men	Eros			19	19	47	15
13 East Street	Eros	4	7	26	37	26	
The Frightened Man	Eros	9	13	22	35	8	13
The Dark Light	Exclusive			5	19	52	24
Black Widow	Exclusive		8	13	21	33	25
Cloudburst	Exclusive	3	3	30	30	19	15

Title	Distributor	Grading expressed as a percentage of total appraisals					
Second features		E	AB	A	B	P	VP
A Case for PC 49	Exclusive			29	39	26	6
Death of an Angel	Exclusive		4	26	22	35	13
Whispering Smith Hits London	Exclusive		19	37	16	19	9
Two on the Tiles	Grand National			17	22	35	26
Four Days	Grand National			22	36	28	14
Myrte and the Demons	H&S		25		25		50
Night Was Our Friend	Monarch		4	21	16	46	13
Life in Her Hands	UA		5	24	19	28	24
Featurettes							
Mirth and Melody	20th Century-Fox				9	27	64
Africa Wakes	Adelphi			29	28	29	14
Harvest of Sunshine	Archway			20	40	40	
Tiffy	Arrow			20		40	40
Norwegian Holiday	British Lion	20	30	40	10		
Madeira Story	Butcher's			40	10	40	10
Dollars to Spend	Butcher's			28	14	44	14
Land of My Fathers	DUK			50		17	33
Across Deep Waters	Famous				25	75	
The Case of the Missing Scene	GFD					20	80
Trek to Mashomba	GFD			50		25	25
Looking for Trouble	GFD				12	38	50
The Man with the Twisted Lip	Grand National				6	37	57
Keep Moving	H&S					33	67
Tales of Two Cities	New Realm			25	17	58	
A Willing Horse	New Realm			14		72	14
No Sail	New Realm			14	29	57	
Beyond the Heights	New Realm		22	56	11	11	
Playing the Game Down Under	New Realm				20	20	60
London Entertains	New Realm			20	30	30	20
Out of True	Regent				29	71	
David	Regent		10	40	10	10	30
Waters of Time	Regent		17			50	33

Faced with this choice, the management of the Plaza in Stockton-on-Tees, County Durham, threw in the towel and showed only 3.5 per cent of quota films in its supporting programme. Moreover, its attitude towards Board of Trade investigations was totally unco-operative: 'They had snapped their fingers at the Board and had given no particulars or information of value to assist inquiries.' During the successful prosecution, representatives of several distributors gave evidence that their quota films had been rejected by the cinema. In defence, managing director Frederick Ewing said: 'I tried to pick out the best British films and take a chance with them, but in most cases I came unstuck.' The Plaza's patrons were 'very choosy' about second features and were not prepared to put up with any 'rubbish'.[155]

The gathering storm broke at the 1952 CEA summer conference, where one distinguished delegate described the supporting-feature quota as 'a filthy racket' designed to peddle 'trash' to exhibitors and extract money from the Eady fund, while another advocated militant rejection of legal obligations. He appealed to fellow exhibitors to put the entertainment interests of their patrons first, and to keep 'B' films that are unworthy of being labelled 'British' off their screens.[156] One that rallied to the cause was the Sussex exhibitor A. R. Gordon, who took a 'personal stand' against the monstrous regiment of quota quickies: 'I refuse to show films of poor quality. Many of to-day's second-features are rubbish. The public will not stand for them and neither will I.'[157] His CEA branch was fully in sympathy, calling for a 10 per cent supporting-feature quota and insisting that Eady money should not be wasted on 'rubbishy second-features'.[158] This really was fighting talk, but the Film Council were unmoved, and remained committed to the 25 per cent supporting quota. They were probably quietly confident that the Eady Levy was beginning to have a marked effect in improving the quality of second features, a judgment supported by Sussex's neighbours the Kent CEA branch, which cited Anglo-Amalgamated, Apex and Exclusive as making genuine improvements in their output.[159] Generally, however, the CEA remained suspicious that the money raised from their patrons was being ploughed into cut-price productions which they would not appreciate.[160]

By this time, though, the work of the producers' organisations was beginning to bear fruit. The Board of Trade was coming under increasing pressure to take determined action on quota defaulters and, more particularly, to purge its advisory body, the Film Council, of members representing defaulting cinemas. As if to demonstrate official resolve, a prosecution was brought against one of the West End flagships of the Rank empire, the Gaumont, Haymarket, which, while exceeding its first-feature quota, had shown less than half of the supporting-feature quota in 1950–1. Humiliatingly, J. Arthur Rank himself was obliged to appear in court to explain his company's lapse. His defence was the familiar one that there were not enough good British second features and that it was commercially impractical to show bad ones.[161] J. Arthur had the last laugh when the case was dismissed by the Chairman of the Metropolitan Magistrates who roundly criticised the Board of Trade for bringing a 'mischievous proceeding'.[162] The case provoked a biliously hysterical editorial in *The Cinema*:

> [T]he combination of Quota and Eady has re-animated the production of Quota Quickies ... [T]he serious question of the moment is should quota be modified to include only *meritorious* British films or should it be considerably reduced until the industry as a whole has its feet on firm ground again? *The Act must be modified.*[163]

In truth, however, the worst of the production shortage was already over. Supporting-programme defaulters were down in 1951–2 from 2,340 to 1,901, and the average showing for British films on the supporting programme was a respectable 24 per cent, helped in no small part by the major circuits which showed an impressive 29.5 per cent.[164]

The Yanks Are Coming (Again)

In part, this upturn was a consequence of an injection of American cash, personnel and know-how. United Artists stumbled onto the field of British 'B' movie distribution with Godfrey Grayson's *The Fake* (1953), in which Dennis O'Keefe played an American shamus on the trail of a painting stolen from the Tate Gallery. There being little to note in terms of direction or performance (although Cedric William's low-key photography was effective), critical praise was largely reserved for the film's authentic London locations. Encouraged by the new Eady fund, MGM British began producing its own curtain-raisers, rather superior supporting features designed to form packages with the company's Hollywood product. An early example was the comedy-thriller *The Hour of 13* (1952), an affectionately nostalgic revisiting of the tradition of the Victorian gentleman thief, which presented the sort of foggy, horse-drawn-hansom London entirely familiar to American audiences. Hollywood's Peter Lawford and Dawn Addams led a cast which included a wealth of home-grown talent like Derek Bond, Leslie Dwyer and Michael Hordern. It was efficiently directed by Harold French. *Time Bomb*

Pointing the direction for British second features: Glen Ford in MGM's *Time Bomb* (1953)

(1953), directed by Ted Tetzlaff and starring Glenn Ford and Anne Vernon, quickly followed. This story of a Canadian engineer called upon to defuse a saboteur's bomb on a goods train was a slickly made suspense thriller with a twist in the tail that really pointed the direction for British second features over the next decade. Its compact story, clear narrative trajectory, convincing location work and engaging central performance augmented with entertaining character studies, all provided a template for smaller British production outfits looking to give their films some international appeal.

One such enterprising company was Hammer/Exclusive, which began to forge co-production and distribution deals with American independents. Deals like these transformed the economics of 'B' production, enabling higher budgets facilitated by overseas earnings and improved domestic booking prospects. Such deals invariably involved the importation of Hollywood actors to play leading roles. Hammer director Francis Searle had no illusions about the use of American actors, claiming that US distributors would say, '"You put him in the film and we'll buy it." So whether they fitted the casting or not didn't matter. We just had to twist everything around to fit the artist.'[165] This transatlantic turn caused Derrick de Marney, who was seeking a distribution contract to make his adaptation of the best-selling *A Chorus of Echoes*, to remark sourly: 'If I were to import three American stars and were to alter my script to make it un-British I would not have any difficulty about distribution at all ... I cannot alter my script to make it suitable for Americans, and the number of stars I employ is naturally governed by my budget.'[166]

His frustrations were shared, not only by colleagues in the film industry, but some tabloid journalists who viewed the prioritising of American talent as an affront to national pride. Ray Nunn of the *Daily Sketch*, for example, after watching the filming of Hammer's motor-racing thriller at Goodwood, complained about the casting of Richard Conte and fellow American Mari Aldon in the leading roles: 'I thought what an ideal story and setting it would make for British stars. But Hammer had other ideas ... It was galling to see the camera film close-ups of Conte seated at the controls of a racing car – and then see Britain's Geoffrey Taylor double for him in the action scenes.'[167] Plots and dialogue were also Americanised, so that the US press book for Hammer's *The Saint's Return* (1953), released by RKO in America as *The Saint's Girl Friday*, reassured exhibitors that 'a competent Hollywood director' had been engaged 'to make certain there would be no heavy British accents to bother American audiences'. A picture like Hammer's plodding *Face the Music* (1954, USA: *Black Glove*) seemed like a Los Angeles private eye story transposed to London, complete with forced wise-cracking exchanges and women regularly referred to as 'chicks'. Even its American trumpeter protagonist (Hollywood's Alex Nicol, playing dubbed by Kenny Baker) appeared to be a firm nod to Michael Curtiz's *Young Man with a Horn* (1950, UK: *Young Man of Music*). Its climax was set at the London Palladium, but to those who, like Anthony Asquith, had struggled long and hard to establish an indigenous industry that was culturally British, this was a betrayal of their hopes. Not so the film's producer, Michael Carreras, a jazz enthusiast who can be seen playing in Nicol's band. Sometimes the critics seemed blind to the Americanness of these crime films. Hammer's *Women Without Men* (1956) – a women's prison story of the type favoured by American exploitation cinema – boasted the charms of Hollywood 'B' queen, Beverley Michaels, but a trade review could still describe it as 'Altogether one of those characteristically British productions whose familiarity is as comforting as the sight of an all-night bus on a rainy night in Clapham.'[168]

With the injection of American cash and talent, re-issues, which had been a crucial part of the staple diet of the circuits in 1951, began to disappear.[169] The BFPA claimed that in the four months

A young man with a horn: Alex Nicol in *Face the Music* (1954)

beginning 1 October 1952, forty-one second features over 5,000 feet in length had been completed, a substantial increase on the same period in the previous year. They also pointed to the growing number of circuit bookings as evidence of the increasing quality of production effected with the help of the Levy fund.[170] However, there was still disquiet about poor British quota films among exhibitors, as the new president of the CEA, J. W. Davies, made clear: 'For many of our members, quota is more than a problem, it is a running sore which weakens them in their battle against falling attendances.'[171] There were also some very gloomy clouds on the horizon as far as the producers of second features were concerned. In September 1953, the MGM Chairman, Sam Eckman, predicted the early demise of the double bill as the Hollywood studios concentrated their resources on fewer and longer films, and the circuits attempted to confine their programmes to two-and-a-half hours.[172] Of course, the death of the double bill had been announced many times over the previous twenty years, and smaller studios were quick to cast doubts on this latest declaration, but its plot of earth was gradually being prepared. A combination of widescreen extravagance and the closure of independent cinemas would eventually bury the two-feature programme; the real question was 'How long could it survive?'

For the time being, however, things were fairly healthy on the circuits which exceeded their supporting feature quota by 6.5 per cent in 1952–3.[173] In the following year, cinemas defaulting on their supporting-programme quota fell by almost one third to 1,116.[174] The number of supporting features (3,000–6,500 feet) increased from thirty-five in 1952–3 to forty-eight in the following year, mainly at the expense of shorts.[175] In 1954–5, the number rose again to fifty-five. That year, exhibitors easily exceeded their quota, showing 31.2 per cent British supporting films.[176] British Bs were also beginning to face less competition from the USA, which was steadily scaling down production and striking co-production deals with British independents. Allied Artists and 20th Century-Fox, for example, both used the services of Charles Deane, formerly of Merton Park and Ealing (but with experience producing in the early days of US television), who knocked up a couple of thrillers for the visiting Hollywood actor, Richard Arlen. He starred with Greta Gynt and Donald Houston in the drug-running story *Devil's Point* (1954, USA: *Devil's Harbor*), directed by Montgomery Tully.[177] Deane then over-reached himself by writing, producing and directing the hackneyed released-prisoner-proves-innocence drama, *Stolen Time* (1955, USA: *Blonde Blackmailer*, 1958), which *Kinematograph Weekly* described as a 'shoddy and untidy crime pot-boiler' and 'a sorry case of one person attempting too much'.[178] Although it had to wait three years for American release, it still demonstrated a transatlantic demand for British 'B' product of whatever quality.

The largest three circuits showed an impressive 38 per cent of British Bs in 1953–4. Though this was partly a consequence of the diminution in American production, it was also persuasive evidence that indigenous second features were now finding a genuinely appreciative audience. The demand for second features was sufficient to encourage Gaumont's Specialised Film Unit, which had previously made advertising shorts and technical training films for the armed services, to try its hand at 'B' films.[179] The work of the Children's Film Foundation, the best of which trade critics had often recommended for release beyond the Saturday morning kids' shows, also came under consideration by the circuits.[180]

Quota Defaulters, 1949–55[181]

Year	First features	Supporting features	Total
1949	1,474	1,381	2,855
1950	2,335	2,195	4,530
1951	771	2,340	3,111
1952	1,042	1,901	2,943
1953	884	1,626	2,510
1954	734	1,116	1,850
1955	529	642	1,171

In 1956 the number of supporting-programme defaulters fell again to 551. Most failed only narrowly to meet their obligations, and the quota was easily exceeded (29.5 per cent) overall.[182]

However, with television beginning to consume more and more screenplays, it still became increasingly difficult to keep up an adequate supply of good scripts for 'B' films, even with the influx of experienced left-wing screenwriters from Hollywood following the McCarthy witch-hunts.[183] Television also began to commandeer more and more studio space. A procession of studios closed or were turned over to television. Highbury, Isleworth, the Gate, Islington, Marylebone, Riverside,

Teddington and Manchester were all lost to 'B' film-making. As the launch of ITV became imminent, Wembley and Southall were added to the list. Both were making television features and advertisements by New Year 1955.[184] At Bushey, where 50 per cent of production was given over to television, Rayant's Anthony Gilkison commented: 'We think of ourselves as picture people, but while the distributors are not asking for supporting stuff we like to eat, and eating unquestionably comes from TV nowadays.'[185] Effectively, only three studios remained consistently available for modest independent productions: Beaconsfield, Merton Park and Nettlefold – six stages in all. There was also Bray available for the 'exclusive' use of Hammer, and six further stages sometimes available to second features at Brighton, Viking, Carlton Hill and Bushey, which was to be taken over by Rayant Films. As studio space became scarcer, renting rates rose further. In February 1955, American independents, the Danziger brothers, lost their tenancy at MGM Elstree and were left to cast around for short-term leases. The prospects began to look bleak for the low-budgeteers:

> The producer who, yesterday, was making second features that, in some situations, could get by on a double feature bill, has just about had it. Not so much because the exhibitors will not take it any more, but because there is not the studio space in which to make such films. Nowadays, you either make first features or you try to find the space to make half-hour films for television.[186]

The future for the second feature was seen as the revamping of the half-hour featurette, which could neatly slot into a supporting role on a programme with one of the longer first features, and might go on to a second life on TV. But what was needed, warned *To-Day's Cinema*, was not a return to the 'fishing-in-the-North-Sea or housing-the-workers-in-the-back-of-beyond stuff' which had been done 'ad nauseum'.[187] Instead, Merton Park's *Scotland Yard* series was leading the way in 'perking up' the supporting programme. The game was up for the orthodox second feature, the perpetuation of which 'must do more harm than good in the long run, particularly as the TV audience grows'. It was 'time to build up the popularity of the cinema by sweeping away all the rubbish'. There would be no point, suggested *To-Day's Cinema*, in waiting 'until the competitor is showing the same kind of quickies already being prepared for it'.[188]

In truth, the standard British black-and-white 'B' product was beginning to look distinctly dowdy beside the growing number of colour, and even widescreen, shorts that were being produced to accompany the longer Hollywood films. Blacklist refugee Cy Endfield, for instance, frankly admitted: 'I cannot see how the "B" picture is going to draw the people away from their television screens. The demand is for big pictures.'[189] At the annual meeting of ACT Films in March 1955, General Manager Ralph Bond argued that the turn to widescreen films was having a disastrous effect on the production of second features. Demand was falling and 'We may find that the considerable output of British second features and the employment given may, within the next twelve months, nearly cease altogether.'[190] A further blow to the morale of Britain's 'B' film producers was dealt by the results of an audience survey which were published in *The Observer*. The survey suggested that the reasons for dwindling box-office returns were to be found not so much in the overwhelming appeal of television but 'the declining quality of films' and, in particular, 'the poorness of the second feature'.[191] One response was the production of flexible programmers, fitting anywhere on the bill, according to the prestige of the cinema that screened them. This multifunctionality was recognised in the name given to the production company formed by Bertie Ostrer and Albert Fennell to make films for Eros at Nettlefold: B and A Productions.[192]

A related strategy was to increase production values and extend a film's appeal to developing European markets by shooting footage overseas. Although this was never a common practice, there were examples, such as Kenneth Hume's *Sail Into Danger* (1957), an action-adventure picture produced by Steven Pallos and filmed partly on location in Barcelona. Previously, overseas filming for the supporting programme had been largely confined to travelogues, which were designed to appeal to the curiosity of domestic audiences. However, some of the longer offerings in this genre often tried to develop a dramatic or comedic strand in their location work. Inevitably, production standards, particularly sound recording, were below the normal standards even for second-feature work. One example was the comedy travelogue narrated by Bonar Colleano, *No Love for Judy* (1955), covering the amorous adventures of a man-hunting London model (Zoe Newton) on the French Riviera. Significantly it was made by the dubbing specialist Jacques De Lane Lea, who also started to shoot featurettes in colour and 'Scope'.[193] With no suitable studio space available, his musical *Five Guineas a Week* (1956) was shot at a public swimming baths. A year earlier, Hammer had been the first company to explore the potentialities of CinemaScope for the supporting feature. Young producer Michael Carreras had embarked on a series of colour and widescreen musical featurettes: 'Of course we have made shorts previously ... But the average returns for such films were £4–5000 over five years! The return should be more immediate with these CinemaScope films. They *are* needed for programmes. CinemaScope films are as long – in running time – as they are broad in view.'[194]

Two for the Price of One

Towards the end of 1955, *To-Day's Cinema* headlined the announcement by Michael's father, James Carreras, that 'The Old Second Feature is Dead':

> A growing and grave shortage of British second features is evidenced in the present tendency for producers who hitherto specialised in this field to go in for more ambitious subjects; to make featurettes of the half-hour variety; or to desert the industry altogether for television production.[195]

Regular producers like Hammer and Tempean were increasingly looking towards co-features, while Archway turned to a series of colour featurettes starring Robert Newton in his role as Long John Silver.[196] The independent production and distribution companies were being obliged to re-think their marketing strategies. Some began packaging their wares into double-feature programmes that offered not only increased value for money to exhibitors and audiences, but also more favourable trading conditions within the supply chain of the film industry. At the end of 1954, Adelphi parcelled up *The Happiness of Three Women* (a romantic comedy set in rural Wales) and *The Crowded Day* as a British comedy programme for the Odeon circuit. The following year, Eros began to offer struggling independent showmen co-feature packages which combined a British low-budget feature with a foreign genre film. Examples included *Handcuffs, London* with the Italian peplum *The Queen of Sheba* (1955), *No Smoking* with *Gangbusters* (1955) and *Not So Dusty* with *Seminole Uprising* (1956), the latter billed as 'The Big NEW Programme for Independent Exhibitors'. By supplying an entire programme to a circuit or independent exhibitor, the medium-sized producer/distributors could distribute the differential rates paid for 'A' and 'B' films across their production budgets and escape the ruinously low returns paid for second features. With the cost of studio rental rising as television production expanded, the independent producers and distributors needed to raise their own fees to the

Package deals from Eros: trade advertisements for two double-bill releases from 1956 and 1958, each teaming a British and foreign film

exhibitor. However, here they encountered the weakest link in the chain of production and consumption. With their customers deserting to television, the exhibitors – particularly those operating outside the main circuits – were unable to raise their seat prices lest they accelerate the rate of desertion. Squeezed between the rock of the quota and the hard place of suppliers with escalating costs, these exhibitors fell back on the agreements they had previously negotiated with distributors. If producers of 'B' pictures needed a greater return to finance their activity, the only solution within the hands of the trade lay in adjusting the percentage of rental income towards the supporting feature and away from the main. This would be a bitter pill for the producers of main attractions to swallow, but, as James Carreras explained, it might ultimately be in their best interests because: 'How many producers would let even their big films go into circulation without a support? I venture to say none.'[197]

Meanwhile, the new production crisis deepened. Between the beginning of April 1955 and the end of September only twenty-two films of 4–7,000 feet were registered for quota as opposed to thirty during the same period in the previous year. In March 1956, the rumour began to circulate that the NFFC was no longer going to assist in the making of second features. In a letter to the BFPA, the Corporation pointed out that, of the twenty-seven second features it had financed in the previous three years, sixteen were estimated to have made a loss of approximately £90,000, and the remaining eleven had recovered only £38,000. Only two of the ten films that had failed to secure a major circuit release had been profitable. The others had lost an average of £8,000 each. Part of the problem remained the rising studio costs which made it increasingly difficult to produce a second feature for less than the benchmark figure of £15,000.[198] The NFFC was inclined to believe that the British second feature afforded no really worthwhile employment, failed to boost the prestige of the national cinema, and did little to help the balance of payments. However, it was content merely to let it be known that it was going to be more careful in choosing the 'B' features it was prepared to support, scrutinising proposals to see if a decent return could be assured.[199] This was a test of the cinema trade's commitment to the two-feature programme, which, it firmly believed, cinemagoers had come to expect and demand, and which it was certainly not yet prepared to abandon. *The Cinema* was in no doubt: 'The cry at the start of the anamorphic era, that the second feature was dead, has not been substantiated by a continued policy of giving the public what it is alleged to want, namely, two pictures whatever the length of the "big" one. The demand is still for a second picture to complete the programme.'[200] As James Carreras put it: 'The public will always patronise the theatre with the double bill and stop away from the house that is showing merely a single feature. They will shop for the full three-and-a-half hour programme.'[201]

Carreras was supported by Nat Miller of ORB Film Distribution, who wrote to *The Cinema* in defence of the double bill: 'As a booker for some years, my experience definitely shows that the supporting feature has its value and has been the saving of many programmes ... No, sir, now is not the time to cut programme values for the vast majority of our audiences.'[202] Independent exhibitors remained steadfastly loyal to the second feature, even going so far as criticising Hollywood films like *Giant* (1957) for being too long and allowing no space for the supporting programme. Many continued to prefer a 7–8,000 ft main attraction with a 6,000 ft support.[203] Concerns remained, however, about the current shortage of supporting features of reasonable quality. The *Kinematograph Weekly* audience survey in 1956 revealed that there were frequent complaints about bad 'B' films, but that these were far outweighed by the annoyance caused by advertising films, long sales intervals and chatter among cinema staff.[204] Circuit bookers actually noted a general rise in standards, but a particular shortage of comedies among the stream of 'murder mysteries and dramas about the seamy side of life'.[205]

The issue was now becoming urgent enough for *The Cinema* to make it the subject of its lead story: 'Deep concern is felt throughout the second-feature production market at the doubtful prospects of being able to continue this class of film making without practical reassurance from exhibitors of a more lucrative return on investment.'[206] However, the British Film Producers Association was not prepared to wait on the goodwill of hard-pressed exhibitors. They quickly prepared a proposal for the Board of Trade which would give second-feature productions a higher Eady Levy subsidy (one and a half times the standard Eady rate for films over 5,000 feet booked on a flat-rate basis). It was a measure designed to bolster the traditional hour-long supporting feature rather than the resurgent half-hour featurette, but the cash-strapped 'B' film producers within the ranks of the BFPA were inclined to believe that more drastic government action might be required if they were to avoid further insolvency.[207] The production figures for British features in 1955/6 made dramatic reading. The number of films under 6,500 feet was down by 57 per cent on the previous year, and those under 3,000 feet by 70 per cent.[208]

Walton Studios also did its bit to ease the situation by offering an economy rate to what had always been its regular customers – the cash-strapped producers of second features. However, this was something of a pyrrhic victory for the producers because the favourable rates were only made possible by the regular income afforded to Walton by Sapphire TV Films, which kept two of the studios' four stages in continuous use making the popular series *Sir Lancelot, Robin Hood* and *The Buccaneer*. Dennis Shand and Maxwell Munden eased the shortage of studio space a fraction when they opened the St John's Wood Studios, close to London's West End, in the summer of 1957. The pair had been operating for ten years as the production company Film Workshop, making documentaries, but now saw a market opportunity in switching to second features. Shand believed it was time for 'a bit of honest-to-goodness showmanship' and that a little more vulgarity in films would not go amiss. Their first film at the new studios, directed by Munden, was the creepy thriller *The House in the Woods* (1957), the story of a novelist (Michael Gough) and his wife (Patricia Roc) who seek solitude in the country house of a murderer (Ronald Howard).[209]

The production difficulties were doubly frustrating at a time when there were real prospects of distribution in the USA. Cutbacks in 'B' productions by Hollywood meant that many cinemas in small America towns were short of programme pictures. Even a company like Republic, which had been a leading force in 'B' movie production, had moved on to bigger pictures and was now looking to Britain to provide cheap programme-fillers for small-town distribution. However, the project was quickly overtaken by Republic's insolvency. According to Cy Roth, the director of the delightfully trashy *Fire Maidens from Outer Space* (1956), a British 'B' film with transatlantic appeal might secure 3–5,000 bookings in the USA, and could earn $300,000.[210] Roth was one of a number of experienced Hollywood film-makers who kept a close eye on British production facilities and the ways in which they might be used to take advantage of market opportunities. Billy Boyle and Burt Balaban (son of Paramount's chief, Barney Balaban) were two others. They made the rambling revenge thriller *Lady of Vengeance* (1957), starring Dennis O'Keefe and film debutante Ann Sears, for United Artists. Afterwards, with American television using up cheap scripts at a prodigious rate, Boyle continued to search (largely fruitlessly) England for 'quick action stories' to transform into £40,000 pictures to be made in Britain.[211] However, the pressure from his American distributor, Arthur Mayor, was towards bigger pictures and so Boyle's next production, a melodramatic tale of prospectors trapped by a snowdrift in the Canadian Rockies called *High Hell* (1957), was a more lavish affair with location filming and imported American stars (John Derek and Elaine Stewart). Critics thought it *High* as a rotting kipper and *Hell* for the audience. They would have preferred a more useful programmer.

The trade in scripts also flowed in the other direction. Billy Wilder's brother, W. Lee Wilder, brought a William Grote story entitled *The Curse of Nostradamus* with him from the USA. In three weeks, Guido Coen then turned it into the severed-head horror *The Man Without a Body* (1957), starring the Hollywood actors George Coulouris and Robert Hutton. Eros gave it the full exploitation treatment: 'Science's most frightening experiment! Behind closed laboratory doors they brought this 400-year old head to life … and then it ran amok! The incredible creature with an age-old head and a man's desires!' Although Wilder probably took a hand in the direction, the film was credited to Charles Saunders, who bemoaned the apparent shift in tastes associated with the growing predominance of teenagers in the audience. 'Comedies are my cup of tea,' he stated, but he was obliged to make an accommodation to new trends and available stories. Eros wittily teamed it with *Half Human*, and the trade pronounced it 'sure-fire for addicts of eerie shockers'.[212] For their next collaboration, Coen and Saunders retained the services of Coulouris to play another mad scientist in *Womaneater* (1958), a deliciously far-fetched tale about a carnivorous 'devil' tree with an appetite for Vera Day. It went out as part of an unashamedly exploitative double bill with *Blonde in Bondage* ('In the spotlight she Strip-teased. In the shadows she collected her pay-cheque in shame!'). The programme's unabashed trade tagline – 'It's X! It's Sex! It's Box-Office!' – offered a direct assault on Puritan sensibilities and signposted a new direction for low-budget film-making in Britain.[213] Coen

ROBERT HUTTON
GEORGE COULOURIS
JULIA ARNALL
The Man Without a Body CERT X

'Science's most frightening experiment!' confronts Julia Arnall in Eros's *The Man Without a Body* (1957)

and Saunders' executive producer was Harrison Reader, an American independent film-maker responsible for delivering Hollywood actors and arranging distribution deals in the USA. In the spring of 1957, Reader set up his own company, Peak Films, to make bargain-basement pictures in Britain. At £15–20,000, the production budget was so low that Reader had to reject the services of Hollywood actor Steve Cochran, with whom he had worked in the States, and adopt Forrest Tucker as a cheaper option. The thoroughly obliging Tucker also agreed to write the script for the first Peak film.[214] Increasingly, British Bs were made to order to fit unpredictable gaps in American release schedules. While Herman Cohen's Anglo-Amalgamated were making *Horrors of the Black Museum* (1959), for example, Cohen received a call from AIP's James Nicholson in Hollywood to say that if Anglo could supply a suitable supporting feature in black-and-white 'Scope' to accompany *Black Museum* a large Texas circuit would book the double bill and others would follow suit. Consequently, a comedy-chiller, *The Headless Ghost* (1959), was written in two weeks and filmed in a further three for £35,000, using a lot of the sets left standing from *Black Museum*.[215]

An Indian Summer

Eventually, the Board of Trade came to the rescue of the beleaguered 'B' film producers. The British Film Producers Association had long been campaigning for payments from the Eady production fund to second features (films booked at a flat rate) to be calculated at double the percentage applicable to other long films. But the BFPA's recommendation went unheeded when the Board published new Eady Levy regulations in summer 1957. In a front-page article headed 'Second Feature Producers Must Not Be Allowed To Disappear', *The Cinema* quoted the BFPA's vice-president, Arthur Watkins speaking in support of 'B' film-making as a vital recruiting ground for directors and technicians: 'If they were to disappear off the map, it would not be a very good thing for the industry ... We thought these boys deserved some assistance – we all know they don't get a great deal out of the till, we are disappointed it has not been given.'[216] Undaunted, the BFPA continued to fight for a better deal for the second-feature boys, and an increasing number of voices joined the association's call. Butcher's Jack Phillips, for instance, publicly bemoaned the lack of financial assistance from the Government to make good second features for which there was still considerable audience demand, not to mention a legal requirement.[217] The call was finally heeded in the summer of 1958 when, following a recommendation by the Cinematograph Films Council, the Board of Trade agreed to extend double Eady funds to second features.

The effect of this financial boost (operative from late 1959), coupled with the collapse of competition from American 'B' movies, was to create a brief Indian summer for the British supporting film. By March 1960, *Kinematograph Weekly* was able to tell its readers:

> The second feature, long the poor relation of the production industry, suddenly springs into the Very Important Picture bracket. A year ago small picture production was at rock bottom. Today, dignified by such new titles as 'co-feature' or 'hour-long feature', the small film accounts for a large part of the activity in British studios.[218]

Following the lead of Anglo-Amalgamated and Eros, new companies like Bryanston began to produce or commission 'B' films to package with their 'A' features. The Danzigers started to make supporting features in colour (for instance, *Escort for Hire* and *A Taste of Money* [both 1960]), even without the assurance of a pre-production distribution contract. They hardly needed one, because the two major circuits were snapping up anything serviceable and, in 1959–60, their supporting programmes were 43 per cent British.[219]

At the same time, the fledgling British cinema of exploitation was beginning to flap its wings, encouraged by liberal classifications from the BBFC, which gave 'A' certificates to 'naturist' films including *Nudist Paradise* (1958, USA: *Nature's Paradise*), filmed extravagantly in Eastman Color and 'Nudiscope' with an on-screen endorsement from the Duke of Bedford, *Travelling Light* (1960), with its naked underwater ballet sequences,[220] Michael Winner's *Some Like it Cool* (1961) and George Harrison Marks's West-Country travelogue *Naked as Nature Intended* (1961). Most of these films were around an hour long, but their status as 'gimmick' pictures enabled them to top the bill at specialist venues, often with a dubbed Continental film in support.[221] Although they came under fire from the Federation of British Sun Clubs for 'debasing' naturism by emphasising its 'sexual rather than the health-seeking undertones',[222] the nudist films offered a way forward for hard-pressed independent exhibitors in urban areas, as well as opportunities for new exploitation entrepreneurs and established distributors of Continental 'art' films. Such sights, of course, could not be viewed on the rival medium of television.

One section of the audience least in thrall to TV was further targeted by films that incorporated the sounds and celebrities of the pop music culture of the young. Rock-'n'-roller Tommy Steele made his screen debut in a conventional 'B' thriller *Kill Me Tomorrow* (1957) before starring in his own blockbusting biopic, and, by the early 1960s, pop stars were increasingly being used to attract young cinemagoers and possibly lift low-budget features to a higher position on the double bill. Singers like Adam Faith and Jess Conrad found that they could also pursue acting careers, the former in 'A' films and the latter mostly in Bs like Lance Comfort's *Rag Doll* (1961). The full-blown rock 'n' roll/pop picture was the creation of producer-distributor E. J. Fancey, who made *Rock You Sinners* as a supporting feature in 1957 and in 1960 added *Climb Up the Wall*, compèred by the television DJ, Jack Jackson, and written and directed by the precocious Michael Winner. While its performers – the likes of Russ Conway and Craig Douglas – were rather more sedate than those of the earlier film, it was still recommended as 'just the thing for the Espresso coffee bar trade'.[223] The taste for 'trad' jazz, which was by no means confined to teenagers, was catered for in the Acker Bilk vehicle *Band of Thieves* (1962), a very British take on Presley's *Jailhouse Rock* (1957).[224] Following Val Guest's lively satire of the creation of pop stars, *Expresso Bongo* (1959), the 'B' film eventually had its own lampoon with the featurette *Meet Mister Beat* (1961), produced by David Cummins and directed by Ivan Barnett.

The clear blue sky of the 'B' film's Indian summer began to cloud over in 1961. Concerns were again expressed, notably by the Boulting brothers and by the BBC's *Picture Parade* programme, about the quality of the crop of Eady-subsidised supporting features and the continuing assumption that the public demanded the double bill. At British Lion, the Boultings backed up their critique of 'the appalling trash that is being inflicted on the patient public, week in week out' by trying to demonstrate what a really good second feature should look like.[225] Their own attempt at a 'B' movie, *Suspect* (1961), was competent enough, but their policy of blooding new talent bore fruit with Cliff Owen's directorial debut, *Offbeat* (1961), a work of genuine ideological dissonance which questioned the conventional wisdom about crime and punishment. As *Kine Weekly* put it: 'The picture expresses sentiments that may raise some eyebrows' but 'carries a kick of one twice its size'.[226] However, from the response to the Boultings' complaints, it was clear that really for the first time a substantial number of exhibitors were beginning to question the utility of the double bill. In an attempt to retain the family audience, many began to look to shorten their programmes to allow early evening television viewing.[227] In these circumstances, it became increasingly difficult to expand the proportion of rental revenue paid to the supporting feature, a measure still desperately needed if production was to be put on a sound commercial footing and standards were to be raised.[228] As the president of the BFPA put it, making second features was 'no hayride' and help in the form of further enhanced Eady payments was urgently required.[229] The Board of Trade agreed to enhanced payments in the summer of 1962, but it was really too little too late. Moreover, one of the primary functions of the 'B' film, the testing of new talent, was now being usurped by television production. Ironically enough, British Bs from Anglo-Amalgamated and Butcher's were attracting some of the best notices from trade reviewers that they had ever achieved, but the chorus of disapproval from exhibitors continued to swell: 'Many of the supporting features today, instead of being an *hors d'oeuvre*, are a very large indigestible mass that leaves the customer with very little appetite for the main feature.'[230]

The curtain for the supporting feature began to come down at the end of 1961 with the announcement of the closure of New Elstree Studios. Built by the American Danziger brothers at a cost of £700,000, the studios had been operational for only six years, during which they had turned out 'B' films at the rate of more than one per month, as well as a number of very successful television series. Harry Danziger told the press:

It's quite simple. Being an independent producer with a studio does not pay any more ... We have been making 16 [second features] a year at approximately £15,000 to £17,000 a piece. They helped to keep the studios going and a large proportion of them were good in themselves irrespective of their cost. But ... we have had to take the sort of critical beating that should be reserved for producers whose films cost ten or twelve times as much as ours. Plainly, the industry does not want to pay for second features. The proof is that the market is diminishing so sharply that there is no point in making them anymore.[231]

The number of studios accommodating supporting-feature production continued to contract, as did the genre range of the films themselves. The smaller stages of Shepperton and Pinewood were occasionally used, but Merton Park and Twickenham were the last remaining specialist 'B' studios. The crime film became virtually the only game in town, an issue taken up in talks between the CEA and the BFPA towards the end of 1962. Exhibitors requested more variety and originality and shorter running times.[232] The major circuits in particular showed a preference for series films like the highly successful Anglo-Amalgamated Edgar Wallace supports. These films, released on roughly a monthly basis, catered to an audience now used to the rhythms of television programming, by employing regular scheduling, careful product-branding and quality control.

Willy Rushton chasing 'tail' in the colour musical *It's All Over Town* (1964)

Length of Registered British Films (including Commonwealth) by Year[233]

Year	Over 72 mins	33.33–72 mins	Percentage of 33.33–72 mins
1945	40	36	47
1946	39	61	61
1947	48	58	55
1948	68	101	60
1949	77	53	41
1950	74	49	40
1951	67	47	41
1952	79	42	35
1953	86	46	35
1954	93	51	35
1955	82	40	33
1956	81	29	26
1957	96	33	26
1958	89	35	28
1959	80	43	35
1960	79	44	36
1961	77	43	36
1962	71	45	39
1963	72	39	35
1964	70	29	29
1965	69	22	24
1966	70	16	19
1967	70	13	16
1968	71	17	19
1969	71	14	16
1970	85	11	12

By 1964, the few remaining supporting features were being budgeted at £20–£22,000, unless, like the musical revue *It's All Over Town* (1964), they were being shot in colour.[234] This film, directed by Douglas Hickox, made it poignantly clear that cinema was now looking to stars and celebrities created in other media – notably television and recorded music – to make its productions viable by giving the audience the added value of colour presentation. These levels of expenditure could no longer be sustained by the flat-rate payment system and, with overall box-office revenue continuing to decline, producers of first features remained understandably reluctant to reduce the size of their slices of cake. A desperate experiment by producer/director Gerry Levy to make an ultra low-budget 'B' on a co-operative basis using deferred payments – *Where Has Poor Mickey Gone?* (1964) – also proved unsustainable.[235] Thus, by 1965, although occasional supporting features continued to be made, their time as a regular part of the cinema programme was effectively past. *The Times* wrote their obituary early in 1967, when it reported the estimate of the Film Producers' Association that the minimum cost of a second feature was £24,000, but the maximum that could be recouped in the UK was £16,000.[236] But let us now rewind the troubled history of the Bs to see who was making these films in the twenty years after the war.

3 The 'B' Factories

Companies, Studios and Producers

I have always believed that it is upon the small men in films that a healthy industry will alone be built up. Not merely the producers of films who come outside the organised groups, or the technicians who may one day graduate to become notable producers or directors but the few who make the persistent efforts to meet a demand for second-feature entertainment within their severely limited means.

C. B. H. 'Willy' Williamson[1]

Most film historiography still approaches the continuities and discontinuities of film-making via the figure of the director, but the volume, regularity and conventionality of 'B' film production directs attention towards more industrial considerations. This is not, of course, to deny that directors are primarily responsible for setting the tone of a picture, interpreting the script and making the immediate decisions that affect the actions of actors and technicians. The producer's contribution to what we see on screen is less easy to pinpoint, except perhaps in such general terms as, say, Balcon's gently leftist (and chauvinist) ethos at work in so many Ealing films or Korda's propensity for lavish production design. Nevertheless, it is impossible to understand the director's product and its relation to other works without addressing the imperatives, facilities and constraints set in place by the producer, the production company and the studio. With the 'B' film – perhaps more than with other, relatively luxurious, forms of picture production – it is this sphere of business practice and industrial creation that is key to interpreting the trajectories of film-making.

Although work on this sphere has been extensive in the USA, covering not just the large Hollywood studios, but also 'Poverty Row' production, research in Britain has focused almost exclusively on the largest and most prestigious of producers and studios. In the historiography of British cinema, only two production companies on the fringes of the respectable core of British cinema have received detailed consideration (largely from amateur historians): Mancunian and, overwhelmingly, Hammer/Exclusive. The pre-war activities of Julius Hagen have had some discussion and the present authors have previously done their best to shine lights in various dark corners of studio production,[2] but it has proved difficult to unearth company records that might facilitate more sustained and detailed study.[3] The main sources for telling the stories of the 'B' producers, companies and studios are the reminiscences of the personnel who worked for them and the cinema trade papers. When the fan magazines, such as *Picture Show* or *Picturegoer*, occasionally ventured on to the sets of 'B' films, they tended to concentrate on the stars.[4] Here, then, is a run-down of the main players in the field of British second-feature production 1945–65 and the work for which they were responsible.

Butcher's

Butcher's Film Services, founded by the Blackheath chemist William Butcher during the Boer War, was by far the oldest company regularly producing low-budget first and second features in the post-World War II period. It was fiercely proud of its Britishness, having survived the competition at the lower end of the market from American renters in the 1930s, and made and distributed pictures that unashamedly addressed national cultural tastes and interests. The war intensified the company's patriotism, as we can easily see from the way it introduced one of its early post-war releases:

> At a time when Great Britain's efforts to secure her rightful share of the Film markets of the world are a matter of National importance ... this company stands firmly in the foremost ranks of film-makers sending its products to all corners of the earth and keeping the British flag flying on the screens of the world.[5]

From its production base at Nettlefold Studios, Walton-on-Thames, where Ernest G. Roy directed operations, Butcher's output in the late 1940s and early 1950s trod the line between the first and supporting feature. Its market had always been the small independent cinemas in the industrial heartlands of the country, and their aging audiences continued to be addressed in explicitly nostalgic featurettes like *Those Were the Days* (1946) and *For Old Times' Sake* (1948), both of which looked back to the Edwardian music hall. But the days of those cinemas and their patrons were numbered, and Butcher's began cautiously to branch out from its accustomed mix of music, mirth and sentimentality in search of new audiences.

In 1947, with the supporting programme likely to feature in revisions to the Quota legislation, Butcher's embarked on a programme of second features, using a variety of small production companies. Vandyke used Viking Studios for *The Hangman Waits*, Grossman-Ardied-Cullimore utilised Carlton

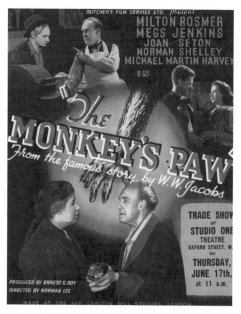

Nettlefold nail-biters: trade advertisements for two thrillers from Butcher's

Hill for *The Clouded Crystal*. Carlton Hill was also the venue for Richard Gray's *Eyes That Kill*, a story suggesting the escape to England of Nazi hierarch Martin Bormann (Philip Stainton). *The Cinema* clearly found its 'facile melodramatics' distasteful, and felt the picture would fail to have 'any marked appeal to the average cinema-goer of to-day'.[6] Norman Lee's *The Monkey's Paw* (1948), on the other hand, was much more popular. A remake of the classic study of the uncanny by W. W. Jacobs, it was filmed in seven weeks at Carlton Hill and Walton with location shooting at New Cross Speedway. It was adopted as a feature by the ABC circuit, perhaps because of the relevance of its storyline – involving the violent death of a son – to so many post-war families. The words uttered by the father in the film, Milton Rosmer, to Megs Jenkins after he has meddled with fate, were full of contemporary resonance: 'Mother, let's go on just as we did before. Life hasn't been so bad for us, although we hadn't realised it. If only we could have the days and the hours back again. We can't. Wishing won't do any good.'

The Monkey's Paw caught the public's imagination sufficiently to play as a first feature, and the same was true of *The Story of Shirley Yorke* (1948), a Maclean Rogers film made at Walton in which Dinah Sheridan starred as a nurse and to which the Middlesex Hospital gave considerable assistance. When Maclean Rogers again directed Dinah Sheridan in the gothic mystery *Dark Secret* (1949), however, *Kinematograph Weekly* complained that, at eighty-five minutes, the film was fifteen minutes too long because it was only of 'B quota picture' quality.[7] The company seemed unsure of which direction to take, and even released a European resistance drama set in Holland and directed by Edmond T. Gréville, an Anglo-French film-maker who rarely shirked controversial subject matter. *But Not in Vain* (1950) updated the biblical story of Abraham by having a Dutch Jew (Raymond Lovell) sacrifice his Nazified son to save refugees and resistance workers.[8] It was not very Butcher's at all; and neither was Lewis Gilbert's *Once a Sinner* (1950). Jack Watling starred as a bank clerk who caddishly jilts his wholesome girlfriend (Joy Shelton) to marry a shady barmaid (the alluring Pat Kirkwood), who turns out to be a single mother with a reform school background. The trade press was cautious, because of the film's sordid themes, but recognised the audience appeal of Pat Kirkwood, particularly to 'the industrial ninepennies'.[9]

Continuity among this pot-pourri was provided by a series of co-features directed by Maclean Rogers and featuring the popular radio sleuth Paul Temple. By 1952, however, the series had lost a little of its lustre, and Butcher's looked to replace it with a new series starring John Bentley, this time based on John Creasy's character, The Toff, a gentleman detective in the nineteenth-century tradition. The series launched with *Salute the Toff* (1952), directed by Maclean Rogers. Its story of insurance fraud hardly broke new ground, but the trade critics recognised a tried and trusted formula that would appeal to Butcher's core audience: the 'industrialites and the provincialites'.[10] *Hammer the Toff* (1952) followed almost immediately, but bookings must have been disappointing, because Butcher's turned back to their earlier series with the appropriately titled *Paul Temple Returns* (1952), again in the hands of Maclean Rogers. It also retained John Bentley as Francis Durbridge's sleuth, in a tale of multiple murder centred on docklands. As well as Patricia Dainton as Mrs Temple, the cast also included Valentine Dyall and the still largely unknown Christopher Lee. It went out as a second feature on the Gaumont British circuit.

In 1953, as television licence-holders passed the 2 million mark, Butcher's began to turn to the rival medium for inspiration. Martyn C. Webster's *The Broken Horseshoe* (1953) was adapted from a TV play about a horse-doping gang and had a strong cast headed by Robert Beatty and Elizabeth Sellars. Some brisk direction ensured that the film rose above the average supporting mystery thriller.

Sordid stuff: Lewis Gilbert directs Pat Kirkwood in *Once a Sinner* (1950)

Butcher's second television adaptation, *Operation Diplomat* (1953), a topical espionage thriller, benefited from a taut script and the reliable direction of John Guillermin. Perhaps most entertaining of all was Wolf Rilla's *Marilyn* (1953, a.k.a. *Roadhouse Girl*), adapted from a stage play, rather than a teleplay, by Peter Jones. This sultry revisitation of J. M. Cain will be discussed in Chapter 8, but we might just note here that it was a fitting swan-song for the Ernest G. Roy era at Walton. In March 1954, Bill Chalmers and Jack Phillips took over Butcher's Film Service, renaming it Butcher's Film Distributors. Over the next three years, the company made seven films, each of which gained a full circuit deal and overseas distribution: *The Black Rider*, *Stock Car*, *It's a Great Day*, *All Good Fun*, *Assignment Redhead*, *You Pay Your Money* and *Cloak Without Dagger*.

Wolf Rilla's motor-bike mystery *The Black Rider* (1954) was a *Boy's Own* story with gothic trappings that starred Jimmy Hanley as a gung-ho investigative reporter, Leslie Dwyer as his irascible boss and Rona Anderson as the journalist's love interest. Wilfred Burns supplied a sub-*Genevieve* score, Geoffrey Faithfull's day-for-night photography simulated some attractive moonlit seascapes, and the film's cowls, castles and smuggled atomic weapons – with a strong dash of comedy – went down well with reviewers. The production company, Balblair, followed it up with Wolf Rilla's *Stock Car* (1955), which cashed in on a new sporting craze by swapping bikes for bangers, and gave television's curvaceous 'dumb' blonde, Sabrina, her first film role alongside Paul Carpenter, Rona Anderson and Susan Shaw. Plot and characterisation were far from original, but the settings were fresher, and Rilla did a workmanlike job with the materials to hand.

John Warrington's *It's a Great Day* (1956) was a spin-off from the first television soap opera, *The Grove Family*. Although the series' legion of devotees virtually guaranteed the film a ready audience, there was little in this homely, domestic material that justified the expanded resources and possibilities of the cinema screen.

Maclean Rogers' *Assignment Redhead* (1956) was made as a second feature on an appropriate budget, in spite of a running time of over eighty minutes. As producer Bill Chalmers commented: 'Films which finally go into the kinema as a co-feature programme are usually first-feature productions which have not made the grade, but if the second features I am presently producing turn out to be worthy of co-billing then, of course, I shall be delighted.'[11] Rogers was at the helm again for *You Pay Your Money* (1957), an out-of-the-rut story set in the rare book trade, which saw Honor Blackman kidnapped by fanatical Arabs. This was the sort of treatment to which she would become accustomed a few years later as Cathy Gale in ATV's *The Avengers*. Impressed by its 'efficient direction, vigorous playing and quick moving events', *To-Day's Cinema* pronounced the film an 'enjoyable 60-odd minutes of boisterous action'.[12] Rank bought the distribution rights for the Walton-made *Cloak Without Dagger* (1956, USA: *Operation Conspiracy*) a light-hearted spy story with a dash of romance, written and produced by A. R. Rawlinson and directed by Joseph Sterling. Mary MacKenzie starred as a fashion journalist trying to protect the life of her former boyfriend (Philip Friend returning after seven years in Hollywood), an MI5 agent.

PHILIP FRIEND
MARY MACKENZIE
LESLIE DWYER
in
Cloak Without Dagger (U)

Mary MacKenzie finds herself in barrels of trouble in the Nettlefold espionage thriller *Cloak Without Dagger* (1956)

As other studios were turned over to television, regular production continued at Walton with films like *The Man from Tangier* (1957, USA: *Thunder Over Tangier*), with the dependable Lance Comfort guiding Robert Hutton and Lisa Gastoni through a formulaic story of passport forgers who enlist an unwilling girl. Butcher's began to dip their toes into European markets with Maclean Rogers' carelessly plotted Cold War thriller *Mark of the Phoenix* (1957). When shooting began at Walton in April 1957, Bill Chalmers had already been to Belgium to scout locations. Then, as rock 'n' roll began to captivate Britain's youth, Butcher's spent a little more on the Terry Dene vehicle, *The Golden Disc* (1957, USA: *The In-Between Age*), in order to market it as a topical first feature. Jack Phillips, however, was quick to assure the trade that Butcher's was not deserting second-feature production and distribution.[13]

To supplement their Walton productions, Butcher's also commissioned films from independent producers. Chelsea Films made *Them Nice Americans* (1958), directed by Tony Young, and featuring Bonar Colleano as a GI who overcomes some rural anti-Americanism towards his marriage to a local lass (Vera Day). Ronald Kinnoch produced and directed *The Secret Man* (1958), a straightforward Cold War drama about espionage at a research establishment. Parroch productions were responsible for Terry Bishop's *Life in Danger* (1959), a thriller about community vigilantes and an innocent man (Derren Nesbitt) mistaken for an escaped child-killer. Josh Billings' review of the box-office performance of British films in 1959 indicated that these last two films, together with *Mark of the Phoenix*, had enjoyed greater popular appeal than other Butcher's offerings like Pennington-Eady's portmanteau picture *The Crowning Touch* and their Shirley Eaton and Tony Wright thriller *In the Wake of a Stranger*, although even these had 'served a useful purpose'.[14]

The Walton studios closed in 1961, but the family business of Butcher's pressed on with supporting-feature production a little longer, under the leadership of Jack Phillip's son John. He made some of the company's most commercially successful Bs in circumstances of diminished competition. Films like Peter Maxwell's *Serena* (1962), Francis Searle's *Gaolbreak* (1962) and Charles Saunder's *Danger By My Side* (1963) used facilities at Shepperton and Twickenham, and all gained advantageous circuit distribution deals: the last named, for instance, supported *Cape Fear*, although its embarrassingly clichéd dialogue and unconvincing characterisations hardly warranted such a distinction.[15] Butcher's regular producer in this period was Tom Blakeley (1916–1984), son of Mancunian filmmaker John E. Blakeley. After working as assistant director on several of his father's regional comedies in the later 1940s, he began producing with two co-feature comedies: Francis Searle's *Love's a Luxury* (1952) and John Harlow's *Those People Next Door* (1952). Blakeley entered into a partnership with Butcher's in 1960, producing Searle's *Trouble with Eve* (1960), praised by *The Daily Cinema* as a 'refreshingly buoyant comedy',[16] and the tough, criminal-centred 'B' *The Marked One* (1963), made at the MGM Studios, Boreham Wood. His main work for Butcher's, however, was in the thrillers he made with director Lance Comfort. *Rag Doll* (1960) and *The Painted Smile* (1962) are above-average melodramas, but *The Break* (1962) and, especially, *Tomorrow at Ten* (1962) are very superior second features. William Lucas, star of *The Break*, praised Blakeley as 'an extremely nice guy. He had no pretensions or anything like that, he was happy making the films he did.'[17]

Highbury and Rank Productions

The Highbury Studios in North London were built in 1937 by Maurice J. Wilson who founded the company Grand National Films Ltd, which continued to distribute films, mainly 'B' movies, until

1970.[18] They were later acquired by the Rank Organisation, which repaired the bomb damage they had suffered in 1944. Rank originally earmarked Highbury as a special effects department and a home for its 'Company of Youth' talent school under the guidance of the formidable Molly Terraine. However, they were quickly promoted to a full production facility where Rank's novice contract artists and technicians could develop their skills. The impetus came from continued agitation in favour of small production units by the ACT. Particularly influential was an article written by Andrew Gray in *Film Industry* in which he advocated forty-five- to sixty-minute programme-fillers to encourage promising technicians and performers and save dollars spent on American second features.

Convinced by the logic of Gray's arguments, Rank appointed Ealing's John Croydon to run the new production unit, called Production Facilities (Film). The unit made nine second features which, if not generally of any special distinction, were at least slightly different from the routine 'B' movies of the period. Adrian Worker, Henry Passmore and Frank Sherwin Green were the studios' associate producers, Green also acting as production manager, and veteran Weston Drury as casting director. John Croydon (1907–1994) was a quiet and studious man who had entered the industry as an accountant with Gainsborough, going on to be an assistant studio manager at Gaumont British and construction manager at MGM-British, before joining Ealing as production supervisor and associate producer during World War II. He was quite clear in his plans for production at Highbury:

> Our idea is to watch promising technicians and players at the various Rank studios. These will be sent to me ... Those who succeed will return to the larger studios for better jobs. Those who fail will return to their old jobs until recommended to come up to me for another chance ... We'll cover a wide range of subjects. ... I'll skip who-dun-its, but don't mind a straight-forward crime story. Comedy will not be forgotten. This will be subtle and broad. I don't mind slap-stick, and I have an idea that we shall endeavour to discover new comedy material for these, both on the writing and directing sides.[19]

The first of the Highbury 'curtain-raisers' went into production in July 1947 on a five-week shooting schedule and a budget of around £20,000. *Colonel Bogey* (1948), a satirical ghost story with a cast of character actors and an unmemorable central pairing of Jane Barrett and John Stone, is now chiefly of interest for its director, Terence Fisher, a film editor who was given his first directorial opportunity as part of Croydon's policy of testing out potential talent. Fisher, of course, would go on to be indelibly associated with the Hammer horror films of the 1950s and 60s. He replaced the slated director, E. V. H. Emmett, for Highbury's second, *To the Public Danger* (1948), an adaptation of Patrick Hamilton's shock radio drama about the dangers of roadhouses and drunken driving, and probably the studios' finest hour (or three-quarters of an hour, to be exact). The working-class couple in the death car – played by Susan Shaw and Barry Letts – were reckless, but the blame was placed firmly on their 'social betters', the irresponsible Captain Cole (Dermot Walsh) and his tipsy friend, Reggie – played by the future host of radio's *Desert Island Discs*, Roy Plomley. *To the Public Danger* divided the critics. *To-Day's Cinema*, for example was impressed by the pace, vivid characterisation and realism of the story,[20] but the downbeat and cynical tone of the film did not endear it to other critics, one of whom likened it to a dramatisation of the Highway Code. 'At least it's short, if not sweet,' was his verdict.[21]

Penny and the Pownall Case (1948) was a comic-strip story of an artist's model who helps Scotland Yard nail an organisation aiding Nazi war criminals. It was naively directed by Slim Hand,

Drunk driving: Susan Shaw realises her mistake in Terence Fisher's *To the Public Danger* (1948)

a production manager at Ealing. The female lead was Peggy Evans, who had her one moment of serious screen notice as Dirk Bogarde's girlfriend in *The Blue Lamp* (1949). The film's main attractions, however, are two fellow Charm School graduates in early performances: Diana Dors and Christopher Lee, well before he became an established monster for Fisher in their Hammer glory days. Lee recalled that the cast were shown no daily rushes, and he first, rather reluctantly, witnessed his performance at the film's premiere at the Odeon, Tottenham Court Road: 'We were forced to attend these showings. I wished that a crevice might have opened up in the stalls that I might have toppled into it.'[22] Lee again appeared in a supporting role as a night-club owner in Terence Fischer's romantic melodrama *Song for Tomorrow* (1948). Something of a poor woman's *The Red Shoes* (1948), the film raises late 1940s issues relating to women's careers and how these may or may not be adjusted to the claims of romantic love.

Charles Saunders, an experienced editor, was entrusted with piloting *Trouble in the Air* (1948) safely through its schedule. The plot of this mildly anarchic comedy starring Jimmy Edwards involved problems with a radio outside-broadcast. *Kinematograph Weekly* appreciated the film's earthy Englishness, but *To-Day's Cinema* was disappointed to see Highbury reverting to the kind of comedy formulas and laboured situations that it thought had been swept away with the war.[23] It was followed by a rather static domestic comedy about children leaving home, *Fly Away Peter* (1948), also directed by Charles Saunders. The work remained within the family, because his brother Peter had handled

Highbury 'curtain-raisers': Rank press books for two 1948 releases

the earlier theatre version of the play by A. P. Dearsley. Peter Hammond and Margaret Barton repeated their stage roles.

Although Highbury never produced a film of real distinction, its efforts reached their nadir with John Irwin's *A Piece of Cake* (1948), a feeble fantasy co-written by Margaret Lockwood's brother Lyn, and featuring radio's purveyor of odes Cyril Fletcher, whose rhymes come to life in the form of a good fairy and Satan. If we were feeling charitable, we might say it was an original concept, but, of course, the same might be said of conjuring underwater: inventiveness without rationale. A supporting cast of Jon Pertwee, Sam Costa, Douglas 'Cardew' Robinson and Betty Astell (Fletcher's wife) did its best to salvage something from the debacle, but failed 'to invest the sorry affair with a vestige of genuine entertainment'.[24] *Kinematograph Weekly* did not beat about the bush: 'the stuff palmed off here as wit is completely beyond redemption. The film is one of Highbury Studio's worst nightmares.'[25] It hardly mattered, because the decision had already been announced to abandon Rank's 'B' film experiment. The closure was part of a raft of measures designed to cure the company's insolvency crisis. As Adrian Worker, the producer of the penultimate Highbury film, put it, 'we were the first one to suffer when Rank started to close things down'.[26] The official reason, however, stressed the removal of the 1947–8 Hollywood film embargo and, consequently, the reduction in demand for British supporting features.[27]

The last two films were *Love in Waiting* (1948, working title *At Your Service*) and a remake of one the most successful films of the pre-war quota-quickie era, *Badger's Green* (1949). *Love in Waiting*, a romantic comedy directed by Douglas Pierce (his directorial debut after being assistant director on

The Wicked Lady), was a piffling story of three waitresses who become involved with the black market as well as in romantic relationships. It boasted a strong cast, with Peggy Evans, Elspet Gray and David Tomlinson, but was let down by weak direction, low production values and an indifferent script. John Irwin's *Badger's Green*, starring Garry Marsh and Kynaston Reeves as a couple of self-important pillars of a local community, was the Highbury unit's swan-song. It was successful in relation to Highbury's mission to blood new talent, as the film's female lead, Barbara Murray, graduated to a part in Ealing's *Passport to Pimlico* (1949), but it failed as a contemporary comedy-drama. Fifteen years before, its whimsical story of a group of villagers putting aside their differences to unite against a threat to their way of life in the form of a modernising developer had put its finger on the concerns of a rural public. In 1949, however, although prefiguring the sorts of past–future tension that would come to underlie such 1950s films as *Laxdale Hall* (1953), *The Maggie* (1953) and *Rockets Galore* (1958), it seemed unnecessarily reactionary.[28] The 'theme seems old-fashioned these days', commented *To-Day's Cinema*, and a cricket match (filmed at Littlewick Green, Maidenhead) as a finale provided insufficient excitement for contemporary audiences.[29] As if to acknowledge its error, Rank's next second feature was Alfred Roome's *It's Not Cricket* (1949, discussed in more detail in Chapter 8), a Gainsborough comedy vehicle from the writers of *A Piece of Cake* for the notoriously cricket-loving Basil Radford and Naunton Wayne. Here, however, the leather-on-willow action is restricted to a farcical finale, while the narrative is driven by the duo's counter-espionage role as private detectives. The critics were suitably bowled over and recommended the film as superior supporting entertainment.[30]

Terence Fisher was the only one of the Highbury directors who went on to have a career in main features, and his films are clearly the best, although, as Peter Hutchings argues, they exhibited 'a certain conventionality' because there was simply not enough time, money and resources for them to be anything else.[31] Nevertheless, Geoffrey MacNab is right when he says that the venture was 'an initiative taken with the long-term interests of the industry in mind which probably deserved to succeed but was smashed by short-term business demands'.[32] In this he was echoing Rank's first biographer, Alan Wood, who also claimed that the venture 'deserved much better success'.[33]

Although Highbury was closed, Rank did not entirely abandon the supporting feature. The low-budget film still provided an effective screen-test for young hopefuls, and kept studios and technicians ticking over. It could also provide a laboratory for technological experimentation. Basil Radford and Naunton Wayne lent their talents to T. J. Morrison's strange feminist fable *Stop Press Girl* (1949), which starred the young Sally Ann Howes alongside Gordon Jackson, and was photographed using the new 'Independent Frame' method.[34] The idea behind the film was a novel one that invited allegorical interpretation: a girl from 'a village bypassed by progress' whose presence stops machinery – including cinema projectors – and who can tell the time without recourse to watches, while her fiancé, who makes them, leads a life regulated by time. However, the film's development of its central premise is thoroughly idiotic. The inexperienced Michael Barry never seemed at home in the director's chair, and the critics gave a unanimous thumbs down to the Independent Frame and to Sally Ann. Milton Shulman declared in the *Evening Standard* that there are 'more laughs in a mausoleum', while Leonard Mosley in the *Daily Express* complained: 'it is a film about a girl who stops all forms of machinery 15 minutes after coming in contact with it. Alas, it took 78 minutes to stop the film.'[35]

The reviewers were no kinder to the next of Rank's 'Independent Frame' offerings, Frederick Wilson's *Poet's Pub* (1949), an adaptation of an Eric Linklater story about an Oxford graduate who tries to revitalise a country inn by staging an Elizabethan masque in its garden. 'Few sensible people buy a picture for the frame,' quipped the *Daily Graphic*'s Elspeth Grant, 'and I won't buy this one.'[36] Making the villain of the piece an American did nothing for the film's transatlantic prospects. Whether *Don't Ever Leave Me* (1949) was intended as a second feature is open to some doubt, but it was certainly cheaply made by Rank standards, and judged by the trade to be of supporting-feature quality. It gave a directorial chance to cinematographer Arthur Crabtree and a leading role to Petula Clark, but neither capitalised on their opportunities as effectively as it must have been hoped. The story of a fake kidnapping was slight and, in the opinion of *To-Day's Cinema*, fit only to 'while away an hour for less sophisticated audiences'.[37] However, it was a work of some gravitas in comparison to its stablemate, Ralph Thomas's *Helter Skelter* (1949), a madcap farrago based on the attempts of a girl (Carol Marsh) to cure a persistent bout of hiccups. True, the film managed to extract some amusement from lampoons of silent comedy and the production culture of the BBC, but even the combined comic talents of Terry-Thomas, Jon Pertwee, Jimmy Edwards and Richard Hearne could not fully rescue the film from unimaginative direction and an undistinguished script.[38] All in all, it was a dismal period for Rank's more modest productions, which struggled against an increasingly hostile and outspoken press. It was hardly surprising that, in the 1950s, the company stuck to distributing second features rather than making them.

Exclusive/Hammer

Founded in the 1930s as a distributor and producer of quota pictures by Will Hammer and Enrique Carreras, Exclusive resumed activities after the war as a family business with the demobilisation of the founders' sons, Anthony Hinds (b. 1922) and James Carreras (1909–1990). The latter was soon joined by his own son, Michael (1927–1994). Exclusive's entry into post-war film production was at the behest of the booking manager of the ABC circuit, who was desperately short of British programme-fillers. Ben R. Hart's featurette *Crime Reporter* (1947) was Exclusive's first post-war production. Made at the end of 1946 and billed as a Knightsbridge-Hammer film, it was a ripped-from-the-headlines story of London's black market. Mainly filmed silent in documentary style with occasional dialogue sequences, the picture was narrated by the eponymous journalist played by John Blythe. While the atmosphere was realistic, the plot was rather more fanciful. Ben Hart's follow-up picture was *River Patrol* (1948), again featuring John Blythe, this time as an undercover customs officer who rounds up a gang of nylon-smugglers, surprisingly led by the usually lovable Wally Patch. Set against a background of Thames-side warehouses, the film was a traditional crime melodrama with few pretensions to originality, but made a convenient programme-filler during the American product embargo.

Exclusive moved into Marylebone Studios in January 1947 to make *Death in High Heels* (1947), adapted from the whodunit by Christianna Brand, in which mystery surrounds the poisoning of a woman working in a dress shop. The trade reviews were less than kind to 'Tommy' Tomlinson's film: 'Poor entertainment for any but most uncritical audiences.'[39] Things got worse for Exclusive when the CEA General Council decided to ban the showing of their second Marylebone film, *There is No Escape*, which starred a notorious jewel thief called Stanley Thurston. The grounds were that 'no person who had achieved notoriety through the Courts should be featured in a film'.[40] Exclusive were obliged to disguise Thurston by re-naming him Charles Stuart, give a fictional gloss to its docu-drama, and retitle it *The Dark Road*, which eventually crept out on release some eighteen months later. Critics, though, still doubted the appropriateness of this biography of a criminal, even though his end was sticky. A more talented director might have got away with it, but Alfred Goulding was lambasted

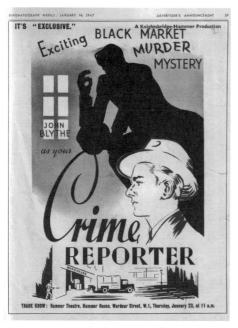

Exclusive releases: trade advertisements for two early post-war films from the company that, as Hammer, would become synonymous with horror

for the weakness of his handling, 'half-hearted attempts at comedy', poor casting and a failure to secure competent performances from his cast.[41] Nevertheless, Exclusive pushed on and began to try out new talent. Anthony Hinds was given his first chance to produce a film when the producer of *Who Killed Van Loon?* (1948) pulled out of the project. Some idea of the gung-ho approach to independent film-making that prevailed at the time can be gauged from Hinds' willingness to take over even though no script was available and a story had to be devised that would not only fit the footage that had already been shot, but would take account of the fact that most of the original cast were no longer available (indeed one had committed suicide!).[42]

Fortunately, Exclusive's confidence was boosted by their coup of securing the film rights to *Dick Barton*, the hit radio serial. Alfred Goulding's *Dick Barton – Special Agent* (1948) was of conventional supporting-feature length (sixty-nine minutes) and made at Marylebone for a mere £12,000, but the extraordinary popularity of its hero ensured that it topped most double bills: 'Cast-iron title attraction for the masses and juveniles,' as *To-Day's Cinema* put it, although it also conceded that, 'Candidly, the actual story is confused, the action crude, and the general presentation hardly up to slick modern standards. Yet the magic name of Barton nullifies all this.'[43] Dashing Don Stannard as Barton proved himself to be an India-rubber man of ludicrous durability, surviving all attempts to kill him before saving the community from a cholera plague. By early June 1948, Exclusive had secured 1,400 bookings for the film.[44]

The next 'Barton' to be filmed at Marylebone was actually the last to be released. It took more than two years for *Dick Barton at Bay* (1950, working title *Dick Barton Versus the Death Plague*) to fight its way off Exclusive's shelves. With Godfrey Grayson replacing Goulding as director, this effort was a little more sophisticated, although its Cold War story was even more fantastical, involving a secret radar device that can destroy aeroplanes in flight. The film gave an early opportunity to Patrick MacNee whose subsequent television character, John Steed of *The Avengers*, would become as famous as Barton. Made at Viking Studios, the third in the series, *Dick Barton Strikes Back* (1949), in which our intrepid hero saves the world from atomic destruction, was originally to be directed by Mario Zampi, but when he dropped out at the eleventh hour, Godfrey Grayson stepped back in.[45] This time Barton survives a gas chamber and a room filled with deadly snakes before a spectacular (and dangerous to film) climax with a death ray on the top of Blackpool Tower, in what was clear cinematic improvement on his first adventure: 'the final sensation, with the incessant screaming of the atomic apparatus, may well prove too much for all but the stoutest nerves. It is punched over with stern resolution by Don Stannard as the implacable Barton.'[46] Sadly, Stannard had thrown his last punch as Barton: he was killed in a car accident on leaving a party hosted by Exclusive in July 1949.

Encouraged by lighting cameraman Cedric Williams, James Carreras began seriously to look for alternatives to conventional studio production. One solution was to use a boat as a floating studio, which was tried by commissioning yacht-owner Vernon Sewell to make *The Jack of Diamonds* (1949), a story of treasure-hunting in the sea off Deauville. However, the film still had to be completed at Carlton Hill Studios.[47] A more practical solution was found by hiring a twenty-three-room country house, Dial Close, at Cookham Dean on the banks of the Thames. Here Exclusive, now operating as the production company Hammer, put its initial windfall from the NFFC to use with the first of a proposed series featuring Ernest Dudley's urbane radio sleuth *Dr Morelle*, played by Valentine Dyall. The film was made at the new 'studio', and the direction was entrusted to Godfrey Grayson. The story put a novel spin on Wilkie Collins' pioneering detective novel *The Moonstone*, and provided another money-spinner which could expect to top many bills.[48] A break-down of expenses prepared for the NFFC showed remarkable savings on a five-week schedule, and reveals much about the economics of low-budget production of this type.[49]

Dr Morelle: Production Costs

Expenditure	£
Five weeks' rent of furnished house	200
Technicians	4,730
Artists	2,111
Equipment (hire and purchase)	2,200
Film rights and script	1,500
Laboratory charges	700
Film stock	500
Music	400
Properties and dresses	400
Insurance, legal costs	400
Miscellaneous costs	1,028
Total	14,169

Celia (1949) was another adaptation of a now-forgotten radio series. Francis Searle directed Hy Hazell in this light comedy-drama of an actress who poses as a charwoman in order to help a private detective solve a mystery and earn herself a bonnet. Anthony Hinds was upbeat about shooting the film at Dial Close: 'We take advantage of this house in every possible way. Soon there won't be a corner left which has not been put to use in one production or another.'[50] It all sounded very simple, but Searle later recalled the restrictions imposed by working in such conditions:

> We had to re-write it with the knowledge of what rooms we had available ... In those circumstances – working in confined spaces trying to make something that cost nothing look like a hundred dollars – a director couldn't go around shouting and blaspheming and waving his bloody arms about. You really had to nurse the artists along.[51]

Recognising the effective way in which *Celia* overcame its economic restrictions, one satisfied critic described it as 'a utility outfit with a smart West End cut'.[52] It was quickly followed by more radio capers in the form of *The Adventures of PC 49: The Case of the Guardian Angel* (1949), sixty-five minutes of artless action directed by Godfrey Grayson and recommended as a 'Gilt-edged proposition for popular showmen'.[53] Hugh Latimer played a university-educated constable in continuous danger in a film that few beyond kindergarten age could take too seriously. Unfortunately, the BBFC in its wisdom awarded this juvenile caper an 'A' certificate. This might explain why, on its ABC circuit release, it was bizarrely teamed with Hitchcock's *Under Capricorn* (1949). Grayson also directed *Meet Simon Cherry* (1949), an unambitious adaptation of the BBC's *Meet the Rev.*, whose country house setting required little set construction at Exclusive's panel-lined accommodation. With its clergyman sleuth (Hugh Moxey) and contrived whodunit plot, it now seems dull and dated, but its trade reviewers praised it as 'an excellent illustration of the fact that films can be made on a modest and economical scale and still be really entertaining'.[54]

In the summer of 1949, the Exclusive production team moved on to another mansion, Oakley Court at Bray, where Francis Searle made *The Man in Black* (1950), in which a plot is hatched to drive a girl (Hazel Penwarden) mad via things that go bump in the night. Unsurprisingly, the film had a country house setting. *The Cinema Studio*'s 'Willy' Williamson paid a visit, commenting that the unit 'has proved that it can make second-features with a production quality comparable to many big films' and 'that its product can be first-featured in many locations with undoubted success'.[55] Valentine Dyall was the sinister storyteller for the film, as he was on the radio, and Betty Ann Davies took the acting honours. Dyall returned for a slightly more ambitious radio adaptation (it included an improvised crane shot!), *Room to Let* (1950), directed by Godfrey Grayson and scripted by John Gilling. Enthusiastically greeted by the trade, this sombre Jack-the-Ripper melodrama, co-starring Jimmy Hanley and Constance Smith, was the first in what would prove to be a long and lucrative line of period chillers. The next Hammer film, Francis Searle's comedy-drama *Someone at the Door* (1950, tagline: 'Let yourself in for a Big Laugh'), was period only in the sense that it was a remake of a 1930s quota quickie. Like many of its predecessors, it took full advantage of the Gothic mansion that served as its studio, with secret passages concealed behind its oak panelling.

Alone among the independent producers, Hammer/Exclusive had maintained a steady output throughout the production crisis of 1948–9, turning out four films at Dial Close – despite the concerted protests of local residents furious at the noise and nuisance caused – before agreeing to transfer the operation to Oakley Court.[56] Exclusive's films cost £14–15,000 each and were profitable on a flat-rate fee to exhibitors, with around 1,500 bookings apiece. The production schedule averaged more than 2.5 minutes of screen time daily, well above the target recommended by the Board of Trade's 1949 Working Party on Film Production Costs.[57] Jimmy Sangster has referred to the 'repertory company atmosphere' at Cookham Dean and Bray, where many of the workers 'lived in'.[58] It was such a successful period for Exclusive that *Kinematograph Weekly*'s Josh Billings was able to state categorically: 'They are absolutely in a class of their own with their handy-length British films, all of which had box office titles and well-founded publicity credentials.'[59]

The first production of 1950 was Grayson's culture-clash (some might say racist) comedy *What the Butler Saw* (1950), completed in a sprightly four weeks. The Butler (Henry Mollison) spies an under-clad stowaway princess from the 'Coconut Islands' (Mercy Haystead), who emerges from a packing case in (inevitably) his English country mansion. 'Get an eyeful of this' ran the film's crass tagline. Another adaptation from radio, the satirical crime comedy *The Lady Craved Excitement* (1950) was next on the production line, once more teaming scriptwriter John Gilling with director Francis Searle. Musical sequences featuring Hy Hazell and Michael Medwin as a couple of cabaret artists were shot at the ballroom of Bray's Hotel de Paris, but the most iconic scene in this madcap movie was the one involving an attempt by a demented painter (Andrew Keir) to decapitate Hy Hazell during a reconstruction of the execution of Anne Boleyn.[60] Once again, the reception was enthusiastic: 'Amiable nonsense, appropriately interleaved with tuneful songs, it earns full marks for making it snappy. Other British producers should take a leaf out of the Exclusive manual.'[61] Searle also directed *The Rossiter Case* (1951), a ripe family melodrama based on a stage play (by co-screenwriter Kenneth Hyde), and it showed its origins in the verbose script and studio-bound settings. Lacking a star name (although the then-unknown Stanley Baker had a walk-on part) and the usual radio associations, it had to wait some time in the queue for circuit release and fairly indifferent reviews.

The continuing success of Hammer/Exclusive can be gauged from the announcement by James Carreras in March 1950 that, in the midst of the production crisis, the company would increase its own output by 50 per cent. Twelve pictures were scheduled for the following twelve months, with production facilities extended to the Gilston Park Country Club, recently used by Vandyke Films.[62] As it turned out, Exclusive's wings were clipped later in the year by a shortage of space on the ABC circuit's two-feature programmes. Following (rather appropriately) the completion of Godfrey Grayson's *To Have and to Hold* (1951), film-making was held up for the last four months of 1950 while the queue of pictures awaiting circuit release was cleared. Eventually shown on the Odeon circuit, *To Have and to Hold* was a love triangle melodrama set among the English gentry. Patrick Barr played the paraplegic husband and Avis Scott the wife in love with an American guest (Robert Ayres). Any allegorical associations with the British cinema, its domestic audience and Hollywood were purely coincidental. After two years and seven films with Exclusive, Godfrey Grayson then left to form his own production company. Before Exclusive's enforced break, production was completed on Vernon Sewell's thriller *The Black Widow* (1951), and begun on Sewell's *The Dark Light* (1951).[63] While Gilston Park provided the lighthouse interiors, the most memorable scenes in the film were the stormy seascapes shot on location near Portsmouth. However, these simply provided an opportunity for the critics to launch their nautical metaphors: 'shipping water', 'all at sea' and the like.[64]

The production break gave Exclusive time to cement its new partnership with the Alexander Mutual production/distribution company in the USA, and secure the services of Hollywood's Robert Preston for the sombre revenge thriller *Cloudburst* (1951) scripted by Leo Marks, the former spymaster who would go on to write Michael Powell's *Peeping Tom* (1960). It was Exclusive's most ambitious production, although it was shot on the regular five-week schedule at the new Down Place Studios at Bray, which would be Hammer's home for the next decade and a half. *Cloudburst*, sold with the tagline 'The Torment of a Man's Split Mind', was expected to achieve at least 'co-feature billing in the major halls', but it had to accept supporting-feature status on the ABC circuit. However, it was Exclusive's first post-war film to achieve distribution in the USA, via the prestigious United Artists. This aspiration became standard for Exclusive following a deal concluded with Sol Lesser whereby his son, Bud, would co-produce with Anthony Hinds nine pictures over the next three years, and a further deal with the US independent Robert Lippert ensuring the availability of American stars and distribution. 'We will not be making any more of those domestic pictures,' declared James Carreras, but 'definitely making a slightly bigger size with American artistes'.[65] The size of Exclusive's achievement in securing American distribution for its product should not be underestimated at a time when many bigger-budget pictures struggled to convince US exhibitors of their merits.[66]

It seemed that *The Black Widow*, *A Case for PC 49* (1951) and *Death of an Angel* (1951) would be the last of Exclusive's 'domestic' pictures. *The Black Widow* was based on the BBC serial *Return*

Whistle while you work: police constable Brian Reece gets a blast from screen fiancée Joy Shelton in *A Case for PC 49* (1951)

from Darkness, a melodrama concerning a wife's murderous plot to exploit her husband's amnesia and marry his best friend. The well-upholstered Christine Norden and the rugged Robert Ayres took the leading roles in a rather more far-fetched version of the sort of noir thriller popularised by J. M. Cain. *A Case for PC 49* was a further adventure of Brian Reece's intrepid constable, now not only a BBC serial, but a comic strip in the new boys' paper *The Eagle*. Christine Norden put in a further appearance as femme fatale in this copper caper of already proven box-office worth. Both films received ABC circuit release. Charles Saunders' *Death of an Angel* was a talky rural whodunit that again featured Patrick Barr. It was not Exclusive's finest hour, but it quietly made its way on to the Odeon circuit.

Rather more impact was made by Exclusive's next, a co-production with Robert Lippert titled *Whispering Smith Hits London* (1952, USA: *Whispering Smith Verses Scotland Yard*). Richard Carlson played an American private eye on a visit to England who is persuaded by the charms of Greta Gynt to investigate a suspicious death. The prolific John Gilling wrote the script, and Francis Searle supplied workmanlike direction for a picture the trade press recommended as 'the safest of bets.'[67] It was followed by *The Last Page* (1952, USA: *Man Bait*), James Hadley Chase's story of how a girl who works in a bookshop (Diana Dors) is coerced into blackmail and then murdered by a crook (Peter Reynolds). With a budget of £40,000, modest Hollywood appeal was supplied by George Brent as the blackmailed bookshop owner and Marguerite Chapman as his assistant. It was Terence Fisher's

Don't tell them the ending: Diana Dors is silenced in *The Last Page* (1952)

first directorial assignment for the company with whose name he would become indelibly associated. 'Its popular pulp fiction has both punch and sheen,' commented *Kinematograph Weekly* approvingly.[68]

As it turned out, however, Exclusive was not quite ready to make a complete break with the 'B' films of its past. At the end of August 1952, a deal was signed with the prominent north-western exhibitor James Brennan to co-produce a series of supporting films at the now vacant Mancunian Film Studios. James Carreras explained that 'It will be our second unit', and placed it in the care of his son Michael.[69] Shooting began on Francis Searle's *Never Look Back* (1952), an Old Bailey trial melodrama, the following month. The film was unusual in having as its protagonist a female barrister (Rosamund John), and was distinguished by some accomplished performances from veterans like Henry Edwards, a matinee idol of the 1920s. At the same time, the 'first unit' moved into Riverside Studios to film Terence Fisher's *Wings of Danger* (1952, working title *Dead on Course*) with Robert Lippert supplying Hollywood's Zachary Scott for the starring role as a pilot for a charter airline. The cast was the most distinguished that Exclusive had yet assembled and included Robert Beatty and Kay Kendall, as well as promising newcomers Naomi Chance and Diane Cilento. James Carreras said of the move from the cramped conditions of Down Place: 'We have been making pictures the hard way and gaining the quality. Now we are going to do it the easy way, with equal quality.'[70] In spite of its relatively brief running time and indifferent trade reviews, the film duly played as a first feature on the Gaumont circuit, and was thus a milestone in Hammer's progress.

Fisher moved straight on to *Stolen Face* (1952), a fanciful crime melodrama about a plastic surgeon's attempts to mould the face of a criminal into the likeness of his lost love, a concert pianist. It starred Paul Henreid and Lizabeth Scott in a dual role as patient and pianist, and was conventionally directed by Fisher. Its American-sourced story, however, attracted unwelcome attention from *Picturegoer*'s Paul Ridgway, who attacked its fantastical premise in a feature article.[71] The input from America became even more pronounced with the disappointing *Lady in the Fog* (1952, USA: *Scotland Yard Inspector*), for which not only was Cesar Romero imported but the directorial duties were given to Sam Newfield.[72] He immediately startled the Exclusive boys at Riverside by setting a daily record of twenty-five camera set-ups and nine minutes of screen time – and this for a film expected to play as a first feature.[73] Dane Clark crossed the Atlantic to star as a socially ambitious card-player in Pat Jenkins and Sam Newfield's *The Gambler and the Lady* (1952, working title *The Money*) alongside Naomi Chance. However, the picture's essay in social climbing was greeted by indifferent reviews, which suggested that Exclusive still had more to prove before it could fully live up to its name and be accepted in the best circles. Paul Henreid was reunited with Terence Fisher for *Mantrap* (1953, USA: *Man in Hiding*), the story of a convicted murderer (Kieron Moore) who escapes from gaol to find the real killer with the help of a suave private eye (Henreid). Kay Kendall, in a supporting role that was hardly commensurate with her talent, caught most eyes, but the film itself broke little new ground.

Hammer spiced its diet of crime with the occasional foray into science fiction like *Spaceways* (1953) and *Four-Sided Triangle* (1953), the latter billed as 'The most Amazing and unusual film ever made!' It imported the controversial Hollywood actress Barbara Payton for a far-fetched story of a scientist's attempt to duplicate the object of his affections (who, inconveniently, is married to his colleague) with predictably disastrous results. As film-makers, Hammer were less adventurous than the scientists in their pictures, remaining cautious about changing a successful formula, particularly one that had made them the blue-eyed boys of the Eady fund. Barbara Payton stayed on to make an adaptation of Max Catto's novel *The Flanagan Boy* (1953, USA: *Bad Blonde*), directed by Austrian-American Reginald LeBorg. She was perfectly cast as the wanton wife of a boxing promoter (Frederick Valk) who ensnares her husband's protégé (Tony Wright in his debut film) with deadly results. 'Enthralled by a woman's possessive passion, he sacrificed everything,' announced the press book.[74] It was the sort of steamy sex drama usually associated with America film noir, and, despite its wages-of-sin denouement, its 'lurid structure' was consequently viewed with some suspicion by the critics at a time of British moral regeneration.[75] Terence Fisher's seriously under-resourced *Spaceways* was an altogether more wholesome offering, and was recommended as a 'Sure-fire box-office attraction for popular showmen, with unlimited exploitation potentialities'.[76] However, even this maiden excursion in space fiction could not escape the gravitational pull of the crime genre. Howard Duff's American scientist is falsely accused of murdering his wife and her lover and hiding the bodies on an orbiting rocket. The film orbited Britain on the ABC circuit.

Hollywood exile Louis Hayward returned to Britain to star as Leslie Charteris's debonair detective in Seymour Friedman's *The Saint's Return* (1953). Naomi Chance and Sydney Tafler were his co-stars in a light and nimble thriller, but it was Diana Dors in a supporting role as a gangster's moll who grabbed most of the publicity. Another ex-pat, Tom Conway (actually born in Russia), played Naomi Chance's leading man in the private-eye thriller *Blood Orange* (1953, USA: *Three Stops to Murder*). Terence Fisher took charge of this competent but conventional mystery set in the world of fashion design, as he did *Face the Music* (1954), an American-style noir designed to please jazz as well as thriller fans. Hammer's co-production/distribution deal with Robert Lippert continued to guarantee them a ready supply of American 'B' movie actors like Dane Clark, who teamed up with Paul

British production (with a little help from across the Atlantic). Although these UK trade advertisements stress the patriotism of these pictures, they played as American films in the USA

Belinda Lee comforts Dane Clark in *Murder by Proxy* (1955)

Carpenter, for Montgomery Tully's *Five Days* (1954, USA: *Paid to Kill*), and then with the young Belinda Lee in Terence Fisher's co-feature *Murder by Proxy* (1955, USA: *Blackout*, 1954), a pretty hackneyed story of a murder suspect who strives to find the real killer. By the time it was released in Britain, after a year or two on the shelf, Lee was Rank's newest and most glamorous 'discovery'.

The wider distribution of Hammer films was also guaranteed by a production deal with AB-Pathé for four to six pictures, beginning with Ken Hughes' *The House Across the Lake* (1954, USA: *Heatwave*).[77] Hughes' steamy Lake Windermere noir featured Hollywood talent in Alex Nicol and Hillary Brooke, and *Picture Show* devoted an entire page to a gossipy production report of the film,[78] and later rated it as 'well-acted and directed and full of atmosphere'.[79] There was also praise for Terence Fisher's dark mystery *The Stranger Came Home* (1954, USA: *The Unholy Four*) which was the swan-song of Hollywood's Paulette Goddard. It was recommended as a 'reliable co-offering anywhere' by virtue of its 'fine camera observation', 'rough, tough climax with a surprise twist' and its 'careful, methodical direction' (very typical of Fisher, that).[80] Next came Montgomery Tully's *Thirty-Six Hours* (1954, USA: *Terror Street*) with a sombre Dan Duryea as another visiting American – this time an Air Force pilot on a thirty-six-hour pass looking for his missing wife and finding he has been framed for her murder. Though clumsily worked out, with too much exposition, it was gratefully received as a useful programmer.[81]

Fisher's *Mask of Dust* (1954), a motor-racing drama partly filmed on location, imported Richard Conte and featured the schoolboy's hero Stirling Moss. Its trade reception, however, was disappointing: 'has speed but gets nowhere'.[82] More or less the same was said of Daniel Birt's *Third Party Risk*

(1955, USA: *The Deadly Game*), which boasted Lloyd Bridges as an American songwriter who finds himself involved in the battle over a new drug formula. The film contained an exciting fight in a burning barn, but nothing could really transcend a lifeless script and conventional plot. Jimmy Sangster recalled: '[I]n spite of the fact that most of the movie was supposed to take place in Spain, we never left the studio. Don't ask me how we did it! A couple of bullfight posters, a mantilla for the leading lady, Maureen Swanson, and rattle some castanets on the score ... Olé!'[83] There was a little more enthusiasm for Montgomery Tully's colourful *The Glass Cage* (1955), featuring John Ireland and Honor Blackman. In an age of *Big Brother* and other versions of reality television, the picture's theme of a man trying to break his own record for fasting in public seems remarkably current, even if the setting of the event – a circus tent on a bombed site – does not. It was, at least, a fairly original idea, but it was also the last of the Hammer-Lippert co-productions and virtually the end of the company's era of supporting-feature production.[84] The female prison drama, *Women Without Men* (1956, USA: *Blonde Bait*) ended the sequence of second features with American leads (Beverley Michaels in this case), and although Hammer continued to make a few shorts, some in colour and 'Scope', it would make only one fleeting return to the black-and-white Bs: *Cash on Demand* (1963), probably the best of the company's supporting features.

Exclusive had specialised in what James Carreras termed 'the dual-purpose feature', which he defined as 'pictures which play on the right-hand side of the bill on the circuit and independent six-day houses and as first features at independent three-day houses'.[85] The production of this type of film, he argued, had been made possible by the Eady scheme, which had boosted the general standard of low-budget film-making. By the end of 1952, Exclusive had received approximately £100,000 in bonus payments from the scheme, allowing budgets to increase by 50 per cent over those in place in the 1940s. The dual-purpose features were averaging 2,000 play-dates, half as first features.[86] At the same time, Hammer/Exclusive were beginning to kiss goodbye to supporting-feature production and moving upmarket into co-features and first features, releasing their first colour picture, the very profitable *Men of Sherwood Forest*, at the end of 1954.

Tempean

It may well be that the production record of Tempean Films outdoes for consistent quality any of the other 'B' movie companies. The twenty-odd second features it made in the 1950s are usually fast-paced, lively and characterful, and have the ability to look more expensive than they were. They also look like the work of people who knew absolutely what they were doing and the market demands they were meeting, sometimes surprising with the bonus pleasures they would offer in excess of their undoubtedly formulaic narrative patterns.

Tempean was founded in 1948 by Robert S. Baker (b. 1916) and Monty Berman (1913–2006), not to be confused with the costumier of the same name. Berman entered films in 1930, as a camera assistant at Twickenham Studios, before becoming a camera operator at Teddington (1934–8) and Ealing (1938–40), and lighting cameraman for Michael Powell's *The Edge of the World* (1936). Baker began as a keen amateur director, winning prizes for short documentaries before working as assistant director on a short musical film called *Night in Havana* (1937). Baker and Berman met in the African desert during the war, when both were transferred to the Army Film Unit. During the retreat from Gazala to Alamein, they were given a lift by Dicky Leeman, an RAF driver with whom Berman had already worked on *The Edge of the World*. The three decided that 'when we got out of the army we were going to make our own pictures. We were demobbed at roughly the same time and we begged, borrowed and stole to get finance together to make a picture.'[87] They set up Tempean together, although Leeman made only one film for the company before leaving to work in television variety. Their contract screenwriter was Carl Nystrom, who wrote three screenplays for them. They were lucky enough to enlist the services of Terry-Thomas and Jean Carson for their first production, the musical *Date With a Dream* (1948), a story with autobiographical undertones, as ex-servicemen who have seen action in North Africa stage a reunion variety show. It was made at Viking, a tiny studio in Kensington, and on location at Brixton Station, Edgware Road and Collins Music Hall, Islington, where three cameras were employed simultaneously to capture the spontaneity of the variety routines.[88] Most notable, perhaps, was the first screen appearance of the then almost-unknown Norman Wisdom, who had been spotted by Monty Berman at the Brighton Hippodrome, where he was filling in for an indisposed comic.[89] *To-Day's Cinema* was congratulatory:

> The presentation lacks nothing in verve and vigour, and it is this very atmosphere of unabashed joviality which, together with the Terry-Thomas individuality, should assure the appreciation of the masses. A further asset is the quintette of songs composed by Vic Lewis, whose orchestra contributes specimens of that strident syncopation beloved by our modern jeunesse.[90]

Baker and Berman realised the importance of securing a regular outlet for their films and, after distributing their first one through Grand National, they approached Phil and Sydney Hyam at Eros. The forging in 1949 of a long-running and mutually profitable deal with Eros, which would buy in American films and show them with a Tempean support, is symptomatic of the industrial savvy that made Baker and Berman such a successful team. Eros promoted Tempean's second film, *Melody Club* (1949) as 'A laugh-a-minute comedy of crime detection'. It was again written by Carl Nystrom and directed by Bob Baker at Viking and again starred the toothy grin of Terry-Thomas, who appeared in a variety of guises as a private eye employed to save the eponymous club from the machinations of racketeers. This time, Thomas lacked the quality of support he had enjoyed in the earlier picture, but his suave urbanity concealing that underlying tendency to panic was just about enough to keep most critics on side. The company's early musicals, however, were a misleading pointer to its future work, which was overwhelmingly in the crime thriller genre, with the occasional comedy – generally mild affairs like Henry Cass's *The Reluctant Bride* (1955) in which the plot about children trying to effect a romance between a paternal uncle and maternal aunt is given a bit of gloss by its (minor) Hollywood stars, John Carroll and Virginia Bruce.[91]

Tempean's real distinction is in the line of brisk thrillers it turned out regularly until 1958, after which Baker and Berman, ever astute at reading climatic changes in the industry, realised that television was likely to make the 'B' movie obsolete and turned their attention to, first, several 'A' movies and then to television itself. In September 1950, they released their first two thrillers, which were both set in London and featured Dinah Sheridan. The titles, *No Trace* and *Blackout*, she once indicated should have pointed to 'well-deserved oblivion'[92] but she was too severe on these proficient entertainments. The former was directed by John Gilling who would become the Tempean house director. Baker took over the directorial duties for *Blackout*, a story of a temporarily blind man (Maxwell Reed) who stumbles over a crime and, with his sight restored, rounds up a gang of currency racketeers. *Kinematograph Weekly* accepted it as a 'saleable pot-boiler'.[93] As a change from London settings,

EROS FILMS present

HUGH SINCLAIR · DINAH SHERIDAN (A)

"NO TRACE"

'Well-deserved oblivion'? Dinah Sheridan calls her agent in Tempean's *No Trace* (1950)

John Gilling took his unit to Romney Marshes in September 1950 to make the smuggling story *The Quiet Woman* (1951). *Picture Show* found it an 'unpretentious but entertaining drama ... notable for its beautiful settings'.[94] Tempean's sixth film, *The Frightened Man* (1952, working title *Rosselli and Son*), again written and directed by Gilling, began location shooting on 19 February 1951 and moved into Riverside Studios a week later. Charles Victor gave a moving performance as an Italian second-hand dealer who turns to crime to finance his work-shy son (Dermot Walsh), and the film won considerable praise for being authentically staged, effectively directed, 'thrilling and human'.[95] It was followed in April by another very well-received picture, *13 East Street* (1952), scripted by Gilling and starring the husband-and-wife team of Patrick Holt and Sonia Holm. Under Bob Baker's direction, the film followed the dangerous path of an undercover detective who goes to jail in the pursuit of a criminal gang.

By this time, Tempean were beginning to develop a reputation for consistency and for quality on a budget. Bob Baker explained to a visiting reporter how it was achieved:

> There are nearly always two ways of doing a thing in film-making – the perfect way and the compromise. We aim at good production values, and we use the best technicians available, but we usually accept the compromise in our stage work, and I am sure that very few members of the audience notice the difference.[96]

'Thrilling and human': a press book for Tempean's *The Frightened Man* (1952)

David Macdonald's *The Lost Hours* (1952) was another efficient little murder mystery from a Gilling screenplay, but significant in at least two respects. The first was the descent of the starry Jean Kent into the netherworld of 'B' films. The second was the introduction by a company that had hitherto relied on indigenous talent, of an American leading actor in Mark Stevens who gave a relaxed performance as an American pilot in London who is framed for murder. There were to be American leads in many other Baker and Berman films, bringing a gloss of otherness to, and reducing the parochialism of, the average 'B' feature. Baker praised the efficiency of Stevens, and this melodrama of jealousy, with a hero drugged into amnesia, certainly benefits by the transatlantic casting.[97]

John Gilling directed his own story *The Voice of Merrill* (1953), a modestly produced 'women's thriller' boosted to co-feature status by its BBC backgrounds and the coolly composed presence of Valerie Hobson as a scheming wife intent on making her lover's name by stealing her husband's radio scripts. *Recoil* (1953) went on location in November 1952 before settling into the Riverside Studios. John Gilling directed a cast headed by Kieron Moore, Elizabeth Sellars and Edward Underdown in a story of how a woman gathers evidence against her father's murderer by pretending to be in love with him. It was not the most plausible of plots, but it was effectively handled. 'The picture tells a meaty tale, and what's more, serves it hot,' enthused *Kinematograph Weekly*.[98] Gilling's *Three Steps to the Gallows* (1953, USA: *White Fire*) took another walk on London's wild side, this time in the company of a visiting American seaman huskily played by Scott Brady. His leading lady was another minor Hollywood star, the Rita Hayworth look-alike Mary Castle. Although formulaic, the action was brisk and often violent, and the settings, as usual, were authentic – including a sequence at the British Industries Fair.

While most producers might have regarded three or four pictures per year as verging on the unmanageable, it was not enough for Baker and Berman who, in late 1952, set up a second production company called Mid Century to combine with the Kenilworth company owned by Alf Shipman, the controller of the Riverside, Southall and Twickenham studios. Mid Century was a 'loss company' bought up so that any profits Tempean made could be written off against that loss. Within just over a year, Kenilworth and Mid Century were responsible for five second features. While Gilling was working on *Recoil* for Tempean, Baker and Berman hired Charles Saunders to provide quiet direction for *Black Orchid* (1953), a conventional murder mystery (apart from a suggestion of unrequited lesbian desire) with a twist ending.[99] Director of choice Gilling was called in for the next Kenilworth-Mid Century production *Deadly Nightshade* (1953). He was handed a screenplay by Lawrence Huntington that stretched credulity with its Cold War story of doppelgangers in a Cornish village: one an escaped convict and one a foreign saboteur and both played by Emrys Jones. However, Gilling managed to wring enough suspense from the tale to satisfy the trade reviewers. He was now so busy that he was reduced to adapting scripts from old quota quickies like *Double Exposure* (1937). His new spin on the old chestnut had the reliable John Bentley and Rona Anderson in the leading roles. The critics were kind: 'a brisk specimen of British whodunit entertainment made up of the usual displays of high-powered sleuthing, fistic rough stuff, romantic backchat and colourful villainy'.[100]

There was another backward glance to films past in Gillings' *The Embezzler* (1954), a modestly effective reworking of the theme of *The Passing of the Third Floor Back*, Jerome K. Jerome's morality play which was filmed in 1935. *The Embezzler*, a rather low-key tale of a worm turning, provoked an equally low-key response when it was trade-shown in July 1954, although one reviewer was prepared to admit that its 'smooth interplay of characters offsets its theatrics'.[101] John Harlow's *Delayed Action* (1954), appropriately enough, followed a few days later to rather greater critical opprobrium. Robert Ayres, Alan Wheatley and June Thorburn did their best to bring to life a standard pulp plot of a man saved from suicide by a criminal gang in order to use his identity, but could not prevent *Kinematograph Weekly* condemning their efforts as 'third-rate quota' with 'neither a thrill nor a laugh', making it just about Baker and Berman's biggest dip in form.[102] It was further proof that Tempean's success owed a lot to John Gilling, and it was he who wrote and directed the more effective noir, *Escape by Night* (1953), with Bonar Colleano as a hard-drinking journalist on the trail of the Rossini gang, led by Sid James affecting a heavy Italian accent. This thriller also featured the father and son team of Ted and Andrew Ray, but the Tempean films would increasingly showcase American talent, following a co-production deal brokered by Robert Goldstein. He arranged for Larry (*The Jolson Story*) Parks to star opposite the Hollywood-adopted colleen Constance Smith in *Tiger by the Tail* (1955, USA: *Cross-Up*).[103] They made a winning combination, with Smith described as 'pert and courageous' in her role, in a tense thriller with the usual atmospheric London backgrounds.[104] It fully justified its Odeon circuit booking.

Some idea of the feverish pace of Tempean production planning can be gleaned from the fact that Constance Smith began filming the Gilling-scripted *Impulse* (1955, working title *Rebound*) on another stage at Walton even before she had finished *Tiger by the Tail*. Scenes had to be carefully dovetailed.[105] Within an hour of finishing *Tiger*, director John Gilling was preparing *The Gilded Cage* (1955), which began shooting the following morning, and by lunch-time he already had three

EROS FILMS LTD. Presents

BONAR COLLEANO · ANDREW RAY · SYDNEY JAMES

" ESCAPE BY NIGHT "

with SIMONE SILVA Patrick Barr Peter Sinclair and TED RAY (GUEST STAR) **A**
A TEMPEAN PICTURE

Sid James gets tough as an Italian gangster in Tempean's *Escape by Night* (1953)

minutes of screen time in the can.[106] He did well enough for the film to be assessed as a 'sound and workmanlike action job'.[107] After this, he was given a rest from directing, but was kept busy scripting, rather atypically, a gentle comedy called *Windfall* (1955, working title *The Crime of Arthur Lee*), another thinly disguised re-hash of an old quota quickie (originally made by George King in 1935) about a man who discovers some money on a bus. This did not prevent *Kinematograph Weekly* hailing the film as a 'little gem' and the performance of its star, Lionel Jeffries, as 'immense'.[108] It was one half of a pair of comedies which Henry Cass made with Jeffries at Southall in August–October 1954. The other was *No Smoking* (1955), involving a cure for nicotine addiction and co-starring the glamorous Belinda Lee. Television comedian Reg Dixon provided the odd song and *Kinematograph Weekly* described the whole thing as 'a harmless, typically English romp'.[109]

As well as the stars, British or American, the Tempean films make notable use of that remarkable resource, the British character actor. It was another aspect of Baker and Berman's astuteness to work with a kind of rep company of players who would understand their methods and thus save time. Actors like Charles Victor, Thora Hird, Dora Bryan, Michael Ward, John Horsley, Michael Balfour and Michael Brennan all appear in several Tempean films, giving them that reputation for dependable character work that makes them still so enjoyable to watch. These and others like them, along with more than usual care in scripting and an economical but judicious use of locations, ensure that

Tempean's productions seem to have a richer texture than might be expected, given their modest budgets and exigent schedules.

One Wednesday morning in April 1955, Tempean completed their twenty-fifth film in seven years, *The Reluctant Bride*; but there was no pause for celebration, as their twenty-sixth, *Barbados Quest* (1955, USA: *Murder on Approval*) started after lunch.[110] However, there were pressing new challenges for the company. First, they could no longer depend on their ace director/scriptwriter John Gilling, who was now in demand from bigger outfits like Warwick Films. He had already directed his last film for the company, and his last 'B' script would be for Henry Cass's *Bond of Fear* (1956), a *Desperate Hours*-inspired story of a middle-class family threatened by a gunman (John Colicos) in their holiday caravan.[111] Second, Baker and Berman were becoming acutely aware of the threats and opportunities posed by new media and formats. Bob Baker told the press that there were plans to shoot in colour in the near future, and he would not rule out the use of 'Scope'.[112] There was also the issue of television, to which their colleague, Dicky Leeman, had already departed as the producer of the BBC's *What's My Line?*. Arguably, possible future sales to television influenced the decision to try to develop a series character in Manning O'Brine's Duke Martin, a suave and unflappable private eye played by Tom Conway. He made his first appearance in *Barbados Quest*, which RKO released as a support for their *Pearl of the South Pacific* (1955).[113] On arriving in England, Duke takes up with a shady former wartime chum, Barney (Michael Balfour, cheerfully shifty as ever). What follows is a lively enough account of philately, forgery and duplicity of several kinds. In Duke's second adventure, *Breakaway* (1956), Conway was supported by Honor Blackman, Michael Balfour and Bruce Seton, better known to television viewers as Fabian of the Yard, but this time playing the villain. Opening in East Berlin with a dying Soviet scientist, it comes on like a Cold War thriller, but the missing formula to cure metal fatigue is only a mcguffin to get the characters from one punch-up to the next. Still, *To-Day's Cinema* thought it 'slickly manufactured crime entertainment', and admired director Henry Cass's ability to ensure that 'his audience are whisked around sufficiently to get the idea they have been through a pretty hectic experience'.[114]

Tempean also embraced their distributor Eros's policy of offering co-feature programmes which could be marketed not only in Britain, but also on the American drive-in circuits. In *Passport to Treason* (1956), American tough guy Rod Cameron cracked a neo-Nazi spy ring with the aid of Lois Maxwell as a female MI5 agent; while in C. Pennington-Richards' *Hour of Decision* (1957) the obligatory American leading man was Jeff Morrow, playing the almost obligatory investigative reporter, with Hazel Court as the regulation cool, classy example of British femininity recruited to offset his rugged masculinity. Both conformed to the established Tempean template of action and intrigue with strategic injections of comedy and romance with a London backdrop. George Pollock's *Stranger in Town* (1957) might have been a generic title for the many American actors who found themselves in British film studios, taking the leading role in a 'B' movie. This particular stranger at Tempean was big, blond Alex Nicol who was more familiar with the local production methods than many of his compatriots, having already starred in three Hammer thrillers. Here he played yet another American newspaper man – this time on holiday in rural England – who investigates the death of a young composer. Apart from the setting, it was routine stuff for Tempean, which was now rather in danger of treading water for too long.

By the summer of 1957, however, Baker and Berman had spotted a growing audience taste for horror. They had hired Hammer's Jimmy Sangster as scriptwriter and, with the enthusiastic backing of Eros, had embarked on a new X-certificate path. First, they adapted Peter Key's television sci-fi-horror serial *The Trollenberg Terror* (1958), a cautionary tale about a radioactive cloud in the Swiss Alps. Directed by Quentin Lawrence, a man more used to television production, and mostly confined to two or three sets, the film starred Forrest Tucker, Janet Munro (very effective as a young psychic), future Labour MP Andrew Faulds and some classic bug-eyed monsters straight out of *Amazing Stories*. Eros teamed it with a ripe slice of continental smut, *Call Girls* ('Vice at a Price!'). Baker and Berman then went on to their highest-budget production, the Eastman Color *Blood of the Vampire* (1958), starring Donald Wolfit as a vampiric doctor with a taste for Barbara Shelley's blood group. This shocker, made on a five-week schedule as a first feature, was directed, at some remove from his Moral Rearmament sensitivities, by Henry Cass, who told a trade reporter that horror films were 'great fun to do', adding, 'and if you succeed in scaring the girls in the audience into the arms of their boy friends then you have done your job well'.[115] While Bob Baker commented: 'It's so easy to make horror films cheap and nasty, but that is a short-term policy. Horror in itself is not good enough. You've still got to have a good story. You've still got to make a good motion picture.'[116] However, Baker and Berman had not quite abandoned their staple crime Bs. Astonishingly, they managed to slip Peter Maxwell's *Blind Spot* (1958) past the trade reviewers without their ever noticing that it was a remake of Gilling's *Blackout*, which Tempean had filmed only eight years before. Robert Mackenzie took the part originally played by Maxwell Reed, of the blind man who has his sight restored. Reviews, in fact, were better the second time around.

From then on, though, Tempean embarked on 'A' film production, and its logo appeared on the war film *Sea of Sand* (1958), the horror films *Jack the Ripper* and *The Flesh and the Fiends* (1959, USA: *Mania*) and the unusual tale of anarchists in London, *The Siege of Sydney Street* (1960), among others.[117] The launch of Baker and Berman's TV career came in 1962 with *The Saint*, which ran from 1962 to 1969. They also produced the series *Gideon's Way* (1964–5) and *The Persuaders!* (1971–2), simply transferring their proven skills in low-budget film-making to the new medium. However, Tempean has a modest but secure place in British film history. Baker and Berman, even more than most 'B' movie producers, understood exactly what they were doing: that it was up to them to bring in efficiently made films on time and within budget constraints, and to ensure adequate distribution, in the USA if possible: in other words, to meet a market demand, and in doing so to achieve a level of production expertise which made it worth sitting through the first half of the double bill.

The Danzigers

The name, Dangizers, unfairly or not, has become virtually synonymous with bottom-of-the-barrel slipshoddiness in film production. It became a common warning in the acting profession of the 1950s that, if you weren't careful or lucky, you might end up working for the Danzigers. The stories told about this pair of American brothers, Edward (1909–1999) and Harry (1913–?), are colourful and legion. Margaret Tyzack, who appeared in their *Highway to Battle* (1960), recalled that 'It was said that the Danzigers' mother wrote their scripts!'[118] Actor Vincent Ball (also in *Highway to Battle*) claimed that, 'Doing a Danziger was really the end of the line, but I had a wife and kids and a mortgage to pay.'[119] Undoubtedly the brothers' methods were rough-and-ready and their attitude to film-making was strictly commercial. They also remained, apart from an occasional sortie upmarket, obdurately committed to the bottom half of the double bill, but they nevertheless sometimes ensured that what was available there would exceed expectations. Certainly, Dermot Walsh was pleasantly surprised by the results of their labours: 'I started making second features for them and they were quite good: they used to pinch stories and reshape them into good plots!'[120] The music publisher Jerry Kruger also had fond memories of the brothers: 'Harry Lee was my particular friend and confidant whilst Eddie was the tougher businessman and harder to know, but always treated me with respect. ... [T]hey were into deal after deal and everything always had to be done immediately if not sooner, but whilst tough, they were fair with me.'[121] The Danzigers produced about seventy films (three-quarters of them in the crime genre), as well as being the most financially successful independent television production company in the 1950s, so they must have been doing something right.[122]

The brothers had produced several US films in the late 1940s/early 1950s, including a controversial picture about racial prejudice, *Jigsaw* (1949), Bernard Vorhaus's reform school drama, *So Young, So Bad* (1950), and two films by the now-cult director Edgar Ulmer: *St Benny the Dip* (1951) and *Babes in Bagdad* (1952). Why they then decided to relocate to England is also unclear, but the McCarthy witch-hunts may have been a consideration. Certainly, on finally moving into Riverside Studios in March 1953 to make a series of thirteen television films for Paramount under the working title *Calling Scotland Yard*, one of their first appointments was the blacklisted Joseph Losey as script editor. As we shall see, a number of these teleplays were anthologised for cinema release in Britain, linked by introductions from the irascible television celebrity, Gilbert Harding.

Subsequently, they filmed at a range of studios including Brighton, Shepperton and MGM, making features as well as television series such as *The Vise*. Their first single-purpose British 'B' film was Paul Dickson's *Star of My Night* (1954), for which a strong cast that included Kathleen Byron and Hugh Williams was assembled.[123] It portrayed the love of a cynical sculptor (Griffith Jones) for a ballerina (Pauline Olsen), and was all too 'arty-crafty' for *Kinematograph Weekly*, which slammed its fake bohemian atmosphere: 'Cliché-ridden from start to finish, it'll exasperate the highbrows and bore the lowbrows.'[124] It would be some time before the Danzigers ventured into that sort of territory again. Instead they tried their hand at the increasingly fashionable science-fiction genre, producing the high-camp classic *Devil Girl from Mars* (1954). *Devil Girl* was a considerable hit, and the brothers would go on to make a bigger-budget, if less-successful, space opera, *Satellite in the Sky* (1957), but for the time being they settled for more standard second-feature crime fare such as *Alias John Preston* (1955), starring Christopher Lee, who claims to have been paid the princely sum of £75 for his leading role, a 'by no means atypical Danziger fee'.[125]

Failing in their bids to buy Beaconsfield Studios or to lease Twickenham, the Danzigers decided to build a studio in Watford Road, Elstree, to be called the New Elstree Studios. In part, they converted buildings erected during the war by the Ministry of Supply as aero-engine testing bays. They moved in at New Year 1956. The complex, which became the home of Danziger Productions Ltd, comprised five or six sound stages and employed over 200 personnel. Key figures included the directors Ernest Morris, Godfrey Grayson, Max Varnel, David Macdonald, Frank Marshall, cinematographer James (Jimmy) Wilson, writers Brian Clemens and Mark Grantham, music directors/composers Edwin Astley and Bill Le Sage, art director Norman Arnold, editors John Dunsford, costume supervisor Rene Coke, and continuity 'girl' Phyllis Townshend, among others. In front of the camera, there are recurring actors of varied competence, but the films benefit distinctly from the presence of such as Francis De Wolff or Colin Tapley, and, as leads, Francis Matthews and Lisa Daniely, who all give

The £75 star: Christopher Lee gives murderous expression to his frustrations in the Danzigers' *Alias John Preston* (1955)

some sense of reality to the often-flimsy cut-outs they are asked to vivify. The Danzigers were not in the business for art; they were in the business for business; and within these unpretentious parameters they ran an efficient studio from 1956 to 1962, letting some of their sound stages to other producers, and striking distribution deals with a surprising variety of renters, including United Artists, Paramount and British Lion.

During their ownership of New Elstree, as well as making television series, the Danzigers turned out a remarkable number of second features, almost invariably between sixty and seventy minutes in length, and costing between £15,000 and £17,500.[126] Vincent Ball recalled that 'They used to make films every ten days and I'd go from one set to another. ... If I finished one film at Friday lunchtime, I'd walk to another set and start the next one that afternoon, changing my jacket or whatever for the new character.'[127] The Danzigers were perhaps just more shameless than most, Edward once being quoted as saying: 'We make the cheapest films and TV series in the world. Nobody makes 'em cheaper.'[128] Their reluctance to part with money is attested to by Vincent Ball: 'The Danzigers had the reputation of being a bit "fly", some actors having had trouble getting paid. The problem was solved by actors insisting on getting paid in cash daily.'[129]

Most of the early production at New Elstree was devoted to television work and to the Cinema-Scope and colour (Georges Périnal, no less) extravaganza *Satellite in the Sky*, but a string of tele-plays was released as twenty-five-minute shorts by Pathé or Republic, and full-length supporting features gradually began to be added to the studio schedules. Tom Conway was cast against type as the murderous owner of a private hospital in Ernest Morris's *Operation Murder* (1957), one of Brian Clemens' earliest scripts for the Danzigers. The picture provoked the sort of review for which New Elstree's product would become notorious: 'Both surprise and punch are lacking ... The staging, too, leaves something to be desired, and so does the dialogue. Definitely made on a frayed cuff.'[130] Between episodes of the Mark Saber television series, Ernest Morris also found time to make the noirish *Three Sundays to Live* (1957) for distribution by United Artists. Kieron Moore played a condemned band leader, framed for murder, who escapes from prison to find a vital witness to the crime (Sandra Dorne). Clemens' next script was the equally noirish *The Depraved* (1957), directed by Paul Dickson, in which an American Army officer (Robert Arden) falls for a femme fatale (Anne Heywood) and agrees to a plot to murder her husband. Though the story was far from original, *The Cinema* was sufficiently impressed by its 'convincing detail' and 'smooth and fluent' direction, dialogue and camerawork to recommend it as a 'useful quota support'.[131]

Ernest Morris's *Son of a Stranger* (1958) starred *Cosh Boy*'s James Kenney cast very much to type as a young thug who beats up old ladies. The reviewers were in no mood for this sort of sordid melodrama and duly flushed it down the critical toilet, while admitting that Kenney put in a creditable performance in a decidedly unsympathetic role, and that the film might make a useful 'fill-up for industrial areas'.[132] The Danzigers' product began to turn the corner, as far as the critics were concerned, with Morris's *On the Run* (1958). It had another screenplay by Brian Clemens, and a vigorous performance by Neil McCallum as an ex-boxer hunted by thugs. He was supported by the reliable William Hartnell. Clemens switched genres for *A Woman Possessed* (1958), a family melodrama directed by Max Varnel. Margaretta Scott gave this one a touch of class as a rich mother whose possessiveness towards her son (Francis Matthews) almost has fatal consequences. Clemens and Varnel's next thriller, *Moment of Indiscretion* (1958), was also regarded as a 'woman's film', in which Lana Morris played a barrister's wife wrongly accused of murder. Again, the reviews were largely sympathetic. Varnel also pleased the critics with *Links of Justice* (1958), a tense courtroom drama with a surprise ending, but Ernest Morris rather blotted his copy-book with *Three Crooked Men* (1958), featuring Gordon Jackson and Warren Mitchell as a couple of unlikely comrades battling bank robbers. The film tries to hold the interest mainly through more attention than usual to characterisation, but can never quite avoid being what *Kinematograph Weekly* called 'a bit of a botched job'.[133]

As the Danzigers found their feet at New Elstree, the pace of production got faster and faster. Managing Director, Eric Blakemore, did his best to present speed as a virtue:

At New Elstree we can perhaps compare our work with lightning sketches of a good artist who, capable of creating masterpieces, can, with adjustments, bring his talent to the production of quick satisfactory work without shedding his inspiration. ... Artistic talent, yes, but we harness it to commercial deadlines ... Really fast shooting means ironing out foreseeable snags in advance; and if you want to ensure against all but fantastic complications, try building a resident production team. People who know each other well work well together. ... Operating at speed means every facility or service being readily available.[134]

Speed was also enhanced by the judicious recycling of standard footage and plot elements across the brothers' television and film production, not to mention the (not always very subtle) lifting of narrative ideas and scenarios from published literature and previous movies. *So Evil, So Young* (1961), for example, shamelessly re-hashes the reform school drama *So Young, So Bad*, made before the Danzigers

Anton RODGERS **PART-TIME WIFE** Henry McCarthy
Nyree Dawn PORTER   Mark Singleton   A BRITISH LION PRESENTATION
Kenneth J. WARREN   *Produced by THE DANZIGERS • Directed by MAX VARNEL • Story by M.M.McCORMACK*   Neil Hallett   *through*
                                                                Susan Richards

The future star of BBC's *The Forsyte Saga* (1967) gets some screen experience in the Danzigers' *Part-Time Wife* (1961)

left America; while *Return of a Stranger* (1961) owes a considerable debt to John D. MacDonald's 1957 novel *The Executioners*, even though it was completed before J. Lee Thompson's official adaptation, *Cape Fear* (1962).

It is not easy to make very clear distinctions among the films directed by the Danziger regulars, but tentatively it might be suggested that, at his best, Ernest Morris showed somewhat more ambition than the others. *The Tell-Tale Heart* (1960), at seventy-eight minutes pushing at the upper limits of the 'B' movie, is a genuinely unsettling version of the Edgar Allen Poe story, filmed with real imagination; *The Court-Martial of Major Keller* (1964) quite skilfully alternates courtroom drama with military action; and *The Spanish Sword* (1962), set in the England of Henry III and Simon DeMontfort, is an unusual foray into costume drama. The pedestrian Godfrey Grayson, on the other hand, was entrusted with the company's Technicolor productions, *The Spider's Web* (1960), a very lame, eighty-nine-minute adaptation of Agatha Christie, and the dubious *So Evil, So Young*. His other Danziger films were more modestly conceived. Frank Marshall made five largely unexceptional features, including the feeble comedy-mystery, *The Gentle Terror* (1962); and Max Varnel made a dozen or so workmanlike thrillers, rising to the occasion if the material was slightly above the ruck, as with *A Woman Possessed*, and sinking with it when it was as ludicrous as *Part-Time Wife* (1961).[135] These aforementioned directors, together with David Macdonald, accounted for the vast majority of the Danzigers' New Elstree output, though there were also minor contributions from a few others: veteran

Montgomery Tully made three films for the Danzigers, including the mildly twisty *Man Accused* (1959), which has in Carol Marsh a more distinctively distraught heroine than most, and Ramsey Harrington made two: *Compelled* (1960), notably under-nourished in motivation and characterisation, and *The Nudist Story* (1960), a ninety-minute naturist epic distributed by Eros.

Most of the Danzigers' films involve crime in one form or other, and among these there is a surprising sense of what has been called 'a world of hopeless nihilism and brutal economy, offering a more accurate picture of contemporary British middle-class life than most would care to admit'.[136] The last moments of Marshall's *Gang War* (1962) encapsulate just such a bleak world-view. A war between gangs over a fruit-machine racket ends with a shoot-out in a sleazy club, with one operator shooting another in the back, after which the young lovers walk out into the night to a moody jazz accompaniment, and the film ends on an overhead shot of a body on the floor of the club. Even when the closure is with a romantic pair apparently in place, there is an unusually pervasive sense of a grim society, from which romance could offer little escape. In Marshall's oddly compelling *Feet of Clay* (1960), set in a world of prison, drab night streets and stuffy private hotels, once the final flurry of fisticuffs is over, the young lovers embrace, but the acrid atmosphere of the film still hovers over their union. The contribution of cinematographer James Wilson is one of the strongest assets of the Danziger oeuvre and is always influential in creating this sort of unillusioned grimness.

The distraught heroine: Carol Marsh, once the star of *Brighton Rock* (1948), finds herself in a Danzigers' movie

More gloom hangs over Grayson's *The Durant Affair* (1962), which has a well-played heroine (Jane Griffiths) with a convincing air of struggling to contain past sadness, while Varnel's *Sentenced for Life* (1959), with a persuasive performance from Francis Matthews, goes back to the war period to initiate a tale of ruined lives. Another drama looking back to the war is Varnel's *The Silent Invasion* (1961, released 1967), in which personal feelings are made to conflict with loyalty to the Resistance in a French village in 1942; while Morris's *Highway to Battle* is set ominously in the German embassy in late-1930s London.[137] In fact, this downbeat tendency is not peculiar to the Danzigers' output but is commonly found throughout British 'B' movies; however, in the 'brutal economy' of the Danzigers' world it seems especially potent. Even a superior entry like *The Court-Martial of Major Keller*, though the hero is predictably exonerated, ends in a curiously muted way. Keller may be cleared, but he has killed and the acceptable motive for this wartime killing leaves little scope for exhilaration as he walks off with the dead officer's wife.

Although crime was meat and potatoes to the Danzigers, they sometimes ventured, usually unwisely, into comedy and other genres. The comedies include: Grayson's excruciating *She Always Gets Their Man* (1962), a witless spin on the provincial-girl-at-large-in-London theme; his marginally more amusing mother-in-law comedy, *The Battleaxe* (1962), with Joan Haythorne making the most of her chances as the eponym; Max Varnel's *Part-Time Wife*, straining credulity at every turn, despite a hard-working performance from Anton Rodgers; and Marshall's *The Gentle Terror* (1962), which offers a pale echo of John Ford's *The Whole Town's Talking* (1935), with a meek clerk-type being mistaken for a crook. In the crime films, all that was required was to keep the action moving briskly but the comedies lack the snappy dialogue and farcically inventive situations they need.

The Danzigers' more generically ambitious work included science fiction, historical romance and supernatural horror, but the budgets they were working with tended not to favour these generally more expensive ventures. However, as we shall see in Chapter 8, their version of Edgar Allen Poe's chilling tale of the supernatural, *The Tell-Tale Heart*, overcame the limitations of budget to surprisingly powerful effect. And, as noted, *The Spanish Sword*, while hardly a competitor for, say, the MGM-British costume dramas, doesn't look too cheese-paring in the matter of sets, costumes and camera set-ups. The settings, whether in unusually varied locations or studio sets of taverns, village square and baronial hall, testify to art director Roy Stannard's skill in making a little go a long way, as indeed did Danzigers' regular designer Norman Arnold in *The Silent Invasion*. All that one would want to claim is that, even in these daunting circumstances, it was still occasionally possible to produce superior work, and that, as for much of the rest, there is an unpretentious speediness in the storytelling and a clear-eyed acceptance of a tough, bleak world.

Merton Park and Anglo-Amalgamated

To many people of a certain age, 'Merton Park' is synonymous with the Edgar Wallace mysteries that poured out so prolifically between 1960 and 1965 or with the *Scotland Yard* and *Scales of Justice* thirty-minute features that kept the studio busy from, respectively, 1953 to 1961 and 1962 to 1967. These are considered in Chapter 6, but here we will look at the rest of Merton Park's output to show that there was a good deal more to the studio at Kingston Road, London SW19, than trench-coated detectives getting in and out of Wolesey police cars and the sonorous voice of Edgar Lustgarten.

In the 1930s, the Merton Park Studios were briefly used to accommodate the overflow of Twickenham Film Studios productions.[138] The first actual Merton Park Studios Ltd production

ANGLO AMALGAMATED FILM DISTRIBUTORS Present
"ASSASSIN FOR HIRE"
with SYDNEY TAFLER · RONALD HOWARD

'You're nicked': Sydney Tafler has his collar felt in Michael McCarthy's debut film *Assassin for Hire* (1951)

seems to have been a five-minute Stanley Holloway monologue, *Albert's Savings* (1940). After the war, the company produced several children's films, directed by Cecil Musk (*Circus Boy*, 1947, and *Trapped by Terror*, 1949) and William C. Hammond (*Jean's Plan*, 1946, *The Secret Tunnel*, 1947, and *Looking for Trouble*, 1951). Hammond also directed the company's first adult feature, the melancholy romance of post-war adjustment, *The Fool and the Princess* (1949).

It was towards the end of 1950, however, that Merton Park studios began their association with the company that would be responsible for so much of their output over the next fifteen years: Anglo-Amalgamated, run by Nat Cohen (1905–1988) and Stuart Levy (1907–1966). Anglo had begun as a distribution company, often packaging British featurettes with American 'A' movies, but with criticism of the featurettes mounting along with a growing demand for full-length supports, Cohen and Levy formed a production company with Julian Wintle, a young producer at Merton Park who had recently completed Jeffrey Dell's *The Dark Man* (1951).[139] The partnership operated under a number of names, principally Merton Park Productions and Insignia Films. The latter name would appear on a dozen or so modest entertainments during the decade, including blacklisted Joseph Losey's first British film, *The Sleeping Tiger* (1954, direction attributed to Victor Hanbury), Guy Green's first directorial assignment, *River Beat* (1953), the first of the *Carry On* series, *Carry On Sergeant* (1958), and the Tommy Steele vehicle *The Duke Wore Jeans* (1958). Anglo's first full-length feature was *Assassin for Hire* (1951). Adapted from his own teleplay by Rex Rienits, the film was shot in fifteen days by a director of Army training films, Michael McCarthy, who was making his first fiction feature. The film told the story of a criminal of Italian origin (Sidney Tafler) who pays for his younger brother's violin lessons by acting as a hit man. He eventually confesses to the police in the belief that he has accidentally eliminated his cherished musical sibling. While *Picture Show* praised Tafler's 'convincing performance', it summed up with 'Competent production suffering from too much talk.'[140] However, the film was well received by exhibitors who were chronically short of British second-feature product and even got some distribution in the USA via William Home and David Dietz, the first of a string of one-off deals with small American independent renters like Realart and Lippert.

Tafler stayed on to play the lead in the next two Anglo-Amalgamated films: as a sleuthing crime writer in McCarthy's *Mystery Junction* (1951), a twisting whodunit with a touch of *The Ghost Train* about it,[141] and as a spiv in *Wide Boy* (1952). The latter film announced the arrival of a director who would quickly make a name for himself in the crime genre, Ken Hughes, and established his trademark directorial style: briskly paced and authentically staged. Anglo's gloomy *Crow Hollow* (1951) took the floor at Merton in August 1951, with Michael McCarthy returning to the director's chair for an old-dark-house mystery with Natasha Parry playing a typical imperilled gothic heroine.[142] More significant, though, was the production that followed, because it heralded a fruitful partnership between Anglo and the director Vernon Sewell. As he recalled: 'I went to two young people starting off called Nat Cohen and Stuart Levy and they – well they let me do what I liked more or less! And I made half a dozen films for them, using very much my steam yacht.'[143] The yacht, *Gelert*, made an immediate appearance in the supernatural tale *Ghost Ship* (1952), which went into production in May 1952 on location near Brighton. Husband-and-wife team Dermot Walsh and Hazel Court took the leads, as they did in Sewell's next directorial assignment, although the yacht was left at the dockside. In the aftermath of the defection of Burgess and Maclean, *Counterspy* (1953) abandoned the chiller in favour of the Cold War. Dermot Walsh played an accountant who unwittingly becomes involved with a spy ring, while Hazel Court played his anxious wife. The action was kept moving by Sewell at a lively pace, with a chase round the Big Dipper in the Festival Gardens fun fair. It was well received by reviewers as a topical thriller with unusual impact.

In 1952, following Exclusive's lead, Anglo struck a production/distribution deal with an American independent – in this case Bob Goldstein. The first production, *Street of Shadows* (1953), imported Cesar Romero to star with Kay Kendall in a thriller aimed at the first-feature market. Their second co-production was *Dangerous Voyage* (1953) a yachting tale right up Vernon Sewell's sea lane, and billed as 'The

Brine and spirits: Anglo's press book for Vernon Sewell's *Ghost Ship* (1952)

Screen's most Explosive Thriller of the Sea!'. William Lundigan was brought over from America to star opposite Bath-born Naomi Chance in a film that was shot partly at Deauville. He played a holidaying writer who stumbles across a nest of ruthless uranium thieves at the Sussex seaside. It was formulaic but graced by some good camerawork. Reviews were encouraging, and it was booked by the ABC circuit. American talent was replaced by a home-grown cast for Sewell's next, *The Floating Dutchman* (1953), which was not the seafaring yarn it sounds, but a London underworld drama – the title deriving from a body in the Thames. Dermot Walsh played a special investigator, and Sydney Tafler his quarry in a lively thriller. This film had a generous budget, by 'B' film standards, of £30,000, but Sewell was on shorter rations for another tour of London by night – this time by taxi. *Radio Cab Murder* (1954) starred Jimmy Hanley, the plucky young copper from *The Blue Lamp* (1950), and moved brightly around its locations. The trade appreciated its humorous characterisations and 'credible dialogue'.[144]

Radio Cab Murder was one of a trio distributed by Eros in 1953–4. Eros had already handled *River Beat*, a swift-moving diamond-smuggling thriller that starred American actress Phyllis Kirk and the ever-reliable John Bentley as a river policeman. It gave Guy Green his first directorial opportunity, and shows the benefits of direction from someone long experienced as a cinematographer.[145]

The other Eros release was Wolf Rilla's *Glad Tidings* (1953), adapted from a play by R. F. Delderfield. It was a lively family comedy that teamed Raymond Huntley (in a rare starring role) as a widowed colonel with the vivacious Barbara Kelly as his new American bride-to-be. It was successful enough for Anglo to continue ploughing Delderfield's bucolic furrow with another comedy, *Where There's a Will* (1955). Somewhat surprisingly, Vernon Sewell – not a director noted for comedy – was assigned to this, but, with a cast that included Kathleen Harrison, Dandy Nichols and George Cole, it was hardly likely to be short of belly laughs, and was judged a 'good British double-bill'.[146] Rilla was also given further rustic duties with *The Large Rope* (1953). Scripted by Ted Willis, it was an examination of prejudice against an ex-con (Donald Houston) who tries to pick up his life in a village community. Essentially a Western in disguise, it was made by Insignia for United Artists distribution, partly at Nettlefold and partly on location in the village of Turville near Henley. Of the rest of Insignia's output, Willa's *Noose for a Lady* (1953) at least rescued the archetypal 'B' movie heroine, Rona Anderson, from the confines of the nice girls she typically played and gave her the chance to be a bad lot.

Although Anglo-Amalgamated had already lifted its sights with *Street of Shadows* and *Sleeping Tiger*, its real breakthrough films were the Ken Hughes' thrillers, *Little Red Monkey* (1955, USA: *The Case of the Red Monkey*) and *Confession* (1955, USA: *The Deadliest Sin*), both surprise international hits. Hughes, who had established himself on Anglo's *Scotland Yard* series, had also filmed the co-feature *The Brain Machine* (1955), a lively mix of 'science', kidnapping and drugs, executed with much better production design (George Haslam) and smarter editing (Geoffrey Muller) than was usually found in 'B' movies. However, the stars, Elizabeth Allan and Maxwell Reed, had enjoyed only minor Hollywood exposure. *Little Red Monkey*, on the other hand, could boast Richard Conte, a well-known American leading man, in the sort of espionage story which had international appeal. *Confession*, a tense thriller of a priest marked for murder after hearing a killer's confession, starred Charlie Chaplin's son Sydney and Audrey Dalton, both beginning to forge Hollywood careers. It was followed by a succession of first/co-features with American leads in the crime genre, some with science-fiction trappings. Zachary Scott and Faith Domergue were imported for Montgomery Tully's

Man in the Shadow (1957, USA: *The Shadow Man*), for which exteriors were shot in Italy. It was a lurid enough tale of murder and blackmail, but it looked relatively wholesome beside its fantastical Eros stable-mate, *Invasion of the Hell Creatures* (1957). Perhaps the most significant of this sequence of British features with American stars was *Intimate Stranger* (1956, USA: *Finger of Guilt*), which was directed by Joseph Losey (although initially credited to producer Alec Snowden) and written by fellow blacklist victim Joseph Koch (as Peter Howard), who had been partly responsible for the screenplay of *Casablanca* (1942). Appropriately, *Intimate Stranger* was the allegorical story of an ex-pat American film director whose life is disrupted by the allegation of an unknown woman. There were also three co-features with supernatural or science-fiction overtones: Alfred Shaughnessy's *Cat Girl* (1957) and Montgomery Tully's *Escapement* (1956, USA: *Electronic Monster*) and *Timeslip* (1956, USA: *The Atomic Man*), which we will consider in a later chapter.

At the beginning of 1957, as the general shortage of British 'B' films became acute, Anglo announced that it would help to fill the gap with a series of supporting features to be made at Merton Park at the rate of one per month, mainly destined for the ABC circuit. The first was *The Key Man* (1957), shot on a three-week schedule by Montgomery Tully, who made sure there was plenty of action, including a cross-London car chase. Lee Patterson was a safe choice as the reporter protagonist and the trade was happy. Patterson was retained to star with Anglo contract artist Kay Callard in Compton Bennett's *The Flying Scot* (1957), a train-robbery story which turned out to be one of the most compelling 'B' thrillers of the decade. *The Daily Cinema* reviewer described it as a 'gem of a thriller ... packing far more suspense and tension than many an "X" horror'.[147] Montgomery Tully travelled further for Anglo's *Strange Awakening* (1958), a romantic crime thriller set in the South of France, before returning to London for *The Long Knife* (1958), featuring Joan Rice as a nurse who gets involved with extortion racketeers and is aided by an American lawyer (Sheldon Lawrence). *A Man With a Gun* (1958) was more of the same – Tully directed and Lee Patterson starred in a crime drama with a night-club background – but this picture was notable for its debutant scriptwriter, a young man just making his way in the world of film-making: Michael Winner. The reviewers were kind about a fairly standard slice of pulp fiction that was 'more robust than subtle'.[148] Patterson was again the lead in Lawrence Huntington's *Deadly Record* (1959), a standard wrongly accused-man-finds-real-killer scenario; and Peter Reynolds was teamed with Lisa Gastoni for Vernon Sewell's brisk heist film, *Wrong Number* (1959).

After this brief burst of activity, Anglo-Amalgamated largely abandoned non-series supporting features in favour of the sixty-minute Edgar Wallace adaptations which could be more conveniently sold to television. These and the shorter *Scotland Yard* series were fitted around Anglo's 'A' feature production, beginning with a trilogy of topical rock 'n' roll films made in conjunction with Sydney Box at his Beaconsfield Studios: *The Tommy Steele Story* (1957, directed by Gerard Bryant), *The Duke Wore Jeans* (directed by Gerald Thomas), with Steele again, and the pop revue, *6.5 Special* (1958, directed by Alfred Shaughnessy). Insignia produced the first of the *Carry On* films, and Anglo-Amalgamated distributed several of the series, until, according to producer Peter Rogers, the company started going upmarket and attending to directors like John Schlesinger.[149]

The names most tenaciously associated with Merton Park, apart from Lustgarten's, are the producers Alec C. Snowden and Jack Greenwood. Snowden (b. 1901) had been in films since 1919, as assistant director at Stoll Studios. After a spell in theatre management in New Zealand, he returned to Britain in 1931, working as production or business manager for several companies. He joined

Merton Park as studio manager in the late 1940s and produced the first twenty-six episodes of its *Scotland Yard* series between 1953 and 1957. He also produced several lively full-length features, including Hughes' *The Brain Machine* and *Confession* and Tully's *Escapement* and *The Hypnotist* (1957). Greenwood (1919–2004) had documentary experience before joining Merton Park as studio manager, and, from 1958, as prolific producer of the studio's three main series: *Scotland Yard* (thirteen half-hour features), *The Mysteries of Edgar Wallace* (forty-seven hour-long features) and *Scales of Justice* (thirteen half-hour features). Like Snowden, he occasionally moved out of the formulaic rut to do somewhat more demanding work, and produced Arthur Crabtree's stylish *Horrors of the Black Museum* (1959), Joseph Losey's *The Criminal* (1960) and Alan Bridges' very superior 'B' movie, *Act of Murder* (1964). Snowden and Greenwood were the backbone of the Merton Park operation in its most productive years.

Adelphi and Advance Films Ltd

Adelphi Films was active in distribution and production for about ten years after World War II and is best remembered for a string of broad comedies that starred some of the most popular comedians of the period, including Max Bygraves and the members of the Goons. The head of Adelphi Films, Arthur Dent (1888–1956), was an actor and publicist before moving into production and distribution, becoming the managing director of Wardour Films in the 1920s and a founding director of ABPC. He resigned in 1940 to work as an independent producer. As Advance Films, he made *Comin' Thru' the Rye* (1947), a biopic of Robert Burns written by the MP Gilbert McAllister, an authority on the Scottish bard, and given full co-operation by the Burns Federation. Looking at it now, it is surprising that Advance survived its first film. Directed by an old ABPC friend, Walter Mycroft,

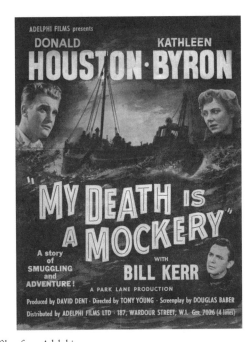

Arthur Dent presents ...: trade advertisements for a bundle of films from Adelphi

it is a picture overburdened with cliché and literalism. It offers sixty-one minutes of hagiography in which Burns (Terence Alexander) is so whitewashed that sexual rapacity is airbrushed into 'romance'. There are also some excruciating moments, as when a plump tenor sitting in a chair just sings 'My love is like a red, red rose' to a woman doing needlework. However, it was seen very differently at the time and, ironically, qualified for renters' quota on the basis of 'special entertainment merit' as assessed by the Films Council.[150] Thankfully, Dent's planned biopic of Shakespeare never materialised.

Early in 1949, Dent acquired the distribution business, as Adelphi, and produced four quota films: three comedies – *Bless 'em All*, *Nitwits on Parade* (both thought to have been made at Bushey), *Melody in the Dark* – and one thriller with a ballet background, *I Was a Dancer* (both Southall Studios' productions). Like John Blakeley at Mancunian, Dent understood that many 'industrial audiences', particularly in the north of England, wanted to relax with undemanding comedies that could be made very cheaply and yet still play as first features, providing popular music-hall comics occupied the staring roles. The service comedy, *Bless 'em All*, made on a 'B' film budget but featuring the much-loved comedian Hal Monty, was a huge hit in many parts of the country.[151] With some films, however, Dent was prepared to settle for supporting-feature status: Robert Jordan Hill's *Nitwits on Parade* was a simple variety featurette with no attempt to introduce a narrative element. Hill's *Melody in the Dark* – billed as 'The Anti-Gloom Film' – starred exuberant 'rubber-necked' comedian Ben Wrigley in a knockabout excuse for the presentation of variety acts in the inevitable country house setting (this one was supposedly haunted). As one review put it: 'The low but lively nonsense is bound to tickle the industrial masses.'[152] It was followed by a second Wrigley vehicle, *High-Jinks in Society* (1949), a comedy involving jewel thieves in the grand tradition of the quota quickie. The critics also responded positively to John Guillermin's debut thriller *Torment* (1949, USA: *The Paper Gallows*), which showcased the work of three actors who would become staples of the 1950s 'B' film: Dermot Walsh, John Bentley and Rona Anderson. The theme of a crime writer who murders in the style of his novels would be re-used in films like *Horrors of the Black Museum*, and here it supported a climax that was exciting enough to boost the film's claim to better than supporting-feature status.

Adelphi lost the magic touch in entering into a co-production deal with the spectacularly untalented Frank Richardson to make *Bait* (1950), with star of 1930s musicals Diana Napier improbably cast as a gang leader. Richardson had perpetrated some of the most incompetent quickies of the 1930s, and *Bait* showed few signs of improvement. The reviews were so bad that Adelphi recalled the film for re-editing, cutting 1,500 feet before letting it out for further scrutiny.[153] According to Adelphi's records, *Bait* managed a miserable 143 bookings at a time of product shortage, compared to an average of almost 2,000 for the Ben Wrigley films. Arthur Dent should really have known better, having viewed the results of Richardson's work on *I Was a Dancer*, which was finally released over a year later to predictable reviews: 'Old-fashioned setting and dialogue and slipshod camerawork ... Few will be able to follow, let alone get a kick out of it.'[154]

Of rather greater significance than the Richardson farragoes were two films that introduced a genuine comic talent in Peter Sellers, *Let's Go Crazy* (1949) and *Penny Points to Paradise* (1951, working title *Double or Quits*), both recently restored. The latter is a comedy about a football pools winner pursued by crooks in Brighton that featured most of the team that would shortly constitute the 'Goons': Peter Sellers, Spike Milligan and Harry Secombe (billed as part of 'the greatest array of radio and vaudeville stars ever assembled in one film'). Inspired by Carol Reed's *Penny Paradise* (1938), the film was directed by Tony Young, who would later be responsible for *The Telegoons* TV puppet series in the 1960s. The future Goons are in exuberant form, and are well supported by Alfred Marks and Bill Kerr as counterfeiters. *To-Day's Cinema* described it as 'another of those breezy, unsophisticated entertainments, produced efficiently on a modest scale, that have so often proved a reliable booking in the smaller popular hall, especially in the provinces'.[155]

Few could have predicted that this unassuming picture would one day be thought an important milestone in the history of British comedy. At the time, it took its place among Adelphi's roster of comedies and revues like *A Ray of Sunshine* (1950), in which established comic Ted Ray and a parade of variety turns like Ivy Benson's all-female band and Wilson, Keppel and Betty offered an unpretentious hour's entertainment that trade reviewers were prepared to endorse for unsophisticated audiences. *The Kilties are Coming* (1952), was another populist revue, but one that acknowledged the growing significance of television by purporting to be staged in a TV studio and employing the services of the BBC presenter McDonald Hobley. Its 'stars' were members of the Royal Kiltie Juniors, an enthusiastic troupe of youthful variety acts. Maclean Rogers' *Alf's Baby* (1953) was another comic offering, an adaptation of a stage farce, and really the original *Three Men and a Baby*. Jerry Desmonde led the cast in a carefree story of a trio of protective bachelors who 'inherit' an infant who quickly grows into an eligible young woman (Pauline Stroud). And there was more dubious parenthood in Adelphi's comedy *Don't Blame the Stork* (1954), in which a stage-struck girl (Veronica Hurst) poses as the mother of a baby left on the doorstep of a famous actor (Ian Hunter). *Kinematograph Weekly* thought it 'neither original nor particularly witty', but (in the casual sexism of the day) that it 'should amuse the womenfolk'.[156]

Although Adelphi focused on comedy and revues, it did release the occasional programme-filler in alternative genres. *Death Is a Number* (1951) was a melancholy tale of an old English family cursed by a gypsy and subsequently dogged by the number nine. It was short on stars, but considered 'worth a gamble' for exhibitors.[157] Numerology was replaced by palmistry in the esoteric *Hands of Destiny* (1954), an hour-long drama-doc directed by Tony Young about the palmist Dr Josef Ranald. *To-Day's Cinema* commented that the two dramatised episodes from the doctor's casebook were 'presented so artificially as to delight sceptics and embarrass converts'.[158] Tony Young also directed the salty noir *My Death is a Mockery* (1952), produced by David Dent (b. 1922), son of Arthur. During filming, Dent reserved judgment on whether it would be a supporting feature: 'We'll see. The film will go out on its merits, and what those will be we shan't know until the picture is finished.'[159] In fact the film just had a chance of topping the bill at small suburban and provincial cinemas, and would achieve some notoriety as the picture viewed by Christopher Craig before being involved in a shoot-out with police on a Croydon rooftop a year later. Starring Donald Houston and Kathleen Byron, it was a story of brandy-smuggling and the murder of a policeman. Considered by *Picture Show* 'Well-handled and told',[160] and narrated in flashback, the tale is bleak and melancholy, documenting the problems of an ex-serviceman trying to make his way in the post-war world and ending up in the condemned cell. The ending is downbeat: the post-war world is not a land fit for heroes and shows little compassion for men with problems.

Adelphi's other jobbing directors included Denis Kavanagh who made the American-flavoured crime featurette *Dollars for Sale* (1955). Production values were unpretentious, to say the least, but it remains of interest for its casting of the black actor Earl Cameron as the villain. John Guillermin, Adelphi's greatest directorial 'find', contributed *The Crowded Day* (1954), perhaps the company's best-regarded programmer. Finally, most of Adelphi's bigger productions were entrusted to Maurice Elvey, wildly prolific since silent days: *My Wife's Lodger* (1952), *Is Your Honeymoon Really Necessary?*, *The Great Game* (1953), *What Every Woman Wants* (1954) and the first 'Scope' feature by a British independent *You Lucky People* (1955). Each produced by David Dent, these were five of Elvey's last films, and are rough-and-ready, amiable co-features with middling stars (e.g., Tommy Trinder well past his prime in *You Lucky People*, or Brenda De Banzie in *The Happiness of Three Women*) or character actors in the leads (e.g., Thora Hird and James Hayter in *The Great Game*, with Diana Dors for decoration). The *Picturegoer* reviewer felt that *Is Your Honeymoon Really Necessary?* 'packs quite a few laugh spots – even though you know what they're going to be well before they arrive'.[161] The production activities of Adelphi/Advance effectively ended with the death of Arthur Dent in 1956, by which time its films had moved determinedly into first-feature territory with the colour and 'Scope' musical *Stars in Their Eyes* (1956).

ACT Films and Group 3

The production hiatus that saw the majority of British studios vacant in the late 1940s was the catalyst for the launch of two experiments in the organisation of film-making. Both took their inspiration from the spirit of the post-war Labour Government, in attempting to develop a methodology that placed the welfare of people and the development of talent before short-term profits and commercial exploitation. They differed, however, in the way they approached this aim and in their willingness to conform to the conventional generic practices of commercial cinema. Initially both took their aesthetic lead from the style of Britain's most influential 1940s studio, Ealing, then on the crest of its wave, but while one, Group 3, clung to the ebbing Ealing formula and was ultimately left high and dry, the other, ACT Films, was obliged to abandon it and flow with the prevailing currents of 'B' feature production.

ACT Films was founded by the film technicians' union, the Association of Cinematograph Technicians, in May 1950 with the primary aim of countering unemployment in the industry. However, according to Sidney Cole, the union 'did not have anything directly to do with the running of the Company, though its Board of Directors included some members of the [executive committee], such as myself'.[162] The Board also included such well-known industry names as Ralph Bond, documentary director and sometime studio manager at Blackheath Studios for John Grierson, Ralph Brinton, Desmond Dickinson, George H. Elvin, Jack Harris, R. J. Minney, Adrian Worker and, most illustrious and influential, Anthony Asquith who was elected chairman. Cole emphasised Asquith's importance as a 'quality' director with a long and impressive track record. He not only brought artistic clout, and industrial muscle, he also directed a film for the company – *The Final Test* (1953), a mildly engaging comedy of cricket- and poetry-lovers – and thus, Cole believed, encouraged other directors to do the same.[163] ACT made twenty-five pictures. Four of them, including Asquith's, were minor 'A' features, the rest were a workmanlike batch of supporting films, mainly in the category of crime-thriller. It may not be a record of distinction to rival Ealing's, but ACT Films remains an interesting phenomenon: it represents not simply an industrial response to a difficult situation, but a rare attempt to produce films for the commercial cinema on a non-profit-making basis. It is also unusual in having left at least a partial record of its operations, now lodged in the BFI's Special Collections.

The new company, with Henry Passmore as production manager, began ambitiously with a would-be 'A' feature backed by the NFFC. Made over ten weeks extensively on location in Norfolk and the Romney Marshes, *Green Grow the Rushes* (1951) was an Ealing-style comedy adapted from

Howard Clowes best-seller and directed by Derek Twist. Now chiefly remembered for an early performance by Richard Burton, it was a story of how three men from the Ministry become involved in the smuggling activities of Anderida Marsh, and how the Marsh's inhabitants make use of their ancient charter to exonerate themselves. However, the title *Green Grow the Rushes* could also be read as a statement of optimism by the company: the 'rushes' in this case being the celluloid kind. Unfortunately, this optimism turned out to be misplaced. Almost a year after the delivery of the film to its distributor, it was still awaiting a booking, and therefore had not returned any of its £95,000 budget to the NFFC.[164] It was finally trade-shown in November 1951, and the boot went in immediately, aimed directly at the pretensions of a union rising above its 'station':

> It tries hard for laughs at the expense of bureaucracy and tradition, but fails dismally. Outmoded and completely lacking in showmanship, its box-office potentialities are slight ... Produced by the ACT, its shortcomings could have been partly redeemed by expert cutting, but the editing, like the script, is untidy. However good the technician, he is lost without the right 'blueprint'.[165]

Three years later, ACT would finally accept the judgment and cut the film down to sixty-seven minutes for release as a second feature by Equity British with a new title, *Brandy Ashore*. 'At first our company met with some hostility from sections of the film trade,' commented Ralph Bond, 'and our first production *Green Grow the Rushes* did not secure a major circuit booking.'[166]

Conditions imposed by the NFFC in respect of further loans obliged the struggling new company to negotiate a contract with Monarch for a series of second features.[167] The first, trade-shown only a month after *Rushes*, was Michael Anderson's sombre *Night Was Our Friend* (1952), made at Viking Studios and based on a typical West End matinee play by Michael Pertwee. Anderson, who went on to direct such popular films as *The Dam Busters* (1955) and *Around the World in 80 Days* (1956), here demonstrated a flair for the orchestration of melodramatic elements, helped in no small measure by Charles Hassé's superior editing. He took the tragedy of the return and subsequent suicide of a man (Michael Gough in a familiar scenery-chewing performance) who had been missing in the Amazon jungle, and stirred in some nervous romance and a female protagonist (very well played by Elizabeth Sellars) tormented by guilt. The result, though a cut above the usual second feature, reassured the trade that the union had settled for a more humble production role. It also proved something of a hit with bookers, playing the Odeon circuit and convincing the company that this was the most viable way forward. It was even distributed in the USA, as were ACT's next two films, by Modern Sound Pictures of Nebraska.

Night Was Our Friend was followed by a surprisingly hard-hitting exposé of local government corruption *Private Information* (1952), directed by former editor, Fergus McDonell. This film, which was booked to the ABC circuit, proved that ACT Films was bringing something fresh to the second-feature market and is of sufficient interest to be given a more extended analysis in Chapter 8. For their third 'B' film, however, ACT played safe with Daniel Birt's *Circumstantial Evidence* (1953), a conventional but well-crafted murder mystery with Patrick Holt and Rona Anderson. Reassuringly, it was praised as a 'workmanlike and polished job', with the comment: 'There'll be no more groans about shoddy quota "seconds" if producers take their cue from *Circumstantial Evidence*.'[168] ACT took the hint and engaged veteran film-maker Maurice Elvey to make a yet more conventional country mansion murder mystery *House of Blackmail* (1953) with William Sylvester, a RADA-educated American, and nineteen-year-old Mary Germaine. This time, it failed to excite the trade press – 'Unassuming direction; routine acting; modest production work' – although it was taken up for distribution by 20th Century-Fox in the USA.[169]

The company now stood at a crossroads: it could continue to keep ACT members in gainful employment by making pictures to a proven formula in popular genres, or it could explore themes which other companies, not to mention American distributors, were likely to avoid. In the spring and summer of 1953, with preparations for the Coronation in full swing, ACT Films began pre-production for a film on the Tolpuddle Martyrs, pioneering union activists who had been punished with transportation to the 'colonies' by the Crown. Synopses were commissioned, including one from Ted Willis, the creator of *Dixon of Dock Green*, which, instead of the activists as protagonists, viewed the events through the eyes of a 'handsome, vigorous' young doctor.[170] Sidney Cole complained that 'the original story has been so glossed over that nothing is left of it', and warned of a likely hostile climate among financiers and distributors, including the NFFC, but was willing to let Willis go ahead with a revised treatment.[171] Willis seems to have been discouraged by the response, prioritised other work, and eventually pulled out of the ill-starred project, turning his attention instead to *Burnt Evidence* (1954), a more contemporary story of ordinary people in extraordinary circumstances. It was directed by Daniel Birt, who could be be an ardent melodramatist but here opted for a somewhat more realistic representation of lower-middle-class life, and in Jane Hylton and Duncan Lamont chose leads who often endowed such protagonists with a feel of reality. Lamont played Jack, a conscientious working man, heavily in debt, who gets involved in a murder charge when his wife's would-be lover is burned to death in a fire in Jack's paint factory. Trade reviewers, unfortunately, found the whole affair a bit dull.[172]

While negotiations continued on the Tolpuddle Martyrs project, general manager Henry Passmore pressed on with the established sequence of crime thrillers. Shooting began on *The Blue Parrot* at Walton in June 1953. It was directed by John Harlow who had turned out a run of lively thrillers and melodramas in the 1940s, but in the new decade made none but second features. The film is set in a world of spivs and black-market liquor, of pawnbrokers and police wearily on the lookout for villains living above their means. Instead of importing an American leading man, ACT used Dermot Walsh to play an American detective, who naturally proves more effective than Scotland Yard in solving the murder. There is little to distinguish this from numerous other urban-set thrillers, but its pacey editing (Robert Hill) and cast of reliable character players carries one over the less probable plot manoeuvres. Similar themes were again to the fore in Harlow's *Dangerous Cargo* (1954), written by the crime correspondent of the *Daily Express*, Percy Hoskins. Jack Watling and the up-and-coming Susan Stephen starred in a lively topical *roman policier* inspired by the recent Heathrow bullion-heist. The film, with its authentic locations, touches of comedy and exciting climax, found favour with the trade reviewers.[173]

In Terence Fisher's *Final Appointment* (1954, working title *Death Keeps a Date*), the next picture off the ACT production line, John Bentley and Eleanor Summerfield played newspaper reporters who track down a murderer after careful surveillance around London. It was tongue-in-cheek, but managed a fairly convincing atmosphere, and *To-Day's Cinema* thought it 'a neat and enjoyable British job' with 'lively performances from bright young stars'.[174] ACT Films then experienced a brief production hiatus when Henry Passmore left to form his own independent company with his old Highbury colleague John Croydon, to make rival supporting features for Monarch at Walton.[175]

During Passmore's tenure, all but two ACT second features had received circuit bookings and most were profitable. The new general manager, Ralph Bond, briefly tried something different with *Room in the House* (1955), an adaptation E. Eynon Evans' homely rural comedy-drama *Bless This House*, but the market seemed more interested in crime and new screen formats. Bond thus thought it best to revert to type, so the same swatch used for *Final Appointment* was again rolled out for *Stolen Assignment* (1955), once more directed by Terence Fisher and produced by another of Hammer's regulars, Francis Searle. John Bentley resumed his role as a reporter, while the vivacious Hy Hazell replaced Eleanor Summerfield as his girlfriend in another sprightly crime picture with plenty of humour. Fisher was retained for *The Last Man to Hang?* (1956, working title *The Jury*), a not particularly distinguished Old Bailey trial drama with a twist ending, that boasted an unusually strong cast including Tom Conway, Elizabeth Sellars, Victor Maddern and Freda Jackson. The cast gave ACT a lucky break. Originally conceived as a primarily domestic release and costing well under £30,000, the film was suddenly guaranteed bookings in 6,000 American cinemas thanks to its adoption by Warwick Films and Columbia looking for supporting product for their latest CinemaScope movies. However, it is doubtful that ACT saw much of this income, as the film was probably sold for a flat fee to Warwick.

Rank distributed *Suspended Alibi* (1957), another of those thrillers in which a journalist hero (Patrick Holt) is caught in a web of circumstantial evidence. However, this one benefited from the

Press association: John Bentley and Hy Hazell as reporters-in-arms in Terence Fisher's *Stolen Assignment* (1955)

'The uninspiring romantic duo': Robin Bailey and Susan Shaw in *The Diplomatic Corpse* (1958)

grace of Honor Blackman, cast as his wife, and some crisp and confident debut direction from Alfred Shaughnessy.[176] His film is a story of sexual frissons among the middle class, and much faster, more frantically and densely plotted than most 'B' movies. The familiar race-against-the-clock to save the condemned man produces some well-sustained tension, and, if the ending is never in serious doubt, Shaughnessy's brisk storytelling and Robert Hill's editing sustain interest in the crowded narrative. *To-Day's Cinema* commented: 'Here's one of those brisk, efficiently made pieces of quota entertainment which fill their modest place in the programme so worthily. Modestly produced, it nonetheless provides an hour of very honest enjoyment.'[177]

There was a similar reception from *The Cinema* for Maurice Elvey's advertising agency comedy *Second Fiddle* (1957), starring Adrienne Corri, Thorley Walters and Lisa Gastoni: 'the ACT appear to have found a formula which can hardly fail ... As clean, fresh British lightweight comedy, this rings the bell.'[178] However, in spite of a string of favourable notices for its films, ACT's finances were in a sufficiently parlous state for rumours of a take-over by the distributors, Eros, to circulate in May 1957. Part of the company's problem was the shortage of studio space for modest productions created by the growth of television and advertising film-making. By September, ACT's state was desperate enough for Ralph Bond to write to the Board of Trade to warn of the 'very serious situation for smaller independent producers' needing to find affordable studio space. His own company was unable to book any accommodation before Christmas.[179] Bond eventually managed to book time at the new

St John's Wood Studios to make *The Diplomatic Corpse* (1958), another tale of sparring reporters written, like *Final Appointment* and *Stolen Assignment*, by Sidney Nelson and Maurice Harrison, but this time directed by Montgomery Tully. Happily, considerable documentation on this production survives, and it gives us the opportunity to trace the development of a fairly typical supporting feature. The story begins in February 1957, when Bond invited Nelson and Harrison to submit a new treatment on the relations between investigative journalists which had previously proved popular. In April, he informed A. I. Callum of Rank Film Distributors that ACT had a follow-up to *Suspended Alibi*, which he described as 'a thriller with a light touch'.[180] Callum commissioned the film, subject to approval of the final script, the producer, director and main cast, and offered a meagre £15,000 in remuneration. On the basis of this guarantee of circuit distribution, Bond was able to raise a further loan from the NFFC, and commission a shooting script for £400 on 8 May. This was duly delivered at the end of June, but, because of its break-even policy, ACT Films already had liquidity problems, which were exacerbated by the lack of available studio space in which to make the next film and thus maintain cash-flow. With Eros keeping the company afloat, Bond was turned away by Shepperton, Southall and Twickenham studios and eventually had to settle for the bijou St John's Wood, although even these studios were not available until late October. The film had now been in pre-production for nine long months and costs were mounting. Bond was sufficiently concerned to go cap-in-hand to Rank for more money:

> You are paying us £15,000 for this film when it is delivered to your satisfaction, and I have just worked out a budget which shows that if we are lucky and there are no unforeseen snags we may come out of it with a profit of £200 to £300. I think you will agree that this is a very narrow margin indeed and does not provide much of an incentive to make further films of the type at that price ... It seems that most exhibitors still want second features and the public wants its double-feature programme. If the admitted demand is to be met somehow or other, the return for this type of picture needs to be increased.[181]

Rank eventually agreed to up the price by £250 and the production was finally green-lit.[182]

Bond had already submitted the scenario to the BBFC, where it was turned round in a week and given a clean bill of health.[183] There had been competition from directors to secure the job, notably from Compton Bennett, who reassured Bond that he was 'not scared of short schedules and low budgets'.[184] Compton Bennett was initially offered the director's chair, but then declined just a month before filming began. In the meantime, approved producer Francis Searle had been busy casting. Robin Bailey was perhaps an unfortunate choice to play the dynamic reporter and seems to have been signed with the budget in mind as he accepted the role for only £25 per day, more usually the fee of a supporting artist and considerably less than Harry Fowler was paid on this film. His co-star was the sophisticated Ursula Howells, but scripts had also been sent to Diana Decker and then to Rona Anderson.

The Diplomatic Corpse finally went on the floor on 21 October 1957 on a fifteen-day schedule and an average daily shooting target of 4.2 minutes. On the first day, almost six minutes were shot, but there were already problems looming. Ursula Howells was suffering from a back problem and a respiratory infection when filming began, and had to withdraw from the production after the first week, necessitating the re-shooting of sixteen minutes with a new actress, Susan Shaw, who was brought in at two days' notice and a hefty salary of £50 per day.[185] Most scenes were shot in the studio (between 8.30am and 6.20pm), with brief location work at the Guinness Trust Residential Club, Avenue Road, an office in Soho Square and Television House, Kingsway. Filming was eventually completed after twenty-three days, eight days over schedule because of Howells' illness and a camera breakdown. It included 116 scenes in a rough cut of seventy minutes and cost a shade over £19,785. One hundred and thirty-two production stills were prepared for the film's publicity. A fine cut of *The Diplomatic Corpse* was shown to the ACT Board and to its distributors at Rank's Wardour Street Theatre on 10 December 1957, just fifty days after the cameras first rolled. The following week, Bond wrote an appreciative letter to Montgomery Tully: 'We had some very bad luck on the film and I felt particularly sorry for you when you were confronted with the necessity of re-shooting almost half the film. I greatly admired the way you buckled down to it and everyone, including the distributors, is pleased with the result.'[186] His film was trade-shown on 24 February 1958 – which meant that ACT had gone a whole year without a release – and went onto the Odeon circuit on 17 March 1958 as the support for *A Tale of Two Cities*.

Unfortunately, the film was disappointing. A pair of sparring reporters (Robin Bailey and Susan Shaw) is meant to be striking sparks of sexual interest, but Bailey in particular is quite lost in this sort of role. Shaw's character gets shut up in a foreign embassy which has been used for drug-smuggling, and the best of the film is in its exploitation of the plucky-girl-in-dangerous-situation (there are lots of plucky, not to say foolhardy, girls in 'B' movies) and in the thriller potential of the idea of the embassy's having diplomatic immunity. But the characters are thinly written – apart from the uninspiring romantic duo. However, the *Monthly Film Bulletin*, though judging it 'mainly naive and stereotyped hokum', still felt that 'lively presentation made this an entertaining second feature'.[187]

Following *The Diplomatic Corpse*, ACT again tried its hand at a couple of modest first features budgeted at around £60,000. George Pollock's *Don't Panic, Chaps* (1959) was a genial Jack Davies comedy filmed at Walton and on location in Surrey, with George Cole and Dennis Price in the leading roles. The more interesting of the two was *The Man Upstairs* (1958) in which a deranged scientist (Richard Attenborough) barricades himself in his lodging-house room. *Films and Filming*'s Derek Conrad urged his readers to 'Go and see ... [this] unheralded and tightly-budgeted British thriller', claiming that it 'poses questions that are very rarely asked in British pictures today'.[188] He elaborated these as issues of our responsibility for each other, and this sort of humane concern is what Roy Fowler, long-time member of ACT, suggests when he wrote of the company that 'If there were a policy it was, I guess, an old-fashioned decency and humanitarianism.' There was no point in expecting that ACT Films, on the strength of its union affiliations, was going to be doing anything very radical, especially not at the 'B' movie level. As Fowler went on to say, 'I don't think there was a consistent political platform. It [ACT Films] was intended to make showable films and give employment to members. Remember the circuits and the censor were very reactionary and would not have touched anything much "leftwing".'[189]

The 1950s ended with a string of ambitious projects that stalled in development, including a co-production deal with Yugoslavia to make a film on the Chetniks, and a television series, *The Virgins of Victoria Street*, for Lew Grade. A similar fate befell an attempt to make Dymphna Cusack's novel *Heatwave in Berlin*, which ACT optioned in 1961, when no British or German distributor proved to be interested. Instead, the company reverted to second features. Montgomery Tully's *Dead Lucky* (1960) used another of Sidney Nelson's scripts in which a reporter (Vincent Ball) and his fashion-journalist girlfriend (Betty McDowall) investigate a murder. The film's background was illegal

Payments to Cast and Crew: The Diplomatic Corpse (ACT Films)

Cast		Crew	
Name	**Earnings (£)**	**Name**	**Earnings (£)**
Robin Bailey	500	Francis Searle (Producer)	450
Susan Shaw	300	Montgomery Tully (Director)	450
Liam Redmond	245	Ralph Bond (Production Supervisor)	665
Andrew Mikhelson	150	Robert Daring (Production Manager)	138
Charles Farrell	130	John Pitcher (1st AD)	88
(Ursula Howells)	106	C. Mansbridge (2nd AD)	90
Harry Fowler	100	Frank Smith (3rd AD)	65
Nicholas Bruce	90	Olga Marshall (Continuity)	95
Bill Shine	80	Philip Grindrod (DP)	257
Maya Kouman	72	Michael Bayley (Camera Operator)	139
Others	225	A. Gatward (Focus)	63
		D. Milsome (Clapper)	70
		J. Connoch (Editor)	287
		E. Jefferies (1st Assist. Ed.)	60
		E. Mountjoy (2nd Assist. Ed.)	116
		Frank Turner (Make-up)	134
		Helen Brown (Hair)	104
		Joseph Bato (Art Director)	220
		William Eyles (Draughtsman)	104
		J. Morris (Sound Mixer)	138
		D. Drinkwater (Boom)	97
		P. Matthews (Sound Crew)	107
		Derek Mark(?) (Sound Crew)	95

gambling clubs, and Ralph Bond's letter to British Lion's E. M. Smedley-Aston shows that it was influenced by current events, notably, the forthcoming Betting and Gaming Act: 'I think this story is now more topical than ever in view of the Government's proposed new gaming laws which are likely to rouse considerable controversy.'[190] Smedley-Aston eventually gave the project the green light, but not without quite extensive and detailed comments on the treatment.[191] The film was then made for £17,000, and in it Chili Bouchier made her last screen appearance. The *Monthly Film Bulletin* found the film 'Bright and ingenuous [claiming it] ... breezes along in such a way as to disguise much of its triteness of story and dialogue'.[192]

CONFIDENTIAL

F I N A L
STATEMENT OF PRODUCTION COST

Production Company......**A.C.T. Films Limited**......................... Period............ended.............

Title of Film...............**"THE DIPLOMATIC CORPSE"**   **A.C.T.** **19.**

COST HEADING	Cost this Period	Total Committed Cost to Date	Estimate to Complete	Estimated Final Cost	Budget	Over (Red) Under (Black) Budget
	£	£	£	£	£	£
A STORY AND SCRIPT	410. 15. 2.					
B PRODUCER & DIRECTOR FEES	900. 0. 0.					
C PRODUCTION UNIT SALARIES :—						
1. Production Management and Secretaries ...	1433. 18. 0.					
2. Assistant Directors and Continuity ...	367. 3. 8.		Total Advances			
3. Technical Advisers			made by			
4. Camera Crews	562. 8. 2.		N.F.F.C.		14,696.	0. 0.
5. Recording Crews	560. 3. 2.					
6. Editing Staff	446. 2. 5.		Cash received			
7. Stills Camera Staff	80. 15. 0.		from Messrs.			
8. Wardrobe Designer and Staff ...	8. 8. 6.		C.T. Bowring		6,271.	10. 0.
9. Make-up Artistes	136. 13. 4.		(Insurance			
10. Hairdressers	100. 0. 0.		Claim)			
11. Casting						
12. Production Accountancy					20,967.	10. 0.
13. Projectionists...						
14. Other Staff		11. 9.	Less:			
15. Foreign Unit Technicians			Cash at Bank		1,182.	3. 1.
D SET DESIGNING & SUPERVISORY STAFF ...	437. 13. 0.					
E ʼTISTES :—					£19,785.	6. 11.
1. Cast	1997. 10. 0.					
2. Stand-ins and Doubles	171. 19. 5.					
3. Crowd	356. 9. 3.					
F ORCHESTRA & COMPOSER	129. 17. 6.					
G COSTUMES & WIGS	41. 2. 0.					
H MISCELLANEOUS PRODN. STORES (Ex. Sets)	76. 14. 10.					
I FILM & LABORATORY CHARGES	2235. 7. 3.					
J STUDIO RENTALS	2378. 7. 3.					
K EQUIPMENT	234. 8. 11.					
L POWER	257. 5. 9.					
M TRAVEL & TRANSPORT :—						
1. Location						
2. Other	380. 13. 7.					
N HOTEL & LIVING EXPENSES :						
1. Location						
2. Other	31. 7. 9.					
O INSURANCES	275. 10. 11.					
P HOLIDAY & SICK PAY SURCHARGES ...	133. 13. 11.					
Q ʵLICITY SALARIES & EXPENSES ...						
R MISCELLANEOUS EXPENSES	344. 9. 2.					
S SETS & MODELS :—						
1. Labour—Construction	944. 12. 4.					
2. Labour—Dressing ·	176. 8. 2.					
3. Labour—Operating	500. 17. 1.					
4. Labour—Striking						
5. Labour—Lighting	603. 1. 5.					
6. Labour—Lamp Spotting ...						
7. Labour—Foreign Unit Labour						
8. Materials—Construction ...	644. 7. 8.					
9. Properties	446. 5. 6.					
T SPECIAL LOCATION FACILITIES	40. 4. 6.					
TOTAL DIRECT COST :	17,845. 6. 4.					
Y FINANCE & LEGAL CHARGES	1,440. 0. 7.					
Z OVERHEADS	500. 0. 0.					
TOTAL PRODUCTION COST ... ...£	19,785. 6. 11.					

PRODUCTION CONTINGENCY

£

Approved by..

FORM S.P.C.   **GENERAL MANAGER.**

Copies of form S.P.C. can be obtained from Metcalfe & Cooper Ltd., 41/42 Wool Exchange, Coleman Street, London, E C 2. Telephone : MONarch 5175

By the early 1960s, changing trading conditions meant that ACT was fighting a losing battle to stay in business. It had a critical hit with Sidney Cole's adaptation of Arnold Wesker's multicultural play, *The Kitchen* (1961), directed by James Hill (replacing Don Chaffey), but the cost of the film (at £27,500 it was £1,000 over budget) was excessive for second-feature profitability.[193] Despite strong performances from the likes of Carl Mohner, Eric Pohlmann, Tom Bell, James Bolam and Sean Lynch, and a song from Adam Faith, *The Kitchen* failed to gain a major circuit release, flopped in the USA, and took until 1967 to recoup its negative costs, mainly from foreign sales.[194] 'The kitchen looms around and encloses them all', said the publicity, and the film was unable to break away from its theatrical origins, just as ACT was unable to extricate itself from the claustrophobic confines of 'B' film production. Sadly, according to Roy Fowler, 'It ended up a mess, thru the usual incompetence, corruption and lack of managerial skill, and racked up a very sizeable deficit which the union had to settle.'[195]

This is not quite the whole story, however. ACT Films' last release was Muriel Box's *The Piper's Tune* (1962), an adventure set in Napoleonic France and made in association with the Children's Film Foundation.[196] It was still not, however, the last film made by the company. That distinction goes unworthily to *Dilemma* (1962), a disaster that finally closed ACT Films and tarnished its reputation for producing serviceable works of modest quality. By 1962, television was consuming the output of scriptwriting talent at an alarming rate and affordable good source material was becoming increasingly scarce for those production companies still clinging to the raft of the supporting feature. The stress of this situation perhaps clouded Ralph Bond's judgment when, in May 1962, he received a treatment from the literary agent Eric L'Epine Smith. The briefest synopsis of *Dilemma*'s plot – suburban wife of schoolteacher leads double life as ruthless drug-dealer – should have left him in no 'dilemma' about its unsuitability as a piece of serious crime fiction. Under pressure, however, he came to the unsustainable belief that the scenario could be rendered plausible. He wrote back to Smith:

> I was considerably intrigued with this story up to about page 20, but I must confess to being puzzled and completely unconvinced by what follows thereafter. I do not believe that an average audience would accept without any question the guilt of the wife as it is presently scripted. There is absolutely no motivation or explanation as to how or why she was involved in a drug racket with the murdered man. The basic idea is an intriguing one, but I don't think it has been sufficiently worked out.[197]

There it should have ended, but Bond was desperately cultivating a relationship with Bryanston Films, one of the few distributors still handling second features.[198] To keep them happy, he sent the treatment for *Dilemma* to one of Bryanston's executives, the illustrious Michael Balcon, pitching the project as 'sufficiently different and original to make a rather good second feature film'.[199] Bryanston must have been desperate too, because its Projects Sub-Committee approved the treatment in July, in the knowledge that the BBFC saw no problem with an 'A' certificate. Clive Donner was suggested as potential director. He turned it down on seeing the treatment, but news that ACT had clearance to make another 'B' film quickly leaked out to the lengthening soup-queue of starving directors eager to get back to work in a field of production that was contracting daily. Once proud, but now finding what casual labour they could in television, these men now lined up with begging bowls at Bond's door. They included Peter Maxwell, who wrote to Bond: 'Since my return in January 1961 from Australia, where I spent 16 months directing *Whiplash*, I have suffered much unemployment, due, I think, to having been forgotten. An engagement with ACT will help a deserving case.'[200]

It was a sad and sorry procession from which the promising John Lemont was selected. By the end of August, he too had thought better of it and withdrawn. When a shooting script was delivered in September by the writers Pip and Jane Baker, it was immediately clear that little had been done to rescue the plot from the realms of the fantastic.[201] The poor producer, Ted Lloyd, immediately hired the reliable Vernon Sewell as script doctor, indicating to Bond that Sewell 'is certainly a more creative thinker than the people we have had on it to date'.[202] Sewell was horrified by what he found and likened his job to a 'suicide pact'. Peter Maxwell, the new director of choice, felt much the same way.[203] However, nothing could stop the juggernaut as it rolled inevitably towards Twickenham Studios, fuelled by a £21,000 budget from Bryanston. The film, starring Peter Halliday, Patricia Burke and Ingrid Hafner, wrapped on 5 November after the scheduled thirteen days in the studio and two on location at Ormond Cresent, Hampton-on-Thames. On seeing the rough cut, its original writers, the Bakers, immediately requested that their names be removed from the credits on the grounds that 'the film they saw the other day, other than the main storyline, is not their work'.[204] But Bond had already paid £105 for the titles and credits, and angrily dismissed their petition: 'I have gone to enormous trouble to ensure that this film was made, despite considerable early difficulties with the screenplay. I was so confident that the subject was worth making that I even had to change directors.'[205] Bond would pay dearly for this error of judgment. On seeing the finished product, the distributors realised their mistake and quietly left it on the shelf.

In the summer of 1964, with ACT Films now wound up, Bryanston's G. L. Wheatley finally wrote to Bond to tell him the fate of the film he had misguidedly championed:

> It has been absolutely impossible to place this film with the circuits, and it is apparent from their reactions that there is a basic fault in the story. In view of this, it has occurred to us that ACTT [having taken over ACT Films] might like to give some thought to the possibility of some drastic re-cutting of this film, and if necessary, the re-shooting of several scenes.[206]

Dilemma never achieved theatrical distribution in Britain, but was sold to television, and has recently had a Channel Five screening and a DVD release. Thus it lives on as an ironic memorial to a rare experiment in the ownership and control of a film-producing company that survived against the odds for a dozen years, provided much-needed employment for many, and even if it ultimately failed to call the tune, it at least made a few films that piped some fresh notes.

While the roots of ACT Films were firmly in the unionised workforce of commercial film production, those of Group 3 were to be found in the documentary movement that had flourished in wartime, but was now experiencing the chill winds of austerity. Sponsorship was declining and the possibilities for exhibition dwindling daily. Although this movement had recruited from most strata of society, its primary constituency was a left-liberal intelligentsia for whom commercial cinema was less a source of employment than an object of reform. Group 3 represented an attempt at an alliance between this serious-minded coterie and progressive elements from conventional feature-film-making. The potential of this alliance was formidable, but realising that potential was never going to be easy.

From its inception in the spring of 1951, Group 3, based at Southall Studios with British Lion as its distributor, was treated with suspicion by the trade press and resentment by its commercial competitors, on the grounds that a production company was being given unfair assistance by the state. In *To-Day's Cinema*, 'Onlooker' admitted that his doubts 'stemmed from the thought that the Group was likely to cultivate a lot of long-haired intelligentsia who would have a high old time at the public expense'.[207] There was also cynicism about its ever carrying out its mission of being purely a training ground for new talent. However, the company's executive earned some respect by acknowledging that this aim was unrealistically idealistic and that some attention should be paid to box-office appeal. The opposition of competitors was also moderated by the possibilities of using the Group's productions as a free laboratory for testing the potential of directors and young technicians. Nevertheless, there was a widespread feeling in the trade that, in spite of budgets that were twice those of commercial second features, Group 3 was really in the business of making 'B' films.[208]

Group 3's fractious Board included luminaries like the Establishment-approved Sir Michael Balcon and the volatile and opinionated John Grierson, who stressed that the Group had been set up for the encouragement of talented young film-makers who, 'harassed by the present condition of the industry, might otherwise desert their vocation'.[209] More accurately, it allowed a number of documentary film-makers to try their hands at feature films. Solidly backed by the NFFC, work started with production controller John Baxter's *Judgment Deferred* (1951), based on an idea by Baxter's long-time collaborator C. G. H. Ayres, and with a cast headed by Hugh Sinclair, Helen Shingler and Leslie Dwyer. Baxter maintained that he was simply 'blooding' the studio for the young directors who

Pony-trekking: delivering the liquor in Group 3's *Brandy for the Parson* (1952)

would follow.[210] The first of these was John Eldridge, a documentarist making his feature debut with the smuggling comedy *Brandy for the Parson* (1952), which was an unused Ealing script scaled down by Eldridge and Alfred Shaughnessy (former assistant to Thorold Dickinson). If Group 3 had been quicker in green-lighting the project, the film would have had Audrey Hepburn as its leading lady; but delays meant that it had to settle for Shaughnessy's wife, Jean Lodge.[211] Filming took place over seven weeks on location in Salcombe and Dorchester. Executive producer Grierson described the results as 'a sweet lemon of a picture' that had the feel of 'old oak and seaweed'.[212] Grierson, however, was a problematic choice as skipper of the Group 3 ship, at least if it intended to find safe harbour in cinema circuits, as Shaughnessy explained:

> [H]e really detested the 'commercial cinema' ... He had plenty of time for Pabst, Bunuel and Jean Vigo but very little for Carol Reed, David Lean or Hitchcock. Like all documentary-minded film-makers, Grierson loved the realism of ordinary people on film, non-actors, photographed dramatically against a brooding sky; the lined, granite faces of very old weather-beaten North Sea fishermen, ploughmen, shepherds, railway signalmen, Covent Garden porters and so on. He had a sort of contempt for actors in films and a deep distrust of the artifice of film studios and sets.[213]

Grierson put the emphasis firmly on freshness of approach and opportunities for relatively unknown players and film-makers. This policy happily led to the engagement of struggling young actor Kenneth More for a leading role in *Brandy for the Parson*. He never looked back. The film itself was modestly well received, with *Picture Show* finding it 'well acted against a delightful background of English scenery, beautifully photographed'.[214]

John Guillermin's whimsical frolic about a children's magazine writer *Miss Robin Hood* (1953) was also well received as a 'diverting romp for the populace'.[215] Like so much of Group 3's output, *Miss Robin Hood* pits the idiosyncratic and the individual against the conformist and the corporate, but by 1952 this Ealing-type sentiment had all but passed, along with the Labour Government of the immediate post-war years. A similar reception was given to John Eldridge's *Laxdale Hall* (budget £56,000), Alfred Shaughnessy's adaptation of Eric Linklater's novel about a parliamentary delegation to an isolated Scottish village. This sort of comedy of the subverting of a pompous dominant culture by a subordinate one based in a rural region had been better done by Ealing, but there was enough wry humour in Group 3's film to make it a respectable contribution to this sub-genre. And this was also true of Lewis Gilbert's *Time Gentlemen Please!* (1952), which was a satire of village life and its institutions from alehouse to almshouse. Its appeal was built on the rich variety of character performances, from Eddie Byrne's lovable Irish rogue to the well-modulated turns of Hermione Baddeley, Sid James, Thora Hird, Dora Bryan et al. Group 3's incorrigible infatuation with whimsy plumbed new depths with C. Pennington-Richards' *The Oracle* (1952, budget £43,000), the mildly engaging tale of a clairvoyant creature (with Gilbert Harding's voice) which lives at the bottom of an Irish well. Ealing 'fantasy' at its best, as in *Passport to Pimlico*, was rooted in reality, but Group 3 was apt to overlook the value of this texture of the everyday. The ABC circuit, which had a representative on Group 3's Board, felt obliged to book its films and grudgingly gave them 40–50 per cent billing, although it was unhappy with most and consequently offered the leanest of distribution deals.[216] Grierson, who was held in contempt by Balcon and blamed for much of the Group's failure, stood down as Executive Producer in September 1952.

The move of the loss-making Group 3 to the state-controlled Beaconsfield Studios in 1953 was part of a wider strategy of provision for a 'State of Emergency', as a company policy document, probably written by Michael Balcon, made evident:

> Without doubt, Beaconsfield is the one studio that should be kept active and fully prepared to meet any emergency that might confront the Government of the day, when films would be an important factor for propaganda purposes. It was, after all, re-developed for this purpose as a centre for the Crown Film Unit.[217]

While awaiting such an emergency, John Baxter realised that, if the new studios were to be kept in continuous production, he would need to mix major productions like the successful *The Conquest of Everest* (1953) with shorter featurettes. The Group's first attempt was an experimental ballet fantasy, *All Hallowe'en* (1953), directed by Michael Gordon and written, designed and produced by Joan Maude and Michael Warre. It was not exactly what the trade was looking for. *To-Day's Cinema* found the picture 'emptily arty' and suitable only for hard-core ballet fans.[218] John Baxter was not the most likely producer to move with the times, as he demonstrated with *The End of the Road* (1954), a film about a skilled craftsman (Finlay Currie) who is compulsorily retired and is nearly driven to madness as a result. It could have been a metaphor for the plight of Group 3 itself, which, unable to find a place in the changing landscape of film production and consumption, folded shortly thereafter.

E. J. Fancey, New Realm, DUK

Edwin John Fancey (1902–1980) was head of a family business that included the distributors DUK and New Realm and the production company Border. In 1940, E. J. Fancey began making short musical films with the Irish director Denis Kavanagh, with whom he would collaborate for nearly two decades. Fancey's first experiment with longer material was a comedy starring two radio comediennes in the mode of the Waters sisters: the lanky Ethel Revnell and the diminutive Gracie West. In the Redd Davis-directed *The Balloon Goes Up* (1942) they masqueraded as WAAFs and helped to uncover a nest of fifth columnists. They were supported by the reliable Ronald Shiner and the singer Donald Peers. The film proved popular enough for a further adventure of Revnell and West, *Up With the Lark* (1943), to be made as a co-feature. It was directed by Phil Brandon and shot over five weeks at Merton Park and on location at a farm in Sutton, where Revnell and West masqueraded as land girls to round up some black-marketeers. The film introduced Fancey's eight-year-old daughter, Adrienne Scott, as well as several well-known boxers, and was recommended by *Kinematograph Weekly* as 'Rollicking fare for the masses with clear-cut stellar pull'.[219]

Fancy's distribution business started in a small way, handling overseas (often Continental) product and British shorts and featurettes. From an early stage, Fancey's product showed a willingness to exploit the topical and the mildly salacious that was at odds with attempts to promote British cinema's claims to seriousness, quality and wholesomeness. For example, New Realm distributed – or at least attempted to distribute – E. W. White's critically derided variety featurette *Wot, No Gangsters?* (1947), forty-five minutes of dancing girls, contortionists and smutty bedroom jokes under the pretext of demonstrating a TV set. Such a combination of suggestiveness and television promotion was a red rag to the critical bull, and it was not slow to charge:

It is difficult to imagine any type of audience deriving any enjoyment from this crude farrago ... a series of turns mostly barren of wit or taste, and certainly devoid of any clean, honest fun. ... Such a production does the poorest of service to the growing prestige of British films.[220]

Fancey also provided distribution for the more ambitious work of Federated Films, the company headed by Harold Baim, a producer, like Fancey himself, with a background in film rental. Baim produced Denis Kavanagh's *Night Comes Too Soon* (1948, USA: *The Ghost of Rashmon Hall*), a creepy country house ghost story which traded on the hit radio series *Journey Into Fear*, to which Valentine Dyall lent his lugubrious tones. It was shot at a mansion said to be haunted by James I: Bittacy House in London's Mill Hill.[221] Kavanagh could bring little that was fresh to the accustomed 'nocturnal groans, demoniacal laughter and spiritual manifestations'[222] of this ponderous and portentous version of Lord Lytton's play *The Haunted and the Haunters*. Unusually, however, it was picked up for distribution in the USA by the independent MC Pictures.

Night Comes Too Soon must have demonstrated to Fancey that saleable results could be obtained on cheap films shot unconventionally outside a studio setting. Consequently, he got together with documentary film-maker Cecil H. Williamson to devise ways in which actuality footage could be incorporated into perfunctory dramatic scenarios. From *Beyond Price* (1947) and *Appointment with Fire* (1947), Williamson introduced a more prominent narrative thread into his featurettes. Almost inadvertently, Fancey found himself making a minor contribution to a tradition of reality filmmaking that linked British wartime propaganda films to the extra-studio shooting practices that had become an essential part of Italian cinema. *Held in Trust* (1949), was an account by former associates of the reformation of a criminal by the fostering of his artistic talents after a spell in the army and a spot of hiking in the Lake District. The little-known picture, narrowly distributed by DUK Films, was a liberal humanist intervention in the urgent debate about crime and its cures in the late 1940s. '[M]orally sound and sentimentally disarming', was *Kinematograph Weekly*'s verdict.[223] Williamson's *Soho Conspiracy* (1950), also released by DUK, might sound like a late contribution to the post-war spiv film cycle, but it was nothing so predictable. Instead, it recycled footage of Italian opera singers from Continental films and grafted on a story of a young man's attempt to stage a benefit concert for a Soho church rebuilding fund. It was not hard to see the joins in the footage, especially when the audience is asked to believe that a London gymnasium could be transformed for the concert into something that looks suspiciously like La Scala or La Fenice. Williamson dished up another minestrone of drama and recycled footage with *The Clown* (1950), a featurette on the theme of *Pagliacci*.

Fancey and Williamson moved on to a full-blown neo-realist methodology with *Hangman's Wharf* (1950), a murder mystery with a largely unknown cast and based on a BBC radio serial. It made good use of locations like the Thames, Falmouth and St Mawes.[224] The story was padded to seventy-five minutes, and production values were relatively low, but the film had a freshness that made it a reasonably attractive proposition for the independent exhibitor. Fancey's documentary featurette comparing London with Paris, *Tales of Two Cities* (1951), partly narrated by Richard Dimbleby, was also thought a 'useful addition to popular programmes'.[225] So too was his Alpine avalanche story *Beyond the Heights* (1951), which cashed in on a recent disaster at Lanterschalp with considerable success. It was narrated by the equally familiar Eamonn Andrews, and made a rare turn from travelogue to suspense drama.

Fancey's *London Entertains* (1952) was the story of an escort agency called 'At Your Service' set up by some girls from a Swiss finishing school to profit from visitors to London for the Festival of Britain. It was the sort of theme that Fancey would exploit rather more pruriently in later years, but in this 'U' film it provided a way of linking a travelogue and a string of night-club acts. Stops included the Windmill Theatre and the recording of a radio show featuring the Goons. Milligan and Co. returned in the starring roles in the lunatic service comedy *Down Among the Z Men* (1952), the eightieth film directed by Maclean Rogers, who was briefly New Realm's resident director. Fancey made sure that the antics of the Goons were bolstered by a stimulating 'leg show' from the Twelve Toppers. Rogers followed it with the considerably less stimulating presentation of grumpy Gilbert Harding as a crime reporter in the documentary-style *Behind the Headlines* (1953).

In October 1953, with something of a fanfare, New Realm unveiled a double-header of films directed by Maclean Rogers: the crime comedy *Flannelfoot*, starring Jack Watling and Ronald Howard and based on the activities of a legendary 1930s housebreaker, and the musical comedy *Forces' Sweetheart*, with Hy Hazell, Harry Secombe, Michael Bentine and Freddie Frinton. *Kinematograph Weekly* liked *Flannelfoot*, in spite of its old-fashioned story of a peer and a jewel thief, and was generously indulgent towards the inanities of *Forces' Sweetheart*, pleading only to be spared a few minutes of its barmy boxing-match finale. The reviewer must have owed E. J. Fancey a favour, as he even singled out for praise the performance of Fancey's daughter, Adrienne Scott, as a sweater girl.[226] Adrienne went on to star opposite Cardew (The Cad) Robinson in Maclean Rogers' *Calling All Cars* (1954), a poor man's *Genevieve* (1953) filmed at the Dover Harbour car terminal.

Pulp realism: an example of the E. J. Fancey approach to using locations from one of two 'B' films titled *Behind the Headlines*. This is the 1953 release

Fancey reverted to travelogues for most of 1955, before producing Denis Kavanagh's spy thriller *Flight from Vienna* (1955). John Bentley essayed a pukka English officer in what was a talky but quite convincing drama. Inevitably, there was a part for Adrienne. Michael McCarthy's thriller *Shadow of a Man* (1955), starring 'B' film stalwarts Paul Carpenter and Rona Anderson, was given a seal of approval by the trade press, with particular praise for Carpenter's performance.[227] Though the film's narrative moves are often arbitrary and perfunctorily motivated, the central relationship is more attractively shaded than usual and good use is made of the Hastings locations. There were also plenty of real settings – including Fancey's own office – in *They Never Learn* (1956), directed by Denis Kavanagh. It offered a rare look at the work of London's policewomen, and featured Adrienne Scott going undercover to unmask a gang of international forgers which included Jackie Collins. Production values were low and the direction 'staccato'.[228] Kavanagh went on to direct Adrienne in *Fighting Mad* (1957), produced by Fancey as 'Edwin Scott' and shot, as usual, on location, appropriately enough, in the Scottish Highlands. It was a lumber-camp thriller about a Glaswegian boxer (Joe Robinson) who takes refuge in Canada after accidentally causing the deaths of two opponents. Jennifer Wyatt's script failed to reach literary heights, but there was enough rough stuff and spectacular background scenery to keep audiences entertained for fifty minutes.

In September 1956, E. J. Fancey lost his younger brother and partner in New Realm, S. A. Fancey. He responded by reasserting his commitment to production by founding Fantur Films to make *The Traitor* (1957) at the Danzigers' New Elstree Studios. Michael McCarthy wrote and directed the film, a thriller about the search for the betrayer among a group of former members of a wartime underground group during a reunion. It starred Robert Bray, recently seen in *Bus Stop* (1956), Donald Wolfit and Jane Griffiths, with a supporting cast that included Anton Diffring and Christopher Lee. The critics generally concurred that, although talky, it was sufficiently gripping and well filmed to be given first-feature status. E. J. Fancey, Denis Kavanagh and Adrienne Scott were reunited for the ultra-topical *Rock You Sinners* (1957), made at the close of 1956. Although it was eventually beaten to general release by *The Tommy Steele Story*, this was actually the first British film to address the new craze for rock 'n' roll music. Its production values may have been meagre and its performances less than accomplished, but it carried a genuine sense of authenticity, as one trade review noted: 'World of sweaters and jeans, curious vocabulary, and uninhibited acrobatic dancing admirably conveyed ... The screen fairly jumps with life as the oddly garbed adherents go into explosive "dancing" routines to the accompaniment of music played by some of the hottest out- fits in the land.'[229] The semi-documentary approach to exploitation film-making developed in pre- vious pictures was continued in the featurette *It Could be You* (1957), this time directed, one imagines, by Fancey himself as Edwin Scott. This exercise in wish fulfilment described a trip to Germany by two British models (Adrienne Scott and Jackie Collins), and won faint praise for 'plenty of pretty scenes'.[230] It paved the way for prissy-but-suggestive pictures like Alfred Travers' Technicolor co-feature *Girls of the Latin Quarter* (1960), which posed the question 'How you gonna keep 'em down on the farm after they've seen a Parisian-style striptease revue?' Travers also directed the surprisingly entertaining 'B' feature *The Primitives* (1962), a thriller with cabaret backgrounds, but by this time, the Fancey family business was moving unashamedly towards exploitation cinema. New Realm made a killing with Arnold Miller and Stanley Long's twenty- seven-minute *Nudist Memories* (1959), costing less than £1,000 and notorious as the film starring Anna Karen, who would become famous on television in *On the Buses*, and narrated by *The*

A naturists' picnic from the Adrienne Fancy production *It's a Bare, Bare World* (1963)

Gentle Touch's Jill Gascoine.[231] Fancey commissioned a follow-up, *Some Like it Cool* (1961), from Michael Winner, whose directorial debut, *Shoot to Kill* (1960), he had sponsored. Adrienne Fancey (Scott) began her career as producer with *Some Like it Cool* and the featurette *It's a Bare, Bare World* (W. Lang, 1963), featuring the bare, bare breasts of Vicky Kennedy (Margaret Nolan). Eventually Adrienne would succeed her father as MD of the family businesses.

Vandyke

Vandyke was one of the more prominent of the small production companies that mushroomed in the late 1940s following demobilisation. It was founded in 1947 by old-Etonian and former pilot Roger Proudlock (b. 1920) and his brother Nigel (b. 1925). The company was responsible for a dozen or so second features before the brothers went their separate ways in film and television. Unfortunately, most of Vandyke's early films are unavailable for viewing, although the larger-budget pictures of the mid-1950s are accessible. Roger Proudlock had cut his producer's teeth on *The Hangman Waits* (1947), a gruesome slice of *Grand Guignol* written and directed by A. Barr-Smith. It told the story of the pursuit of a limping cinema-organist, wanted for the killing and dismembering of an usherette, her body deposited in a trunk at Victoria Station. Before plunging to his death from the top of a newspaper building, the hunted man manages to do away with a fellow-organist in a church. Somewhat unconvincingly, its distributors, Butcher's, tried to emphasise the film's factual and educational credentials: 'An absorbing and thrilling exposition of Newspaper life showing how

Torso in a trunk: Butcher's press book for the Vandyke production *The Hangman Waits* (1947)

crime news is collected and presented in its various stages', claimed the poster. Reviewers were less than convinced and could recommend this only for the unsophisticated. Turning instead to comedy, the Proudlocks gave Peter Graham Scott, the young editor of *Brighton Rock*, his first opportunity to direct with *Panic at Madame Tussaud's* (1949), experimentally filmed mainly on location at the famous waxworks after closing time. The result, distributed by Exclusive, was fifty minutes of knockabout fun, loosely organised around a crime caper at the waxworks where the numbskull crooks pose as exhibits. Scott handled the madcap proceedings in a tongue-in-cheek way that won faint praise from the trade reviewers. More important, however, was Scott's demonstration that considerable production savings could be achieved by the use of 'factual locations' (in spite of the interruptions caused by traffic sounds and other 'noises off').[232]

Vandyke's 'B' films followed no recognisable pattern. In a single year, their productions for Grand National ranged from Alfred Travers' *The Strangers Came* (1950), a satirical Irish comedy, to John Gilling's *A Matter of Murder* (1950), billed as 'The Drama of a Man who couldn't escape his conscience'. The latter film was Gilling's own story of a bank clerk (Barry Brigg, a.k.a. John Barry) who is driven to embezzlement by a gold-digger and is then implicated in her murder. He eventually finds redemption by sacrificing his life to save that of a policeman.[233] Following the successful experiment with factual locations, the film was shot mainly in a former girls' private school in Kensington, which was dressed as a boarding house, and at Paddington Station as well as Viking Studios. *The Strangers Came* also used factual backgrounds, including the Gilston Park Country Club near Harlow for the interiors and Irish locations for the exteriors. The film was an Ealing-style yarn of a self-important Hollywood producer (Tommy Duggan) who goes to an Irish village to make a film of the life of St Patrick. Naturally, he is no match for the wily locals. Alfred Travers certainly had hopes that his film might merit first-feature status at some cinemas.[234] Vandyke switched to Eros for its next production at Riverside Studios, a thriller titled *The Six Men* (1951) directed by Michael Law, a veteran of the Naval Film Unit. It starred Harold Warrender as a Scotland Yard Inspector who brings a gang of thieves to justice one by one, using his daughter (Olga Edwardes) as a pawn. Although it involved considerable location work in Soho and Mayfair, Victoria Station and Northolt Airport, *The Cinema* still found the atmosphere 'unconvincing'.[235]

In the summer of 1950, Vandyke lined up three consecutive productions for Walton Studios. All were directed back-to-back by John Guillermin: *Smart Alec* (1951) was a comedy-thriller about an acquitted murderer who subsequently confesses to his crime in the belief that he cannot be retried.

Trade reviewers singled out Guillermin's 'imaginative' direction for particular praise.[236] Guillermin also provided lively direction for *Two on the Tiles* (1951), a farce revolving around matrimonial indiscretions starring Hugh McDermott, Brenda Bruce and Herbert Lom as a blackmailing butler. *Four Days* (1951) was another well-received story of marital infidelity, this time involving amnesia and attempted murder in which Hugh McDermott and Kathleen Byron were joined by the star of *Smart Alec*, Peter Reynolds. Guillermin achieved yet more critical success with *Song of Paris* (1952, USA: *Bachelor in Paris*), an Adelphi-distributed co-feature starring Dennis Price as an indigestion pill salesman who brings a cabaret star back from the French capital. Here clearly was an example of the usefulness of modest programmers in allowing a talented director to experiment and develop his powers.

The same could not be said of Dallas Bower's adaptation of Pinero's *The Second Mrs Tanqueray* (1953). Although the director borrowed the multiple camera techniques of television production to complete filming in just eight days at Riverside Studios, the result was an ultra-conservative transposition of the Victorian domestic melodrama from stage to screen. This sort of photographed theatre with few concessions to ideas of the cinematic had not been witnessed since George Bernard Shaw policed the filming of his *How He Lied to Her Husband* (1931). *Kinematograph Weekly* rightly described it as a 'Museum piece'.[237] It remains a curious anomaly in Vandyke's output. The company was back on more familiar crime territory for *Black 13* (1953), made for distribution by Archway, but adopted by 20th Century-Fox for release in the USA. It was directed by Ken Hughes, a rising talent, at the newly reopened Wembley Studios on a four-week schedule. The script – an adaptation of an Italian 'A' certificate film *Gioventu Perduta*, concerning the exploits of a juvenile delinquent – had been closely scrutinised by the censor following the moral panic about cosh boys, and originally rejected as unacceptable in an English setting. Vandyke were obliged to raise the age of the protagonist, make him an accidental killer and give the documentary style of the Italian original a more theatrical feel.[238]

Although severely under-capitalised, Vandyke Productions managed to set up their own studio, a converted 500-seat cinema in Barnes.[239] It remained, though, a shoestring operation. Don Chaffey was obliged to manage a shooting schedule that allowed the stars of *Time Is My Enemy* (1954) extensive time off to work on other commitments: Dennis Price on television, Susan Shaw and Renee Asherson in the theatre, and Patrick Barr on another 'B' film.[240]

Val Guest lent his considerable talents to Vandyke's *They Can't Hang Me* (1955), based on a topical tale of nuclear science secrets by the film critic Leonard Mosely. 'A Thrill-a-Minute Story Behind Today's Atomic Headlines!' enthused the tagline. The presence of Guest in the director's chair, and of his wife Yolande Donlan and the Rank contract artist Terence Morgan in the cast, signified that this was a superior 'B'. However, it was rated no more than 'an average programmer' by *Kinematograph Weekly*.[241] Hanging may have been avoided, but Vandyke failed to survive the adverse trading conditions that suppressed 'B' film production in 1956–7. However, Roger Proudlock made a brief solo return to 'B' features when conditions improved in 1960.

Brighton Studios

Brighton Studios was the more successful of two attempts to diversify the sites of film production: to offer alternatives to the intense concentration of production facilities in the north and west of London and its suburbs, and create the opportunity for film-making by the seaside where, after all, it had all begun. The other venture at Paignton in Devon was an expensive and protracted disaster.

Filming at the seaside: trade advertisements for two early Brighton Studios' productions

With the name of the Sussex resort in the public eye following the release of *Brighton Rock* (1947), the first plans for a new studio were laid by Managing Director Jack Norman, a man-about-Wardour-Street with a film library, and Production Director 'Tommy' Tomlinson, an independent producer. The studios were eventually opened by Sid Field in September 1948, unfortunately, in the midst of the worst production crisis since the mid-1920s. They were designed primarily for modest independent films or as overspill accommodation for larger studios.[242] Their advantage, announced an advertisement in *The British Film Yearbook*, 1952, was that they were 'compact' studios 'situated under ideal conditions by the seaside and South Downs in Sussex, and therefore affording unsurpassable location facilities'.

Between 1949 and 1956 the studios produced at least thirteen second- and co-feature films, in addition to numerous shorts. The first production took the floor early in January 1949 on a five-week schedule, with Edward G. Whiting producing and directing the comedy-drama *The Adventures of Jane*, based on the celebrated *Daily Mirror* cartoon strip – strip is the operative word as the eponymous heroine spent much of the time losing her clothes. Made for distribution by Eros, the film starred the authentic artist's model for Pett's cartoon, Christabel Leighton-Porter, in what was hoped would be the first of a popular series. Unfortunately, the script was disastrously short of comedy, drama and, crucially, undressing. *The Cinema* lamented its 'incomprehensible welter of narrative loose ends', as well as the film's 'weak direction', 'moderate production values' and 'unsubtle portrayal'.[243] Christabel Leighton-Porter's name was conspicuously absent from the film's publicity, and for this she may have been grateful, as all *Kinematograph Weekly* was prepared to say was that 'her legs, shapely as they are, fail to make up for her lack of acting ability'.[244]

A front-page ad was placed in *The Cinema Studio*, declaring Brighton Studios 'The Bright Spot in British Film Production!' and stressing the 'High sunshine record' of the town;[245] but, in fact, the clouds were already gathering. The studios would be left searching for tenants for the next twelve months. The production of the second *Jane* film was cancelled, and cameras did not turn again until April 1950 for a series of documentaries. *Penny Points to Paradise*, the film that put the Goons on screen, followed towards the end of the year, but it would be a further ten months before the studios secured another feature booking. Adelphi's *My Death is a Mockery* moved in early in November 1951. Donald Houston had to fit filming round his stage commitments in the West End, but the picture was completed within five weeks.[246] The studios went through another period of inactivity in the first half of 1952 – taking the opportunity to renovate and update – before Lance Comfort moved in to make *The Girl on the Pier* (1953, working title *Palace Pier*), the debut feature of John Temple-Smith's Major Productions.[247] The film's trailer dramatically juxtaposed the two sides of Brighton's image, contrasting the legend 'Playground for Holidays' across a sunny panorama, with 'Background for Murder' emblazoned across a menacing nightscape. The story follows the sleuthing of Charlie (Anthony Valentine), the son of a police inspector, who discovers that the manager of Brighton's wax-works exhibition (Campbell Singer) is being blackmailed because of his criminal past by an ex-confederate (Ron Randell). Disguised as the waxworks' laughing clown, the manager murders his tormentor before, chased by the police, like Pinkie in *Brighton Rock*, he falls to his death from the end of the Palace Pier.[248] The same theme of a child exposed to crime in a holiday setting is present in a rather more prestigious colour production from Brighton Studios, *The Secret* (1955), which featured Sam Wanamaker, an American actor fleeing McCarthy's purges. He played Nick, a struggling hustler trying to raise his fare back to the USA, and the emerging child star, Mandy Miller, was Katie, the girl whose teddy bear is stuffed with her mother's diamonds. As in so many other films of this type (*Hunted* [1952], *Tiger Bay* [1959], for instance), the child charms and ultimately reforms the adult exploiter. The film won praise for its direction by another blacklist émigré, Cy Endfield, who quickly became a significant force in the British industry with films like *Hell Drivers* (1957) and *Zulu* (1963).[249] Enfield, directing under an alias, had already worked at Brighton, on *The Master Plan* (1954), a Cold War espionage thriller set at an international meeting of political leaders. *To-Day's Cinema* found the story a little incoherent, but was impressed by the 'top-speed direction'.[250]

Under the studios' new head, Derrick Wynne, 1953–5 was the peak period for feature production at Brighton. Geoffrey Goodhart and Brandon Fleming produced a string of thrillers. The first of these, directed by Alfred Travers, was the somewhat far-fetched *Solution by Phone* (1953) in which a self-centred matinee idol (John Witty) murders his lover and then phones her husband (a crime writer played by Clifford Evans) for advice on the disposal of the body. Goodhart and Fleming followed it up with *Alive on Saturday* (1957), another contrived little 'B' thriller, in which Goodhart also appeared, that stood a couple of years on the shelf awaiting distribution. Terence Fisher was then brought in to make *The Flaw* (1955), a thriller with a climax at sea that seemed tailor-made for Fisher's colleague, Vernon Sewell. The plot was no less contrived than the previous two efforts, but at least put Donald Houston back on a boat and gave him a rough-house climax with John Bentley, as a ruthless playboy who tries to execute the perfect murder, only to discover that his victim is still alive. Sewell, whose yacht was moored just down the coast at Shoreham, did finally make a film at Brighton: *Rogue's Yarn* (1957), another essay in the perfect murder. Channel-hopping between Shoreham and La Havre, it was a reasonably rust-free Eros co-feature in which Derek Bond played a wife-killer trying to estab-lish a water-tight alibi, but who is pursued to his doom by a tenacious Scotland Yard bloodhound (Elwyn Brook-Jones). In general, the critics found both films a pleasurable cruise.

It is hard to imagine anyone finding much pleasure in Francis Searle's *The Gelignite Gang* (1955),[251] except for the frequent unintentional laughs provided by its clichéd script and wooden direction. It starred American actor Wayne Morris, and was presumably made while he was in town filming the slightly more accomplished *The Master Plan*. In a film that displays the 'B' movie's usual animosity between the police and the private investigator, Morris rescues endangered secretary Sally (Sandra Dorne) from the clutches of her employer (Patrick Holt, in a rare role as villain). The film's one redeeming feature is a reasonably well-filmed rooftop shoot-out. David Macdonald directed the Danzigers' only film at Brighton: *Alias John Preston*, a story about a schizophrenic murderer (Christopher Lee) masquerading as a rich philanthropist in an English village. It was a pretty botched job, over-played and under-plotted, but *To-Day's Cinema* judged it 'Palatable fodder for the masses'.[252]

It was not all crime and intrigue, however. The Cold War was given the comic treatment in *Take a Powder* (1953) an in-house production directed by Tommy Tomlinson with the help of Julian Vedey. Little more than an extended music-hall sketch, the film was a vehicle for the antics of the now-forgotten Max Bacon, who played a medicine-seller who poses as a kidnapped scientist (played by Vedey) and runs amok in a hospital. Terence Fisher made a weak attempt at comedy with *Children Galore* (1954), a sentimental and cliché-ridden tale of rivalry between aged villagers to see who could qualify for a donated cottage by having the most grandchildren. The intention was to make a 'lovable' film that 'warms the heart',[253] but the result fell a long way short – although it offered an early opportunity to June Thorburn. It was produced by Henry Passmore, who was also responsible for four CFF shorts directed by John Irwin and starring the children's entertainer, Peter Butterworth. The most interesting film of the quartet was *Playground Express* (1955), in which Butterworth is a Brighton fun-fair manager who leads a boisterous crowd of youngsters in a campaign against a killjoy – virtually an allegory of British society as it began to experience a libertarian challenge to the repressive status quo.

After 1955 and the arrival of commercial television, however, Brighton Studios increasingly concentrated on the production of TV ads until the eventual closure of the premises in 1966. Butcher's used the studios for some of its last supporting features, including Ernest Morris's *Shadow of Fear* (1963) and one of the venerable company's best films, *Smokescreen* (1964), which we will consider in more detail in Chapter 8. Lifted by an engaging performance from Peter Vaughan as an insurance investigator who takes nearly as much pleasure in fiddling his expenses as he does in exposing the fraud of others, *Smokescreen* provided doughty support to the Elvis Presley musical *Roustabout* (1964) as it did the rounds of Britain's provincial cinemas.

Apex and Present Day Productions

In 1950, Apex began handling second features from its associate company Present Day Productions and for Target Films. The latter's first film – unusually produced by a woman, Miriam Crowdy – was *Dangerous Assignment* (1950). Directed by Ben Hart and featuring Lionel Murton and Pamela Deeming, it was a story of an American reporter's search for a missing car-dealer. *To-Day's Cinema* criticised its 'weak' story and some 'stilted and over-dramatised' portrayals, but still found it a 'commendable effort' at low-budget film-making, demonstrating 'considerable imagination in production', with 'a seemingly genuine attempt at realism'.[254] There was less enthusiasm for Present Day Productions', *Dark Interval* (1950), the first of a trio of films scripted by John Gilling, produced by Charles Reynolds and directed by Charles Saunders. *Dark Interval* was a contribution to the cycle of brooding depictions of homicidal paranoia in country mansions, in this case Cranbourne Hall, a Country Club in Windsor Forest. It may have been miserablist, but it still secured a coveted place on the ABC circuit. Present Day's next two both gave meaty roles to Sidney Tafler, fast forging a promising career in the Bs. *Chelsea Story* (1951) was a talky noir melodrama of a man on the run (Henry Mollison) after accidentally killing a householder during a burglary. For *To-Day's Cinema*, the film constituted only 'passable supporting entertainment', but it was booked onto the Odeon circuit nevertheless.[255] *Blind Man's Bluff* (1951), which was produced at Braywick House, just near Exclusive's new studios, featured Tafler as a sleuthing crime writer and Zena Marshall as his love interest, but the picture was an uneasy combination of stock characters and complicated plotting.

Kenneth Hume's directorial debut *Cheer the Brave* (1951), made at Southall in less than four weeks, might have sounded like a flag-waving war film, but the conflict turned out to be entirely domestic in this simple comedy of a hen-pecked husband (Jack MacNaughton) and his shrewish wife (Elsie Randolph, a 1930s star wasted in this dim tale). The film was made for Apex by SWH Productions (John Sutro, David Webster and Kenneth Hume). Brendan J. Stafford's *The Armchair Detective* (1952) was made at Viking Studios by Derek Elphinstone's new company, Meridian, and adapted by Ernest Dudley from his popular radio show in which he played the eponymous sleuth. It achieved a circuit release, but the critics thought it better heard than seen. *Kinematograph Weekly* referred to it tersely as a 'flatulent thriller'.[256] Elphinstone took a leading role as a doctor in his next production, *Distant Trumpet* (1952), a romantic drama about medical missionary work in Africa. Director Terence Fisher was able to do little to relieve the talky script and static staging.

David Macdonald's murder mystery/back-stage musical, *Tread Softly* (1952), made at Marylebone Studios, was a 'B' film with some pretensions above its station. Atmospherically set in a derelict theatre (the Granville, Fulham) it was a tall tale of a thespian's deranged widow and hidden jewels. John Bentley played the suave producer who is trying to reopen the theatre, and Frances Day and Patricia Dainton provided plenty of pulchritude as his leading ladies. Kenneth Hume's *Hot Ice* (1953) was cast in a similar entertainment mould, with a little more comedy and fewer thrills. Its story-line (supplied by Alan Melville), of an eccentric who invites an assortment of people to a country house and keeps them captive while he steals their jewels, was a good twenty years out of date; but the trade press seemed happy enough with its melodramatic trappings of concealed switches, hidden microphones and subterranean chamber. Apex, however, had just about exhausted the possibilities of the old dark house and breathed its last early in 1954 after a brief partnership with Brighton Studios.

Guido Coen and Fortress

Italian-born Guido Coen (b. 1915), who finished his career producing Vernon Sewell's horror film, *Burke and Hare* (1971) and Tudor Gates's sex comedy *Intimate Games* (1976), began it at Two Cities Films. He established his own company in 1953 and produced a number of films for Baker and Berman under the Kenilworth banner. However, he is most closely associated with director Charles Saunders and the production company Fortress, founded after Saunders parted from Charles Reynolds.[257] Coen made about a dozen mildly entertaining thrillers with Saunders, best of them perhaps the wise-cracking *One Jump Ahead* (1955) and tough-minded *Naked Fury* (1960), a film which takes the trouble to motivate its crooks and doesn't shirk a bleak ending. Coen and Saunders made films for a number of distributors, including major companies like Rank, Pathé and Columbia, and minor ones like Archway, which distributed Saunders' *The Golden Link* (1954), a lengthy whodunit

PAUL CARPENTER . DIANE HART
JILL ADAMS
in **One Jump Ahead** ·'A'·

Desire in deep focus: Paul Carpenter and femme fatale Jill Adams in Saunders' *One Jump Ahead* (1955)

with co-feature aspirations, made at Riverside. As well as starring André Morell and Patrick Holt, it could boast camerawork by Harry Waxman and the debut of 'Britain's loveliest model', Marla Landi,[258] but it suffered from an excess of talk and too little action.

Rank-distributed films included the thriller *Behind the Headlines* (1956) and the limp crime comedy *The Hornet's Nest* (1955), in which a couple of models (June Thorburn and Maria Landi) rent a barge with loot under the floorboards. Waxman photographed the Thames-side locations to good effect. Rank also took charge of Saunders' engaging worm-turned comedy-drama, *There's Always a Thursday* (1957), starring Charles Victor in one of those performances that made 'B' movies worth watching, and the weaker comedy *Operation Cupid* (1959), set in a matrimonial agency. Pathé had the dubious distinction of distributing Saunders' *A Time to Kill* (1955), described by *Kinematograph Weekly* as a 'tin-pot British whodunit, set in the suburbs'.[259] The combined talents of Jack Watling, Rona Anderson and Russell Napier could do little with their stock characters or Doreen Montgomery's formulaic script. Columbia handled the efficiently nasty *Kill Her Gently* (1959) and *Murder Reported* (1957), in which two journalists (Paul Carpenter and Melissa Stribling) investigate the discovery of a body in a trunk. The American press book described it a little more colourfully: 'Trunkful of Murder Sends Sob Sister and Newsman After Clinch-and-Kill Goon!'

Coen and Saunders were also kept in regular work by Eros, beginning with *The Scarlet Web* (1954), directed by Saunders and featuring the reliable Griffith Jones and Hazel Court as a couple on the run and Zena Marshall as a femme fatale. Leavened with touches of wry, wise-cracking humour, nothing in the film would have been out of place in a hardboiled flick from America except the English accents and the backgrounds. It was just the sort of material young British urban audiences were seeking at the time. Saunders' *The Narrowing Circle* (1956), based on a novel by Julian Symons, had an American thriller writer (Paul Carpenter) attempting to sleuth his way out of a murder charge with the help of a female reporter (Hazel Court). The ending was suitably twisting, but its most innovative aspect was the casting of perennial Yard man Napier as a villain. *Date with Disaster* (1957), scripted by the experienced Brock Williams, employed the talents of American actor Tom Drake, hard-bitten William Hartnell and beautiful Shirley Eaton (her character was described in the film's American publicity as 'a love-hungry rock-and-roll babe'). With its safe-blowing and car chases, it was rated 'a very useful co-feature', with a convincing atmosphere, 'capable direction' and well-handled suspense.[260] Coen and Saunders' next for Eros was a neat little noir which featured Barbara Shelley, fresh from her convincing performance as *Cat Girl*, as a devious femme fatale who manipulates Alan Baxter in an intricately plotted story. The title was *The End of the Line* (1957), but Fortress still had one more for Eros: the schlock horror film *Womaneater* (1958).

Coen once said of the type of film he made on £13,000 budgets in this period: 'Style was of secondary consideration. It had to be made for a price ... You had to live, that's all.'[261] In 1959 the living got a little easier when he took up an appointment as Production Executive at Twickenham Studios

'A love-hungry rock-and-roll babe': Shirley Eaton in bother in *Date with Disaster* (1957)

and was responsible for developing the studio's international profile by attracting major productions including such films as *Saturday Night and Sunday Morning* (1960) and *Reds* (1981).[262] However, he did not entirely abandon Saunders, producing for him *Dangerous Afternoon* (1961) and *Jungle Street* (1961), with their well-realised worlds of, respectively, an old ladies' home and tatty back-street clubland. Coen hated the term 'second features': 'If anybody asks what I am doing I tell them I am making a picture. It is psychologically wrong to tell people, particularly the technicians, that you are making a second feature. Naturally they immediately think in terms of second best ... No ... I simply make a picture which in my mind is the best.'[263]

Bill Luckwell

Bill Luckwell worked as a publicist before producing seventeen 'B' films in ten years, under various production company names like Jaywell, Luckwin and Winwell. Most remain hard to track down but, by all reports, few were memorable. He began with *Miss Tulip Stays the Night* (1955), an Adelphi programmer featuring the fading talents of Jack Hulbert and Cicely Courtneidge and the vivacious charms of Diana Dors. In partnership with his wife Kay and Derek Winn, he went on to remake *Not So Dusty* (1956), a Cockney dustmen comedy, first brought to the screen by Maclean Rogers twenty years before. Rogers again took charge, with the dustmen now played by Bill Owen and Leslie Dwyer, and the title now suggesting that the old jokes are still the best. Winwell Productions engaged ex-Gainsborough cameraman Arthur Crabtree to direct two thrillers at Nettlefold. *West of Suez* (1957, USA: *Fighting Wildcats*), starring Keefe Brasselle and Kay Callard, was a hit with the trade critics and was adopted on the ABC circuit.[264] *Morning Call* (1957, USA: *The Strange Case of Dr Manning*) should have starred George Raft had he not called it off at the last minute. In the event, the Australian actor Ron Randell played the private eye who combines with a police inspector (Bruce Seton) to track down a doctor's abductor. Greta Gynt supplied the glamour quotient as the doctor's anxious wife, but the film failed to excite the bookers. Following the closure of Republic's British production operation, Luckwin took over its scheduled projects, Henry Cass's *The Crooked Sky* (1957), in which Wayne Morris played a US Treasury investigator on the trail of counterfeiters led by Anton Diffring;[265] and *Hidden Homicide* (1958), directed by Tony Young at Merton Park. Luckwell, Winn and Cass also teamed up to make programmers for Eros like *Booby Trap* (1957). The implausible plot, involving an absent-minded professor who loses the fountain pen bomb that he has just invented and becomes involved with a gang of dope smugglers, was further handicapped by 'indifferent acting and haphazard direction' and fizzled out 'like a damp squib'.[266] Francis Searle's *Undercover Girl* (1958), made at Twickenham for Butcher's, was not much better, despite the presence of the reliable Kay Callard in the title role alongside the ubiquitous Paul Carpenter as a photographer on the trail of the man who murdered his brother-in-law. Like so many of the low-budget films of the late 1950s, it had a night-club background and a garnish of strip-tease.

After this burst of activity in the mid-1950s, studio space became harder to find and productions became more infrequent, but Luckwell continued to soldier on with 'B' productions, like the impoverished crook dramas *Ambush in Leopard Street* (1962) and *Breath of Life* (1963), well into the next decade. The last, *Delayed Flight* (1964), was made at Bray after Hammer had graduated to 'A' productions.

Is he a murderer? Maya Koumani and Patricia Laffan don't know what to believe about Griffith Jones in Bill Luckwell's production *Hidden Homicide* (1958)

Independent Artists

Leslie Parkyn (1918–1983) and Julian Wintle (1913–1980) took over Beaconsfield in 1958 when it was sold by Sydney Box. Parkyn had experience in distribution before joining Rank's Highbury experiment and subsequently becoming an independent producer making films at Pinewood in partnership with Sergei Nolbandov. Wintle, originally an editor, had produced films at Merton Park before also working for Rank at Pinewood. The Parkyn and Wintle production company, Independent Artists, had a distribution deal with Rank that enabled them to stay in virtually continuous production for the next five years. This was facilitated by a policy of filling the gaps between major productions with the making of supporting features. 'We didn't call them B pictures, because we didn't like that connotation,' Wintle maintained. 'We always had about half a dozen scripts ready for these shorter films, so that they could roll at a moment's notice. They were made by the same technicians who worked on our major pictures, but they enabled us very often to try out new talent among directors and writers.'[267]

These 'shorter films' are among the most rewarding British 'B' movies and are often unusual in their evasion of genre conventions and their attention to detail, like Sidney Hayers' *Violent Moment* (1958), an unusual psychological study of a man deprived of his son by a corrupt woman. Some sound fascinating but remain frustratingly difficult to view. These include Don Sharp's well-received *Linda* (1960), in which Carol White ushers in the 'swinging 60s' by arriving in Brighton on the pillion of a scooter;[268] Peter Graham Scott's impressively cast thriller *Breakout* (1959); and John Kruse's *October*

CAROL WHITE · ALAN ROTHWELL · CAVAN MALONE · EDWARD CAST

LINDA 'A'

Produced by **JULIAN WINTLE** and **LESLIE PARKYN** Directed by **DON SHARP** Screenplay by **WILLIAM MacILWRAITH**   AN INDEPENDENT ARTISTS PICTURE
Distributed by **BRITISH LION** in association with **BRYANSTON**

Another love-hungry rock 'n' roll babe: Carol White in the title role of *Linda* (1960)

Moth (1959), a grim tale of a mentally retarded man (Lee Patterson) who believes the victim of a motor accident is his dead mother and takes her to his isolated farm on the moors. Other Wintle and Parkyn productions have become 'B' classics, and we will return to them in later chapters. They include Vernon Sewell's genuinely strange *House of Mystery* (1961) and his *The Man in the Back Seat* (1961) with their chilling last moments; Cliff Owen's bracing debut *Offbeat* (1961); and Peter Graham Scott's *Devil's Bait* (1959) and *The Big Day* (1960), refreshing in their emphasis on character and the details of living rather than on hectic plotting. Unfortunately, this impressive sequence petered out with Sewell's unappetising slice of East End life *Strictly for the Birds* (1963), an apparent homage to its contemporary, *Sparrows Can't Sing* (1963).

The more one considers the British 'B' film, the more one comes to agree with Parkyn and Wintle that some tag other than the implicitly derogatory 'B' label is called for, at least in recognition of the best that was achieved in these often austere production circumstances.

4 Behind the Scenes

Directors

The men (there were virtually no women[1]) who made the British 'B' films fall into three clear groups. There are those who made second features while awaiting their chance to direct in the 'A' league; those who had had some 'A' movie experience and turned to the bottom half of the double bill to prolong their careers, if not their reputations; and those whose whole working life was conducted in the lower reaches of the industry. We would want to suggest at the outset that there is no clear correlation between the groupings and the quality of the output: that is, some former 'A' directors responded vigorously to the straitened conditions of the second-feature industry; some who used the latter as a stepping stone to bigger things didn't always reveal their potential in their earlier work; and some who spent their careers on the 'B' movie treadmill could occasionally surprise with the sharpness and freshness of their work.

On the way up

Among those directors who cut their teeth on 'B' movies before going on to more ambitious fare are Terence Fisher, John Guillermin, John Gilling, Ken Hughes, Lewis Gilbert, Peter Graham Scott and Don Chaffey. The present-day equivalent is probably the direction of episodes of television series, in which the likes of Michael Winterbottom and Anthony Minghella worked before making the jump into major features.

John Gilling (1912–1984) entered the 'A' league with a batch of films for Warwick, including action pieces such as *High Flight* (1957), thrillers like *Interpol* (1957) and the musical *Idle on Parade* (1958), efficient, if not especially flavoursome, entertainments aimed at an international audience. After directing his former Tempean boss Robert Baker's 'A' venture, *The Flesh and the Fiends* (1959), a version of the Burke and Hare story, he stayed with the genre and was taken on by Hammer for such mid-1960s numbers as *The Reptile* and *The Plague of the Zombies* (both 1966), as well as several other costume films. Baker remembered him as: 'a writer who directed, basically. He was very good and very conscientious; a little bit tough with actors on the set, but he maintained discipline and turned out some very good pictures.'[2]

Gilling was a Londoner who, at the age of seventeen, had packed up his first job with an oil company and headed for Hollywood. There he scratched a living as a prize-fighter, actor, stage manager and writer before returning to England in 1933 and landing a post as an assistant director with BIP and later with Gainsborough. After naval service, he re-entered the film world via his screenwriting, which drew effectively on his cosmopolitan experience.[3] In the late 1940s he formed a partnership with the producer Harry Reynolds, who had made *Strange Duet* (1948) at the tiny Windsor Studios in central London. The pair began to make thirty-five- to forty-minute films, starting with *Escape from Broadmoor* (1948), shot extensively on location. This was a fanciful melodrama of a homicidal maniac's return to the scene of his crime, where he encounters the ghost of his victim. It is interesting in the way it confronts the themes of loss, guilt, atonement, revenge and the survival of the spirit, that were preoccupations in a variety of post-war genres. The cast included Victoria Hopper, the former protégée and wife of Basil Dean, in her last role, and John LeMesurier, later a character fixture in British film and television, as the maniac. Gilling's other 1940s film, *A Matter of Murder* (1949), unavailable for this study, has been dismissed as a 'tatty programme-filler'.[4]

Tempean, perceptive and lucky in nabbing Gilling, gave him the opportunity to write and direct *No Trace* (1950, working title *Murder by the Book*) at Southall and Riverside studios. Hugh Sinclair, Dinah Sheridan and John Laurie took the leading roles in the story of a crime novelist who murders a blackmailer and then helps the police investigate the crime he has committed. Released from the restrictions he had recently experienced when filming in factual locations, he experimented with the technique then being developed by Hitchcock of long choreographed takes, which, correctly handled, saved studio time.[5] He went on to make standard thrillers such as *Escape by Night* (1953), a tale of hard-drinking newsmen and vice kings,[6] and *The Gilded Cage* (1955), with a plot involving the smuggling of valuable paintings out of the country (and a nicely oleaginous turn from Elwyn Brook-Jones as a night-club owner). However, there are some less predictable entertainments among Gilling's Tempean films, all worth at least brief notice here: *The Quiet Woman* (1951), *The Voice of Merrill* (1953), *The Frightened Man* (1952) and *The Embezzler* (1954).

The Voice of Merrill was made on 'B' movie lines, but played the top half of the bill in some situations. According to Baker, 'It wasn't a very expensive film to make but the distributors [Eros] felt it was too good to go out as a second feature.'[7] Further, in Valerie Hobson, it has a certifiably 'A' level star; and its production values (Wilfred Arnold was art director) were much more lavish than usual in second features. Hobson here gives a stylish and sexy account of an unhappy wife, while James Robertson Justice is typically waspish as the husband. The plot, which moves with exemplary speed and fluency towards its downbeat ending, and Berman's camerawork collude with a strong cast to produce an 'ingenious specimen of murder-mystery drama'.[8] *The Quiet Woman* is a rare 'B' movie with a female protagonist. Usually the leading lady will be a nicely spoken young woman with permed hair, 'new look' clothes and a refined accent, who has got herself into a dangerous situation, her rescue from which will distract the hero from nailing low-lifers with common or, worse, foreign accents at a remove from hers. None of this is true of the arresting Jane Hylton, who made something very interesting of the pub-keeper with an escaped-convict husband and a dashing smuggler boyfriend (Derek Bond). She suggests, often with evocative stillness, a woman whose past is unravelling and whose future she is tentatively trying to make something of. The film also had a strong supporting performance by Dora Bryan, who replaced Diana Dors when Dors fell foul of the director. 'Its salty and cockney humour cover up the flat spots,' commented *Kinematograph Weekly*.[9]

The Frightened Man and *The Embezzler* also offer a good deal more in the way of character, and character interaction, than is common in the 'B' film, and the former furthermore provides a limited but not foolish discourse on matters of class and homophobia. Charles Victor plays Rosselli, a second-hand-goods dealer who has educated his son Julio (Dermot Walsh) above his class level and Julio has rewarded his aspirations by being sent down from Oxford and getting involved with crooks including

Maxie (John Blythe, icon of cheery unscrupulous low-life in post-war British cinema). With considerable care for emotional motivation, *The Frightened Man* works its way through to a very tense rooftop chase in which Julio falls to his death and Rosselli, numb with grief, is led off by his policeman lodger Harry (John Horsley). As well as Victor, who imbues Rosselli with a touching remorse and pain, there is a sharply effective role from Michael Ward, veteran of dozens of prissy cameos but here allowed a chance to develop a (probably) gay character with real intelligence and a certain dignity. Julio's abrasive treatment of him, as Cornelius, Rosselli's knowledgeable assistant, is a surprisingly astute and critical rendering of homophobic disdain to find in a film of the period. *Picture Show* praised it as a 'Simple, sincerely told drama'.[10] *The Embezzler* is ingenuous enough in its well-meaning way, and Gilling allows Charles Victor enough scope to enlist our sympathy with Henry Paulson, who, diagnosed early with a bad heart, wishes 'it wasn't too late ... for getting out of the rut', steals money from the bank he works at, and absconds to an Eastbourne hotel presided over by Mrs Larkins (Peggy Mount). There he atones by sorting out the problems of its residents.[11] Production values are perfunctory, but the strength of the acting and the neatness of the plotting carry it through.[12]

The very least that can be said for Gilling's Tempean films is that they answered a market demand with unpretentious efficiency, that Gilling shows in all of them a capacity for establishing the premises of his plots economically and evocatively, for developing them with clarity and speed, for giving competent players a chance to invest their characters with a feeling and detail that go beyond stereotype, and for making deft use of limited locations and settings. All four of the films discussed above have a convincing sense of place and atmosphere that belies their skimpy budgets. In some of his other Bs Gilling used Hollywood stars such as Scott Brady in *Three Steps to the Gallows* (1953) and Larry Parks in *Tiger by the Tail* (1955), and, while this no doubt secured a certain gloss and wider US distribution for them, the wholly indigenous jobs tend to be more individually flavoured. From Tempean, Gilling would go on to larger budgets but not necessarily to more rewarding outcomes.

Before Terence Fisher (1904–1980) became what has been described as 'arguably the most important director of the Gothic cinema in the second half of the twentieth century',[13] he had directed over two dozen films, mainly 'B' crime movies. He had abandoned a career in the Merchant Navy to become the oldest trainee at Shepherd's Bush studios in the 1930s, and eventually became a fully fledged editor at Warner's Teddington Studios. Joining Rank, he had edited *The Wicked Lady* (1945) and *The Master of Bankdam* (1947) before being rewarded with the chance to direct. *Colonel Bogey* (1948) is a modestly engaging entry in the minor spiritualist strand of 1940s British cinema, and anticipates, albeit in comic mode, Fisher's later interest in horror and the supernatural. A young Victorian couple spends time with the wife's aunt (nicely played by Mary Jerrold) who behaves as if her late husband were still alive and his ghostly voice is heard (ITMA's Jack Train). He is finally shamed into leaving only when it is revealed that his regiment is to take arms against suffragettes. There is some charm and mild comedy at the expense of Victorian manners, perhaps intended to be read in terms of women's changing position during and after World War II, but it is too slight to bear much significance of this kind. With Fisher's Christian Science background and abiding interest in the supernatural, it would be easy to incorporate this film into an auteurist reading of his work, but the director thought that *Colonel Bogey* had no significant influence on his future films. 'I don't talk about *Colonel Bogey* much', he added, 'because it was a comedy, and I am not a comedy director.'[14]

Feminists in bondage: Terence Fisher's debut, *Colonel Bogey* (1948)

At Highbury, Fisher went on to make its only film of any distinction, *To the Public Danger* (1948), as well as the romantic melodrama, *Song for Tomorrow* (1948). He collaborated with Anthony Darnborough on several 'A' films, but his pre-horror career was chiefly in a string of efficient crime-thrillers, mostly for Hammer before it discovered its particular crock of gold in Fisher's *The Curse of Frankenstein* (1957). The thrillers, all with at least one US star of variable voltage, included *The Last Page*, *Wings of Danger*, *Stolen Face* (all 1952), *Mantrap*, *Blood Orange* (1953), *Face the Music*, *The Stranger Came Home*, *The Mask of Dust* (1954) and *Murder by Proxy* (1955). There is not much in these, competent though they are, to presage the horrormeister to come, except for the plastic sur-geon's ambitions in *Stolen Face*. Nor are there such omens in most of the other Bs he made, including several for ACT Films (*Final Appointment*, 1954; *Stolen Assignment*, 1955; *The Last Man to Hang?*, 1956), but the two clear science-fiction programmers he made for Hammer, *Four-Sided Triangle* and *Spaceways* (1953), have at least 'a generic affinity with Hammer horror'.[15] As Andrew Spicer argues, Fisher's early career as a director was in large part dictated by its industrial context:

> The crime thriller was the obvious choice for low-cost entertainment, as it required a limited number of easily constructed and small-scale sets, whose deficiencies could often be disguised by the use of low-key lighting, and which could be accommodated in the cramped space available in the small studios that these companies used.[16]

If Fisher's early directorial trajectory was shaped by market demands and budgetary constraints, from 1957 he would be important in shaping not just his own career but that of perhaps the most profitable production company in British film history.

Among others who moved on to more ambitious territory, John Guillermin (b. 1925) offers one of the most clear-cut career paths. He made ten second features, six of them for the Vandyke company, and followed this apprenticeship with a dozen British 'A' films, including such varied and accomplished genre pieces as the small-town thriller *Town on Trial* (1954), the war film *I Was Monty's Double* (1958), the Gallic romance *Waltz of the Toreadors* (1962) and the all-star Christie whodunit *Death on the Nile* (1978), as well as several big-budget spectaculars in the USA. His 'B' films reflect his ease in moving from genre to genre: there are the usual thrillers, such as *Torment* (1949) and *Four Days* (1951), the excessively whimsical *Miss Robin Hood* (1952) and the well-regarded children's film *Adventures in the Hopfields* (1954). *The Cinema*'s comments on his thriller *Four Days* are typical of the plaudits received by his early directorial efforts: 'John Guillermin's handling of this melodramatic material gives one an impression of surface accuracy and a sense of pictorial composition. He most adroitly introduces moments of genuine suspense and cleverly tones down the more lurid scenes.'[17]

Ken Hughes (1922–2001) made documentaries from the mid-1940s for the MoI and the War Office, mostly writing the screenplays as well. His first feature was a late edition to the post-war 'spiv' cycle, *Wide Boy* (1952). Then at Merton Park in 1953 he embarked on a series of half-hour *Scotland*

Ken Hughes

Windermere noir: Hilary Brooke and Alex Nicol in Ken Hughes' *The House Across the Lake* (1954)

Yard thrillers, which won a reputation for crisp storytelling, often displaying a visual flair at odds with their limited budgets. His other low-budget films included neat thrillers such as *Black 13* (1954) and *The Brain Machine* (1955), both starring Patrick Barr, and, best of his early work, *The House Across the Lake* (1954), starring US imports Hillary Brooke and Alex Nicol, and imbued with film noir stylistics in relation to both narrative and visual sheen. Thereafter, he moved into 'A' features, initially with Mike Frankovich for Columbia. These also favoured the use of American stars (e.g., Arlene Dahl in *Wicked as They Come*, 1956; Victor Mature in *The Long Haul*, 1957) and the noir mode. Arguably, and apart from *The Trials of Oscar Wilde* (1960), his directorial skills are better displayed in the tautness of his earlier films.

Just as Michael Powell developed his powers on pre-war 'quota quickies' before his dazzling work of the 1940s, so directors such as Alan Bridges, Guy Green, Wolf Rilla, Peter Graham Scott and Don Chaffey all made 'B' films before establishing themselves in main features and/or television. Alan Bridges (b. 1927), an often-underrated director, has to his credit one of the very best 'B' films, *Act of Murder* (1964, see discussion in Chapter 8), before making his mark in several eloquent dramas tinged with melancholy (e.g., *The Hireling*, 1973, and *The Shooting Party*, 1984) and the dire miscalculation of the *Brief Encounter* remake (1974). Guy Green (1913–2005), who'd won an Oscar as cinematographer on *Great Expectations* (1946), made his director's debut with the 'B' film *River Beat* (1954), exceptional in its use of docklands locations and pacey action. 'I was lucky to be able to cut my teeth on a small film, make my mistakes and not carry a huge load of responsibility,' Green recalled. 'I remember the film had to run seventy minutes, or something, and the script was ten minutes short of what I needed, so I filled in with this chase down the river.'[18] He went on to main features, including *The Angry Silence* (1960), and, eventually, to Hollywood.

Wolf Rilla (1920–2005) really mixed 'A' films with Bs, such as the touching study of old age *The End of the Road* (1954) and the excellent thriller *The Large Rope* (1953), with an arresting narrative premise and an unsentimental view of the potential mean-spiritedness of village life.[19] *Glad Tidings* (1953) was a comedy of cultural differences and was effectively handled by Rilla, who won critical praise for a 'consistently diverting picture which will quietly captivate most audiences'.[20] Unusually, *Silent Witness* (1959), a 'B' thriller which benefits from tense cross-cutting and music (by Philip Green), was made *after* Rilla had had some success with such main features as *Bachelor of Hearts* (1958). Peter Graham Scott (1923–2006) came into his own with his television work but most of his 'B' films were above average and are worthy of attention. He began his directorial career with producer John Temple-Smith, with whom he made three Bs. Reviewing *The Hide-Out* (1956), a fast-moving and eventful thriller about fur smuggling and anthrax featuring the talents of Dermot Walsh and Rona Anderson, *The Cinema* was impressed by Scott's use of locations in giving 'full dramatic impact' to the film's passages of suspense, and declared the whole thing 'crackling crime entertainment'.[21] *Account Rendered* (1957) featured Honor Blackman in a tale of infidelity, blackmail and murder in Hampstead, but was too stuffed with stock characters and too theatrical to generate much enthusiasm from the critics.[22] Scott and Temple-Smith did better with *The Big Chance* (1957), a cautionary tale of a clerk – played by William Russell, television's Sir Lancelot – who takes the opportunity to embezzle funds, and eventually is relieved to return them. It was a realistic study in criminal temptation that *To-Day's Cinema* was happy to recommend as an 'excellent British supporting feature anywhere, and fit to head the bill in many spots'.[23] Scott's best Bs, however, were probably *Devil's Bait* (1959) and *The Big Day* (1960), both out-of-the-rut in subject and treatment; they will be given more detailed consideration later.

Don Chaffey (1917–1990) began his film career during the war in the art department of Gaumont British, and was given his first directorial opportunity by the Children's Film Foundation in 1949. He went on to make *Time Is My Enemy* (1954), a suspense thriller set in authentic London locales, that was well received by the trade as a 'useful' supporting feature characterised by 'confident performances' and 'breathless' direction.[24] Cresswell Productions gave Chaffey the chance to direct Donald Houston in the well-scripted (Paul Rogers), light-hearted thriller *The Girl in the Picture* (1957) for Eros. Junia Crawford was the girl and the picture was judged '[a] very honest hour's entertainment', although Chaffey's direction was criticised as 'a little erratic'.[25] He worked for ACT on *The Man Upstairs* before making his own ascent to the upper level of film-making with Walt Disney and then the classic fantasy films *Jason and the Argonauts* (1963) and *One Million Years BC* (1965). He is also remembered for his contributions to the television series *The Avengers* and *The Prisoner*.

One might also note briefly three other early directorial efforts. Jack Clayton (1921–1995) made his debut with the critically acclaimed featurette *The Bespoke Overcoat* (1955), tailor-made for Alfie Bass and David Kossoff and filmed using small set-ups at Marylebone Studios. It supported *Brothers in Law* at the Astoria, Charing Cross Road before going on ABC general release.[26] Cy Endfield (1914–1995) came to England in the wake of the McCarthy blacklistings, and made a handful of 'B' thrillers, uncredited on the best of them, *Impulse* (1955). This is an atmospheric noir, starring the US actor Arthur Kennedy, but the director's name on the film is that of Charles De Lautour, though producer Robert Baker confirmed that Endfield was indeed the director.[27] The same situation obtained on *The Limping Man* (1953), made for Banner but distributed by Eros, which also handled most of Baker's output. This remake of the Anthony Verney story of narcotics and murder had Lloyd Bridges in the leading role and a British cast that included Moira Lister, Leslie Phillips and Alan Wheatley. It was hoped that twenty years was a sufficient gap for audiences to have forgotten the unlikely twist in the tail. Both Clayton and Endfield shortly after went on to direct major features, including, respectively, *Room at the Top* (1959) and *Hell Drivers* (1957). Finally, proof that the humble featurette gave opportunities to considerable directorial talent is provided by the case of a little Cornish fantasy called *The Starfish* (1952). This story of a young fisherman (Kenneth Griffith) who saves a group of children from a vindictive witch largely missed its juvenile audience thanks to an 'A' certificate from the BBFC, but it was co-directed – 'rather hazily', according to *To-Day's Cinema* – by John Schlesinger, future luminary of the British New Wave.[28]

On the way down

Having acquired some reputation for main-feature work in the 1940s, or even earlier, directors such as Lance Comfort, Lawrence Huntington, Maurice Elvey, David Macdonald, Arthur Crabtree, Leslie Arliss, Bernard Knowles, Montgomery Tully and Vernon Sewell all had a further ten to fifteen years' work in the neglected corner of the field of production where 'B' films were made. In some cases, Comfort and Sewell particularly, they did some of their best work on the tight budgets and unforgiving schedules of the 'B' movie world. Of course, most of them also found a lucrative haven in the television series which were becoming prolific in the 1950s.

Lance Comfort (1908–1966) arguably achieved the most commendable track record in 1940s 'A' features. Certainly, he adapted with more consistent success than the others to the 'B' film world to which, following the commercial failure of *Portrait of Clare* in 1950, he was relegated. During a long apprenticeship dating back to the 1920s, he performed a range of functions, including work in the 1930s as a sound recordist, editor, 'technical supervisor', assistant director and maker of children's films, before starting his career as director with the pedestrian biopic *Penn of Pennsylvania* (1941). He scored a success with his second feature, *Hatter's Castle* (1941), which made clear where his gifts lay: in the confident exercise of melodramatic impulses in the interests of illuminating character and relationship, in a decorative visual style to serve these impulses, and in giving their heads to a string of dominant actors. He made a series of popular films in the 1940s, notably the wicked-woman thriller *Bedelia* (1946), his atmospheric masterwork *Temptation Harbour* (1947) and the eerie *Daughter of Darkness* (1947). In the 1950s, he did a good deal of work for television series, including over sixty stints as director or producer of half-hour playlets in the *Douglas Fairbanks Presents* (1953–7) series.[29] He was in fact immensely busy in the 1950s, directing nine second or co-features, and producing several others, and his 'B' film career continued into the 1960s with a further eleven as director and two more as producer.

His 'B' films contain some of his most assured work, suggesting that the skills honed in the preceding decade stood him in good stead when it came to making the best use of limited budgets and rigorous shooting schedules. He applied himself to a surprising range of genres. Although the crime thriller was his staple, there were also comedy spoofs (*Make Mine a Million* and *The Ugly Duckling*, both 1959, taking swipes at, respectively, commercial television and Hammer horror), and a couple of cheery teen musicals starring the young David Hemmings, *Live It Up* (1963) and *Be My Guest* (1965). However, what may well be his most interesting post-1950 film is hard to classify in the usual genre terms: *Bang! You're Dead*, released as support for Guy Hamilton's *An Inspector Calls* (1954), involves two boys and a murder in one of the strangest settings in a British film of its period. The beauty of the surrounding woodlands is alloyed with a strong sense of the sinisterly confining. The woods are also contrasted with the congeries of Nissen huts which make up most of the shanty town where Perce Boswell (Jack Warner), a scruffy, negligent father and his small son Cliff live. These unlovely buildings are a visual correlative for the after-effects of war, and obliquely for the careless Americanisation of the country – and the countryside – since it is an American revolver left lying around that precipitates the film's chain of events. It is a picture that leaves one somewhat uneasy because its narrative ultimately eschews easy resolution.

Among the thrillers, *Tomorrow at Ten* (1962), perhaps Comfort's finest, a taut kidnap thriller with a cunningly developed plot, is discussed in Chapter 8, but there are at least a couple of others worth noting here. *The Break* (1962) has a striking pre-credits sequence (a device not then very common) involving a criminal's leap from a train, a murder and an arrest. Comfort typically takes the film out of the stagy interior setting, avoiding that airless, studio-set claustrophobia which so often bedevils British budget film-making, and the action sequences are handled with real flair. The narrative shifts to a farmhouse run as a hotel by an edgy married couple who are also involved in a smuggling racket. The setting-and-character mix sometimes recalls old-fashioned three-act plays, but a strong cast (including Sonia Dresdel as a grimly enigmatic cook and William Lucas as the fugitive) gives point to the film's relationships. *Touch of Death* (1962) similarly responds to the director's urge to get his film out of the studios. After a petrol-station robbery and its aftermath, all executed with economy and suspense by Comfort working from a trim screenplay by one of his

Lance Comfort directs Jess Conrad in *Rag Doll* (1960)

William Franklyn hits the roof in Comfort's *Pit of Darkness* (1961)

regular collaborators, Lyn Fairhurst, the two thieves (David Sumner and William Lucas again) board a houseboat where they hold its attractive young owner (Jan Waters) hostage. Meanwhile, the police have discovered that the notes stolen from the garage are contaminated with potassium cyanide and launch a frantic search for the thieves. Comfort alternates with real skill between the police search and the riverside events, and the latter are given far more than usual character interest by the growing rift between the robbers.

There are inevitably some journeyman pieces in the Comfort CV, but even minor programmers such as *The Man from Tangier* (1957), *Rag Doll* (1960) and *Pit of Darkness* (1961) reveal compensations that lift them above the formulaic routine of the second feature. These three all have protagonists whose naiveté or other traits render them vulnerable to criminal intentions; and are marked by a little more concern for detail of character than was common at this level. In the first, the fading US actor Robert Hutton is the victim of hapless coincidence and plays with easy authority; Christina Gregg is fresh and touching as the provincial girl led astray in London in *Rag Doll*; and William Franklyn, as an amnesiac plunged into fraud and worse, gives substance to *Pit of Darkness*. These central performances are all offset and/or surrounded by character actors whose effortless inhabiting of their (sometimes stereotypical) roles give touches of unexpected textural richness to these routine thrillers. *Rag Doll* and *Pit of Darkness*, too, make Comfort's characteristic use of locations, with the final shoot-out of *Rag Doll* on a hillside at dawn, with a village church bell ironically heard in the distance, and a striking use of a bombsite setting in *Pit of Darkness*. Both were shot by veteran cinematographer Basil Emmott, and benefit greatly from his black-and-white images of urban threat and delusive rural calm. All Comfort's films are persuasive narratives, marked by absence of sentimentality and the whiff of human reality, by a feeling for melodramatic tension and

for thematic contrasts underlined by a visual style which can move into the expressive and the
metaphoric.

Among those who laboured on the direction of post-war 'B' films Vernon Sewell (1903–2001)
perhaps has the strongest claim to auteur status in that his films exhibit certain consistencies of
theme and treatment that are distinctive among his peers and across different production companies. In particular, he displays abiding interests in the sea and the uncanny which, while not present in all his work, give many of his better pictures an unusual flavour. Notably, his willingness to
embrace the uncanny furnishes chilling finales to *The Man in the Back Seat* and *The House of
Mystery* (1961), while the two themes combine effectively in *Ghost Ship* (1952), filmed on the
director's own yacht. 'Dead Men Spoke to Solve the Secret of the Sea!' ran the chilling tagline, and
the film's unusual mixture of brine and spirits fired the imagination of the critics: 'The picture
weighs anchor with alacrity, drifts a little between flashbacks, but cleverly avoids the rocks of obscurity and finally makes port in exciting circumstances ... The authentic nautical roll adds immea-
surably to conviction.'[30] However, he was not limited by these interests and could turn his hand to
more prosaic land-bound thrillers when required, as his co-feature *Strongroom* (1962), a tautly
structured account of a bank robbery and the immuring of two staff in the eponymous vault,
proves. This excellent race-against-time thriller, with a bleak ending, made for Theatrecraft Films,

Woman in a dressing gown: Carol White and Derren Nesbitt wonder what to do with *The Man in the Back Seat* (1961)

Oxy-acetylene-fuelled suspense: Vernon Sewell's *Strongroom* (1962)

scores for its admirable use of a limited setting and its attentive acting, especially from Colin Gordon and Ann Lynn.[31]

Sewell, too, had had a long apprenticeship in the 1930s, coming into his own as director on the still-gripping wartime feature *The Silver Fleet* (1943), but his period in 'A' features was less notable than Comfort's. *Latin Quarter* (1945), which he also co-wrote, has some genuinely gothic frissons, and *The Ghosts of Berkeley Square* (1947) is a fantasy with some charm and wit, but most of his work is in the 'B' territory of succeeding decades. Apart from those mentioned above, there is plenty of competently routine stuff like *Dangerous Voyage* and *Radio Cab Murder* (1954), but even here there are touches of class. *Radio Cab Murder*'s only real point of originality is in the idea of a woman (Sonia Holm) holding up a bank and initiating the chain of events that involve taxi-driver Fred (Jimmy Hanley), but there is a social edge to the attitude that suggests that because he has once stepped out of line this should not be held against him forever. Sewell provides well-staged chases through London streets and Peter Graham Scott's fluent editing breaks up the dialogue sequences. *Picture Show* rated it an 'action-packed crime thriller' with 'commendable performances' from its stars who are 'well supported in this neatly made film'.[32] There are also some ventures into slightly less formulaic material in such films as *Johnny, You're Wanted* (1956), which mixes lorry-driving, dope gangs and show business, and the well-meaning anti-racist drama *The Wind of Change* (1961).

Strongroom suggests what Sewell might have achieved if he'd been in a better position to choose his material: at his best, he seems to have had, in Bourdieu's term, a 'feel for the game',[33] but, for whatever reason, he never quite capitalised fully on either his pictorial skills or his capacity for creating a tightly suspenseful narrative. He certainly knew how to make a little go a long way. According to Sewell, the budget for *The Floating Dutchman* (1953) was around £30,000, necessitating the greatest of care in managing the shooting schedule of five weeks and prompting his comment: 'you see a low-budget director has got to be a cleverer man than a big-budget director'.[34] Sewell revelled in the challenges offered to his ingenuity by his work for companies like Anglo-Amalgamated, and felt no compulsion to return to bigger features: 'I was making enough money to live on and I didn't have to worry about anything, and I liked the stories, that was the main thing, I liked the story, and I thought I could make it entertainment.' Like Comfort, he was undoubtedly helped by having Basil Emmott as his regular cameraman. Eventually, though, Cohen and Levy decided that they could no longer indulge Sewell's enthusiasm for his yacht: 'I ran her for nine or ten years. Then they wouldn't take any more of my bloody yacht films, they said, "Vernon, your yacht ... Out! Out! No more!" '[35]

One of the most prolific 'B' movie careers was that of Montgomery Tully (1904–1988), who had had only a minor brush with main feature-making in the 1940s. However, the titles point to a certain versatility: *Murder in Reverse* (1945) was a well-received, uncompromising thriller; *Spring Song* (1946) was an ingenuously attractive musical; *Mrs Fitzherbert* (1947) was a touching period romance; and there was also the Borstal-set social-problem film, *Boys in Brown* (1949), made on Rank's Independent Frame process. The diversity may also indicate a director looking for his true metier which, in second features, he established as the crime-thriller. There were odd brushes with comedy (*I Only Arsked!*, 1958, from a TV hit series; and *She Knows Y'Know*, 1962, described by one reviewer as 'one more conveyor-belt North Country farce'[36]) and, finally, with science fiction (the colour co-features *The Terrornauts*, 1967, and *Battle Beneath the Earth*, 1968). However, crime was always going to be Tully's forte, on the strength of his best 1940s work, *Murder in Reverse*.

Having worked on documentary shorts for Merton Park in the war years (e.g., *Behind the Guns*, 1940), he spent a good deal of time there in the 1950s, when he made over a dozen short mysteries in the *Scotland Yard* series, as well as several longer films, including the co-features *The Hypnotist* (1957), *Man in the Shadow* (1957), *The Counterfeit Plan* (1957) – the latter two starring former Hollywood lead, Zachary Scott – and *Dial 999* (1955). David Quinlan believed *Dial 999* to be Tully's best film: 'A taut thriller about a man on the run, it made

Montgomery Tully

its audience grip the sides of their seats in suspense, stretching one's nerves tighter and tighter.'[37] *Kinematograph Weekly* described it simply as 'colourful pulp crime fiction, attractively bound.'[38] Another co-feature, *Escapement* (1957), a crime and fraud yarn with sci-fi trimmings, also had faded Hollywood starlings in Rod Cameron and Mary Murphy. It gets off to a swift start with a film star crashing a car in the south of France, and the ensuing action involves a clinic which treats patients with 'deep relaxation' techniques after which they 'wake up into an entirely different world'. The film, in fact, generates a genuine strangeness of atmosphere through its use of electronic music and special effects.

Among Tully's crime programmers made at Merton Park was *Strange Awakening* (1958), a quite accomplished thriller which rather wittily cast Lex (Tarzan) Barker as an amnesiac assault victim, who spends much of the picture in a wheelchair. If there were any twisted vines to swing from, they were to be found in J. MacLaren-Ross's ingenious, if far-fetched, screenplay. This film also had the benefit of Wilfred Arnold's superior set design, and the 'exotic' settings supply the whiff of otherness which keeps the parochialism of so many 'B' films at bay. The trade critics were enthusiastic, being particularly smitten with Barker's femme fatale, Lisa Gastoni.[39] Tully also filmed several times for Hammer, including *Five Days* (1954), another neatly contrived thriller, again with an American lead, Dane Clark, who gives an energetic centre to the film, commanding the screen effortlessly as a financier who has arranged his own death and then tries to get out of the plot he has made when his circumstances change. The film won instant admiration from *To-Day's Cinema* for its 'go-ahead direction',[40] and *Picturegoer* thought that its 'finely judged direction' made it a British second feature 'with that bit extra in the way of precision planning that should make it worthy export material'.[41] John Ireland in *The Glass Cage* (1955) and Dan Duryea in *36 Hours* (1954), both for Hammer, are two further cases of minor American stars lending that touch of authority that, say, Robin Bailey so signally fails to provide in *The Diplomatic Corpse* (1958), the problematic newspaper comedy-thriller Tully made for ACT Films.

In general, though, Tully brought a practised skill in keeping a narrative moving briskly to the unassuming mysteries and thrillers which came his way for Merton Park, Hammer and, in a burst towards the end of his career, for a company called Eternal, distributed by Grand National.[42] His first for Eternal was *The House in Marsh Road* (1960), which offers an unusually frank picture of a grim marriage, with a heavy-drinking husband with a wandering eye (Tony Wright, with the statutory shirtless scene to sustain his beefcake image), before it settles into being a haunted house mystery with (not rare in British Bs) a downbeat ending. *Jackpot* (1960), with its cop-killer antagonist, has echoes of *The Blue Lamp* (1950), which grow louder with the final trapping of the fugitive in a sports stadium – in this case, Highbury, the Arsenal Football Club ground. Of the other Eternal pictures, *The Third Alibi* (1961) is a tense enough variant on the theme of marital discord and murder, involving the use of tape recorders, a pair of well-contrasted jealous sisters (Patricia Dainton and Jane Griffiths) and, as a bonus, Cleo Laine singing 'Now and Then'. If Tully never made 'B' movies as accomplished or distinctive as Comfort and Sewell at their best, his is at least an admirable record of persistence in often-unrewarding territory, and there are enough signs of directorial insights, both thematically and stylistically, to make him worthy of further study.

Maurice Elvey (1887–1967) had perhaps the longest career of any British director, with well over a hundred silent films, a string of popular entertainments in the 1930s (several with Gracie Fields) and a collaboration with Leslie Howard on two wartime pictures. His last major film was *Beware of*

Maurice Elvey

Pity (1946), a tragic romance adapted from Stefan Zweig's novel, starring Lilli Palmer as the crippled heroine, and *The Late Edwina Black* (1951), though a taut version of a stage thriller, signals the onset of the double bill for Elvey. He kept busy in the 1950s, albeit in co- and minor 'A' features with middle-rank comics. One of the unequivocally 'B' films is ACT's *Second Fiddle* (1957), a film which raised significant gender issues and also demonstrated to *The Cinema*'s satisfaction that, when 'handled properly by the right people' a three-week schedule could produce perfectly adequate entertainment.[43] *The Harassed Hero* (1954) is mildly amusing in its artless comedy-thriller way, and also interesting in its depiction of the police in much less respectful terms than usual: they are very sure of themselves and very wrong. Some of Elvey's old expertise is on display in the way he keeps the idiotic plot moving (helped by Anne Barker's brisk editing and Frank Chacksfield's sometimes comically jaunty music); *To-Day's Cinema* thought the direction 'straightforward', but *Kinematograph Weekly* and *Picture Show* raised a little more enthusiasm.[44] *Room in the House* (1955) gave a rare starring role to the great character actress Marjorie Rhodes, but *Monthly Film Bulletin* found 'the entertainment is generally very tame' and the performances ranged from 'eminently presentable to extremely indifferent'.[45] Elvey was not always blessed with the best 'B' film material, but generally managed at least an efficient job as befitted his experience.

David Macdonald (1904–1983) had enjoyed considerable success with main features in the late 1930s and the 1940s, particularly with the wartime documentaries, *Desert Victory* (1943) and *Burma Victory* (1946), and the sombre melodrama *The Brothers* (1947). However, after rumoured personal difficulties and some unfortunate career choices (including *The Bad Lord Bryon* and *Christopher Columbus*, both 1949), he was largely reduced to 'B' movies and dual-purpose film/television pictures for the Danzigers in the 1950s, returning only once more to 'A' films with *The Moonraker* (1957) and *Petticoat Pirates* (1961). However, Macdonald made some entertaining low-budget films including *Devil Girl from Mars* (1954), the lively comedy *Small Hotel* (1957) and the back-stage chiller *Tread Softly* (1952). The latter had all the elements to make popular entertainment, although, as critics noted, none of them was particularly well-handled by Macdonald, and the film suffered in comparison to Val Guest's more authentically staged *Murder at the Windmill* (1949).

Leslie Arliss (1901–1987) entered films as a writer in the 1930s and came to prominence as the director of the groundbreaking Gainsborough melodrama, *The Man in Grey* (1943), following this with two more for the studio – *Love Story* (1944) and *The Wicked Lady* (1945) – all starring Margaret Lockwood at the peak of her popularity. His decline in the late 1940s was rapid, precipitated by the ludicrous disaster of *Idol of Paris* (1948), with its notorious whip-cracking heroines (although some might argue that the British Bs would have benefited from a bit more of this sort of thing). In the next decade most of his work was for television, with a few 'B' movies sandwiched among such fare. These included *Miss Tulip Stays the Night* (1955), an absurd comedy-thriller with a slumming Diana Dors, four shorts, made for Park Lane/ABPC (including *Insomnia is Good for You*, 1957, with Peter Sellers) and Hammer/Eros (including *Danger List*, 1958, with Honor Blackman) and several features cobbled together from TV playlets, such as *Forever My Heart* (1954).

Forever My Heart also had a contribution from Bernard Knowles (1900–1975), who, after a distinguished career as one of Britain's finest cinematographers, spent the second half of the 1940s making 'A' features for Gainsborough (including *A Place of One's Own*, 1945; *The Magic Bow*, 1946; and *Jassy*, 1947). Most of his subsequent work was for television, with a couple of slightly upmarket Bs, starring Hollywood's Tom Conway, *Park Plaza 605* (1953, USA: *Norman Conquest*) and *Barbados Quest* (1955, USA: Murder on Approval). *Park Plaza 605* has a strong cast, and Eric Cross was its far-from-negligible cinematographer; while *Barbados Quest* has at least the characteristic Tempean efficiency. Knowles keeps the film moving fast, the plot has enough twists to keep the viewer guessing, and the Hollywood star and the domestic rep company do all that is needed to sustain interest and suspense over seventy minutes. Knowles's 'B' career, though, was not generally distinguished, finishing with two minor science-fiction pieces, the UK/German co-production, *Der Fall X 701* (1964, a.k.a. *Frozen Alive*) and *Spaceflight IC-1* (1965), with burned-out US star Bill Williams, alongside young British actress Linda Marlowe. It is a similar story with Arthur Crabtree (1900–1975). After working as cameraman on such diverse films as *Waterloo Road* (1944) and *Fanny by Gaslight* (1944), which his lustrous images help to make the classiest of the 1940s Gainsborough melodramas, he got the chance to direct several of the Gainsborough films, including *Madonna of the Seven Moons* (1945). Unfortunately, his 'B' films, which include *Morning Call* (1957) and *Death Over My Shoulder* (1958), are largely without distinction, although his work for Republic's *Stryker of the Yard* series is well crafted. Apart from two horror films, *Fiend without a Face* (1957) and the stylishly nasty *The Horrors of the Black Museum* (1959), Crabtree spent most of the rest of his career in half-hour television films.

Two others who had fleeting 'A' film experience in the 1940s but quickly slipped to the bottom half of the double bill in the 1950s were Lawrence Huntington (1900–1968) and Daniel Birt (1907–1955). Huntington had had a busy enough time in the 1930s, working across the decade's genre range – crime-thrillers, a musical, melodrama, farce – and in the mid-1940s he had a run of superior melodramas, starting with the spy thriller, *Night Boat to Dublin* (1946) and including *Wanted for Murder* (1946), *When the Bough Breaks* (1947), *The Upturned Glass* (1947) and, best of all, *Mr Perrin and Mr Traill* (1948), which combined psychological insight with absorbing character clash in a school setting. His career in the subsequent decade began with some adroit co-features, *The Franchise Affair* (1951), from Josephine Tey's ingenious mystery, and the comedy-thriller *There Was a Young Lady* (1953), both starring Michael Denison and Dulcie Gray. After that, it was largely a matter of short films made for Douglas Fairbanks Productions and welded together to make supports, and a few genuine but unmemorable Bs, including *Deadly Record* (1959) and *The Fur Collar* (1962), starring regular 'B' leads Lee Patterson and John Bentley respectively. There was also the Eastman Color co-feature *Contraband Spain* (1955), and what looked like a doomed attempt to return to 'A' features with *Death Drums Along the River* (1963), a hopelessly dated remake of *Sanders of the River*, and a piece of sub-standard science fiction, *The Vulture* (1967), a UK/US/Canadian co-production.

ORB presents
DEATH OVER MY SHOULDER
STARRING 'A'
KEEFE BRASSELLE . BONAR COLLEANO
and JILL ADAMS

Jill Adams in the sort of 'baby doll' nightie that would become commonplace in the Norman Hudis-scripted *Carry On* films

Huntington had an enjoyably melodramatic flair in the 1940s but was unable to transfer the skills then honed to meagre budgets and punishing schedules.

Daniel Birt had only three goes at 'A' features in the 1940s, but one of these at least – *The Three Weird Sisters* (1948) – is a gothic piece that stays in the mind, if only for the way in which he gave three notable character actresses (Mary Clare, Nancy Price and Mary Merrall) their leads as the eponymous sisters.[46] His 'B' career began with two competent thrillers for ACT Films: *Circumstantial Evidence* (1952) and *Burnt Evidence* (1954). The latter is a film which puts working-class lives at the centre of the drama, rather than, as was more often the case, the comic or villainous periphery. On the other hand, Birt's *Three Steps in the Dark* (1953), made at Viking, was an ultra-conventional hour's entertainment in the company of Greta Gynt and Hugh Sinclair: another wealthy eccentric, another country house, another murder with a host of suspects, another amateur sleuth, another predictable set of talky stereotypes.[47] It was scripted by the usually reliable Brock Williams, as was *The Night Won't Talk* (1952), a thriller staged among the artist's of London's Chelsea, a paint-flick from the Viking Studios in Kensington. Birt, who certainly had some flair for melodrama, died young, and his last film, posthumously released, was the UK/Danish co-production *Laughing in the Sunshine* (1956), a romance filmed in Technicolor, which enhanced the look if not the drama of the co-feature.

Two distinguished documentarists also found themselves making 'B' pictures towards the end of their careers. Paul Rotha (1907–1984) turned his attention to the crime 'B' film with an adaptation of John Creasy: *Cat and Mouse* (1958). With Lee Patterson starring and Eros distributing, the picture's only other obvious claim to difference was the cinematography of Wolfgang Suschitzky, a specialist in location work who would go on to film *Get Carter* (1971). In a foreword to his script, Rotha insisted that the style of the film should be that of extreme realism, with exteriors filmed in whatever weather conditions presented themselves. He put an unusual amount of preparation into what he regarded as 'a very personal picture', including the recording of authentic American dialogue that could then be used in scripting the central part of a US Army deserter (Patterson) who terrorises a young woman (Ann Sears). Rotha was keen that his actors should 'be the characters and not just play act them'. To this end, during two weeks of intensive rehearsals, he even went shopping with Patterson and Sears to buy the clothes they would wear in the film and then made them remain in the chosen attire until the cameras rolled on the grounds that 'the clothes had to *belong*'.[48] Unfortunately, all this meticulous attention to detail ultimately fails to lift *Cat and Mouse* much above the level achieved by the regular directors of second features, although it does point the way towards a more extensive use of suburban and provincial locations over the next six or seven years.[49] Pat Jackson (b. 1916), the celebrated director of wartime docu-dramas like *Western Approaches* (1944), had an 'A' film career as director and screenwriter in the 1950s, which included the hospital dramas *White Corridors* (1951) and *The Feminine Touch* (1956), before working on some well-crafted Bs. For Julian Wintle and Leslie Parkyn he made *Snowball* (1960), a tale of the tragic consequences of a schoolboy's lie, and the crime melodrama *Seven Keys* (1962). Both benefited from good casting, particularly Dennis Waterman (later of TV's *Minder*) as the schoolboy in the former, and the musical-comedy star Jeannie Carson in the latter. For producer Derick Williams, a commercials-maker based at Marylebone Studios, he turned out the effective perils-of-puberty tale *Don't Talk to Strange Men* (1962) and another schoolboy-in-trouble picture *Seventy Deadly Pills* (1964).

Stuck there

Directors such as Ernest Morris, Francis Searle, Charles Saunders, Maclean Rogers, Godfrey Grayson and Michael McCarthy either never had a serious chance at the prestige level of production or fluffed it when they did. However, some of these responded to the rigours of 'B' movie production to produce unpretentious thrillers (mainly) and comedies which provide a richly revealing social barometer of their times.

Ernest Morris (1913–1987) entered the film industry in 1934, working in the construction department at Gaumont British, and on Gainsborough films throughout the 1940s, from 1944 as assistant director on several pictures including *Madonna of the Seven Moons* and *Jassy*. When he finally got his chance to direct, after some television experience in the 1950s, it would always be in 'B' films, of which he made twenty-two in eight years. Most of his directing career was spent at Danzigers, with three for Butcher's (*Echo of Diana* and *Shadow of Fear*, 1963; *The Sicilians*, 1964) and, finally, *The Return of Mr Moto* (1965) for Lippert. Morris's name has become almost synonymous with 'B' film perfunctoriness, but, like not a few working at this underprivileged level, he could still surprise on those rare occasions when he was given the chance to do something a little different from the run-of-the-mill crime fodder. His best film, *The Tell-Tale Heart* (1960 – see Chapter 8), starring Laurence Payne, is a revelation to those who think of Morris as a mere hack. The *Monthly Film Bulletin*'s assessment as a 'modest but surprisingly effective little film' seems unnecessarily restrained.[50] Laurence Payne also starred in another of Morris's more ambitious projects, *The Court-Martial of Major Keller*

(1964), which alternates skilfully between courtroom drama and wartime flashbacks. In court, Keller is defending himself against a charge of deliberately causing the death of his commanding officer Winch (Ralph Michael), justifying his actions on grounds of security, but his defence is complicated by the fact that he is in love with Winch's widow (Susan Stephen). The film arrives at a rather contrived ending, but the courtroom scenes are sufficiently well written and acted to confer a certain veracity on the proceedings. Production values, too, are well above the Danziger average and the film moves confidently among its various settings.

This last comment is also true of *The Spanish Sword* (1962). This medieval romp, generically unusual among 'B' films, is quite lavishly set (the sets, in fact, were left over from the Danzigers' *Richard the Lionheart* television series), though its tale of treacherous knights rebelling against kingly authority is barely convincing and some of the acting is wooden.[51] Nevertheless, Nigel Green, as Breauté, is an entertainingly robust villain and the action sequences achieve a certain realism through a quite fluid camera, which is at odds with the often static-looking dialogue sequences of this and many another 'B' movie. There is, in fact, a convincing viciousness about the fighting, and there are moments when the screen takes on a modest vigour and engagement, such as the sudden expansiveness of an overhead shot during the film's final duel.

Apart from these somewhat more ambitious numbers, Morris worked primarily in crime movies (and his comedy, to use the term loosely, *Three Spare Wives*, 1962, is excruciating), of which several have the virtues of economical storytelling even when plausibility is strained. This is true of *Three Sundays to Live* (1957), which makes good use of varied settings, including the prison exercise-yard, the lawyer's country house and the Old Bailey (the courtroom scene is quite inventively done with music and dissolves from face to face but no spoken words).[52] Of the other crime films, *The Sicilians* tries to inject some life into its kidnapping plot by darting about between the USA (Manhattan skyline), Paris (Eiffel Tower) and London. The excellent Ursula Howells lifts the level of the film's flat dialogue exchanges but the whole thing is padded with terrible cabaret acts, and the paper-thin characterisation includes caricatures of a chattering woman on a plane (Patricia Hayes), a tetchy stage doorman (Michael Balfour) and a 'gallant' Frenchman (Alex Scott).

Butcher's *Echo of Diana* mixes espionage and missing-person elements in what the *Monthly Film Bulletin* praised as 'An unassuming but swift spy thriller, which is sufficiently intriguing to make its unconvincing and melodramatic denouement seem comparatively unimportant.'[53] *Shadow of Fear*, also made for Butcher's, starts in Baghdad, with some reasonably convincing back projection, and there are good production values throughout as the plot moves back to London and Sussex. There is an immense amount of talk but the cast is more than competent and Morris keeps the intricate plot moving reasonably smartly. The best of the bunch, though, is *Night Train to Inverness* (1959), which generates genuine suspense from a neatly plotted screenplay by Danziger regular Mark Grantham. A released prisoner, Roy (Norman Wooland) abducts his son, Ted (twelve-year-old Dennis Waterman in his debut), to Scotland, unaware of Ted's need as a diabetic for insulin injections. This race-against-time element is common enough in 'B' films, but it is rehearsed here with some freshness as Roy deliberately leaves a false trail, and it has the advantage of another of Jane Hylton's thoughtful performances as Roy's former girlfriend (called, Marion Crane! She even looks a little like Janet Leigh). It seems unlikely that anyone will ever want to mount a case for Ernest Morris as an auteur, but one might easily venture that he was a proficient storyteller with some gift for the creation of suspense.

It would be absurd to make major claims for directors such as Morris or Francis Searle (1909–2002). In fairness, though, it needs to be said that they filled a market demand with a workmanlike approach that sometimes yielded enjoyable results, occasionally even flashes of real cinematic flair. Of Searle, David Quinlan wrote: 'There can be few more dogged purveyors of programme-filler material.'[54] While the 'dogged' part is certainly true of a career that spanned three-and-a-half decades, it doesn't do justice to what Paul Quinn has called 'some of the very best small films of the 50s and 60s.'[55] After a decade-long apprenticeship in the industry, including many short documentaries (for Gaumont British and others), he made his feature debut as director for Sydney Box with *Girl in a Million* (1946), a comedy about a dumb wife who gets her voice back, and followed this with an Aldwych-type farce, *Things Happen at Night* (1947). Thereafter, comedies were rare for Searle – *Love's a Luxury* (1952), *Trouble with Eve* (1959), which has a breezy performance from Hy Hazell but little else to commend it, and some featurettes at the end of his career. Most of the time, he was involved with crime material, often with American stars and sometimes showing a surprising interest in character and in film noir stylistics. Interviewed in 1995, Searle was under no illusions about the rigours of schedule and budget, or about why most of his output was in crime films: 'it's not my taste at all. It was all the market, because comedy is so much more difficult, and particularly with the low-budget support feature.'[56] He was a journeyman director for hire. For example, when the young stage producer John Ainsworth was offered the director's chair for *Murder at 3am* (1953), to be made at Bushey, the ACT stepped in with a veto.[57] The production company, Henley, moved Ainsworth to the producer's role and recruited the experienced Searle as director.[58] A downwardly mobile Dennis Price played the man from the Yard, while Philip Saville took a dual role as the murderer and his half-brother in what *To-Day's Cinema* described as an 'efficient specimen' of the mystery thriller.[59] The Gaumont circuit booker agreed.

Most of Searle's best work was for Hammer in its pre-horror days. Even an early one such as *The Man in Black* (1949), absurd as it is in some of its narrative turns, is really quite an enjoyable shocker. 'Danger stalks her in this house of terror', warned the publicity, and Sidney James as the house owner, Betty Ann Davies as the ruthless wife and Sheila Burrell as her greedy daughter enter whole-heartedly into the gothic spirit of the thing. Even in this nonsense, Searle shows some capacity for generating tension and for building up an atmosphere of threat and fear as the wicked women try to drive Joan mad. For his next Hammer film, *Someone at the Door* (1950), Searle would have one of those moments of genuine inspiration all too rare in British Bs, for its title sequence, filmed in the grounds of Oakley Court. After introducing the cast, each walking through a door, the camera pulls back to reveal the set, which is then lifted clear and we see the crew gathered behind. Searle would never do anything quite so unconventional again.

As its resident director, Hammer entrusted Searle with its first Anglo-American production, *Cloudburst* (1951), and with imported American star, Robert Preston. In *Whispering Smith Hits London* (1952), Searle had American Richard Carlson paired with regular British 'B' movie leading lady, Rona Anderson and with 1940s 'A' film vamp Greta Gynt. Anderson hires US detective Smith, holidaying in London, to investigate the 'suicide' of her boss's daughter, and he uncovers a conspiracy involving Gynt and Herbert Lom, as duplicitous a pair as were to be found in British movies at the time. It is a fast-moving and efficient thriller, though it is arguable that nothing is quite as much fun as its opening minutes at London airport when Dora Bryan, as a mink-coated film star, tells waiting reporters that she wants to get 'closer to nature ... far from the maddening crowd'. In *Never Look Back*

Doomed Man: Bryan Forbes contemplates the inevitable, watched by Patric Doonan and Sandra Dorne, in Searle's *Wheel of Fate* (1953)

(1952), an upmarket cast, headed by Rosamund John, Hugh Sinclair and Guy Middleton, with a flamboyant cameo late in the film by Brenda De Banzie, gives some real edge to a sinuous melodrama, which draws on then-current debates about women trying to manage marriage and career. As Hammer turned to 'A' productions, Searle eked out a living as a producer/director for companies like Major, ACT and Kenilworth for whom he made perhaps his most memorable 'B' thriller, *Wheel of Fate* (1953), based on a rather crudely plotted play by Alex Atkinson. It was received without much enthusiasm at the time,[60] but now seems an entertainingly gritty piece of English noir. Bryan Forbes played Ted, a gambler and dance-hall habitué with a flashy tie and a greasy quiff in love with a torch singer (Sandra Dorne) who, he thinks, is heading for 'the big time', but who becomes involved in murder. Ted turns to his more stable and artistic older brother (Patric Doonan) and his disabled father, but ultimately cannot escape his doom. There is a resourceful use of the slightly unusual setting of a garage with upstairs living quarters and some care taken in establishing the relationship between the two contrasting stepbrothers. Released in the summer of 1953, this bathetic tale of austerity struggles and frustrated ambitions offered an astringent antidote to the rose-coloured romantic chauvinism of the Coronation. *Wheel of Fate*'s down-at-heel atmospherics are in stark contrast to the artificialities of *Profile* (1954, Major), a lame murder mystery set in the world of magazine publishing. Here Searle's leaden direction of a tortuous plot squanders the talents of Kathleen Byron and John Bentley.[61] He made a better job of *One Way Out* (1955), a strongly cast police procedural with

The sombre finale to Searle's *Freedom to Die* (1962)

a carefully detailed central performance from Eddie Byrne, that was again made for John Temple-Smith's Major Productions.

Eventually, Searle gravitated to Butcher's, one of the last companies making second features in the early 1960s. There he made a handful of efficient Bs, including *Freedom to Die* (1962), an unusually sombre thriller with a grim ending, starring Canadian Paul Maxwell; *The Night of the Prowler* (1963), with Patrick Holt again atypically cast as a murderer trying to pull off a company fraud; and the race-against-time thriller *Emergency* (1962), a remake of Lewis Gilbert's 'A' film *Emergency Call* (1952).[62] The quality of Searle's output was undeniably uneven, but it takes real aesthetic snobbery not to admire what he was often able to do with more or less formulaic material.

There are several other directors who made their careers substantially in the 'B' corner of the production field and whose work might also have repaid more detailed treatment than there is space for here. They include such names as David Eady, Charles Saunders and Michael McCarthy who all made at least three or four second features worth noting. David Eady (b. 1924), son of the man who gave his name to the Eady Levy, had a background in documentary and experience as an editor with London Films before directing an episode of *Three Cases of Murder* (1955). He subsequently made *The Heart Within* (1957), an early, well-intentioned and certainly, in 'B' movie annals, rare cinematic intervention in the area of racial problems; *Zoo Baby* (1957), an oddly affecting tale of a lonely small boy who kidnaps a coati mundi bear from a London Zoo; and the very amusing *The Man Who Liked*

Funerals (1959, see Chapter 8), full of droll characters and more fun than most plushier comedies of the period. Charles Saunders (1904–1997) also had experience as editor and assistant editor and, with Bernard Miles, co-wrote and co-directed the charming pastoral *Tawny Pipit* (1944) before starting as a solo director at Rank's Highbury Studios in the late 1940s. Among his run-of-the-mill second features there are several worth noting. He was quite adroit at presenting sparring male–female reporters and others involved in crime investigation, as in *One Jump Ahead* (1955), *Find the Lady* and *Behind the Headlines* (1956), generated some sexual tension in the murder-triangle of *Black Orchid* (1952), took trouble to motivate his villains in *Naked Fury* (1960), which has some moments of surprising ferocity, and, in the best of his 'B' films, *There's Always a Thursday* (1957), a comedy-drama of inhibited mundaneness and unexpected possibilities, he has the advantage of a fully realised character study from Charles Victor. This story of a hen-pecked clerk's exploitation of a false reputation as a ladies' man (via meetings with Frances Day) was received by critics – and probably by audiences – as a fresh and unusual slice of comedy, 'glib and frisky'.[63] Saunders essayed a similar character study of a couple of genteel con-men in *Strictly Confidential* (1959), but by then, he had waded into the fresh waters of exploitation cinema with *The Man Without a Body* (1957), *Womaneater* (1958) and *Nudist Paradise* (1959). He ended his film-directing career with Butcher's, and his penultimate film, *Jungle Street* (1961), a co-feature set in a Shepherd's Bush strip club, remains a piece that is wonderfully evocative of its era, and a decidedly superior film to Ernest Morris's similarly themed *Strip Tease Murder* (1963).[64]

Michael McCarthy (1917–1959) was on the verge of an 'A' film career when he died very young. His last films included the domestic comedy-drama *It's Never Too Late* (1956), starring Phyllis Calvert, and *Operation Amsterdam* (1959), starring Peter Finch, and about which the *Monthly Film Bulletin* claimed: 'Michael McCarthy's considerable experience in the documentary field is well in evidence.'[65] His first 'B' is *Assassin for Hire* (1951), which, despite a rather talky screenplay, achieves some real depth of characterisation in Sydney Tafler's assassin, who maintains a family life and supports his young brother's violin training on the proceeds of his criminal activities. Tafler is again the star of *Mystery Junction* (1951), also made at Merton Park, and set largely on a train speeding through the night with an accused murderer on board (the ever-oily Martin Benson), and Tafler as a mystery novelist and somewhat unlikely hero (it is always hard to accept him as being unequivocally on the side of the law). The plotting is perfunctory, but the performances are enthusiastic and the direction is efficient. McCarthy's other 'B' films, include the unusually gloomy grim-old-house mystery *Crow Hollow* (1952), with a new wife trying to find her way in a treacherous domestic set-up, and *Shadow of a Man*, which involves a diabetic killer and some excellent location shooting, including a Hastings pier finale. Christopher Lee, who worked with McCarthy on *Douglas Fairbanks Presents* and on *The Traitor* (1957) in the uncomfortable conditions of the Danzigers' New Elstree Studios, offered the highest assessment of his ability: 'young and brilliant and soon to die. Had he lived he would have been one of the great directors.'[66]

There are other now more or less forgotten directors who made their careers virtually exclusively in 'B' films. One of the most prolific is Godfrey Grayson (1913–1998), among whose two dozen films as director a brace of Hammer's *Dick Barton* thrillers are probably the best remembered. Only a couple of the others (a leaden version of Agatha Christie's *The Spider's Web*, 1960, and the art fraud thriller *The Fake*, 1953, with US leads, Dennis O'Keefe and Coleen Gray), even approached co-feature status. Grayson had experience as assistant editor and worked on Army Film Unit documentaries, but his 'B' film credits show little sign of either background role. As director, he began by adapting radio material for Hammer. The results, all in the vein of hearty thick-ear crime adventures, were sporadically lively in their undemanding way. His Jack-the-Ripper speculation, *Room to Let* (1950), was atmospheric, and together with the contrived but intricate family melodrama *To Have and to Hold* (1951) is perhaps his most enjoyable film of this period. In the later 1950s, after stints in television, he turned to Danzigers and the films he made for them are almost uniformly appalling.[67] The few near-exceptions are *An Honourable Murder* (1960), a modern, board-room version of *Julius Caesar*, given a boost by Norman Wooland and Margaretta Scott; *Escort for Hire* (1960), which is at least pacey and has the surprising gloss of Technicolor; and *The Lamp in Assassin Mews* (1962), a sub-Ealing crime-comedy that spotlights resistance to the sort of local-government modernising programmes that destroyed so much of value in the 1960s. The rest, including such utterly dire pieces as the comedy, *She Always Gets Their Man* (1962), and the derivative and clichéd girls' reform-school melodrama *So Evil, So Young* (1961), are beyond reclamation, although *Kinematograph Weekly* judged that the latter at least avoided 'descending into the squalor of its Continental counterparts'.[68]

Terry Bishop (1917–1981) was also from a documentary background (he won an Oscar for the CFU's *Daybreak in Udi*, 1949), but in his case it showed in much of his second-feature work. He made ten modest 'B' films, beginning with the co-feature *You're Only Young Twice* (1952) for Group 3, and including several neat, unpretentious thrillers, such as the realistic *Life in Danger* and the more fanciful *Model for Murder* (1959), *Danger Tomorrow* (1960) and *Cover Girl Killer* (1960), and the comedy *Hair of the Dog* (1962), all for the company Parroch. *Cover Girl Killer* is memorable for the unlikely casting of *Steptoe and Son*'s Harry H. Corbett as a sexually repressed psycho-killer, and looks pretty ridiculous beside such contemporary treatments of the theme as *Psycho* and *Peeping Tom* (both 1960), but in its breathless naiveté it is highly evocative of a key moment of transition in British attitudes towards sexual display. Corbett played a kidnapper in Bishop's *The Unstoppable Man* (1960), a picture which won rare praise from the *Monthly Film Bulletin* for its 'sharply drawn' characters, 'authentic backgrounds' and 'slick and resourceful' direction.[69] *Bomb in the High Street* (1961), a late entry in the cycle of films in which disillusioned ex-servicemen use the skills that the state has taught them in the quest for personal profit, begins well and creates an atmosphere of promising strangeness. If it doesn't quite fulfil this promise, it still offers a more interesting critique of prevailing social attitudes and values than many films of the period.[70]

Oswald Mitchell (1890–1949) is remembered largely for his direction of a string of films starring Arthur Lucan as Old Mother Riley. These were made on 'B' film schedules and very modest budgets, but were lifted to 'A' or co-feature status by the popularity of the character. Mitchell had begun his career in quota quickies, and was one of the few directors to continue to make low-budget programme-fillers during the war years. At the time of his premature death, he was still turning out melodramatic programmers in the bargain basement of British cinema. *Black Memory* (1947), made at Bushey, was South African-born Sid James's film debut. It was shot in the depths of the twentieth century's coldest winter, and the cast and crew could probably have done without location scenes at Cricklewood's ice rink. Mitchell's sombre Victorian melodrama *House of Darkness* (1948) gave Laurence Harvey an early starring role in a film that took its place in a post-war cycle that dealt with madness, hauntings and old dark houses. George Melachrino's atmospheric score enhanced the film's macabre feel. Harvey found himself in another madhouse in Mitchell's next film *The Man From Yesterday* (1949). Harry Reynolds produced this doom-laden drama of a family's disintegration under

Harry H. Corbett sizes up his next victim in Terry Bishop's *Cover Girl Killer* (1960)

the malign influence of a mystic guest (Henry Oscar). In the face of indifferent reviews, Renown's publicist gave it the full treatment: 'A new British Mystery Film that *really* mystifies! A thriller that *really* thrills! – The story of a strange *vengeance* – with the year's biggest surprise ending!' That sort of hyperbole invites debunking, so we do not mind telling you that this disquieting tale of murder, defenestration and the transmigration of souls turns out to be nothing more than the bad dream of the daughter of the house (Gwyneth Vaughan). Unfortunately, Oswald Mitchell's own soul was not long for this world: he became the 'Man from Yesterday' at the end of April 1949. Mitchell's last film, *The Temptress* (1949, working title *Dr Leroy's Secret*), was made at Bushey for Gilbert Church's Ambassador Film Productions (for whom Mitchell had recently made *The Greed of William Hart*, 1948). Filming began in November 1948 with Arnold Bell in the leading role, and Don Stannard (who would barely outlive Mitchell) in support. It is the story of a wealthy invalid whose murder is abetted by his wife (Joan Maude). Set in the South of France, the picture was described by Ambassador as their most ambitious to date and, at eighty-five minutes, certainly had ambitions to top the bill in some locations.

It may be tempting to think that those who spent their entire feature careers in the 'B' wilderness fetched up there because of inherent inadequacies. In truth most of them, for most of the time, do not show marked flair of the kind one expects to find in the work of 'A' feature directors. Nevertheless, it is still possible at this level to be struck from time to time by how a director has encouraged a cinematographer to lift the narrative with a little visual inventiveness; sometimes an editor who cared beyond merely linking events comprehensibly will create a surprising tension or an economical montage; and there is often the pleasure of watching actors doing more than the screenplay may have required, giving a touch of real character interest, and recalling the words of Nanette Newman who made several 'B' films at the start of her career: 'at the time, you go into this thinking, "I shall make something of this." It's an actor's eternal optimism.'[71] Well, sometimes that optimism is rewarded, even in the films of these directors who worked exclusively in largely unrewarding production circumstances.

Screenwriters

Given the often formulaic nature of British 'B' movies, one can't help wondering if the screenwriters were aiming less at originality than at variations on an accepted pattern. There is undeniably, too, a recurring set of characters (smart reporter who out-sleuths the police, nicely spoken girlfriend, corrupt night-club owner, etc.), and there are too many occasions when the films grind to a halt for long dialogue passages of exposition, the cheapest kind of sequence to film. Nevertheless, it is worth *not* succumbing to generalities because, as is the case with the directors, there are some 'B' movie screenwriters whose output repays closer inspection.

One doesn't perhaps expect flights of wit in the comedies, though even then an exception will surprise, as in Margot Bennett's often-amusing screenplay for *The Man Who Liked Funerals* or Peter Blackmore's broad satire on commercial TV, the co-feature *Make Mine a Million* (1959). And maybe one doesn't expect detailed character-drawing but, again, in films such as *The Impersonator* (1961, co-scripted Kevin Cavander and Alfred Shaughnessy) or *Act of Murder* (scripted Lewis Davidson) one

can be surprised at the degree of subtlety and complexity in the material the actors are given to work on. Or, if one is not usually aware of 'B' movie screenplays which aim to place their characters in a convincing relation to their occupations, then it is still possible to find films which, like *Cash On Demand* (1961, co-scripted David Chantler and Lewis Greifer), *Devil's Bait* (co-scripted Peter Johnstone and Diana K. Watson) or *The Big Day* (scripted Bill McIlwraith), do just that. It may not be on the cards for ideologically radical elements to figure prominently in 'B' movie screenplays, but even here, there is the very occasional exception such as the critical criminology of Peter Barnes's script for Cliff Owen's directorial debut, *Offbeat* (1961).[72] As in other matters pertaining to the British 'B' film, it is not wise to adopt easy formulations.

Some of those named above wrote only one or two screenplays, sometimes going on to

Alfred Shaughnessy

careers in television, but there are also several who laboured away to some purpose in the 'B' movie corner of the production field, building up, in Bourdieu's terminology, economic capital (maybe not even a lot of that) rather than cultural.[73] Crime writer James Eastwood, about whom little is known beyond the fact that his career stretched from the 1940s to the 1970s, contributed over fifty screenplays for second features, mainly for Anglo-Amalgamated's *Scotland Yard* and *Scales of Justice* series, after cutting his scriptwriting teeth on Danzigers' productions like *Devil Girl From Mars*. He then seems to have returned to novel-writing. Other names to consider in this respect include Brian Clemens, Mark Grantham, W. E. C. Fairchild, Lyn Fairhurst, Brandon Fleming, Allan Mackinnon, Geoffrey Orme, Paul Tabori and Brock Williams. John Gilling is a special case of one who became an established director virtually at the same time as he was becoming one of the most proficient 'B' movie screenwriters. Others better known as directors, such as Francis Searle, Vernon Sewell and Montgomery Tully, contributed some smarter-than-average screenplays to their own films, and there are odd names, notable for other reasons, who wrote the occasional 'B' movie – people such as novelist Arthur LaBern and playwrights Ted Willis and Philip Mackie. We shall look more closely at the careers of the first two listed here: Clemens and Grantham, and at Gilling, whose importance as a 'B' movie *director* has already been discussed.

Articles about Brian Clemens (b. 1931) invariably, and unsurprisingly, concentrate on his career as a prolific screenwriter for such high-profile television series as *The Avengers* and *Danger Man*.[74] They skim over the years he spent churning out scripts for the Danzigers where he honed the professional skills that enabled him to meet television's exacting schedules. Without the 'B' movie experience, he might never have acquired his formidable reputation in the newer medium. He worked in advertising, interrupted by National Service; but, after having a radio play produced by BBC television in 1955, he attracted the attention of the Danzigers. He spoke affectionately of the time he spent with the brothers, and remembered how, before they built their own studios at New Elstree, they would use standing sets left over from bigger films: 'they'd come to me and say, "Look, we've got two weeks to shoot, so we want you to write something for these sets, a 70-minute second feature, and it must have the Old Bailey, a submarine and a mummy's tomb in it."'[75]

His first film for Danzigers was the critically derided *Operation Murder* (1956), a hospital-set tale of dual alibis which the *Monthly Film Bulletin* dismissed by saying: 'The familiar crime-and-detection formulas are applied in a manner conventional to the point of dullness.'[76] It was directed by Ernest Morris, for whom Clemens wrote the screenplays for his best 'B' movies, including *The Tell-Tale Heart*, examined in more detail in Chapter 8. As for Clemens' other films for Morris, *Three Sundays to Live* and *Three Crooked Men* (1958) are each seventy-one minutes of mistakenly attributed guilt and last-minute revelation. *Kinematograph Weekly* was a little harsh in dismissing the former as 'cheap pulp fiction'.[77] The *Monthly Film Bulletin* also could find in it 'no redeeming feature',[78] but conceded that *Three Crooked Men* 'builds up some suspense as a crime melodrama'.[79] These brief reviews never actually mention Clemens by name; nor did *Picturegoer*, which dismissed *Operation Murder* with: 'Clinical claptrap, this effort lacks both thrills and conviction,'[80] and said of *Three Sundays to Live* 'the strain on the viewer's credulity reaches breaking point some time before the end'.[81] As a fan of Hollywood movies, Clemens was happy to plunder them for inspiration: 'I don't use the word plagiarism,' he once assured an interviewer, 'I call it an homage.'[82] Morris's venture into medieval costume, *The Spanish Sword*, was certainly a homage to *High Noon* (1952), although Fred Zinnemann might not have been flattered. The dialogue scenes are notably static, with noble

A doctor in distress: Tom Conway in *Operation Murder* (1956), Brian Clemens' first script for the Danzigers

sentiments such as 'All I can do is stay here and fight for the King in my own way' and 'I have orders
to bring peace out of bloodshed', but perhaps actor Ronald Howard wasn't the man to make them
seem to belong to either history or drama. The court-room drama *The Court-Martial of Major Keller*
depends a good deal, as one would expect, on the quality of the dialogue and on the processes of alter-
nation by which the screenplay reveals the events which have led to the present situation, and here
Clemens does a much slicker job. As well as ten films for Morris, Clemens also wrote four that fell to
Godfrey Grayson's lot and eleven for Max Varnel, and neither of these directors could usually be
counted on to make a screenplay seem or sound better than it was. Many of his screenplays are co-
credited to 'Eldon Howard'. This was the alias of Edward Danziger's mother-in-law, Mrs Guggenheim,
who acted as a script editor.[83]

Clemens went on to serious fame as one of television's leading writers, and later still as a director
in both Britain and the USA. Mark Grantham (b. 1931), his exact contemporary, wrote some
episodes for TV's *Richard the Lionheart* (1962–3), starring Dermot Walsh, and intended to exploit
the success of the *Robin Hood* series, but he seems not to have had an extensive post-Danzigers writing career. Perhaps the reason is that, at Danzigers, he worked chiefly for Godfrey Grayson, which
cannot have been advantageous. Though several of Grayson's films for the brothers are in colour, they
are generally the kinds of film that attract such obloquy to British 'B' movies. *Escort for Hire* is mildly
entertaining, but the plot is full of coincidences and perfunctory causality, for which presumably
Grantham is responsible. Whatever the script of the cautionary tale *So Evil, So Young* may have had

Reform-school girl: Jill Ireland behind bars in *So Evil, So Young* (1961), scripted by Mark Grantham

going for it, woefully inept acting (apart from a cherishable display of eye-rolling sadism from Ellen Pollock as a reformatory wardress), characterless sets and silly, insistent music sink it – a shame, because the screenplay makes unusual acknowledgment of female sexuality as an issue in the drama. Grayson's *She Always Gets Their Man* is about as inane as a film can be. A provincial-girl-in-London comedy, it is sexist, full of stereotypes about girls who can't live without men, and who have nothing on their minds *but* men, and plot convolutions that are both preposterous and unamusing. Nevertheless, it still has something to tell us about the attitudes and mores of the period.

Grantham fared slightly better in the films he wrote for Frank Marshall. They are unremarkable, certainly, but at least lack the foolish pretensions of the Grayson films. Three that reveal Grantham writing in different modes are *Feet of Clay* (1960), *Gang War* (1962) and *The Gentle Terror* (1962). The last-named is a feeble enough comic variant on the mouse-mistaken-for-a-lion theme, which Grantham treats in a mildly jokey tone, well suited to leading man Terence Alexander's light touch. *Gang War*, which has a background of fruit machines and pop music, creates a quite interesting contrast between two brothers, one straight, the other crooked. There is the odd touch of wit in the writing and the rival gang chiefs are convincingly drawn, but it settles too often into the common 'B' movie failing of too much talk. *Feet of Clay* is unusual in its protagonist (Hilda Fenemore) – a middle-aged woman who is a probation officer but also involved in a dope ring. It is all penuriously shot in cramped studio sets but there is just enough interest in character (the police are less cosy, more hard-nosed than is common) to see it through its fifty-five minutes. As supporting features, they are no worse than average, and have moments of invention that lift them intermittently above that level.

Of the dozen or so Grantham wrote for the Danzigers,[84] the best may be *Night Train to Inverness*, directed by Ernest Morris and mentioned above. There is perhaps something mechanical about the way the strands of the plot are brought together in this suspenseful tale, but the writing catches the right social class; Norman Wooland is surprisingly convincing as the ex-convict father of the imperilled boy, and the denouement has a quietly humane quality. Grantham was under no illusions about his paymasters, however: 'The smell of profit could send the Danzigers rooting for truffles at strange trees.'[85]

Another Danziger alumnus, Hungarian Paul Tabori (1908–1974), naturally worked for Alexander Korda for several years (1943–8) as a contract writer. Apart from writing the ponderous romantic melodrama, *Star of My Night* (1954), he wrote several pre-horror Hammers, including the nicely tense *Five Days*, with Dane Clark as a businessman desperate to stop the hit man he has paid to kill him. The plot is neatly contrived, there is more than usual attention to the male–female relationships at the film's core, and the film ends on a surprisingly and satisfyingly subdued note. *Picturegoer* highlighted its 'excellent story' and 'convincing characters'.[86] Another of Tabori's Hammer films, *Four-Sided Triangle* (1953), might be scientifically naive, but again has something to say about gender relationships. After Hammer, he opted for the swift and sure, if not munificent, returns of the Danzigers, where his record is less extensive than Clemens' or Grantham's, although the psychiatric melodrama *Alias John Preston* (1955) at least provides an early opportunity for Christopher Lee to reveal his charismatic contact with the camera. Tabori also wrote some episodes for the Danzigers' TV serials, including *Richard the Lionheart*, but his career was finished by the mid-1960s.

The career of John Gilling (1912–1984) as director has been discussed, but a note should be added here about his equally prolific career as a screenwriter, and not just for his own 'B' movies. He was responsible for the screenplays of nine of the films he directed for Baker and Berman, including such superior Bs as *The Quiet Woman*, *The Frightened Man*, *The Embezzler* and the co-feature *The Voice of Merrill*. All of these are marked by well-drawn characters, and the excellent actors who played them are given material sufficiently detailed to engage their and our attention. It is not just the leads who get this sort of attention in some of Gilling's screenplays. It is probably true that actors like Thora Hird, Sam Kydd, Dora Bryan, John Horsley and Michael Ward only needed two words on the back of an envelope to devise eye-catching cameos, but in the films Gilling wrote they are apt to be given that little extra that distinguishes a character from a 'turn'.[87]

As well as writing the screenplays for the films he directed, Gilling also wrote for Tempean three very trim pictures which Robert Baker himself directed, *13 East Street* (1952), *Blackout* (1952) and *The Steel Key* (1953), the fast-moving American-serviceman-back-in-England thriller, *The Lost Hours* (1952), directed by David Macdonald, co-authored the compelling noir-influenced *Impulse*, and wrote Henry Cass's moderately inventive thriller *Bond of Fear* (1956).[88] It seems likely that, in Baker, astute as he was about schedules and budgets, Gilling found more creatively sympathetic support than the Danzigers' authors could count on. In fact, Gilling in his dual function as writer-director now seems one of the key elements in accounting for the continued success of Tempean. He also wrote screenplays for, among others, Oswald Mitchell (*House of Darkness*), Francis Searle (*The Man in Black*) and Charles Saunders (*Blind Man's Bluff*, 1951). In fact Gilling was so prolific as a writer that he actually had no less than three screenplays going into production in May 1951: *13 East Street* for Tempean, *Whispering Smith Hits London* for Exclusive and *Blind Man's Bluff* for Present Day Productions. By the mid-1950s, however, the regularity of scripting contracts meant that he increasingly fell back on recycled plots from old films. He regained some more original inspiration for his own upmarket jobs (e.g., the Warwick-produced *High Flight* and *The Bandit of Zhobe*, 1959), but it is at least arguable that his skills as a screenwriter, like those as a director, are most favourably represented by the unpretentious care of his best work for Tempean.

Norman Hudis (b. 1922), who once described himself as having 'the shiniest and most aggressive ego in the industry', is another writer who graduated from supporting features to more prestigious projects.[89] Before writing the first six *Carry On* films and making a long and successful career in American television, Hudis turned out a dozen 'B' films and co-features between 1955 and 1958. Born in Stepney, he began a career in local journalism and as a war reporter before working for Rank as a publicist and trainee screenwriter in the early 1950s. When Rank failed to adopt any of his scripts for production, Hudis went freelance and found a ready market for his work among production companies like Tempean, Butcher's and Anglo-Amalgamated. 'Scripts never took longer than two to three-and-a-half weeks,' he recalled, and his screenplay for the box-office smash *The Tommy Steele Story* (1958) – which he expected to be 'a sterling support film' at best – actually took a mere ten days.[90] Hudis's first scripts for Baker and Berman were often adaptations or collaborations with other writers such as John Gilling, Alfred Shaughnessy and Brock Williams. *Breakaway* (1955) and *Passport to Treason* (1956) were both adaptations of stories by Manning O'Brine, and *Stranger in Town* (1957) was based on a novel by Frank Chittenden. As he explained: 'I establish with the producer the reason he bought the property. It might be the story as a whole; it may be one filmic gimmick it contains ... Having once fixed the particular aspect he wants to develop I give myself up almost solely to the characters.'[91] His work for Bill Luckwell (*West of Suez*, 1956, and *The Crooked Sky*, 1957) and for Vicar (*Death Over My Shoulder*) were solo efforts, as was the best of his second features, *The Flying Scot* (1957), for Anglo-Amalgamated. It demonstrated a talent for thriller writing, but the runaway success of the *Carry On* series meant that Hudis found his real metier in comedy.

Among other 'B' film screenwriters who should be mentioned here are W. E. C. (later William) Fairchild (1918–2000), who, before going on to a more illustrious career in 'A' films, including *Morning Departure* (1950) and *Malta Story* (1953), wrote four of the Highbury supports, including Terence Fisher's *Colonel Bogey* and *To the Public Danger*, and Geoffrey Orme (1904–1978), who wrote many forgettable comedies but also two modest dramas that are worth recalling. First is Wolf Rilla's *The End of the Road*, which Orme co-wrote with James Forsyth (author of the original story), a rare and sensitive account of a working man's difficulties in adjusting to retirement, which *Picturegoer* praised: 'The story's entertaining – and it also makes you think. Quite a worthy combination.'[92] The other is David Eady's *The Heart Within*. This, taken from a story by John Baxter, the populist director with whom Orme had often worked, is a crime-thriller with irreproachable attitudes to racial problems at a time when these were surfacing in Britain. Jim O'Connolly (1926–1987), who began his career as an assistant director at Ealing, went on to direct several efficient 'B' films, including *The Hi-Jackers* (1963) and *Smokescreen* (1964), both of which he also wrote. He was producer or associate producer on nearly twenty films, moving into minor 'A' pictures, including *Berserk!* (1967) starring Joan Crawford no less, but the screenplays for the two 'B' films named perhaps show him at his best: they are trim, twisty crime tales, both with well-written roles for actor Glyn Edwards. Allan Mackinnon (b. 1912) had pre-war success with Roger MacDougall in writing the popular thrillers *This Man Is News* (1938) and *This Man in Paris* (1939), but post-war, after a stint at Gainsborough (e.g., on *Traveller's Joy*, 1949), he settled to writing 'B' films. In the 1950s he wrote several times for

ACT Films: the thrillers *Circumstantial Evidence* and *The Blue Parrot* (1953), and, elsewhere, a further thriller *House of Blackmail* (1953) and the breezy comedy *Second Fiddle* (1957), both directed
by veteran Maurice Elvey. He also wrote three films for director Charles Saunders, none of them
among Saunders' best – *The Golden Link* (1954), the idiotic *The Hornet's Nest* (1955), a comedy-
thriller bereft of laughs or excitement,[93] and *Behind the Headlines*, with journalist outsmarting police
and rival woman reporter.

Brock Williams (1894–1968) directed two films, both unremarkable (*The Root of All Evil*, 1947,
and the little-seen B, *I'm a Stranger*, 1952, a comedy-drama which he also wrote), but scripted over
ninety, as well as episodes in television series. His screenwriting credits embrace several dozen across the
1930s genre range when he worked for Warner Bros. at Teddington; he was scenario editor at
Gainsborough in the mid-1940s and wrote there the pleasing ghost drama *A Place of One's Own*; wrote
and co-produced the mildly amusing tilt at child psychology *Tony Draws a Horse* (1950); then more or
less settled into writing for 'B' films. In truth, many of his 1950s scripts are pedestrian and cliché-bound,
particularly those he wrote for Daniel Birt like *Three Steps to the Gallows* and *Meet Mr Malcolm* (1954),
an incoherent murder mystery of a kind that was rather fresher when Williams learned his trade at
Teddington.[94] Nevertheless, several of Williams' other screenplays are worth noting: *The Gilded Cage*
(directed by John Gilling) is a proficient Tempean thriller; *The Harassed Hero* is a mildly amusing
comedy-thriller, with paper-thin characters and absurdly complicated plot, but with some genuinely
funny moments; Francis Searle's *Trouble with Eve*, despite its shop-worn late-of-the-West-End look,
moves along breezily and the competent actors make the most of their amusing lines; and Lance
Comfort's cautionary tale *Rag Doll*, which Williams co-wrote from his own story, has quite sharply
etched characters and holds the attention. There are also half a dozen thrillers and comedies for director Charles Saunders, usually for Alliance, the best possibly being *Naked Fury*, a genuinely hard-boiled
heist thriller which required cuts to gain a 'U' certificate and a supporting berth on the ABC circuit.[95]

Williams's body of work, at 'A' and 'B' levels, holds up respectably, but that is probably more than
can be said for the 'B' movie screenplays of A. R. Rawlinson (1894–1994), father of one-time
Attorney-General Peter Rawlinson. His pre-war work on such films as *The Man Who Knew Too
Much* and *Jew Süss* (both 1934) can scarcely have prepared him for the rigours of the 1950s 'B' movies
in which he finished his career. There are several thrillers and comedies for Godfrey Grayson (*What
the Butler Saw*, 1950, and *Meet Simon Cherry*, 1950) and Francis Searle (the facetious thriller *Someone
at the Door*); the intricate Cambridge-set co-feature *The Scarlet Thread* (1951) for Lewis Gilbert
(well-acted by a superior cast including Kathleen Byron and Laurence Harvey); and a hectic mix of
espionage and fashion in Joseph Sterling's too-talkative thriller *Cloak Without Dagger* (1955).

Another who warrants a mention is Brandon Fleming, an actor and producer who wrote screenplays such as *Dangerous Afternoon* (1961), *Womaneater* – which producer Guido Coen dismissed as
'rubbish' – and *There's Always a Thursday*, Charles Saunders' low-key comedy-drama of a hen-pecked
man who becomes involved with blackmail and a woman far more attractive than his virago wife.
Coen thought this an entirely different plate of meat:

> Brandon Fleming was forever in search of money, and he used to read all the papers in the world because
> he took ideas from the papers. But the one picture which Brandon Fleming wrote with great effort, and
> I worked with him a great deal on it, was *There's Always a Thursday*, which was superb ... and we made
> it for peanuts.[96]

Hack work: Brandon Fleming scripted this story of a carnivorous tree. Eros press book for *Womaneater* (1958)

When Charles Victor's protective agent finally allowed him to see the script, Victor phoned Coen and simply said 'When can we start? I've waited 25 years for this.' On receiving the £30,000 finished product, Rank's Chief Executive, John Davis, immediately screened it for his producers at Pinewood to show them 'how to make a comedy'.[97]

One of the few women screenwriters among the 'B' film ranks was Doreen Montgomery (1913–1992), who had worked at Gainsborough during its bodice-ripping heyday in the early 1940s and would go on to write much television and to create the character of Emma Peel in TV's *The Avengers*. In between these phases of her career, she scripted about ten 'B' films, specialising in the investigative journalism sub-genre mainly for Fortress films, in which she was a co-director with Guido Coen and Charles Saunders. Her work is uneven, ranging from the highly convention-bound *A Time to Kill* (1955), through the solidly professional *The Scarlet Web* (1954), to the entertaining *One Jump Ahead* with some lively sparring between Paul Carpenter and his two leading ladies, Adrienne Corri and Hazel Court. Schooled in melodrama, her scripts are usually interesting in the prominence that they give to spirited female characters, but sometimes strain credulity. A good example is her screenplay for Wilfred Eades' *You Can't Escape* (1956), in which a young woman (Noelle Middleton) falls for a successful novelist (Robert Urquhart) and finds herself involved in scandal and blackmail.

There was also a small army of American writers scripting British low-budget films and television series. Many of these were hiding out from the McCarthy witch-hunts and writing under pseudonyms. One interesting case in point is *Night of the Full Moon* (1954), a Cold War thriller with possible supernatural undertones directed by Donald Taylor and starring Philip Saville as an American secret agent with Dermot Walsh and Kathleen Byron as a farmer and his wife. The script was credited to the German writer-director Carl Koch (his only British credit), but the picture is so full of the paranoia of the age – with a lonely English farmhouse put under nocturnal siege by a group of Eastern European agents – that it might easily have been the work the McCarthy refugees. One is tempted to speculate that 'Carl Koch' might even conceal the hack work of Oscar-winners Carl Foreman and Howard Koch, both writing under pseudonyms in Britain at the time. Significantly, perhaps, the film was released by United Artists, the liberal American company co-founded by 'fellow traveller' Charlie Chaplin, who was also exiled from the USA.[98] There were also some American screenwriters of British Bs who continued to work in the USA. This was probably the case with New Yorker Richard Landau (1914–1993), whose scripts Robert Lippert regularly supplied to Hammer. His most celebrated contribution was the adaptation of *The Quatermass Experiment* (1955), but he also worked on co- and 'B' features like *Stolen Face*, *Spaceways*, *The Flanagan Boy* (1953), *Murder by Proxy*, *The Glass Cage* and *Women Without Men* (1956), re-working Hollywood genre formulas and ensuring that the Hammer product would be intelligible and acceptable to American audiences. Landau was not a writer of startling originality, but he knew how to ring the changes on standard genre plots and conventions, as he later demonstrated in a highly prolific career as a writer for US television.

Among directors who sometimes wrote their own screenplays were Vernon Sewell, Francis Searle, Alfred Shaughnessy, Montgomery Tully and Ken Hughes. These have all been discussed earlier as directors but in each case there is at least one screenplay worth highlighting. Sewell's *House of Mystery* has a central premise that invites our interest (why is this apparently attractive house so cheap?), develops the contrast between the rational young couple and the strange woman who shows them through (Jane Hylton, compelling as usual) and involves a medium (Molly Urquhart) who is written and played without caricature. Even the usually snooty *Monthly Film Bulletin* thought that 'the narrative is ingeniously worked out, giving full credit to the supernatural'.[99] In two contrasting films, the violent thriller *Cloudburst* and the romantic melodrama *Never Look Back*, Searle collaborated to good effect on the screenplays, though, admittedly, his co-writer Leo Marks is probably more crucially responsible for the tensions of *Cloudburst* and its use of wartime coding practices, but the detail about motivation and relationship may be fairly enough shared with Searle.

The writing in *The Impersonator*, one of the best of British 'B' movies, is of a quality that helps explain Alfred Shaughnessy's subsequent success as the chief writer on the popular television series, *Upstairs, Downstairs* (1971–5). Shaughnessy's abilities as a writer had, in fact, already been signposted by his Group 3 work and particularly by *Cat Girl* (1957), an American script which he substantially rewrote to emphasise the psychology of the main character. The film's star, Barbara Shelley, was in no doubt that its quality was primarily attributable to Shaughnessy's input:

> It was very lucky that Alfred Shaughnessy, who was associated with the studio in those days, stepped forward and wanted to direct it, because I think that Alfred's taste and discretion and his re-writes and the way he directed the picture and the final picture that was shown was completely due to his talent.[100]

Montgomery Tully, in his prolific career as director of 'B' and minor 'A' films, collaborated on the screenplays of two of his neatest second features: *The Third Alibi* and *No Road Back* (1957), both starring Patricia Dainton. *No Road Back*, co-written with Charles A. Leeds, is an unlikely but gripping story of a deaf-blind woman (Margaret Rawlings) who acts as a fence; it holds the viewer by the care in plotting and performances. Finally, Ken Hughes wrote half a dozen scripts for the *Scotland Yard* series he directed for Merton Park, as well as the screenplay for his ingeniously twisty film noir, *The House Across the Lake*. Sarah Stoddart, writing of this in *Picturegoer*, commended Hughes for fashioning 'a tense, convincing drama', that was 'a fair copy of the best American import'.[101] It is not surprising that Raymond Chandler was Hughes' favourite author.[102]

Occasionally, too, a writer whose main reputation lay elsewhere would bring a momentary distinction to the 'B' movie scene. Playwright Philip Mackie (1918–1985), whose 1955 play *The Whole Truth* was adapted to the screen (but not by him) in 1958, wrote half a dozen or more Edgar Wallace mysteries for Merton Park, and Frederick Knott (1916–2002), author of stage hits *Dial M for Murder* (1952) and *Wait Until Dark* (1962), wrote the script for Terence Fisher's *The Last Page*, an efficient melodrama of blackmail and murder. Novelist Arthur LaBern (1909–1990), author of the books on which *It Always Rains on Sunday* and *Good Time Girl* (1947) were based, also wrote several of Merton Park's Edgar Wallace mysteries and Francis Searle's *Freedom to Die*, with its very grim ending and some of LaBern's well-known feeling for scenes from scruffy life.

The pioneer director George Pearson once wrote that 'the secret of every fine film is enshrined in the script, which should never go to the floor till every second of time entailed in its screening has been proved necessary and rightfully used'.[103] Pearson had plenty of experience of the quota quickies of the 1930s, and must often have been aghast at the kinds of screenplay that did get filmed. In the post-war decades of the 'B' film, there would be plenty of occasions when the screenplay clearly needed more work than the budget could allow: too often, characterisation is perfunctory, motivation sketchy and plot causality pushing credibility. As well, they are often madly talkative, recalling Robert Baker's comparison with US films: 'Americans will cut out dialogue if they possibly can, relying on the action. In England we tend to use six words when two would do.'[104] At their best though, they show what can be done under the most rigorous writing conditions: plots get underway swiftly, care is taken to fill out a sense of character and of relationship, and there are revealing little glimpses of the state of things at the time when the writing takes the trouble to focus on the sort of detail that is in excess of the formula. Let Brian Clemens have the last word: 'The short shooting time meant that rewrites had to be done instantaneously. The result was a crash course in writing to order and producing the best quality, if occasionally bizarre, output possible.'[105]

Cinematographers

Occasionally a cameraman who had established a reputation elsewhere would confer a touch of distinction on the 'B' movie scene, as, say, Erwin Hillier did on the co-feature *House of the Arrow* (1953) for his frequent collaborator, director Michael Anderson, or as Harry Waxman did on a handful of Bs, such as *The Golden Link*. A few cinematographers, like Nicolas Roeg (*The Great Van Robbery*, 1958, as camera operator,[106] and *Information Received*, 1961) and Arthur Grant, went on to 'A' feature work, Grant graduating to become one of Hammer's most respected craftsmen after honing his skills on such 'B' movies as *The End of the Road*. However, the names that recur belong to men who spent virtually their whole careers shooting 'B' movies. These most often did so in constraints of schedule and budget that wouldn't have allowed them much scope to be adventurous, and that might have encouraged them to minimise the number of set-ups and to rely on what Karel Reisz described as 'photographs of people talking'.[107] These are the men (there are no women) who are responsible, for better or worse, for the look of the British 'B' film. Some of the names worth lingering over for a moment are Monty Berman, Basil Emmott, Walter J. Harvey, Stephen Dade, Cedric Williams, Geoffrey Faithfull and James (Jimmy) Wilson. None of these rates an entry in Duncan Petrie's valuable monograph on British cameramen,[108] but each has shot films that, among their other qualities, are worth looking at. They took what came along, and they sometimes gave cheaply shot films a sheen that made them look more expensive than they were.

Monty Berman, one of the founders of Tempean Films, also shot most of their films. His low-key lighting gave budget items like *No Trace* and *13 East Street* an aptly dishevelled look. The quality of location shooting in the Romney Marshes for *The Quiet Woman*, praised even by the *Monthly Film Bulletin*, brought a whiff of reality to its tale of smuggling and a convict on the run.[109] Baker later regretted that they hadn't the money to shoot all he wanted on location and was dissatisfied with the 'technically imperfect' back projection,[110] but the look of the film is well above second-feature functionality. In

Nicolas Roeg's camerawork brought some distinction to the Danzigers' *The Great Van Robbery* (1958)

Escape by Night, the camera's decisions and angles contribute significantly to the well-staged fight which constitutes the film's penultimate sequence. The rooftop chase (chases are endemic in these films) which brings *The Frightened Man* to its bleak finale is even better: it colludes with Andrew Mazzei's skilful production design to make night and height the perilous antagonists of Julius Rosselli's attempt to evade a richly deserved capture. Berman's strength may be best shown in the way he shoots crucial events such as this, but in quieter moments he knows how long to hold a close-up to register, say, the face of Charles Victor as Rosselli Sr, numb with pain and grief as he contemplates the body of his son. In other circumstances, Berman can give a gloss to the comparatively high life of *The Voice of Merrill*, as well as getting it off to a teasing noirish start with legs moving on a dark, wet street, and finishing it with a potent bleakness. Again, in Quentin Lawrence's science-fiction thriller *The Trollenberg Terror* (1958) Berman's camera draws us into the film's atmosphere with an opening high long shot of a snow-covered mountain valley, pulling up to a cloud-swathed peak before a man shouts, then falls, as the camera cuts to the close-up of a fraying rope. He knows how to make *dramatic* use of awe-inspiring scenery, so that it becomes something more than mere setting.

It is not that Berman is a mute inglorious Gregg Toland or Robert Krasker, but it is true that his care often made a conventional plot less predictable, more engaging to the eye than a mere journeyman might have. The same is true of Basil Emmott (1894–1976), who has nearly a hundred credits, not all of them for 'B' films. For instance, in 1929, he made his name for shooting the seminal documentary *Drifters*, and he is responsible for the pre-noir images of Arthur Woods's highly regarded thriller *They Drive by Night* (1939). By the 1950s, most of his work was in 'B' territory, especially in the films of Lance Comfort. His moody images reinforce Comfort's unsettling view of the world in such thrillers as *Rag Doll, The Break, Tomorrow at Ten, The Painted Smile* (1962) and *Blind Corner* (1964). All Emmott's work for Comfort has moments of distinction, moments when what might be a merely formulaic thriller offers something genuinely disturbing. *Rag Doll* is an unremarkable morality tale about how the big city nearly ruins a provincial girl, but Emmott's camera gives an authentic touch of drab ordinariness to the roadhouse she quits, of urban danger to the city she innocently samples, and imbues the pastoral setting of the final chase with an undertow of shabbiness. Emmott contributes importantly to the baffling, atmospheric opening of *The Break*, the explanation withheld until a close-up of handcuffs is revealed as a light is accepted for a cigarette. In *The Painted Smile*, the early shot of an unknown figure mounting stairs is angled for maximum suspense, and the final sequence, shot in a stretch of bleak countryside, isolates its characters as the camera pans the surrounding hills. And in *Tomorrow at Ten* Emmott's camera poignantly foregrounds the kidnapped boy's predicament as it backtracks down the corridor and stairs of the empty house where he is held before dissolving to the elegant balustrade of his father's home.[111] Vernon Sewell, whose work also benefited from Emmott's incisive eye, summed up his abilities: 'He was very good! He would get on with me well. He was very quick, he didn't mess about. And you know Basil Emmott did all the work that Grierson got the credit for.'[112]

Of the other cinematographers named above, none has a 'B' movie filmography of the sustained quality of either Berman or Emmott. However, each has done some more than merely routine work. Stephen Dade (b. 1909), who did striking black-and-white work for Gainsborough in the 1940s, and would go on to such big-budget features as *Zulu* (1964), gave distinction to several 'B' films. He sets the edgy tone of Pat Jackson's *Don't Talk to Strange Men* with the opening sequence in a deserted village street at night, with a young woman walking in long shot as a car cruises by her, and in Maurice Elvey's co-feature *The Late Edwina Black* he registers the affluence of the Victorian interiors and through well-modulated chiaroscuro creates some genuine frissons of unease. With a hundred films to his credit (as well as television) Walter J. ('Jimmy') Harvey (1903–?) was one of British cinema's most prolific cameramen, starting in 1930. There were some upmarket occasions, including *The Quatermass Experiment*, but the bulk of his work was in 'B' movies. These included four of Rank's Highbury films, and several for Francis Searle (*Cloudburst*, in particular has a sombre look to it that accentuates the grim violence of its plotting), Terence Fisher (*The Last Page, Wings of Danger, A Stolen Face*) and Charles Saunders (Harvey responds well to the shoddy urban ambience of *Jungle Street*). His most notable 'B' film work, though, is probably in the noir sheen he gives to Ken Hughes's co-feature, *The House Across the Lake*: to say that he makes it look indistinguishable from an American film noir is to acknowledge his contribution to what is clearly the film's overall intention. Much of the rest of Harvey's work is purely functional, but every now and then he would show his calibre: for instance, the grainy, grimy look of the crumbling warehouse setting in *Naked Fury*, and the roadhouse, desolate station and uninviting countryside in *The Hi-Jackers*.

Men like Harvey and James ('Jimmy') Wilson were the work-horses of the British 'B' movie industry. Wilson shot about 125 films in his career, which spanned the decades from 1918 to 1966, his most high-profile work being on John Baxter's *Love on the Dole* (1941) and Lance Comfort's *When We Are Married* (1943), which suggested his versatility in lighting and shooting two very different worlds. Virtually all of his post-1950 career, though, was spent in 'B' movies, including masses of routine crime-thrillers for Danzigers and more than a dozen in Merton Park's Edgar Wallace series. Even so, there are several of more than average interest. His mobile camera gets Alan Bridges' *Act of Murder* off to a teasing start and continues to assist in creating an erotic tension that eventually gives way to ferocity and sexual capitulation, and ends with a strikingly enigmatic overhead shot. *Monthly Film Bulletin* acknowledged the unusual quality of its photography, writing of the 'camera restlessly prowling and panning', and drawing attention to the 'long, languid close-ups [that] convey the dreamy sensuousness of the wife'.[113] For Ernest Morris, Wilson provided a strikingly effective rendering of Edgar Allen Poe's horror tale *The Tell-Tale Heart*, in which superior production values are shown to best advantage by Wilson's imaginative camera. In scenes of the protagonist's torment, Wilson obliges by a large close-up that says much more than words might, and in fact the most powerful aspect of the drama is in this kind of intimate shot, as, for instance, in the way Edgar's growing paranoia is registered in his reactions to the tick of a clock's pendulum or to a dripping tap. It wasn't always just business-as-usual for the likes of Wilson and Harvey.

One of British cinema's longest careers is that of Geoffrey Faithfull (1893–1979), who actually played one of the 'cards' in Hepworth's *Alice in Wonderland* (1903), before shooting Hepworth's *Tansy* (1921). Fifty years later he had been director of photography on at least 130 films, including about forty 'B' movies in the 1950s. He worked often for such directors as Charles Saunders, Montgomery Tully and Maclean Rogers, and if there is nothing very distinguished about his contribution to their films they are all at least efficiently lit by someone who, after a great deal of work at all levels, knew absolutely what he was doing. In fact, some of his films, particularly *Marilyn* and *The Large Rope* benefit significantly from the noir imagery he was able to bring to bear on their sombre plots.

Arthur Grant (1915–1972) moved definitively into 'A' territory when he became one of Hammer's most notable cameramen, and, with Val Guest, did much to develop the art of black-and-white anamorphic cinematography. In 'B' movieland he made his contribution to the tensions of *The Spaniard's Curse* (1957) and, particularly, to *Cash on Demand*. In the latter, his restrained approach gave the provincial bank in which the action is set a repressive ordinariness which is crucial to this excellent low-key thriller. With a strong background in documentary, Jonah Jones (b. 1913), who had co-shot *Night Mail* (1936) and *London Can Take It* (1940), turned to 'B' films after 1950, doing competent work on such films as *The Limping Man* and *The Embezzler*, and something more than competent on *Impulse*. Jones's camera, in matters of lighting quality and angles of vision, is crucial to *Impulse*'s contrasts of the everyday securities of a legal practice in a provincial town and the heady temptations of a noir version of London. Ernest Palmer (1901–1964), whose finest hour coincided with Britain's (he shot *San Demetrio, London*, 1943), turned to 'B' movies in the 1950s, and his unaffected lensing of two films for David Eady, *Zoo Baby* and *The Heart Within*, enhanced their humane appeal and helped keep their potential for sentimentality at bay. Cedric Williams (1913–1999), who spent most of his career in 'B' movies, helped to account for the genuinely scary moments of Mario Zampi's *The Fatal Night* (1948), but did his best work on location: he makes the garish charms of the Blackpool tower an element to reckon with in *Dick Barton Strikes Back* (1949), for example.

All those mentioned above, and probably quite a few others, left their mark on routine material, lifting it, even if briefly, out of the rut. They were almost never working with colour, though when Jimmy Wilson was allowed this extra expense for *Escort for Hire*, *Kinematograph Weekly* affirmed that 'The settings … all benefit from Technicolor.'[114] Generally, though, they worked under conditions that would have severely taxed, say, a Walter Lassally or a Jack Cardiff: they hadn't the luxury of experimenting with set-ups, and they were often forced, by the rigours of budget and schedule, to make do with the least demanding ways of visualising the action. However, even in these rigorous conditions, some of them managed, for at least some of the time, to make the action interesting to the eye. They took advantage of the opportunity to encapsulate a series of narrative moments in an imaginatively shot montage, or they used the angle of their camerawork to disturb the viewer's expectations, or they made a little bit of location work, most of it economically near the studios, go a long way. At their best, they could make one unaware that every penny and every minute had to be accounted for.

Composers

'Musical accompaniment should never be consciously heard,' Louis Levy (head of Gaumont British's music department) once suggested, but rather should 'play subtly on the emotions and never intrude on the story.'[115] Until recently, the musical score has been as unobtrusive in film analysis as it was in Levy's theory of film-making, and the music of 'B' films must be the least noticed of all. We should not assume, however, that scoring second features was simply a matter of selecting the appropriate discs from a commercial sound library. Some companies such as ACT Films relied mainly on stock music composed by jobbing musicians like H. M. Farrar, but most of the regular 'B' producers commissioned custom-made work. Many of the early post-war featurettes, for example, could call upon the services of distinguished composers and sizeable orchestras. The score for Paul Rotha's *The World is Rich* (1948) was composed by Clifton Parker and recorded at Watford Town Hall by the Philharmonia Orchestra under the direction of John Hollingsworth. The music contained novel rhythmic passages in unusual tempi such as 7:4 and 5:4, as well as a parody of the type of library music favoured by the travelogues of the period. Parker contributed some fine complementary scores to documentary and semi-documentary films like the CFU's *Life in Her Hands* (1951), but his greatest challenge was to find appropriate sounds to accompany the footage of the Hiroshima explosion. His solution was simply to sound the bass wires of a piano with soft tympani sticks.[116] ABFD's deluxe, hour-long documentary *Three Dawns to Sydney* (1949) boasted a score by William Alwyn.[117] The film was an elaborate travelogue covering the stops on a three-day passenger flight from London to Australia – the sort of journey that was being contemplated by more and more Britons in mental or physical flight from their austere post-war society. Low-budget, black-and-white 'B' films, of course, were emblematic of that austerity, but music could sometimes give them some richness or plain old excitement: critics, it was said, were kept awake only by the 'vigorous musical background' of Alfred Goulding's indifferently directed spy story *The Devil's Jest* (1954), which featuring a motley collection of British character actors and was rated as strictly for 'unexacting patrons'.[118]

As post-war 'B' production gathered pace, a number of popular and specialist film composers were employed on low-budget as well as more prestigious film-making. Temple Abady (1903–1970) was a typical example. He began composing for Rank in 1947, working on both 'A' films like *Miranda* (1948) and curtain raisers like *Love in Waiting* (1948). Later, he also worked for Group 3, and provided a thundering score for the Rank-distributed *Wheel of Fate*. Rank's Highbury Studio's, with a little more to spend than most independents, could afford a specially composed score for *Colonel Bogey*, written by Norman Fulton and played by the London Philhamonia Orchestra conducted by John Hollingsworth. However, some studios were too small to accommodate large orchestras, and scores had to be recorded elsewhere. Wembley Town Hall, for instance, housed a fifty-piece ensemble to record George Melachrino's suitably haunting rhapsodic score for *Strange Duet* (1947).

Frank Spencer (1911–1975) was Exclusive's musical director in the 1940s. His scores were generally fairly sparse and composed in a classical register. Francis Searle commented:

> Frank Spencer did the music on most of my films for Exclusive and I used to like working closely with
> the composer. Something I found very helpful was being a dance band drummer in my early days ...
> Because of my musical experience, Frank Spencer and I would go to the local pub and he'd go through
> his scenes on the piano. We'd then have a few sherbets, kick it around, and that's how we'd do the
> composition side of the music![119]

Spencer left Exclusive in 1951, and the company used a variety of composers and arrangers, including Doreen Carwithen (1922–2003), who had scored Terence Fisher's *To The Public Danger*, and, perhaps most successfully, Ivor Slaney (1921–1989), who composed a tumultuous orchestral score for *Spaceways*.[120] As budgets rose, Hammer was even able to afford Malcolm Arnold (1921–2006), who scored *Stolen Face*, *Wings of Danger* and *Four-Sided Triangle*. Eventually John Hollingsworth (b. 1916) was appointed musical director in 1954. Hollingsworth was a respectable concert-hall figure who had conducted operas at Covent Garden and ballets at Sadlers' Wells, and was an associate director of the Proms. His role was one of coordination and arrangement rather than the contribution of original scores.[121]

Many of the early Tempean films were under the musical supervision of John Lanchbery (1923–2003) who supplied original compositions as well as selecting library music. Baker and Berman also employed the versatile talents of Stanley Black (1913–2002), whose jazz-infused scores regularly won praise from critics.[122] Noting that Black's scores 'were often of a quality that was unmatched by the films themselves', Kevin Donnelly, in his book on *British Film Music*, singles out Black's work on *Recoil* as particularly noteworthy: 'The score is for a small orchestra and uses a musical language that habitually involves the unresolved dissonance that had become a characteristic feature of twentieth century concert music, aiming for psychological impact through eschewing the use of memorable themes.'[123] Black had entered the 'B' field at the behest of Mario Zampi, composing for *The Fatal Night*, and he stayed with Zampi as he graduated to first features.[124] Some of Black's earliest work had been at Nettlefold on, for example, *The Monkey's Paw* (1948), but the composer most closely associated with the studios was Wilfred Burns (1917–1990) and his Film Orchestra. Burns composed for the *Toff* films, *Marilyn* and *The Black Rider* among others. Stanley Black was a well-known BBC dance-band leader who mixed 'A' and 'B' film work throughout the post-war years, but, until the late 1960s, Burns worked almost exclusively in 'B' production, contributing music to well over thirty films in this class.

At Merton Park, Anglo-Amalgamated turned to Eric Spear (1908–1966), who did atmospheric work on *Ghost Ship* and produced memorable themes for *Wide Boy* and *Street of Shadows* (1953). Like most of his contemporaries, Spear freelanced for a variety of companies, contributing to the disturbing atmosphere of *Bang! You're Dead*, and providing a sonorous organ and violin score, typical of his work in the gothic idiom, for *Murder at 3am*. The Danzigers hired Edwin Astley (1922–1998) to compose and conduct the London Philharmonic for *Star of My Night*. Astley, the future father-in-law of The Who's Pete Townsend, was one of the most prolific composers and arrangers on the low-budget production scene, and could always be relied upon to provide a sympathetic and unobtrusive score that would enhance the action. His jazzy score for *Naked Fury* is an excellent case in point. He moved regularly between film and television work for a large variety of companies, including Hammer, Baker and Berman and the Danzigers. The brothers also gave regular compositional work to Albert Elms (b. 1920), whose television work would range from *The Prisoner* to *The Benny Hill Show*.

Other maestros of the Bs included William Trytel (1894–1964), whose long association with low-budget film-making began with quota quickies from Julius Hagan like *The Ghost Camera* (1933) and *The Last Journey* (1936). He turned from composing to producing with *A Sister to Assist 'Er* (1948). Birmingham-born Ray Terry (1906–?) scored some early television series and a handful of Bs, including *The Girl on the Pier* and *The Hide-Out*, and provided the rather overly jaunty accompaniment to *Find the Lady*. E. J. Fancey's composer of choice was generally Jackie Brown, while Kennedy Russell worked regularly for John Baxter from the mid-1930s onwards. Most of those who toiled on 'B' film scores were hardly household names, but even the humblest of productions could occasionally boast a star turn. *The Flamingo Affair* (1948) had a performance by Stephane Grappelli, *Kill Me Tomorrow* gave Tommy Steele his screen debut, while perhaps the most memorable aspect of *The House in the Woods* (1957) was its sinister theme tune by harmonica wizard Larry Adler.

ANTHONY OLIVER   MAUREEN CONNELL   ALAN TILVERN
with BILL NAGY and SONIA CORDEAU in
"**DANGER BY MY SIDE**"
Directed by Charles Saunders   Produced by John I. Phillips

Cert "A"

Martin Slavin wrote the catchy title song for this typical Butcher's offering from 1963, *Danger By My Side*

As the connection between the film and popular music businesses became closer in the 1960s, Butcher's began to embellish its crime narratives with songs that it hoped might appeal to younger audiences and might also provide lucrative recording spin-offs. The songs, often by Martin Slavin, offered the further possibility of publicity through radio broadcasts, which Butcher's courted assiduously and with some success. The BBC's *Movie-Go-Round* show regularly aired songs from Butcher's Bs during the summer of 1963.[125] Producer Jim O'Connolly also jumped on the beat bandwagon with *Farewell Performance* (1963), a crime melodrama, directed by Robert Tronson, with a pop-star protagonist (David Kernan) and a guest spot for The Tornados (of 'Telstar' fame). However, as we know, even the 1960s beat boom could not prevent the 'B' film from going bust.

5 On the Screen

I was starring in one of those Neolithic happenings known as the British second feature. We made them on what was known as a 'tight schedule' … and talent was measured by an actor's ability to say the right lines on the first take without benefit of rehearsal and above the noise of the carpenters building the next set on the same stage.

Bryan Forbes, on filming *Wheel of Fate* (1954)[1]

Actors

As with directors, some actors got their start in 'B' films, others declined from 'A' features into the less prestigious 'B' movie corner of the production field, while yet others made almost their whole careers there – some, like Tod Slaughter, dying in harness.[2] In the first of these categories, one finds perhaps more ambitious actors, not content simply to soldier away in these often-unregarded films, but making efforts to find work in plusher circumstances. Often, though, they lacked sufficient distinctiveness to carry more expensive features. Many moved between main and second features, few actors ever being in the position of turning down work. Starring in the Renown programmer *Port of Escape* (1956), for instance, we find Googie Withers and John McCallum – the headlining couple of Ealing's *It Always Rains on Sunday* (1947). Their performances in this Docklands melodrama were praised, but the film could only be rated a 'fair to middling quota second'.[3] Among leading actors in 'B' films, one needs also to note the distribution-led prevalence of minor Hollywood stars, supported by teams of reliable British character players.

Leading men

There are certain names that immediately conjure up the British 'B' film of the 1950s and 1960s. Try John Bentley, Patrick Barr, Paul Carpenter, Derek Bond, Clifford Evans, Patrick Holt, Donald Houston, Ronald Howard, William Lucas, Lee Patterson, Conrad Phillips, Peter Reynolds and Dermot Walsh. Two were Canadians: Lee Patterson (b. 1929) spent most of his career in Britain, where he had supporting roles in the odd main feature, such as *The Story of Esther Costello* (1957). However, he was most often to be found playing Americans in such bottom-of-the-bill crime films as *The Flying Scot* (1957), as well as the lead in Paul Rotha's only venture into this territory, *Cat and Mouse* (1958). Patterson, with his luxuriant quiff and air of virility, was a useful presence in such films. For example, his performance in Lawrence Huntington's *Deadly Record* (1959) was singled out by *The Daily Cinema*: 'Due mainly to the efforts of the experienced Lee Patterson, as the innocent implicated in a murder … the story sustains interest.'[4] The paper had a similar reaction to Sidney Hayers' *The*

LEE PATTERSON in "THE WHITE TRAP" Cert.'U' with CONRAD PHILLIPS
ANGLO AMALGAMATED FILM DISTRIBUTORS LTD.

The beefcake of the Bs: Lee Patterson in Sidney Hayers' *The White Trap* (1959), another harrowing tale from Independent Artists

White Trap (1959): 'Another big asset is the photogenic face and likeable personality of Lee Patterson, as the [prison] escapee.'[5] His fellow Canadian, Paul Carpenter, elicited similar praise from the trade press, *Today's Cinema* noting: 'Paul Carpenter is always a smooth addition to a production of this type.'[6] This particular production was Charles Saunders' *Murder Reported* (1957), but Carpenter made over three dozen British films in the post-war decades, most of them 'B' pictures, such as *Diplomatic Passport* (1954) and *One Jump Ahead* (1955), to which he brought an easy, likeable authority that seemed more difficult for British actors to achieve.

Some British leading men had got started in 'A' films of the 1940s: Ronald Howard (1918–1996), son of the famous Leslie, starred in the Asquith-Rattigan comedy, *While the Sun Shines* (1946), co-starred as the irresponsible younger brother in *My Brother Jonathan* (1947) and had a run of service-able supporting roles in such films as *The Queen of Spades* (1949) and *The Browning Version* (1950). Despite his blond good looks (and resemblance to his father) and his agreeable demeanour, he lacked genuine star quality. He was convincing as doctors (*Black Orchid*, 1952) and policemen (particularly as the shrewd inspector in *Assassin for Hire*, 1951), and was cast interestingly against type as a crook disguised as a bomb-disposal officer in *A Bomb in the High Street* (1961), but he never again had the lead in a main feature, though he went on acting until 1973. Ealing gave Derek Bond (1919–2006) his best chances, including the title role in *Nicholas Nickleby* (1947) and gallant Captain Oates in *Scott of the Antarctic* (1948). In the 1950s, however, he worked primarily in television and second features, including *The Quiet Woman* (1951), which traded on his rangy handsomeness and breezy manner in his role as painter and smuggler, but even in his 'B' movies he was apt to play second fiddle to such American imports as Dale Robertson (*The High Terrace*, 1956) and John Ireland (*Stormy Crossing*, 1958).

Donald Houston (1923–1991) starred opposite Jean Simmons in his first film, *The Blue Lagoon* (1949), but subsequently moved easily between first and second features. He had leads in such superior examples of the latter as Wolf Rilla's *The Large Rope* (1953) and Terence Fisher's *The Flaw* (1955), in which his playing of the dull lawyer who loves the heroine defined the limits of his persona. More usually, he was cast as a countryman or a young man of the sea. He continued to work in more upmarket productions until the 1980s. Conrad Phillips (b. 1930), was also in a few 'A' films, such as *Sons and Lovers* (1960) and *The Secret Partner* (1961), but is better remembered as a serviceable doctor hero in *Strangers' Meeting* (1957), as a plucky reporter in *The Desperate Man* (1959), or as a playboy lawyer in *The Durant Affair* (1962). He made nearly thirty films, mostly Bs, but his real fame came as TV's William Tell in the late 1950s. Patrick Holt (1912–1993), older than the others, started before his distinguished war service, came back to play second leads for Rank in such films as *When the Bough Breaks* (1947), but didn't register a strongly individual enough screen personality. Consequently, by the 1950s, he had become a reliable 'B' film leading man in *13 East Street* (1952) and *There's Always a Thursday* (1957), as well as, surprisingly because he always seems so upright, the

Donald Houston plays the persecuted ex-con in Wolf Rilla's rural noir, *The Large Rope* (1953)

villain in *The Gelignite Gang* (1956). His later films, in fact, including *Guns at Batasi* (1964), tended to aspire higher, and he was still purveying elderly dignity as late as 1986's *Playing Away*. The other Patrick, Patrick Barr (1908–1985), was well established in supporting roles before the war. Post-war, he never became a star in main features, though he appeared in plenty of them, usually as solid authority figures, and, middle-aged, he settled into 'B' films in the 1950s, typically as doctors (as in *Death of an Angel*, 1951) and senior detectives (as in *Black 13*, 1953). 'Decent but dull' might have summed up most of his 'B' film leads.

Potentially more interesting were those whose personae suggested that they could not be wholly trusted. You generally knew where you were with, say, Houston or Howard or film and TV's 'Stryker of the Yard', Clifford Evans (though he could surprise you by turning venal in *The Heart Within*, 1957). William Lucas (b. 1925), on the other hand, brought a much more dangerous edge to the 'B' movie leads he played, notably in two tense thrillers for Lance Comfort, *Touch of Death* and *The Break* (both 1961), as criminals on the run in each case. He was the older Morel son in *Sons and Lovers*, but, apart from some middling 'A' features (e.g., *Payroll*, 1961), his is essentially a career in 'B' movies – and they were lucky to have him. As for Peter Reynolds (1925–1975), he was the archetypal spiv, unreliable boyfriend, unscrupulous blackmailer, the smoothie ever ready to light a lady's cigarette. In *The Bank Raiders* (1958), for instance, he is described by one writer as 'a flashy crook',[7] and that, enjoyably, was exactly his main function in most of his thirty-odd films, overwhelmingly second features.

More equivocal than any of the above was Dermot Walsh (1924–2002), very recognisable with his dark hair and its white blaze. Somehow, this physical detail managed to suggest something other than the straightforward heroes he often played. Perhaps, though, one's lingering doubts about his probity derived partly from the roles he'd had in such 1940s films as *Hungry Hill* (1947, as Wild Johnnie) and *To the Public Danger* (1948). In the latter, he played the caddish ex-Captain Cole, who is responsible for luring Susan Shaw away from her nice boyfriend and to her death. Walsh had starring roles in a couple of other 1940s films but was not securely enough established to ride out some dud films for Rank (e.g., *My Sister and I*, 1948) or what he later considered to be Charles Crichton's tricking him out of a lead in Ealing's *Dance Hall* (1950): 'In effect, you see, they'd ruined my career in first features,' he claimed in 1994.[8] Subsequently, the promising young leading man of the 1940s was more or less relegated to second features, but he undeniably made the most of them, often imbuing their formulaic plots and stereotyped heroes with a nicely ambiguous aura. As a rather meek accountant in Vernon Sewell's *Counterspy* (1953), he surprises by the suppression of his customary dashing qualities, while in the excellent Tempean thriller *The Frightened Man* (1952), he mines a vein of real nastiness, as the antique dealer's son who has been educated out of his class. Having worked for John Guillermin in the latter's very early film *Torment* (1949), Walsh made the point that Guillermin never wanted to use him again when he had become famous, and contrasted this approach with that of his Tempean producers, Robert S. Baker and Monty Berman, who remembered him when they made their first venture into 'A' features, with *Sea of Sand* (1958).[9] It was too late for him to become a star, but he went on for another quarter-century in films, mainly Bs, some of them of more than routine value, particularly Ernest Morris's imaginative version of *The Tell-Tale Heart* (1960). His relegation to 'B' stardom was at least compensated by his marriage to Hazel Court, a co-star in films like *Ghost Ship* (1952). Together, they became the celebrity couple of the second features. Walsh also maintained a stage

Perks of the job: trench-coated newsman Dermot Walsh grills the chorus girls in the Danzigers' production, *A Woman of Mystery* (1957)

career, and starred in twenty-nine episodes of TV's *Richard the Lionheart* (1962–3), but his is above all a competently maintained 'B' film career.

However, if there is a single actor who, more than any other, conjures up the British 'B' film of the 1950s in particular that is John Bentley (b. 1916). Apart from playing the colourless romantic lead in *The Happiest Days of Your Life* (1950) and an unproductive one-movie fling in Hollywood, with the aging Errol Flynn in *Istanbul* (1956), he almost never left the 'B' film turf. In the memory, he seems forever to have been tracking down thugs of every hue, usually as private or even amateur detectives, inevitably quicker off the mark than the plodding police. The conventionally handsome Bentley entered films in the dim Irish-set musical *The Hills of Donegal* (1946), one of the few in which he failed to 'get the girl'. She was Dinah Sheridan and she played his wife in *Calling Paul Temple* (1948) and *Paul Temple's Triumph* (1950), second and third of the film spin-offs from the popular radio series based on the exploits of the titular sleuth.[10] Bentley was smoothly accomplished as Temple and in the subsequent Maclean Rogers' films that featured him as the Toff, becoming in the process 'the second-feature detective par excellence'.[11] He also played numerous other trench-coated scourges of the criminal population, combining an easy authority with the touch of necessary ruggedness that made him ideal casting for these budget thrillers. His debonair assurance makes programmers like *Double Exposure* and *Final Appointment* (both 1954) seem more compelling entertainment than they might otherwise be. There were plenty of other examples of Bentley doing what must have been

The reliable John Bentley gets on the blower in Montgomery Tully's *Dial 999* (1955)

second nature to him; but there were also several films which allowed him to undermine the smoothly charming persona. In *Black Orchid*, he is neither hero nor villain, just a cheerful travel-writer with a benevolent interest in the solving of a murder; in *The Lost Hours* (1952), he is unmasked as a murderer, who has been foiled in love; and in *The Flaw*, he is a dashing racing-driver planning to murder his rich wife (Rona Anderson). In the last, he is able to suggest the possibility of violence which enables him to transcend a limited screenplay and 'thoroughly convinces as the villain' in a film *Kinematograph Weekly* regarded as 'stoutly carpentered'.[12] Bentley seems wholly to have understood the genres and production levels he was working within and gave a professional sheen to all his appearances. There were one or two somewhat more ambitious ventures, including the three African-set adventures – Brendan Stafford's *Men Against the Sun* (1953) and two for director George Breakston (*The Scarlet Spear* and *Golden Ivory*, 1954) – but his real contribution was to the supporting film, helping to render respectable what might otherwise have seemed merely shoddy. *Kinematograph Weekly* summed up Bentley's appeal when it commented that he has 'an easy way with him'.[13]

There are two other categories of male leads that need to be mentioned in relation to the kinds of masculinity habitually on display in these films. First, there are some striking leading roles played by actors not generally associated with 'B' films. There is, for instance, a very notable study in prissy tyranny from Peter Cushing as a provincial bank manager in *Cash on Demand* (1961). Duncan Lamont, primarily a character actor in main features, gave a couple of eloquent performances in 1954 as working-class protagonists in *Burnt Evidence* and, especially, *The End of the Road*. And several actors associated with the suave end of British stage and screen gave a lift to the lower depths: think of Hugh Sinclair, dangerous as only a man in a smoking-jacket can be, in *No Trace* (1952), but a sympathetic lover in *Never Look Back* (1952), in which Guy Middleton is properly ousted from Rosamund John's affections. Middleton's raffish smoothies were often in films of high prestige (e.g., *The Rake's Progress*, 1946), but he brought a touch of class to a few 'B' comedies, such as *The Harassed Hero* (1954) and *What Every Woman Wants* (1962). Eddie Byrne, more often seen in supporting roles in 'A' features such as *Albert RN* (1953), had a couple of agreeable co-feature leads: as the layabout blot on his village's escutcheon in *Time Gentlemen Please!* (1952), and as the police superintendent on the brink of retirement who is pressed back into service when his daughter is involved in a crime in *One Way Out* (1955).[14]

Second, and more important in industrial terms at least, there was a steady influx of American leads, not major stars by the 1950s if they ever had been, but still names sufficiently known in the USA to guarantee distribution there. An astute producer like Robert S. Baker knew the value of these stars trained in a more high-powered studio system in which their careers depended on their efficiency: 'They knew the camera and consequently their performances were always very, very smooth. In that way, they gave a lift to British co-features – plus the different accent helped to make the picture more universal.'[15] They were not, as a rule, actors with a stage background: everything they knew about performing had to do with film, and they frequently brought with them a gloss, a whiff of the international world, that the British actors were less likely to be able to offer. For example, George Brent, never perhaps a real headliner in Hollywood, but a popular co-star for the likes of Bette Davis and Miriam Hopkins, brought a star's (albeit an aging star's) presence to the trim thriller *The Last Page* (1952). Some of these Americans, though, had indeed been stars of some magnitude who, in the first half of the 1950s, began to feel the heat of Senator McCarthy's witch-hunt for communists and fellow-travellers. Britain thus became a useful bolthole in difficult times. Larry Parks, prior to his blacklisting, had been riding high on the success of his two Al Jolson biopics; but by 1955 he was no doubt glad to accept the lead in the sleek Tempean co-feature, *Tiger by the Tail* (1955).

Often the presence of these Hollywood players would be explained by their having been in Britain during the war or by their being Canadians. One of the most quietly persuasive and valuable uses of such actors was in Arthur Kennedy's performance in the noirish *Impulse* (1955), as a small-town lawyer, who, we assume, has stayed on after the war. This detailed and un-showy study of a man tempted away from a comfortable but dull rut is one of the subtlest to be found in the 'B' film ranks. Other American actors who starred in these films, mainly in the 1950s, include Lloyd Bridges (*The Limping Man*, 1953; *Third Party Risk*, 1955), Scott Brady (*Three Steps to the Gallows*, 1953), Dane Clark (*The Gambler and the Lady*, 1952; *Five Days*, 1954; *Murder by Proxy*, 1955 – and famously disliked by his British colleagues for his apparent arrogance), Alex Nicol (*The House Across the Lake*, 1954; *Face the Music*, 1955; *The Gilded Cage*, 1955; *Stranger in Town*, 1957); Tom Conway (not American but long resident there – *Park Plaza 605*, *Blood Orange*, 1953; *Barbados Quest*, 1955; *Breakaway*, *The Last Man to Hang?*, 1956; *Operation Murder*, 1957), Robert Hutton (*The Man from Tangier*, 1957; *The Secret Door*, 1962; *The Sicilians*, 1964); Richard Denning (*Assignment Redhead*, 1956); Mark Stevens (*The Lost Hours*; *Frozen Alive*, 1964, UK/German); William Sylvester (some As but mainly Bs such as *Dublin Nightmare*, 1958, and *Blind Corner*, 1963; his British career preceded his US work); and Wayne Morris (*The Master Plan*, *The Green Buddha*, 1954; *Cross Channel*, 1955; *The Gelignite Gang*; *The Crooked Sky*, 1956). None of these was ever a major Hollywood star,

WAYNE MORRIS
KARIN BOOTH
in
THE CROOKED SKY (U)

Hardboiled hero: American import, Wayne Morris, takes no nonsense in Henry Cass's *The Crooked Sky* (1956)

but they brought to these unambitious thrillers a rougher kind of masculine authority, or in some cases a suaver demeanour, than the likes of Bentley or Walsh might have conveyed. Many also embodied the sex appeal that large sections of the British female audience had come to associate with American masculinity.

One Hollywood import with considerable star value, particularly in the context of the crime genre, was George Raft, who was brought over to star alongside Britain's Sally Gray in *Escape Route* (1953), directed by the Anglo-American partnership of Peter Graham Scott and Seymour Friedman. It was a London-set Cold War thriller in which British and American agents, working together, track down the kidnappers of some important boffins. The film made outstanding use of London locations from the West End to docklands, but the suspense was not augmented by the emotional monotone of Raft's performance, which was as wooden as his floating namesake. Sometimes, American leads seemed under-prepared for the culture shock of British film-making. William Lundigan, for instance, was actually expecting to star in a motor-racing film when he discovered that he had to take to the ocean for Vernon Sewell's *Dangerous Voyage* (1935). He had to be virtually press-ganged onto Sewell's boat from his comfortable suite at the Dorchester Hotel.[16] As the British 'B' film reached its terminally decadent phase in 1963, Lawrence Huntington directed American actor Macdonald Carey in the highly self-referential *Stranglehold*. In a fitting swan-song for the importation of transatlantic 'B' players, Carey played a Hollywood actor specialising in gangster parts who is employed to make a film in a British studio. Ironically, although these tough, wise-cracking Yanks often looked out of place in the English suburbs and shires, they were needed to bring a sense of genre authenticity to British attempts to emulate the sort of hardboiled crime cinema that been developed in Hollywood rather than Boreham Wood.

Leading women

There are fewer 'B' film leading actresses who established a toe-hold in main features. Among those who started in 'A' films were such Rank contract players as Rona Anderson, Honor Blackman, Hazel Court, Sonia Holm, Jane Hylton, Lana Morris, Barbara Murray and Susan Shaw, most of them alumni of the much-derided Charm School, and most of them deserving to be better remembered than that. Honor Blackman (b. 1925), after second leads in such Gainsborough numbers as *So Long at the Fair* (1950), drifted into Bs in the 1950s, providing a touch of cool in *Suspended Alibi* (1956) and *Account Rendered* (1957), though neither role tapped the sexiness she would demonstrate in the next decade in *Goldfinger* (1964) and TV's *The Avengers* (1962–4), when she escaped for good from the 'B' film trade. Red-headed Hazel Court (1926–2008) appeared in ten 'A' films of the 1940s, including the young female lead in the popular *Holiday Camp* (1947), without quite becoming a star. She then spent most of the 1950s in 'B' films, including two for Vernon Sewell (*Ghost Ship*; *Counterspy*, 1953,

A 'white telephone' film, British style: Hazel Court stars in the Edgar Wallace mystery *The Man Who Was Nobody* (1960)

both with then-husband Dermot Walsh) and three for Charles Saunders (*The Scarlet Web*,1954; *The Narrowing Circle, Behind the Headlines*, 1956), before finding a niche as Technicolor queen of several horror films, including Hammer's *The Curse of Frankenstein* (1957), before leaving Britain for Hollywood in the mid-1960s. The waif-like Susan Shaw (1929–1978) made a stronger impression in her dozen films of the 1940s, exhibiting a sulky, spiky tenacity that differentiated her from many of her contemporaries. For Rank, she was a Huggett daughter in four films, starting with *Holiday Camp*, and foolishly beguiled by Dermot Walsh's posh manner in *To the Public Danger*; and for Ealing she was very vivid as Googie Withers' disputatious step-daughter in *It Always Rains on Sunday*. By the early 1950s, however, she had slid into 'B' films, never to emerge from them again up to her sadly early death. In fact, she is not a very interesting leading lady in the dozen or so she made, perhaps because character parts were her real forte, and she is best served by two which gave her something less pallid than the usual 'B' film heroine: *The Large Rope*, as the girl who hasn't waited for her imprisoned boyfriend's return, and *The Big Day* (1960), as the wife sick of hearing of her husband's work aspirations. While Blackman, Court and even Shaw tended to play virtuous heroines, glamorous Sandra Dorne (1925–1992) was the vamp of the British Bs, so often cast as the blonde with dangerous intentions, most notably in *Marilyn* (1953), where she is as near to a home-grown noir femme fatale as was to be found in 1950s British second features. Occasionally, even she was cast as a heroine, as in *The Gelignite Gang*, but much more often she was the girl who was not to be trusted and likely to come to a bad end.

All those women named above had something going for them, but once out of the 'A' league they tended to find their roles in the second features too formulaic to do much with them. Dorne apart, they were often girlfriends, doing foolish things that distracted the men from their more serious crime-solving activities, or wives patiently being dutiful. Someone like Barbara Murray (b. 1929) had shown real style and promise in her late 1940s/early 1950s films, such as *Passport to Pimlico* (1949), and would do so again on television, as in *The Pallisers* (1974), but the 1950s was no decade for a seriously elegant and perhaps witty leading lady. Kay Kendall grabbed what was going in that line, and Murray was largely confined to 'B' films. She had fair chances in *Mystery Junction* (1951) and *The Frightened Man*, bringing some spark of life to thinly written female leads. In Stephen Clarkson's *Death Goes to School* (1953) she and Gordon Jackson wholesomely scotched any salacious interest that might have attended the girls'-school background of this efficiently made whodunit about the murder of a monstrous teacher (Pamela Alan). Pert Lana Morris (1930–1998) was off to an even better start in the 1940s, very much noticed in *Spring in Park Lane* (1948), *Trottie True* (1948) and *The Chiltern Hundreds* (1949), but, for whatever reason, was unable to sustain the momentum, and spent most of the 1950s in such Bs as *Radio Cab Murder* (1954) and *Moment of Indiscretion* (1958), emerging twice to co-star with Norman Wisdom, her vivacity suppressed in the conventional roles she found. Similarly, Zena Marshall (b. 1926) got off to a busy start with Rank, in late 1940s films such as *Sleeping Car to Trieste* and *Miranda* (both 1948), and hung on long enough to resurface from the 'B' film field as Miss Taro in *Dr No* (1962), but in between was unmemorably marooned in second features, including several for each of John Gilling (*The Embezzler*, 1954, gives her a decent part, and she is Emrys Jones's loyal girlfriend in *Deadly Nightshade*, 1953), Charles Saunders and Francis Searle. Inevitably, there were some established leading ladies of the 1940s whose career began to slip away in the following decade. One such was the Gainsborough star, Phyllis Calvert, who was obliged to accept a position on the bottom half of the bill in Associated British's rather cruelly titled

Starry Phillis Calvert realises she is in a 'B' film in *A Lady Mislaid* (1958)

comedy drama *A Lady Mislaid* (1958, directed by David Macdonald). The reviews for this tale of a respectable home disrupted by rumours of a buried corpse were respectful, if bland, and studiously avoided any reference to the Gainsborough lady's decline.

Those almost wholly associated with 'B' films, usually as heroine, included Jane Barrett, Susan Beaumont, Mary Germaine, Jane Griffiths, Mary MacKenzie, Felicity Young and Dorinda Stevens (the last two, contrasting sisters in Charles Saunders' shoddy *The Gentle Trap*,1960); and half a century later it is hard to find anything very distinctive about them or their roles. So, Barrett was brunette, Germaine blonde, Mackenzie graceful, Beaumont was the least memorable thing about the surprisingly funny and inventive *The Man Who Liked Funerals* (1958) and Griffiths never had another comparable opportunity after co-starring with Gregory Peck in *The Million Pound Note* (1953), though she was unexpectedly poignant in the Danzigers' *The Durant Affair* (1962). More interesting were Adrienne Corri and Ursula Howells, who tended to look as if they were slumming in 'B' films, though Corri brought real character to *The Tell-Tale Heart* and as reporter Paul Carpenter's bantering opposite number in *Behind the Headlines*; and Howells endows Griffith Jones's faithless wife in *Account Rendered* and duplicitous Mme Perrault in *The Sicilians* with her intransigently stylish demeanour. These two were too smart to settle into 'B' film leading-lady status.

Two who did and who repay closer attention, partly because they represent contrasting demeanours in second features, are Rank alumni Rona Anderson and Jane Hylton. In 1994, Rona Anderson (b. 1926) said: 'You know, I think if you did second features it didn't really do you much

Vanishing point: the ethereal Jane Hylton in Vernon Sewell's *House of Mystery* (1961)

good. It looked as if you hadn't made it.'[17] Perhaps, and once she had settled into 'B' films in the 1950s she only once again emerged in a main feature – in her last film to date, *The Prime of Miss Jean Brodie* (1969). However, she brought a real freshness and naturalness to her second features. There were probably too many Rank 'young ladies' in the late 1940s for her to make a stronger impression, though she made the most of the nervous Joan in *Sleeping Car to Trieste*. Later, she said she was always playing Joan or Mary and they never had much fun in British films: to be exact, she was Joan again in *Torment* and Mary in *Floodtide* (1949), *The Twenty Questions Murder Mystery* (1950) and *The Black Rider* (1954), but there were also several Anne, Barbara and Betty characters who were 'Joan or Mary' in all but name. She was essentially crisp and wholesome, in her open Scots prettiness, and brought a proper spirited resourcefulness to these assorted plucky heroines, making them a good deal more endearing and credible than the screenplays deserved. Reviewers allowed that she 'does well' in *Double Exposure*[18] and that she 'pleases as the comely and courageous Julia' in *Little Red Monkey* (1955).[19] However, she was described by *The Cinema* in its review of *The Hide-Out* (1956) as 'anybody's idea of the sort of girl to go through hell and high water for'.[20] If there had been a Scottish film industry in place then, one can imagine her being fashioned into a serviceable star; as it was she is attractive company in all those stereotyped 'B' thrillers, and she achieves convincing rapport with such leading men as Dermot Walsh (*The Hide-Out*), Jimmy Hanley (*Black Rider*), Paul Carpenter (*Stock Car* and *Shadow of a Man*, 1955) and especially John Bentley (*Torment*; *Double Exposure*; *The Flaw*). She and

Sideways glance: Rona Anderson keeps her eye on a distracted Patrick Holt in Daniel Birt's *Circumstantial Evidence* (1952)

Bentley are relaxed, easily inhabit and enlarge the contours of often thinly written leads, and they persuade one of their ordinariness in often very melodramatic circumstances.

One had only to sight Jane Hylton (1927–1979) in late Gainsborough melodramas, such as *Dear Murderer* (1947, as a maid) and, far more prominently, as Jack Warner's mistress in *My Brother's Keeper* (1948), to realise that Rank had potentially a major talent on its books. She had quite unusual intensity and a real capacity for depicting working-class lives, displayed amply in her Ealing films, *Passport to Pimlico* and *Dance Hall*. Unfortunately the film that seems intended to have showcased her talents, *It Started in Paradise* (1952), was a romantic melodrama of the fashion world, with the most tenuous links to the kind of reality Hylton was so adept at suggesting.[21] Her last clear 'A' film, the women's-prison drama *The Weak and the Wicked* (1953), for ABPC, gave her a better chance as Babs, who says: 'I'm no good. I like men too much', and is punished for her sexuality. Hylton imbued her with the kind of social and sexual veracity that she would bring to some less rewarding 'B' film scenarios. Virtually everything she did is worth watching, for her if sometimes for little else. Five 'B' films that show her at her best are: *The Quiet Woman, Burnt Evidence, Devil's Bait* (1959), *Night Train to Inverness* (1960) and *House of Mystery* (1961). Every one of these, admittedly better-than-average supports, benefits from the instinctive humanity, the sense of her characters' having a past and a place in the world, which she brings to them. The working-class women to whom she gives such commendable substance in *Burnt Evidence* and, particularly, as the baker's wife in *Devil's Bait* are convincingly rounded figures in what was so often a cardboard world; and in the quite compelling fantasy of *House of Mystery* she is properly and arrestingly strange as the narrator/protagonist. She died at fifty-two, having scored successes on television, as in Peter Graham Scott's *The Four Seasons of Rosie Carr* (1964), and on stage at the National Theatre, just before her death, in a fine revival of Harley Granville-Barker's *The Madras House* (1977). Main-feature fame eluded her, but she made many a second feature flicker into unwonted truth and reality.

Since the 'B' films were overwhelmingly of the crime genre, and by convention therefore male-dominated, it is not surprising that comparatively few female Hollywood imports are to be found topping their cast lists. The visiting male stars brought an un-English toughness to the job, but there wasn't the similar demand for American women. Three who came trailing clouds of film noir deviance and ambiguity to Hammer Studios were Lizabeth Scott, her days of major stardom over, Hillary Brooke, never a major star but an enjoyable 'A' movie 'other woman' and the notorious Hollywood 'bad girl' Barbara Payton. In *Stolen Face* (1952), Scott appeared as concert pianist Alice and as scarred working-class ex-convict, who is given Alice's face to satisfy the longings of the surgeon Ritter (McCarthy-fled Paul Henreid), and she later co-starred with another Hollywood émigré, Steve Cochran, in Val Guest's co-feature *The Weapon* (1956), bringing her husky 'otherness' to bear on the

Femme fatale: the notorious Barbara Payton gets her hands on Tony Wright in the boxing noir *The Flanagan Boy* (1953)

British scene. Brooke smouldered away with practised ease in Ken Hughes' *The House Across the Lake*, one of Britain's most enjoyable films noirs, and it benefits considerably from her long cinematic career in adulterous deceit.[22] Barbara Payton's brief English sojourn from the Hollywood scandal magazines saw her ideally cast as a dangerous blonde in the boxing noir *The Flanagan Boy* (1953) and, less comfortably, as a perfect partner for cloning in Fisher's *Four-Sided Triangle* (1953). She quickly returned to California, a life of addiction and prostitution, and an early death at thirty-nine.

Ten years after her memorable role in Powell and Pressburger's *A Matter of Life and Death* (1946), Columbia arranged for the rather more wholesome Kim Hunter to co-star with Gary Merrill in Edward Sutherland's *Bermuda Affair* (1956). Filmed on location in the Caribbean, this was a more exotic picture than the average British 'B', and its story of the marital problems of air charter pilots was targeted at a female audience. Critics, however, were far from impressed: 'The picture teems with contrived situations ... and not one of its characters wins sympathy ... Kim Hunter displays little depth as career woman Fran ... To make matters worse, the authentic Bermuda backgrounds are robbed of colour by poor camerawork.'[23] It is hard, though, to imagine most of the other US imports to the 'B' film scene generating much audience excitement, though such women as Mary Castle, Marguerite Chapman, Faith Domergue, Marsha Hunt, Phyllis Kirk, Carole Matthews and Mary Murphy, were all attractive and competent enough for what they were asked to do.[24] Above all, like their male counterparts, they may never have been big box-office attractions at home but at least their names were known, and they did have a certain studio-type glamour about them. You couldn't imagine any of them in a hand-knitted cardigan, unlike the indigenous 'Joans' and 'Marys'. On the other hand, they were sometimes no match for the British second leads, such as Sandra Dorne, more vivid than Betta St John in *Alias John Preston* (1955), or Diana Dors and Eleanor Summerfield, both more memorable than Chapman in *The Last Page* (1952).[25] Overall, though, the presence of American stars, albeit of the second rank, had the effect of opening up the British 'B' films in ways that were helpful, giving them the sort of anti-parochial shot in the arm that the sudden smart use of location shooting sometimes did – getting them away, that is, from the confines of the suburban studios in which they were typically made.

The same could also be said for those 'Continental' imports, such as Lisa Gastoni, decorative and possibly duplicitous in the likes of *The Man from Tangier*, a sexy threat to the hero's marriage in *Second Fiddle* and a witness intimidated by mail-van robbers in *Face in the Night* (all 1957); Simone Silva, consorting with low-lifes in *Escape by Night* (1953) when she's not singing of being 'Haunted, taunted' in the night club to which her type belongs; and Marla Landi, a photographic model in the dim *The Hornet's Nest* (1955). All these, in their descents to the lower depths, brought a touch of Mediterranean exoticism that the 'B' movie regulars couldn't be counted on to supply. Still others, such as Julia Arnall and Ingrid Hafner, Eva Bartok, Yvonne Furneaux, Helene Cordet and Nadja Regin brought un-English whiffs from respectively Austria, Hungary, France, Switzerland and Yugoslavia, in careers that hovered between first and second features, Bartok enjoying a higher profile than the others. These Continental sirens also helped to open up European markets as these became increasingly important to 'B' film profitability in the latter years of the 1950s.

They also serve …: the character players
British cinema has always had a strong tradition of character acting, and the 'B' film output, perhaps to an even greater extent than the main features, often depends on a gallery of familiar faces

for providing an illusion of a 'real world' in which the films' hectic plotting is meant to be taking place. It is hard to write of these stalwarts without lapsing into sentimental gratitude for their usually unsung services in supporting the lead pair (there is almost invariably a pair, though not as invariably as one might expect destined for a final clinch). Among the men, there are, of course, numerous policemen, epitomised at the upper levels by Russell Napier, John Horsley, John Stuart or Ronald Leigh-Hunt, with the lower echelons represented by, say, bulky Martin Boddey or beaky Campbell Singer. Perhaps Russell Napier as Duggan in the *Scotland Yard* series was the police inspector par excellence, but he is rivalled by John Horsley (b. 1920) who represented the Law in countless Bs of the 1950s, either trench- or tweed-coated according to his level of seniority. Such actors did not typically receive much critical attention, but the film-makers knew whom they could trust and used them repeatedly. Horsley made a half-dozen films for John Gilling at Tempean, and producer Robert Baker said of such casting, in 1995:

> They were what you would call our repertory company. We knew them, and if a suitable part came up for one of them, we would give it to them. John Horsley, for instance, played in a lot of our pictures; we liked his style, he was easy to work with, he was flexible, so we tended to use him. Probably we weren't as adventurous as we might have been, but we never had casting directors in those days ... We knew they were reliable so we tended to use them again.[26]

This type of casting was no doubt based primarily on physical suitability: there would not have been time allotted in the screenplay for, say, the dignified Horsley to establish himself as a weaselly black-mailer. The obverse would have been true for short, scruffy Michael Balfour, enjoyable company as any number of fly characters and sidekicks sailing close to the legal wind, but hard to accept as, say, a corrupt banker or Scotland Yard higher-up. What such actors did was to set up expectations arising from their physical presence, which became familiar to filmgoers, even if their names did not; and then quite artfully filling out their usually short screen time with the kind of detail that bestowed a fleeting individuality. Among the criminals, one could hardly imagine, for example, the hangdog look of Edwin Richfield (quite memorable as the lugubrious, apparently mute houseboy Moses in *The Break*) or bulky, thuggish Danny Green, or slyly insinuating Harold Lang, or the dodgy persona of the ubiquitous Sam Kydd slipping round to the virtuous side of the law. There is also a sub-category of saturnine 'heavies' such as Bruno Barnabe, Elwyn Brook-Jones, Martin Benson, or Sydney Tafler, all treacherously smooth, all nature's night-club owners, each though subtly different from the others. Tafler occasionally had leads, as the eponymous *Assassin for Hire* or hero in *Mystery Junction*, for exam-ple, but he was hard to accept in 'respectable' roles, having acquired such an image of shifty black-market entrepreneur. And there were well-spoken crooks, like those epitomised by Alexander Guage, as a suave, effete, Sydney Greenstreet type in *Counterspy*: *Variety* wrote of his 'scenery-chewing mas-terminding of the spy ring'.[27] Other criminal types were vividly represented by Kenneth Griffith, a fixture in British films for sixty years, in 'B' pictures most noticeably as sleazy crooks, as in *Rag Doll* (1960) and *The Painted Smile* (1962), and very memorably by John Salew as a murderous pantomime dame in *The Impersonator* (1961).

As well, there are toffs, corrupt or otherwise, swiftly delineated in accent and demeanour by such regular exponents as Kynaston Reeves (in main and second features from the early 1930s), or Basil Dignam (solid but equivocal in *The Spaniard's Curse*, 1958, or the Danzigers' *Sentenced for Life*,

Supporting actor: Michael Balfour allows Tom Conway and Delphi Lawrence to upstage him in Bernard Knowles' *Barbados Quest* (1955)

1959), or extravagantly moustachioed Bill Shine (as party-giving Colonel Shellaby in *The House in the Woods*, 1957), or Hugh Latimer, reeking of unreliable old-boyism in a dozen or so 'B' films, after starting as a posh policeman in *The Adventures of PC 49* (1949). Put-upon types, husbands of strong-minded women or subservient clerks, for example, were incarnated by the likes of Eric Chitty, who doddered his way through several Bs after starting as a ballistics expert in *Time Is My Enemy* (1954); or diminutive, bespectacled Ian Wilson fussing his way briefly in As and such Bs as *The Last Page*; or Cyril Smith, ordered about by employers and finally playing the most put-upon husband in *Sailor Beware!* (1959). One of the men who ordered Smith about was Garry Marsh in *The Lost Hours*, and he was often cast in a very long career as bounders but also as professional men, presumably because of his imposing stature. As for other such professional types in 'B' films, their name was legion – or, more specifically, Ronald Adam, Howard Douglas, Brian Oulton and John Welsh. Foreigners were almost invariably sinister, and they were played by the likes of Eric Pohlmann, Arnold Marlé (often pathetic rather than dangerous, as in *The Floating Dutchman*, 1953), Karel Stepanek, Roger Delgado, Ferdy Mayne, George Pastell and Trinidadian Frank Singuineau: it hardly mattered where such actors actually came from: what counted, in these often xenophobic narratives, was that they were 'foreign', and were either in the pay of, or fleeing from, enemy powers.

There is real character richness among the supporting casts of British 'B' films, which, while television was getting itself established, kept large numbers of utterly competent, if not specially versatile, character actors in steady employment. The types referred to above by no means exhaust their ranks: there were, for instance, honest and/or rough-hewn working types like those enacted by Patric Doonan, John Slater, Glyn Houston, Wally Patch, George Woodbridge (police sergeants, farmers, taxi-drivers all fell to his lot) and Charles Victor (he gave some of his best performances in such Tempean films as *The Frightened Man* and *The Embezzler*). There was, too, a string of juveniles, mostly boys, in these films, played by such actors as David Hannaford (pleasingly natural in *The Last Load*, 1948, and *End of the Road*), Andrew Ray, who went from the prestige of *The Mudlark* (1950) to several substantial 'B' film roles (as in *Escape by Night*, playing at being a gangster, or as the besotted schoolboy in *Too Young to Love*, 1959) and David Hemmings, who cut his teeth on such films as the well-meaning racial conflict pieces, *The Heart Within* and *The Wind of Change* (1961), before going on to serious swinging-60s stardom.

There is perhaps a slightly narrower range of female character roles on display in the 'B' films, but nevertheless there are plenty of colourful landladies, barmaids, secretaries, cleaners and other servants, vamps, motherly types, dotty old ladies and bossy and/or sophisticated upper-class types to enliven the corners of the formulaic thrillers and comedies that occupied the bottom half of the double bill. Those landladies, cleaners, housekeepers and nosy neighbours, as often as not with hair in turban, a fag hanging out of the mouth and an ear cocked for scandal, ensured moments of pure pleasure from such as Beatrice Varley (*The Black Rider*), Irene Handl (*The Fool and the Princess*, 1948), Dandy Nichols (*Time Is My Enemy*), Avril Angers (*Be My Guest*, 1965), Thora Hird (*The Frightened Man*), Doris Yorke (*Account Rendered*, as a very suspicious landlady) and Joan Hickson (*Deadly Nightshade*). Given that the heroines were often just nice girls who'd got themselves into difficulties but who were not notable for character interest, one valued those sharp-talking secretaries, models, barmaids, or just plain vamps and floosies, sometimes played by the likes of Marianne Stone (who could be nicely ambiguous as in *Echo of Diana*, 1961), Delphi Lawrence (*Blood Orange*), or the great Dora Bryan, a considerable actress who no doubt made valuable pocket-money from such 'B' film sketches as the barmaid in *The Quiet Woman* or the insinuating neighbour in *13 East Street*. And there was a stable of dotty old ladies like those played by Nora Nicholson and Christine Silver in the *The Hornet's Nest*, or Nicholson and May Hallatt as a pair of old lags in *Dangerous Afternoon* (1961).

All of these were busy in 'A' films as well, but the second features needed them more. In interviewing actors who had appeared in the Bs, one realises that they were as often as not doing whatever was offered. Nevertheless, in doing so they were equally obviously filling out their roles, however consciously, with the fruits of their observation of the types they were assigned, and sometimes contrived to give these a more individual life and flavour than the screenwriter may have had in mind.

Genres

Why were some genres, especially crime-thrillers and comedies, favoured over others? The reasons governing genre choices in this area of the field of cultural production are likely to be intricately tied to market demand, to budgeting and to audience acceptability. Even the most cursory scanning of the pages of Denis Gifford's *British Film Catalogue*[28] will leave one in no doubt that crime films constituted the most popular genre in 'B' film-making in the post-war decades. The table below bears this out. We have used here forty minutes as the minimum requirement for second-feature status. The upper limit has been generally taken to be eighty minutes, though on a few occasions slightly longer films known to have been screened on the bottom half of the cinema programme and reviewed (by *Picturegoer*) as 'double bill' have been included in the count.

Year	Crime	Comedy	Drama	Fantasy	Musical	Other
1947	10	1	1		2	5
1948	13	6	4	8		5
1949	16	6	2	1	3	5
1950	35	10	2		1	6
1951	18	10	4	1	1	3
1952	31	14	3	2	1	4
1953	37	9	2	4		9
1954	32	8	1	2		7
1955	23	13				5
1956	25	9	1	3	2	8
1957	36	6	2	1	2	6
1958	21	4			1	13
1959	25	6	4	2	1	6
1960	21	10	8	3	1	6
1961	37	2	3			14
1962	38	12	5		2	8
1963	30	2	3	1	4	5
1964	15	2	1	2	1	8
1965	7	3	2	1	2	4

There is undoubtedly a certain arbitrariness in this tabulation, but, even allowing for this, the trend is clear. This 'arbitrariness' means that, for example, the thirty-minute *Scotland Yard* thrillers have not been included; if they had, the balance would have been even more decisive in favour of crime films as the crucial genre.[29] The column in the table headed 'Other' includes the sparse representation of such other genres as adventure, children's, horror, nudist, religious, revue, romance, sport and war. We have retained Gifford's genre names, though they sometimes may be said to elide distinctions: for instance, his category of 'Fantasy' also includes what might be more commonly labelled 'Science Fiction', and the 'Drama' category seems to be used for films which resist other labels. Despite all such minor reservations about how we have used Gifford's *Catalogue* to arrive at the table above, it still may be said to summarise the main generic trends of the British 'B' movie over nearly twenty years.

Crime

The enduring popularity of 'B' movie crime is partly a reflection of preferred genres at more ambitious levels. In Britain, as in Hollywood, there has been a long tradition of crime films.[30] There was a prolific output of crime pictures, usually of second-feature status in the 1930s, and, while there was a falling-off in the war years, post-war saw such major examples of the genre as *Brighton Rock* and *They*

Made Me a Fugitive (both 1947). In the 1950s, there is a sprinkling of main features, but it is essentially the 'B' movie in which crime provides the narrative impetus. There are nearly 300 of the genre among the second features. Only 'Comedy' with about a hundred 'B' movie titles in the same period was remotely as popular with film-makers at this level. Tempean's Robert S. Baker, responsible for a string of about thirty proficient thrillers (and a few comedies) during the 1950s, maintained this was a matter of market demand:

> A thriller is always acceptable. It's very difficult to make a soft romance as a second feature, it needs something harder. I don't know why. The public appetite was in favour of thrillers rather than comedies, but you *could* make a comedy or a thriller – anything else was very dubious! ... With a murder there's something to interest you, whether it's a question of whodunit, or someone's life in jeopardy, or someone on the run from the law or from the villains. It's easy to hook an audience with a thriller, not so easy to hook them on a romantic plot. It was demand, basically. Thrillers were easier to sell and therefore easier to set up.[31]

Contemporary crime narratives could economise on production design and, provided gross brutality was avoided and just deserts were eventually handed out to the villain, the censor was usually content.[32] Crime stories also offered a vehicle for addressing contemporary issues and fears as this trade review of Montgomery Tully's *Jackpot* (1960) makes clear: 'Crime drama of this type has been popular for a long time with cinema audiences and here a story that rings almost topically true to life and has been as efficiently and effectively told as the best of its kind to be made in Britain.'[33] Consequently, the Bs were, as Rona Anderson put it, 'mostly cops and robbers' stuff.[34] Some were evidently inspired by the themes and stylistics of film noir, but most managed to inflect their stories with indigenous elements. Horace Shepherd's *The Flamingo Affair* (1948), made at Viking Studios, was one of the most faithful adaptations of American film noir narrative to a British context. It contains all the classic ingredients – a scheming spider woman (Colette Melville), a demobbed serviceman ripe for seduction in a corrupt post-war world (Denis Webb) and lashings of flashbacks – but ends in *Boys' Own* fashion with the reassertion of wartime camaraderie as ex-commandoes rout the forces of decadence.[35] There was more hardboiled melodrama in the Dublin-set *Stranger at My Door* (1950), directed by Brendon J. Stafford and Desmond Leslie. Narrated in flashback, it told the familiar post-war cautionary tale of another former commando (Joseph O'Connor) forced to turn to crime to protect his girl (Agnes Bernelle) in the inhospitable peace. Its noir credentials were further reinforced by casting 'The Man in Black', Valentine Dyall, as a menacing blackmailer. What, though, are the typical formulas of the British supporting pictures in the crime genre? From the sample for this study, of about 160 'B' thrillers of the period, random in the sense of their being dictated by availability, the following are some of the characteristics which emerge:

(a) The crime on which the film's plot essentially rests has either been committed 'before the film begins' or in its first twenty minutes, very often in the opening segment. Many begin on deserted streets at night: in Michael McCarthy's *Assassin for Hire* a pedestrian on a lonely street is shot by an unseen hit man; in Charles Saunders' *Behind the Headlines*, a blonde, bent on blackmail, strides purposefully through a lamp-lit street; in John Gilling's *Panic* (1965) a frightened girl runs through darkened city streets; Godfrey Grayson's *Dick Barton at Bay* (1950) starts with a man being pursued down

Waterfront skulduggery: a press book for Vernon Sewell's *The Floating Dutchman* (1953). Albert Lewin's *Pandora and the Flying Dutchman* (1950), with its ghost ship, must have been a film close to Sewell's heart

a street at night; and in Pat Jackson's *Don't Talk to Strange Men* (1962) a car cruises threateningly beside a young woman in a night street. Many others begin on busy urban streets in daytime, the quotidian reality almost invariably on the point of disruption by some criminal activity. Such films include: *Burnt Evidence, The Embezzler, Time Is My Enemy, The Gentle Trap, Dangerous Afternoon, Touch of Death* and many more. Almost as common is the film which opens on a stretch of river, usually the Thames, as in *The Steel Key* or *The Heart Within*, with its initial sequence of Tower Bridge opening, the Bridge also featuring in the opening shot of *Three Steps to the Gallows, Tiger by the Tail* and *The Floating Dutchman*, which (anticipating Hitchcock's *Frenzy* by nearly twenty years) begins with a dead body found floating past.[36] There are also more than a few that start with an aircraft arriving, as often as not flying in an American to sort out criminal matters which elude the British constabulary: *vide* Lloyd Bridges in *The Limping Man* or Paul Carpenter in *Diplomatic Passport* or Tom Conway in *Barbados Quest*.

These films waste no time in getting down to business and are economical in their storytelling procedures: a recognisable ambience is quickly established, in just enough detail for audience orientation. The physical setting is in fact no more than this in most cases. We are not required to make careful connection between the character, whether criminal or victim, and, say, a humdrum or soulless or corrupting environment, as the New Wave films did. In this respect, movies such as Charles Saunders' *Jungle Street* (1961) or Vernon Sewell's *The Wind of Change* are unusual in their correlating of, respectively, youthful unrest and inter-racial animosities to the urban environments. In general, the 'B' movie didn't aspire to such explicit social commentary. The kinds of crime are essentially 'personal', growing out of individual greed or ambition, rarely reflecting in any *direct* way the contemporary political or social scene.[37] One should note, however, that engagement with pressing contemporary issues was by no means common even in the British 'A' films of the period.

(b) There will usually be at least one other crime committed. The culprit is either an individual *or* a gang: on the basis of the sample, crime is as likely to result from the actions of disaffected individuals as from the machinations of a group. Whether one or many, the executor of the crime in these films is, in most cases, just that: an executor, with a clearly defined Proppian *function*,[38] with perfunctorily sketched motivation and unencumbered with much psychological interest. The British 'B' film shows little aptitude for examining the criminal mind and its motivations, or for the Hollywood skill in representing the criminal group, though Lance Comfort's *Tomorrow at Ten* (1962) gestures towards the former and Jim O'Connolly's *The Hi-Jackers* (1963) the latter. The villain may be a racketeer night-club owner (e.g., Sydney Tafler in *The Floating Dutchman*, Elwyn Brook-Jones in *The Gilded Cage*, or Kenneth Griffith in *The Painted Smile*) or a pawnbroker (Clifford Evans in *The Heart Within*) – or a foreigner like Arnold Marlé's fence in *The Floating Dutchman* or the embassy official (André Mikhelson) in *The Diplomatic Corpse* (1958) or John G. Heller as a wartime spy in *Cloak Without Dagger* (1956).

Villains are more often suave than crude, though they may have low-life henchmen at their disposal. Structurally, as is the case with so much action genre film-making, the narrative moves towards a showdown of one kind or other between the hero and the chief villain. In the British 'B' film, the outcome is also very often influenced by matters of class: the protagonists are almost invariably middle class, whereas villains may be decadently upper class (André Morell in *Cash on Demand*, or Guy Middleton in *Never Look Back*), or lower-class criminal types (such as Derren Nesbitt in Sewell's *The Man in the Back Seat*, 1961, and *Strongroom*, 1962), or middle-class traitors to their class (Hugh Sinclair in *No Trace*), or, straying in from film noir, the occasional femme fatale, such as Constance Smith in *Impulse* or Hillary Brooke in *The House Across the Lake*. It is not in the usual way of 'B' movies to allow much time to detailed character-drawing, so these assorted villains will normally have to establish their credentials through unmistakable signifiers of accent, dress and demeanour. These, allied in many cases to occupation, were sufficient for audiences to sniff out quickly whom to suspect and where their sympathies should lie. One would never, for instance, trust a man in a smoking jacket or a woman smoking at a bar in a 'B' movie – or even a woman with a decent dressmaker.

(c) The hero of these films is sometimes a policeman: for example, bland Ronald Howard in *Assassin for Hire*, or cop-about-to-retire Eddie Byrne in *One Way Out*. More usually, though, the police are there to disbelieve the hero and come to his aid at the end. Typically, the hero is a private detective, such as John Bentley in *Double Exposure*, Dermot Walsh in *The Floating Dutchman*, or investigator (Walsh in *The Hide-Out*, or Philip Friend in *Cloak Without Dagger*), or reporter (Paul Carpenter in *Behind the Headlines* and *One Jump Ahead*, Conrad Phillips as the reporter on holiday in *The Desperate Man*, 1960), or other professionals such as doctor (Ronald Howard in *Black Orchid*, Donald Houston in *Find the Lady*, 1956), author (William Lundigan in *Dangerous Voyage*, Robert Ayres in *Delayed Action*, 1955), or even a bank official (Peter Cushing in *Cash on Demand*, Griffith Jones in *Account Rendered*). Although the character of The Saint was briefly revived in Seymour Friedman's *The Saint's Return* (1953), by the 1950s, the reformed gentleman crook was more or less obsolete as far as the 'B' film was concerned. Such heroes seem to belong to the pre-war era, to even less egalitarian times. However, though high society is now no longer the preferred location for the 'B' thriller, it cannot be said that the egalitarian spirit has often spread below the middle classes. Duncan Lamont's conscientious debt-ridden working man in *Burnt Evidence* and Geoffrey Keen's harassed baker in *Devil's Bait* are among the very rare exceptions in which the working or lower middle classes have functions other than comic relief or low-life villainy in British 'B' thrillers. They would be exceptional at any level of British film-making, of course, until late in the 1950s.

(d) There is almost always a romantic action accompanying the crime story. The most typical heroine is the nice middle-class girl, whose plucky support for the hero's attempts to track down the criminals often leads her into dangerous situations which complicate his efforts. In *The Diplomatic Corpse*,

MONARCH FILM CORPORATION LTD. presents
DERMOT WALSH • JACQUELINE HILL
IN
" THE BLUE PARROT "
AN A.C.T. FILMS PRODUCTION

Ⓐ

Dangerous situation: Jacqueline Hill is tied up in an underground chambre by the dastardly John LeMesurier in ACT's *The Blue Parrot* (1953)

Susan Shaw, as a reporter, gets herself trapped in a foreign embassy from which she has to be rescued by boyfriend Robin Bailey; while in *Find the Lady*, intrepid model Beverley Brooks is tied up in an underground hide-out by criminals before being saved by the village doctor played by Donald Houston. An identikit romantic couple for such films would be a composite of Dermot Walsh/Hazel Court (of Sewell's *Counterspy* and *Ghost Ship*) and John Bentley/Rona Anderson (of Gilling's *Double Exposure* and Fisher's *The Flaw*). He is purposeful, more insightful than the police or his newspaper boss, handy with his fists and with a practised line in bantering with women. She is pretty, spirited, with a touch of venturesome recklessness, and practised in parrying banter. They behave essentially as chums or sparring partners rather than lovers; there is scarcely a suggestion of sexual feeling between the leads in these films, even when they end in each other's arms.

Adrienne Corri, a more potent female and sexual presence than is usual in British Bs, nearly gets a hen-pecked tourist clerk (William Russell) to leave his nagging wife in Scott's *The Big Chance* (1957). The wife is called 'Betty', so we can be sure whose side the film will have to come down on – whatever Corri is called, she must be relinquished in favour of domesticity, however drab. Scott's 'B' films were more likely than most to be sexually motivated, at least in part, as in *Account Rendered*, its plot based on an illicit affair and the murder of a faithless wife (Ursula Howells), or in the non-thriller

The Big Day, which opens on a moment of erotic intensity unusual at *any* level of British film-making at the time. Sexually wandering wives, like Mary Laura Wood in *Black Orchid*, rarely live to see the closing credits, and heroes generally manage to channel their libidos into intimate dinners at the local bistro. In sexual-romantic terms, the 'B' film resolutely upholds the status quo of British cinema: men may be tempted but they go home to dull wives; more adventurous spirits are not likely to be rewarded with last-scene embraces; sexual impulses are either played down in the manner validated at a higher level by *Brief Encounter* (1945) or are deployed into a wise-cracking repartee which offers the faintest echo of the 'Thin Man' comedy-thrillers of the 1930s. Their American counterparts did not go to bed before our eyes in those days, but the films often found ways of suggesting that that was where they were going – or where they had been.

(e) The *Scotland Yard* series of police procedurals apart, the solving of the crime is not usually the result of the patient and ingenious sleuthing one finds in the detective fiction of the time. One of the virtues of these films is that they move along quite smartly as a rule and this kind of narrative pace means that they depend more on action than on the sifting of evidence. They are at their least effective when they allow themselves to become burdened with a lot of expository talk. Whatever the specificities of setting or the nature of the action, the forces of law and order invariably assert their supremacy in a sequence of confrontation with the offenders. The middle-class upholders of various kinds of authority (mainly police, but also newspapers, the judiciary, medical and other science, occasionally the church) may seek to use other investigatory procedures, but in the end the disorderly elements are routed in much more basic, physical ways. The chase is the commonest means of bringing the narrative to a close. One third of the thrillers viewed utilised a chase, through streets or deserted buildings or at sea, or perhaps most strikingly in a church in Ken Hughes' 1955 co-feature *Confession*. The others make use of physical confrontations of various kinds, such as the scuffle in a flat in *The Floating Dutchman*, or on the parapet of a castle in *The Desperate Man*, or on a barge in *The Hornet's Nest* or, perhaps most commonly of all, in a shoot-out in a warehouse.

What is a little surprising is the bleakness of so many of the endings. At the close of Terry Bishop's *Cover Girl Killer* (1959), an overhead shot observes the young couple (Spencer Teakle and Felicity Young) walk off into the night as the body of the Man (Harry H. Corbett) is left spreadeagled in the street. The last shot of Michael McCarthy's co-feature *The Traitor* shows the treacherous Joseph (Anton Diffring) playing the piano madly as soldiers arrive to arrest him. *The Embezzler* ends with the death of its sympathetic eponym, played by Charles Victor, who is also grief-stricken at the death of his wastrel son at the end of *The Frightened Man*, while the girl (Barbara Murray) walks off into the night. Lance Comfort's *Rag Doll* ends on a very downbeat note with its star, Jess Conrad as a pop-singer turned burglar, lying dead in a field, his young wife bending over him, and on the soundtrack the film's theme song, 'Why am I Living?'. And the last image of Frank Marshall's *Gang War* (1962) is an overhead shot of a dead body prone on the floor of a club. There were, of course, plenty of last-minute clinches, but there are enough examples of the kind mentioned to indicate a curious strand of nihilism at work in the British 'B' thriller.

Comedy

Apart from the crime thrillers, the only other genre with substantial numbers is one that could be broadly labelled comedy. The label is broad because it needs to include: farces, comedies of character, romantic and domestic types, personality pieces built around well-known comics, and satires and parodies. In other words, comedy at this level tends to fall into categories which also exist at the top half of the double bill where they have the advantage of superior production qualities, better scripts and stronger casts and directors. In a very general way, one might say that if there is a prevailing paradigm of the 'B' comedies it is one in which the central comic figure (there is sometimes a pair) overcomes some obvious bogey, such as pompous officialdom or heartless materialism. Such oppositions were, of course, much explored at the 'A' level of the film-making hierarchy, but in the 'B' films the battle lines are apt to be drawn more crudely. In the farces, for instance, the comedy is at the expense of caricatured prudery (e.g., the belligerent mother-in-law in *Fast and Loose*, 1954, or *The Battleaxe*, 1962), or, in the parodies, of the pomposities of the official guardians of the nation's culture (the thinly disguised BBC in the co-feature *Make Mine a Million*, 1959).

Unlike the thrillers, the comedies tend to spread the character interest across the genders: virtually none of the crime-thrillers exhibits a narrative instigated by or driven by a woman. In almost none of them is there a character so centrally responsible for the working of the narrative as those played by Margaret Rutherford in *Miss Robin Hood* (1952) or *Aunt Clara* (1954) or by Kathleen Boutall in *Fly Away Peter* (1948). In terms of class, while the 'B' comedies certainly offer no threat to the middle-class hegemony which prevails in British cinema in this period, they are at least a little more likely to focus on either lower middle-class life than the 'B' thrillers do (or British cinema in general does) or, in the case of certain personality comics, to be anchored in no particular class. There are quite clearly different narrative paradigms at work in, say, the farces which depend on frantic comings and goings and mistaken intentions and identities, on the one hand, and the character comedies which depend on major and sometimes unexpected attitudinal shifts in their protagonists. Thus, it is more useful to consider the films briefly in relation to their sub-genres, bearing in mind that there are often elements of more than one sub-genre in any given film.

Farce in the sense of the term established by such playwrights as Georges Feydeau and Ben Travers had a very lean innings in the period examined in this book. The 1930s had been rife with screen adaptations of stage farces, especially of those made famous at the Aldwych Theatre, mostly by Travers and starring Tom Walls, Ralph Lynn, Mary Brough and Winifred Shotter. These were very often directed by Walls and bear all the marks of their stage origins: conventional character groupings, patently artificial studio settings, high jinks among the upper classes and all manner of absurd confusion in the action. Such films had virtually disappeared in the war years, and never again constituted a numerous sub-genre. Editor Alfred Roome and cameraman Freddie Young have attested to the difficulties of giving such films any kind of cinematic fluency.[39] Gordon Parry's co-feature *Fast and Loose* is one of the few examples of this kind of theatrical farce on the screen in the post-war period. (Saunders' *One Wild Oat*, 1951, is another.) An adaptation of Travers' *Cuckoo in the Nest* (previously filmed in 1934), it involves the series of accidents which bring a young husband (Brian Reece) together with a glamorous old flame (Kay Kendall) in compromising circumstances at a country inn, where in due course they are joined by the rest of the cast, including his wife (June Thorburn, regular 'B' lead), her parents and an eccentric cycling vicar. In the tradition of such farces, everyone having converged on the site of maximum confusion, the denouement finds each restored to the appropriate spouse. It was, however, a tradition that seemed more or less played out by the mid-1950s and this strongly cast but unimaginatively filmed version was unlikely to resuscitate the genre. Like others of its ilk, it harks back to a British comic never-never-land, and shares a conventional British farcical attitude to sex: the idea of men as either overgrown schoolboys in their leering approach to women or the hen-pecked victims of domineering wives, and the essential failure of anything sexual actually to happen.

Of the others which might be claimed for the farce sub-genre, Ralph Thomas's *Helter Skelter* and Alfred Roome and Roy Rich's *It's Not Cricket* (both 1949) come from Gainsborough, a studio which produced few 'B' films, at least intentionally, during the 1940s. Both are derived from original screen-plays: *Helter Skelter*'s is the work of Patrick Campbell, Jan Reid and Gerard Bryant, and the result, apart from a few moments of comic liveliness, is deplorably silly; *It's Not Cricket* is written by Bernard McNab, Lyn Lockwood and, again, Bryant, and the result is often one of inspired comedic invention. *Helter Skelter*, a series of wild incidents in the search for a cure for a young girl's hiccups, affects a *Hellzapoppin* style[40] of crazy comedy, but its scattergun approach ensures that there is no building of farcical structure and expectation. There are odd funny moments, some of them involving in-jokes about the film industry (including an extended spoof on *Forever Amber*, 1947) and a mother-ridden hero, Nick Martin (David Tomlinson), as a parody of detective Dick Barton. The film's procedure is that of anything-for-a-laugh, whereas *It's Not Cricket* develops its central idea – a mad ex-Nazi leading a pair of private detectives a dance through southern England – firmly enough to provide a real framework for its comic set-pieces.

The personality comedies depend for their appreciation on one's response to the comedians around whom they are built. For instance, Charles Saunders' *Trouble in the Air* (1948) was a

Dinner for one: Freddy Frinton serves Jimmy Edwards in Charles Saunders' topical comedy *Trouble in the Air* (1948)

Highbury Studios vehicle for Jimmy Edwards, a radio and television comic who never really acquired a popular film following, and there were two minor pieces built around Margaret Rutherford, Anthony Kimmins' *Aunt Clara* and John Guillermin's *Miss Robin Hood*, for Group 3. Edwards's characteristic bluster and innuendo, so funny in radio's *Take It From Here*, on screen seems to be too knowing, to be working too hard. Certainly, *Trouble in the Air*, ostensibly based on a clash of old ways (bell-ringing) and new (the radio programme presided over by Edwards) with a dash of post-war spivery (in the person of Bill Owen), is so ramshackle in its plotting, so hit-and-miss in verbal and visual jokes, that Edwards can scarcely be held responsible for its collapse into inanity. Ironically, the personality who catches the eye is Freddie Frinton, rehearsing the role of a butler for which he would later receive adulation in Continental Europe when he starred in *Dinner for One* (1961). The case is different with Margaret Rutherford, very often, of course, a star or major character player in 'A' films. The co-features referred to above do not give her major opportunities, but by the time she made them her screen persona was firmly established and she had shown herself an actress who could do more than repeat a personality 'turn'. The stocky figure swathed in haphazardly chosen garments, the wobbling chins, the genteel but wild-eyed zealot's doggedness: these were elements of her stock-in-trade, and they meant that she was an immediately identifiable presence. However, as the eponymous Aunt Clara she tempers eccentricity with a mixture of innocence and moral aggression that gives a dimension of reality to the heroine who has been made her uncle's sole legatee because she will look after the only people he cared for. *Aunt Clara* is admittedly written (by Kenneth Horne) and acted with more skill and care than the Edwards vehicle, but, unlike Edwards, Rutherford had learned to accommodate a larger-than-life personality to the intimacy of the screen's scrutiny. She manages even to give a bumbling reality to the dim sub-Ealing goings-on of Group 3's *Miss Robin Hood*, in which, as a middle-aged fan of an author of adventure stories for girls, she helps to retrieve a stolen whisky formula. All agog, wide-eyed with admiration and outrage, with frizzy fringe, flowered dress and dangling earrings, she is the very picture of eccentric obsession. Rutherford, as well as being a remarkable comic presence, could also carry a moral weight when given half a chance, which is what *Aunt Clara* gives her and the feebly imagined *Miss Robin Hood* does not.

Satire does not flourish in the British 'B' film, whereas it is a very common tonal element in the upper reaches of production, even though its intentions seem generally less than lethal. Lance Comfort cannot do much with the very broad satire at the expense of commercial television, and the advertising which sustains it, in the co-feature *Make Mine a Million*. Comic Arthur Askey, then coming to the fag end of a prolific screen career, plays an accident-prone TV make-up man who helps market-stall holder, Sid Gibson (Sidney James) to get his detergent, Bonko, advertised on national television. Jokes good and bad ('Bonko contains a very high concentration of supercilious acid') and slapstick incident (Askey dressed as a nurse at Ascot and taken off to attend a woman in labour) succeed each other at such a pace as to defy serious criticism, but the satire on television tends to get lost. The image of the National (= BBC) as the purveyor of high culture and of commercial television's preoccupation with advertising revenue could have been used to pull together the film's plot since each wants the gormless Askey for its own purposes. However, the satire is limited to a few barbs at the expense of the BBC's high-cultural pretensions ('It will take three poetry readings and a visit to Glyndebourne,' laments one of the National's directors, to reclaim audiences after their exposure to an ad for Bonko); whereas the power of commercial television is mocked by an early dismissal of Bonko: 'It can't be much good, it hasn't been advertised on the telly.' In fact, the most telling criticism of 1950s television is unwitting – in the parade of guest stars whose turns make one wonder that TV entertainment (romantic duets, ballroom dancing, Denis Lotis, Sabrina et al.) was ever so blandly inane.

The romantic comedies among the 'B' films are as dismal as any films ever made in Britain. They are apt to be neither romantic nor comic. From Highbury came *Love in Waiting* (1948), comic-book fiction, dealing wholly in stereotypes (camp dress designer, man putting on glasses to signify shyness, etc.). Its perfunctory plotting has a country girl leaving home to make her way in London, meeting two city girls with whom she shares a flat and with whom she becomes a waitress, unmasking the vine-gary manageress (Patsy Drake) as engaged in illicit traffic in foodstuffs, and all three girls romantically attached by the film's end. The reference to the black market in still-rationed food is this talkative little film's only connection with the realities of life in 1948 Britain – as distinct from those with the Rank Company of Youth. At least the hour-long *Love in Waiting* has brevity on its side, whereas two other so-called romantic comedies of this post-war period – John Paddy Carstairs' *Fools Rush In* and Michael Barry's *Stop Press Girl* (both 1949) – each dawdle along for almost another twenty minutes. These two dire pieces, the first dealing with the threat to a girl's marriage by the return of her dashing, divorced father, and the second with the antics that ensue from a girl's power to stop machinery, both star Sally Ann Howes, whose film career never recovered from this double exposure. She is co-starred in each with Rank hopeful Nigel Buchanan, as jilted (later reclaimed) fiancé in the former and stuffy businessman suitor who loses out to enterprising journalist Jock (Gordon Jackson) in the second. Both films may be said to come down on the side of the free spirits: the divorced father (Guy Rolfe) rather than the mother's pompous titled suitor Charles (Raymond Lovell) in *Fools Rush In*, and Jock who is prepared to parachute from a plane, rather than the hidebound Roy in *Stop Press Girl*. *Fools Rush In* recalls, to its great disadvantage, such notable Hollywood comedies of divorce as *The Awful Truth* (1937) and *The Philadelphia Story* (1940); unlike them, it suggests no vein of real feeling, only the non-stop flow of brittle West End dialogue. Just one line is genuinely funny – and revealing. The old nanny (Nora Nicholson) of the heroine and of her mother before her rebukes the daughter for asking if her mother had been swept off her feet by passion. 'Certainly not. I will not stand here and listen to you accuse your mother of passion.' Sadly, the film does not follow through this witty insight into the nature – or at least the typical representation – of English love and marriage.[41]

The remaining sub-genres – the domestic and the character comedies – tend to overlap. However, David Eady's *The Man Who Liked Funerals* and Lewis Gilbert's *Time Gentlemen Please!*, two of the most attractive 'B' films, are both clearly 'character comedies', built around a character rather than an established personality; Terence Fisher's *Children Galore* (1954) and Charles Saunders' *Fly Away Peter* are clearly 'domestic' in the source of their comedy; whereas Saunders' *There's Always a Thursday* com-bines elements of both in roughly equal parts. What these films have in common is a sympathy for either the ordinary or the opponents of conformism and/or materialism, acknowledging a binarism at the structural heart of a good deal of 'B' comedy. *The Man Who Liked Funerals* (see Chapter 8) centres on the efforts of an amiable printer, Simon Hood (Leslie Phillips, well outside his regular womanising persona), to raise £4,000 to renew the lease of a Boys' Club: 'the only civilising influence in their lives', says Simon. He is motivated by a benevolence that sets him at odds with some of the key institutions of his society; but it is indolence rather than benevolence which sets Dan Dance (Eddie Byrne) apart from the officious in the Group 3 comedy *Time Gentlemen Please!*. The village of Little Hayhoe has a 99.9 per cent employment and productivity record; its problem is the 0.1 unemployed,

'The flowering of George Potter': Charles Victor and Frances Day in Charles Saunders' *There's Always a Thursday* (1957)

Dan, who must be got out of the way before a visit by the Prime Minister. The solution – to pack Dan off to the almshouse – allows gentle satire at the idea of welfare: the benefactor of the almshouse is a grim-faced old man, Dan is decked out in the absurd costume of the pauper and subject to every penalty the mean-faced almoners (Thora Hird and Ivor Barnard) can invoke. The character of Dan is to some extent sentimentalised: he is allowed too easily to be a lovable old codger who understands the birds, and his Irish resistance to British authority is typical of a recurring Celtic strain in British films. However, as played by Byrne, he provides a firm centre for the kinds of satire that give the film its edge. The village setting, attractive as it is, is seen as a hotbed of snobberies, gossip and corruption. Of course, everything about the film's attack on aspects of the Establishment is mild, but, like *The Man Who Liked Funerals*, it has the advantage of an amusing screenplay (by Peter Blackmore, from a novel by R. J. Minney), a central character engaging enough in concept and execution to hold the narrative together and one of those prodigally rich casts of British character actors (add Raymond Lovell, Sidney Tafler, Edie Martin, Sidney James, Hermione Baddeley, Dora Bryan, Joan Young and the young Ian Carmichael to those already listed) which can make much worse British films than this enjoyable. It was, as *To-Day's Cinema* put it, 'commendably off the beaten track',[42] and *Picture Show* allowed it 'brightly acted and told, with agreeable settings.'[43]

In the domestic comedies humour arises from what are essentially home/family-based situations and incidents. Typical of the sub-genre, Montgomery Tully's corset comedy *Girdle of Gold* (1952) was unfortunately no great rib-tickler. The film featured Maudie Edwards as a cash-starved wife, and poked gentle fun at the stuffy provincialism of Welsh village life. What little humour there is in *Children Galore* derives from the more or less absurd premiss of aristocrats quitting a village and leaving a cottage to the couple with the most grandchildren, so as to maintain the family name in the village. This gracious gesture from their betters leads to some vulgar competition from the lower orders, especially between two notably warring families, the Arks and the Bunnions, whose husbands are secretly friends and whose young (June Thorburn and Richard Leech) offer a lower middle-class version of Romeo and Juliet before facing their squabbling mothers with the fact of their secret marriage. The cottage is finally won by the work-shy Zacky (Eddie Byrne in a variation of his role in *Time Gentlemen Please!*) and an old flame Mrs Gedge (Ealing's Grace Arnold), the film coming out clearly in opposition to materialism and acquisitiveness, as so much English comedy does. These unattractive qualities are here linked firmly to the petit bourgeois, rather than to the bountiful aristocracy whose gift is seen to bring out the worst in the class a couple of rungs down.

Charles Saunders' *Fly Away Peter*, one of the best of the short-lived Highbury Studios experiment, has a serious theme – the attempts of a growing family to fly the parental nest and of the mother to come to terms with this – which gives the comedy a little more ballast than is the case elsewhere. Unfortunately, in its warm and wholesome way, it fails to flesh it out. It is at crucial moments fatally underwritten, short on the detail that would have anchored it more firmly to reality. Saunders depends very much on the sturdy performances of Kathleen Boutall as the mother who can't bear to see the children leave and Frederick Piper as her quietly perceptive husband, and the raucous comedy of Margaret Barton as the youngest child Myra and Peter Hammond as her bullied boyfriend. The situations in which the older children find themselves (wanting to marry or to take a job in Nigeria) are thinly written and such Rank contract artistes as Elspet Gray, Nigel Buchanan and Patrick Holt haven't the personality to remedy this. The story was taken at face value by the trade reviewers, but had obvious allegorical connotations as the 'children' of Empire began to achieve their own independence. The associations of its message, identified by *To-Day's Cinema* as 'it is time for the once possessive mother to give her blessing to the last of her departing children', should really have been evident in the year following India's independence.[44]

The last in the batch to be considered here is Saunders' *There's Always a Thursday*, part domestic comedy, part character comedy. It opens on the close-up of a boiling electric kettle, then a nagging voice is heard as the browbeaten husband George (Charles Victor) comes down to prepare tea The domestic setting is quite briskly evoked and the excellence of these character actors gives some credibility to the not very original goings-on. In fact, the film's major strength is in the performance of Charles Victor as the worm who turns.[45] Mistaken for a dangerous ladies' man, George relishes the attention he attracts as a result, in the family and among his office colleagues. A new professional life opens up to him, his now *soignée* wife has a new respect for him, and his previous boss's mistress (Frances Day) is happy to see him as a replacement. The film is quite neatly structured but, without the coherence which Victor's sympathetic understanding of the central character gives, it would seem much thinner than it does. Its comedy centres on the drabness of an oppressive domestic situation and, in the flowering of George Potter, what may be lost in unthinking conformity to a routine.

Few of the comedies in this sample rises impressively above the limits of skimpy budget: screenplays which, however promising their central premisses, lack the density of 'felt life', predictably stagy settings or village locations, insipid young leads defeated by inadequate dialogue or direction. Yet, if there are films to be salvaged, it is almost invariably due to the reserves of character acting, much of it theatre-trained and used to filling in the contours of a lightly sketched role. It is the performances of Leslie Phillips, Charles Victor and Eddie Byrne, for example, which illuminate, respectively, the eccentricity, the sudden efflorescence and the shyster whimsicality of their respective starring roles in *The Man Who Liked Funerals*, *There's Always a Thursday* and *Time Gentlemen Please!*, in screenplays more comically inventive and structurally sound than is common.

Musicals

Although British 'B' films frequently feature diegetic musical interludes, often in the form of night-club performances, there are surprisingly few fully fledged musicals. In the late 1940s and early 1950s one finds the occasional revue-style featurette, as well as a few more ambitious attempts to integrate narrative and musical performance such as Tempean's first release, *Date with a Dream* (1948), John Guillermin's *Melody in the Dark* (1949) and Mario Zampi's *Come Dance with Me* (1950). The latter took the tradition of Variety, which had sustained so much of British production aimed at 'industrial halls' in the 1930s and 1940s, and gave it an upmarket tweak by setting it in an exclusive night club. The film also retained the pre-war convention of class masquerade, for the linking romance between a valet (Gordon Humphris) and a maid (Yvonne Marsh) who both pose as aristocrats. In addition to the clowning of Max Wall and the singing of Anne Shelton, the picture's main interest lay in the appearance by zither-player Anton Karas, a hit in the previous year's *The Third Man*. Knightsbridge Films made *It's a Wonderful Day* (1949), a vehicle for Lou Sherman and his orchestra with a Devon setting. Directed by Hal Wilson, it packed no fewer than eight numbers into its fifty-minute running time. *Kinematograph Weekly* appreciated its 'wholesome atmosphere' and 'ear-tickling tunes'.[46] These films, however, are hardly an equivalent for the cheerful minor musicals produced by Columbia in the 1940s, starring the likes of Ann Miller or Jinx Falkenberg.

As John Mundy has noted, it was surprising, given the previously extensive exploitation of pop-ular music stars, that there was a general hiatus in British musical film-making in the early to mid-1950s.[47] With the exception of Peter Graham Scott's *Sing Along with Me* (1952), an ill-fated attempt to establish singer Donald Peers' screen career,[48] practically the only supporting pictures on offer which used the talents of singers like Alma Cogan or dance bands such as those of Cyril Stapleton, Eric Winstone and Edmundo Ross were shorts or featurettes.[49] Music achieves major significance in British 'B' films only with the arrival of rock 'n' roll and other youth-oriented styles like trad jazz and skiffle, and the gradual desertion of older audiences. In fact, it is a 'B' feature, Denis Kavanagh's *Rock You Sinners* (1957), that captures (albeit crudely) the first enthusiastic scrabbling of young people for a music that was genuinely their own, but the initiative is then used by a company like Anglo-Amalgamated to bolster its attempts to break into the 'A' feature market by exploiting the popularity of home-grown rocker Tommy Steele, as we have already noted. There are a few attempts to turn pop singers into thespians and to build a narrative around the limited acting abilities of Acker Bilk's jazz band (*Band of Thieves*, 1961), The Shadows (the dire colour featurette *Rhythm and Greens*, 1964) and the Spencer Davis Group (the haunted house romp *The Ghost Goes Gear*, 1966), but popular per-formers like Cliff Richard, Adam Faith and Billy Fury could command a star billing in 'A' pictures. True, pop impresario Jeffrey Kruger managed to assemble a collection of musical non-entities for the (ironically titled?) *Sweet Beat* (Ronnie Albert, 1959), a warning of the moral dangers awaiting ambi-tious pop singers. It was never likely to be a main attraction, but by 1962, the modestly budgeted,

Rock and romance: a trade advertisement for the original British 'teen-pic', *Rock You Sinners* (1957); and a press sheet for the romantic drama of post-war adjustment, *The Fool and the Princess* (1948)

seventy-three-minute *It's Trad Dad* (1962), with Helen Shapiro, Chubby Checker and other pop stars, could expect to transcend even co-feature status and head straight for the top of the bill. It helped, of course, to have the dynamic young director Dick Lester at the helm, and his efforts to weave the songs into a slight story won praise even from *Monthly Film Bulletin* for 'sheer zest and invention'.[50] From 1945 to 1965, there are no more than twenty-four musicals which could be described as 'B' movies in the usual time range of fifty to eighty minutes, and some of these played as co- or main features.[51] While Dick Lester and Sidney J. Fury put The Beatles and Cliff Richard at the top of the cinema bill, Douglas Hickox (1929–1988) laboured over thirty musical shorts and a handful of jazz/pop supporting features like *Four Hits and a Mister* (1963). Briefly, it must have seemed that the 'beat boom' might rescue the ailing 'B' film, but as musical tastes among the young began increasingly to fragment, putting music on screen became too risky a proposition.

Romance

This genre possibly depends for audience involvement on the presence of major stars of certifiable appeal, and such stars are not likely to be found working in low-budget films. Further, in the limited running time of the 'B' movie, it was important that attention was caught at once and that plot developments unfolded briskly: the rendering of romance is apt to be a more gradual process. Consequently, 'B' romances are few in number and, it has to be said, of no particular distinction. The main exception is William C. Hammond's *The Fool and the Princess* (1948). Produced by Frank Hoare and based on a story by Stephen Spender, *The Fool and the Princess* was described as the first 'supporting programme' film to be made by a documentary or specialised producing company. It had its origins in an initiative by Stafford Cripps, the President of the Board of Trade, who was concerned at the dearth of British entertainment films of five reels in length. As a consequence, Rank invited three producers to submit scripts. The Merton Park proposal was accepted for guaranteed Rank distribution. Unusually for a supporting feature, the film attracted the attention of the Fleet Street reviewers, who also admired it for its intelligence, naturalism and honesty.

It was a topical story of the disruption caused to an English suburban marriage by wartime experiences. In a rarely employed strategy, a woman is given access to the film's overt narrational voice, as she so memorably was in *Brief Encounter*, of which *The Fool and the Princess* is a briefer reminder. The voice belongs to Kate (Lesley Brook) whose marriage to Harry (Bruce Lester) is foundering as a result of his experiences while attached to a displaced person's camp in Germany. As Kate sits prosaically sewing, while Harry listens to music, the film slips into flashback as he recalls Maura (Adina Mandlova), the displaced 'Princess' whom he has helped and with whom he has fallen in love. He returns to Europe, reaches an understanding with Maura, who reveals that she is not a real princess. There is much high-flown dialogue about love and need and betrayal, the upshot of which is that, in the film's last scene, Kate receives a letter from Harry saying, 'This time darling I'm coming home because I want to'. Despite the stiffness of some of the lines and the acting, this is at least a 'B' film that attempts more than most. Its similarities to *Brief Encounter* are numerous, and spotting them becomes part of the film's appeal for cineastes.[52] As in Lean and Coward's film, the choice between a conventional suburbia and the wilder shores of love is finally reduced to the safe and the dutiful, quotidian demands suppressing more exigent emotions. On to this romantic structure is grafted an element of those adjustment-to-the-peace films,[53] contrasting a husband whose horizons have been widened by the experience of war and the climate of intellectual self-improvement promoted by the post-war government, with a wife whose world has been constrained by the privations of the home front. In reply to her husband's assertion that he has 'acquired a keener sense of value, a better appreciation of things', she poignantly retorts: 'But I've been at home coping with the baby, queues, ration books and all that Britain-can-take-it stuff.'

A. E. Wilson in *The Star* believed *The Fool and the Princess* represented 'a new approach to the making of British supporting features, an endeavour to provide pictures of adult interest at modest cost', and the *Daily Telegraph*'s reviewer also saw it as 'a refreshing attempt at originality, made inexpensively but not cheaply'. The *Daily Graphic*'s Elspeth Grant was unashamedly moved by the film, commenting: 'I think you will approve of this film – and I believe even Sir Stafford Cripps will applaud the economy and enterprise of Messrs Hoare and Hammond.'[54] *The Cinema* had also acknowledged its attempt at verisimilitude: 'we realise that here is a real problem, even though its solution is really left in the air'.[55] *Picture Show* praised it: as 'unpretentious but sincerely acted'.[56] *The Fool and the Princess* has enough going for it for one to wish it had been a little more ambitious, but it is still unusual enough at its level to be worth noting, both for itself and for its way of reflecting both the times of its production and more prestigious works in the contemporary cultural field.

As far as the other romances are concerned: Paul Dickson's *Star of My Night* (1954), strains to break out of the 'B' film formulas, but for the most part succeeds only in being rather arty and turgid. Its characters are essentially stereotypes: they include Michael (Griffith Jones), the cynical, moody artist; Iris (Pauline Olsen), the fragile ballerina with whom Michael's oldest friend Carl (Harold Lang) is in love; the worldly Eve (Kathleen Byron), Michael's former mistress; Eve's suave current lover, Arnold (Hugh Williams); and even a comic charlady. A competent cast struggles to breathe life into the plot which hinges on Michael's approaching blindness which leads him to pretend still to be in love with Eve so as to make Iris believe he is indifferent to her. And so on. It ends with the deception exposed and Iris committing herself to Michael, the willing fulfilment of Eve's bitchy but feminist-friendly accusation of him: 'You always did resent women who had a life of their own.' No more than any 'A' film of the time does it think of exploring such a notion; the line itself is typical of the promise the film sets up at various points then fails to develop. The film is often on the verge of full-blown melodrama (in a more elaborate *mise en scène* and with a lusher score than usual), then pulls back as if this were foreign to its pretensions.

Terence Fisher's *A Song for Tomorrow* (1948) has been noted as one of Rank's Highbury Bs. With its romantic plot complicated by amnesia, it has such cinematic forebears as *Random Harvest* (1942) and *Woman to Woman* (1929), and in its opera singer heroine's career-vs-love dilemma it recalls *The Red Shoes* (1948), released a month later. In its deliberate espousal of 'B' film-making procedures, it is very much a poor relation of the earlier films, indigent in matters of setting and scripting. Its hero Nick Wardell (Shaun Noble) recovers from an operation following war wounds and, now amnesiac, falls in love with Helen (Evelyn McCabe), the contralto whose singing is his only 'bridge to the past'. If the ending is somewhat unpredictable – Nick tells her backstage (between Acts of *Samson and Delilah*) that he is going back to his pre-amnesia fiancée whom we never see – this is largely because the threadbare screenplay offers no preparation for such a move. The film ends with Helen subduing her grief to sing 'Softly Awakes My Heart' on a very tatty Covent Garden set to a very skinny Samson in a leopard-skin cloth. Most of the acting by such Charm School enrollees as Noble (who had his brief moment in *Black Narcissus*, 1947) and Christopher Lee is stiffly uninvolving; and like most British 'B' films it is devoid of visual flair. And yet, it is not without a certain idiotic, ingenuous charm: it simply trusts its audience to recognise a post-war problem when it sees one and to be happy to listen to Evelyn McCabe singing well-loved arias. Reviewers were certainly charmed by her singing, but were largely unmoved by the drama and unimpressed by the 'economical setting', the 'amateurish' acting and the 'novelettish' script.[57]

Costume adventures and war films

If the musical and romantic drama are under-represented among post-war British 'B' films, some genres – particularly those which require more expensive production values to ensure suspension of disbelief – are hardly represented at all. Costume adventures are especially thin on the ground, perhaps surprisingly given the preponderance of historical series on television from the mid-1950s to the early 1960s. Robin Hood makes an appearance in a few colour but inexpensive 'A' films, but only Ernest Morris's *The Spanish Sword* (1962) utilised sets and costumes from the Danzigers' television productions. Ideologically, although the Robin Hood adventures generally managed to combine some radical politics with the ultimate submission to traditional authority, *The Spanish Sword* is more thoroughly conservative. Dealing with rebellion in the time of Henry III, it upholds royal authority against 'rough justice'.

The most ambitious venture into costume adventure, however, was mounted by Monarch when it explored previously unknown regions for the sixty-odd-minute picture with Brendan J. Stafford's *Men Against the Sun* (1953). This film was a naively approached adventure melodrama dealing with the building of a railway in Uganda in 1890. Although the picture employed regular 'B' actors John Bentley and Zena Marshall, it was filmed against authentic African backgrounds and displayed the sort of scenes of lion attacks and battles with Arab slave-traders more usually characteristic of expensive main

Rough justice: Ronald Howard and Nigel Green in *The Spanish Sword* (1962) realise what might happen to the actor in a Danzigers' film who requires too many takes

features. The suspicion must be that some cine-recycling may have taken place. In any case an 'artless and makeshift plot' and 'sketchy' continuity ensured that the film had little chance of fighting its way out of the supporting-feature jungle.[58]

If historical adventures were too expensive for most 'B' film budgets, one solution was to buy them in cheaply from the Commonwealth. Such imports (which counted as quota) included Randall C. Hayward's New Zealand-made *The Last Stand* (1949), an early sketch for depiction of the slaughter of plucky colonial natives later rendered in glorious colour in *Zulu* (1963). Here the year was 1863 and the victims of the sharp end of British steel were the 'misguided yet ever gallant Maoris'. The reviewer in *To-Day's Cinema* admired its historical fidelity and was particularly impressed by the 'hoards of authentic looking Maoris jabbering and gesticulating to the manner born.'[59]

War films, so significant in production at the 'A' level, are almost non-existent among the Bs, perhaps *not* surprisingly when one considers the logistics and expense of mounting combat sequences on screen. Among the handful of Bs are Max Varnel's *Silent Invasion* (1961, but not released until 1967), economically focused on German occupation of a French village rather than on lavishly staged battle scenes, and described by *Monthly Film Bulletin* as 'Glumly unconvincing wartime melodrama';[60] and Robert Lynn's *Blaze of Glory* (1963), criticised for its 'coincidence-ridden story' and for articulating its anti-war theme in 'vague, theatrical terms.'[61] Best of a small bunch is Ernest Morris's *The Court-Martial of Major Keller* (1961, released 1964), which works through a series of alternations between court-room scenes and military episodes leading up to the eponymous trial. It establishes more character interest and is more elaborately staged than one expects at this level, and the war footage, if not exactly evoking *Saving Private Ryan* (1998), is adequate to the occasion.[62]

Fantasy: horror

Until the mid- to late 1950s, there is no tradition of low-budget horror film-making in Britain of the kind that flourished in Hollywood at such studios as Universal and RKO. The British Board of Film Censors battled long and hard to prevent this particular menace infecting the studios of its homeland. While lurid horror was discouraged, the Board was prepared to allow the occasional excursion into the uncanny in the shapes of the traditional English ghost story and the old-dark-house chiller. These excursions were at their most frequent in the late 1940s when a vogue for spiritualism and the practical logistics of filming in country houses combined to facilitate the investigation of things that go bump in the night. In 1948 alone, examples range from the light-hearted *Colonel Bogey* to the creepier *Night Comes Too Soon* and *Escape from Broadmoor*. Hammer, the studio that would later become known for its gothic chillers, offered one or two early essays in the macabre, including the gaslight thriller *Room to Let* (1950), but mainly turned out crime films. Bona fide horror was left to a young, cash-strapped independent film-maker called Ivan Barnett (b. 1925). In 1947 he ambitiously began work on an adaptation of Poe's *The Fall of the House of Usher*, using a country house in Sussex. Three years later, the results of his labours finally earned one of the few 'H' certificates issued to British productions. The film, which gave a rare starring role to the otherwise perennial supporting actress Gwen Watford, suffered from budget inadequacies and directorial inexperience, but it still managed to capture an authentic gothic atmosphere and to evoke a few genuinely shocking thrills. It achieved a number of top-of-the-bill bookings, and its success with audiences, particularly in that graveyard for London-made supporting features, the North-West of England, pointed a possible direction for Hammer.[63] However, despite much critical disdain, especially from those writing for 'quality' papers and journals, Hammer's horror films were not designed for, nor consigned to, the bottom of the bill: for their predominantly younger audience, they were the essential attraction of the programmes on which they appeared.

The British horror films sponsored by Eros were usually released as co-features. They included the schlock horror of *The Trollenberg Terror* (1958), a spin-off from a television serial, and the entertainingly absurd *The Man Without a Body* and *Womaneater* (both 1957). *Cat Girl* (1957), released with *The Amazing Colossal Man* and billed as 'Breathtaking in Their Tremendous Power', was the best of them. Although owing a considerable debt to Jacques Tourneur's RKO chillers of the 1940s, Alfred Shaughnessy's film was a genuine contribution to British gothic cinema, with memorable atmospherics and what *The Daily Cinema* called a 'blood-curdling' central performance by Barbara Shelley as the feline eponym.[64] 'A hectic amalgam of savagery and sex', was how *Kinematograph Weekly* summed it up,[65] and that was exactly what the film's American backers, AIP, were looking for, as Shaughnessy explained:

> *Cat Girl* was made in 1957 when the new X-certificate was enabling the makers of what were even then known as 'exploitation' films to combine the ingredients of erotic sex and violent horror in the same picture. My brief was to achieve just this. However, there was still a limit beyond which the censor would not allow a director to go on both counts ... So we used to shoot both a British and a Continental version of all naughty scenes.[66]

Students without a cause: the teenage trio register shock at the sight of *The Headless Ghost* (1959)

Cat Girl received little critical attention at the time, but was later championed by David Pirie in his pioneering early 1970s study *A Heritage of Horror*.[67] More recently, Charles Barr has acknowledged the film's 'eerily sexy qualities',[68] and the eroticism of Shelly's performance, unusual for its period, has assured it a permanent niche in the history of British horror cinema.

As for the ghost stories that continued into the early 1960s, Peter Graham Scott, can make nothing of the inanities of *The Headless Ghost* (1959). Shot in 'Scope' and geared to the sensibilities of the American drive-in circuit, it has three college students, led by Richard Lyon as the 'humourist' of the trio, spend a night in a haunted castle and help the titular ghost to be reunited with his head. Like Scott's other films, this moves along quite smartly, but this time there is virtually nothing worth moving. Clive Revill provides a touch of campy style as the ghost of the fourth Earl who steps down from his portrait, the special effects are simple but adequate, but the overall impression is one of meagre inventiveness and the unlikeable young leads suffer from a terribly damaging echo of the Dean-Wood-Mineo trio in *Rebel Without a Cause* (1955). The essays in the uncanny by Vernon Sewell are rather more impressive. The final moment of *House of Mystery*, when the storyteller and protagonist (Jane Hylton) fades from sight, has absolutely the mysterious quality the film has hinted at and makes one feel that the special effects of huge-budgeted Hollywood films, so bent on dazzling us, miss the mark by sheer extravagance and overkill. Sewell, not without reason, thought 'The ending was sensational – the audience was absolutely stunned.'[69] Actually, though it has more style and a more convincingly pervasive sense of the inexplicable, *House of Mystery* offers a dry-land parallel to Sewell's maritime fantasy *Ghost Ship* made nine years earlier. Both involve young couples ready to make purchases – of, respectively, a house and a ship – and in each case they find that the object of their proposed ownership has a sinister reputation. The rationality of the young couples (Nanette Newman and Maurice Kaufmann in *House of Mystery*, Dermot Walsh and Hazel Court in *Ghost Ship*) is brought to the point where it must accept the idea of an otherness at odds with everyday reality. In each film there is a medium (Mignon O'Doherty, in the earlier film, Molly Urquhart in the later) who proves influential in helping them to get at the truth and who is presented with a surprising lack of patronage. The mystery in each case has to do with a passionate triangle which has led to murder and to the interment of one or more bodies. Further, in narrational terms, there is the parallel of much of the 'inner' story's being told in flashback by the medium, so that the principal couples offer no more than a frame for the central mystery to be revealed, their own relationship being in no sense affected by the past events. And in *House of Mystery*, indeed, the main character interest is focused on Stella who not only tells the frame story of the young couple but also the story-within-the-story of which she is the female protagonist. *House of Mystery* benefits from superior performances, especially from Jane Hylton, who suggests quite potently the strangeness of the woman from the very beginning, and from the camerawork in which close-up imbues ordinary objects such as lamps with mystery. *Ghost Ship* has some narrative clumsiness, some awkwardly obvious editing and some amateurish scenes and performances, but also some touches of plain, unpretentious and sometimes imaginative film-making. There is more evidence of efficiency and imagination in Sewell's unusual uncanny crime film *The Man in the Back Seat* (1961).

Fantasy: science fiction

In American cinema of the 1950s, science fiction is the quintessential genre of the 'B' film. Stuffed with concealed Cold War paranoia, these audacious pulp programmers are valued for their idiotic plots and crude special effects. Happily, British low-budget production could boast a handful of pictures to rival the most gloriously absurd examples of Hollywood paracinema. The Danzigers' *Devil Girl from Mars* (1954) has all the lovable characteristics associated with the Hollywood science fiction 'B' picture. Piloted to Earth with tongue pressed firmly in cheek by the experienced David Macdonald, it has all the kitschy bizarreness that any devotee of cult strangeness could require. The *Monthly Film Bulletin* reviewer was certainly captivated by its 'charm' when commenting: 'There is really no fault in this film that one would like to see eliminated. Everything, in its way, is quite perfect.'[70] Patricia Laffan is at her imperious best as Nyah, a Martian woman who arrives at a Scottish inn to abduct healthy specimens of native manhood for her planet's sexual regeneration programme. Clad as a dominatrix in leather cap, cloak and stiletto boots, she is a genuinely shocking figure in the staid world of British film-making of the time: it is as if the underworld of S&M fetishism had suddenly surfaced, and with it the collective unconscious of the nation. Backed by the mechanised might of her faithful robot (resembling a fridge on legs) she imparts a sexual charge that the film's scenario struggles to contain, and gives a wholly different spin to the desire expressed by another of the inn's visitors, the prodigal metropolitan model played by Hazel Court, to 'spend more time in the country, find the right man, have children'. Nyah is an eroticised threat to a patriarchy that was increasingly troubled in the post-war years. She comes to turn the proud men of Earth into sex slaves for her matriarchal order, the result, apparently, of a bitter gender war over 'many of your Earth years'. She is thus a contradictorily coded warning (sexy and scary) of the consequences of allowing women's emancipation to go 'too far'. *Devil Girl from Mars* is, therefore, not only a camp classic but an ideologically

A 'B' film in spirit only: Patricia Laffan and her faithful robot round up some virile males in the camp classic *Devil Girl from Mars* (1954)

significant moment in 1950s British cinema.[71] One would dearly like to claim it for the pantheon of British Bs, but, unfortunately, it is a 'B' film only in spirit: it was never intended as a supporting feature, or even as one half of a double bill, despite its modest running time of only seventy-six minutes. It opened at the Metropole, Victoria on 2 May 1954, and at the Odeon, Tottenham Court Road, on the 10th. It was described in the trade press as 'the first major outer space film to be made in this country, and the trade reviewers treated it with due seriousness, praising not only its maintenance of suspense, but also its 'convincing' technical qualities (convincing?).[72] It is, however, one of the earliest examples of British exploitation-film making, a mode to which the 'B' film is historically and aesthetically linked.

Nevertheless, there are other films featuring visitors from outer space that did play as second or co-features. Eros's *Stranger from Venus* (1954) was more likely to play as a supporting feature, but was certainly less entertaining, even though it could boast the presence of Patricia Neal, who had recently starred in one of the classics of science-fiction film, *The Day the Earth Stood Still* (1951). The Venusian *Stranger* offered a similar grim warning to mankind to curb its atomic experiments, but director Burt Balaban failed to extract any excitement from what was a pretty dreary script. However, *To-Day's Cinema* was surprisingly appreciative of Balaban's 'concise direction' and attempts to generate suspense, as well as the film's mixing of fantasy and realism.[73] *Kinematograph Weekly* was nearer the mark with its judgment that the picture failed to compete technically with the 'slap-up, stream-lined American coloured pseudo-scientific jobs': 'Grounded by dialogue, its story of flying saucers' was 'too wordy for the industrial element and too far-fetched for the intelligentsia'.[74] As exhibitors, Eros had spotted the popularity of American sci-fi films with audiences, and had decided to encour-age the production of British contributions to the genre. Their next effort was another story of extra-terrestrial visitation, Gilbert Gunn's *The Strange World of Planet X* (1956). As usual, the alien (prosaically named Smith) is on a mission to save the world from the arrogant pretensions of science in the service of the military, and much of the action again centred round a pub. The film's class-B special effects did manage a flying saucer and a mutant spider, with French import Gaby André tan-gled in its giant web, but the picture hardly lived up to the publicity hype: 'Unknown Terror from Outer Space! Giant Insects Threaten the World! Deadly Rays Turned Men into Maniacs! Science Fiction's Greatest Thrill!'[75] The strangest world revealed here was that of British social life and gender relations.

Inter-planetary miscegenation is very much in the offing in the amazingly ridiculous *Fire Maidens from Outer Space* (1956), another Eros essay in cult badness.[76] In this cod-Freudian space opera from American director Cy Roth a spacecraft carrying five scientists lands on the thirteenth moon of Jupiter, which is terrorised by a monster, and where a lot of nubile young women (clad in what look like gym tunics from ancient Greece and conveniently speaking English) are presided over by an aged patriarch (Owen Barry). The maidens, the last of their race, perform a modest bump-and-grind to the strains of 'Stranger in Paradise', and the thirteenth moon looks suspiciously like the Home Counties. The serpent in this paradise is 'The Creature', a monster of the id, half-man, half-beast, who embodies the lustful desires of the astronauts. By killing the patriarch, The Creature releases the libidos of the spacemen and of the fire maidens, who proceed to establish their own matriarchy. The monster is indescribably tatty, the space travel does not even reach comic-book realisation; and the dialogue provides a delirious mix of banality and portentousness: 'It was foretold in the sands of time that we should meet,' says leading fire maiden Hestia (Susan Shaw) to 'top nuclear scientist' Luther Blair (Anthony Dexter). It is tempting but unnecessary to quote more. Shot in ten days for $120,000, this exercise in male wish-fulfilment was released as a co-feature package with *Superman Flies Again*, and dubbed 'The Double-bill with the Fantastic Thrill'. *To-Day's Cinema* viewed the whole proceed-ings with an indulgent eye, appreciating its tongue-in-cheek direction: 'Audiences will doubtless gargle down the technical bait, goggle at the girls and giggle at the meandering Neanderthal.' It was thought suitable for 'cloth-cap districts'.[77]

In comparison to the juvenile pulp released by Eros, Hammer's early forays into science fiction look positively sophisticated. While Terence Fisher's *Stolen Face* (1952) gives a technological make-over to the Pygmalion myth, adding fears about class mobility to its fears about female independence, *Four-Sided Triangle* reconfigures the *Frankenstein* fable as an erotic troika. Based on a book by William F. Temple, the film warns against men's attempts to employ science to flout the God-given laws of biology. Less overtly, the film associates the blasphemies of science and gender transgression with the effects of Americanisation. Lena, played by the notoriously promiscuous Hollywood actress Barbara Payton, is the love object of Bill (Stephen Murray) and Robin (John Van Eyssen), two scien-tific prodigies. When Robin finally wins her, Bill decides to adapt a machine designed to 'transform the world into a place of peace and plenty' to replicate Lena for his own use. The cloned Lena's body becomes Bill's to possess, but her romantic thoughts continue to be of Robin, and she is killed in the attempt to empty her mind of past attachments. Ultimately it is Lena's excessive desirability, enhanced by a visit to the USA, that perverts scientific altruism, and which resists all attempts at masculine control.[78] Hammer had a bash at putting some Brits (and Eva Bartok) into orbit in Fisher's *Spaceways* (1953), but the success of Val Guest's *Quatermass* pictures quickly raised Hammer's sci-fi aspirations, and their subsequent films in the genre aimed higher on the bill than a supporting role. *X The Unknown* (1956), for instance, was released as a co-feature with *Les Diaboliques*, although the *Monthly Film Bulletin* feared that 'enthusiasts may find [it] … rather tame when compared with' *The Quatermass Experiment*.[79]

Anglo-Amalgamated generally stayed Earth-bound, but they did acquire the rights to two works by sci-fi writer Charles Eric Maine. Montgomery Tully's co-feature *Escapement* (1957) was a fairly conventional murder thriller with a few exotic trappings: a French Riviera setting and a mysterious clinic which experiments with hypnosis. The publicity cranked up the film's qualities of bizarreness: 'Strange and Fantastic Murder in a World of Dreams!' Executive producer, Richard Gordon, recalled that Nat Cohen and Stuart Levy were never really committed to the sci-fi genre:

Nat and Stuart did not see the picture this way but rather as another thriller … with two leading roles (hero/heroine), once again to be played by American artists. For this purpose, I was able to sign Rod

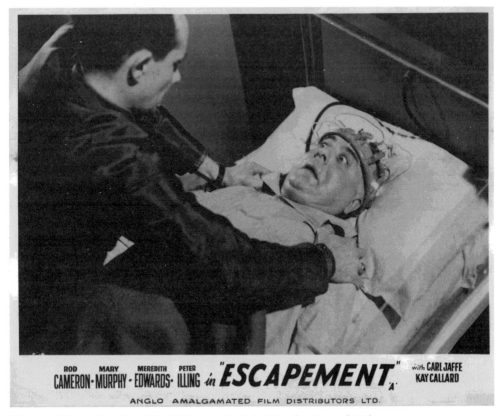

'Strange and Fantastic Murder in a World of Dreams!': inside the clinic of *Escapement* (1957)

Cameron and Mary Murphy. The screenplay was written by Maine to Nat and Stuart's specifications and the film was released in England under the original title. Unfortunately, it failed at the box office because it was not good enough as a thriller and certainly did not qualify as a horror or science fiction. In order to try and salvage it in the United States, we re-edited the film after considering – and rejecting – the idea of re-shooting the dream sequences which would have been too costly.[80]

By retitling the film *The Electronic Monster*, Gordon was able to sell it to Columbia for distribution in America as a co-feature with *Womaneater*. Ken Hughes directed the second Maine adaptation, *Timeslip* (1956, USA: *The Atomic Man*), about a man whose 'radio-active brain' enables him see seven seconds into the future. The leading actors were again American, Gene Nelson and Faith Domergue, but, at ninety-one minutes, it seems likely to have been intended as a first feature.

Realist drama

What might be thought of as realist drama fares rather better at the 'B' level: low in incidence, its exemplars tend to draw on some of the characteristic strengths of British film-making at the main-feature level. They focus on small-scale but humanly significant situations; their central plotting is bolstered by the neatly observed verisimilitude of their representation of daily life. In the early post-war years, they are also inspired by the more radical approach to the depiction of ordinary lives then being explored in Italian cinema. But, although critics were generally respectful or enthusiastic, exhibitors were often sceptical of the virtues of adopting films without conventional entertainment values for the purpose of programme-building.

Exhibitors had little stomach for screening the work of the Free Cinema movement, which might have revitalised some of their more tired and predictable programmes. Most of the movement's films had to rely on NFT screenings, although a few were trade-shown. Lorenza Mazzatti's BFI-financed *Together* (1956), an atmospheric examination of friendship and disability in London's East End, was judged by *To-Day's Cinema* an 'Interesting avant-garde piece of film-making that will undoubtedly attract serious students of the cinema.'[81] However, bookers were deterred by its lack of dialogue and downbeat tone. Similarly, Lindsay Anderson's celebrated Ford-sponsored portrait of Covent Garden market, *Every Day Except Christmas* (1957), was praised for its photography, but criticised on the grounds of repetition and length, which, at forty minutes, broke the conventions for the commercial short film.[82] The only Free Cinema picture that *The Daily Cinema* was prepared to endorse as 'a welcome programme-builder' was Karel Reisz's *We Are the Lambeth Boys* (1959), although it was recommended primarily for 'sophisticated audiences who are most likely to appreciate the issues involved.'[83]

In times of product shortage, Eros, a distributor usually committed to stars and genres, was prepared to pick up an occasional social realist film like Herbert Marshall and Fredda Brilliant's *Tinker* (1949), an examination of a boy's induction into the fraternity of colliers. Commissioned by the new National Coal Board, the film had caused a stir at the Edinburgh Film Festival. It was shot in the Durham mining village of Easington – later the setting for *Billy Elliot* (2000) and the final scenes of *Get Carter* (1971) – and had used local children for its cast. Remarkably, the climax of the film directly anticipates that of *Get Carter* with the bullied Tinker (Derek Smith) carried out to sea on the trolley system used to dump colliery waste that also conveys the body of Carter's last victim (Ian Hendry) to its resting place.

Two young Australians – actor Don Sharp and documentary-maker Frank Worth – were responsible for Pathé's *Ha'penny Breeze* (1950), the story of the post-war regeneration of an east-coast fishing village which was shot over twelve weeks on location at Pinmill near Ipswich, where the third partner in Storytellers Productions, actor Darcy Conyers, owned a yacht. Billed as 'The *different* film of the year!', it was shot in factual locations, including barge interiors, pubs, boat sheds and village shops, and starred Sharp, Gwyneth Vaughn (who had appeared in the Welsh neo-realist drama *Blue Scar*) and Edwin Richfield. Their performances were accompanied by folk tunes played on an antique concertina.[84] The film cost just £8,000, mostly raised from a Leeds auctioneer, and its publicists were happy to describe it as 'entertainment on a shoe string', emphasising that it employed the 'methods of Italian film production'.[85] So, too, did Anthony Mavrogordato's *Born of the Sea* (1949). This fable of fishing in Cornwall suggested that what the ocean gives up (in this case, a baby boy), it will eventually take back (the boy grown up). We might easily relate the picture's use of members of a remote fishing community as actors to its Italian neo-realist contemporary *La Terra Trema* (1949), but, in truth, the earth failed to move for its reviewers. To them, its artless silent footage overlaid with commentary simply seemed a throwback to a less sophisticated era of cinema.[86]

The realist films made by Philip Leacock, on the other hand, were more accomplished, if hardly more commercial. He made two docu-dramas for the Crown Film Unit, *Out of True* and *Life in Her Hands* and the jewel in the Group 3 crown *The Brave Don't Cry* (all 1951). All three of these attest to Leacock's training in documentary before the war and with the Army Kinematograph Unit during the war. In *Life in Her Hands*, made to encourage recruitment to the nursing profession, Kathleen Byron played a young widow who, tormented by the unfounded thought that she might have been responsible for her husband's car crash, becomes a nurse as a means of atonement and discovers her vocation. In showmanlike fashion, the film was marketed as 'A Great Film of a Great Profession: Dramatic – Powerful – True', but the trade was cautious: 'The hospital detail is authentic', commented *Kinematograph Weekly*, 'but who wants to see a close-up of a caesarean operation? Least of all the expectant mother.'[87] *Out of True* was also made, at the Government's behest, 'as an answer to *The Snake Pit* ... to allay people's fears about [mental hospitals]'.[88] Jane Hylton convincingly portrayed a working-class wife driven past breaking point, but the film's theme made it a tricky proposition as a curtain-raiser. *The Brave Don't Cry* (at ninety minutes, probably intended as a first feature) records without false dramatics or sentimentality the processes of rescue in a Scottish coal-mining disaster. In all three cases, Leacock was interested in avoiding the more obvious neatness of narrative patterning in favour of exploiting the realism of actual settings and, in some cases, of supplementing actors with non-professionals. Subsequently Leacock graduated to such popular 'A' productions as *The Kidnappers* (1953) and *The Spanish Gardener* (1956).

In a similar vein, it is worth mentioning Clive Donner's more sentimental *Heart of a Child*, made for Rank and picturesquely set in the Tyrol in 1918. Jean Anderson plays a spinster who rekindles an old romance with a vet in the process of helping a small boy to save his dog from his brutal father (Donald Pleasence) who plans to sell the dog to the local butcher during the wartime meat shortage. Though the film has many of the elements of routine boy-and-his-dog films, Donner directs on location with a briskness and visual imaginativeness not common in British 'B' films and one wishes its budget might have run to Technicolor. If one can understand the scarcity of 'B' films in those genres which cry out for more lavish production values, it *is* surprising that more use was not made of the low-key attractiveness of this realist vein, drawing on the extraordinary wealth of character players, who were the staple of the English repertory of the period, and making enjoyable use of real locations.

Whatever the genre though, the films suffer from meagre budgets, the latter only rarely acting to catalyse the film-makers' imaginative resources as it seems to have done with, say, Edgar Ulmer. The pleasures of American 'B' films are most commonly to be found in their energy and in the ways that they will subvert the prevailing dominant ideology to suggest darker possibilities and dangers for nice young couples and families (see Anthony Mann's *Desperate*, 1947, and *Raw Deal*, 1948, or Ulmer's *The Naked Dawn*, 1956). They are seriously alert to urban corruption or rural poverty or the boredom of the road, as the case may be. It is harder to make such a case for the British 'B' film. Instead, almost invariably staying within the middle-class ideological parameters of the period without submitting them to much scrutiny, it offers a revealing barometer of what was conceived of as normality. One is usually obliged to search deeper below the surface of these texts to discover the suppressed desires and fantasies that they can barely acknowledge, let alone endorse. This only really begins to change in the final years of the Bs, with the loosening of censorship in response to declining cinema attendances and a liberal turn in social mores.

Never the subject of serious critical discourse at the time (or since), these films were not encouraged to be anything more ambitious than they were. The 'B' movie scenario is virtually never mediated by creative idiosyncrasy, let alone iconoclasm. On the rare occasions this did happen, there was much scratching of heads. In October 1954, Film Traders offered exhibitors what would now be considered an 'art film', in spite of the presence in the cast of the popular husband-and-wife team of John LeMesurier and Hattie Jacques. *The Pleasure Garden* was an off-beat critique of social repression set in the grounds of Alexandra Palace and directed by James Broughton. The film's cavalier approach to the conventions of commercial second features left the trade reviewers nonplussed. 'Amateurish and somewhat precious' with a cast 'overwhelmingly untalented as ... pantomimists' was the verdict of *To-Day's Cinema*, 'direction too pretentious and heavily underlined to free symbolism from plain whimsy'. All in all, like any film that challenged audiences' expectations of their curtain-raisers, it was a 'doubtful proposition'.[89]

6 The Men from the Yard

And it just goes to show that crime does not pay.

Narrator ex-Detective Inspector Tom Fallon, *Stryker of the Yard*, 1953

If there was one perennial theme in the post-war 'B' film, it was the activities of Scotland Yard. Moreover, the criminal investigation was the common denominator that opened up a second, and economically crucial, market for the second-feature producer, and allowed the development of a dual-purpose product for cinema and television. As far as the 'B' film was concerned, this double market lasted for a dozen years or so, from the early 1950s to the early 1960s, although it would, of course, endure for much longer for film-makers as a whole.

Police stories had been a staple of English popular culture since the establishment of the Metropolitan Police in 1829. A century later the 'Big Four' detective superintendents at Scotland Yard had become household names, thanks to a constantly inquisitive newspaper press and a growing vogue for police memoirs. Although the newsreels periodically took an interest in current cases, contemporary crime-fighting was largely absent from cinema screens in the 1930s, thanks to the British Board of Film Censors (BBFC) which prohibited the fictional representation of actual crimes and criminals. The vigilant attention of the BBFC meant that few pre-war films attempted to tackle the realities of criminal activity or policing. Crime stories were only acceptable as morality plays in which audiences were shielded from the more sordid aspects of the tales. However, the wedding of documentary techniques to storytelling, encouraged during World War II, opened new possibilities for the crime narrative. Ronald Haines' British Foundation Pictures spent most of the war making informational shorts, but as peace approached, Haines turned his attention to criminal matters. His attempt at making a full-length second feature based on a story by Roland Daniel – *The Man with Magnetic Eyes* (1945) – was a dismally dated depiction of the tracking down of a crudely disguised criminal mastermind, who, in violation of genre convention, turns out to be a character previously unknown to the audience. Of greater significance, however, were the shorts and featurettes which Haines made in 1943–4. These began with the *What Price Crime?* series of shorts: crudely produced and plotted CID investigations into *The Soho Murders*, *The Safe Blower* and the *Murder in Mayfair* (all 1943). They continued with the *Quiz Crime* series of potted murder mysteries, and culminated in an attempt to launch a series of featurettes based on George Goodchild's detective, MacLean. His initial adventure was a formulaic English detective story concerning the theft of jewels,[1] but its title, *The Man from Scotland Yard* (1944), anticipated the scores of police investigation dramas that would form the backbone of the supporting programme in the 1950s.

With the end of the war, the escalating figures for indictable offences gave a new urgency to the post-war battle against crime. The second of Rank's popular *This Modern Age* series, definitively titled *Scotland Yard* (1946), was part of the Metropolitan Police's public relations offensive, detailing the steps being taken to combat the spread of criminality:

> Throughout the world, the police are faced with the crime wave that follows war. The Commissioner of Police, Sir Harold Scott, refers to unsettled conditions, scarcity of goods, the black market and the under-the-counter deals, which are all leading to major crimes. All countries recognise Scotland Yard as crime-fighting machine number one. This is the authentic story of The Yard at work ... The film shows accurately how the various sections of Scotland Yard are brought in on a murder, how they go over the scene of the crime, check and re-check evidence, using the latest methods of science, and how the whole vast machine is employed against the individual criminal. [2]

The Yard's drive to win the hearts and minds of post-war society and to fill the vacancies in its own ranks would climax with Basil Dearden's *The Blue Lamp*, the biggest domestic hit of 1950, but it was preceded by Paul Barralet's *The Girl From Scotland Yard* (1948), which followed the career of a woman police officer in what was a full-blown recruiting poster for the Metropolitan Police.[3] *Kinematograph Weekly* appreciated its 'authentic detail' and recommended it as a 'fascinating, exciting and unusual subject'.[4]

This cinematic celebration of the Metropolitan Police provided the context and set the tone for the first films with the dual purpose of television and cinema screenings. In the autumn of 1949, while *The Blue Lamp* was awaiting release, Parthian, bankrolled by the National Film Finance Corporation, began production of dual-purpose pictures at Carlton Hill and Viking Studios and shortly after at the small Windsor Studios on London's Cursitor Street. The producer was John Austin, a former Chief of Indian Information films, and the basic unit of production was a twenty-six-minute programme for American television. The aim was then to package two or three of these together for the British second-feature market. The first film, *Too Sweet* (1950), was completed for less than £2,000 in five days in the studio with additional footage shot at London airport.[5] Early in 1951, International Distributors released Parthian's *Files from Scotland Yard*, combining three television stories. Made on a minimal budget and shot in a stilted and largely uninspired fashion by director Anthony Squire, these stories were deemed passable for the small independent exhibitor. *The Cinema* commented: 'What is all right for TV does not always make good cinema.'[6] In fact, these tales, dealing with murder, breach of promise and bigamy and starring Reginald Purdell as a Chief Inspector, did not even make good TV: Parthian was wound up in July after its films proved unsaleable in the USA because of characters' excessively English accents and a general failure to adapt the programmes to the taste of the American market. The NFFC was left to write off most of its £50,000 loan. However, although the series proved an early set-back for British ambitions to produce for the transatlantic television market, for the cinema it pointed the way to what would become the decade's most successful supporting feature genre: the case-file police procedural.

Small distributors, such as Grand National, Archway, Ambassador and New Realm, also became interested in the dual-purpose idea, without hitting on a winning formula. In 1951, Grand National attempted to launch a series of Sherlock Holmes featurettes. *The Man With the Twisted Lip* (1951) was unpretentiously directed by Richard M. Gray and starred John Longden in the deerstalker hat.

Watson was played by Campbell Singer, and Holmes' antagonists were a gang of ruthless dope smugglers. However, critics (and probably audiences) had seen quite enough of Holmes over the previous two decades and were looking for fresher and more contemporary thriller entertainment. Archway offered theatrical distribution to *The Wallet* (1952), an episodic thriller produced and directed by Morton M. Lewis and starring John Longden and Chili Bouchier. It was designed by writer Ted Willis to be divided into three parts for American television, and *Kinematograph Weekly*'s Josh Billings praised it as a 'quart in a pint pot'.[7] Gilbert Church's production unit at Bushey experimented with a series of short films featuring the venerable barnstormer Tod Slaughter as arch criminal Terence Riley, pitted against Morley of the Yard (Patrick Barr). These had future television sales in mind, but were gathered into two anthologies for cinema release: *King of the Underworld* and *Murder at Scotland Yard* (both 1952).[8] Few bookers expressed much interest in such old-fashioned fare. E. J. Fancey developed a light-hearted detective series around John Laurie as a meek Scotland Yard clerk named Edward Potter, but it ran to only three episodes.[9] Moreover, the influence of television on British 'B' film scenarios was further extended by the shift from adapting radio drama to transposing BBC television productions. Both *The Broken Horseshoe* and *Operation Diplomat* (both 1953) were adaptations of television serials and Group 3's whimsical fantasy *The Angel Who Pawned Her Harp* (1954) began life as a TV play.[10]

It must have seemed relatively straightforward to link together two or three short stories into a feature film. There had been a vogue for anthology films of this type in the post-war period, notably those based on Somerset Maugham stories.[11] However, this format would prove to be more difficult to accomplish successfully at the 'B' film level. Furthermore, production for US television, which began in earnest in British studios in 1952–3, required a detailed knowledge of American cultures and industrial practices, so native practitioners were generally better equipped to make these films than their British counterparts. Thus, the three initially successful producers of dual-purpose films were all American: the Danziger brothers, Douglas Fairbanks Jr and Hannah Weinstein, although the last named quickly abandoned attempts at theatrical distribution and concentrated on television programmes.

The Danzigers Call in The Yard

Television was initially conceived by the Danzigers as a secondary market. The thirteen featurettes they made at Riverside in 1953 were designed primarily as a series of supporting features that might then be sold to television on both sides of the Atlantic. The first fruit of their labours was the anthology *Gilbert Harding Speaking of Murder* (1953), directed by Paul Dickson and distributed by Paramount as the support for its Charlton Heston Western *Pony Express* (1953). The notoriously grumpy and outspoken BBC celebrity, Harding, was used to link and commentate on three fanciful stories of murder, two of which had theatrical backgrounds – one involving a Shakespearean actor and the other a dramatist (Hubert Gregg) who, in anticipation of *Theatre of Blood* (1974), takes revenge on a critic (Laurence Naismith). The short stories were from writers such as Paul Tabori and James Eastwood (friends who had begun their writing careers with a co-authored history book), and *To-Day's Cinema* thought the compilation an 'agreeable dramatic novelty, assured of wide popular appeal', and it was prominently advertised in the trade press with the tagline: 'Dramatic Star Value + Dramatic Production Value = Dramatic Box-Office Value!'[12] Another trio was packaged as *A Tale of Three Women* (1954), again introduced by Gilbert Harding. Two were murder stories and one a

Calling Scotland Yard: Alan Wheatley stars in Paul Dickson's *The Javanese Dagger* (1953), an early entry in the Danzigers' dual-purpose film and television series

comedy, and the three women were Hazel Court, Gene Anderson and Patricia Owens. However, the chief interest of the compilation is a fourth woman, Thelma Connell, who received a co-director credit with Paul Dickson. She was almost the only woman to be given a directing opportunity in the post-war 'B' film. The Danzigers' police stories were also given theatrical release in America as single featurettes and subsequent screening on the NBC network as the *Calling Scotland Yard* series. However, Gilbert Harding was considered unsuitable for American audiences and was replaced as narrator by Paul Douglas.

For their second series, the brothers hired a narrator acceptable to both US and UK audiences, the Australian Ron Randell. It is not clear if *The Vise* (filmed 1954–5), made up of playlets concerning people trapped in desperate situations, was ever intended for screening in American cinemas, or to go straight to television. In Britain, though, the episodes were either released singly as shorts, or packaged for cinema exhibition, distributed mainly by Republic. Most were directed by David Macdonald, including the double dose of macabre criminality released as *The Yellow Robe* (1954). Clifford Evans and Honor Blackman starred in the superior second story, a satire on business competition. A trio directed by David Macdonald was boxed-up as *Three-Cornered Fate* (1955), to the derision of the critics. Indifferent direction and 'banal dialogue' resulted in a picture that was 'crummy, to put it mildly'.[13] The trio was accompanied by a duet of thrillers, *The Final Column* (1955), with casts that included Sandra Dorne and Christopher Lee, but equally novelettish scripts and direction lacking in 'finesse'.[14] They were sheepishly followed by a pair of double-barrelled crime thrillers under the titles *The Count of Twelve* and *One Just Man* (both 1955). The former, directed by Paul Dickson (as Paul Gerrard), was counted out by the critics, floored by 'uneven acting and direction, to say nothing of cramped staging'.[15] The latter, from David Macdonald, was marginally better received; with praise for Alexander Knox's performance as a hanging judge and even some congratulations for Macdonald for 'the vigour he brings to [a] weak story'.[16] Overall, though, *Kinematograph Weekly* thought that 'few will be thrilled'.[17] Generally, the single shorts – *Diplomatic Error* (1955), *The Very Silent Traveller* (1954), *Murder of a Ham* (1955) and *Death Walks by Night* (1955) (all directed by David Macdonald) and *Stranglehold* (1963, directed by Ernest Morris) fared better. With fewer pretensions as far as programme-building was concerned, and some attractive star names leading the casts (Dennis Price and Linden Travers, for example) these single releases were given a rather easier ride by the trade reviewers. The Danzigers must have come to understand, however, that dual-purpose production across the cultural divide that separated Britain and America was impractical. Henceforth, they produced either for television or for the supporting-feature market, recycling scripts, actors and sets at New Elstree as appropriate.

Colonel March

Hannah Weinstein (1911–1984) was another of the producers who began to operate at the interface between cinema and television, but quickly opted to concentrate on the small screen. Weinstein, who would later have enormous success producing hit television series such as *Robin Hood*, was a left-wing journalist and publicist who had left America to avoid McCarthyite persecution. Her production company found a berth at Southall Studios – then the home of Group 3, which was sympathetic to Weinstein's politics – and provided a safe haven for a number of fellow exiles and blacklisted writers operating from the USA. In the winter of 1952–3, Weinstein secured the services of Boris Karloff to star in a series based on the character of Colonel March, a partly psychic sleuth who had appeared in John Dickson Carr's *The Department of Queer Complaints*. The writing of the politically conservative Carr was hardly fertile ground for Weinstein's band of displaced radicals, but blacklisted screenwriters like Walter Bernstein and Abraham Polonsky did what they could with it.[18] Three pilot episodes for *Colonel March of Scotland Yard*, which would become the first British-made crime series to be shown on the new Independent Television in 1955, were entrusted to the direction of the talented McCarthy refugee Cy Endfield. They were combined into the anthology film *Colonel March Investigates* (1953), but the trade reaction was not overly encouraging. *To-Day's Cinema* halfheartedly recommended it as an 'acceptable novelty for popular halls'.[19] The subsequent decision not to offer any of the further twenty-three episodes for theatrical distribution, though, was probably influenced by the response to the offerings of fellow American dual-purpose producer, Douglas Fairbanks Jr.

Douglas Fairbanks

Production for American television went largely unreported in the trade press, both because sponsors and potential customers in the USA would not want their programmes thought of as 'B' films and because British distributors would not want their films thought of as cheap television shows. In the wake of the Parthian fiasco, the film trade was, in any case, suspicious. As Willy Williamson, the Studio Correspondent of *To-Day's Cinema* put it:

[S]ome of the TV stuff when seen on cinema screens reveals a hardness in its photography and often a lack of quality in its general production values that is likely to add fuel to the fire of criticism already being heaped by exhibitors on some of the films they are expected to accept to make up their supporting programme quota. The budgets of most of the producers of featurettes do not allow for such an expensive item as publicity but the idea that none is called for may prove to be a little short-sighted – particularly if such films have to combat this kind of TV stigma ... if they are to be made down to a level that is suitable for TV then we don't want to see them on British cinema screens at all.[20]

Douglas Fairbanks had just reopened the National Studios at Borehamwood for dual-purpose production under the direction of Harold Huth. The unit appears to have appreciated the wisdom of Williamson's remarks and, after the release of its first compilation of two stories, *The Accused* (1953, directed by Lawrence Huntington and Charles Saunders), invited him to pay a visit. The ploy worked. Having watched a day's shooting on one of the five-day productions, talked to its stars, James Hayter and Wilfred Hyde-White, and viewed a completed twenty-four-minute film directed by Lawrence Huntington, he concluded:

[T]hey were demonstrating that good results could be achieved working at a very high speed with minimum expenditure (under existing labour conditions) in a first class studio, without skimping sets but without demanding costly effects. I decided that here was scope for testing new talent, for developing it until such time as it was ripe for stardom in major product. And, in view of the fact that these films will be seen by millions in America here is the very thing to develop their appreciation of British talent and get them familiarised with many of our artistes.[21]

A couple of months later, British Lion duly unveiled the second of the Douglas Fairbanks' anthologies, *The Triangle* (1953). Its three stories could boast the directorial talent of Lance Comfort, Leslie Arliss and Bernard Knowles – all of whom had enjoyed notable successes in the previous decade – and, although genuine star names might have been in short supply, there were plenty of good character actors. The stories all had interesting premises and were effectively filmed. The trade press had no hesitation in recommending them as a 'varied and versatile popular offering', giving a positive emphasis to their diversity: 'three stories for the price of one: entertaining contrasts of character, setting and situation: good acting: efficient production work'.[22]

When they went on general release, however, the Fairbanks films were the subject of an exposé in *Picturegoer* by Paul Ridgway. In an article hysterically titled 'Beware! These Films are Dangerous', he warned readers that 'a new type of British film' was heading their way, and that the British cinema screen was in danger of becoming 'a second-hand window' for American commercial television interests:

Is it right that the British picturegoer should be asked to pay to see something that the American televiewer will be offered for nothing? From what I've seen of these films I answer with an emphatic no. Their scope is limited and the settings, when seen on the cinema screen, are cramped. Distracting background shots have to be avoided, and a cosy, between-you-and-me intimacy maintained.[23]

Taking *The Triangle* as an example, Ridgway went on to question the wisdom of awarding these films quota status and supporting them with precious Eady money. When Fairbanks responded, he stressed the thought and care that went into each of his films. Each was explicitly 'designed for cinema presentation, but, of course, with the proviso that it should be right for TV, too'.[24] He also reminded *Picturegoer* that the purpose of the Eady fund was to facilitate profitable production in British studios. In this case it was helping to bring in dollars. When marketing the third in the series, *Three's Company* (1953), British Lion, was careful to give the impression that the anthology films were made first and foremost for the cinema. 'Showmen! *This* is what you have been waiting for!', announced the press book. 'Sell the stars – sell the comedy – sell the drama! A terrific star cast combining to give you terrific entertainment in three big pictures rolled into one.'[25]

Three's Company, in fact, was again enthusiastically received by trade reviewers. This trio of stories was directed by regular 'B' film men, Terence Fisher and Charles Saunders. In retrospect, the principal interest of this second anthology lies in its final story in which Fairbanks and Constance Cummings play an unhappy couple who rent a house haunted by a scream which proves to be an omen of the husband's murder of his unfaithful wife. This could easily have been a Terence Fisher excursion into the uncanny, but, in fact, the segment was the one directed by Saunders. Fairbanks seemed to acknowledge the trend towards crime stories in the second-feature market with the title of his fourth anthology *Thought to Kill* (1953), but actually, the three stories were essays on the commonplace rather than the criminally exceptional, with Leslie Arliss, Lawrence Huntington and Bernard Knowles dramatising stories of ordinary people in problematic situations. This threesome was hailed by reviewers as the best so far.[26] The fifth in the series, *The Genie* (1954), was equally well received. All three stories – directed by Lance Comfort and Lawrence Huntington – dealt with problematic romantic relationships, notably in the title story in which a French girl (Yvonne Furneaux) acquires a magic lamp and manages to turn the genie (Fairbanks himself) into a mortal lover.

The anthologies reached their zenith with the release, in the summer of 1954, of *The Red Dress*. *To-Day's Cinema* hailed it as 'Certain entertainment no matter where', praising Lawrence Huntington's 'highly skilled direction', coupled with 'Grade A dialogue and top-of-the-class performances'.[27] *Kinematograph Weekly* agreed, finding it 'amusing and gripping all-round entertainment',[28] and the enthusiasm extended to fan magazines like *Picture Show*, which described the film as a 'Neatly directed omnibus feature, well-balanced with drama, comedy and thrills',[29] and to the *Monthly Film Bulletin*, which described its three stories with their 'last minute plot twists' as 'quite capably written and directed'.[30] British Lion's follow-up Fairbanks compilation was *Destination Milan* (1955), directed by Huntington, Leslie Arliss and John Gilling and featuring the work of Christopher Lee as well as Fairbanks himself. Lee can be scathing about some of his low-budget work, but he found working with Fairbanks 'the kind of experience actors dream about':

> I was successively a Swedish circus-proprietor, a Russian lion-tamer with a clawed face, an American leading people to safety through the lines of the war, a Moroccan pimp, a half-witted Jugoslav soldier in a Dalmatian Laurel-and-Hardy act, a Mongol in the People's Army and many other descendants of Babel.[31]

Destination Milan was more equivocally received by the trade, with *To-Day's Cinema* recommending it to exhibitors as 'varied and satisfying entertainment',[32] but *Kinematograph Weekly* finding that it lacked 'the polish and crispness' of its predecessor.[33] A shorter compendium of Fairbanks stories, *The Last Moment* (1955), directed by Lance Comfort, raised doubts about whether 'two comparatively ordinary tales are better than one good one'.[34] For the first time, Fairbanks' performance – as a suicidal scientist – was criticised, particularly in comparison to Cyril Cusack's crowd-pleasing Irish imbiber.[35] There were ten Fairbanks anthologies in all, released over a three-year period, but, like the Danzigers, Fairbanks eventually abandoned the attempt to market the same product to British cinemas and American television stations. Most of the 180 half-hour television programmes which he made at Boreham Wood remained just that. Ultimately, he was obliged to acknowledge an incompatibility between big and small screen products at a particularly difficult historical moment in their relationship: 'Certainly television is the cinema industry's deadliest opponent at the moment,' he commented. 'But ... I'm sure the conflict will eventually reconcile itself.'[36] Nonetheless, Fairbanks' dual-purpose output made more than $4 million in overseas earnings, thanks to his acute awareness of international markets: 'It's all a question of packaging,' he explained. 'We pick only a certain type of story – one that is universally understandable. Anything too localised is out. We take care to avoid over-English accents ... Americans just don't understand the Mayfair drawl.'[37]

Acknowledging the vogue in the supporting-feature market for celebrations of the Constabulary, Fairbanks made his own contribution with the full co-operation of the Metropolitan Police. In this case, however, it was the pooch from the Yard: Derek Twist's *Police Dog* (1955) starred PD Rex III, and was snapped up by the Gaumont circuit.[38] Eros continued to try to market anthologies of dual-purpose films to cinemas during 1955, but eventually had to admit defeat. American actor Lorne Greene starred as Mitch, the skipper of a small cargo boat, in twenty-six half-hour *Sailor of Fortune* films produced at Elstree by RKO for US television. Eros released a couple of double doses of Mitch's adventures in exotic parts of the world as supporting features under the titles *Dust and Gold* and *Double Jeopardy* (both 1955). Reviewers found some merit in these tall tales, especially in the strong casts and the acting of Lorne Greene, but the circuit bookers were not persuaded. Within a film industry that predominantly viewed television as a deadly competitor, there remained considerable unease about any meeting of the two media. The compilation films could be viewed as a way of encouraging exhibitors to help cut their own throats by using their own screens to publicise and further popularise the television series. The patrons that came to their cinemas and enjoyed these television samplers today would stay at home and watch further episodes tomorrow. *To-Day's Cinema*'s 'Onlooker' clearly regarded the compilation films as illegitimate cinema:

The other day I picked up one of those so-called features about which there has been so much talk, and which, starting as subjects for commercial television, have been literally thrown together to make up a quota feature for British cinema consumption. If the British Quota Act, coupled

JOAN   TIM   SANDRA   CHARLES
RICE   TURNER   DORNE   VICTOR
and introducing Scotland Yard's Wonder Dog
REX III

POLICE DOG

Distributed by EROS FILMS LTD. 111 Wardour Street, London. W.1.

The pooch from the Yard: PD Rex III stars on the cover of the press book for Derek Twist's *Police Dog* (1955)

with a shortage of product, is encouraging the release of this kind of thing on our screens, then it is time there was an amendment to the Act to exclude them from registration. They're infinitely worse than the bad old 'quickies'. They are bad advertisements for the studio that made them whose label appears prominently in the credits, and most damaging to any good feature that is unfortunate enough to be coupled with them in the programme. The example I saw consisted obviously of three films intended to be shown quite separately on TV, but which had been joined quite incongruously to provide about the most boring hour and a half it has ever been my misfortune to suffer. Even the players' (you can't call them stars) limited talent was thoroughly wasted ... Not in all the years of trade reporting have I heard any film get the bird so pointedly: it was practically laughed off the screen, and I am sure that, had the audience had the energy, they would have given it that devastating kiss of death, the slow clap.[39]

More than likely, this was one of the Douglas Fairbanks anthology films which had drawn so much critical praise from his colleagues. 'Onlooker' was not alone in his loathing for TV-film hybrids. The South and East Lancashire branch of the CEA called for them to be banned from cinema exhibition. The Chair explained: 'The trouble is, if we book them, the producers will not make the supporting quota films for cinemas only.'[40]

Police Procedurals

By 1955, all that exhibitors were prepared to accept were the police featurettes that audiences seemed to crave as appetisers for their main features. Thirty-minute police procedurals were already popular on British television when they began to appear on cinema screens,[41] summoned by the runaway success of *The Blue Lamp*, a Home Office blitz on vice following the election of Churchill's Conservative Government and an insistent demand for law and order provoked by the cosh-boy panic and the Craig/Bentley case in 1952. No less than three rival series of featurettes about the work of London police detectives went into production in the early months of 1953, as Britain awaited the Coronation of its new sovereign and the birth of a new age of peace and prosperity that would surely follow: *Fabian of the Yard* was filmed at Carlton Hill for theatrical release by Eros; *Stryker of the Yard* was filmed at Nettlefold Studios by Republic Pictures' British production company for British Lion release; and *Scotland Yard*, the longest running and most commercially successful of the series, was made at Merton Park for distribution by Anglo-Amalgamated.

The *Fabian of the Yard* series starred Bruce Seton as the eponymous detective, and was produced by the enigmatic Anthony Beauchamp (Winston Churchill's son-in-law and suspected Soviet spy). It would eventually run to thirty half-hour episodes on BBC television between 1954 and 1956. Its case files were given the stamp of authenticity by the appearance of the real Chief Inspector Robert Fabian to endorse proceedings at the close of each episode. As Susan Sydney-Smith argues, the series was made with export sales firmly in mind and was at pains to offer a portrait of Britain appropriate for the Coronation celebrations:

Fabian promotes a postwar reconstructive ideology, explicit in the series' moral tone and documentary aspect. The sense of a united nation is attached to the sense of a unified past in the depiction of landmark London, reinforced by the travelogue style as the narrator guides the viewer past tourist sights, including 'the Tower of London, started by William the Conqueror in 1078'.[42]

A nice cup of tea: Ann Hanslip plays an undercover policewoman in the controversial 'Bombs in Piccadilly' episode
included in the compilation *Fabian of the Yard* (1954) for theatrical exhibition

Three early episodes directed by John Harlow were combined in the anthology, *Fabian of the Yard*
(1954). *To-Day's Cinema* praised the 'first-rate documentary reconstructions, full of intent and mystery', and declared its combination of 'convincing performances' and 'original' backgrounds 'excellent
whodunit entertainment for most spots'.[43] Production shifted to Twickenham in 1954, with John
Larkin producing for the BBC. Bernard Knowles directed the three episodes selected for the
Handcuffs, London (1955) compilation, all written by Brock Williams. Reviewers gave cautious
approval, but, following the broadcasting of the first TV episodes in November 1954 and questions
raised in the CEA General Council, Larkin felt it necessary to reassure exhibitors that the six stories
used in two feature-film compilations released by Eros 'will not be seen on British television for
several years, if at all'.[44]

In February 1953, the President of Republic Pictures, Herbert Yates, announced plans for a series
of half-hour featurettes to be made by a British production team for theatrical release. Interestingly,
he declared that he was responding to 'a world shortage of "B" pictures' rather than the needs of the
new medium of television.[45] However, Yates was already aware that television sales were vital to the
profitability of his company, having sold $3 million-worth of old Republic films to the networks in
the previous year. By September 1953, as Republic watched the market for its 'B' movies continue to
shrink – by more than 50 per cent since the arrival of TV – Yates was forced to announce that public
reaction 'demanded' that theatres and television must find common ground to serve the public.[46]

Significantly, there were fourteen *Stryker of the Yard* featurettes produced by William 'Billy' N.
Boyle during 1953 and 1954: just enough for a television season and a pilot episode. They would

Police procedurals: press sheets for two of the popular *Scotland Yard* series from Anglo-Amalgamated

eventually air on Republic's Hollywood Television Service in slightly attenuated versions in 1957, and on ATV in Britain in 1962–3. All episodes starred Clifford Evans as the sleuthing policeman and George Woodbridge as his faithful helper. The first seven were directed by Gainsborough's ace camera-man Arthur Crabtree, who had just finished work on *Colonel March of Scotland Yard*, also filmed partly at Nettlefold. The remaining episodes of *Stryker* were handled by John Krish, a film editor who had begun his career on classic wartime documentaries like *Target for Tonight* (1941) and *Listen to Britain* (1942). The writing team consisted of the Australian Kenneth Hayles, who had four productive years scripting supporting features before moving on to television, Patricia Latham, who worked mainly for the Children's Film Foundation, Guy Morgan and Lester Powell. The editor was John Seabourne, who had cut his teeth on Tod Slaughter melodramas and had done sterling work on Powell and Pressburger films during the war.

The first featurette in the series was trade-shown in July 1953 to positive reviews which noted its 'crisp direction' and 'realistic portraiture'.[47] *The Case of Express Delivery*, a tale of van robberies, co-starred Donald Houston as the victim of a wayward femme fatale (Sandra Dorne), and, like the *Fabian* series, it was given a stamp of authenticity by an introduction from an ex-detective inspector, in this instance, Tom Fallon. However, it was yet to establish its identity as a series. In spite of acknowledging the disciplinary mood of the time, it would prove to have something of a 'soft centre'. This is most strikingly revealed in the second instalment, *The Case of Uncle Harry* (1953), the sentimental tale of an aged Robin Hood figure who forges money for what he believes is the public good. When the series came to focus on the hot topic of juvenile delinquency, *The Case of Gracie Budd* (1953) attributed the behaviour of its reform-school girl to the dislocation of her upbringing during the war. Joan Dowling played the eponymous Gracie, who falls under the influence of a murderous army deserter (Patric Doonan, one of the young tearaways in *The Blue Lamp*). Stryker, of course, tracks down the deserter who dies in an escape attempt while the redeemable Gracie Budd is only injured. The film's morality was carefully tailored to ease the social fears of Coronation year, and the featurette was given the thumbs-up by reviewers. The nightmares of the film-makers, though, were best exemplified by the self-referential robbery film *The Case of the Studio Payroll* (1953).

After a summer break, *Stryker* went on the floor again in September 1953 with John Krish's *The Case of the Second Shot* (1954), which also illustrated the relatively liberal orientation of the series. Crime was to be explained more often by circumstance than by evil, and in this story a man turns to crime to finance the treatment of his sick wife.[48] 'Criminals' were sometimes themselves the victims of conspiracy or misfortune, like Kenneth Haigh in Krish's *The Case of the Two Brothers* (1954). The

NAT & STUART present *The latest* SCOTLAND YARD *action Thriller*
"*THE SILENT WEAPON*"'u' *featuring* EDGAR LUSTGARTEN

Helping the police with their enquiries: Geoffrey Keen is the investigator in this 1961 *Scotland Yard* story of greyhound doping

series really hit its stride with Krish's *The Case of Diamond Annie* (1954), in which Marjorie Rhodes played the leader of a gang of robbers tracked down by the redoubtable Stryker via the usual criminal habitat of pawn shop and amusement arcade. *To-Day's Cinema* appreciated its 'energetic star portrayals', 'ingenious' story, 'enterprising direction' and 'good photography and dialogue',[49] and was equally complimentary about *The Case of the Bogus Count* (1954): 'Realistic, interesting story is told with great economy, direction is firm and clear ... Neatly constructed popular entertainment.'[50] A viewing of the film, however, suggests that this is a fairly generous appraisal. The plot, involving a singer who works for a shady night club, lacks originality and relies on contrivance, clues are heavily emphasised when they appear, and the development is slow by modern standards. Moreover, the character of Stryker is fairly flavourless, and he doesn't have to work too hard to trap criminals who effectively convict themselves.

The *Stryker* featurettes were ideal for slotting into a bill to accommodate the longer films now being produced in Hollywood. However, Republic ensured that its product could also support films of more conventional length by doubling up individual *Stryker* stories in two portmanteau packages lasting seventy minutes each. 1953's *Stryker of the Yard* parcelled up *Studio Payroll* and *Uncle Harry*, while 1954's *Companions in Crime*, released simultaneously with *Diamond Annie*, combined *The Case of the Black Falcon* and *The Case of the Two Brothers*, which *Picture Show* reviewed as 'a thriller in two parts, based on true-life happenings'.[51] This may have been correct, because Arthur Crabtree's earlier *The Case of the Burnt Alibi* (1953) was based on an actual investigation of identity swapping from the 1930s. *The Case of the Pearl Payroll* was trade-shown in October 1954 to the usual positive reviews,[52] and the final *Stryker*, *The Case of Canary Jones*, followed a month later to applause that was a little more muted.[53]

After the completion of the *Stryker* series in the summer of 1954, Republic began to make sixty-five- to seventy-five-minute features at Nettlefold, with Billy Boyle as associate producer. The house director, supplied by the parent studios, was R. G. ('Bud') Springsteen, who had overseen the early *Stryker*s. Springsteen had been schooled in Republic's budget- and speed-conscious style of working, and made sure that every penny spent was up on the screen. He was known as a director 'who knew what he wanted and got it in a take', without wasted footage. Scripts were rigidly followed, and last-minute changes avoided.[54] The first of the Springsteen films was *Track the Man Down* (1954), a race-track-robbery thriller that brought over Kent Taylor to star with Ursula Howells and Petula Clark. It was followed by Kent Taylor and Kathleen Byron in *Secret Venture* (1954), a Cold War, kidnapped-scientist story in which loose cannon Kent typically decides that the case cannot be left to Scotland Yard. Hard on its heels came *The Green Buddha* (1954), which featured the imported American 'star' Wayne Morris and the German actor Walter Rilla in the tale of the theft of an art object. The story was 'implausible' and the direction 'unpretentious', but the film was notable for its use of Battersea fun fair for some of its more dynamic sequences.[55] Wayne Morris stayed on to play the owner of a boat-for-hire in the jewellery-smuggling melodrama *Cross Channel* (1955). Like the other British Republic pictures, it is unavailable for viewing today, but by all accounts it was a weak vessel, subject to a good deal of drift. Its dialogue was clunky and its fights clumsy.[56] Although Springsteen was responsible for most of the directorial duties, John Lemont was credited as director in an attempt to circumvent the quota on foreign directors which had been instituted by the ACT. However, the union was not fooled for long, and was informed that Lemont had directed only location and process shots. The Ministry of Labour was notified and, consequently, Springsteen was recalled to the USA towards the end of October 1954 and Republic's British production, which had been intended to run into 1956, was suspended.[57]

Stryker fulfilled Republic's aims for dual-purpose film-making, but the real hit among the plethora of police series was Anglo-Amalgamated's *Scotland Yard* series. While the moral climate of the time might have influenced the themes and treatments of the series, it owed its existence to hard-nosed economic considerations concerning both the changing make-up of the cinema programme and the rhythms of studio production. Anglo's chairman, Stuart Levy, was well aware that, although nine out of ten 'big' pictures continued to need hour-long supporting features to fill out the programme, a new breed of super-productions was on its way:

> Since undoubtedly there will be a number of features which, by reason of their magnitude ... will not permit of a full-length feature in support, and as the ordinary, commentated documentary is as dated as the hansom cab, there is a need for first-class shorts, such as our action thrillers in the 'Scotland Yard' series.[58]

The series would also guarantee continuity of production at Merton Park, as producer Alec Snowden would fit the making of films in the series to gaps in the studios' schedule.[59] Anglo's statement was carefully timed to steal the thunder of the rival *Stryker* series, due to take the floor that week, and was indicative of the shrewd promotional work that distinguished the Anglo-Amalgamated product from most of its competitors.

Scotland Yard was a great success from the outset in 1953, winning ABC circuit release and enthusiastic reviews. Ken Hughes wrote and directed the first five films (and four later ones), developing a brisk storytelling flair and creating as much visual interest as possible within the austere budget limits. After the reception given to the first of the series, *The Drayton Case* (1953), Anglo's publicists pulled out all the stops for the release of the second, Hughes' *The Missing Man* (1953), announcing: 'The Most Thrilling Crime-Series Ever Made! No1 ... Acclaimed by all ... The Best Supporting Feature of All Time! No2 ... Even Better!' It was a big claim for a quiet story about a retired vicar trying to trace an absent son with the aid of the Yard, but the film was gratefully received by the trade as an '[e]ntertaining and useful filler'.[60] Hughes immediately hit on a winning formula, embellishing the depiction of painstaking forensic investigation with touches of expressionism borrowed from the noir school, low-life *mise en scène*, and the sort of directorial flourishes that would later be revisited in television series such as *Trial and Retribution*. All this was stitched together by the sometimes wry, sometimes ghoulish commentary of the barrister-crime writer Edgar Lustgarten, his air of authority enhanced by seating him at his study's desk.

The third and fourth in the series, *The Candlelight Murder* and *The Blazing Caravan*, were released in the winter of 1953–4, and *To-Day's Cinema* reported that the featurettes were 'proving extremely popular with the trade and public alike in the West End'.[61] The trade advertisements for the series quoted Peter Noble's comment on radio that they were 'The best second features now being made in Britain', as well as a string of positive endorsements from the trade press. With the fifth in the series, *The Dark Stairwell* (1954), the endorsements included many of the top reviewers for the national dailies like Reg Whitley of the *Daily Mail* and Peter Burnup of the *News of the World*.[62]

These early films were indeed based on actual murder cases. *The Drayton Case*, for example, sticks closely to the 'blackout murder' of Rachel Dobkin by her husband during the London blitz of 1941. *The Blazing Caravan* draws its inspiration from the murder of a vagrant by Alfred Rouse. However, fact is always mixed with fiction, and, as Dave Mann has demonstrated, the stories sometimes also reference quasi-mythical historical crimes whose realities had already been overlaid by ballads and melodrama, such as the case of Maria Marten and the red barn, which is evoked in *The Missing Man*.[63] In fact, the guidelines laid down by the BBFC at the time explicitly prohibited the depiction of recent criminal cases, as Exclusive had discovered when it tried to film the life story of Stanley Thurston. Anthony Beachamp, the producer of *Fabian of the Yard*, summarised the censors' policy towards crime reportage thus:

> Any films on a recent criminal case which would be identifiable in the public mind, do not get certificates. One reason is that it might cause pain to the relatives of the people concerned ... [Moreover], in the board's view it is not a good thing to increase morbid public interest in actual crimes by allowing them to be commercialised.[64]

Actuality was obliged to give way to fictionalisation and increasingly did so when the inflexibility of censorship regulations became clear. The post-Hughes films, mostly written by James Eastwood and often directed by Montgomery Tully, had looser roots in the reality of crime.

Indicative of the success of *Scotland Yard* was the decision taken by the series' regular bookers, the ABC circuit, to support the Hollywood blockbuster *Seven Brides for Seven Brothers* (1955) with *Passenger to Tokyo* (1955). Nat Cohen was quick to point out that the choice of his featurette 'to support such a great film' was further evidence of 'the tremendous popularity with the trade and the public' of the series.[65] The films also appear to have done valuable export business, playing well in France, Spain, Holland and even the Far East.[66] Anglo claimed to have sold the series in fifty-one countries.[67] The combination of the *Scotland Yard* story *The Drayton Case* with Anglo's more ambitious feature *Street of Shadows* (1953) was highly successful in Norway, for instance,[68] while *The Dark Stairwell* was accepted as an official entry at the 1959 Moscow Film Festival.[69] Between 1956 and 1959 the sales of British films in Continental Europe doubled[70] and the export success of *Scotland Yard* is indicative of this. The expanded market began to influence content. Announcing the release of *Wall of Death* and *The Case of the River Morgue* in the spring of 1956, Stuart Levy commented that Anglo-Amalgamated were concentrating on commercial films 'especially tailored for the overseas markets'. Much of the action in both films takes place in France, and includes French dialogue, ensuring a particular appeal to Continental and North African audiences.[71] *Destination Death* (1956) continued to build in a Continental appeal with backgrounds in France and Portugal, and there were more European settings in *The Grand Junction Case*, *Crime of Honour*, *Wings of Death* and *Night Crossing* (1960).

Within three years of its launch, the *Scotland Yard* series was familiar enough to cinemagoers for the Goons to release a spoof version *The Case of the Mukkinese Battle Horn* (1956), made for £6,000 at the home of the series, Merton Park, by Jon Pennington, Harry Booth and Michael Deeley's Cinead (a company that had been set up to make advertising films). Directed by Joe Sterling and scripted by Spike Milligan, the film substituted Dick Emery for regular Goon Harry Secombe and was advertised in 'Schizophrenoscope: the new split screen process'.

The films varied from twenty-six to thirty-three minutes in length, and were made in under a week by two units shooting simultaneously. As C. H. B. Williamson reported, they relied on the speed of skilled technicians in erecting and dismantling sets:

> I was told that something like twenty-four sets are used on the Merton stage in a matter of four days ... art director George Haslam, who knows the limits of the Merton Park stages, can get effective and pleasing results whilst fitting in a number of sets in the manner of a jigsaw puzzle.[72]

Whatever problems the logistics of production posed, the *Scotland Yard* films maintained an enviable consistency, even as their production sector contracted around them. Reviewing Montgomery Tully's *The Case of the River Morgue*, *The Cinema*'s reviewer observed:

> This series ... has built a reputation for itself of realism and ingenuity of plot, and this production is one of the most polished and ingenious. Far from holding up the action, the use of explanatory narration by criminologist Edgar Lustgarten helps largely to sustain the documentary effect as well as preventing the plot from becoming too tangled.[73]

Similarly, *Person Unknown* (1956) was garlanded in praise by *Kinematograph Weekly*: 'The acting is first-class, the direction resourceful and atmosphere impeccable. Headline stuff, it'll intrigue and grip all types of audiences.' The same publication assured its readers that on *Inside Information* (1957), 'Not a foot is shot in vain'.[74] By August 1957, the series had been running for twenty-one episodes. *To-Day's Cinema* pronounced it 'the most consistently popular series of featurettes released on the British market'. The explanation for this, it was believed, lay in the convincing realism of the stories, authenticated by their criminologist presenter: 'it is this authenticity combined with all-out action and lack of "padding" which has maintained an unflagging demand for the series from exhibitors and public alike'.[75]

In half of the films in this series, the man from the Yard was Russell Napier, who, as Inspector (later Superintendent) Duggan, became an iconic personification of the quiet, tireless investigator, but also of the inevitability of justice and retribution. Duggan, though, was only the visible representative of a vast investigative network that extends beyond Scotland Yard and even the wider police force to other state and municipal organisations, and ultimately to the dutiful citizen. The message is clear and repetitive: crime can never go undetected, no matter how resourceful the criminal or minimal the incriminating evidence.

In January 1958, Jack Greenwood took over from Alec Snowden as the series' producer. With him came a subtle process of updating, as Dave Mann points out:

> There is a sense in which the Yard's old stalking grounds are being overwritten by the modern city and that crime now feeds off the new consumerism. Increasingly the crime location is a feminised space and the criminals and those that pursue them are women. Ironically it emerges that the biggest threat to the hegemony of the plainclothesmen was the emerging presence of the not-so-plainly clothed woman.[76]

Women become more prominent in the series, both as offenders and as crime fighters, notably in Peter Maxwell's *The Ghost Train Murder* (1959), which featured Jill Ireland, Mary Laura Wood and Diane Aubrey, and appeared to draw its inspiration from *Brighton Rock* (1948). It provoked one trade reviewer to applaud it as a 'further example of how well produced and directed' the films in the series were, and remark that they maintained 'a much higher standard than any of the kind that can be seen on TV'. The reviewer also suggested that the frequency of the series might be increased so that exhibitors might offer patrons the kind of regular weekly diet appreciated by the television audience.[77] In fact, though, the pace of production was slowing, and would grind to a halt early in 1961 with *The Square Mile Murder*. The following year, Associated British acquired a 50 per cent stake in Anglo-Amalgamated and began negotiations to buy the television rights to the thirty-nine *Scotland Yard* films for ABC Television.

By the late 1950s, experience of working in television production was beginning to feed back into film-making for the big screen, just as the experience of wartime actuality filming had influenced the trend towards shooting in authentic locations a decade earlier. Terry Bishop, who had worked in both documentaries and TV, summed up the impact of the latter during the making at Shepperton of his co-feature, *Model for Murder* (1959):

> One virtue of television is that it makes other work a piece of cake, at least as far as the time factor is concerned. This picture, for instance, has only a three weeks' schedule, yet compared with television it is almost leisurely. ... Everyone in the industry knows that much time and money can be saved by working out all the possible camera angles, script problems, and so on, beforehand ... yet often the cinema industry doesn't take advantage.[78]

By the time *Scotland Yard* was bought for television, however, most of the 'B' film-makers had thrown in their lot with the rival medium, but Anglo-Amalgamated were undeterred. They continued to produce featurettes and second features in series for cinema exhibition, but they were conscious of the second life promised to products that were also designed to be television-friendly. In the early summer of 1962, Anglo began a new series of 'fact-based' featurettes again with criminologist Edgar Lustgarten.

The Scales of Justice

The films in the new series, each shot in a week to ten days by a close-knit team of technicians, were designed by Jack Greenwood to feature 'lighter content' than *Scotland Yard*: 'They may concern comparatively trivial offences which have, for instance, an interesting point of law,' said Greenwood launching the series, 'and, consequently, there may be more of a humorous element.'[79] This desire to bring lightness into the treatment of crime narratives sat uneasily with the solemnity of the series' pre-credits declaration:

> Wherever men live and work, one priceless possession makes civilised life possible: the Rule of Law. Here in London, at the heart of the City, are the very buildings that symbolise this tradition: the Law Courts in The Strand; the historic Inns of Court where for centuries lawyers, both for the prosecution and the defence, have prepared their cases to put before judge and jury; and The Old Bailey. Dominating the City stands the figure of Justice: in her right hand, the sword of power and retribution; in her left, the Scales of Justice.

The tension set up between the traditional rhetoric of discipline and punishment which inflects this introduction and the need to acknowledge the libertarian wind of change blowing through the 1960s would surface throughout the thirteen-part series. Two films in particular, both scripted by James Eastwood and presented in September 1963, illustrate this. In *Position of Trust*, the spotlight is turned on those ungrateful sons and daughters of privilege, students. Presenter Edgar Lustgarten, hardly an appropriate voice for more liberal times, cautiously identifies the problem: 'University students today are generally hard-working, serious-minded, fully aware that it is a privilege to attend one of Britain's historic colleges. But there are exceptions.' Son of a knight of industry, Simon Dennington (Derrick Sherwin) drops out of university and the life his father has planned for him, picks up a French girl (Imogen Hassall) and heads for a Brighton hotel room, only to find himself the victim of a blackmail plot hatched by his father's manservant (Edward Atienza). Clearly, the old certainties have dissolved and nothing can be taken for granted in the post-Profumo age. This protean quality of 1960s society extended to the designed environment of the new town, which Lustgarten prowls around in *The Undesirable Neighbour*. This world of supermarkets and housing estates turns out to be one of the front lines in the decade's culture wars. A housewife (Bridget Armstrong) who moonlights as a photographic model in conflict with a nosey neighbour (Vanda Godsell) provides director Gordon Hales with an opportunity to explore challenges to conventional morality. Predicably, Lustgarten's conclusion is unequivocal: new surroundings do not change human nature.

The early films in the series were short of box-office names, but more effort was made after 1965 to boost star values. Jack Greenwood did his best the assemble casts that combined experienced 'B' players such as Dermot Walsh (*Infamous Conduct*, 1966) with new talent (e.g., Alexandra Bastedo,

The Haunted Man, 1966), and faces familiar from television, such as Keith Baron and James Ellis (*The Haunted Man*). There was also an attempt to address new social problems such as hire-purchase debt (*Payment in Kind*, 1967) and revisit others such as drunken driving (*The Material Witness*, 1965), first exposed in *To The Public Danger* (1948). However, while *Scotland Yard* had been firmly rooted in its times, *The Scales of Justice* struggled to stay in touch with the sprightly spirit of its age, weighed down, as it was, by the censorious and authoritarian presence of Lustgarten. No amount of updating, including filming the last four contributions in Eastman Color, could rescue an old-fashioned format. The jaunty theme music by The Tornados, so up-to-the-minute in the days before The Beatles' first LP, sounded increasingly tinny in the wake of *Revolver*. Nor could the series' unquestioning faith in the unimpeachable quality of British justice, and its guarantee that the Rule of Law would ensure 'the rights and freedom of all', survive the coming iconoclasm of 1967's Summer of Love. The series' swan-song, *Payment in Kind* was a valiant attempt by director/screenwriter Peter Duffell and cinematographer Jimmy Harvey to experiment with more expressive treatment of grittier subject matter, and is commendable in achieving a certain measure of psychological realism reminiscent of Roman Polanski's *Repulsion* (1965).

The Scales of Justice series was the last made at Merton Park for cinema exhibition, and quietly made its way onto Independent Television in the early 1970s, but there is one final series of second features we must consider before we move on to look at how British society was represented in the 'B' film. The series concerned was the most substantial, and probably the most successful, of all, and even constituted a primary attraction for some cinemagoers, who continue to look back on it with affection: the Edgar Wallace mysteries.

Edgar Wallace Mysteries

When Nat Cohen and Stuart Levy acquired the screen rights to the work of England's most prolific thriller writer of the twentieth century from Sydney Box, Jack Greenwood put nine adaptors, including authors of the calibre of Arthur LaBern, to work on what would become a series of forty-seven one-hour dramas, released virtually monthly between 1960 and 1965.[80] All were produced by Greenwood – apart from *The Malpas Mystery* (1960, directed by Sidney Hayers), which was farmed out to Julian Wintle and Leslie Parkyn – and his adapters generally did a remarkable job in transferring stories written four or five decades earlier to a contemporary setting. The first in the series, Allan Davis's *The Clue of the Twisted Candle* (1960), like the *Scotland Yard* films, was released on the ABC circuit, but a number of subsequent entries were Rank releases. This was an indication of just how popular and ubiquitous on cinema programmes the Edgar Wallace mysteries became in the early 1960s. The stories had no significant shared locations, and only one set of characters – a senior detective (Bernard Lee) and his retinue of underlings – that made occasional reappearances, but they were effectively branded by the Wallace name and the 'Man of Mystery' theme music, which was a hit for The Shadows.

Eight films had been completed by June 1961, with six released.[81] The responses from reviewers and audiences were enthusiastic from the outset. Nat Cohen was never slow to promote his company's products, but in this case he was fully justified in claiming: 'already these one-hour supports are not only fulfilling exhibitors' demands, but they are undoubtedly proving an actual box-office attraction by dint of their excellent production values, and the unflagging popularity of the Edgar Wallace stories'.[82] Confirmation followed immediately with the release of *The Clue of the New Pin* (1961), directed by Allan Davis, which was judged by the press a 'Taut and tense tale' with 'good characteri-sation, slick direction, smooth dialogue, thrilling finale'.[83] Two weeks later, Peter Duffell's *Partners in Crime* (1961), an updating of Wallace's *The Man Who Knew*, was praised as 'A quart in a pint pot, decanted against realistic backgrounds, it'll make the crowd smack its lips.'[84] Davis's *The Fourth Square* (1961) was described as a 'Skilfully wrought thriller, unfolded against appropriate London backgrounds' and an 'ideal curtain-raiser'.[85] These reviews were typical of the praise the series won from trade critics for its twisting narratives, polished presentation and crisp dialogue.

Naturally, individual Wallace adaptations varied in quality. Three Edgar Wallaces were trade-shown in the same week of March 1962. *Kine Weekly* hailed Gerald Glaister's *The Shareout* (1962), a tale of dishonour among thieves, based on Wallace's *Jack O' Judgment*, as the best of the bunch, and of the series to that point.[86] It was helped by an efficient screenplay by Philip Mackie, and by the pres-ence of Bernard Lee as Supt Meredith and Moira Redmond as a sympathetic racketeer. However, even in reviewing one of its less accomplished stable-mates, Alan Cooke's *Flat Two* (1962), a tale set among the new casinos legalised by the recent Betting and Gaming Act, *The Daily Cinema* was keen to stress the virtues of the series:

> These modest screen thrillers, with the Edgar Wallace trademark, have achieved such a high standard of feature entertainment that it's more noticeable perhaps when one doesn't square up by comparison. Here too much of the plot is left to the three-man discussion at the end and the climax hasn't the expected punch. But the production's as adroit as ever, the suspense satisfying and the key performances thor-oughly workman-like ... The winning appeal of the series should certainly ensure a gathering of the fans.[87]

It is rare for a supporting feature to be considered to have 'fans', but there is evidence that the films in this series were sought out by some cinemagoers as primary attractions. A retired friend has told us that he used to go to see the latest Wallace, rather than the film it was supporting, while, in 1962, Anglo-Amalgamated received a letter from a Mrs Audrey Myles of St John's Wood asking for the play-dates of two Wallaces she had missed and indicating that she was prepared to travel up to a hundred miles to see them.[88]

If we take the Wallace films released in 1961 as examples, we can see that some of the uneven qual-ity of the series can be attributed to differential directorial talent. Royston Morley, responsible for *Attempt to Kill*, shows no particular aptitude for the task, whereas Gerard Glaister is more at home in handling *The Clue of the Silver Key*, as is Allan Davis with *The Fourth Square*. However, the quality of original story and adaptation can produce considerable variations within the work of the same direc-tor. Of the three directed by Robert Tronson – *Man Detained*, *Never Back Losers* and *Man at the Carlton Tower* – the first-named is the smartest. Based on Wallace's novel *A Debt Discharged*, it gets off to a lively and involving start as a secretary (sprightly Elvi Hale) discovers a theft of money that proves to have been counterfeit. The police investigation, led with convincing authority by Bernard Archard, is thus at odds with the wishes of the secretary's dodgy boss. *Monthly Film Bulletin* properly praised it as a 'Taut and vivid addition to the Edgar Wallace series' and drew attention to its 'smart pace'.[89] *Man at the Carlton Tower*, with a screenplay by dramatist Philip Mackie, also gets off to a zippy start and has the benefit of quite luxurious settings (courtesy of the then-new Carlton Tower Hotel, which is given a credit) and of a nicely ambiguous performance by Maxine Audley. Unfortunately, the plot, to do with a Rhodesian criminal and a London jewel robbery, is perfunctorily developed, and the ending is unconvincing. Adapted from Wallace's *The Green Ribbon*, a tale of race-track skulduggery and the death of a popular jockey who refuses to throw a race, *Never Back Losers* has Tronson's characteristic virtues of moving the story along swiftly and making good dramatic use of his contrasting settings (in this case, stuffy insurance offices, sleazy clubs and the turf).[90] However, the director can do little about an over-wordy script by Lukas Heller, which validates Robert Baker's view that 'In England we tend to use six words when two would do.'[91]

Although the series used handy locations, often to good effect, whenever the limited budgets would allow, the cramped studio conditions restricted set design and sometimes give a claustrophobic atmosphere to the proceedings. Gerard Glaister's *The Partner* (1963), while perhaps not one of the most distinguished of the series, had the added interest of intrigue and infidelity against a film studio background, and gives us an opportunity to see the lot and sound stages on which this and the other Merton Park series were shot. Nevertheless, some directors managed to transcend these limitations, and John Moxey (b. 1920) in particular managed a film which ranks among the finest of British Bs. Moxey had signalled his emerging talent in September 1960 with the release of a pair of features: the wartime spy thriller *Foxhole in Cairo* and the occult chiller *City of the Dead*. It may have been something of a Mario Bava pastiche, but the latter film demonstrated that Moxey was capable of the sort of visual stylistics that were rare among jobbing British directors. He contributed five films to the Edgar Wallace series, but *Face of a Stranger* (1965) is distinguished by its cinematic invention and its absorption of the currents flowing through European film-making at the time. With the termination of the series perhaps already announced, Moxey may have felt free to experiment. Certainly, he was prepared to rip up the rule book for second features and deliver a film of considerable bravery that stripped away extraneous dialogue and exposition and granted extraordinary freedom to cinematographer Jimmy Wilson and his camera operator, the appropriately named Peter Allwork. Like *City of the Dead*, the film has a Continental look, although here the influences are French rather than Italian, but it is the screenplay by Jimmy Sangster (as John Sansom) that is as remarkable as anything about the picture. *Face of a Stranger* eschews the usual conventions of 'B' narratives: there is not a policeman in sight, sentimentality is clinically excised and the only sympathetic character is brutally betrayed and slaughtered in a blazing car. This is a study of human venality in which the typical victim figure of the conventional thriller, the blind woman (Rosemary Leach, cast against type), turns out to be as ruthless and immoral as the hardened criminal played so convincingly by Jeremy Kemp. Moxey's direction gives the film an hallucinogenic quality that

The *nouvelle vague* crashes over the British Bs: a press sheet for John Moxey's extraordinary Edgar Wallace thriller *Face of a Stranger* (1965)

Small beginnings: Michael Caine accepts a bit part as a heavy in the Edgar Wallace adaptation *Solo for Sparrow* (1962)

reaches full delirium at its climax as close-up follows close-up, resting on Leach's sightless eyes as she screams hysterically 'Give me the money' and, finally, on Kemp's unbelieving stare as he blows her away with a shotgun. In the sheer bleakness and desperation of its vision, it is a film which anticipates the final scene of Michael Reeves' more celebrated *Witchfinder General* (1968).[92]

The series relied on dependable character players and actors usually cast as second leads in 'A' films rather than stars, but they could be very effective, particularly as the sort of duped anti-hero essayed by Barry Foster in Quentin Lawrence's *Playback* (1962). The series also managed to give a leg up the ladder to one or two future film luminaries such as Michael Caine, who played a small supporting role in the enthusiastically received *Solo for Sparrow* (1962), based on Wallace's novel *The Gunner*. Gordon Fleming's *Five to One* (1964) was notable for an early screen appearance by John Thaw, who would later emerge as a major television star, as would Harry H. Corbett, who worked up a sweat in *Time to Remember* (1962, directed by Norman Harrison). As the series made inroads into European markets, an increasing number of Continental actors were introduced into the casts, beginning with *Candidate for Murder* (1962), which featured Hans Borsody and Erika Remberg.[93] Margit Saad was given top billing as a frau fatale in *Playback*, and the addition of Yvonne Monlaur to the cast of the under-par *Time to Remember* caused *Kine Weekly* to describe the film as a 'vest-pocket crime melodrama with French dressing'.[94] There were also periodic engagements for Bernard Lee who was particularly popular in France, where he was hailed as 'the English Maigret'.[95] It was probably the success of the films in Continental Europe that gave them the financial viability that the Danzigers' output had failed to find. Jack Greenwood commented:

> In France, Italy and Germany they are proving so popular that they are not only dubbed into the language of the country but exhibited as a first-feature by joining two films together with a specially filmed introduction and linking sequences, so that they make a 95–100 minute feature.[96]

The films were also great successes in Australia and New Zealand, consistently reliable markets for British 'B' films.[97] The series was conceived primarily for theatrical exhibition, but was eventually shown on American television as the *Edgar Wallace Mystery Theatre*. Some of the early films were also screened in 1962 as the *Invitation to Murder* series.

The dual-purpose cops-and-crime series is, in many ways, emblematic of post-war British 'B' films. This genre of film-making was the first to acknowledge the compatibility of cinema and television, where the sort of low-budget production methods practised in the 'B' sector would eventually find a more secure home. These films-in-series survived most 'one-off' second features and provided a bridge to the small screen, even as most of the film industry was throwing up barriers against the 'menace' of television. Moreover, these pictures take the temperature of society in a period of rapid change. Born in an age of wishful thinking, in which the 'Man from the Yard' represented the stability and disciplined consensus of the new Elizabethan age, they died in the gathering cultural maelstrom of the 1960s in which the old, taken-for-granted certainties were under severe strain. It is to the representation of Britain in these changing times that we now turn.

7 Britain in the Bs

For the first time since the film spoke our pictures are representative of us and not a pale imitation of the American product. They show our way of life in a manner as *true* to life as possible ... We are trying to portray on the screen life as it is lived and not as the militant American churchwoman would like it lived ... Our pictures are succeeding because they are *English*. A very large section of the public both in England and overseas goes to see them because of that special quality.

Anthony Asquith[1]

It is sometimes easier to gauge widely held views of the period from 'B' films than from the more prestigious productions that attracted the attentions of directors with highly individual styles. 'B' films, generally intended to fill an hour of the audience's time while they waited for the main feature, are less likely to be espousing controversial attitudes to aspects of contemporary life. Relatively unmediated by directorial intervention or other powerful collaborative input, guided by what the 'B' movie market wanted, and dependent on regular sales as distinct from box-office percentages, they may offer a fair indication of what ideas and representations were widely acceptable. In the 1950s, it must be said, acceptability was often a function of censors in America as much as in Britain, particularly as far as crime films were concerned.

However, despite their often seeming to be settling for predictable values, and being ideologically revealing in doing so, 'B' films are also quite surprisingly studded with critical insights about the nature of contemporary society. Even such modest programmers as *Penny and the Pownall Case* (1948) or *The Adventures of PC 49* (1949) touch on the Cold War and post-war malaise as they go about their comic-strip narratives. There is not the space here for a thorough analysis of gender representations in the Bs, but in the mid-1950s, for instance, there were a number of 'B' films in which women were the protagonists or significant antagonists. While in the 'A' features of the time women were so often wives or nurses, in the supporting features of 1956 they were in the police force (*They Never Learn*), the prison service (*Women without Men*), journalism (*Behind the Headlines*), or even MI5 (*Passport to Treason*). C. Pennington-Richard's *Stormy Crossing* (1958) actually centres on a woman swimming the Channel. There may be an argument to be made that films of female agency like these became the flip-side of the male-centred war films that became such a feature of 'A' film production after 1954.

To consider the kinds of ideological and sociological 'information' revealed by British 'B' movies, 250 films have been analysed, dating from roughly 1945 to 1965, but concentrated in the 1950s (161 derive from that decade). What emerges is, of course, not 'hard' statistical evidence but a series of tendencies which tell us something about what large numbers of people were prepared to accept. If it is sometimes surprising to find what can slip in, whether overtly or covertly, consciously or otherwise, it is equally surprising to see what scarcely gets a look-in. There is, for example, no reference in the sample under discussion to the Suez crisis or to National Service or to the shifts emerging in attitudes to sexual behaviours (the implications of the Wolfenden Report aren't felt at all). There is little sense of the social iconoclasm chronicled in plays such as *Look Back in Anger* (1956) or novels such as *Lucky Jim* (1954): film, with its vast popular following, has tended to trail behind the other arts in such matters, even at the 'A' feature level; in the 'B' films, there are a few Teddy Boys to be glimpsed, being rude to their elders or behaving with modest abandon in coffee bars, but nothing very disruptive.

Religion, too, is hardly visible except in the form of, say, a comic and/or ineffectual vicar (as in *The Man Who Liked Funerals*, 1957, or *The Late Edwina Black*, 1951) or the odd prison chaplain (as in *My Death Is a Mockery*, 1952). More surprising, perhaps, is how insignificantly sport figures in these films: in the 250 films considered, there are scarcely more than a dozen in which sports play a role, whether for purposes comic or serious, and there are a couple which register in passing anti-blood-sports agitation (*Home to Danger*, 1951; *Don't Talk to Strange Men*, 1962). Football, that 'expression of the ordered and disciplined society' in Jeffrey Richards' words,[2] is almost invisible, apart from TV coverage in *Emergency* (1962). Dog-racing is comically exploited in *One Wild Oat* (1951), and treated more seriously in *Wheel of Fate* (1953), *The Man in the Back Seat* (1961) and *Never Back Losers* (1961). Golf is just registered as a spare-time activity in *Four Days* (1951), *The Lost Hours* (1952), *Alias John Preston* (1955) and in *Strongroom* (1962). Bob McNaught's *Grand National Night* (1953), with Nigel Patrick and Moira Lister, was a murder-without-crime drama with a realistic horse-racing background. It was appreciated by the trade press as an excellent programmer, but supporting features interested in sport became increasingly uncommon during the 1950s. For example, the English obsession with cricket, strongly enough represented in 'A' films,[3] makes an early showing in second features (*Badger's Green*, 1949; *It's Not Cricket*, 1949; *Death of an Angel*, 1952; *Four-Sided Triangle*, 1953) and then virtually disappears. One can only speculate on the reasons, but the consideration given to the female and American audiences (from about 1952) in conceiving the 'B' scenario is likely to be a significant factor.

The ways in which the 'B' films represent the social order of the period – and it is a period of immense changes – and the relationships between individuals and between classes and other groups are essentially conservative. That said, though, and it *is* dangerous to generalise, trends and shifting contours do surface in even the most anodyne enterprises, because ideological content is not an optional extra. A film can't decide *not* to have any views on such matters: they will seep through at one level or another, in an image or a casual remark. It would be difficult to view these 250 films without noticing how much does filter through in relation to matters such as housing, work, politicians and bureaucrats, social organisation and class, international relations, post-war unease and adjustment, the rise of a youthful population with money in its pockets – and so on.

Law and Order

It is appropriate to start with how these films deal with crime, since thrillers constitute the overwhelming majority of the 'B' film output of the period. As several social historians have pointed out, there was a significant increase in crime in the decade after the end of World War II. John Montgomery, for instance, attributes this to 'frustrated emotional drives and social ambitions,'[4] while Arthur Marwick adduces statistics to support his claim that the accelerating crime rate from the mid-1950s onwards was most significant among younger age groups.[5] Of the 250 films under study here, 191 can be classified as 'crime'. Murder, in spite of its statistical infrequency in the crime statistics, was the most common crime on screen, its narrative roots very often being found in family affairs, whether of infidelity or inheritance, or jealousy of one kind or another. In this respect the 'B' films were echoing the classic detective fictions of the Christie-Allingham school dating back to the 1930s, so it is hard to pinpoint anything startlingly new about the motivations attributed to the murderers. Adulterous wives in several of these films – *Black Widow* (1951), *The House Across the Lake* (1954), *Account Rendered* (1957), *The House in Marsh Road* (1960), *Blind Corner* (1964) – hardly constitute a case for a slackening of the marital fibre of the nation, nor does the death of a model in each of *Blood Orange* (1953) and *Cloak Without Dagger* (1956) point to a dangerously corrupt profession, though in all these cases there is a sense that the protagonists – victims and assailants – live at some remove from the safety of quotidian middle-class mores. In this sense, they do differ from the Christie formulas which almost invariably located their culprits and victims among the well heeled.

In fact, as far as crimes go, murder is less revealing of the period than some of the other narrative starters. For instance, there is considerable incidence of smuggling as a post-war phenomenon, in films such as *Dick Barton – Special Agent, Love in Waiting* (1948), *Blackout* (1950), *The Quiet Woman* (1951), *My Death Is a Mockery, The Limping Man, River Beat, Three Steps to the Gallows, Wings of Danger* (1953), *The Black Rider, Diplomatic Passport* (1954), *Johnny, You're Wanted* (1956) and *The Heart Within* (1957). Sometimes, the smugglers are dealing in luxury goods such as whisky (as in *The Quiet Woman*) or furs (as in *The Hide-Out*, 1956), or in black-market foodstuffs in the comedy *Love in Waiting*, or in short-supply currency as in *Wings of Danger*, or 'drugs' as in *Johnny, You're Wanted* and *The Heart Within*. Most often there is a suggestion of the war hovering in the background of these films, whether because they highlight goods in short supply in the period of post-war austerity or because they point to a restlessness, a failure to adapt to peacetime, after the heightened excitements of the war years. Drugs and 'dope gangs' also featured in such films as *Home to Danger, Shadow of a Man* (1954), *Third Party Risk* (1954), *The Brain Machine* (1955), *The Diplomatic Corpse* (1958) and *Feet of Clay* (1960), but it would take almost another decade before 'drugs' acquired both higher profile and dangerous glamour. These films treat the subject with a certain obliquity as if the filmmakers really only had second-hand knowledge of it at best, and their comparative rarity and usual marginal plot function, perhaps reflected British officialdom's complacency at having 'preserved the country from the horrors of the illicit drug trade which went on in the United States'.[6] The 1960s would change all that.

There is also an immense amount of robbery fuelling the plots of the 'B' pictures, much of it directed at jewellers. This is more likely a reflection of the post-war fascination with luxury beyond attainment for most people, rather than some kind of subversive critique of a growing preoccupation with material goods. Diamonds were the commonest object of 'B' movie larceny, as one finds in films such as *The Frightened Man* (1952), *Impulse* (1955) and *No Road Back* (1957), but hard cash accounted for several mailbag robberies, as in *The Flying Scot* (1957) and *Wrong Number* (1959). Banks were perennially attractive to small gangs, rather than individuals, and two brilliantly sustained suspense jobs near the end of our period – *Cash on Demand* (1961) and *Strongroom* – use the invasion of banking premises to investigate the kind of relations that might exist between those at different places in the hierarchy of their institutions. These crimes are essentially small scale in conception and operation, at some remove from what one commentator diagnosed as the 'multi-million pound enterprises, conducted on the margin of legality'[7] that came to dominate financial scandals in the 1960s. For the most part, individual greed, working through a few associates, was behind 'B' movie robberies, though single embezzlers were at work in *The Big Chance* (1957), *Dublin Nightmare* (1958) and *The Embezzler* (1954). Other finance-related crimes recurring in the 'B' film scenarios involved currency and counterfeiting rackets of various kinds (often involving international villains – see below) and insurance fraud: all part of what Marwick, in a riposte to Harold MacMillan's oft-quoted bromide, called the 'acquisitive aspect of having it so good'.[8]

There are many 'private investigators' and representatives of US law enforcement agencies among the male protagonists of the 'B' films. In deference to possible American exhibition, such actors as Zachary Scott (*Wings of Danger*; *The Counterfeit Plan*, 1956), Larry Parks (*Tiger by the Tail*, 1955), Richard Denning (*Assignment Redhead*, 1956), Robert Hutton (*Man from Tangier*, 1957) and Rod Cameron (*Escapement*, 1958) were given the opportunity to unmask counterfeiting schemes, often stumbling on other crimes in the process. These American leads frequently bring with them the accoutrements of their trade and their culture: a 'fresh' approach to women, a facility with wise-cracking repartee and a (probably unlicensed) revolver. Other films whose narratives involve, with varying degrees of centrality, forgery and distribution of coveted currency include *Blackout, Four Days, River Beat, Delayed Action* (1954), *The Harassed Hero* (1954), *The Breaking Point* (1961), *Man at the Carlton Tower* (1961) and *Man Detained* (1961). The eventual collapse of demand for British Bs in the USA allowed greater opportunity for cultural verisimilitude, as in Peter Vaughan's convincing portrayal of an insurance investigator at work in *Smokescreen* (1964).

If the interest in smuggling and stealing luxury goods noted above may be seen partly as a flow-on from wartime and post-war austerity, spivs being ever-ready to supply such needs for a price, there was also a smaller number of films in which crimes were more directly connected to wartime events or to the leavings of the post-war world. Both *The Traitor* (1957) and *The Court-Martial of Major Keller* (1964) engage with the notion of wartime treachery in the Allied ranks, and one could speculate that such a subject might not have been felt appropriate in the years immediately following the war. These uncharacteristic moments of critique modify a little one's sense of the innate conservatism of the second feature. Other 'B' films treating crimes related to wartime conduct but dealt with post-war include: the comic-book adventure *Penny and the Pownall Case*, in which the disappearance of Pownall is linked to his tracking down of war criminals; and *The Bay of St Michel* (1963), in which three ex-commandos, with mixed motives, work to recover art treasures looted by the Nazis. First features were, of course, much preoccupied with wartime exploits during the 1950s, but usually in more celebratory mode than this batch of modest 'B' films exhibit. More generally, the aftermath of war serves as a backdrop to the challenges of the peace. This is symbolically expressed in the iconography of bomb damage, where devastated buildings pose a physical and moral danger to the young (as in *One Jump Ahead*, 1954, and *The Heart Within*, for instance). The discarded service revolver is another potent symbol of the legacy of war, most notably in *Bang! You're Dead* (1954), where, as part of the post-conflict detritus, it is the cause of death and minor felonies.

'B' films like *Bang! You're Dead* and *The Flamingo Affair* (1948) are, however, unusual in tackling in a serious way the kinds of post-war malaise one finds treated in a range of first features that includes *They Made Me a Fugitive* (1947), *Cage of Gold* (1950), *The Intruder* (1953) and *The Ship That Died of Shame* (1955). There are inevitably times, however, when the mundane struggles of life in austerity Britain, which form the context of these films, are evident in their scenarios and *mise en scènes*.

A pint and a pipe: Jack Warner relaxes in Lance Comfort's unusual rural thriller, *Bang! You're Dead* (1954)

Francis Searle's *Wheel of Fate* is a good example of a 'state of the nation' crime film. It is a story of damaged people seeking happiness while living in quiet desperation. Their tough and stoical fronts conceal a sensitivity we know lies beneath. The ailing patriarch of the family at the centre of the narrative is unable to adjust to changed post-war circumstances, and his sons are confused about the prioritising of duty and personal ambition, battling against constraining circumstances to discover themselves and their talents. In contrasting the staid world of work-a-day enterprise with the glamour of dance halls, gambling, bottle blondes and sudden violence, *Wheel of Fate* suggests a nation at the crossroads, riven by moral dilemmas and temptations. Unsurprisingly, the film finally advocates the righteous path: the spirit of self- and social discipline fostered during the war and predictably represented here by a policeman.

The threat posed to enduring national values and ways of life in the 'B' films is often expressed as an external one. The threat constituted by Americanisation can rarely be explicit in crime pictures that are increasingly required to be compatible with transatlantic distribution, and it generally remains more or less subliminal in the *mise en scène* or dialogue: criminals who sport flashy ties, drive Yankee automobiles and address as 'sister' women who are certainly not their blood relations. However, the deteriorating East–West relations of the Cold War offered greater possibilities to contrast virtuous Britishness with a heinous Otherness. Foreigners of all kinds are deeply suspect in these films, recalling Herbert Lom's comment in another context, 'in English eyes all foreigners are villains,'[9] and this view can be endlessly substantiated through the annals of the British 'B' movie. The representation of foreigners and the post-war European situation surfaces in various ways, but here it is worth noting a number of 'B' films which foreground crimes of espionage and attempts at world destruction. Schoolboy blood-and-thunder pieces such as *Dick Barton – Special Agent* and *Dick Barton at Bay* (1950) and the comedy *It's Not Cricket* (a mad Nazi at large in the Home Counties) point to the post-war preoccupations with foreigners as a necessary 'other'. Supposedly more serious were second features such as: *Devil's Jest* (1954), with MI5 on the track of a German baron in Scotland; *Counterspy* (1953), exposing a young accountant to foreign crooks with secret jet plans; Anthony Squire's naive *Doublecross* (1956) in which a Cornish fisherman (Donald Houston) gets into deep water, as it were, with Soviet spies; *Suspect* (1960), whose scientists fear their discoveries may, in the Cold War climate, bring harm; and *Echo of Diana* (1961), with reporters uncovering an international spy ring and a double agent. Films like these kept such actors as Anton Diffring and Karel Stepanek in steady work for years as they provided the chilly faces of Britain's enemies past and present.

As there had been in the quota quickies of the 1930s, there was a lot of blackmail about, in films such as *The Limping Man, House of the Arrow* (1953), *Man in the Shadow* (1957), *Stranger in Town* (1957) and *The Man Who Liked Funerals* (for comic effect). Its aim was, as ever, to produce profit

The shape of things to come: a prominently placed television set indexes the challenge to the 'B' feature in this still from Ernest Morris's espionage film *Echo of Diana* (1963)

from shameful secrets in a society which still valued personal privacy and social respectability. Another ingredient far from novel, the escaped convict, had surfaced in many earlier films and in such British 'A' films of the period as *Great Expectations* (1946), *It Always Rains on Sunday* (1947), *The Small Voice* (1948) and *Floods of Fear* (1958), where he was apt to provoke a questioning of values. In the 'B' films, the escapee sometimes exerts the same influence on the narrative, as in the period piece *Room to Let* (1950), when he terrorises a conventional family, or *Bond of Fear* (1956) when he disrupts a family holiday and exposes middle-class vulnerability, or *The Break* (1962) in which he causes havoc in an apparently cosy English guest house, or *Clash by Night* (1963) which raises the issue of undeserved sentences.[10] There is also a batch of films which deal with kidnapping (virtually unknown in Britain at the time) and the holding of hostages, whether as a result of the sinister interventions of foreign powers, as in *The Man in the Road* and *Dick Barton at Bay*, or of international smugglers as in *Diplomatic Passport* and *River Beat*, or as part of a Mafia-revenge plot in *The Sicilians* (1964). In *The Unstoppable Man* (1960), as in similar thrillers, the kidnapping of a child signals a challenge to the due processes of law and policing, and the reversion to more 'primitive' forms of retribution, giving an opportunity to an ordinary, middle-class man to become an action hero (with a home-made flame-thrower in this case) in defence of his family. The two tautest kidnap/hostage thrillers are *Tomorrow at Ten* and *Touch of Death*, both 1962 and both directed by Lance Comfort, who gives the characters a little more background to account for their actions than is often the case.

Few of the crime films of the 1950s paint a particularly realistic picture of the criminal underworld. When these films are not trying to unravel the sort of complex puzzles beloved of Agatha Christie, they are over-reliant on the melodramatic formulations of Edgar Wallace, with their mysterious masterminds seen only in shadow. Maxwell Munden's *The Bank Raiders* (1958) is typical in presenting what Robert Murphy has described as 'a singularly unconvincing depiction of life in the English underworld'.[11] Rank had hoped to cash in on a spate of well-publicised robberies, and its press book encouraged exhibitors to play up the crime prevention angle: 'Remember, today, tomorrow, at any moment, events in your town could parallel this drama. From the quiet of a peaceful day violence could suddenly flare to leave a vicious scar.' Audiences in the tranquil shires may have taken some convincing, despite Rank's earlier attempt, in *Find the Lady* (1956), to persuade them that mild-mannered Mervyn Johns could be the leader of a gang of desperadoes intent on breaking into a village bank. It is not until the end of the decade that the literary blinds begin to be raised and a cold light is shed on organised crime. Bs like *Naked Fury* (1960), *Offbeat* (1961) and *The Hi-Jackers* (1963) are at last able to present the morals, mores and motivations of those on the wrong side of the law with some sense of authenticity, even if they do not go as far as depicting criminals as 'ordinary people trying to make a living', as one of the characters in *Offbeat* describes them.

As to who was dealing with the crime so endemic in the 'B' films, the answer is, for the most part, a sympathetically presented police force, uniformed or trench-coated and trilby-hatted, or even undercover (as in *13 East Street*, 1952; *The Floating Dutchman*, 1953; *The Frightened Man*). Whatever the variation from the regular police force as the agency for bringing wrongdoers to justice, it is a fair generalisation that the police are not, in this decade following *The Blue Lamp*'s idealisation of them, submitted to any serious scrutiny, let alone criticism. Montgomery may be right in saying that 'The image of the police had changed. No longer the guardians of liberty in the eyes of the civilian population, they had become identified with Puritanism and the prevention of having a good time,'[12] but there is almost no sign of this diminution of respect in the 'B' films of the 1950s. It

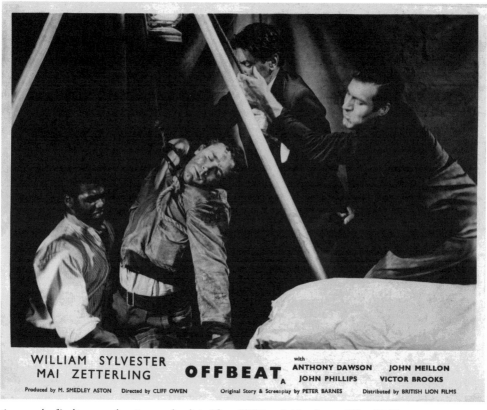

WILLIAM SYLVESTER
MAI ZETTERLING
OFFBEAT A
with
ANTHONY DAWSON   JOHN MEILLON
JOHN PHILLIPS   VICTOR BROOKS

Produced by M. SMEDLEY ASTON   Directed by CLIFF OWEN   Original Story & Screenplay by PETER BARNES   Distributed by BRITISH LION FILMS

An example of 'ordinary people trying to make a living' from Cliff Owen's debut feature *Offbeat* (1961)

is an unshakable convention that the inspector will always get his man, without recourse to any questionable or underhand methods. The iconography of Bobbies on the beat, detectives arriving in limos and a police box on the corner is everlastingly reassuring. One has to wait until *Offbeat* for any significant questioning of the 'copperolatry' of the post-war crime film. The worst that might be said of the police as they are represented in these films is that they are slower than some of the extra-Constabulary professionals and amateurs that are also inclined to do a bit of sleuthing in these pictures: ordinary citizens who are dragged into criminal investigations by force of circumstance (as in *Home to Danger* or *The Man from Tangier*), or private eyes (as in *Barbados Quest*, 1955), or secret agents of various hues (the *Dick Barton* trio), or insurance investigators (see above), or reporters (as in *Behind the Headlines*; *The Girl in the Picture*, 1956; etc.). As Paul Carpenter, the journalist in *One Jump Ahead* puts it: 'I'm one jump ahead of the police, but they'll catch up, they always do.' The police are generally at their slowest when their investigative competition is American as it is in, say, *The Blue Parrot* (1953), *The Gelignite Gang* (1956), *Breakaway* (1956) and *The Impersonator* (1961).

Work

There is plenty of evidence in the 'B' film of police and other investigators going about their callings, but as to the population at large, little sense of their regular paid activities beyond the extent to which these are interrupted by criminal incursions. The importance of work is emphasised in the garage setting of *Wheel of Fate*, where the wheels of the nation are literally kept turning by the repair of tyres. A few other Bs take the idea of work seriously, notably Wolf Rilla's *The End of the Road* (1954). This heartfelt account of an old factory hand's unwilling retirement is remarkable in its questioning the place of work in life. *Picturegoer* applauded 'a screenplay [by James Forsyth and Geoffrey Orme] that knows what it's saying ... it also makes you think'.[13] The film opens with a small boy kicking a football in sight of factory smoke; the siren blows and inside the factory the works manager (Edward Chapman) makes a jocose speech as he presents the retiree, Mick-Mack (Finlay Currie in a rare starring role) with 'a small token' for the fifty years he has 'pass[ed] in and out of our gate'. Disconsolately, the old man walks to his son's house through homely streets and past non-picturesque canals, but his family is preoccupied with its own affairs and doesn't notice Mick-Mack's unhappiness, while he cannot find an appropriate time to tell them.[14] Consequently, they push him off to work as usual, where, after further tribulations, he is finally offered the position of time-keeper at the factory. Certainly, the narrative finds too neat a closure, but the film is characterised by a real feeling for cramped working-class life and for the gap left when suddenly one is no longer required to be anywhere on a regular basis. If in the end it evades the problem it has raised, it is also true to say that almost no other 'B' film (and not many As for that matter) even begins to deal with a matter of such common human significance. *Kinematograph Weekly* rightly praised it as 'provocative and purposeful entertainment. Of and for the masses.'[15]

Although *The End of the Road* is rare among 'B' films in being interested in the ways in which characters go about their everyday working lives, a great deal of information relating to the sorts of employment available inevitably impinges at the edges of the narrative plotting, even when it doesn't especially influence the outcome of that plotting. Protagonists need some sort of context and part of that context is provided by their work situation, however sketchily it may be represented. When one considers the incidence of this or that job or profession, there are some surprises. One would expect to find several dozen reporters and journalists, often outstripping the police in their investigations, but it is perhaps less predictable that there should be such a sprinkling of actors and other entertainers or of writers and publishers. Since most 'B' films have an urban setting, one doesn't get much sense of rural life. Not more than about a dozen films in our sample concern themselves with country life: *Bang! You're Dead* offers a surprisingly bleak view of post-war scruffiness in a woodland setting; *Comin' Thru' the Rye* (1947), a deeply ridiculous biopic of Robert Burns, has a montage of rural activities to give a suggestion of the poet's background; *David* (1951) and *The Valley of Song* (1953) show rural life in Wales; and *Where There's a Will* (1955) has a cockney family inheriting a run-down farm. There are plenty of village streets and some attention to local activities in the comedies *Stop Press Girl* (1948), *Badger's Green*, *Time Gentlemen Please!* (1952) and *Trouble with Eve* (1959), in which Hy Hazell tries to run a tea shop. Inevitably, the village and its small-scale enterprises are made to stand for traditional values and morals under challenge from modernising and 'progressive' forces. *Trouble in the Air* (1948) casts a satirical eye at the decline of the squirearchy, contrasting a world of bell-ringers and faithful retainers with a rising nouveau riche culture almost indivisible from spivery. There are more campanologists in the Cornish fishing village that is the setting for *Doublecross*. Most of the thrillers, when they venture into the countryside, barely leave the manor house, but a few show people going about village occupations (shopkeepers, publicans, vicar, doctor, etc.), although these are not central to the narrative action. They include *The Large Rope* (1953), in which a former convict returns to his village to clear himself, and *Death of an Angel*, in which a banker murders a doctor's wife.

There are many pubs, cafés, restaurants and roadhouses scattered through the Bs, employing barmen and barmaids, waiters and waitresses, cooks, but only rarely are these premises and their employees more than context. Most of the pubs are announced by 'olde' architecture and quaint inn signs. They are, of course, sometimes used for the carrying out of more or less nefarious activities: in *My Death Is a Mockery*, the corruption of a former naval officer begins in a pub, when a smuggling proposition is put to him; and, in semi-comic vein, pub-keeper Gordon Harker colludes with poachers in *Bang! You're Dead*. The most serious outcome of pub culture is probably that depicted in *To the Public Danger* (1948), in which too much drinking leads to tragic results. More often, though, as in such entertainments as *Fools Rush In* (1949) and *Miss Robin Hood* (1952), pubs are as innocuous as tea rooms. *Assassin for Hire* (1952) has Soho cafés as a setting for an Italian hit man going about his vocation to support his brother's musical career. In the piffling *Love in Waiting*, the restaurant is the scene of crime, but as well there is at least a whiff of the actual work of the place, as there is in the roadhouses of *Marilyn* (a.k.a. *Roadhouse Girl*, 1953), *Rag Doll* (1960) and *The Hi-Jackers*, and in the small country trust house from which *Small Hotel* (1957) takes its title. We should also note *The Impersonator*, in which a café proprietor and her small son are vital figures in the drama and the café itself is important in the life of the small town near a US Air Force base.

Other kinds of business premises include banks, warehouses and shops at various levels of opulence. In *The Frightened Man*, the protagonist's antique shop is central to the drama of inter-generational conflict, as will later be the Hatton Garden jeweller's on which the larcenous son has set his sights. Jewellers were targets for thieves in other films such as *Cat and Mouse* (1958), *Stranger in Town* (1957) and *Time Is My Enemy* (1954); a bookshop is the slightly surprising setting for murder in *The Last Page* (1952); the ex-boxer's shop in *Three Crooked Men* (1957) is the scene of his frustration and of criminal invasion; village shops give verisimilitude to such films as *The Large Rope*, *Doublecross* and *Time Gentlemen Please!*; and the world of fashion is glimpsed in *Death in High Heels* (1947), *Cloak Without Dagger* and *Blood Orange*. As for banks, they provide the setting for two of the best of all 'B' movies, *Cash on Demand* and *Strongroom*: in both, the relations between manager and staff are as important as the attempted robberies. Bankers and/or their underlings are important to *Account Rendered*, *The Bank Raiders*, *Cat and Mouse*, *Death of an Angel*, *The Embezzler* and *Three Crooked Men*, in which the robbers wear suits and ties as even crooks did in this period.

Among the professions most commonly represented in the British 'B' films are medicine (including a few psychiatrists), the law, the press and science. Doctors are of course frequently called in to assist with investigations of crimes normally perpetrated by the lower orders, as in such films as *The Man in Black* (1949), *The House Across the Lake*, *Find the Lady*, *Dangerous Afternoon* (1961) and *Never Back Losers*. The doctors in the two thrillers involving small boys who have been abducted, by father in *Night Train to Inverness* (1959) and by kidnapper in *Tomorrow at Ten*, have significant and authoritative roles to play. However, in at least a handful of 'B' films, the medical profession is called into moral question: doctors are suspected of murder in *Death of an Angel* and *Black Orchid* (1952); the plastic surgeon in *Stolen Face* (1952) is up to some pre-Hammer-horror tricks; the tetchy doctor in *Smokescreen* (1964), cross at being interrupted while tending his roses, asks five guineas for 'professional advice'. This sort of behaviour hardly justifies the bludgeoning with a poker of the psychiatrist in *Alias John Preston*, but equally, these 'B' representations hardly support the common assertion that the National Health reforms brought new respect and reverence for the medical profession. Bizarrely, journalists seem to be more trustworthy than medics in the British Bs. So too, on balance, are the lawyers: for example, in *House of Darkness* (1948), the family lawyer (John Stuart), charged with administering the hero's mother's will, tries to warn him against accumulating debts, while the conscientious country solicitor (Donald Houston) in *The Flaw* (1955) will ultimately win the heiress he loves when her wastrel husband conveniently drowns. Judges are invariably fair-minded and authoritive, even if they occasionally have to don the black cap. The *institution* of the law and justice is usually observed with uncritical respect, and its representatives are customarily played by actors of commanding dignity.

As for scientists, they were frequently in the service of foreign powers – or in the service of the horror and science-fiction genres. This is the period – the mid-1950s – of C. P. Snow's famous *New Statesman* essay, 'The Two Cultures',[16] in which he controversially claimed that science came an unde-servedly poor second in Britain, after what he saw as an unadventurous literary culture. Much scien-tific activity in Britain in the post-war years was directed towards either the development of nuclear power or to the prospect of space travel, and in neither field was Britain a world leader. However, for the purposes of the 'B' movie, the controversial work of scientists at least made them targets for the machinations of unscrupulous foreign powers, as in *Dick Barton at Bay* and *The Man in the Road*, in which a scientist is abducted to work behind the Iron Curtain. *The Steel Key* (1953), a hectic thriller, at least foregrounds the work of its scientists in their research for a process that will harden steel, while, more fancifully, in tackling *The Trollenberg Terror* (1958), a Swiss professor and a UN science investigator (American Forrest Tucker) actually spend more time convincingly at their research than most. Probably the most sustained account of a scientist at work is in the Boulting brothers' superior 'B' *Suspect* (1960), in which a young researcher faces the dilemma of aiming to save lives while fear-ing that misuse of his work, if it falls into the wrong hands, will kill people. In general, though, it cannot be said that the spectacle of scientists going about their work is treated with much seriousness in the 'B' films, reaching its nadir in *Mother Riley Meets the Vampire* (1952) in which Bela Lugosi plays an evil scientist who aims at world domination by means of radar-controlled robots.

Clearly, it is not possible here to deal with all the jobs and professions that surface, however sig-nificantly or marginally, in the 'B' movies. There are numerous secretaries and receptionists, efficient or merely sassy, landladies, bossy (*The Embezzler*) or merely nosey (*The Hornet's Nest*, 1955), a few garage workers (*Marilyn*, *Wheel of Fate* and *Touch of Death*) and several who work the waterways, whether as fishermen (*Doublecross*, *My Death Is a Mockery*), bargees (*Painted Boats*, 1945) or boat-builders (*Touch of Death*).[17] But, apart from policemen, the most over-represented occupational group in these films are workers in what we would now term 'the creative or cultural industries': actors, entertainers, musicians, artists, models and night-club workers. They add colour to the proceedings in cameos like Dennis Shaw's stereotypical Left-Bank artist in *Trouble with Eve*, but they are also at the narrative heart of some films: in the gloomy *Star of My Night* (1954), a sculptor is going blind while working on the statue of a ballerina with whom he falls in love, then using an actress friend to help promote his romance; in *The Impersonator* an actor is unmasked on stage as a killer; and a London actor tries to persuade an ex-actress to stop mouldering away in a rural retreat with her hus-band in the triangular drama *Act of Murder* (1964). The whole plot of *Live It Up* (1963) and much of *Be My Guest* (1965) revolves around the aspirations of a pop group calling itself 'The Smart Alecs'; and a Covent Garden singer furthers the plot in Highbury's romantic melodrama *Song for Tomorrow* (1948), as does a promising violinist in *Assassin for Hire*. Singers and showgirls in night clubs are con-stant and dangerous objects of desire in the British 'B'. They included Mary Castle singing 'No Way

Out' in *Three Steps to the Gallows*, with Simone Silva in *Escape by Night* (1953), Constance Smith as the seductive Lila in *Impulse* and Jill Ireland driving real-life husband David McCallum to murderous distraction in *Jungle Street* (1961). Showgirls are also involved in murder in the likes of *Tread Softly* (1952), *Wheel of Fate, Johnny, You're Wanted* and *The Painted Smile* (1962). These women are invariably more knowing, more worldly and sexier than the usual 'B' film heroines, perhaps reflecting both social change in Britain and an urge to Americanise the 'B' thriller for wider acceptability.

Given that every film begins with a scriptwriter, it is perhaps not so surprising that alter egos crop up frequently in the Bs, even though writing has limited visual appeal. Their romantic need for seclusion to get on with literary work is perhaps hinted at in such titles as *The House Across the Lake*, *The House in the Woods* and *The House in Marsh Road* (1960), in each of which a writer is deflected from his work by crime and mystery, with a suggestion of adultery as well in the first, a nutty neighbouring painter in the second and a poltergeist in the third. Crime writers are to be found in *The Gold Express* and *The Man in the Road*. Publishers are also on show in *Cover Girl Killer*, in which sleazy magazine publishing is at issue, comically in *Miss Robin Hood* and straight in *Black Orchid*, without any of these yielding much impression of the *work*. At least writing and its publication are not seen to be slackers' jobs, though they are subject to some gently funny satire in *The Man Who Liked Funerals*.

The modern business organisation is scrutinised in a couple of unusual Bs: Godfrey Grayson's *An Honourable Murder*, a brave and imaginative adaptation of Shakespeare's *Julius Caesar*,[18] and Peter

Et tu, Brute: Brian Clemens' adaptation of *Julius Caesar* for the Danzigers, *An Honourable Murder* (1960)

Graham Scott's *The Big Day* (1960). In *An Honourable Murder*, the Danzigers' regular screenwriter Brian Clemens has transposed the central action of *Julius Caesar* from the running of a country (the republic of Rome) to the running of a company, Empire Petroleum, which is in the middle of a negotiation to merge with the Pompey Shipping Line. There is a basic problem with this analogy in the circumstances of the play/film: one might admire a man who puts loyalty to his country above that to a friend; such a discrimination becomes more problematic when country is replaced by 'company'. Nevertheless, the film concerns itself with this play of loyalties and establishes briskly a network of ambition, friendships and treacheries which will tax those loyalties. Julian Caesar (veteran John Longden) is voted off the Empire Petroleum board by the other members of the board, led by the 'lean and hungry' Cassius figure (Douglas Wilmer) who knows their coup will only work if they have the upright Brutus Smith (Norman Wooland) on their side. 'And you, Brutus!' cries Caesar, when Brutus raises his hand to vote. Caesar dies almost immediately after the coup from a heart attack, while Brutus's slide into remorse and illness is more protracted. There is also a spirited shareholders' meeting at which Mark Anthony (Philip Saville) sways the feeling of the crowd, spurred on by Caesar's secretary Paula (Lisa Daniely). One has to admire the Danziger brothers' cheek.[19]

The Big Day offers some surprisingly sour insights into the workings of a small business – and even sourer ones into the personal relationships of the three men who are up for a possible promotion. Selkirk (William Franklyn) is a smooth bully, who is smugly confident, having already undermined the chances of another competitor, Jackson (Harry H. Corbett). Jackson has the further burden of a nagging wife Mabel (Betty Marsden), who is the sister-in-law of the company chairman, Baker (Colin Gordon). She is not above using this connection against the third aspirant, Partridge (Donald Pleasence), a weak man who is having an affair with his young secretary, Nina (Andrée Melly). However, when the mediocre Partridge is finally chosen, not for any positive qualities, but because he poses the least threat to Baker's position of power, Baker instructs him to 'get rid of your typist immediately'. We have been encouraged to think there is something genuine in the feeling between Partridge and Nina, but he has no compunction in sacking her: 'I don't want to be saddled with a failure,' he tells her, and boasts to the wife he's been cheating on, 'I'll have my name on the company's notepaper.' His wife's response – 'The job doesn't seem worth it' – sums up the film's critical attitude to the dehumanising effects of workplace competition. There is no attempt to soften the emptiness of the 'yes-man's' victory; indeed, in human terms it is represented wholly as loss. Like a remarkable number of British 'B' films, it doesn't end on an upbeat note: in fact, there is, arguably and paradoxically, a greater degree of honesty in these programme-fillers, intended to satisfy an undemanding market, than big-budget films could have afforded. *The Big Day* gives a very sober sense of what work is worth and how it relates to the other aspects of living, particularly to the way it connects with the emotional lives of those engaged in it.[20] The *Monthly Film Bulletin* justifiably praised the film for its 'serious exposé of manners and morals within the confines of a closed little society'.[21]

Leisure

The short running time and hectic narrative schedules of 'B' films do not as a rule allow for extended depictions of leisure-time activities. However, they do reveal much about the taken-for-granted aspects of cultural life in the twenty years after World War II. There is a great deal of casual alcohol consumption – pub beer for working-class characters, spirits or cocktails for their 'betters', who are almost incapable of entering a living room without crossing straight to the drinks cabinet – and

A slinky blonde on a bar stool: Hollywood's Gene Nelson strikes a light for Kay Callard in *Dial 999* (1955)

smoking: so much, in fact, that it is scarcely worth cataloguing their appearances. There is also an immense amount of tea-drinking, often more ritualistically presented than the intake of alcohol and cigarettes. The preparation and drinking of tea is regularly the occasion for unthinking solace (*The Large Rope*) or reflecting on a quarrel (*Valley of Song*). Much ado is caused in *Trouble with Eve* about the wish of a woman of questionable reputation to turn her cottage into 'Willow Teas', while the build-up of tension in *Emergency* has to overcome endemic tea-breaks. The 'nice cup of tea' is a leit-motiv throughout the 'B' movie corpus, its restorative properties even recommended as a cure for the shock revelation of extraterrestrial life in *Devil Girl from Mars* (1954). Its omnipresence is actually articulated in *Impulse*: 'Why do the English resolve everything with a cup of tea?' when the protagonist's life is about to be much more seriously disturbed; and in *The Late Edwina Black* the police inspector (Roland Culver) tells his assembled suspects that 'There are few moments in life when a cup of tea isn't welcome,' before using the ceremony of serving the beverage to unmask the guilty party. As to coffee, it is one of those alien influences that threaten to subvert 'Britishness'. When Banner (Paul Carpenter) in *One Jump Ahead* asks for coffee after a night on Maxine's (Diane Hart's) couch, she can only reply 'You Canadians!' No self-respecting Englishman would wake to anything so *outré*.

Coffee bars, a growing phenomenon associated with the bohemian young, were only a step away in decadence-potential from the extraordinarily numerous night clubs in which the denizens of 'B' movie Britain got into so much trouble. In the first two post-war decades, the superficial 'luxury' of

'There are few moments in life when a cup of tea isn't welcome': Roland Culver unmasks the person responsible for the death of *The Late Edwina Black* (1951), watched anxiously by Geraldine Fitzgerald, David Farrar and Jean Cadell

these nocturnal spaces answered subliminally a need for liminal relief from the austerities of daily reality. In dramaturgical terms, night clubs provided a non-domestic meeting place for leisure and crime, a venue for the seduction of innocents by the glossier habitués, and a rationale for the staging of modest musical production numbers thought to enhance the films' audience appeal. There is no denying how often they appear in the 'B' movies, at least fifty times in the sample under discussion. Here, typically, the sound of Anglicised mambo played by bored combos accompanies the half-hearted routines of chubby dancers. There are some deeply suspicious-looking owners, such as Sydney Tafler, proprietor of Skinner's Supper and Dancing Club in *The Floating Dutchman*, or Elwyn Brook-Jones in *The Gilded Cage* (1955), or Bruno Barnabe at the Blue Baboon Club in *Pit of Darkness* (1961). It is hard to think of an amiable, let alone honest, club owner in the British Bs, and this may point to a general community dubiety about their activities, which the 1961 film *Jungle Street* renders with a strong sense of their tattiness and iniquity potential. By this time, the night club is increasingly a strip club and songs are supplemented by gyrating tassels and enough wobbling cellulite to cause disquiet among the censors of Soho Square.[22] *Jungle Street*'s dive is a fully designed and carpentered set, but many of these films settle for a flimsy plywood bar and a few chromed stools – enough to accommodate a slinky blonde with an extravagantly cantilevered bosom and a cigarette in need of a light.

Dancing venues are found in many films, ranging from the 'Palais' in *Wheel of Fate*, to the American Air Force base in *The Impersonator*, to the comparative wholesomeness of the boys'-club hop in *The Man Who Liked Funerals*. Visits to, and scenes set in, theatres are also common, indeed, they provide the entire setting for many of the musical revues of the late 1940s and early 1950s. That tradition is updated in the pop films of the 1960s, such as *Live it Up*. *Song for Tomorrow* stages part of its action at Covent Garden, while Christopher Lee confirms his image as a sophisticate by attending a classical concert in *Alias John Preston*. The provincial-town pantomime is convincingly re-created in *The Impersonator*, in which the theatre is presented as a popular site of the town's leisure. It is also, of course, associated with a deranged killer (in this case a pantomime dame), as it had been in first-feature fare like *Stage Fright* (1950) and *Murder at the Windmill* (1949), and in the 'B' *Tread Softly*, which otherwise is given a lift by the performance of Frances Day, a stage-trained actress and revue artiste.

In their hurry to get on with the narrative, these films don't dwell on domestic relaxation – they are too anxious to get out on to the night streets for that – but there are occasional glimpses of people working their gardens (as in *Smokescreen* or *Live It Up*) or lingering over dinner (in evening dress in posher situations, as in *To Have and to Hold*). The concept of dining out (as in *Small Hotel* or *An Honourable Murder*) or holding a dinner party at home (*Home to Danger*) is insufficiently in evidence to warrant conclusions about its place in the social lives of urban Britain. Getting away from the home for holidays, so prominent in the travelogue featurettes of immediate post-war Britain, is less in evidence in the full-length 'B' films. A family is heading off on a caravan holiday to France in *Bond of Fear* when events overtake them; *Dick Barton – Special Agent* is on a chaps' holiday before the inevitable crime distracts him; the unhappy lovers in *The Late Edwina Black* are headed for Italy at film's end; a gaggle of teenagers on holiday fetches up at a haunted castle in *The Headless Ghost* (1959); people staying at an isolated guest house in *The Break* will wish they weren't; and *The Trollenberg Terror* unnerves travellers in an alpine resort. But the more conventional British leisure resorts – for instance, the seaside, the countryside of hill, river and canal, or the holiday camp (famously featured in Ken Annakin's 1947 film) – only occasionally make their presences felt in these films, most likely because their restricted budgets didn't encourage extensive location shooting. The main exceptions are the films made at Brighton Studios which often include shots of holidaymaking in the town. The pier of neighbouring Hastings provides a fitting venue for the climax of *Shadow of a Man*.

In 1956, Wolf Mankowitz wrote scathingly of television as being '[piped] into the home like warm water from an atomic pile', reviling it as 'The cultural equivalent of the atom bomb' and adding that because 'subject to mass approval for its success, it must necessarily accept and promote mass standards'.[23] Despite this, there is remarkably little attention paid to it in the 'B' films. Could this possibly be a matter of self-protection? In the sample on which this chapter is based, there is virtually no incidence of television-viewing as a leisure activity before *The Limping Man* (1953), in which it is sardonically presented as a form of addiction, and *Radio Cab Murder* (1954), in which there is talk about aerials as a new phenomenon. Experiments in the name of scientific 'progress' jam local TV signals in *The Strange World of Planet X* (1956), itself a television adaptation, but, by and large, characters in the Bs are far too busy to watch TV.

Sex

Britain in the period under review was a society which still clung officially to the notion of marriage as the only proper site for sexuality and to the superior status of the male. As Kenneth Morgan wrote in relation to 1961, 'The official view of the Inland Revenue that the woman, whether as wife or

ADRIENNE CORRI   THORLEY WALTERS   LISA GASTONI
in **"SECOND FIDDLE"** 'U'
with **RICHARD WATTIS**   an A.C.T. FILM   Produced by **ROBERT DUNBAR**   Directed by **MAURICE ELVEY**
In charge of Production **RALPH BOND**   Screenplay by **ALLAN MACKINNON** and **ROBERT DUNBAR**
From an original story by **Mary Cathcart Borer** and **Arnold Ridley**   Distributed by **BRITISH LION FILMS**

Career girl: Adrienne Corri poses problems for her boss in Maurice Elvey's ACT film *Second Fiddle* (1957)

daughter, was the dependant of the male bread-winner, was the dominant stereotype,'[24] a statement utterly reinforcing the acceptance of marriage as the basis of social and sexual organisation. This view is echoed by Cate Haste when she writes of the situation in the latter 1950s: 'The domestic ideal of life-long marriage as a partnership of breadwinner and housewife still put women at the centre of the home and the family.'[25] However, she also allowed that 'beneath this apparent stability, strong cross-currents of social and political conflict were forming'.[26] These currents, as well as the limits of their flow, are sometimes evident in 'B' pictures like ACT's *Second Fiddle* (1957), which is built around the theme of women's conditions of employment: Debbie (Adrienne Corri), a brilliant executive in an advertising agency, struggles successfully to overturn a ban on the employment of married women only to give up her work when she becomes pregnant. On the other hand, a film like *She Always Gets Their Man* (1962) reinforces every stereotype of women at work or in society. Interestingly enough, some of the most 'progressive' representations of working women (who constituted one in three of the workforce by the end of the 1950s) are to be found among the foreign female scientists of the sci-fi programmers *Spaceways* (1953) and the aforementioned *The Strange World of Planet X*. Although initially viewed as disturbing intrusions into the masculine work culture of cutting-edge research, the capable and independent scientists played by Eva Bartok and Gaby André win the recognition and respect of their male colleagues, and for more than the fit of their fully fashioned lab coats.

Gaby André's Michelle also has a nice line in sexual innuendo when discoursing on the inexhaustible capabilities of her machine, but, generally, the dialogue of 'B' films and their depiction of erotic situations was carefully policed. Although during the 1950s violence was the most pressing issue, the minutes of the British Board of Film Censors contain a catalogue of exceptions taken to any suggestions of sexual activity. In September 1954, for example, Tempean were instructed to make a number of cuts to Reel 2 of John Gilling's *Tiger by the Tail*, in which Lisa Daniely played Anna and Larry Parks played Desmond:

> Delete from dialogue Anna's remark 'In the lonely hours – fun!' Delete whole sequence of embrace at door, with overcoat dropped etc. Delete all references, next morning, both by Jane at office and receptionist at Desmond's hotel, to his having been out all night.[27]

If a commercially damaging 'X' certificate was to be avoided, sex outside marriage – and even sex within matrimony – was simply not to be suggested. Any hint at masturbation was also to be eradicated, as the instructions to Tempean for cuts to their Belinda Lee comedy *No Smoking* (1955) attest: 'Delete man's suggestive snigger after Miss Tomkins' [Lee's] remark "I'd love to see you fiddle". Delete all shots of man standing in doorway of house, his hands in his trouser pockets, watching Miss Tomkins going to chemist's shop.'[28] Things had not changed a great deal by 1960, when the Mancunian risqué comedy *Trouble With Eve* struggled to win an 'A' certificate:

> Remove the lines 'Pity to let the crumpets get cold' and 'I can't wait to get at the crumpets'. Remove shots of maid on chair, and of Axbridge clutching her dress. Remove the line 'Be careful what you do with it' (after reference to Louise's form). Remove all the dialogue about the groundsheet. Remove 'I spent all night with George in a turnip-field and all he would do was talk about his turnips'. Remove all the dialogue about Monsieur Duclos' having been in Eve's room at night ... Remove Eve's line 'He tried to take me over' (in conversation in Maitland's house). Shorten scene in which George is embracing Louise in chair. Shorten shadow-scene on blind, and the watchers' reaction to it, and in particular remove silhouette of man kissing girl on neck.[29]

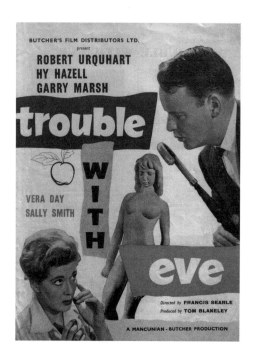

Talk of crumpets and turnips and kisses on the neck were clearly markers on the slippery slope to permissiveness, and had no place on the bottom half of the bill. A main feature, such as *Room at the Top* (1958), could trade on its 'X' certificate and set a new standard in sexual frankness – pre-marital sex, adultery tacitly

Crumpets and turnips: the press book for Francis Searle's risqué comedy *Trouble With Eve* (1960)

condoned, the ultimate marriage not depicted as the happy answer to everything – but the 'B' film could hardly dare to be so outspoken. Its reflection of changing sexual mores was necessarily more oblique.

In the British 'B' movies from 1945 to 1965, there is some suggestion of a shift in the representation of sexuality and social attitudes to its manifestations, but not as much as one might suppose. This was, after all, a period of major change, particularly from the later 1950s, when the Wolfenden Report was causing such a stir. In the earlier two-thirds of the period, though, sex was mostly subsumed and softened into 'romance'. As Paul Ferris writes of the early 1950s, 'Marriage was the thing, then as always. Engaged couples might have sex before it, but "living together" was rare. It meant loose morals, an affront to decency.'[30] There is little to challenge these perceptions in the decade immediately following the end of the war.

As a rule, the romantic action in these films is a pretty aseptic affair; equally, though, it needs to be noted that the couples do not move as predictably to the final clinch that was endemic in their Hollywood counterparts. There is mildly sexy banter in the light-hearted thrillers featuring the Paul Banner character, *One Jump Ahead* and *Behind the Headlines*, starring Paul Carpenter as a journalist who, in each case, is investigating a murder. In both films he is involved with two women (Diane Hart

Intimate revelations: the truth begins to be exposed in *Strip Tease Murder* (1963), one of a number of films exploiting the craze for 'exotic dance' clubs

and Jill Adams in the first, Adrienne Corri and Hazel Court in the second). In *Behind the Headlines*, there is the quite unusual 'B' film situation of the two women both with Banner in their sexual sights, leading to reporter Pam (Corri) resignedly getting the story as 'consolation prize' for losing Banner.

For more 'serious' depiction of sexual relationships, one generally has to look towards the films of later in the period under discussion, though such earlier films as *The Fool and the Princess* (1948), *The Rossiter Case* (1950), *Four Days* (1951) and *Five Days* (1954) are posited on the reality of sexual attraction. In the first, the protagonist is erotically obsessed by a woman he encountered in a displaced person's camp. In *The Rossiter Case*, a paralysed woman discovers that her husband is in love with her sister-in-law, and the film ends both surprisingly and austerely. The neglected wife of *Four Days* (played by Kathleen Byron who typically suggested more sensuality than most of the 'B' film female protagonists) has an affair with her husband's business partner who taunts him with, 'What did you expect her to do? Take up knitting?' In *Five Days*, three male–female relationships are sketched in somewhat more detail than usual, and again arrive at a subdued ending. Characteristically, women who evince the kind of sexual responsiveness that passes almost unnoticed in men can scarcely expect to arrive at happy endings. A key film in this respect is *Marilyn* (a.k.a. *Roadhouse Girl*), discussed in Chapter 8, in which the dissatisfied wife of a bullying garage owner strikes out for a more pleasurable life and is left alone and without hope.

In the latter film Marilyn loses her last support when her clearly lesbian maid finally deserts her, tired of being used. There is a slightly more veiled suggestion of a maid's love for 'madam' in *Black Orchid*, in which Sheila Burrell as Annette avenges the murder of her mistress (Mary Laura Wood), and in *The Late Edwina Black*, an actual declaration of love by the housekeeper (Jean Cadell) of the deceased Edwina. Lesbian representation was barely visible and generally limited to the sort of butch dragon-type played by Judith Furse in, for example, *Mother Riley Meets the Vampire* or *Not a Hope in Hell* (1960), though Stephen Bourne may be right in attributing 'lesbian feeling' to the relationship between characters played by Margaret Rawlings and Patricia Dainton in *No Road Back*.[31] Notions of how sexuality might be dramatised on screen were changing in the last third of these post-war decades, but explicit reference to homosexuality, while it might be accorded serious treatment in the 'A' film *Victim* (1961) and *The World Ten Times Over* (1963),[32] was still unlikely to surface in the lower depths – or, rather, that is where it would stay.

Nevertheless, there are several examples of gay encoding which audiences must surely have twigged at the time, such as Murray Matheson's ultra-aesthete preoccupations in *The Fool and the Princess*, Philip Gilbert's stroking a cat as he speaks of his admiration for the banker played by Griffith Jones in *Account Rendered* and, most evidently, Peter Sellers' camp rendering of Assistant Commissioner Jervis Fruit in *The Case of the Mukkinese Battlehorn* (1956). Michael Ward, a gay actor, has a typically stereotyped cameo in the inane *Stop Press Girl* as a hairdresser fussing about how his dryer has stopped, but he is permitted a much more sympathetic role in *The Frightened Man* as an antiques expert who excites the homophobia of the son of the shop's owner. He had more conventional material in *Tread Softly* as the camp son of theatre-owning Nora Nicholson. Arthur Howard, as an actor in a flashy suit in *Never Look Back* (1952), and Brian Oulton, as secretary to a flamboyant star in *It's Not Cricket*, are typically effeminate theatrical 'types'.

As the 1950s merged with the 1960s, the gradual relaxation of censorship allowed the sexual dimension of psycho-pathology to become more evident in films like *The Impersonator*, *Urge to Kill* (1960), *Don't Talk to Strange Men* (1962), *The Tell-Tale Heart* and *Cover Girl Killer*. *Rag Doll* suggests strongly that sexual abuse is the motivation for the fleeing of its heroine to London, and the compelling drama of workplace competitiveness *The Big Day* opens on a striking scene of what looks like the sexual enslavement of an older man for a much younger woman and which proceeds to a passionate kiss. There *is* some small evidence that the 'B' movie film-makers took notice of a somewhat more liberated attitude to sexual matters in the wider culture. In *Cover Girl Killer*, there is overt acknowledgment of sex magazines, of strippers plying their trade, of awareness of sex as an industry and of a permissiveness that points to the pornographic arm of 'X' certificate film-making. *So Evil, So Young* (1961), no doubt unconsciously, draws attention to the notion of sexuality in a girls' reformatory. By 1964, *Act of Murder*, *Blind Corner* and *Smokescreen* all treat sexual infidelity as crucial narrative factors, without trying to soften the impact or being notably judgmental about this state of affairs. Sex is rarely at the centre of 'B' film narratives, but equally it can't help surfacing in one way or other, whether it is a matter of sexual dissatisfaction in the middle-class life depicted in *The Big Chance* (1957) or of young English women turned on by the prospect of Americans as in *Cat and Mouse* or *The Impersonator*.

Class

In British cinema, at 'A' and 'B' levels, the ever-present cultural determinant is apt to be class rather than sex, and until the New Wave of the late 1950s it was very often taken for granted in films. Even so, in the large batch of 'B' films on which this study is based, there is still a thin trickle of films in which some vestigial critique of class organisation can be felt. For instance, in *The Big Chance*, Bill (William Russell), a travel agent, frets against the constraints of middle-class life and wife, and nearly takes up with the upmarket Diana (Adrienne Corri), who later says disparagingly of his wife, 'She's only a little shopgirl person, isn't she?' The film will end by endorsing the simpler values, but that kind of overt class-based comment is extremely rare. The middle-class ambience of so many of the films is simply a given: in Charles De Lautour's superior thriller *Impulse*, the 'bland life-style of middle-class England', is given unusual attention.[33] It is implicitly critiqued, almost held responsible for the dangerous waters into which the protagonist (Arthur Kennedy) plunges in response to the noir allurements of a sexy stranger (Constance Smith). Far more often, though, the kind of middle-class household and expectations of such films as, to choose a cross-genre handful, thrillers *Death of an Angel* and *Emergency*, the domestic comedy-drama *Fly Away Peter*, the romance *The Fool and the Princess* and the comedy *Miss Robin Hood*, is presented with a sense of affirmation, whatever minor constraints it may seem to offer. Even as late as the 1965 comedy-musical *Be My Guest* this holds good.

The upper- and upper middle-class households which run to servants and in which people still dress for dinner are amply represented. Of the three films Terence Fisher directed for Highbury, *Colonel Bogey* (1947) is set in a grand house in the country, and it is possible for one character to say 'Pas devant les domestiques', in *Song for Tomorrow* a son dresses to dine with his mother in her chintzy upper middle-class set-up, while *To the Public Danger* alone offers any sense of class critique as the former officer makes off with the pretty girl he meets in a pub and embarrasses her boyfriend. Upper-class mansions replete with servants are found in *House of Darkness*, *Meet Simon Cherry* (1949), *Four Days*, *The Gambler and the Lady* (1952, in which an American aspires to the upper social echelon's ways and in which there is more explicit talk of class than is usual), *Home to Danger*, *The Voice of Merrill* (1952, in which the butler brings in coffee to elegantly dinner-dressed Valerie Hobson and James Robertson Justice) and *Night Was Our Friend* (1952), and even *Mother Riley Meets the Vampire* sports a butler and maid. Was there around the late 1940s/early 1950s, where these films are clustered, a sneaking nostalgia for the pre-war images of how toffs lived? And what does one make of *Children Galore* (1954) in which the local lord and lady offer a cottage as a parting gift to the village family with most grandchildren? The incidence of upper- and upper middle-class families with resident staff dwindles somewhat during the 1950s, but as late as *Three Spare Wives* (1962) and *Tomorrow at Ten* they are still to be found. Overall, from films such as these, one would scarcely be aware of any move towards a more egalitarian society or of the kinds of social changes that characterised the post-war years.

On the other hand, there are some instances of working-class and lower middle-class life, sometimes evincing aspiration to higher things, sometimes comfortably satisfied with things as they are. Films with working-class protagonists include *Burnt Evidence* (1954), *Devil's Bait* (1959), *Doublecross* (with its sense of comfortable working-class life, albeit involved with Iron Curtain spies), *The End of the Road* (which takes the pressures of work and retirement seriously), the chilling *Man in the Back Seat* (1961, with a wife anxious about her husband's associates) and *The Impersonator* (which convincingly imagines a mother and small son living behind the café she runs). *Jungle Street*, with its images of urban sleaze, also embraces the idea of aspiring to other kinds of living, as do *The Flamingo Affair*, *One Way Out*, in which a fence is described as having 'come a long way ... up from the slums', and *The Frightened Man* and *No Road Back* have in common sons of receivers who have been educated beyond their parents' illicit practices. So, there is some sense of the class mobility that began to make itself felt in the 1950s, though no one would claim that the 'B' movies were ever exactly subversive in their responses to, and representation of, a long-entrenched class system.

Race and Ethnicity

Like the rest of British cinema in the period, the Bs overwhelmingly presented an ethnically homogeneous vision of the nation. The principal exceptions were the Jewish characters (predictably, often businessmen or tailors, as in *The Bespoke Overcoat*, 1956), Mediterranean types (frequently cast as café owners, waiters or gangsters) and Irish people (almost inevitably depicted as light-hearted, humorous and tuneful). There had been films targeted at the substantial Irish diaspora since the arrival of sound, and these made periodic appearances in the post-war years. Like Henry Cass's *Professor Tim* (1957), they often employed the talents of the famed players of Dublin's Abbey Theatre. The trade press thought that its 'artless humour and sentiment' was 'certain to delight in the many areas with an Irish population'.[34]

There is very little sign in the contemporary cinema of the increase in immigration from the Commonwealth, particularly the Caribbean, that was such a controversial aspect of Britain in the post-war years. The issue of racial prejudice was slow enough to make itself felt in first features (e.g., *Sapphire*, 1959; *Flame in the Streets*, 1961), and hardly surfaces in the Bs. One exception was David Eady's quite thoughtful dockside-set thriller *The Heart Within*, dealing with what the trade press called 'the West Indian problem'.[35] This unpretentious film concerns itself with the difficulties of docker Victor Conway (Earl Cameron),[36] who goes on the run when suspected of murdering a spiv. He is eventually instrumental in the demise of a drug-smuggling gang, with a little help from Danny, a newspaper boy played by the young David Hemmings. In what must have seemed quite outspoken dialogue at the time, Victor tells Danny 'A coloured man's always guilty till he's proved innocent,' and is reviled by another black man who claims, 'It's folks like him gets us all a bad name.' Overall, the film

JAMES HAYTER
CLIFFORD EVANS
EARL CAMERON in
THE HEART WITHIN (U)
Released by
Rank Film Distributors Ltd.

Heart's desire: Earl Cameron and Gloria Simpson in David Eady's sensitive drama *The Heart Within* (1957)

offers a very sympathetic picture of West Indians in dockside London: 'a good job and a decent living' is all Victor has wanted, and he fears his girl, who has a somewhat middle-class air when she arrives from Trinidad, will not find his work as a crane-driver impressive enough. Home-grown bigotry surfaces in remarks such as that passed by the policeman who wants to 'send the whole lot packing'.

The two main plot-lines involve the efforts of Danny and his grandfather (James Hayter) to help Victor prove his innocence and the police efforts to counter the drug smuggling in which corrupt men, both black and white, are caught up. The casting of Clifford Evans, famously 'Stryker of the Yard', as a pawnbroker who deals also in narcotics adds a nice balance to the film's moral texture. The film wants to make clear that colour and morality have no necessary connection. Apart from its invoking of inter-racial tensions (and moments of rapport), the film's chief claim to distinction is in the persistent and imaginative use of its locations. There are definite echoes of Ealing's *Pool of London* (1950) in *The Heart Within*'s wharves, shabby streets, bomb-sites and allotments which situate actions and attitudes in a real sense of time and place, and which must have enhanced the film's feeling of relevance for contemporary audiences.[37] Director Eady had worked uncredited on *The Third Man* (1949), so he knew the value of location shooting. He and producer Jon Pennington were keen to establish themselves as serious film-makers who wrote their own material, and claimed the picture was 'a complete breakaway from the cop and robber type of thing'.[38] Even the usually grudging *Monthly Film Bulletin* allowed that 'the film has a more convincing air than most thrillers of its type'.[39] The

Daily Film Renter gave it 'Good marks ... for attempting, as it tells its simple story, to put the problem of West Indians in this country into some sort of sympathetic perspective.'[40] Not to make too-extravagant claims for the film, it is certainly true to say that its heart within is in the right place, as one might expect from an original story by John Baxter and direction from the liberal-minded Eady. It was made before the Notting Hill riots of 1958, which no doubt led to a more serious attempt by the British film industry to put black faces on the screen and to address some of the issues raised by the riots against the West Indian community in West London. Subsequently, the black actor Tommy Eytle was cast as one of the more sympathetic gang members in *Naked Fury*, a role that might easily have been filled by a white player.

On 3 February 1960, Prime Minister Harold Macmillan in an address made to the South Africa Parliament declaimed: 'The wind of change is blowing through this continent.'[41] Shortly afterwards, a rare 'B' movie which has racial hatred as its mainspring took its title from Macmillan's speech. In *The Wind of Change* (1961) young Frank looks surlily at a black youth who comes into a coffee bar, turns off the juke-box, and snarls, 'You get your filthy black face out of here.' If it is all a bit didactic and strident in its indictment of racial prejudice and the crime it gives rise to, at very least it is interesting to see its being treated at all at this level of film-making. It suggests an ideological step forward from all those 'B' crime-thrillers that either recall Agatha Christie or anticipate the TV series that were about to displace them. Nevertheless, it remains the case that characters in the British Bs were overwhelmingly white, a set of representations that, even in the more racially homogeneous 1940s, 1950s and early 1960, hardly reflected social reality.

8 The Best of the Bs

I have seen small second-features that have been little gems of screencraft, demonstrating that this particular producer, director or producer-director was a man of undoubted ability. Knowing their handicaps
and the conditions under which the film was produced, it has been easy to realise that they achieved what
they set out to do – and even more. ... Even the worst of these small films can teach us something, be it
only that money is not all that counts.

The editor, The Cinema Studio[1]

This final chapter will offer analyses of fifteen superior 'B' movies, each from a different director, to
substantiate our case that they have been unjustly neglected, that real merit was to be found even when
film-makers were working on very tight budgets and schedules. We wish to argue that such films have
an intrinsic value as entertainment as well as offering insights into what was socially or industrially
revealing. We might have added many more to this section: there is, for example, no Tempean film
included here, on the grounds that several of these (e.g., *The Frightened Man*, 1952, *The Quiet Woman*,
1951, *Impulse*, 1955) have been discussed elsewhere in this study). The choice-making process for such
a chapter has inevitably a strongly personal element, but our purpose here is no more than to suggest
that the term 'B' movie has tended to elide real workmanship. Although the business of film-making
may have been driven by market demand and commercial considerations, Guido Coen spoke for many
of the producers, directors and writers of the British 'B' film when he remarked: 'There was a certain
amount of pride always: trying desperately to make it as well as possible, as elegant as possible, because
your name was on there. Without enthusiasm, you'd better get out of this business.'[2]

It's Not Cricket (1948)

'Here's a really funny and thoroughly English comedy,' proclaimed *Picture Show* of Alfred Roome's *It's
Not Cricket*, starring the leather-and-willow-loving character duo of Basil Radford and Naunton
Wayne.[3] Sixty years later, it can still raise a laugh. Although Roome, who had had long experience as
an editor, insisted he was really 'a back-room boy by nature', and 'not too keen on dealing with the
foibles of actors',[4] he succeeded in encouraging his players to produce some of the most humorous
moments in a British film of the period.

    Radford and Wayne play a pair of incompetent officers who, when demobbed, set up as private
detectives. Their efforts, during a charity matinee, to locate the leading lady's little dog and a mad Nazi
on the loose, cause havoc on stage. The trilling pair (Jane Carr and Patrick Waddington) sing gamely on
of 'Sweet moment of spring' as the dog races on stage, and the revolve button is pressed by mistake, and

trapdoors open beneath them. The Nazi, Otto Fisch (Maurice Denham), in turn presses (appropriately) the thunder and lightning switch, causes the stage to revolve and drenches the stars with the sprinkler system, in a sequence which, as slapstick goes, is undeniably hilarious. Fisch is on the track of a diamond which is hidden in a cricket ball which in turn finds its way to a country cricket match and ... Oh, there's no point going on with an account of the lunatic plot, which takes in an evening in a country house in which certain mistaken identities occur, and a cricket match in which Fisch and fellow-Nazi Felix (Alan Wheatley) try to retrieve the ball – it is enough to applaud its comic invention. There are some flattish patches in between the set-pieces, and Roome was probably right to speak of 'all the terrible, boring romance stuff with Susan Shaw',[5] but not many Bs maintain this film's speed and laughter quotient. Even the Susan Shaw 'stuff' has its moments and provides opportunity for jokes about cricket, described by Fisch as 'a very dull game – these decadent English patting a little ball to each other'.

A lot of the credit is due to Maurice Denham's extravagantly mad Fisch in contrast with the phlegmatic incompetence of Radford and Wayne, and the whole film bears witness to the period's profligate casting of character actors doing enjoyable turns. Just consider the rollcall here: it includes, apart from those named, Diana Dors, Leslie Dwyer, Edward Lexy, Mary Hinton, Margaret Withers, Frederick Piper, Brian Oulton and Hal Osmond. With a few moments each, they and the leads can almost guarantee that an hour and a quarter will pass painlessly – and, indeed, most often with pleasure for the viewer. While acknowledging that 'Susan Shaw ... has not much of a part,' *Picturegoer* allowed that 'she and the cast as a whole play the game with a zest which is contagious and enthusiastic'.[6]

The Late Edwina Black (1951)

For obvious budgetary reasons, period dramas are very scarce among the ranks of British 'B' movies, where the resources for re-creating the costumes and settings of an earlier era were strictly limited. For this reason, if for no other, it is worth noting Maurice Elvey's adaptation of *The Late Edwina Black*, the West End success by William Dimner and William Morum, which had also been staged for television. Elvey was into the last decade of his immensely long career (it had begun in 1913) and was tapering off into second features and co-features like this one.

The unseen Edwina Black, the village schoolmaster's wife, is dying when the film opens, and the severe housekeeper Ellen (Jean Cadell) sows the seeds of suspicion as to the cause of her beloved mistress's death. The doctor who has attended Edwina at the end has been dissatisfied as to the cause of her death and this leads Inspector Martin (Roland Culver) to order an exhumation which reveals arsenic in her body. Her husband Gregory (David Farrar) and her companion Elizabeth (Geraldine Fitzgerald) are both suspects since both stand to gain by Edwina's death, and the film records the growth of tension between them. They have been in love but Elizabeth now says, 'I knew it. I knew Edwina would stop us.' In the play version there are only the four characters and a single set, but the film employs the facilities of a country house, and adds several minor characters, including the doctor (Harcourt Williams), the enjoyably sharp-tongued Lady Southwell (Mary Merrall) and the vicar (Charles Heslop) forced into pious hypocrisies at Edwina's funeral. Nevertheless, the burden of the film falls on the original four and this is where the film's strength lies: few character actresses can do mean-faced malevolence better than Jean Cadell; Roland Culver for once drops his gentleman's demeanour and accent for the shrewd Inspector; and David Farrar is a virile and compelling Gregory. Best of all, the beautiful and underused Geraldine Fitzgerald is particularly fine as the companion who begins to suspect the man she loves.[7]

This is very much an actor's film. The dialogue (Charles Frank and David Evans's screenplay hews closely to the play) has a kind of stagy edge to it that needs the skill of the actors to give it some feeling of conversation in the demanding mimesis of film. But there is real interest too in the corrosion of the relationship between the would-be lovers as they are forced to doubt each other, and as Ellen works her vengeance, indicating possibly a lesbian attachment to her late mistress. The Victorian mores are suggested not only in George Provis's handsome production design, which creates an atmosphere of upholstered oppressiveness, but also in the ways in which the young woman's situation in the household becomes problematic after Edwina's death. Elizabeth also longs for a honeymoon in Venice, recalling other plays and films in which the Mediterranean becomes a symbol of romantic freedom from constraint. Elvey's long experience is attested to in the build-up of tension, and in maintaining enough pace to mute the film's theatrical origins. One responds to such touches as the cut from the jingling wind chimes to the fanciful black plumes of the funeral as an insistence on the presence of the late Edwina, owner of the former and cause of the latter. Later those chimes will be seen shaking in the breeze as though Edwina were laughing at Gregory and Elizabeth, who embrace, saying, 'All we've ever done is to fall in love.'

The film was not especially well received at the time, but has worn better than many that were. *Picture Show* thought it 'well-staged but rather grim,'[8] but gave it a centre-page spread of stills; *Variety*, under the US title of *Obsessed*, felt that 'Dialog and situations are ... frequently creaky and cliched,'[9] and the *Motion Picture Herald* considered 'It is surprising, in view of the competent cast, that the picture did not turn out better.'[10] The *Monthly Film Bulletin* summed it up as 'An unpretentious thriller which succeeds in being thrilling.'[11] A recent commentator, alert to the film's antecedents, characterised it as 'draw[ing] on a sturdy mixture of conventions from the classical detective genre, film noir, and gothic fiction'.[12] Too slow a melodrama for contemporary American tastes, it seemed to be better appreciated at home – and with reason.

Private Information (1952)

This trim hour-long film, the second of the ACT Films to be released, is rare among British 'B' pictures in that it is a social drama, one that addresses itself to matters of municipal corruption as manifested in a shoddily constructed post-war council housing estate. Adapted from a play by Gordon Glennon, who co-authored the screenplay with John Baines and producer Ronald Kinnoch, it is really a small-scale English version of Ibsen's *An Enemy of the People* – or, to come more nearly up to date, *Erin Brockovich* (2000). Its director, Fergus McDonell, had a long career as an editor (from 1934 to 1973, with a spell in Canada as both editor and director of shorts and documentaries), but he directed only three British features: *The Small Voice* (1948), *Prelude to Fame* (1950) and *Private Information*. In all of them, he displayed a sensitive regard for human relationships and for the ways in which the pressure of circumstance highlights aspects of character. He also had a knack for obtaining striking performances from his leading ladies.[13] In *Private Information*, Jill Esmond plays Charlotte Carson, a council-house tenant who takes on the town hall, accusing mayor and surveyor of knowingly permitting inadequate drainage specification, in return for a little palm-greasing.

For most of its modest length, *Private Information* develops its issue with the venalities of local government and sub-standard housing in calm and sufficient detail to establish its seriousness of purpose. This is also quite skilfully interwoven with the elements of personal drama that develop when Charlotte sees a confidential report about the problems of drainage and construction which her son

Hugh (Jack Watling) has submitted to his superior, Freemantle, the borough surveyor (Norman Shelley). This leads Charlotte to attack the mayor and council in a crusade that accrues the backing of the community. Perhaps the drama is over-determined in the way that the screenplay presents Hugh, as assistant borough surveyor, as (1) prospective son-in-law of Freemantle and (2) nephew to the mayor (Lloyd Pearson), brother to Charlotte's late (clergyman) husband, as well as being Charlotte's son. However, this makes for a reasonably intricate network of loyalties – and obstacles to plain speaking. It could also be argued that the typhoid outbreak which threatens the life of Charlotte's daughter, Georgie (Carol Marsh), provides one of what the *Monthly Film Bulletin* described as an 'overly melodramatic choice of incidents',[14] and *The Daily Film Renter* called 'a rather overdrawn climax'.[15] The film is certainly all neatly tied up at the end, with the daughter recovering, Hugh reconciled with fiancée Iris Freemantle (Mercy Haystead) and Charlotte finding comfort with an émigré journalist, Alex (Gerald Heinz). One might counter such criticisms by adding that the screenplay seems to have been worked on with rather more care than was routinely the case with 'B' films, in the sense that character and event have more connection than usual.

There was also criticism at the time of the film's staginess: *To-Day's Cinema* considered that it was talky and 'rather obviously theatrical in conception'.[16] Again, there is some basis for this criticism but the film's strengths also go some distance to offsetting the theatrical origins. It has an apt look of unadorned ordinariness in its production design in recreating Charlotte's jerry-built home, which she has sought to mitigate with a few pleasing pieces from her past, and this contrasts well with the pretentious authority of the council chambers, both interior and exterior, and with the sense of temporising bureaucrats at work. What most critics singled out for praise was an earnest, carefully observed performance as Charlotte from Jill Esmond, a fine, undervalued stage actress whose comparatively rare films invariably evince an easy naturalness before the camera. Her Charlotte has just the right look and demeanour of middle age and she suggests admirably a quiet woman who finds unexpected reserves of strength. *Picturegoer* claimed that 'her performance prevents propaganda from getting the better of straight drama' and found the film 'both stimulating and holding'.[17] Some of the supporting players and their material are weak, but it is surprising to find a film at this level which is at least ready to address a theme of some social significance. Ultimately, then, it is the bravery and sincerity of *Private Information*'s critique of local government that is its enduring interest. A recent commentator has attributed the way in which McDonell was able to mount this critique 'from a citizen's point of view' to the fact that the picture 'was produced by the company set up by the film workers' union, the Association of Cinema Technicians'.[18] For this and other reasons noted above, this is a second feature of more than usual interest.

Marilyn (Roadhouse Girl) (1953)

Marilyn, an adaptation of a play by Peter Jones, was produced at Nettlefold. It is a lurid roadhouse story, very much on the lines of James M. Cain's *The Postman Always Rings Twice* (1946), of how a dissatisfied young wife's (Sandra Dorne) seduction of Tom, a garage hand (Maxwell Reed), leads to the death of her domineering husband, George (Leslie Dwyer). Marilyn is clearly intended to evoke Lana Turner's Cora in *The Postman*, and Tom, in black leather jacket and luxuriant quiff, is the sexy young mechanic in whom she sees the chance of a more exciting life, as Cora once did in John Garfield's drifter. She quickly deserts her lover, seeking more glamorous horizons of the kind that the dubious Nicky (Ferdy Mayne) seems to offer, and the steamy drama ends with her betrayal by her previously faithful maid Rosie (Vida Hope).

Roadhouse girl: a trade advertisement for Wolf Rilla's steamy tale of desire and exploitation *Marilyn* (1953)

The film gets off to a promising start with credits and moody soundtrack over a long straight road, with trucks hurtling past, before the camera comes to rest on George's combined petrol station and café. Tom arrives almost at once, is brusquely given a job by George and is clearly the kind of trouble Marilyn is looking for. Dorne, a Yorkshire lass, described her role, perhaps a trifle optimistically, as 'a Bette Davis part at her finest', and Marilyn is certainly an Americanised figure, signalled not least by her devotion to the juke-box. The plot develops swiftly as Tom responds to Marilyn's obvious advances, and George is so firmly established as a bully in relation to Marilyn (and, indeed, to Tom) that our sympathies are apt to be with her from the start. But, like a good film noir heroine, she will all but lose them as a result of her uncompromising pursuit of materialist goals. Dorne, in a series of enticing 1950s costumes, and Reed, elsewhere often inclined to woodenness, convincingly suggest a couple who, for somewhat diverse reasons, come together sexually, and fall out because of their different needs. Dwyer, the perennial working-class comedy support in dozens of British films, is here given a uniquely unsympathetic role which he plays with some relish. Most surprising is Vida Hope's study in repressed lesbianism: 'I would have died for you,' she tells Marilyn at the end, adding 'but tonight you were ready to leave without me.' There is certainly some crudity and over-simplification in both plot and character development, but what the *Monthly Film Bulletin* called 'unusually heavy-handed' playing and direction only serve to heighten the film's camp appeal.[19]

For reasons not wholly clear, Butcher's held the film back from general release to be re-edited, and it was finally released in May 1954, having lost three minutes or so, under the new title *Roadhouse Girl*. It was symptomatic of a transatlantic turn in the British 'B', and it was duly released in the USA by the Astor Pictures Corporation. Its president, Robert M. Savini, called on exhibitors to give the picture the hardest of sells: 'In *Roadhouse Girl* we know for a fact that we have the year's biggest *exploitation special* ... Sure, you can make a feeble effort by stencilling a sidewalk or sending out postcards ... but with this baby you must do more than that and she will pay off handsomely.'[20]

First-time director Wolf Rilla had learned his craft in television, and this was another pointer to the future. He would go on to make some of the most creditable 'B' films, including *The Large Rope* (1953) and *The End of the Road* (1954). In *Marilyn* he shows already a capacity for economical storytelling and a willingness to deliver subversive goods without descending to the merely sensational. Perhaps *Picture Show* had this sort of quality in mind when it described the film as 'Forthright drama.'[21] Like its contemporary, *Wheel of Fate* (1953), this film has a pervasive sense of dissatisfaction with things as they are which is undiminished by the dawn of the new

'Elizabethan age'. In this, it anticipates the New Wave that would break in British film and theatre a few years later.

The Flying Scot (1957)

An unusually unsympathetic pair of protagonists is only one of the distinguishing marks of this tense thriller set largely on an overnight train from Edinburgh to London. A tantalising opening sequence, involving thirteen minutes without any dialogue is another. Throughout, there are signs of an expertise well above the routine 'B' movie level, and an attention to detail that one would appreciate at any level.

Perhaps modestly recalling the famous silent heist episode in *Rififi* (1955), Compton Bennett's trim thriller opens with an assured overhead shot of a large railway station where the London-bound train is soon to depart. A young man and woman settle into a compartment, pasting up 'Just married' and 'Reserved' signs on the windows and have obviously tipped the guard to ensure they are not disturbed. After changing their clothes and, in his case, removing his moustache, they are joined by the second man. The robbery is effected by dismantling the back of the compartment's seat to give access to the van where mailbags stacked with banknotes are secured; the bags are then thrown out of the train window where they are caught by a waiting accomplice at an appointed bridge. The young

Lee Patterson tries to drill his way to a fortune in Compton Bennett's accomplished thriller *The Flying Scot* (1957)

couple then leave the train separately and the film cuts to a bar at a resort in the south of France. The thirteen-minute sequence (one fifth of the film's running time) has been the acting out of a proposed mailbag-robbery, while the audience has been tricked into thinking it has been watching the real thing. The film's original narrative hook is then to see how far the actual robbery will follow the proleptic images of the sequence without dialogue.

The actual train journey is introduced by the same overhead shot. The cocky Ronny (Lee Patterson) and blonde waitress Jackie (Kay Callard) talk to and tip the guard (Gerald Case), who promises to be very discreet, while Phil (Alan Gifford) is joined in his compartment by a middle-aged woman reading a journal called *Crime*. When the time comes, Phil joins the other two in their compartment and the robbery plans are set in motion. This central section of the film is executed with considerable tension, as the trio run into various obstacles such as the unyielding nature of the back of the compartment's seat, but especially because of the increasing pain Phil is suffering from a possibly perforated ulcer. The sheer arduousness of the enterprise is registered with persuasive realism. The understanding guard finally tumbles to what is going on and alerts the police who appear on the train before the robbers can disembark.

The matter of Phil's health is worked neatly into the plot via a discussion with the woman in his compartment (played with quiet realism by Margaret Withers): she has been a nurse, recognises and is solicitous about his ulcerous condition. This detail, with no actual bearing on the narrative, is typical of the individuating touches which Bennett and his scriptwriter, Norman Hudis (soon to be enmeshed in the *Carry On* series), have brought to bear on both character and plot. Among the other characters are a man with a drink problem heading to London for treatment, with a wife who is quietly observant but not a caricature of disapproval, and a small boy Charlie (Jeremy Bodkin), who is a nuisance but not outrageously so, and whose parents hold divergent views on corporal punishment. Both the drunk (Kerry Jordan) and Charlie add to the film's tensions but are also intrinsically endowed with just enough personal detail to catch our attention.[22]

It is easy to exaggerate the merits of a 'B' movie that rises above our usual – and usually wellfounded – expectations. It is nevertheless important to acknowledge that such merits are to be found. Here, the overall contours of the plot are more sturdily and freshly conceived than is often the case. Further, the film doesn't lose its nerve to try to involve us with Ronny and Jackie as a couple, and Patterson and Callard, stalwarts of the British 'B' movie, respond with a crispness and opportunism that is as convincing as it is unendearing. With some subtlety, the film allows her a modicum of sympathy with Phil's condition, whereas Ronny is only concerned with his capacity to do the job. When the contributions of the director and the convincing cast are duly acknowledged, much of the credit for this must go to Hudis's taut, twisting and ingenious screenplay. *The Daily Cinema* got pretty close to this film's appeal when it wrote: 'We are fascinated as we watch the unforeseen difficulties and unimagined contingencies arise.'[23] This, indeed, is a film not just of suspense, but of real fascination.

Compton Bennett had a major hit with *The Seventh Veil* (1945) over a decade earlier. He subsequently made the gloomy but holding melodrama *Daybreak* (1948), had some modest success in Hollywood (*King Solomon's Mines*, 1950) and returned to Britain in the early 1950s, when he made some largely unremarkable 'A' features (e.g., *The Gift Horse*, 1952) before drifting into Bs. It is at least arguable that *The Flying Scot*, shot in just three weeks on a budget of £18,000,[24] contains his most proficient work since *The Seventh Veil*: he seems to respond admirably to the challenges of relating a tense story in an unexpected way and to finding rewarding moments of humanly telling interaction.

Small Hotel (1957)

There is no point in wondering how thin this gentle comedy might be in less assured hands than those of its chief cast members – Marie Lohr, Gordon Harker and Irene Handl – who do with consummate ease what they had in their respective ways done so often before. It was directed by David Macdonald whose 'A' film career had foundered in the 1950s, possibly because of his being unfairly associated with such expensive duds as *Christopher Columbus* and *The Bad Lord Byron* (both 1949), 'unfairly' because it is arguable that no one could have salvaged that pair. He took whatever was going in the 1950s, and, if *Small Hotel* is no rival to his smart, fast-moving early successes *This Man Is News* (1938) and *This Man in Paris* (1939), it certainly benefits from the lighter touch he brought to those 1930s comedy-thrillers.

Based on a modestly successful play by Rex Frost, *Small Hotel* was clearly a vehicle for Gordon Harker, a popular comedian from the late 1920s, when he appeared three times for Hitchcock. Here he plays Albert, an amiably scheming waiter at a small country hotel, whose job is threatened when Finch, a head office inspector (John Loder), arrives and intends to install the bossy upstart Caroline (Billie Whitelaw) as waitress, and to smarten up the place. The play has been only vestigially 'opened out', with the odd shot of a car arriving at the hotel: most of the action takes place in the hotel's dining-room, with brief scenes in its office, lounge and kitchen.

The catering corps: Irene Handl, Marie Lohr, Janet Munro, Billie Whitelaw and Gordon Harker make up a highly distinguished cast in *Small Hotel* (1957)

There is a sub-Ealing touch about the central situation in which Albert connives to get the hotel's resident guest, the upper-class Mrs Samson-Box (Marie Lohr), on side against the testy bureaucratic Finch and flashy Caroline. His other allies are the young couple who run the hotel, the inept young waitress Effie (Janet Munro), who has been up before the Bench presided over by Mrs Samson-Box, and the fiery outspoken cook Mrs Gammon (Irene Handl). The ending is never in doubt as the unlikely home team routs the unsympathetic outsiders, Mrs Samson-Box blackmailing Finch about her influence with 'Head Office'. As with Ealing, the latter are there to be routed; what is not so like Ealing are the very conservative viewpoints regarding the status quo and, in particular, the mildly reverential tone allowed to the old gentry represented by Mrs Samson-Box. However, this is to make heavy weather of what may be no more than, in *Picturegoer*'s words, 'a gentle, inoffensive farce'.[25] The film moves along quite briskly and smoothly, the young couple, played unremarkably but competently by Francis Matthews and Ruth Trouncer, providing an adequate ordinariness against which the more colourful cast members do their stuff. Harker, in his second-last film, plays arch-fiddler Albert with an ease born of decades of sly technique; Lohr brings her own West End-honed technique to bear as the stately resident, and even achieves a moment of not unaffecting pathos ('Underneath, she's a great lady,' Albert tells Effie); Handl, all dangling earrings and malapropisms, is a broadly comic cook; and Loder, once a dull leading man, is more enjoyable as the officious Finch. As distinct from veterans like these, two relative newcomers, Billie Whitelaw, who had played a few very small roles, and Janet Munro, in her first film, more than hold their own, as contrasting waitresses – the 'smart' one with her lapses of grammar, and the hapless one with lapses of decorum but whose heart is in the right place. Munro, would have a brief but distinguished career in 1960s British cinema before dying tragically young at just thirty-eight. Whitelaw would build an impressive career in cinema and television lasting more than fifty years.

It is worth stressing the acting, since this is what gives entertaining flesh to Wilfred Eades' screenplay and Frost's play, whose bone density needs attention. Macdonald's direction may lack imagination but it at least allows some very able actors to do the sorts of things one expects of them, and Norman Warwick's cinematography is aptly clear and shadowless. When so many 'B' films were routine crime-thrillers, this 'unassuming but unquestionably entertaining screen version',[26] as one trade paper assessed it, makes an agreeable change. Ironic, perhaps, as the film itself depicted the triumph of the forces of inertia, a theme that was doubtlessly of appeal principally to the dwindling band of older cinemagoers that may have begun to feel threatened the tide of modernisation.

The Man Who Liked Funerals (1959)

True comic inspiration is rare in British 'B' films, but is evident in David Eady's *The Man Who Liked Funerals*, which, not much liked at the time,[27] now seems fresh and gently funny. Eady, son of Sir Wilfred who introduced the Eady Levy, had a background in documentary and then in feature films as editor and assistant director before making a batch of slightly off-centre 'B' films in the 1950s. *The Man Who Liked Funerals* benefits from a much wittier screenplay than was common in second features. This was the work of actress Margot Bennett, from a story by Cecily Finn and Joan O'Connor, the trio also responsible for Eady's next film, *The Crowning Touch* (1959). Its basic idea is simple but flexible enough to allow for some genuine comic variety.

Simon Hurd (Leslie Phillips) runs a church boys' club which will lose the lease to its premises unless £4,000 can be found quite smartly. 'We've got to think of something new, something bold, something daring,' he urges, to his girlfriend Stella (Susan Beaumont) and the wet, pipe-smoking vicar (Shaun O'Riordan). What he comes up with is the idea of running off at the publishing house where he works as a printer the supposed embarrassing memoirs of recently deceased persons and then subtly blackmailing their not necessarily grieving relatives. His first victims are the family of a military man, whose widow, Lady Hunter (the droll hatchet-face, Anita Sharp-Bolster), is very shocked, telling Simon that 'My late husband regarded the artistic temperament as the sign of a diseased mind'. As one seeking information of decadent tastes, she asks Simon, 'Tell me, Mr Hurd, do many people read?' before telling her blustering son to write him a cheque for £500.

Hurd's subsequent efforts involve him with: the twittering widow (Mary MacKenzie) of the Bishop of Harchester, supposed author of scandalous love poems (shocked, she tells Hurd, 'My husband was almost unreasonably sane'); a senior Communist Party official (Alastair Hunter), stunned by his ex-leader's terrible novel; two schoolmistresses (Hester Paton-Brown and Thelma Ruby) at Lowdean School for Girls, whose late headmistress apparently authored a volume to be called 'Sex and How to Get It'; and most dangerously a gang of Soho criminals who aren't as bereaved as they want to have it believed, and whose dear departed is said to have written fairy stories. This last strand to the plot opens in church with a coffin (later proved to be empty), covered in wreaths with inscriptions such as 'To a loyal customer from the United Razor Manufacturers (British Goods are Best)' and 'To Nick, a good son and a fine gangster, Your Ma'.

'Innocent' as Hurd's blackmailing activities are, the film must of course end happily and it does so, with all the victims being invited to the club dance at which Hurd foils the vengeful mafia family, secures the future of the club and Stella's loving admiration. The film dissolves to their wedding as they come out of the church, with Mendelssohn strident on the soundtrack, and Simon, now addicted to funerals, wanders off from the bridal party to pay his respects to a melancholy passing procession. If there is nothing remarkable about any of this, it is consistently amusing, its plot worked out with some wit and its cast, amiably led by Phillips at the start of his starring career, enters into the spirit of the joke. There are neat swipes at the institutions of the church, the army, education, politics (when the communist leader settles for a knighthood and to marry a lord's daughter, he suggests to his secretary that it would be more apt if she addressed him as 'Sir Comrade' in future) and the criminal underworld. Even if one reviewer did find it a 'tepid farce [which] fails to live up to the promise of either its original idea or its intriguing title',[28] overall, it is a great deal more fun than many of those Technicolored Pinewood and ABPC comedies set in the Home Counties and recounting the privations of middle-class couples and their servants.

Devil's Bait (1959)

One synopsis of Peter Graham Scott's *Devil's Bait*, made for Wintle and Parkyn's Independent Artists, reads: 'Suspense thriller about a rat-catcher who leaves cyanide around a bakehouse and the frantic efforts of the baker and his wife to avoid fatal consequences.'[29] This may not give much sense of the main pleasures of the film, but, it does point up the film's narrative command and the source of its tension. The film opens well with a close-up of rats among flour bags, and the attempts of baker Joe Frisby (Geoffrey Keen) to take to them with a broom handle. His wife Ellen (Jane Hylton) secures the services of a hard-drinking and ironically named rat-catcher Love (Dermot Kelly), and when the job is done she inadvertently bakes loaves in a tin contaminated with the cyanide he has been using. What follows has elements of such films as the American movies from 1950, Earl McAvoy's *The*

Bread of death: Geoffrey Keen discovers he has baked a lethal loaf in *Devil's Bait* (1959)

Frightened City and Elia Kazan's *Panic in the Streets*, and the subsequent British drama, *80,000 Suspects* (1963, directed by Val Guest): that is, a random but deadly threat to the community.

One could say that *Devil's Bait* is improbably slow in involving the police in the search for anyone who might have had access to the contaminated bread. On the other hand, Peter Johnstone and Diana K. Watson's script draws attention to a lower middle-class fear of the police, as encapsulated in the remark 'We wouldn't like an inquest or anything like that.' This is characteristic of the film's concern with details of behaviour, most notably in the way it reveals Joe and Ellen's daily lives, and how their livelihood is threatened by this dangerous mishap. The Frisbys' conflict is between telling the police the truth and saving their business. The excellent performances of Hylton and Keen create a wholly convincing sense of two people whose relationship is under the strain of everyday irritations and who are imperceptibly drawn closer by the near disaster in which they are caught up. 'It's a long time since you called me Ellie,' she says to him: it's a small moment which suggests a tiny but real turning point in a long married and working life.

As a thriller, the film works efficiently enough. After the initial discovery of rats in the bakehouse, Scott steers the film smartly between the bakery, the Town Hall where Ellen gets the name of a rat-catcher and the latter's landlady (a neat, unpatronising sketch from Molly Urquhart), and this kind of pacey shift between well-observed locations is characteristic of the rest of the film. The film's editing (by the reputable John Trumper) often works to effect rapid transitions and to cut in unexpected ways. When the careless Love is boozing away in the pub, his blurred vision of an ice-tray gives way to the contaminated bread tin. A little later, the film cuts from a close-up of the dead rats to one of Love's face when he has fallen drunkenly down a railway siding in the dark. There is more conventional suspense in tracking down the picnicking girls who may be victims of the poisoned bread, when the Frisbys and the police sergeant (Gordon Jackson) are held up by a bus on their way to the picnic site, but, conventional as it may be, it does move the film forward to a satisfyingly taut end – and one which leaves both narrative and character interests gratified.

Scott described how he worked with the writers 'on the script to make it much tighter, less verbose, and ... [to give] the policeman, played by Gordon Jackson, much more character. Similarly the two girls who go off on a picnic, and one of whom is poisoned, had no depth at all in the original script.'[30] He also recalled persuading Julian Wintle not to cast Leslie Dwyer as Joe, believing that Dwyer was too closely associated with Cockney types, whereas Geoffrey Keen was a more protean actor who might bring a sturdier sense of character and individuality to the role.[31] The finished film bespeaks the kind of care that Scott was ready to bring to this modest enterprise, and even the *Monthly Film Bulletin* was forced to admit that: 'Here is a reasonable attempt to depart from the stereotyped and do something more unusual in the field of the second-feature suspense thriller.'[32] Peter Graham Scott went on to become a noted director of television drama, making his name on series such as *The Onedin Line* and the teleplay *A Separate Peace*. In his memoirs, he dismisses both *Devil's Bait* and his *The Big Day* (1960) quite briskly, saying only that 'both with tight, well-written scripts, attracted the right sort of attention'.[33]

The Tell-Tale Heart (1960, released 1963)

An opening title offers a warning to 'those who are squeamish or react nervously to shock, we suggest that when you hear this sound ... [amplified heartbeat on black screen] you close your eyes and do not look at the screen again until it stops'. This pre-film alert may seem a cynical gimmick, but in fact the film is a surprisingly alarming experience.

Adapted from Edgar Allen Poe's chilling story, Brian Clemens' screenplay[34] gets off to a striking start. A carriage hurtles through a night street and when the camera cuts to an interior it reveals a young man, Edgar, who wakes up screaming. His friend gives him medication as his landlady watches and Edgar refuses to have a doctor to see him. In the next episode, Edgar is attracted to a girl at a neighbouring bar, but leaves hurriedly when she makes up to him, and the film makes clear that suppressed sexuality is at issue. The screenplay gives Laurence Payne as the obsessed Edgar dialogue that both complements his tormented face and, in its ordinariness, makes his obsession humanly credible. 'How do you get to know a girl?' he asks his more sophisticated friend Carl, and the effect is touching rather than banal. Poe's tale had been adapted for the screen in 1934 by Brian Desmond Hurst, who had drawn out a gay subtext and used it to explore his own sexuality. In contrast, Clemens' screenplay is stridently heterosexual.

As well as Clemens, Ernest Morris's adaptation employs the talents of other regular collaborators, art director Norman Arnold and cinematographer Jimmy Wilson. Arnold and set decorator Peter Russell create a studio-bound world which provides a resonant ambience for Edgar's increasing paranoia. The chief actors, Payne as the timid Edgar, Dermot Walsh as the debonair friend Carl and Adrienne Corri as the object of Edgar's passion and of Carl's dalliance, all enter intelligently and wholeheartedly into the melodrama of obsession and murder, and Payne's somewhat haggard features mirror

Something beating beneath the floorboards!: Laurence Payne struggles to retain his sanity in the Danzigers' adaptation of Poe's *The Tell-Tale Heart* (1963)

his torment, and the contrast with Walsh's easy demeanour and charm works potently to propel the conflict. Payne gives a convincing sense of a man whose life is about to be interrupted. Edgar is a shy reference librarian (not among the excitements of fiction) and his hobby is chess. Everything about his life suggests a retreat from the world, whereas Carl has all the worldliness he lacks.

In visualising the nature of Edgar's growing obsession, Morris reveals himself as a director in sympathy with his material: as Edgar, having murdered Carl, drinks, he imagines the carpet heaving in time with Carl's heartbeats below the floorboards. Most of Edgar's increasing agony of mind is achieved in giant close-ups: he registers horror at the drip of a tap [pre-dating Losey in *The Servant* by a couple of years] or the tick of a clock: but it is all far more subtly achieved than one expects in 'B' movies. There is in fact a rare and real sense of gothic horror as Edgar loses control at the 'beating of this infernal heart'. He begins to drink in his room and to wander the streets at night; and, as the climax of his paranoia draws near, Morris does without words, focusing on anguished close-ups of Edgar's face and details such as the chess pieces rattling. The *Monthly Film Bulletin* confessed that: 'The tell-tale heart itself is particularly effective, where the whole house ... seems to pick up and magnify the terrifying beating rhythm which haunts Edgar.'[35]

Again and again, in this film Morris shows the instincts of a genuine film-maker. Where possible he avoids the kinds of expository colloquies that, comparatively cheap to film as these were, take up so much running time in 'B' films. In the sequence in which Edgar, having summoned up his courage, takes Betty to dine and dance, Morris opens on a close-up of a violin being played, widens the shot to take in the orchestra, cuts to dancing feet, then moves into an overhead shot before framing Edgar and Betty. Shortly after this, Carl enters and the triangular tensions – Betty is clearly attracted by Carl's charisma; Edgar by contrast seems an over-anxious wimp – are set in motion to propel the rest of this highly proficient piece of film narrative. The *Monthly Film Bulletin*'s reviewer aptly praised the 'excellent playing' of the three leads and 'a script which concentrates intelligently on establishing a credible triangle relationship before moving into the horror, [creating] three-dimensional characters of real interest'.[36] The trade paper *Kinematograph Weekly* was in no doubt that it 'excites the imagination and steadily works up through sex and horror to a salutary and showmanlike climax'.[37] Both commercial and critical criteria seemed satisfied, unlike the British Board of Film Censors, whose confidential minutes record that 'amongst episodes removed or shortened were a brutal murder with a poker, the resurrection of the victim's body from its hiding place and the removal of the heart ... bedroom scenes were shortened'.[38] In fact, in the wake of the controversy that had surrounded Michael Powell's *Peeping Tom* (1960), it was the association of sexual arousal with violence that particularly disturbed the censor, even though the film was being given an 'X' certificate. The Board was not prepared to allow cheapskate film-makers like the Danzigers the sort of leeway granted to the more respectable Powell, and instructions were given to: 'Shorten the scene in which Edgar looks at the girl's legs through the window of a bar and remove shots of his face as he looks at the girl's knees when he is inside the bar and shots of her knees. Reduce shots of nude pictures. Reduce shots of Betty undressing (whilst Edgar watches her). Reduce the episode of Betty sitting on the bed in a seductive pose and reading a book.'[39] This may help to explain why the film's release was delayed for over two years.

The Impersonator (1961)

This exceptionally proficient 'B' movie from Bryanston won nothing but praise for its unpretentious virtues around the time of its release. Penelope Gilliat saw it as a prime example of the way 'several production companies are bending themselves to improving the standard of second features'.[40] Dilys Powell, noting that it was made for £23,000, claimed that 'It has more narrative ingenuity ... than plenty of British thrillers made for many times that sum.'[41] Generally, 'B' movies had a hard time in getting noticed by critics as celebrated as these two, but *The Impersonator* wholly deserves the welcome it was given. Alfred Shaughnessy's direction of the carefully wrought screenplay he co-wrote with Kenneth Cavander maintains a very firm grasp on the mounting tension within and between individual episodes, and welds the strands of the plot firmly together.

The film's opening shots show a young teacher at Northbridge County Junior School, Ann Loring (Jane Griffiths), packing up her belongings, leaving her classroom and then walking out into the night, down a long driveway. She finally catches a bus on which an American airman chats her up before he is interrupted by a sergeant, Jimmy Bradford (John Crawford), who, in *his* own way, imposes himself on her company. When he believes Ann has stood him up after accepting his invitation to a dance at the nearby airbase, he takes café proprietor Mrs Lloyd (Patricia Burke), who is murdered on her way home from the dance by a prowler who has been terrorising the town. In the astute and economically plotted screenplay, the romantic angle and the murder are cleverly connected. Ann is not just the routine girlfriend who gets herself into danger through folly she could have avoided; Jimmy is not just the usual stalwart hero in the John Bentley mould. He is a suspect, indeed the *only* suspect, as a result of a little boy's mendacious testimony (the film in this respect, and in the performance of John Dare as Tommy, Mrs Lloyd's son, recalls better-known films including the famous American 'B' movie, *The Window* [1949, Ted Tetzlaff] and, nearer home, Carol Reed's *The Fallen Idol*, 1949). If there is a weakness in the plotting, it is in its failure to come to any sort of terms with Tommy's reaction to his mother's disappearance and death. Too much emphasis on this might have unbalanced the narrative but a brief reaction to his loss would have added a touch of conviction.

A strength of the screenplay and direction is in the gradual revelation of the 'impersonator'. Not only is Harry Walker (a major role for the excellent character actor John Salew) a man impersonating a woman in his role of Mother Goose in the town's Christmas pantomime, he is also a killer impersonating a facetiously insinuating actor. 'I've always found pantomime dames terribly macabre and slightly sinister,' Shaughnessy recalled, 'a creature apart. Neither man nor woman.' He had originally conceived the dame as a child-murderer, but the censor would only allow the victim to be a woman.[42] A recent commentator concurred: 'a rapist-killer Mother Goose is somehow more transgressive than all those American Santa Claus slashers put together'.[43] The night scenes in which he stalks women in the town are lit with real skill by cinematographer John Coquillon[44] and edited by John Bloom to ensure maximum frissons as Shaughnessy cuts from close-ups to long shots, from tense tracking to sudden stillness. One scarcely sees the prowler at full length so that there is no chance of recognising him when he first comes into Mrs Lloyd's café. Mention of the café recalls what unobtrusively resourceful use the film makes of its market-town settings. *The Impersonator* is much more firmly anchored in place and period than most 'B' films were able to achieve. The film opens on the apparently peaceful town of Northbridge at night, with faintly heard voices singing a Christmas carol. The locations include the school, the café and the comfortable living quarters behind it, the police station, the NATO air force base outside the town, the canal area, residential streets and parklands, the main commercial street – and the theatre. It's as if the film-makers have understood – and stretched their budget to render – the notion that people's daily lives take in more than just a couple of perfunctory studio sets.

The theatre (actually the Metropolitan Theatre, Edgware Road) is of pivotal importance. The 'golden egg' promised by the Dame in the panto becomes a sort of grail for Tommy and, finally, the means of unmasking the killer. Jimmy's superior officer has ordered him, as part of a good-will exercise, to take a party of school children to the panto, an offer turned down as a result of the town's anti-American feeling, but in the film's last (and alarming) sequence all the film's strands persuasively converge on the theatre. Another attractive feature of the film is that it allows the panto enough running time to establish the nature of its appeal: it is performed not with great expertise but without condescension. It is not just set up to be made fun of, and you can see the audience enjoying itself – and why.

The recurring motif of Anglo-American cultural differences roots the film in its period. Sometimes this is lightly and humorously suggested, as when Jimmy, told about the drag act at the heart of the panto, asks, 'Are you sure this show is suitable for kids?', or Tommy begins play-acting as a cowboy after watching television (although this fantasy is also cunningly built into the revelation of the killer). More nastily, it takes the form of xenophobic abuse from some of the locals, anxious to pin the crime on Jimmy. Writing forty years later, Kim Newman called the film 'a gem', claiming that it 'is, at least conceptually, quite a remarkable work ... [with] very creepy nighttime scenes, a seam of perversity located in a semi-sleazy British tradition, and one terrific shock "reveal"'.[45] To these excellences,

Newman might have added the uncommon care with establishing an ambience and some thoughtful performances, especially from Salew but also from Patricia Burke and, as the headmistress, Barbara Cavan. These latter two invest their small roles with a lightly sketched verisimilitude that epitomises the film as a whole.

Cash on Demand (1961, released 1963)

Quentin Lawrence's *Cash on Demand* makes every one of its sixty-six minutes work hard. It is adapted from a TV play by Jacques Gillies, entitled *The Gold Inside*, and perhaps betrays its origins by keeping to the single setting of the provincial bank with just a brief glimpse of the street outside. Arthur Grant's camera moves fluidly and aptly, but without flashiness, around the rooms of the bank: the tellers' counter, the outer office, the manager's office and the vault. The confinement of the scene contributes not a little to the film's tension, as does the fact of its being enacted in real time, with just enough unobtrusive shots of a wall clock to remind one of this.

The film's plot is tight and uncluttered. A suave criminal, Hepburn (André Morell), posing as an insurance company investigator checking on security arrangements, has come to rob the bank's vault of £90,000. He forces the manager, the prissy, unbending Fordyce (Peter Cushing), to do his will by leading Fordyce to believe his wife and child are being held hostage and will be killed if he doesn't open the vault. Fordyce is compelled to act before his staff as if nothing is wrong, and in the end he is saved by the intervention of the staff, whom he has treated with scant humanity, and the arrival of the police. The film's denouement, involving a faked tape recording of the terrified wife, a Father Christmas outside the bank and a not-too-clearly motivated confession from Hepburn, who has been arrested, involves the least satisfactory moments in the film's taut narrative.

What give this picture its distinction are two chief elements. First, and most obvious, is the creation of a very unsettling tension between Fordyce and Hepburn. Fordyce is used to unquestioning obedience from his staff and is forced into a position of helplessness in his own office by the ruthless Hepburn, whose sangfroid never deserts him. Except once, when he slaps Fordyce, and in a thriller which eschews physical violence this is a shocking moment. He also assesses Fordyce accurately when he says: 'You're not a very charitable man, let alone a sporting one.' Second, the gradual breaking down of Fordyce's chilly reserve: under the extreme stress of Hepburn's threat, he reveals a capacity for devotion to his wife and child that would have been a revelation to his staff, and in his need to rely on the support of his clerk, Pearson (Richard Vernon), he is made convincingly to reappraise his attitude to others. There is, of course, a strong echo of Dickens' *A Christmas Carol* here in the kind of transformation wrought in Fordyce, as well as the film's pre-Christmas setting with talk of a staff party which he will not be attending.[46] This Dickensian resonance, felt in the subdued but heartfelt way in which the shaken and chastened Fordyce speaks at the end to the staff whose loyalty he has scarcely deserved, provides a satisfying strand in the film's texture.

This outcome might have seemed simplistic if the film had been less well written, directed and acted. As it is, there is far more attention paid to detail of dialogue, of character, of positions in the bank hierarchy than might have been expected. Above all, it is Peter Cushing's performance of the austere man, to whom efficiency matters most (though the film is subtle enough to allow him a certain integrity as well), and who will be frightened into a warmer sense of humanity, that lifts the film well above the perfunctory levels of much 'B' film-making. Hammer made him a star in many showier roles, but it is arguable that he never did anything finer than this. He is also surrounded by a cast that fleshes out neatly suggested roles, and, in the case of Morell, he and Cushing (who had co-starred in Hammer's *The Hound of the Baskervilles*, 1959) offer a stimulating interaction of jocose criminality and cold rectitude. The other bank staff do what their smaller roles require with quiet conviction, especially Vernon as Pearson, who suppresses his justifiable bitterness to help Fordyce, but even the tiny sketches of Edith Sharpe, Norman Bird and Barry Lowe have an unwonted authenticity.

The director Quentin Lawrence never did anything so accomplished again, but, in the limited critical coverage given to 'B' movies, he was rightly praised here: the *Monthly Film Bulletin* described the film's story as 'watertight, tense and gripping' and found that its 'menace is more pronounced than in many films relying on physical brutality'.[47] *Kine Weekly* also noted that it created 'considerable tension and excitement without any notably violent action and without straying at all from the bank itself'.[48] A quarter of a century later, a reappraisal of the Hammer output wrote of it as 'one of Hammer's lost films ... [which] yet remains a powerful drama'.[49] If the film has indeed been 'lost', it richly deserves to be found again; it is both tensely compelling and humanely rewarding.

Tomorrow at Ten (1962)

Kidnapping, as noted earlier, was a crime quite commonly featured in British Bs, even though it was virtually unknown in the real life of the period. *Tomorrow at Ten* gets off to a very tense start when the usual driver who takes a rich man's small son to school is replaced by the taciturn Marlow (Robert Shaw), who drives the boy to a deserted house in Wimbledon, sets him up with a bottle of milk and a golliwog with an explosive device implanted in its back. He returns then to the home of the affluent

A ticking golliwog: John Gregson confirms that dolls like this are not good for a child in Comfort's tense *Tomorrow at Ten* (1962)

Chester (Alec Clunes), demanding £50,000 in return for a phone call about the boy's whereabouts when he, Marlow, has arrived in Rio. This planning goes astray when Chester interrupts police officer Parnell (John Gregson) just as the latter may be on the point of breaking down Marlow's story and knocks Marlow out. The kidnapper dies before revealing where the boy is and the film moves to its very suspenseful denouement.

There is real tension in the potentially appalling situation that arises when Marlow dies and the boy's life is in danger from the timed explosion, and though the plotting after this point is more perfunctory Lance Comfort maintains a firm grip on its elements. The tracking down of Marlow's parents (guest stars Renee Houston and William Hartnell) leads to some simplistic – but, in the event, adequate – motivation, and there is a predictable race against time, but there has been enough interest and detail in the creation of character and place for this not to matter much at the time.

There is, for instance, a very early scene in which the police inspector Parnell is interviewing a minor crim, Stripey (a knowing cameo from Harry Fowler). This episode has nothing directly to do with the kidnapping plot, but its importance is to establish Parnell's acumen and psychological insight into the criminal mind, qualities that later might have been successful in breaking down Marlow's resistance. Again, Parnell's wife (Betty McDowall) appears only three times and the film avoids stereotype in her responses to his several excuses for not being at home when she expects him. It is not, though, just in the characterisation and the performances (all distinctly superior for 'B' movies) that the film is to be commended. Its production design discriminates clearly and subtly among the houses – the grandiose but derelict one in which the boy is held, Chester's tasteful mansion and Parnell's comfortable middle-class suburban house – and Basil Emmott's cinematography imbues each of these with lighting and angles that reinforce their distinctiveness in relation to each other.

As to the actors, Robert Shaw's Marlow was singled out by several contemporary reviewers, but there is also carefully judged work from John Gregson as the tenacious Parnell, Alec Clunes as the anguished patrician Chester and Alan Wheatley as a social-climbing police commissioner. In fact, all the cast is excellent, imbuing well-written roles with the sort of individuating detail that compels audience belief. The film's outcome is presumably not in doubt but there is a good deal of expertly engendered excitement along the way to it. Peter Millar and James Kelly's original story and screenplay are worked out with considerable care for detail, but the film's real strength is in the direction of veteran Lance Comfort in one of his last films. *Tomorrow at Ten* is one of his finest low-budget features, but was obliged to support the box-office draw *Hud* on its first release.[50]

Unearthly Stranger (1963)

John Krish's *Unearthly Stranger* was one of the last in a string of excellent programmers produced by Leslie Parkyn and Julian Wintle at Beaconsfield. Krish, a documentarist who had gained second-feature experience on the *Stryker of the Yard* series, in fact only took the assignment ten days before filming when the original script by the American writer, Rex Carlton, was rejected by the distributors and the slated director. Krish did a total rewrite over a weekend, rejecting the space monsters of the original and substituting the idea of aliens disguised as humans. He persuaded his friend John Neville to play the lead and pre-production was completed in a week.[51]

Unearthly Stranger has the distinction of being perhaps the most explicit treatment of the 'otherness' of women in British cinema. The film is essentially a male-voiced *I Married a Monster from Outer Space* (1958) in which the screenplay identifies four types of alienness from the point of view

Alien women: Jean Marsh poses a threat to mankind in *Unearthly Stranger* (1963)

of the English Establishment: those deriving from class, gender, nationality and planetary origin. The vetting procedures of the Civil Service are used cleverly to expose the discriminatory practices which perpetuate the public schoolboy club of science and politics. Major Clark (Patrick Newell) has the task of examining the trustworthiness of the wife of scientist Dr Davidson (Neville). 'She's an alien, isn't she?' queries the Major. 'She was born in Switzerland,' replies Davidson, bitter that Clark does not find it necessary to vet his boss's wife because 'she's from a nice respectable English family'. The sweet-chewing Major is merely the exposed tip of an iceberg of misogynistic suspicion that permeates this male bastion. 'As a confirmed bachelor,' he insists, 'I'd rather face the unknown than a face covered in cold-cream at night and pin-curlers over breakfast.'

Davidson tries to distance himself from the chauvinism of his work colleagues and, in the domestic sphere, allows himself to be feminised to a degree, swapping his office suit for sports shirt and soft sweater. What he doesn't know, however, is that his wife Julie (the Italian actress Gabriella Licudi) and secretary (Jean Marsh) are both extraterrestrials, part of a mission to sabotage man's – or rather *men's* – attempt to develop space travel. The infiltrators' impersonation of human women is imperfect – they have no pulse, they are impervious to heat and they sleep with their eyes open – but it seems to take the men a long time to notice. The real clue to the alienness of these women, though, is that they have no blink reflex, and it is their unblinking, interrogative appropriation of the male gaze which is the key metaphor of the film. Although *Unearthly Stranger* appears to draw attention to the performance of femininity, it is male society that is the real object of scrutiny. As for the alien women, they respond differently to their experience of terrestrial gender relations. Julie embraces the human (and not simply feminine) emotions of love and the desire for children, while the secretary, Miss Ballard (a homage to J. G.?), continues to dismiss the idea of love as 'an illusion'.

Unearthly Stranger turns out to be a highly effective fable, which benefits considerably from Krish's astute direction and Reg Wyer's skills as a cinematographer.[52] These combine to create an unsettling atmosphere of dislocation and tension which disturbs our taken-for-granted assumptions about the worlds of office and home. The film ends with a paranoid climax in which Davidson is surrounded by women, any of whom might be aliens.[53]

Act of Murder (1964)

This trim thriller received pretty well uniformly positive reviews at the time, and that means at a time when 'B' films were lucky to receive any sort of attention at all. Even so, there was apt to be an element of patronage in the praise. *Variety*, for instance, was struck by how the 'brief running time ... naturally militates against all but superficial character-drawing, motivation and plot development' and later claimed that the drama 'could probably have been resolved more logically with more running time'.[54] The *Monthly Film Bulletin*, though thinking very well of it, was concerned not to 'make too much of a fuss of this film' and writes of its clearly 'humble origins',[55] while *Films and Filming*, which also liked the film overall, finished its review with 'but the feeling of the studio is far from banished'.[56]

The point of quoting these cavils from generally favourable reviews is just to suggest the grudging reception accorded to even superior 'B' films. In this case, the grudge element seems misplaced as one looks back at the film. Lewis Davidson's screenplay quite deftly weaves its strands of sexual-triangle drama and mystery-thriller to unusual effect. This is a film whose tone is hard to be sure of as it picks its way through a web of obliquely suggested jealousy and a scam involving convincingly improbable frauds.

The teasing nature of the plot is there from the start. In a country cottage, furnished with antiques which have a role in the story as distinct from 'B' movie production designers' routine suggestion of rural retreats, London actor Tim Ford (John Carson) tries to persuade ex-actress Anne Longman (Justine Lord) to return to the stage. 'You're miscast,' he tells her about her function as country house-wife tending her roses and chickens; it's 'a pure waste of God-given talent', he adds with actorly hyperbole, thereby, incidentally, throwing down a challenge to the actress playing Anne. Ralph (Anthony Bate), Anne's husband, observes their erotically charged banter with a certain restraint, calling out to Tim, 'Put that woman down. You don't know where she's been.' Where she's been, we discover much later, is to have had an affair with Tim two years earlier, and the film only makes us privy to this fact when it is three-quarters over, the sexual capitulation between the two handled with a convincing build-up of erotic tension. The outcome of this triangular affair will be a murder and a suicide, shot eerily from high above a London alley.

Alongside this drama is the mystery relating to the Longmans' holiday arrangement to change houses with the Petersons, a London couple. The latter move in as Anne and Ralph drive off to London, immediately empty the bricks from their cases and start stashing away the antiques. They are interrupted in their work by the return of Tim for a bag he's left behind, and by the time Anne and Ralph return, having found the London address non-existent, the cottage appears to have been restored. Except that the chickens, the canary and the Pekinese dog are found to be poisoned. The film brings these disparate elements together with some dexterity, contriving a plausible enough background to the Petersons' scam. As the London policeman (Michael Brennan) tells the Longmans when they report the non-existence of the London address, they'd be surprised how many people such as themselves are 'inclined to hand over the complete contents of their house on the strength of a piece of embossed note-paper'. The cynical remark carries the slightest critique of class affectations, and the Petersons, as played by Dandy Nichols and Duncan Lewis, present as the acme of solid middle-class respectability. They, with the antiques dealer Quick (Richard Burrell), constitute another kind of triangle, with its own enigmatic quality about who is telling whom what to do.

There are some obvious shock moments, like that in which the Longmans return to the cottage at night and a man suddenly looms up inside, proving to be no more than a policeman on duty who's been dozing. But this kind of predictable (if quite scary) effect is minor by comparison with the way in which the erotic triangle is developed. One is struck in the opening sequence with the way Tim pursues Anne through the garden, making as if to grasp her about the hips when Ralph calls out from inside; there is a strange moment when Tim, back in his London flat and in pyjamas, strokes his own body, as he talks to the Longmans on the phone about what has happened at the cottage; and when we first see Anne at Tim's flat they are at opposite ends of a very long sofa which cuts diagonally across the screen in a way that makes it hard to assess their relationship at this point. James Wilson's camerawork, as noted in an earlier chapter, is considerably more venturesome than one usually finds in 'B' movies, and an atypically long-held close-up of Justine Lord's face persuasively establishes an ambiguity in her

As good as a cheap film gets: director Alan Bridges shows just what could be achieved on a tiny budget with *Act of Murder* (1964)

character and her situation. Elsewhere, Wilson prowls through a party of tanked-up theatricals, including the very slow-speaking, basilisk presence of Marianne Stone, creating an unease that suggests things are likely to get out of control soon.

On the strength of this film, the *Monthly Film Bulletin* judged that former television director 'Alan Bridges might become quite an acquisition for the cinema', rightly pointing out that he had 'absorbed his Antonioni and Losey' and had succeeded in using those influences to create a convincing 'atmosphere of strangeness'.[57] *Kinematograph Weekly* praised its 'imaginative direction',[58] and Allan Eyles noted that 'Alan Bridges puts unusual care and thought into the details of staging'.[59] All this praise seems well earned: the actors are encouraged to register a complexity not common in 'B' movies, the camera has been, as noted, instructed to move in ways that foster enigma and tension; and Bridges has not, after refusing to spell out all the connections, shied away from a desolate ending. In the event, his career in first features remained a low-key affair: he generated some wintry frissons with *The Hireling* (1973); he drew remarkable performances from three famous actresses in *The Return of the Soldier* (1982); and the elegiac *The Shooting Party* (1984) impressively 'dissects class attitudes and male aggression on the eve of the First World War'.[60] There are merits in all these films, but it is arguable that *Act of Murder*, with its stunning and disorienting climax, still contains his tautest work on film.

Smokescreen (1964)

This uncommonly neat little insurance racket-cum-murder thriller is essentially the work of director-writer Jim O'Connolly, who had accumulated a decade's experience as scriptwriter and assistant director before getting his chance to direct a couple of smart 'B' thrillers. *Smokescreen* exhibits considerable care in the details of its plotting and characterisation, and combines a real sense of the investigation, which unearths the crime, with a comic thread which proves to be in the service of either rendering the 'felt life' of the protagonist or of furthering his enquiries. In the opening sequence a car in flames goes over a cliff, observed only by a couple of enthusiastic snoggers, and there is a £100,000 insurance policy on the life of the man who, it is claimed, was in the car. Roper (Peter Vaughan, already an authoritative character player, as he would be for the next forty years) is sent by his boss to Brighton to investigate the claim.[61] This brings him in contact with the supposedly dead man's widow Janet Dexter (Yvonne Romain), his former business partner Turner (Gerald Flood) and Baylis (John Carson), the insurer who had sold Dexter the policy. Whether or not Dexter committed suicide or was killed or is still alive are the possibilities the plot keeps healthily alive, until a quite tense stand-off on the same clifftop that opened the film.

The investigation is carried out methodically and without any overt violence until the film's last sequence. The humorous undertow of the film is less in the nature of the standard 'B' movie comic relief, of the kind so often (and enjoyably) provided by the likes of Michael Balfour or Dora Bryan. Instead, it is built into the fabric of the film's main narrative action. Roper is an insurance claims investigator who is well known to his boss, Player, and Player's secretary (John Glyn-Jones and Barbara Hicks) for his apparent thriftiness. There is a running joke about his fiddling his expenses: in a very early scene, as he returns from a job, Player and Miss Breen observe him arriving by bus and are sure he'll enter a taxi expense claim. Elsewhere, he is seen to be very stingy in tipping or walking after enquiring about a taxi fare or eating the free nuts provided at a bar without ordering a drink.

Maximising the expenses: Peter Vaughan questions Derek Guyler in *Smokescreen* (1964)

This seems, at first, no more than a simple characterising trait: then its relevance is seen in two ways. His apparent stinginess is 'explained' in a brief scene that testifies to his reason: he is up against it financially to provide round-the-clock nursing for his terminally ill wife. This humanises the character of Roper and enables us to sympathise with his habits. Later, also in comic mode, we see him entertain at drinks Helen, the secretary of the dead man's partner. She is amusingly played by Penny Morrell (in fact, in Dora Bryan mode), who as she downs several champagne cocktails blows smoke in Roper's eyes and serendipitously indicates to him the purpose of the insurance scam. Roper, thus alerted, races out and leaves her to pay for the several rounds of expensive drinks. Again, the comedy has been made to *work* in the interests of the plot. Just as it does in a brief scene with the dead man's doctor (Derek Francis), in which Roper's subtlety gets valuable information from the curmudgeonly medico when Baylis's tactlessness has failed.

The reviewer who wrote that 'this pleasant little mystery story has a few features that lift it out of the ordinary'[62] was right to draw attention to the originality of 'the central figure' and to 'the refreshingly off-hand police inspector played by Glynn Edwards'. He might also have referred to the film's inventive use of a range of settings – the cliff at the opening and close of the film, several well-differentiated offices and, in Brighton, the Grand Hotel, the railway station and the pier. This is not one of those second features that seems to have been shot in the perfunctorily appointed corner of a disused warehouse (or a tiny studio), and it benefits as well from smart editing and camerawork that knows when to hold a shot a moment longer than purely narrative demands might require.

Thematically, the whole film is held together by the motif of claims, the claims one person might have on another as well as the more formal kinds – of claims made for purposes both serious (whether or not honest) and comic (whether or not there is more to them than that). The last film made at the small studios in Brighton, *Smokescreen* is a breath of fresh sea air and affords the pleasure of watching people making the most of the resources at their command.

Appendix: Revolving Bs

British Second Features on the Gaumont British, Odeon and Rank Circuits

This listing is derived from research on film exhibition carried out by Allen Eyles and reported in the following books published by the Cinema Theatre Association and distributed by the BFI: *Gaumont British Cinemas* (1996), *Odeon Cinemas 1: Oscar Deutsch Entertains Our Nation* (2002) and *Odeon Cinemas 2: From J. Arthur Rank to the Multiplex* (2005). Most second features from Exclusive and Anglo-Amalgamated were shown on the rival ABC circuit.

The main attraction on the programme is noted in brackets after the title of the supporting feature. Co-feature programmes are indicated thus: (Co), and Australian films thus: (Aus).

Date	Odeon	Gaumont British
1940	Young Man's Fancy (Professor Manlock) Full Speed Ahead (The Man in the Iron Mask) An Englishman's Home (Husbands or Lovers) Mr Chedworth Steps Out (Aus) (The Light That Failed) Meet Maxwell Archer (Over the Moon) Return to Yesterday (Laugh it Off) The Chinese Bungalow (Eternally Yours) Mrs Pym of Scotland Yard (Destry Rides Again) Room for Two (Dr Cyclops)	Three Silent Men (Irene)
1941	Pastor Hall (Hired Wife) You Will Remember (Argentine Nights) The Man at the Gate (Nice Girl?) Target for Tonight (The Lady From Cheyenne)	Dad Rudd MP (Aus) (The Long Voyage Home) Old Mother Riley's Ghosts (Kitty Foyle) Target for Tonight (The Devil and Miss Jones) Tanks a Million (The Great Awakening)
1942	The Seventh Survivor (Birth of the Blues) (Co) Penn of Pennsylvania (Sullivan's Travels) Sabotage at Sea (Song of the Islands) Salute John Citizen (The Palm Beach Story)	Old Mother Riley's Circus (Sundown) Ferry Pilot (Appointment for Love) The Night Has Eyes (Weekend in Havana) Frontline Kids (To Be or Not to Be) Suspected Person (To the Shores of Tripoli)
1943	The Brains Trust (Happy Go Lucky) The Volunteer (The Sky's the Limit) World of Plenty (So Proudly We Hail)	Battle of Britain (Rhythm Serenade)

Date	Odeon	Gaumont British
1944	It's in the Bag (Wuthering Heights *Revival*) (Co) Tunisian Victory (Standing Room Only) Minesweeper (The Bridge of San Lois Rey) (Co) Medal for the General (Sensations of 1945) Meet Sexton Blake (I Love a Soldier)	Old Mother Riley Overseas (Jack London)
1945	The Battle for New Britain (Here Comes the Waves) Don Chicago (Salty O'Rourke)	
1946	Whose Baby? (Leave Her to Heaven) The Skipper Puts to Sea (Dragonwyck)	Bothered by a Beard (The Spanish Main) Send for Paul Temple (Three Little Girls in Blue)
1947	All the King's Horses (Notorious) Beyond Price (So Well Remembered) (Co) Dancing With Crime (Dear Ruth) The Royal Weddings *Short* (The Woman in the Hall)	The Loyal Heart (The Strange Woman) Headline (The Ghost and Mrs Muir) The Little Ballerina (Uncle Silas)
1948	(Co) While I Live (Maryland) The King's Navy (Blanche Fury) A Song for Tomorrow (A Double Life) Penny and the Pownall Case (Fort Apache) Colonel Bogey (Night Has a Thousand Eyes) Trouble in the Air (The Exile) Fly Away Peter (An Act of Murder)	Circus Boy (When the Bough Breaks) Death in the Hand (Against the Wind) Black Memory (Blue Skies) Dick Barton – Special Agent (Bandit of Sherwood Forest) A Piece of Cake (A Foreign Affair) The Secret Tunnel (Call Northside 777)
1949	To the Public Danger (You Gotta Stay Happy) Love in Waiting (Red River) Aqua-Show Sports Serenade (Cardboard Cavalier) (Co) Helter Skelter (Reign of Terror) (Co) Murder at the Windmill (Tulsa) (Co) Poet's Pub (Impact) Daybreak in Udi (Down to the Sea in Ships) Proud Canvas (Rope of Sand)	The Fool and the Princess (Tap Roots) Badger's Green (Eureka Stockade) (Co) It's Not Cricket (The Lost Moment) Meet Simon Cherry (Morning Departure)
1950	Stop Press Girl (One Way Street)	Dick Barton at Bay (Broken Arrow) Shooting Stars (The Mudlark)
1951	To Have and to Hold (Rawhide) Assassin for Hire (Follow the Sun) Chelsea Story (On the Riviera) Death of an Angel (The Card)	The Rossiter Case (I Shall Return) The Dark Light (This is My Affair)

Date	Odeon	Gaumont British
1952	Royal Journey (His Excellency) Night Was Our Friend (Viva Zapata!) Never Look Back (Belles on Their Toes) Crow Hollow (Full House) Come Back Peter (The Big Sky) (Co) The Voice of Merrill (The Lawless Breed)	Hammer the Toff (Robin Hood and His Merry Men) (Co) Brandy for the Parson (Scarlet Angel) Mother Riley Meets the Vampire (Untamed Frontier) (Co) The Brave Don't Cry (The Dual at Silver Creek) Distant Trumpet (Just for You) Lady in the Fog (Lure of the Wilderness) Paul Temple Returns (Monkey Business) Potter of the Yard (The Road to Bali)
1953	Gentlemen ... The Queen (The Long Memory) Deadly Nightshade (Tonight We Sing) (Co) House of Blackmail (Titanic) The Broken Horseshoe (Innocents in Paris) The Limping Man (Second Chance)	Hot Ice (Marching Along) Wheel of Fate (Thunder Road) Murder at 3 am (Genevieve) The Saint's Return (White Witch Doctor) Love in Pawn (Albert R.N.) Blood Orange (Casanova's Big Night)
1954	Star of My Night (The Glen Miller Story) Double Exposure (O'Rourke of the Royal Mounted) (Co) The Diamond (Witness to Murder) Johnny on the Spot (Knock on Wood) The Queen in Australia (Carnival Story) Burnt Evidence (Johnny Guitar) The Master Plan (Dance Little Lady) The Embezzler (The Far Country) Delayed Action (The Seekers) The Golden Link (Live it Up) Devil's Point (The Black Knight) Model Girl (The Caine Mutiny) Final Appointment (The Green Scarf) The Clue of the Missing Ape (Aunt Clara) (Co) The Crowded Day (The Happiness of 3 Women) Children Galore (Sign of the Pagan)	Park Plaza 605 (Money From Home) Royal New Zealand Journey (The Love Lottery) (Co) The Runaway Bus (Border River) River Beat (Star of India) (Co) Bang! You're Dead (An Inspector Calls) Dangerous Cargo (Miss Sadie Thompson) The Stranger Came Home (Secret of the Incas) Profile (The Beachcomber) Mask of Dust (The Divided Heart) The Green Buddha (On the Waterfront) The End of the Road (The Belles of St Trinians)
1955	Armand and Michaela Denis Under the Southern Cross (One Good Turn) Secret Venture (The Colditz Story) One Jump Ahead (Captain Lightfoot) Tiger by the Tail (Run for Cover)	Three Steps to the Gallows (The Sea Shall Not Have Them) The Delavine Affair (3 Ring Circus) (Co) Before I Wake (Six Bridges to Cross) Third Party Risk (Man Without a Star)

Date	Odeon	Gaumont British
	Room in the House (Strange Lady in Town)	Armand and Michaela Denis on the Barrier Reef
	The Flaw (We're No Angels)	(As Long as They're Happy)
	The Reluctant Bride (Cast a Dark Shadow)	(Co) Where There's a Will (The Eternal Sea)
	(Co) Timeslip (The Rawhide Years)	Police Dog (Above Us the Waves)
	(Co) A Yank in Ermine (Flame of the Islands)	(Co) The Secret (Escape to Burma)
	Dial 999 (An Alligator Named Daisy)	Barbados Quest (Pearl of the South Pacific)
		Windfall (Escapade)
		The Hornet's Nest (The Shrike)
		One Way Out (Man of the Moment)
		Armand and Michaela Denis Among the
		Headhunters (Touch and Go)
		(Co) The Blue Peter (The Girl Rush)
		(Co) Portrait of Allison (Tennessee's Partner)
1956	The Lilt of the Kilt (The Man With the	(Co) The Gamma People (The Last Frontier)
	Golden Arm)	Cloak Without Dagger (The Benny Goodman
	April in Portugal (Picnic)	Story)
	The Gelignite Gang (Backlash)	Flight From Vienna (The Rose Tattoo)
	(Co) Soho Incident (Hot Blood)	(Co) The Intimate Stranger (Toy Tiger)
	Breakaway (The Iron Petticoat)	Behind the Headlines (Away All Boats)
	The Narrowing Circle (Bandido)	(Co) The Last Man to Hang? (He Laughed Last)
	Home and Away (The Weapon)	Passport to Treason (Child in the House)
	Find the Lady (Written on the Wind)	The High Terrace (Back From Eternity)
		(Co) Bermuda Affair (Nightfall)
		The Hide-Out (Up in the World)
1957	No Road Back (Bundle of Joy)	(Co) The Counterfeit Plan (Don't Knock the
	Suspended Alibi (Battle Hymn)	Rock)
	The Crooked Sky (High Tide at Noon)	There's Always a Thursday (The Hunchback of
	Murder Reported (Interpol)	Notre Dame)
	Hour of Decision (Funny Face)	(Co) The Silken Affair (The Day They Gave
	The Hypnotist (Interlude)	Babies Away)
	The Heart Within (Hell Drivers)	(Co) That Woman Opposite (The Oaklahoman)
	Man From Tangier (Night Passage)	Second Fiddle (Beau James)
	The Big Chance (Campbell's Kingdom)	(Co) Time Lock (After the Ball)
	Stranger's Meeting (Robbery Under Arms)	Account Rendered (Across the Bridge)
	(Co) Not Wanted on Voyage (Men in War)	The Depraved (Time Limit)
1958	The End of the Line (The Sad Sack)	Son of a Stranger (Legend of the Lost)
	The Diplomatic Corpse (A Tale of Two Cities)	The Strange Awakening (6.5 Special)
	The Betrayal (Paris Holiday)	High Hell (St Louis Blues)
	Heart of a Child (The Big Money)	The Spaniard's Curse (Law and Disorder)
	Them Nice Americans (Nor the Moon by	On the Run (Run Silent, Run Deep)
	Night)	(Co) The Man Upstairs (Chain of Events)

Date	Odeon	Gaumont British
	A Woman Possessed (Kings Go Forth)	Links of Justice (Rock-A-Bye Baby)
	Moment of Indiscretion (The Defiant Ones)	
	Dublin Nightmare (Passionate Summer)	
	The Bank Raiders (The Naked and the Dead)	
	Antarctic Crossing (Me and the Colonel)	
1959	The Secret Man (Bachelor of Hearts)	

Date	Rank	National (Rank alternative)
1959	Three Crooked Men (Houseboat)	The Great Van Robbery (Anna Lucasta)
	High Jump (Shake Hands With the Devil)	Broth of a Boy (Subway in the Sky)
	Floating Fortress *Short* (Some Like it Hot)	Model for Murder (Make Mine a Million)
	Royal River *Short* (The Diary of Anne Frank)	The Child and the Killer (Separate Tables)
	A Woman's Temptation (The Bridal Path)	Innocent Meeting (The Hound of the
	This is Malta *Short* (A Hole in the Head)	Baskervilles)
	Life in Danger (This Earth is Mine)	No Safety Ahead (Don't Give Up the Ship)
	This is Burma *Short* (I Want to Live)	Man Accused (The Wonderful Country)
	The Man Who Liked Funerals (Ask Any Girl)	
	Strictly Confidential (SOS Pacific)	
	Devil's Bait (Follow a Star)	
1960	The Awakening (Operation Petticoat)	Web of Suspicion (But Not For Me)
	Night Train for Inverness (A Touch of Larceny)	Murder on Site Three (The Best of Everything)
	Sentenced for Life (Happy Anniversary)	Witness in the Dark (Desert Mice)
	And Women Shall Weep (The League of	Date at Midnight (The Jayhawkers)
	Gentlemen)	Operation Cupid (Please Don't Eat the Daisies)
	Boyd's Shop (Never Let Go)	Hello London (The Siege of Sidney Street)
	Dead Lucky (The Savage Innocents)	The Gentle Trap (Surprise Package)
	Snowball (Make Mine Mink)	Identity Unknown (GI Blues)
	The Man Who Couldn't Walk (Strangers	
	When We Meet)	
1961	A Taste of Money (Tunes of Glory)	Feet of Clay (Never on a Sunday)
	Edgar Wallace: Marriage of Convenience	(Co) Shadow of the Cat (The Curse of the
	(Man in the Moon)	Werewolf)
	The Trunk (The Wackiest Ship in the Army)	(Co) So Evil, So Young (Macumba Love)
	Echo of Barbara (Midnight Lace)	Out of the Shadow (A Raisin in the Sun)
	The Solitary Child (No Love for Johnny)	The Boy Who Stole a Million (Follow That Man)
	The Wind of Change (Double Bunk)	Compelled (The Hoodlum Priest)
	Murder in Eden (No, My Darling Daughter!)	(Co) Mary Had a Little (A Cold Wind in August)
	The Impersonator (Spare the Rod)	(Co) The Kitchen (Room at the Top *Revival*)
	A Question of Suspense (Two Road Together)	(Co) Three on a Spree (Warlord of Crete)
	Edgar Wallace: Partners in Crime (Flame in	
	the Streets)	

	Rank	**National** (Rank alternative)
	The Middle Course (The Young Savages) Thin Ice (Wild in the Country) The Long Shadow (Whistle Down the Wind) Information Received (The Last Sunset) Edgar Wallace: Attempt to Kill (Victim) Dangerous Afternoon (A Taste of Honey) Edgar Wallace: Man Detained (Back Street) Johnny Nobody (The Hellions)	
1962	The Pursuers (The Devil at 4 O'Clock) Part-Time Wife (The Day the Earth Caught Fire) Enter Inspector Duval (The Best of Enemies) Edgar Wallace: Never Back Losers (All Night Long) Freedom to Die (Lover Come Back) Design for Loving (HMS Defiant) She Always Gets Their Man (Sergeants Three) Edgar Wallace: Backfire (Waltz of the Toreadors) Hair of the Dog (Lonely Are the Brave) Two-Letter Alibi (Walk on the Wild Side) Strongroom (Two and Two Make Six) (Co) Captain Clegg (The Phantom of the Opera) Emergency (That Touch of Mink) The Traitors or Gaolbreak (Tiara Tahiti or Billy Budd) Band of Thieves (Life for Ruth) The Lamp in Assassin Mews (The Miracle Worker) The Primitives (The Wild and the Willing)	Terminus (Only Two Can Play *Revival*) What Every Woman Wants (Geronimo) Ambush in Leopard Street (Five Finger Exercise) She Knows Y'Know (The Wooden Horse of Troy) Three Spare Wives (The Vikings *Revival*)
1963	Danger by My Side (Cape Fear) Stranglehold (The Fast Lady) Gang War (I Could Go On Singing) Edgar Wallace: On the Run or The £20,000 Kiss (Call Me Bwana or Doctor in Distress) Mystery Submarine (The Very Edge) The Gentle Terror (Five Miles to Midnight) The Fur Collar (Lancelot and Guinevere) A Guy Called Caesar (The Interns) The Break (The War Lover)	(Co) The Cool Mikado (Red River *Revival*) Master Spy (The Black Bucaneer)

	Rank	National (Rank alternative)

	The Spanish Sword (All This and Money Too)
	 (Co) The Siege of the Saxons (Jason and the
	     Argonauts)
	 The Bay of St Michel (80,000 Suspects)
	 The Bomb in the High Street (A Gathering
	     of Eagles)
	 (Co) Girl in the Headlines (In the French Style)
	 Cash on Demand (Bye Bye Birdie)
	 Live It Up (A Stitch in Time)	

1964	Impact (Father Came Too) (Co) It's All Over Town (Ladies Who Do) Edgar Wallace: The Switch (Hot Enough for June) Strictly for the Birds (Charade) (Co) East of Sudan (First Men in the Moon) Blind Corner (The Beauty Jungle) The Six-Sided Triangle (The Pumpkin Eater)	
1965	A Home of Your Own (A Shot in the Dark) The Sicilians (Kiss Me Stupid or *Various revivals*) Night Train to Paris (Goodbye Charlie) Be My Guest (The Intelligence Men) Edgar Wallace: Never Mention Murder (The Satan Bug) Traitor's Gate (The Knack) Game for Three Losers (Mister Moses) (Co) You Must Be Joking (Cat Ballou)	
1966	Dateline Diamonds (Doctor in Clover) The Murder Game (Stagecoach) The Runaway (The Wrong Box) The Boy Cried Murder (What Did You Do in the War, Daddy?)	
1967	Palaces of a Queen (The Quiller Memorandum) The Crooked Road (Murderer's Row) Just Like a Woman (Accident) Spaceflight IC-1 (Caprice) The Trygon Factor (Stranger in the House) Miss MacTaggart Won't Lie Down (The Professionals) The Plank (The Long Dual) I Like Birds (Pretty Polly)	

	Rank	National (Rank alternative)
1968	Promenade (Planet of the Apes) A Little of What You Fancy (Bandolero!) They Came From Beyond Space (Nobody Runs Forever) (Co) 30 is a Dangerous Age, Cynthia (Interlude) (Co) A Twist of Sand (Inspector Clouseau)	
1969	Submarine X-1 (The Thomas Crown Affair) Naked Evil (The Boston Strangler)	

Notes

Preface

1. *The Cinema Studio*, 17 November 1948, p. 7.
2. Gareth Owen with Brian Burford, *The Pinewood Story* (London: Reynolds & Hearn, 2000), pp. 87–9.
3. Alfred Shaughnessy, *Both Ends of the Candle* (London: Peter Owen, 1978), p. 133.
4. This it succeeded in doing via Continental Distributors of New York.
5. Anon, *Monthly Film Bulletin*, January 1961, p. 18.
6. *The Daily Cinema*, 19 May 1961.
7. Shaughnessy, *Both Ends of the Candle*, p. 134.
8. Steve Chibnall, *Quota Quickies: The Birth of the British 'B' Film* (London: BFI, 2007).

1 Big Ships and Little Ships

1. Quoted in *Kinematograph Weekly*, 9 January 1941, p. 32.
2. For a more detailed discussion of the first two Quota Acts see Rachel Low, *The History of the British Film 1918–29*, and *1929–39* (London: Allen and Unwin, 1971 and 1985); Margaret Dickinson and Sarah Street, *Cinema and State: The Film Industry and the British Government 1927–84* (London: BFI, 1985); Steve Chibnall, *Quota Quickies*.
3. Charles Barr, *Ealing Studios* (New York: The Overlook Press, 1980), pp. 19–22.
4. *Film Report*, 6 January 1940.
5. *The Cinema*, 28 February 1940, p. 14.
6. E.g., 'The situations are made to order and the gags are crude. The would-be comedy "business" falls flat ... The direction and presentation are amateurish'. *Film Report*, 27 January 1940.
7. Letter to *Picturegoer* from Penarth, 3 August 1940, p. 19.
8. *Picturegoer* (19 October 1940, p. 15), however, thought Barnes and Gynt teamed 'quite well' and praised the film for its pace, suspense and romantic comedy.
9. *Film Report*, 23 March 1940, and *Picturegoer*, 12 October 1940, p. 17, respectively.
10. Reviewers were generally unimpressed, with *Picturegoer* (19 October 1940, p. 15) describing it as a disappointing 'bedroom farce without the necessary spice'.
11. *Film Report*, 5 October 1940. The film had been sponsored by the London Co-operative Society. Alan Burton (ed.), *The British Co-operative Movement Film Catalogue* (Trowbridge: Flicks Books, 1997), p. 159.
12. *The Cinema*, 26 June 1940, p. 15.
13. Dickinson and Street, *Cinema and State*, pp. 113–4.
14. *The Cinema*, 10 July 1940, p. 5.
15. *The Cinema*, 24 July 1940, p. 5. Columbia's policy is discussed in Joe Friedman, 'American Renters and Their Policy of British Production', *Kinematograph Weekly*, 14 January 1943, p. 109.
16. *Film Report*, 23 November 1940. *Picture Show* (15 March 1941, p. 14) was a little kinder,

highlighting the excellent supporting performances by Reginald Purdell and Edward Rigby.

17. Ace was one of the quickest off the mark, distributing a documentary featurette on the work of the Royal Artillery titled *The Boys with the Guns* (1940). Other documentary featurettes distributed in 1940 included Avon's statistics-heavy *City of Ships*, the first of a number of studies of the Port of London, and Anglo-American's *African Skyways*, a travelogue charting the role of the aeroplane in improving communications in Africa.

18. *Picture Show*, 23 August 1941, p. 4.

19. Edward Wood, 'Finest War Flying Film Proves Truth is Stronger than Fiction', *Picture Show*, 30 August 1941, p. 11.

20. However, his enthusiasm did not prevent Taylor from offering criticism of *Target for Tonight* for failing to 'dig behind the subject and show the implications of the subject'. *Kinematograph Weekly*, 8 January 1942, p. 30.

21. For an account of the work of the CFU during the war, see James Chapman, *The British at War: Cinema, State and Propaganda, 1939–1945* (London: I. B. Tauris, 1998), pp. 114–38.

22. *Documentary News Letter*, March 1942, p. 46.

23. *Documentary News Letter*, May 1942, p. 68.

24. RKO agreed to pair *Desert Victory* with their hit Cary Grant and Ginger Rogers movie, *Once Upon a Honeymoon*, to give it an Odeon premiere in London. *The Cinema*, 3 March 1943, p. 8.

25. *Evening Standard*, 10 June 1943. While most of the product of the CFU was distributed by British companies, the featurette *Before the Raid* (1943), Jiri Weiss's stirring account of resistance to the Nazis among Norwegian fishermen, was handled by MGM. Another American company, Paramount, distributed Paul Rotha's acclaimed study of global food problems, *World of Plenty* (1943).

26. Walker and Lawson were partners in British National and the production company GHW, and Lawson would have starring roles in the bigger-budget *Hard Steel* and Technicolor turkey *The Great Mr Handel* (both 1942).

27. *To-Day's Cinema*, 14 December 1943, pp. 4–5.

28. *To-Day's Cinema*, 1 May 1942, p. 5.

29. *To-Day's Cinema*, 24 July 1942, p. 15.

30. E.g., *To-Day's Cinema*, 6 August 1943, p. 8.

31. *Film Report*, 11 October 1941.

32. 'Butcher's, Britain's Oldest Producers and Renters Keep Up Tradition', *Kinematograph Weekly*, 8 January 1942, p. 47.

33. Although Nazi spies were a popular theme for film-makers during the early part of the war, the proud boast of MI5 that there were no effective German agents in Britain after 2 September 1939 has been more or less validated, apparently, by captured Nazi documents. See Peter and Leni Gillman, *Collar the Lot: How Britain Interned and Expelled its Wartime Refugees* (London: Quartet, 1980), pp. 36–7.

34. In the morally loosened circumstances of the war on the Home Front, the BBFC was prepared to sanction jokes that were a little more risqué than usual. For example: 'What's that, Madam, something wrong with the keyhole of your bathroom door? OK, I'll look into it.'

35. *Film Report*, 27 September 1941. There was more homely sentiment in Burger's *Rose of Tralee* (1942), whose much-loved Irish ballads enabled it to play as a first or co-feature.

36. *Kinematograph Weekly*, 8 January 1942, p. 90.

37. *Kinematograph Weekly*, 14 January 1943, p. 107.

38. *Kinematograph Weekly*, 14 January 1943, p. 96.

39. *The Cinema*, 5 August 1942, p. 3.

40. For example, two Preston exhibitors were fined £5 and £7 10s (for a second offence) with a guinea costs for failing to make quota returns. *The Cinema*, 2 September 1942, p. 8.

41. *The Cinema*, 2 September 1942, p. 5.

42. One example was John Harlow's spiritualist melodrama, *Spellbound* (1941, USA: *Passing Clouds*), which was trimmed by fifteen minutes and re-released in March 1943.

43. *To-Day's Cinema*, 4 September 1942, p. 2. Second features had already been eliminated in Nazi-occupied France.

44. 'Playing Time Cut May be Avoided', *To-Day's Cinema*, 26 February 1943, p. 3. On the arguments in favour of suspending or abolishing the double bill see Dickinson and Street, *Cinema and State*, p. 127.

45. *To-Day's Cinema*, 26 February 1943, p. 3.

46. See the table in Dickinson and Street, *Cinema and State*, p. 131.

47. *Kinematograph Weekly*, 4 December 1941, pp. 4, 9.

48. *Film Report*, 24 July 1942.

49. Fancey was also responsible for the hour-long *Down Memory Lane* (1943) which compiled old footage of variety acts, linking them with the story of a romance between a music-hall stage manager and a barmaid.

50. *To-Day's Cinema*, 15 January 1943, p. 4.

51. *To-Day's Cinema*, 21 December 1943, p. 15.

52. *To-Day's Cinema*, 11 February 1941, p. 13.

53. *The Cinema*, 16 August 1944, p. 10. *Documentary News Letter* (no. 53, 1946, p. 33), on the other hand, rated the film as a fine example of the combination of actuality and drama.

54. *To-Day's Cinema*, 18 February 1944, p. 24.

55. *To-Day's Cinema*, 6 October 1944, p. 21.

56. *To-Days Cinema* (6 April 1943, p. 18) was clearly underwhelmed: 'the material is put over inoffensively enough to achieve the unambitious goal'.

57. *Rainbow Round the Corner* should not be confused with British National's 'A' film *Heaven is Round the Corner* (1944) trade-shown in the same week.

58. *The Cinema*, 25 April 1945, p. 18.

59. *Film Report*, 22 February 1946. The film, though, was part of a veritable sheepdog cycle that began with Butcher's *Sheepdog of the Hills* and included *The Voice Within* and *The Lakeland Story* (both 1946).

60. See the pull-out ad in *To-Day's Cinema*, 24 April 1945, pp. 16–18.

2 'What's on with it?'

1. *The Cinema*, 30 April 1947, p. 27.

2. *The Cinema*, 8 August 1945, p. 22.

3. *Documentary News Letter*, no. 51, 1946, p. 9.

4. 'Many of the people who appear in *Children on Trial* are duplicating for the screen the roles they play in real life ... All the school sequences were taken in two approved schools – the Leicester Home School for Girls and the Liverpool Farm School ... The interiors of the slum houses were reconstructed in the studio by the Crown Film Unit Art Department from rooms actually seen by Jack Lee when he visited slum areas.' Press sheet, Ealing, 1946.

5. *Documentary News Letter*, no. 53, 1946, p. 33.

6. Ibid. *The Cinema* (29 August 1945, p. 45) agreed that the film was 'good supporting entertainment for all audiences'.

7. *Documentary News Letter*, no. 53, 1946, p. 41.

8. The film's political overtones were made explicit in its publicity: 'The suffering of other nations is illustrated by scenes of Black Market operators and the wealthy living in complete luxury, while a short distance from their comfortable homes the poor are dying like flies from starvation.' Press sheet, British Lion, 1948.

9. Quoted in *To-Day's Cinema*, 30 January 1948, p. 17.

10. *Documentary News Letter*, no. 61, 1948, p. 5.

11. *To-Day's Cinema*, 26 April 1946, p. 29.

12. 'Occasionally one is included in the cinema programmes but it is never an attraction *per se*, and is only utilized in a haphazard and time-filling capacity. You can almost hear the film magnate's "If you must have your two-and-a-half/three hours show, you'll have to sit

through this." ' Leslie Halliwell, 'The Receiving End', *Documentary News Letter*, no. 56, 1947, p. 96.

13. *Documentary News Letter*, no. 58, 1947, p. 115.

14. *This Modern Age*, promotional booklet, J. Arthur Rank, 1947.

15. Issue 5, *Thoroughbreds of the World* (1947), a visit to Lord Derby's racehorse stables, was dismissed as 'twenty minutes of snob-appeal' and 'tranquil to the point of boredom'. *Documentary News Letter*, no. 56, 1947, p. 89.

16. *Documentary Film News*, no. 64, 1948, p. 43.

17. *Kinematograph Weekly*, 18 January 1951, p. 35.

18. Although support for the documentary movement was never official Labour Party policy, the closeness of the Party and the documentarists would later be symbolised by the marriage of future Party leader Michael Foot to Jill Craigie.

19. *To-Day's Cinema*, 17 October 1944, p. 3.

20. *The Cinema*, 22 January 1947, p. 32.

21. *The Cinema*, 15 January 1947, p. 26.

22. *The Cinema*, 19 December 1945, p. 21.

23. *To-Day's Cinema*, 6 February 1948, pp. 14–15.

24. *To-Day's Cinema*, 30 November 1945, p. 3, and 4 December 1945, p. 3. This was not necessarily a view shared by the cinema trade magazines, which often recommended the showing of serious documentaries. For example, *To-Day's Cinema* (19 March 1948, p. 11) recommended that the CFU's *Voices of Malaya* (1948), directed by Ralph Elton, 'be included in every programme'.

25. *The Cinema*, 22 January 1947, p. 26.

26. The involvement of members of the Federation of Documentary Film Units in the campaign against monopoly in the cinema industry did nothing to persuade the controllers of the three major circuits to screen its products. See Dickinson and Street, *Cinema and State*, p. 169.

27. Previously the Association of Short Film Producers.

28. Cripps had already worked with Paul Rotha in 1945 to see if mechanisms might be set up to achieve this aim and to encourage independent film production. See Dickinson and Street, *Cinema and State*, pp. 170–1.

29. *Documentary News Letter*, no. 60 1947, p. 156.

30. Kevin Jackson, *Humphrey Jennings* (London: Picador, 2004), p. 314. The film's explicit depiction of a mining accident led to its being severely trimmed for theatrical release.

31. *Kinematograph Weekly*, 20 January 1949, p. 28.

32. 'Featurettes Deplored in Quota Report to Council', *To-Day's Cinema*, 12 April 1946, p. 3.

33. '50% British Films Under 4,000 ft', *The Cinema*, 26 March 1947, p. 3. A further twenty-six non-fiction featurettes were released in the first three months of 1948.

34. 'More Criticism of Featurettes by Exhibitors', *To-Day's Cinema*, 30 April 1946, p. 3.

35. 'Banish Quota Featurettes: Circuit Plea', *To-Day's Cinema*, 18 March 1947, p. 13. Only a lucky few of these featurettes achieved a major circuit release. One was the Rank-sponsored *Bothered by a Beard* (1946), a quizzical examination of the issue of facial hair that was written, produced and directed by E. V. H. Emmett. Its appeal was boosted by the presence of popular performers like Jerry Verno and Tod Slaughter acting out illustrative vignettes. Another was A. Barr-Smith's *Death in the Hand* (1948), a suspense thriller based on a Max Beerbohm short story and radio play and made at Viking Studios. The story, involving palmistry and a train crash, was unlikely but ingenious, with an unreliable narrator (Esme Percy). It was enthusiastically received by the trade press: 'compactly produced, efficiently directed, and realistically played, this little film is well above the average featurette which too frequently merely masquerades as entertainment'. *To-Day's Cinema*, 17 February 1948, p. 16.

36. *Film Report*, 2 August 1946. Haines' career probably reached its nadir with *Mister H. C.*

Andersen (1950), an hour-long biopic of Hans Christian Andersen which employed crude comic cartoons. Haines was thoroughly rubbished by critics for his amateurishness in delivering an 'overgrown charade' that was 'pathetically incompetent'. *Kinematograph Weekly*, 29 June 1950, p. 23.

37. Letter to *The Cinema*, 17 April 1946, p. 17.

38. Letter to *To-Day's Cinema*, 1 May 1946, p. 22.

39. Letter to *The Cinema*, 8 May 1946, p. 26. The desire to abolish the flat-rate rental system for supporting features was the one issue that united the warring factions of shorts and featurette producers.

40. *The Cinema*, 13 August 1947, p. 14.

41. *To-Day's Cinema*, 28 March 1947, p. 15.

42. *Prisoners of the Tower* press book, DUK Films, 1946.

43. *Film Report* (14 June 1946) offered the surprising and casually sexist comment: 'The film has little interest, its appeal being confined to women.'

44. For example, De Lane Lea's, *Model Girl* (Archway, 1954), featuring the celebrated mannequin Fiona Campbell Walker, was snapped up by the Odeon circuit to support *The Caine Mutiny*.

45. *To-Day's Cinema*, 22 June 1945, p. 20.

46. There was further Thames navigation in New Realm's *Sing as They Flow* (1947). On the desirability of the British countryside in cinema see Andrew Gray, 'Britain's Greatest Star – Her Countryside', *Film Industry*, November 1946, pp. 12–14.

47. *To-Day's Cinema*, 30 January 1948, p. 16.

48. There were at least two featurettes aimed at Naval recruitment: W. J. Hewitson's *Britain's Sure Shield* (1948), and John Haggarty's *The Naval Artificer* (a.k.a. *Tiffy*, 1951). The latter, in spite of its unpromising title, was recommended to exhibitors as a 'very good quota fill-up'. *Kinematograph Weekly*, 8 February 1951, p. 18.

49. Most of the pictures made by the new British Transport Films Unit under Edgar Anstey were shorts, but *Berth 24* (1950), on the unloading and reloading of a cargo ship in Hull's docks, was forty minutes long and stretched beyond what most critics believed was a viable length for the subject matter.

50. Civil aviation had its moment in the documentary limelight with Harold Baim's *Wings Over the World* (1950), a jauntily scored and somewhat repetitive look at the 'Viscounts', 'Brabazons' and 'Comets' that populated the skies in the still privileged world of British air travel. The industrial documentary could also lend itself to propaganda uses. The most striking example is John F. Abbott's *Britain Awakes* (1952), the sort of account of agrarian land use and tractor production one would more often associate with the command economies of China or the Soviet Union. Sponsored by the tractor manufacturer Ferguson's, the film promoted the positive benefits of good labour-management relations and the principle of tying wages to productivity.

51. *The Upstart Crow* was one of a few featurettes released in different-length versions for the convenience of programme builders.

52. Fitzpatrick returned in 1949 to make a further series in black and white and colour for American television and for distribution in British cinemas by MGM. *Kinematograph Weekly*, 28 July 1949, p. 25.

53. *The Cinema*, 19 May 1948, p. 13.

54. *To-Day's Cinema*, 20 October 1950, p. 9.

55. *To-Day's Cinema*, 2 November 1948, p. 10.

56. *To-Day's Cinema*, 30 March 1948, p. 12.

57. *The Cinema*, 22 March 1950, p. 10.

58. *To-Day's Cinema*, 6 January 1948, p. 12.

59. *Kinematograph Weekly*, 6 December 1951, p. 25.

60. *To-Day's Cinema*, 1 July 1949, p. 11.

61. Kearton's career was chronicled in Burt Hyam's *Journey to Adventure* (1947), distributed by

Warner's, and in the anthology *A Million and One* (1948), which was mainly concerned with the social life of penguins.

62. New Realm's *Animal Kingdom* (1950) took cinemagoers to the jungle – but only via a chimps' tea party at London Zoo and a couple of performing seals on the variety stage.

63. *Kinematograph Weekly*, 1 January 1948, p. 17.

64. A chatty commentary by popular broadcaster McDonald Hobely and 'unobtrusively pleasant' background music made it a 'superior quota featurette'. *To-Day's Cinema*, 4 June 1951, p. 12.

65. *It's a Great Game* press book, Ambassador Film Productions Ltd, 1948.

66. It was marketed as 'The Film with a Punch in it'. *Pathway to Fame* press book, Piccadilly Productions, 1946.

67. *To-Day's Cinema*, 26 April 1949, p. 5.

68. *Kinematograph Weekly*, 25 March 1948, p. 20.

69. *To-Day's Cinema*, 5 October 1950, p. 9.

70. Quoted in the digest of reviews in *The Cinema Studio*, 18 January 1950, p. 18. Its success was further enhanced by a BBC television documentary describing how it was compiled. The programme was among the first examples of what would later become its own genre, especially with the arrival of DVD. In June 1949, Pathé had reopened its studio in Wardour Street for the production of its own second features and *Pathé Pictorial* shorts, as well as for rental. 'Second Features Scheduled for Wardour Street Stage', *The Cinema Studio*, 15 June 1949, p. 3.

71. *Showground of the North* press book, Mancunian Film Corporation, 1948.

72. *To-Day's Cinema*, 7 October 1949, p. 8.

73. 'Well-meaning' but 'facile' explanations and solutions, as well as 'stilted acting' robbed it of credibility according to *To-Day's Cinema*, 2 January 1948, p. 10.

74. *Operation Diamond* press book, Renown Pictures, 1948. The story was retold a decade later on a grander scale as *Operation Amsterdam* (1959).

75. *Kinematograph Weekly*, 23 December 1948, p. 16.

76. The film had been co-produced by Sydney Box and directed by Compton Bennett in 1944 to mark the centenary of Rochdale Co-operation, but appears to have taken two years to secure theatrical distribution. Alan G. Burton, *The British Consumer Co-operative Movement and Film, 1890s–1960s* (Manchester: Manchester University Press, 2005), pp. 172–5.

77. *Film Report*, 21 June 1946. *The Cinema* (26 June 1946, p. 15), however, was not unduly impressed by the picture's 'stagey atmosphere and weak dialogue', not to mention 'indifferent direction'.

78. *Kinematograph Weekly*, 21 July 1949, p. 23.

79. *To-Day's Cinema*, 24 July 1951, p. 12.

80. Cf. *The Cinema*, 22 September 1948, p. 14.

81. *Kinematograph Weekly*, 26 January 1950, p. 23.

82. 'No film to our knowledge has so successfully captured the spirit of "bohemia".' *Kinematograph Weekly*, 20 July 1950, p. 34.

83. *Kinematograph Weekly*, 11 June 1953, p. 22.

84. *Kinematograph Weekly*, 5 April 1956, p. 20. United Artist's Eastman Color biopic of Shaka Zulu, *Flame of Africa* (1954), directed by T. V. Bulpin was less warmly received. Its narrative edge was 'blunted by protracted wild-life sequences and interminable close-ups of native women'. *Kinematograph Weekly*, 22 July 1954, p. 27.

85. *Among the Head-Hunters* press book, Rank, 1955.

86. *Kinematograph*, 14 January 1954, p. 20.

87. Angel, however, was no proselytising missionary for the new viewing system, as he told the press: 'If you have got a good picture – good stars, good story and the rest – you have got something: 3-D is merely an additional thing.' *To-Day's Cinema*, 30 March 1953, p. 6.

88. *Documentary News Letter*, no. 58, 1947, p. 121.

89. E.g., *To-Day's Cinema*, 7 February, p. 21.

90. P. G. Baker, 'Box-Office Informationals', *Kinematograph Weekly*, 30 September 1948, p. 7.

91. *The Cinema*, 30 April 1947, p. 27.

92. *To-Day's Cinema*, 20 January 1950, p. 7. For Peter Noble's account of the making of the film see his 'Denham's Little Brothers', *Film Fare*, vol. 2 no. 5, September 1947.

93. *The Cinema*, 12 February 1947, p. 35.

94. It was aimed at a juvenile audience, but in the prevailing conditions of shortage, the trade press deemed this 'terpsichorean tit-bit' suitable as a supporting feature. *Kinematograph Weekly*, 29 January 1948, p. 22.

95. *The Cinema*, 7 January 1948, p. 21. See also the production report in *The Cinema*, 24 September 1947, p. 27.

96. *To-Day's Cinema* (10 May 1949, p. 6) was scathing, calling *Slick Tartan* a 'tedious parade of laboured lunacies'. It had the further misfortune of going on release while the nation was still mourning the death of Don Stannard, the 'real' Barton.

97. Not to be confused with the appalling 1958 feature of the same title starring Sonja Henie

98. Bruton had previously made the featurette *Men of the Mines* (1945).

99. The headlines referred to were primarily those announcing the murder of Alec d'Antiquist, a 'have-a-go hero' who had tried to prevent the getaway of thieves robbing a pawnbroker in London's Charlotte Street in 1947.

100. *A Gunman Has Escaped* press book, Monarch Film Corporation, 1948.

101. Gerald Landau, 'Plan for Progress', *Film Technician*, February 1947, pp. 10–11

102. 'Exhibitor Aid Given to Boom in "Quickies"', *To-Day's Cinema*, 22 August 1947, pp. 3, 8.

103. *To-Day's Cinema*, 22 August 1947, p. 7. It brought a predictably indignant response from Harold Baim, who questioned the wisdom of condemning films before they have even been produced, and deplored the closure of major studio space to 'all but the most wealthy'. Letter to *The Cinema*, 27 August 1947, p. 37.

104. *The Cinema*, 17 December 1947, pp. 18–19.

105. Paul Nugat, 'Film Shortage Means a Boom in Second Features', *Film Industry*, November 1947, pp. 8–9.

106. *Kinematograph Weekly* (3 March 1949, p. 22) thought it was a 'jolly boost for Kent's most colourful seaside resort'. Lewis went on to produce one of the hit films of 1950, *Morning Departure*.

107. Dickinson and Street, in their *Cinema and State* (p. 192), identify a huge increase in second-feature production during the Hollywood boycott. This is more apparent than real, however, as the Board of Trade figures conceal as much as they reveal. On the one hand, over seventy films with running times between thirty-three and seventy-two minutes were offered for rental during the seven months of the boycott. On the other hand, only seventeen were conventional second features, and a number of these were children's films. Forty-four featurettes were offered, supplemented by eleven re-issues of old supporting features. *Film Report*, September 1947 to March 1948.

108. *The Cinema*, 14 July 1948, p. 6.

109. *Vengeance is Mine* was a melodramatic thriller scripted and directed by Alan Cullimore, a young film-maker who had served his time as a camera operator and was now determined to make a quality 'B' feature as an industry calling card. *The Cinema Studio*, 17 November 1948, p. 7. Enlivened by Dyall's performance, it was judged a 'workmanlike pint-size blood and thunder' by *Kinematograph Weekly*, 21 July 1949, p. 17.

110. *To-Day's Cinema*, 12 January 1950, p. 6.

111. *The Cinema*, 16 June 1948, p. 10. Two thousand six hundred independent exhibitors

immediately applied for exemption or relief, representing about three-quarters of all cinemas outside the two major circuits. Over 1,700 were eventually accepted. However, the Board of Trade indicated its intention to scrutinise defaults 'rather more seriously' than had been the case in the past, *The Cinema*, 29 September 1948, p. 22. In fact, there had effectively been a total amnesty for quota defaulters, with not a single prosecution among almost 3,000 cases for the 1946–8 period.

112. *The Cinema*, 7 July 1948, p. 10.

113. *The Cinema*, 22 February 1950, pp. 3, 18.

114. *To-Day's Cinema*, 9 July 1948, p. 10.

115. 'It was essential', Wilson said, 'for the Government to step in and do what the City could or would not do.' *To-Day's Cinema*, 23 July 1948, p. 8.

116. Sue Harper and Vincent Porter, *British Cinema of the 1950s: The Decline of Deference* (Oxford: Oxford University Press, 2003), pp. 12–13. However, a number of supporting features like Present Day Production's *Chelsea Story* (1950) were among the beneficiaries of loans from the NFFC's fund.

117. *The Cinema* (10 November 1948, p. 3) was sufficiently concerned to speak out against what it saw as Government support for the monopolistic practices of the Rank organisation.

118. Letter from Horace Shepherd to *The Cinema Studio*, 8 December 1948, p. 14. Shepherd extended his critique in a polemical article in *Kinematograph Weekly*, again attacking the mistake made by the 1938 Films Act in introducing a minimum cost criterion in awarding quota status to films. 'Forget the Worship of the "Big" Call to the Board of Trade', *Kinematograph Weekly*, 9 December 1948, p. 6.

119. *The Cinema*, 15 September 1948, pp. 3, 30.

120. *Kinematograph Weekly*, 7 April 1949, p. 10.

121. Board of Trade, *Report of the Working Party on Film Production Costs*, HMSO, 1949, p. 32.

122. 'Independent Exhibitors Plan to Make Own Films', *To-Day's Cinema*, 20 July 1948, p. 3. The National Independent Cinema Owners Film Organisation struggled to raise the £200,000 in subscriptions needed to begin production at the Oldway Film Studios at Paignton, which had been leased from Paignton Urban Council in May 1948. Finally, in October production began with a pilot programme for an American psychology series *Shadows of the Mind* which eventually yielded a contract for all fifty-two episodes. By stalling its creditors, Oldway limped along until it was finally forced into liquidation in January 1951, still desperately claiming that the Board of Trade would bail it out, *To-Day's Cinema*, 16 January 1951, pp. 3, 12. The whole sad tale was chronicled by *The Cinema Studio* (see: 19 May 1948, p. 5; 21 July 1948, p. 3, 20; 1 September 1948, p. 5; 15 September 1948, p. 5; 24 November 1948, p. 3; 2 March 1949, p. 3; 20 April 1949, pp. 3, 14; 29 June 1949, p. 3).

123. Board of Trade, *Report of the Working Party on Film Production Costs*, HMSO, 1949.

124. *The Cinema*, 5 January 1949, p. 3.

125. *The Cinema*, 2 February 1949, p. 3. See also *Kinematograph Weekly*, 17 February 1949, pp. 3–7 which put the number of idle studios at eighteen out of twenty-eight.

126. Derrick de Marney, 'The Over-All Programme Britain's Present Need', *The Cinema Studio*, 19 January 1949, p. 5.

127. *To-Day's Cinema*, 11 March 1949, p. 7.

128. *To-Day's Cinema*, 2 February 1950, p. 4.

129. *To-Day's Cinema*, 21 July 1950, p. 7.

130. Trade advertisement for *It's a Grand Life*, *To-Day's Cinema*, 29 September 1953, pp. 4–5. Many critics and, no doubt, some Southern exhibitors, would have preferred to see Mancunian's films trimmed by half an hour to make them useful as second features, as *Kinematograph Weekly* commented on the ninety-four-minute Jewel and Warriss farce

Let's Have a Murder (1950), 'True, it could be vastly improved by cutting ... [but] director John Blakeley is stubborn in his assertion that North Country audiences like their light fare in large lumps, and he should know!', *To-Day's Cinema*, 24 August 1950, p. 22.

131. Paul Nugat, 'Film Shortage ...', pp. 8–9. On the other hand, first features with transatlantic ambitions might cost £200,000 to £600,000, and first features with lower horizons would be budgeted at £50,000 to £200,000.

132. *The Cinema*, 25 January 1950, p. 10.

133. 'A Recipe for £75,000 Box-Office Successes', *Kinematograph Weekly*, 25 August 1949, p. 21.

134. *Castle Sinister* was an unconvincing tale of hooded Nazi agents operating in an old Scottish castle (exteriors were shot at Kingsgate Castle, Thanet). 'Nothing at all exciting happens in the way of action', bemoaned *To-Day's Cinema* (24 February 1948, p. 8), before slamming the 'weak direction, colourless portrayal, undistinguished production qualities'. *The Cinema*, 18 June 1947, p. 38.

135. The pretentious young Harvey was less than grateful for these opportunities in what he dismissed as this 'pseudo world of art and culture'. After making *House of Darkness*, he wrote to his brother: 'In approximately two weeks' time I start work on another film. The story of the first film was bad enough, but the next story is even worse and although I openly refused to do it I am afraid I am bound by a sheet of paper known as a contract which I bitterly regret.' Quoted in Des Hickey and Gus Smith, *The Prince: The Public and Private Life of Laurence Harvey* (London: W. H. Allen, 1976), pp. 43–4.

136. *Kinematograph Weekly*, 10 June 1948, p. 24.

137. 'The Case for Factual Backgrounds by the men who use them', *The Cinema Studio*, 16 March 1949, pp. 9–11.

138. Ibid.

139. Ibid.

140. *The Cinema Studio*, 9 November 1949, p. 4.

141. *Kinematograph Weekly*, 15 December 1949, p. 29.

142. 'Unique Team with the Right Ideas', *The Cinema Studio*, 28 September 1949, pp. 16–17.

143. 'Northern Challenge to Supporting Quota', *To-Day's Cinema*, 14 March 1950, p. 3.

144. *The Cinema*, 7 March 1951, pp. 3, 10.

145. *To-Day's Cinema*, 3 August 1951, p. 8.

146. *To-Day's Cinema*, 18 April 1952, p. 3; 10 July 1952, p. 3. Less obviously, the ASFP's initiative was a gambit in its struggle with the British Film Producers' Association to represent the makers of second feature films. It also proposed to drop 'Specialised' from its title. The BFPA responded by proposing to extend its scope beyond first-feature production by setting up a special section for the 'B' picture producers. *To-Day's Cinema*, 24 April 1952, p. 3.

147. The Eady fund would, in the first instance, be the saviour of the makers of shorts who were awarded 2.5 times the regular payment rate when their impossible financial position was recognised. Harold Baim wrote to the NFFC's Sir Henry French to assure him that the Eady payments he had received for his compilation of amateur shorts *Filming for Fun* (1950) and for *Wings Over the World* had kept him in business: 'without these payments, each and every short we make and distribute through various renting organisations would lose money' (quoted in *To-Day's Cinema*, 13 January 1953, pp. 3, 8). The maximum length of film for qualification for 2.5 times the distributor's gross was reduced from 3,500 to 3,000 feet after 1 August 1953.

148. Circuit booker, quoted in *To-Day's Cinema*, 2 March 1951, p. 4.

149. *To-Day's Cinema*, 14 April 1950, p. 10.

150. *Kinematograph Weekly*, 25 May 1950, p. 20.

151. *Kinematograph Weekly*, 13 July 1950, p. 22.

152. The unfortunate Link Neale had also been the producer of James Corbett's *Meet the Duke* (1949), a country house comedy depicting the misadventures of an American pugilist (Farnham Baxter) who inherits an English dukedom. It contained a sub-text about better understanding between Britain and the USA that was largely obscured by a clutter of unserviceable situations and ideas. As one exasperated trade reviewer complained: 'In all our wide experience, we've seldom seen such a rag-bag or witnessed a more inept attempt to meet quota requirements.' *Kinematograph Weekly*, 21 April 1949, p. 18.

153. *To-Day's Cinema*, 26 May 1952.

154. Adapted from the table printed in *Kinematograph Weekly*, 18 June 1953, p. 6.

155. *Kinematograph Weekly*, 23 September 1954, p. 23.

156. Sir Alexander King and Theo Fligelstone, *To-Day's Cinema*, 10 July 1952, pp. 3, 6.

157. *To-Day's Cinema*, 17 July 1952, p. 3.

158. *To-Day's Cinema*, 20 November 1952, p. 3.

159. *The Cinema*, 3 December 1952, p. 9.

160. 'Discourage Some Quota Supports', *Kinematograph Weekly*, 11 December 1952, p. 3.

161. *To-Day's Cinema*, 1 December 1952, pp. 3, 7, emphasis in original.

162. *To-Day's Cinema*, 4 December 1952, p. 3.

163. *The Cinema*, 10 December 1952, pp. 5, 7.

164. *The Cinema*, 18 March 1953, p. 3.

165. Mike Murphy, 'An Interview with Francis Searle', *Dark Terrors* no. 9, 1994, p. 38.

166. *Kinematograph Weekly*, 4 October 1951, p. 24. While relatively sophisticated Bs, like those made by Hammer, were partly Americanised in their approach, some of the smaller production companies still clung to the type of slight and sentimental British subjects that had been such a feature of quota production before the war. Hugh Wedderburn was the producer, director, author, composer and star of the featurette *The*

Lark Still Sings (1954), which was distributed by Equity British, purveyors of some of the most light-weight quota quickies in the 1930s. This 'complicated and overlong' (at only forty-five minutes) story of a sensitive young man who takes a job at a seaside hotel in order to learn the piano was blighted by 'casual' direction and 'overweighed with dialogue' and the sort of 'melodramatic portrayals' that had been the bane of the quickie. *To-Day's Cinema*, 21 May 1954, p. 12.

167. *Daily Sketch*, 1 April 1954. Quoted in Marcus Hearn and Richard Reynolds, Viewing notes for *Mask of Dust*, Home Entertainment DVD, 2005.

168. *To-Day's Cinema*, 15 June 1956, p. 7.

169. *To-Day's Cinema*, 5 February 1953, p. 5.

170. *To-Day's Cinema*, 12 February 1953, p. 7.

171. 'Act Helps Poor Films', *Kinematograph Weekly*, 12 March 1953, p. 3.

172. *The Cinema*, 16 September 1953, p. 3.

173. *Kinematograph Weekly*, 4 March 1954, p. 3.

174. Allowing for quota relief, the average quota requirement was 23.7 per cent, while 28 per cent was actually achieved overall, up from 26 per cent in the previous year. *Kinematograph Weekly*, 3 March 1955, p. 3.

175. *To-Day's Cinema*, 11 June 1954, p. 3.

176. *The Cinema*, 14 March 1956, p. 3.

177. *Kinematograph Weekly* (9 September 1954, p. 19) rated it 'saleable pulp fiction',

178. *Kinematograph Weekly*, 20 October 1955, p. 18.

179. However, the demands of established clients quickly interfered with the production's tight shooting schedule of *The Gold Express* (1955) when director, Guy Fergusson had to be switched to making a film for the Admiralty on the latest anti-submarine weapons. He was replaced by Colin Bell. The finished film took eighteen months to be released and was panned by the critics.

180. Michael McCarthy's *John of the Fair* (1953), for example, had been recommended by *To-Day's*

Cinema (12 December 1952, p. 16) as not simply a 'first-class bet for juvenile audiences', but a 'useful supporting picture for normal showing'. It was not until October 1954, however, that the Gaumont circuit began an experiment of releasing some CFF films as supporting features on regular programmes. The first of these was Lewis Gilbert's *Johnny on the Run* (1954), which had taken the prize in the children's section of the Venice Film Festival. It was released with *The Purple Plain* (1954), and would be followed by *The Clue of the Missing Ape* (1953).

181. *Kinematograph Weekly*, 3 January 1957, p. 7.

182. *Daily Film Renter*, 20 March 1957, p. 1.

183. Insignia's George Minter, for instance, complained about the dearth of decent scripts for 'modest films' in 1954. *To-Day's Cinema*, 23 August 1954, p. 7. Guido Coen was still complaining about the screenplay shortage early in 1957. *To-Day's Cinema*, 21 January 1957, p. 6.

184. *To-Day's Cinema*, 24 January 1955, p. 3.

185. *To-Day's Cinema*, 11 November 1955, p. 3

186. *To-Day's Cinema*, 14 February 1955, p. 7.

187. Ibid.

188. *To-Day's Cinema*, 18 April 1955, p. 6.

189. *The Cinema*, 14 January 1957, p. 8.

190. *To-Day's Cinema*, 8 March 1955, p. 5

191. *The Observer*, 25 August 1957.

192. Their first was *Park Plaza 605* (1953), an adaptation of one of the Norman Conquest detective thrillers written by Berkley Gray. Almost inevitably, the suave Tom Conway played the immaculate sleuth, while Joy Shelton and Eva Bartok were respectively the safe and dangerous women in this extravagantly plotted adventure with a car-chase finale.

193. This sort of quasi-drama of a pretty girl in an exotic locale, a specialism of De Lane Lea and E. J. Fancey, paved the way for the eventual emergence of the sexploitation travelogues like *Naked as Nature Intended* (1961).

194. 'Bands May Sound Box-Office Jingle', *Kinematograph Weekly*, 13 January 1955, p. 6. In fact, the proprietors of the Regent, Brownhills, tried to excuse their failure to meet the supporting-feature quota by pleading that there were not enough British second features in CinemaScope, the format their cinema had recently been equipped to screen. *To-Day's Cinema*, 15 June 1956, p. 3.

195. *To-Day's Cinema*, 6 October 1955, p. 3

196. Two of these were packaged up as the fifty-minute *South Sea Pirates* (1957), directed by Lee Sholem, and released shortly after Newton's death.

197. *The Cinema*, 14 February 1956, p. 3. If J. M. Phillips of Butcher's is to be believed, adjusting the rates towards second features was a course of action that British distributors were more prepared to take than their American counterparts. Letter from J. M. Phillips to *To-Day's Cinema*, 20 December 1956, p. 8.

198. *Kinematograph Weekly*, 19 January 1956, p. 3.

199. *To-Day's Cinema*, 10 February 1956, p. 3,

200. *The Cinema*, 1 September 1956, p. 7.

201. *The Cinema*, 14 February 1956, p. 3.

202. *The Cinema*, 21 February 1956, p. 8.

203. *To-Day's Cinema*, 4 July, 1957, p. 3.

204. *Kinematograph Weekly*, 13 December 1956, p. 9.

205. *To-Day's Cinema*, 6 October 1955, p. 3. However, one producer of 'B' films was warned by his distributor: 'For your own sake don't get too ambitious and start making good B pictures. The poorer the picture, the better they will do.' The explanation was that a good specimen would be selected by circuit bookers to try to shore up a doubtful first feature. Thus a producer on a percentage deal was likely to see a poor return. On the other hand, an indifferent 'B' film would be slipped into a programme topped by a solid attraction that would earn good money for the 'B' producer on a percentage. *Kinematograph Weekly*, 8 August 1957, p. 18.

206. *The Cinema*, 15 February 1956, p. 3.

207. *The Cinema*, 27 February 1956, p. 3.

208. *The Cinema*, 6 June 1956, p. 3.

209. *Kinematograph Weekly* (21 November 1957, p. 19) was afraid that 'arty-crafty treatment and hifalutin' dialogue' robbed it of 'suspense and mass appeal'.

210. *The Cinema*, 15 November 1956, p. 3.

211. *The Cinema*, 14 January 1957, p. 8.

212. *The Cinema*, 26 April 1957, p. 7.

213. Increasingly, co-feature marketing foregrounded exploitable elements within the programme. Nat Miller, who founded Vicar Productions in June 1957 to make Anglo-American films with Randall Brasselle Productions of New York, explained the thinking behind the partnership's debut film *Death Over My Shoulder* (1957), a private-eye picture directed by Arthur Crabtree and made at Walton: 'We don't intend kidding ourselves. We know that this picture isn't going to be the greatest. But if it's half as good as we expect, we shall be very happy. Our plan is to find a good co-feature, possibly a Continental, and distribute the two as a package programme.' He argued that a picture must have a 'plus' to be successful – in this case, it was the title. 'A title can mean the difference between success and failure at the box-office. Secondly, Brasselle has written a theme tune which is destined for the top of the hit parade. We've also collected together a fine cast. We've even got people like Sonia Dresdel doing two days' work. We are pushing everything, and I mean everything, to get all the production value out of our budget and 4-week shooting schedule. I think it's going to be a picture which will look a lot more expensive than it really is.' *Kinematograph Weekly*, 15 August 1957, p. 30.

214. *To-Day's Cinema*, 1 April 1957, p. 5.

215. Herman Cohen commentary, *Horrors of the Black Museum*, DVD.

216. *The Cinema*, 28 June 1957, p. 1.

217. *To-Day's Cinema*, 23 September 1957, p. 4.

218. *Kine Weekly*, 17 March 1960, p. 29. In 1958–9 British material already constituted just under one third of cinema supporting programmes. *Kine Weekly*, 24 March 1960, p. 3.

219. *Kine Weekly*, 30 March 1961, p. 6.

220. *Kine Weekly* (24 March 1960, p. 27) judged this one 'suitable for both sexes', commenting that it 'so delicately exploits the female form that only minds bluer than the deep Mediterranean, where most of the action takes place, could possibly see anything indecent about it'.

221. *Travelling Light*, the shortest of this quartet, was actually the junior part of an eagerly booked Gala double bill with the French sex melodrama *The Sins of Youth*. *Some Like it Cool* played for months on London's Oxford Street and broke house records in Manchester and Belfast, while *Naked as Nature Intended* played a full year on Windmill Street before being replaced by *My Bare Lady* (1962). The nudist film cycle 1958–63 is discussed in more detail in Simon Sheridan, *Keeping the British End Up* (London: Reynolds and Hearn, 2001), pp. 9–11, 31–42; and David McGillivray, *Doing Rude Things: The History of the British Sex Film 1957–1981* (London: Sun Tavern Fields, 1992), pp. 23–51.

222. *Kine Weekly*, 31 August 1961, p. 6.

223. *Kine Weekly*, 14 April 1960, p. 9.

224. John Mundy, *The British Film Musical* (Manchester: Manchester University Press, 2007), pp. 196–7 offers a useful analysis of *Band of Thieves*.

225. John and Roy Boulting, 'Quality First', *Kine Weekly*, 15 December 1960, p. 7. See also their letter to *Kine Weekly*, 16 February 1961, p. 6; and Nat Cohen's spirited reposte on 23 February 1961, p. 9. The BBC received approximately 200 letters criticising the quality of supporting programmes after the *Picture Parade* item in February 1961.

226. *Kine Weekly*, 26 January 1961, p. 37.

227. Cf. the letter from cinema manager G. Brian Snape, *Kine Weekly*, 2 March 1961, pp. 5, 36; and the report of the Manchester CEA meeting, *Kine Weekly*, 9 March 1961, p. 33. One Burnley exhibitor reported a 15 per cent increase in trade with single-feature programmes. Letter from R. Tattersall, *Kine Weekly*, 30 March 1961, p. 7. The survey of cinema audiences commissioned by the Screen Advertising Association revealed that two-thirds of the average audience were sixteen- to thirty-four-year-olds who constituted just one third of the population. *Kine Weekly*, 23 March 1961, p. 3.

228. E.g., 'Bigger Share is Sought for Second features', *Kine Weekly*, 6 April 1961, p. 3.

229. 'Producers Urge Increased Levy Help for Second Features', *Kine Weekly*, 9 November 1961, p. 7. The general extension of booking runs to Sunday also increased the number of prints of a supporting feature that had to be struck. Butcher's, for example, increased its average number of prints from forty to fifty-four, adding £1,000 to the cost of distributing one of its films. *The Daily Cinema*, 9 April 1962, pp. 3, 6.

230. Letter from R. H. Godfrey, Cheshire County Cinemas, *Kine Weekly*, 29 November 1962, p. 7.

231. *Kine Weekly*, 7 December 1961, p. 20.

232. *Kine Weekly*, 3 January 1963, p. 3. When some more unusual Bs – like Caspar Wrede's Yiddish comedy *The Barber of Stamford Hill* and Bill McLeod's Temperance Seven musical, *Take Me Over* – began to appear in 1963, however, distributors had difficulty in marketing them.

233. Source: Board of Trade.

234. *Kine Weekly*, 13 February 1964, p. 6.

235. The film was made over six days at Carlton Hill (usually used for TV commercials) and five days on location in Soho. *Kine Weekly*, 6 February 1964. Its commercial prospects were perhaps not helped by the unexpected award of an 'X' certificate.

236. 'Second Features Threatened with Film Fade-out', *The Times*, 23 January 1967, p. 9.

3 The 'B' Factories

1. C. B. H. 'Willy' Williamson, 'Small Men ... With the Big Ideas!', *The Cinema Studio*, 7 September 1949, p. 7.

2. E.g., Brian McFarlane, 'Value for Money: Baker and Berman and Tempean Films', in Ian McKillop and Neil Sinyard (eds), *British Cinema in the 1950s* (Manchester: Manchester University Press, 2003). pp. 176–89; 'Pulp Fictions: The British B Film and the Field of Cultural Production', *Film Criticism* vol. 21 no. 1, 1996, pp. 48–70; Steve Chibnall, *Quota Quickies*.

3. These have now been discovered for Adelphi Films.

4. There are occasional minor exceptions, as when a *Picturegoer* columnist draws attention to 'John Baxter, a producer with an impressive record'. Donald Hunt, 'This Outfit Beats the Bankroll', *Picturegoer*, 29 March 1952, p. 16.

5. *Send for Paul Temple* press book, Butcher's Film Services, 1946.

6. *The Cinema*, 27 August 1947, p. 15.

7. *Kinematograph Weekly*, 29 September 1949, p. 12.

8. *To-Day's Cinema* (21 February 1950, p. 7) described it as 'Provocative entertainment for more thoughtful type of patron', but *Kinematograph Weekly* (23 February 1950, p. 18) was entirely unmoved and unimpressed.

9. *Kinematograph Weekly*, 27 July 1950, p. 34. See also *To-Day's Cinema,* 20 July 1950, p. 7.

10. *Kinematograph Weekly*, 3 January 1952, p. 16.

11. *Kinematograph Weekly*, 3 May 1956, p. 102. *Assignment Redhead* starred Richard Denning and Carole Matthews in an enthusiastically reviewed tale of ex-Nazi racketeers: 'Direction secures lively and constant change of scene to help speed the improbable story on its way to a

conventional but exciting finale.' *To-Day's Cinema*, 11 October 1956, p. 8.

12. *To-Day's Cinema*, 14 February 1957, p. 6.

13. *The Cinema*, 23 September 1957, p. 4.

14. *Kinematograph Weekly*, 17 December 1959, pp. 6–7.

15. *Serena* supported *The Password is Courage* (1963), and *Gaolbreak* was programmed with *Tarus Bulba* and *Tiara Tahiti* (both 1962).

16. *The Daily Cinema*, 18 March 1960, p. 9.

17. Philip Martin Williams and David L. Williams, *Hooray for Jollywood: The Life of John E. Blakeley & The Mancunian Film Corporation* (Ashton-under-Lyme: History On Your Doorstep, 2001), p. 130. Blakeley produced two further films for Comfort, *Blind Corner* (1963) and the occult horror 'A' feature, *Devils of Darkness* (1964).

18. Patricia Warren, *British Film Studios* (London: B. T. Batsford, 2001), p. 93

19. Croydon quoted in Andrew Gray, 'Highbury will be the Technicians' Shangri-La', *Film Industry*, June 1947, pp. 6–7.

20. *To-Day's Cinema* 21 September 1948, p. 14.

21. *Kinematograph Weekly*, 23 September 1948, p. 20. The BFI seems to have been rather more impressed, selecting *To the Public Danger* for preservation in the national collection. 'It must be the first occasion upon which a professed curtain-raiser has been selected for this honour,' commented *Kinematograph Weekly*, 3 February 1949, p. 5.

22. Christopher Lee, *Tall, Dark and Gruesome: An Autobiography* (London: Granada, 1978), p. 134.

23. *Kinematograph Weekly*, 17 June 1948, p. 20; *To-Day's Cinema*, 11 June 1948, p. 10.

24. *To-Day's Cinema*, 2 November 1948, p. 10.

25. *Kinematograph Weekly*, 4 November 1948, p. 25.

26. Andy Worker, BECTU Oral History Project Interview no. 51, 19 August 1988.

27. *The Cinema Studio*, 9 June 1948, p. 3.

28. See Christine Geraghty's treatment of this theme in her *British Cinema of the Fifties* (London: Routledge, 2000).

29. *To-Day's Cinema*, 14 January 1949, p. 10. *Kinematograph Weekly* (20 January 1949, p. 22), however, could resist neither the film's nostalgic appeal nor its 'flawless atmosphere', hailing 'a modest but really English film at last!'.

30. *To-Day's Cinema*, 6 April 1949, p. 6.

31. Peter Hutchings, *Terence Fisher* (Manchester: Manchester University Press, 2002), p. 43.

32. Geoffrey MacNab, *J. Arthur Rank and The British Film* (London and New York: Routledge), p. 148.

33. Alan Wood, *Mr Rank: A Study of J. Arthur Rank and British Films* (London: Hodder and Stoughton, 1993), p.172. When the Highbury unit ceased production, Croydon worked as producer or production manager on a further dozen films, mixing second features (*The Delavine Affair*, 1954, directed by Highbury alumnus Douglas Pierce), co-features (Robert Day's *Grip of the Strangler*, 1958) and main attractions, such as Tony Richardson's *The Entertainer*, 1959, as associate producer.

34. Independent Frame, a system which filmed the actors in front of pre-photographed backgrounds, was intended to cut production costs and might therefore have had a special place in 'B' movie history, but it was abandoned (perhaps precipitately) after no more than a dozen features, none of which enjoyed major success.

35. Quoted in the digest of reviews in *The Cinema Studio*, 8 June 1949, p. 14.

36. Quoted in the digest of reviews in *The Cinema Studio*, 13 July 1949, p. 16.

37. *To-Day's Cinema*, 19 July 1949, p. 6.

38. *Kinematograph Weekly* (21 July 1949, p. 18) called it an 'incredible mess' and 'much too barmy for the box-office'.

39. *To-Day's Cinema*, 30 May 1947, p. 20.

40. 'Exhibitors Say "No" to Criminal Star in Film', *To-Day's Cinema*, 13 June 1947, p. 3.

41. *To-Day's Cinema*, 30 July 1948, p. 10.

42. Wayne Kinsey, *Hammer Films: The Bray Studio Years* (London: Reynolds and Hearn, 2002), p. 12.

43. *To-Day's Cinema*, 5 March 1948, p. 9. Budget information from Paul Nugat, 'Film Shortage Means a Boom in Second Features', *Film Industry*, November 1947, pp. 8–9.

44. *To-Day's Cinema*, 16 June 1948, p. 20.

45. Jimmy Sangster, *Inside Hammer* (London: Reynolds and Hearn, 2001), p. 11.

46. *To-Day's Cinema*, 11 March 1949, p. 8.

47. *Kinematograph Weekly* (13 January 1949, p. 17) noted approvingly that the budget might have been small, 'but every cent is on the screen'.

48. *Kinematograph Weekly* (5 May 1949, p. 23) recommended it as a 'Capital British programmer'.

49. Mike Murphy, 'Life Before the Undead:2', *Dark Terrors*, 9 November 1994, pp. 31–3.

50. Ibid.

51. 'The Man in Black-and-White', Francis Searle interviewed by Jonathan Rigby, *Hammer Horror*, 3 May 1995, pp. 34–8.

52. *Kinematograph Weekly*, 25 August 1949, p. 20. *Celia* supported Elizabeth Taylor and Robert Taylor in *Conspirator* on the ABC circuit.

53. *To-Day's Cinema*, 7 October 1949, p. 9.

54. *To-Day's Cinema*, 25 November 1949, p. 8. It supported *Morning Departure* (1950) on the Gaumont British circuit.

55. 'Willy', 'They Have an Assurance Policy Here', *The Cinema Studio*, 14 September 1949, pp. 11–13. It was coupled with *Your Witness* (1950) on the ABC circuit.

56. 'Residents Protest at Cookham Studio', *The Cinema Studio*, 6 April 1949, p. 18; 'The Battle of Cookham Dean!', *The Cinema Studio*, 20 April 1949, p. 6; 'Cookham Dean: Council Views', *The Cinema Studio*, 8 June 1949, pp. 3, 12.

57. 'The Story Behind Exclusive's House-Studio Policy Success', *Kinematograph Weekly*, 3 November 1949, p. 28; 'Willy', 'They Practice What the Report Preaches', *The Cinema Studio*, 7 December 1949, pp. 11–13.

58. Sangster, *Inside Hammer*, p. 13. See also Harry Oakes interviewed by Mike Murphy, *Dark Terrors*, 8 April 1994, pp. 13–17.

59. Josh Billings, *Kinematograph Weekly*, 15 December 1949, p. 12.

60. *The Cinema Studio* 22 February 1950, p. 13. John Bretton, 'The Unit Craved Excitement', *Picturegoer*, 15 April 1950.

61. *Kinematograph Weekly*, 3 August 1950, p. 22.

62. 'Exclusive Production to be Increased by 50 Per Cent', *The Cinema Studio*, 15 March 1950, pp. 3, 6.

63. *The Cinema Studio*, 26 April 1950, p. 19.

64. E.g., *Kinematograph Weekly*, 29 March 1951, p. 13.

65. *The Cinema*, 23 May 1951, p. 18.

66. A trade survey at the end of 1948 had found that 96 per cent of American exhibitors did not book British films, and a further 3 per cent would book them only if the terms were exceptionally favourable. *Kinematograph Weekly*, 30 December 1948, p. 26.

67. *Kinematograph Weekly*, 24 January 1952, p. 24. Hammer's attempt to drop Gilling's script credit in favour of that of the original creator of the Whispering Smith character almost led to a terminal falling out between Gilling and the company.

68. *Kinematograph Weekly*, 24 April 1952, p. 23.

69. *To-Day's Cinema*, 30 August 1951, pp. 3, 8.

70. *Kinematograph Weekly*, 16 August 1951, p. 26.

71. 'The Case of the Stolen Face', *Picturegoer*, 21 June 1952, p. 19.

72. However, the source material was indigenous: another BBC radio serial.

73. *To-Day's Cinema*, 7 April 1952, p. 9. In America, the film played as a support to *Plymouth Adventure* on the Loew's circuit.

74. *The Flanagan Boy* press book, Exclusive, 1953.

75. *Kinematograph Weekly*, 25 June 1953, p. 21.

76. *To-Day's Cinema*, 25 June 1953, p. 6.

77. *To-Day's Cinema*, 1 February 1954, p. 3.

78. Edith Nepean, 'Round the British Studios', *Picture Show*, 6 March 1954, p. 11.

79. *Picture Show*, 26 June 1954, p. 10.

80. *To-Day's Cinema*, 7 July 1954, p. 6.

81. *Kinematograph Weekly*, 9 September 1954, p. 18.

82. *Kinematograph Weekly*, 25 November 1954, p. 16.

83. Sangster, *Inside Hammer*, p. 18.

84. In 1963, Lippert struck a deal with British producer/exhibitor Jack Parsons for a series of low-budget films by Parroch-McCallum Productions that included Gordon Hessler's little-seen chiller *Catacombs* and *Do You Know This Voice?*.

85. 'Thanks for the Right Support for Supports', *Kinematograph Weekly*, 18 December 1952, pp. 18–19.

86. Ibid.

87. Interview with McFarlane, 1995.

88. *The Cinema Studio*, 31 March 1948, p. 12.

89. *The Cinema Studio*, 14 April 1948, p. 3.

90. *To-Day's Cinema*, 5 October 1948, p. 11.

91. Another transatlantic couple, the Canadian celebrity husband-and-wife team of Barbara Kelly and Bernard Braden, starred in Charles Saunders' *Love in Pawn* (1953, working title *The Pledge*), which was based on the unlikely premise of a wife putting her artist husband literally in hock. The future TV comedy luminaries Frank Muir and Denis Norden contributed to the script.

92. Letter to McFarlane, 2002.

93. *Kinematograph Weekly*, 21 September 1950, p. 39.

94. *Picture Show*, 28 April 1951, p. 10.

95. *Kinematograph Weekly*, 6 March 1952, p. 23. *Picture Show* (2 February 1952, p. 10) commended it as a 'Simple, sincerely told drama' with 'A brilliant performance from Charles Victor … [which] dominates the film.'

96. *Kinematograph Weekly*, 29 March 1951, p. 21.

97. Jean Kent recalled that she suggested she should kiss Stevens in one scene, but that he rejected the idea on the grounds that Americans would think it unmanly of him to have the woman initiate the kiss! Interview with Jean Kent, 2000.

98. *Kinematograph Weekly*, 13 August 1953, p. 18.

99. *Kinematograph Weekly*, (19 February 1953, p. 18) thought that, 'for its size, it carries quite a kick'. *Kine* was not usually so easily pleased.

100. *To-Day's Cinema*, 15 March 1954, p. 6.

101. *Kinematograph Weekly*, 22 July 1954, p. 12.

102. *Kinematograph Weekly*, 29 July 1954, p. 22.

103. *To-Day's Cinema*, 22 April 1954, p. 5.

104. *Kinematograph Weekly*, 28 April 1955, p. 22. For an astute analysis of this and other Tempean films of the period, see Dave Mann, 'From Minor Misdemeanours to Ill-Gotten Gains: the Origins and Emergence of Britain's First TV/Film Crime Series', PhD thesis, University of the West of England, 2008, Chapter 3.

105. *To-Day's Cinema*, 12 May 1954, p. 15.

106. *Kinematograph Weekly*, 3 June 1954, p. 29. Meanwhile, Kenilworth-Mid Century switched to Southall to make *One Jump Ahead* (1955).

107. *To-Day's Cinema*, 18 January 1955, p. 11.

108. *Kinematograph Weekly*, 28 July 1955, p. 16.

109. *Kinematograph Weekly*, 3 November 1955.

110. 'Tempean Films to Make Bigger Pictures', *Kinematograph Weekly*, 21 April 1955, p. 37.

111. *Bond of Fear* was a Mid Century production made at Twickenham. *Kinematograph Weekly* (19 April 1956, p. 25) summed up its appeal as 'suspenseful, yet completely innocuous'.

112. *To-Day's Cinema*, 15 April 1955, p. 5.

113. It is one of those Tempean productions labelled CIPA (for tax reasons).

114. *To-Day's Cinema*, 5 July 1956, p. 9.

115. *Kinematograph Weekly*, 31 October 1957, p. 23.

116. Ibid.
117. They retained the services of such actors as Sam Kydd and Dermot Walsh who commented on this generosity of the producers as 'exceptions to the rule ... about people forgetting you when they move on in their careers', Walsh in McFarlane, *Autobiography*, p. 593.
118. Interview with Brian McFarlane, Melbourne, June 2004.
119. Ball in McFarlane, *Autobiography*, p. 55. Gordon Jackson recalled that he was to play a Yorkshire ex-boxer for the Danzigers (in *Three Crooked Men*, 1958): 'I pointed out I was Scots. Danziger said, "You can play it anything but Jewish."' Ibid. p. 322.
120. Walsh, August 1995, in McFarlane, *Autobiography*, p. 592.
121. <www.78rpm.co.uk/tvd.htm>
122. Tise Vahimagi, *The Danzigers*, <www.screenonline.org.uk/people/id/773807/>
123. Paul Dickson (a.k.a. Paul Gherzo and Paul Gerrard), had won acclaim for his documentaries, *The Undefeated* (1950) and *David* (1951), but never fulfilled this promise in his features.
124. *Kinematograph Weekly* 4 February 1954, p. 22.
125. Lee, *Tall, Dark and Gruesome*, p. 188.
126. Peter Pitt, 'Elstree's Poverty Row', *Films and Filming*, September 1984, p. 15.
127. Ball in McFarlane, *Autobiography*, p. 55.
128. Grantham, 'Life on the Cheap ...', pp. 1–2.
129. Ball, letter to Brian McFarlane, 4 September, 2004.
130. *Kinematograph Weekly*, 3 January 1957, p. 15.
131. *The Cinema*, 4 November 1957, p. 4. Typically, *Kinematograph Weekly* (7 November 1957, p. 47) was harder to please: 'The picture, clumsily made with an eye on the American market, is lurid, yet lacks suspense.'
132. *Daily Cinema*, 30 December 1957, p. 7.
133. *Kinematograph Weekly*, 9 October 1958, p. 26.
134. *Kinematograph Weekly (Studio Review)*, 29 May 1958, p. iv.

135. Varnel, who had experience as assistant director for Warwick Films, ventured only once as director into near-'A' territory, with *Mrs Gibbons' Boys* (1962), before leaving for another career in Australian television.
136. Wheeler Winston Dixon, 'Danzigers, The', in Brian McFarlane (ed.), *The Encyclopedia of British Film* (London: Methuen/BFI, 2003), p. 161.
137. *Monthly Film Bulletin* (June 1961, p. 82) properly claimed that it 'does suggest a little of the pressure under which Germans of conscience laboured'. However, *Kinematograph Weekly* (18 May 1961, p. 29) could find nothing to sear the heart in the 'spectacle of Nazis being nasty to Nazis'.
138. Rachael Low, *Film Making in 1930s Britain* (London: Allen and Unwin, 1985), p. 176
139. *The Cinema*, 6 December 1950, p. 18.
140. *Picture Show*, 14 July 1951, p. 10.
141. Reviews were largely positive: 'Modest but by no means cheeseparing, it'll enhance most programmes and disgrace none.' *Kinematograph Weekly*, 4 October 1951, p. 25.
142. It was praised by *Picture Show* (15 November 1952, p.10) as 'well-directed and acted'.
143. Vernon Sewell, BECTU Oral History Project interview, 329, 7 July 1994.
144. *To-Day's Cinema*, 5 October 1954, p. 8.
145. He followed it up with a co-feature for Insignia, *Portrait of Alison* (1957, USA: *Postmark for Danger*), which benefited from Wilkie Cooper's photography and had another American import, Terry Moore, then at the height of her modest stardom after *Come Back Little Sheba* (1952). She played opposite the Canadian Robert Beatty, and a substantial cast of British character players, including the chilly charisma of Alan Cuthbertson as chief villain.
146. *Kinematograph Weekly*, 3 March 1955, p. 18. It only meant that Sewell, who must by now have been pining for his yacht, had to do another comedy, *Johnny, You're Wanted* (1956),

featuring broadcasting stars John Slater and
Alfred Marks.

147. *The Daily Cinema*, 29 November 1957. p. 3.

148. *Kinematograph Weekly*, 4 September 1958,
p. 18.

149. Rogers in McFarlane, *Autobiography*, p. 496.
'I think they got a bit of culture up their
backsides' was Rogers' diagnosis.

150. *The Cinema* (24 December 1947, p. 12)
commented: 'the film has much to commend it,
not least its frequently beautiful Scottish
panorama and its no less often fervent singing
in soli and chorals. It is the familiar Burns
lyrics, however, which provide the
entertainment backbone, and Burns lovers will
be in their element in listening to the twenty or
so songs which have come to us down the years.'

151. One Sheffield exhibitor told a reporter from
the trade press just what a phenomenon it had
become: 'I'm playing it this week, first-feature.
You want to see it? It's unbelievable. All day I'm
packed out. They scream the place down. Up
the road they have a big new American film but
no business.' John Montgomery, 'Why Neglect
a Paying Market', *The Cinema Studio*,
2 November 1949, p. 8.

152. *Kinematograph Weekly*, 10 March 1949, p. 21.

153. *The Cinema*, 12 April 1950, p. 14.

154. *Kinematograph Weekly*, 28 February 1952,
p. 29.

155. *To-Day's Cinema*, 26 April 1951, p. 6

156. *Kinematograph Weekly*, 7 January 1954, p. 17.

157. *Kinematograph Weekly*, 22 November 1951,
p. 20.

158. *To-Day's Cinema*, 16 June 1954, p. 18.

159. *Picturegoer*, 15 December 1951, p. 17.

160. *Picture Show*, 18 October 1952, p. 10.

161. L. C. [Lionel Collier], *Picturegoer*, October 3,
1953, p. 20

162. Letter from Sidney Cole to Brian McFarlane,
5 February 1996.

163. Ibid.

164. *Kinematograph Weekly*, 12 April 1951, p. 11.

165. *Kinematograph Weekly*, 15 November 1951,
p. 23.

166. Letter from Ralph Bond to Hans Gottfurcht,
Secretary of the International Labour Film
Institute, Brussels, 31 December 1958, held in
BFI Special Collections, London.

167. *Kinematograph Weekly*, 28 June 1951, p. 3.

168. *Kinematograph Weekly*, 9 October 1952, p. 27.

169. *To-Day's Cinema*, 20 March 1953, p. 14.

170. Ted Willis to ACT Films' General Manager,
Henry Passmore, 18 November 1953, BFI. The
treatment provoked apoplexy from the General
Secretary of the ACT Union, who was
'appalled' by Willis's 'travesty of history': 'I
cannot believe this is the same Ted Willis who a
quarter of a century ago was a fellow member
with me of the National Advisory Committee
of the Labour Party Legion of Youth.' Letter to
Passmore, 16 December 1953, BFI.

171. Sidney Cole to Passmore, 14 December 1953,
BFI.

172. E.g., *To-Day's Cinema*, 17 May 1954, p. 8.

173. E.g., *To-Day's Cinema*, 19 May 1954, p. 10

174. *To-Day's Cinema*, 27 September, p. 8.

175. Croydon-Passmore's first production,
The Delavine Affair (1954), was cut from the
same cloth as *Final Appointment* – a comedy
thriller about a reporter and his wife on the
trail of a killer, this time directed by Douglas
Pierce and starring Honor Blackman and Peter
Reynolds.

176. Shaughnessy's breakthrough into directing was
facilitated by ACT's chairman, Anthony
Asquith, an old school friend.

177. *The Cinema*, 1 February 1957, p. 8.

178. As producer Robert Dunbar added: 'Three or
four weeks is ample time to make a picture.
Here at Shepperton we have had no trouble
whatsoever with set building, facilities have
been first class. The production has had the
devoted attention of everyone concerned.' *The
Cinema*, 4 February 1957, p. 4.

179. *The Cinema*, 10 September 1957, p. 1.

180. Bond to Callum, 8 April 1957, BFI.

181. Bond to F. Thomas, 11 September 1957, BFI.

182. D. Cubitt to Ralph Bond, 13 September 1957, BFI.

183. 'It does not seem likely at this stage that anything in the script will give trouble for the "U" certificate' (presumably required by Rank). BBFC to Bond, 10 October 1957, BFI.

184. Compton Bennett to Bond, 9 September 1957, BFI.

185. The additional cost was covered by completion insurance.

186. Bond to Tully, 17 December 1957, BFI.

187. *Monthly Film Bulletin*, April 1958, p. 45.

188. *Films and Filming*, November 1958, p. 23.

189. Letter from Roy Fowler to Brian McFarlane, July 2004.

190. Bond to E. M. Smedley-Aston, 3 November 1959, BFI.

191. Smedley-Aston to Bond, 20 October 1959, BFI.

192. *Monthly Film Bulletin*, August 1960, p. 111.

193. Studio rental costs were almost three times higher than they had been for *The Diplomatic Corpse* only four years earlier. *The Kitchen*, Statement of Production Costs, 17 March 1961, BFI.

194. ACT hoped that *The Kitchen* would go out as a first feature, but had to settle for a position on the National circuit as a support to the re-issued *Room at the Top*.

195. Fowler, op cit. In early 1963 a 'Friends of ACT Films' subscription was raised via a promotional letter from Anthony Asquith.

196. The film was praised by the *Monthly Film Bulletin* (March 1962, p. 40) as 'Invigorating, suspenseful and jumping with action'.

197. Bond to E. L'Epine Smith, 18 May 1962, BFI.

198. He had promised Bryanston a treatment of Arnold Wesker's *Chicken Soup With Barley*, but Alun Falconer had been slow to deliver.

199. Bond to Michael Balcon, 22 June 1962, BFI.

200. Peter Maxwell to Bond, 17 July 1962, BFI.

Other applicants were D'Arcy Conyers, Lance Comfort, Franklin Gollings, Charles Saunders, Anthony Squire, Bernard Knowles, Gordon Parry, David Macdonald, Mickey Delamar and Bob Hall. Even Montgomery Tully, with whom Bond had been so impressed on *The Diplomatic Corpse*, had to take his place in the queue after writing: 'I hear that you may be looking for a director for your next picture in October – so just a line to let you know that I am still in circulation.' Montgomery Tully to Bond, 16 July 1962, BFI.

201. In fact, it might have made entertaining science fiction, a genre in which the Bakers later had most success (the television series *Doctor Who* and *Space 1999*), had the wife been an alien rather than a drug-peddler.

202. Ted Lloyd to Bond, 4 September 1962, BFI.

203. Peter Maxwell to Bond, 7 September 1962, BFI.

204. E. L'Epine Smith to Bond, 10 November 1962, BFI.

205. Bond to L'Epine Smith, 11 November 1962, BFI.

206. Wheatley to Bond, 19 August 1964. BFI.

207. *To-Day's Cinema*, 23 July 1954, p. 4.

208. Group 3 Board Paper 19 June 1952. BFI Sir Michael Balcon Collection.

209. *The Cinema*, 13 June 1951, p. 16.

210. Ibid. Baxter had spent the early post-war years making films aimed primarily at a juvenile market. *Nothing Venture* and *The Last Load* (both 1948) were both accounts of schoolkids foiling gangs of crooks, the latter described as 'much more sensible and thrilling than the average "B" picture'. *Kinematograph Weekly*, 27 May 1948, p. 25. Baxter's most ambitious production was *The Second Mate* (1951). Starring Gordon Harker as the skipper of a Thames barge and child actor David Hannaford as his youngest crew member, the production's ingenuousness just about saved it from shipping too much water.

211. Alfred Shaughnessy, *Both Ends of the Candle*, pp. 114–6.

212. Ibid., p. 117.

213. Ibid. Shaughnessy is exaggerating here. Grierson was fully aware of the importance of showmanship and commercial values, but insisted on them being combined with more fundamental artistic or political concerns.

214. *Picture Show*, 2 August 1953, p. 10.

215. *The Cinema*, 10 December 1952, p. 17.

216. Letter from the Associated British representative to J. H. Lawrie of the NFFC, 6 May 1952. BFI Sir Michael Balcon Collection.

217. Anon, 'Notes on Future Policy', 8 December 1953, BFI Sir Michael Balcon Collection.

218. *To-Day's Cinema*, 24 July 1953, p. 6.

219. *Kinematograph Weekly*, 24 November 1943, p. 11.

220. *To-Day's Cinema*, 24 January 1947, p. 28.

221. Baim told an *Evening News* reporter that 'During a scene we heard footsteps and a strange tapping coming from the cellar.' *The Ghost of Rashmon Hall* press book, MC Pictures, 1949.

222. *To-Day's Cinema*, 13 January 1948, p. 8.

223. *Kinematograph Weekly*, 24 February 1949, p. 24.

224. 'Interior scenes, also, have been filmed in the places where they would normally occur, thus giving a somewhat stereotyped story an air of actuality that pulls it out of the rut of the average mystery melodrama.' *To-Day's Cinema*, 16 December 1949, p. 10.

225. *To-Day's Cinema*, 12 April 1951, p. 8.

226. *Kinematograph Weekly*, 15 October 1953, p. 24.

227. *To-Day's Cinema*, 14 January 1955, p. 11.

228. *To-Day's Cinema*, 19 September 1956, p. 10.

229. *The Cinema*, 23 May 1957, p. 6.

230. *The Cinema*, 7 October 1957, p. 10.

231. Stanley Long, *X-Rated: Adventures of an Exploitation Filmmaker* (Richmond: Reynolds and Hearn, 2008), pp. 65–9.

232. *The Cinema Studio*, 30 June 1948, p. 14.

233. 'Dependable action fare for the masses', pronounced *The Cinema*, 7 December 1949, p. 12.

234. *The Cinema Studio*, 7 September 1949, p. 7.

235. However, this did not 'detract from its value to the smaller exhibitor, whose patrons will find in the violent action enough compensation for the lack of continuity, pedestrian dialogue and cheap staging'. *The Cinema*, 18 July 1951, p. 13.

236. *The Cinema*, 28 February 1951, p. 12; *Kinematograph Weekly*, 8 March 1951, p. 36.

237. *Kinematograph Weekly*, 18 December 1952, p. 120B. 'We brought it in for £25,000. Pamela Brown's performance was quite superb.' Bower in McFarlane, *Autobiography*, p. 84.

238. *To-Day's Cinema*, 4 May 1953, p. 7.

239. *To-Day's Cinema*, 26 February 1954, p. 1.

240. *To-Day's Cinema*, 3 March 1954, p. 8.

241. *Kinematograph Weekly*, 20 October 1955, p. 18.

242. The two-stage studios close to Brighton Station were identified, as *Picturegoer* (15 December 1951, p. 17) noted by 'the words "Film Studios" written in huge letters on the red-brick building'.

243. *The Cinema*, 23 November 1949, p. 10.

244. *Kinematograph Weekly*, 24 November 1949.

245. *The Cinema Studio*, 23 February 1949.

246. *The Cinema*, 3 December 1951, p. 5.

247. Major Productions was a partnership with Francis Edge (b. 1923), and was responsible for a further six 'B' films directed by Charles Saunders, Francis Searle and Peter Graham Scott, before Temple-Smith moved on to 'A' pictures in 1960.

248. *Picture Show* (17 October 1953, p. 10, pp. 5–6, 10, 14) not only praised it for 'many comedy touches' and 'authentic settings', but also chose to devote several pages to telling its story.

249. *To-Day's Cinema*, 26 May 1955, p. 10.

250. *To-Day's Cinema*, 7 July 1954, p. 10.

251. Some sources cite Terence Fisher as co-director, but his name does not appear on the film.

252. *To-Day's Cinema*, 18 June 1956, p. 70.

253. *Children Galore* press book, General Film Distributors, 1954.

254. *To-Day's Cinema*, 20 October 1950, p. 10.

255. *To-Day's Cinema*, 22 May 1951, p. 10.

256. *Kinematograph Weekly*, 27 December 1951, p. 17.

257. Other Board members of Fortress were screenwriter Doreen Montgomery and producer Clive Nicholas.

258. *The Golden Link* press book, Archway, 1954.

259. *Kinematograph Weekly*, 3 November 1955, p. 24.

260. *The Cinema*, 16 July 1957, p. 14.

261. Unpublished interview with Andrew Clay, 1997.

262. Warren, *British Studios*, p. 171.

263. *To-Day's Cinema*, 21 January, 1957, p. 6.

264. 'Vigorously acted by a talented international cast, ambitiously mounted and generously flavoured with sex, it hands out plenty of thrills.' *Kinematograph Weekly*, 7 February 1957, p. 14.

265. The plot was less than plausible, but there was enough action for *To-Day's Cinema* (17 April 1957, p. 11) to declare it 'a serviceable British thriller'; Republic distributed the film in the USA.

266. *Kinematograph Weekly*, 11 July 1957, p. 16. At the time, the picture's principal interest was the film debut of the glamorous hostess of Victor Sylvester's television dance show, Patti Morgan.

267. 'Second Nature', interview with Julian Wintle, *Films and Filming*, January 1974, pp. 12–17. See also Anne Francis, *Julian Wintle: A Memoir* (Yeovil: Dukeswood, 1984), p. 60.

268. The *Monthly Film Bulletin* (January 1961, p. 9) thought this 'entertaining little film' was a genuine 'attempt to do something positive and different' and presented its teenage story with 'insight, humour and even charm'.

4 Behind the Scenes

1. Two minor exceptions: Marjorie Deans directed *The Girl Is Mine* (1950) and Thelma Connell co-directed *A Tale of Three Women* (1954).

2. Baker in McFarlane, *Autobiography*, p. 45.

3. 'Gilling has Practical Answers, Too!', *Cinema Studio*, October/November 1950, p. 12.

4. David Quinlan, *British Sound Films: The Studio Years 1929–1959* (London: B. T. Batsford, 1984), p. 229.

5. His camera operator, Eric Besche, had just finished working with Hitchcock on *Stage Fright* (1950).

6. Surprisingly, this was producer Baker's favourite among his Tempean films. Interview with Baker, 2000.

7. Baker in McFarlane, *Autobiography*, p. 47.

8. *To-Day's Cinema*, 2 December 1952, p. 8.

9. *Kinematograph Weekly*, 22 March 1951, p. 22.

10. *Picture Show*, 2 February 1953, p. 10.

11. The film also recalls Henry Cass's *Last Holiday* (1950), from a J. B. Priestley screenplay, in which Alec Guinness, like Victor's character, believes himself likely to die shortly and spends his time doing good to those he meets in a (smarter) hotel.

12. *Monthly Film Bulletin* (September 1954, p. 132) rightly assessed the film as being 'distinguished by the unaffected acting of the principal players, and by a certain humanity implicit in the treatment of the subject'.

13. Wheeler Winston Dixon, 'Fisher, Terence', in McFarlane, *Encyclopedia*, p. 224.

14. Tony Dalton, 'Terence Fisher: Emotional Fairy Tales for Adults', *Little Shop of Horrors* 19, 2007, pp. 52–67.

15. Peter Hutchings, *Terence Fisher* (Manchester and New York: Manchester University Press), 2001, p. 24.

16. Andrew Spicer, 'Creativity and the "B" feature: Terence Fisher's crime films', *Film Criticism* vol. xxx no. 2 (Winter 2005–6), p. 26.

17. *The Cinema*, 29 August 1951, p. 15.

18. Green in McFarlane, *Autobiography*, p. 235.

19. The film's rural backgrounds, untypical of its genre, caused *Kinematograph Weekly* (10 December 1953, p. 16) to describe it, rather unkindly, as a 'barnyard "who-dunnit"' that was 'of and for the sticks'.

20. *The Cinema*, 12 August 1953, p. 10. Sarah Stoddart in *Picturegoer* (October 10, 1953, p. 21) found it 'Entertaining enough in parts, but so theatrical that you can almost hear the rattle of matinee trays.'

21. *The Cinema*, 30 November 1956, p. 8.

22. 'A gleam of originality would have been welcome', wrote *To-Day's Cinema*, 16 August 1957, p. 6.

23. *To-Day's Cinema*, 25 September 1957, p. 9.

24. *To-Day's Cinema*, 10 September 1954, p. 8.

25. *To-Day's Cinema*, 7 January 1957, p. 4.

26. *Daily Film Renter*, 4 April 1957, p. 5.

27. Interview with McFarlane, 2005.

28. *To-Day's Cinema*, 27 October 1952, p. 8.

29. Some were shown in cinemas as parts of anthologies such as *The Genie* and *The Triangle* (both 1953).

30. *Kinematograph Weekly*, 23 October 1952, p. 27.

31. *The Daily Cinema* (25 April, 1962, p. 8) heaped praise on it as a 'small-scale quality thriller' that was 'bang on target for the mass market'. *Kine Weekly* (3 May 1962, p. 19), however, thought it a little long for a supporting feature and would like to have seen the last two reels tightened up. It played second fiddle to the entertaining but inferior *Two and Two Make Six* (1962).

32. *Picture Show*, 4 December 1954, p. 10.

33. Pierre Bourdieu, *The Field of Cultural Production: Essays on Art and Literature* (edited and introduced by Randal Johnson) (Cambridge: Polity Press, 1993), p. 75.

34. Vernon Sewell, BECTU interview.

35. Ibid.

36. *Monthly Film Bulletin*, August 1962, p. 116.

37. David Quinlan, *The Illustrated Guide to Film Directors* (London: B. T. Batsford, 1983), p. 299.

38. *Kinematograph Weekly*, 15 December 1955, p. 190.

39. *Kinematograph Weekly*, 20 March 1958, p. 23.

40. *To-Day's Cinema*, 13 May 1954, p. 7.

41. S. S. [Sarah Stoddart], *Five Days*, *Picturegoer* vol. 28 no. 1012, 25 September 1954, p. 21.

42. All but one of Eternal's output was directed by Tully at Walton or MGM British. Eternal ceased production in 1966.

43. *The Cinema*, 4 February 1957, p. 4.

44. *To-Day's Cinema*, 12 March 1954, p. 12; *Kinematograph Weekly*, 18 March 1954, p. 17; and *Picture Show*, 4 December 1954, p. 10. The picture was produced by Corsair Pictures, the swashbuckling name for a company associated with the veteran pulp screenwriter, Brock Williams, and starred the prolific Guy Middleton and Joan Winmill in her first (and practically her only) leading role.

45. *Monthly Film Bulletin*, August 1955, p. 125.

46. The other two As are *No Room at the Inn* (1948), the grim version of a stage play about the fate of wartime evacuees, and the nicely twisty railway crash melodrama *Interrupted Journey* (1949), starring Valerie Hobson and Richard Todd. In the 1950s, he starred Hobson again in the Group 3 drama of divorce *Background* (1953), a superior co-feature.

47. 'Passable' was *The Cinema*'s verdict (8 July 1953, p. 7). 'Third rate' said *Kinematograph Weekly*, 9 July 1953, p. 21.

48. *Kinematograph Weekly*, 26 December 1957, p. 19, emphasis in original.

49. *Kinematograph Weekly* (28 August 1958, p. 20) disliked the sordid tone of the picture, and was brutal in its condemnation: 'The script is full of loopholes and unimaginative direction, indifferent acting and stodgy dialogue magnify flaws. It neither touches the heart nor thrills.'

50. *Monthly Film Bulletin*, January 1963, p. 10.

51. This latter criticism includes Ronald Howard as upright Sir Richard and June Thorburn, in 1960s beehive hairdo, as Lady Eleanor.

52. *The Cinema* (18 October 1957, p. 5), however, was dismissive: 'Some suspense and capable acting, but the narrative bristles with improbabilities which direction fails to adjust ... A routine thriller that wisely does not pretend to be anything else.'

53. *Monthly Film Bulletin*, December 1963, p. 171.

54. Quinlan, *Illustrated Guide*, p. 267.

55. Paul Quinn, 'Searle, Francis', in McFarlane, *Encyclopedia*, p. 598.

56. Searle in McFarlane, *Autobiography*, p. 526.

57. A similar move that had been attempted two years earlier when J. Lee Thompson was offered the opportunity to direct his own script for *Murder Without Crime* (1951) at Welwyn.

58. *To-Day's Cinema*, 5 January 1953, p. 6.

59. *To-Day's Cinema*, 14 July 1953, p. 6.

60. *Kinematograph Weekly* (23 July 1953, p. 18) condemned it as 'dreary'.

61. However, *To-Day's Cinema* (19 August 1954, p. 6) could still imagine it as 'acceptable fare in [a] supporting slot', and *Kinematograph Weekly* (26 August 1954, p. 22) could even predict that its 'elegant staging' would 'hold most audiences'.

62. They also included *Gaolbreak* (1962), which was cursed with an embarrassingly simple-minded screenplay by A. R. Rawlinson.

63. *The Cinema*, 15 March 1957, p. 6. *Kinematograph Weekly* (21 July 1957, p. 29) praised cast and director for their neat handling of a satirical tale.

64. According to Guido Coen, the film's star, David McCallum, made a substantial input into the direction of *Jungle Street*. Interview with Andrew Clay, 1997.

65. *Monthly Film Bulletin*, March 1959, p. 29.

66. Lee, *Tall, Dark and Gruesome*, p. 192.

67. The trade did not always agree: *Date at Midnight* (1960), for example, was praised as 'Punchy and just right for size' by *Kinematograph Weekly*, 4 February 1960, p. 30. However, *The Daily Cinema*'s (14 May 1962, p. 6) dismissal of *The Durant Affair* (1962) as a poor substitute for *Perry Mason* on TV and 'a pretty flavourless appetiser for the top feature', was more typical.

68. *Kinematograph Weekly*, 25 May 1961, p. 10.

69. *Monthly Film Bulletin*, December 1960, p. 173. It had also praised Bishop for 'maintain[ing] the supernatural atmosphere quite well' in *Danger Tomorrow*. *Monthly Film Bulletin*, June 1960, p. 83.

70. The film is discussed more extensively in Steve Chibnall, 'Ordinary People: New Wave Social Realism and the British Crime Film 1959–1963', in Steve Chibnall and Robert Murphy (eds), *British Crime Cinema* (London: Routledge, 1999), pp. 94–109.

71. Newman in McFarlane, *Autobiography*, p. 435.

72. Chibnall, 'Ordinary People'. Barnes was also responsible for the unusual psychology of *Violent Moment* (1958).

73. Bourdieu, *The Field of Cultural Production*, p. 75. For an informative overview of the field of 'B' film screenwriting, see Dave Mann, 'From Obscurity to Authority? The Changing Status of the Screenwriter during the Transition from "B" Features to TV/Film Series (1946–64)', *Journal of British Cinema and Television* vol. 5 no. 2, 2008, pp. 280–99.

74. For example, Wheeler Winston Dixon, 'The Man Who Created The Avengers: An Interview with Brian Clemens', *Classic Images* no. 287, May 1999, pp. 18–20, 33–5; James Davies, 'Brian Clemens', in *The Tides of Time*, Oxford University *Doctor Who* Magazine, no. 29, 2004, pp. 26–8.

75. In Dixon, 'The Man Who Created the Avengers', p. 19.

76. *Monthly Film Bulletin*, February 1957, p. 20.

77. *Kinematograph Weekly*, 24 October 1957, p. 21.

78. *Monthly Film Bulletin*, December 1957, p. 153.

79. *Monthly Film Bulletin*, November 1958, p.145.

80. R. H. B. *Picturegoer*, 2 February 1957, p. 17.

81. R. H. B. *Picturegoer*, 7 December 1957, p. 15.

82. Unpublished interview with Andrew Clay, 1997.

83. Ibid.

84. He claims in his memoir to have written 'more than twenty for them', some perhaps without credit. Grantham, p. 2.

85. Ibid.

86. S. S., *Picturegoer*, 25 September 1954, p. 21.

87. Think of Ward's effeminate but not stereotypically camp antiques dealer, Cornelius, in *The Frightened Man*. As Charles Victor's assistant, he is allowed to be knowledgeable about his work; he attracts the strange remark from dealer Stone (Martin Benson), 'I like you very much – beautiful manners and you smell nice', prior to his rumbling Stone as peddling stolen goods. 'B' films do not habitually take this much care to establish the individuality of minor characters.

88. Gilling could not resist a little in-joke at the expense of one of his fellow Tempean directors, naming the poor victim of circumstance who just wants to get on with his holiday in France – Mr Sewell.

89. 'Writer in Profile', *Kinematograph Weekly*, 28 January 1960, pp. 27, 32.

90. Ibid.

91. Ibid.

92. L. C. (Lionel Collier), *Picturegoer*, 13 November 1954, p. 21.

93. 'It's contrived and stolid and never really gets funny'. C. A. W., *Picturegoer*, 3 September, 1955, p. 19.

94. *To-Day's Cinema* (8 January 1954, p. 6) could only rate it a 'moderate offering for the readily pleased'.

95. *Kinematograph Weekly*, 11 February 1960, p. 16.

96. Interview with Guido Coen by Andrew Clay, 1997.

97. Ibid.

98. Reviews were less than rapturous: 'indifferent direction, over-emphatic portrayals, moderate technical quality', complained *To-Day's Cinema*, 1 April 1954, p. 6.

99. *Monthly Film Bulletin*, June 1961, p. 82.

100. Interviewed by Al Taylor, *Little Shop of Horrors* 12, April 1994, pp. 101–6.

101. 'Here's Home-made Gloss', *Picturegoer*, 3 July 1954, p. 14. The following year, *Picturegoer* (26 March 1955, p. 21) again lauded Hughes for his director-screenwriter stint on *Little Red Monkey* (1955), calling it 'a first-rate thriller'.

102. Tom Johnson and Deborah Del Vecchio, *Hammer Films: An Exhaustive Filmography* (London: McFarland, 1996), p. 90.

103. George Pearson, *Flashback: The Autobiography of a British Film-maker* (London: George Allen & Unwin, 1957), pp. 193–4.

104. Baker in McFarlane, *Autobiography*, p. 47.

105. Clemens, *Tides of Time*, p. 26.

106. This film has a strikingly bravura opening robbery scene, for which credit is probably owed to Roeg.

107. Interview with McFarlane, London, October 1992.

108. Duncan Petrie, *The British Cinematographer* (London: BFI Publishing, 1996).

109. *Monthly Film Bulletin*, April 1951, p. 252.

110. Baker in McFarlane, *Autobiography*, p. 47.

111. Fine as much of Emmott's work is for Comfort, arguably it is Brendan J. Stafford's cinematography on the co-feature *Bang! You're Dead* (1954) that best serves Comfort's sombre vision. It catches brilliantly the contrast between the vernal freshness of the forest and the scruffy evidence of human intervention in this, and the final night-time search for the missing boy is shot with a mixture of lyricism and brooding danger that help to make this one of the most haunting films of its decade.

112. Vernon Sewell, BECTU interview.

113. *Monthly Film Bulletin*, February 1965, p. 19.

114. *Kinematograph Weekly*, 22 February 1962, p. 21.

115. Louis Levy, 'Music for Every Mood', interview in *Film Weekly*, 7 March 1937, p. 9.

116. *The Cinema*, 30 July 1947, p. 30.

117. Surprisingly, Alwyn later supplied the scores for the humble heist film *The Professionals* (1960) and the thriller *Devil's Bait*.

118. *To-Day's Cinema*, 19 March 1954, p. 8.

119. Interviewed by Mike Murphy, *Dark Terrors*, 9, November 1994, pp. 36–9.

120. Slaney went on to produce experimental electronic scores for Norman J. Warren's horror films of the 1970s.

121. Randall Larson, 'The Music of Hammer', *Little Shop of Horrors*, 10/11, July 1990, pp. 65–88.

122. Cf. *The Cinema*, 7 January 1948, p. 21.

123. K. J. Donnelly, *British Film Music and Film Musicals* (London: Palgrave, 2007), p. 26.

124. Peter Noble, 'The Two Stanley Blacks', *The Cinema Studio*, August 1951, p. 18.

125. *Kine Weekly*, 1 August 1963, p. 4.

5 On the Screen

1. Bryan Forbes, *Notes for a Life* (London: William Collins, 1974), pp. 225–8.

2. Slaughter's last hurrah was *Murder at Scotland Yard* (1954) under the direction of Victor M. Gover, who had become his regular helmsman. The film appears to have stood two years on the shelf, probably an indication of the waning popularity of Slaughter's brand of bloodcurdling theatrics. For *To-Day's Cinema* (8 April 1954, p. 6), this 'lurid tale' was only deserving of a 'quiet booking' in 'small halls'.

3. *Kinematograph Weekly*, 10 May 1956, p. 21.

4. *The Daily Cinema*, 8 June 1959, p. 4.

5. *The Daily Cinema*, 17 August 1959, p. 4.

6. *To-Day's Cinema*, 16 April 1957, p. 16.

7. David Quinlan, *British Sound Films: The Studio Years 1928–1959* (London: B. T. Batsford, 1984), p. 280.

8. Walsh in McFarlane, *Autobiography*, p. 591.

9. Ibid., p. 593.

10. The first was *Send for Paul Temple* (1946), starring Anthony Hulme.

11. David Quinlan, *The Illustrated Directory of Film Stars* (London: B. T. Batsford Ltd., 1981), p. 41.

12. *Kinematograph Weekly*, 18 August, 1955, p. 18.

13. Ibid.

14. Byrne was 'quite a lot younger than the character he played' as Searle recalled in McFarlane, *Autobiography*, p. 525.

15. Baker, in ibid., p. 44.

16. Sewell, BECTU interview.

17. Anderson in McFarlane, *Autobiography*, p. 18.

18. *Picturegoer*, 17 April 1954, p. 17.

19. *Kinematograph Weekly*, 20 January 1955, p. 19.

20. *The Cinema*, 30 November 1956, p. 8.

21. See Hugh Samson, 'Break for One', *Picturegoer*, 16 February 1952, p. 8, about how this film was seen by Hylton as her 'big chance'. He described her as 'a downright, down-to-earth type'.

22. *To-Day's Cinema* (27 May 1954, p. 8.) praised Brooke for 'exploiting her charms, quite properly … for all she is worth and giving a persuasive effect of smouldering passion'.

23. *Kinematograph Weekly*, 18 October 1956, p. 17.

24. Guy Green remembered Phyllis Kirk, whom he directed in *River Beat* (1953), as 'an up-and-coming actress who never became a major star, but she was a very bright, nice girl, whom I was lucky to have,' in McFarlane, *Autobiography*, p. 235.

25. Peter Hutchings is properly appreciative of Summerfield when he writes of how, in films such as this, she 'emerges from undeserved obscurity as the epitome of female sassiness'. Peter Hutchings, *Terence Fisher* (Manchester: Manchester University Press, 2001), p. 61.

26. Baker in McFarlane, *Autobiography*, p. 45.

27. Brog, '*Undercover Agent*' (US title), *Variety*, 25 November 1953, p. 26.

28. Denis Gifford, *The British Film Catalogue 1895–1970* (Newton Abbot: David & Charles, 1973).

29. It also means that famous short films such as Wendy Toye's *The Stranger Left No Card* (1952) and Jack Clayton's *The Bespoke Overcoat* (1955), at twenty-three and thirty-three minutes respectively, have not been included in the count, despite what may have been their exhibition history. Among those hovering around the eighty-minute cut-off, we have counted, say, the Boultings' eighty-one-minute *Suspect* (1960) because it was deliberately conceived and shown as a 'B' film, while two from Charles Crichton, *The Lavender Hill Mob* (1951) and *Law and Disorder* (1958), at seventy-eight and seventy-six minutes respectively, were clearly (in terms of their stars and other credentials) intended, and exhibited, as main features. Nevertheless, some films that played mainly as first features will have been included because they were made on budgets appropriate to a supporting feature. For example, Val Guest's *Murder at the Windmill* (1949) was a modest seventy minutes long, but had realistic ambitions to be at least a co-feature, given the quality of its direction and the reputation of the Windmill girls, described by *The Cinema* (11 May 1949, p. 10) as 'chastely underclad nymphs who also patter pertly in airy dressing-room discussions'. Guest offered an entertaining blend of music, mirth and mystery that was thoroughly enjoyed by the trade reviewers and which exhibitors were happy to play as a first feature. It recovered its costs within three-and-a-half months of general release, with a further six months of domestic bookings and export earnings to come (*The Cinema*, 16 November 1949, p. 17). Brian McFarlane's tabulation in, 'Pulp Fictions: the British B Film and the Field of Cultural Production', *Film Criticism* vol. xxi no. 1, Autumn 1996, p. 51, used a lower cut-off criterion, and cut out at 1963.

30. Steve Chibnall and Robert Murphy (eds), *British Crime Cinema* (London and New York: Routledge, 1999). On Hollywood's crime pictures cf. Thomas Schatz, *Hollywood Genres* (New York: Random House, 1981), pp. 81–2.

31. Baker in McFarlane, *Autobiography*, p. 46.

32. Chibnall and Murphy, *British Crime Cinema*, pp. 16–26.

33. *The Daily Cinema*, 14 March 1960, p. 10.

34. Interview with Rona Anderson, London, July 1994.

35. *The Cinema* (14 January 1948, p. 11) thought it 'a fanciful commentary on post-war life' but suitable for 'easy-going patronage'. It supported Robert Morley and Emlyn Williams in *You Will Remember* on a Grand National package programme.

36. Tower Bridge could also supply a setting for a finale, as it does in Lance Comfort's *Face in the Night* (1957, USA: *Menace in the Night*).

37. The evils of drink-driving in *To the Public Danger*, the whiff of Cold War paranoia in *Dick Barton at Bay*, and the idea of an association to save Nazi war criminals in *Penny and the Pownall Case* are quite striking exceptions.

38. V. Propp, *Morphology of the Folktale* (1928), trans. Laurence Scott (Austin: University of Texas Press, 1968), pp. 22–63.

39. Interviews with Alfred Roome and Freddie Young, London, October 1992.

40. Director Ralph Thomas has acknowledged this influence in Brian McFarlane (ed.), *Sixty Voices* (London: BFI, 1992), p. 209.

41. Nor do those films in the genre that are now unavailable for viewing look any more promising: made in 1949 with higher than usual production values, Gordon Parry's *Golden Arrow* had to wait until 1953 for a release on the Odeon circuit. It was a slight story of how a Frenchman, an American and an Englishman fantasise about a girl (Paula Valenska) they meet on a journey from Paris to London.

42. *To-Day's Cinema*, 17 July 1952, p. 8.

43. *Picture Show*, 25 April 1953, p. 10.

44. *To-Day's Cinema*, 12 October 1948, p. 10.

45. *Picturegoer* (20 April 1957, p. 17) enthused: 'He gets the most out of the farcical situation [and] ... doesn't miss a chance to register comedy – and sometimes pathos, too.'

46. *Kinematograph Weekly*, 26 May 1949, p. 23.

47. John Mundy, *The British Musical Film* (Manchester: Manchester University Press, 2007), p. 166.

48. Peers had previously appeared in New Realm's *The Balloon Goes Up* (1942).

49. Dick Richards in *Picturegoer* (15 October 1955, p. 12), praised '*The Eric Winstone Dance Band Show* – one of Exclusive's first-class dance-music supporting features – [which] cost under £10,000 and needed only four days' shooting'. However, a reader later complained of 'those boring musical shorts. Give us back the ordinary double-bill programme.' *Picturegoer*, February 19, 1956, p. 3.

50. *Monthly Film Bulletin*, May 1962, p. 68.

51. Figures derived from Gifford's *British Film Catalogue*.

52. These connections include: the basic plot of failed adultery and return to the dull spouse, the use of the flashback technique, the significance of Beethoven's 'Apassionata' for Harry (cf. Lean's use of Rachmaninoff to signify Laura's brush with passion), the undertones of homosexuality in the relationship between the male protagonist and his sophisticated friend, and the casting of Irene Handl, the cinema pianist in Lean's film, here playing a gossiping neighbour who recalls the Everley Gregg role in the earlier film.

53. Brian McFarlane, 'Losing the Peace: Some British Films of Post-war Adjustment', in Tony Barta (ed.), *Screening the Past: Film and the Representation of History* (Westport, CT: Praeger, 1998).

54. All quoted in a digest of reviews in *The Cinema Studio*, 12 January 1949, p. 14.

55. *The Cinema* 1 December 1948, p. 15.

56. *Picture Show*, 8 January 1948, p. 11.

57. *To-Day's Cinema*, 4 June 1948, p. 10, and *Kinematograph Weekly*, 10 June 1948, p. 17.

58. *To-Day's Cinema*, 26 June 1953, p. 6.

59. *To-Day's Cinema*, 3 May 1949, p. 11.

60. *Monthly Film Bulletin*, March 1967, p. 46. This film was released in Australia at least in 1961.

61. *Monthly Film Bulletin*, December 1963, p. 170.

62. The Danzigers made a couple of other war films in 1961: Montgomery Tully's gung-ho *The Middle Course* and Ernest Morris's *Tarnished Heroes*, a sort of cheap prototype for *The Dirty Dozen* (1967).

63. *To-Day's Cinema* (26 February 1951, p. 4) recorded notable success in Manchester, Liverpool and Blackpool, as well as in London. The picture was also a seminal influence on the 1970s horror films of Pete Walker. Cameraman-director Barnett went on to make *Robbery with Violence* (1958) and *Meet Mister Beat* (1961).

64. *The Daily Cinema*, 13 November 1957, p. 15.

65. *Kinematograph Weekly*, 14 November 1957, p. 21.

66. Shaughnessy, *Both Ends of the Candle*, p. 126.

67. David Pirie, *A Heritage of Horror: The English Gothic Cinema 1946–1972* (London: Gordon Fraser, 1973).

68. 'Shaughnessy, Alfred', in McFarlane, *Encyclopedia*, p. 607.

69. Sewell in McFarlane, *Autobiography*, p. 531.

70. *Monthly Film Bulletin*, June 1954.

71. The reading of this and other British sci-fi films of the period is discussed at greater length in Steve Chibnall, 'Alien Women: the Politics of Sexual Difference in British SF Pulp Cinema', in I. Q. Hunter (ed.), *British Science Fiction Cinema* (London: Routledge, 1999), pp. 57–74.

72. *To-Day's Cinema*, 30 April 1954. The Danzigers' other sci-fi number, *Satellite in the Sky* (1956), with a similarly strong cast (Donald Wolfit, Jimmy Hanley, Lois Maxwell), but in colour and 'Scope was definitely aimed at first or

co-feature status, and was assessed by *Picture Show* (5 January 1957, p. 10) as 'Realistic [what could it have meant?] and suspenseful'.

73. *To-Day's Cinema*, 5 October 1954, p. 8.

74. *Kinematograph Weekly*, 7 October 1954, p. 24.

75. *The Strange World of Planet X*, press book, Eros, 1956.

76. It is cheerfully described by Harry Fowler, one of its stars, as 'the worst film ever made'. Interview with Fowler, London, 1991.

77. *To-Day's Cinema*, 27 June 1956, p. 8.

78. Peter Hutchings argues that these pictures 'dwell upon some of the more disturbing aspects of male desire, and their conservative but also somewhat contrived conclusions do little to resolve issues raised elsewhere in the films'. Hutchings, *Terence Fisher*, p. 67.

79. *Monthly Film Bulletin*, October 1956, p. 128.

80. *Classic Images* no. 225, March 1994, p. 6.

81. *To-Day's Cinema*, 14 May 1956, p. 10.

82. *Kinematograph Weekly*, 13 February 1958, p. 22.

83. *The Daily Cinema*, 23 September 1959, p. 10.

84. *The Cinema Studio*, 26 October 1949, p. 22.

85. *The Ha'penny Breeze* press book, Associated British-Pathé, 1950. *To-Day's Cinema* (27 October 1950, p. 9) detected a certain 'slowness and obviousness in the telling of the story', but was charmed by its 'unaffected acting' and 'a genuine feeling for the English rural scene'. Darcy Conyers also directed *The Devil's Pass* (1957), a story of a modern-day 'wrecker', which was set in the Devon fishing village of Brixham with plenty of additional action at sea. It was a change of scene from the usually urban-centred 'B' thriller which *To-Day's Cinema* (25 April 1957, p. 9) definitely appreciated: 'A wholesome film which has the tonic effect of a breath of sea air.' For *Kinematograph Weekly* (2 May 1956, p. 19), however, the film's authentic backgrounds hardly compensated for its 'scrappy acting and direction'.

86. *To-Day's Cinema*, 29 April 1949, p. 6.

87. *Kinematograph Weekly*, 7 June 1951, p. 28.

88. Leacock in McFarlane, *Sixty Voices*, p. 154.

89. *To-Day's Cinema*, 12 October 1954, p. 12.

6 The Men from the Yard

1. As *To-Day's Cinema* (12 September 1944, p. 19) noted, 'There is no sustained gangster action, but just a trip to the English countryside, with a careful interrogation of all suspects by the man from Scotland Yard in the usual official way, all evidence pointing in one direction, and ending in a most unexpected solution.'

2. *This Modern Age*, promotional booklet, J. Arthur Rank, 1947.

3. The same topic would shortly be given a fictional treatment in Muriel Box's *Street Corner* (1953).

4. *Kinematograph Weekly*, 25 March 1948, p. 20.

5. *The Cinema Studio*, 21 December 1949, pp. 3, 12.

6. *The Cinema*, 14 February 1951, p. 11.

7. *Kinematograph Weekly*, 29 May 1952. It was re-issued the following year under the more dynamic title *Blue Print for Danger*.

8. A short from the series, *A Ghost for Sale* (1952), which recycled footage from Slaughter's *The Curse of the Wraydons* (1946), was also released.

9. *Potter of the Yard* (1952), *Too Many Detectives* and *Mr Beamish Goes South* (both 1953).

10. *Kinematograph Weekly* (9 September 1954, p. 18) admitted that Diane Cilento made 'a ravishing angel' but still tried to clip her wings by condemning the film as 'too airy-fairy' and overlong. However, she got a much more sympathetic reaction from Fleet Street critics who generally seemed more favourably disposed towards the work of Group 3.

11. *Quartet* (1949), *Trio* (1950) and *Encore* (1951).

12. *To-Day's Cinema*, 3 September 1953, p. 6; 8 September 1953, p. 1.

13. *Kinematograph Weekly*, 3 March 1955, p. 19.

14. Ibid.

15. *Kinematograph Weekly*, 24 March 1955, p. 22.

16. *To-Day's Cinema*, 30 March 1955, p. 10.

17. *Kinematograph Weekly*, 31 March 1955, p. 24.

18. The politics of the series are discussed in Dave Mann, 'Epicurean Disdain and the Rhetoric of Defiance: *Colonel March of Scotland Yard*', *Scope* no. 12, October 2008, <www.scope.nottingham.ac.uk>

19. *To-Day's Cinema*, 23 April 1953, p. 11.

20. C. H. B. Williamson, *To-Day's Cinema*, 7 July 1952, p. 34.

21. *To-Day's Cinema*, 9 February 1953, p. 6.

22. *The Cinema*, 28 April 1953, p. 10.

23. Paul Ridgway, 'Beware! These Films are Dangerous', *Picturegoer*, 4 July 1953, p. 21.

24. Douglas Fairbanks Jr, 'Fairbanks Answers Us', *Picturegoer*, 8 August 1953, p. 13.

25. Press book, *Three's Company*, British Lion, 1953.

26. 'Just as kinematic as *Trio* and *Quartet*', said *Kinematograph Weekly*, 24 September 1953, p. 25.

27. *To-Day's Cinema*, 3 August 1954, p. 6.

28. *Kinematograph Weekly*, 5 August 1954, p. 16.

29. *Picture Show*, 16 October 1954, p. 10.

30. *Monthly Film Bulletin*, September 1954, p. 134.

31. Lee, *Tall, Dark and Gruesome*, p. 170.

32. *To-Day's Cinema*, 23 November 1954, p. 7.

33. *Kinematograph Weekly*, 25 November 1954, p. 16.

34. *Kinematograph Weekly*, 23 December 1954, p. 21.

35. But it was still rated a competent job and recommended as a 'useful, handy-length support for popular halls'. *To-Day's Cinema*, 17 December 1954, p. 7.

36. *Daily Sketch*, 6 December 1955, quoted in Jonathan Rigby, *Christopher Lee: The Authorised Screen History* (London: Reynolds & Hearn, 2001), p. 34.

37. Ibid.

38. Eros also distributed Fairbanks' subsequent co-feature, *The Hostage* (1957), directed by Harold Huth from an Alfred Shaughnessy screenplay. This tall tale of South American revolutionaries was somewhat outside of Shaughnessy's range, and Huth struggled to sustain enough pace and excitement to keep all the trade reviewers satisfied. *Kinematograph Weekly* (20 December 1956, p. 15) was more savage than most: 'Much of it is serial-like and the phoney accent of its lily-white heroine, untidy direction and topsy-turvy topography do little to strengthen realism. Kid's stuff, despite its a certificate.'

39. 'Onlooker', *To-Day's Cinema*, 28 February 1955, p. 6.

40. *To-Day's Cinema*, 19 April 1955, p. 3.

41. Significant television series in this context included *War on Crime* (1950), *I Made News* (1951) and *Pilgrim Street* (1952). See Susan Sydney-Smith, *Beyond Dixon of Dock Green: Early British Police Series* (London: I. B. Tauris, 2002), pp. 62–86.

42. <www.screenonline.org.uk>

43. *To-Day's Cinema*, 6 October 1954, p. 12.

44. *To-Day's Cinema*, 23 February 1955, p. 11.

45. *The Cinema*, 25 February 1953, p. 3.

46. *To-Day's Cinema*, 3 September 1953, p. 3.

47. *To-Day's Cinema*, 17 July 1953, p. 10.

48. *To-Day's Cinema* (2 February, 1954, p. 6) rated it 'acceptable second feature entertainment for crime-thriller addicts'.

49. *To-Day's Cinema*, 12 May 1954, p. 18. The judgment was echoed by *Kinematograph Weekly*, 20 May 1954, p. 21.

50. *To-Day's Cinema*, 18 August 1954, p. 10.

51. *Picture Show*, 17 July 1954, p. 10. *To-Day's Cinema* (15 May 1954, p. 13) admired Krish's 'ambitious' direction, dialogue which was 'crisp and to the point', and the 'natural backgrounds which add to the authenticity of situations'.

52. E.g., *To-Day's Cinema*, 26 October 1954, p. 10.

53. *To-Day's Cinema*, 23 November 1954, p. 7. Having been discharged from his duties as Stryker, Clifford Evans crossed to the National

Studios to star in the title story of the Fairbanks' anthology *The Red Dress*.

54. *To-Day's Cinema*, 20 September 1954, p. 5.

55. *To-Day's Cinema*, 8 October 1954, p. 6.

56. Cf. *Kinematograph Weekly*, 14 July 1955, p. 19.

57. *To-Day's Cinema*, 27 October 1954, p. 4; *Kinematograph Weekly*, 21 October 1954, p. 52.

58. Letter from Stuart Levy to *Kinematograph Weekly*, 15 October 1953, p. 10.

59. *To-Day's Cinema*, 2 March 1953, p. 5.

60. *To-Day's Cinema*, 12 May 1953, p. 8.

61. *To-Day's Cinema*, 24 February 1954, p. 11.

62. Trade advertisement, *Kinematograph Weekly*, 18 March 1954, p. 14.

63. Dave Mann, 'An Industrial and Cultural History of Selected British Crime Supporting Features and Filmed Television Series, 1946–64', Ph.D thesis, University of the West of England, 2008, p. 51.

64. Quoted in Harper and Porter, *British Cinema of the 1950s*, p. 230.

65. ''Tec Featurettes Popular on Circuit', *To-Day's Cinema*, 30 March 1955, p. 11.

66. *To-Day's Cinema*, 2 May 1956, p. 24.

67. 'The Anglo Story', Supplement to *The Cinema*, 20 February 1957, p. vi.

68. *To-Day's Cinema*, 18 May 1954, p. 6.

69. *The Daily Cinema*, 5 August 1959, p. 5.

70. Anon, *A Guide to British Film Production* (London: British Film Producers Association, 1963), p. 20.

71. Anglo's 'A' feature *Confession* (1956) was playing in five Paris cinemas at the time. *Kinematograph Weekly*, 3 May 1956, p. 18d.

72. *To-Day's Cinema*, 14 February 1955, p. 7.

73. *The Cinema*, 14 June 1956, p. 7. Lustgarten's narrative voice has been perceptively described as 'confidential, immodest, a "nudge, nudge, wink, wink" appeal to the listener's attention which implicitly licenses his or her vicarious curiosity in the pornography of violence'. Mann, 'An Industrial and Cultural History', p. 49.

74. *Kinematograph Weekly*, 15 November 1956, p. 24, and 20 June 1957, p. 22.

75. *To-Day's Cinema*, 8 August 1957, p. 7.

76. Mann, 'An Industrial and Cultural History', p. 57.

77. *The Daily Cinema*, 18 December 1959, p. 11.

78. *Kinematograph Weekly*, 18 September 1958, p. 20. By the 1960s, the rival medium was even evident in the *mise en scène* and narrative of some Bs. In Robert Lynn's murder-thriller *Two Letter Alibi* (1962), scripted by the small-screen writer Roger Marshall, TV footage from a Lords' Test Match is used to clear the accused boyfriend of a television personality (Petra Davies).

79. *Kine Weekly*, 19 April 1962, p. 24. The second in the series, *A Woman's Privilege* (1962), for instance, revolved around a law suit brought by a man for breach of promise.

80. The last two in the series – *Strangler's Web* and *Dead Man's Chest* (both 1965) – were not based on Wallace stories.

81. *Kine Weekly*, 1 June 1961, p. 19.

82. Letter to *Kine Weekly*, 23 February 1961, p. 9.

83. *Kine Weekly*, 9 March 1961, p. 31.

84. *Kine Weekly*, 23 March 1961, p. 10b.

85. *Kine Weekly*, 29 June 1961. p. 21.

86. *Kine Weekly*, 22 March 1962, p. 10.

87. *The Daily Cinema*, 26 March 1962, p. 4. The other film in the trio was Paul Almond's *Backfire!*

88. *Kine Weekly*, 16 August 1962, p. 14.

89. *Monthly Film Bulletin*, December 1961, p. 171.

90. 'Sharply characterised, shrewdly directed and realistically staged', was the verdict of *Kine Weekly*, 7 December 1961, p. 25. Robert Tronson (1924–2009) never aspired beyond the second feature, with the one marginal exception of the co-feature *Ring of Spies* (1963), based on the Lonsdale spy case, co-authored by Peter Barnes and Frank Launder.

91. Baker in McFarlane, *Autobiography*, p. 47.

92. Moxey quickly left for America where he worked prolifically, mainly in TV.

93. Jack Greenwood, 'Now for the Next 25', *Kine Weekly*, Studio Review, 27 September 1962, pp. 3, 11.

94. *Kine Weekly*, 12 July 1962, p. 23.

95. 'Anglo Scores in Overseas Markets', *Kine Weekly*, 6 June 1963, p. 18.

96. Jack Greenwood, 'Two and Two Make Four', *Kine Weekly*, Studio Review, 25 January 1962, pp. 3, 9.

97. *Kine Weekly*, 23 January 1964, p. 12.

7 Britain in the Bs

1. *Film Industry* no. 1, July 1946, p. 3.

2. Jeffrey Richards, 'Football and the Crisis of British Identity', in Steve Chaunce, Ewa Mazierska, Susan Sydney-Smith and John K. Walton (eds), *Relocating Britishness* (Manchester: Manchester University Press, 2004), pp. 88–109.

3. See Charles Barr, 'What's Happening to England? Twentieth-century Cricket', in Chaunce et al., *Relocating Britishness*, pp. 110–25. Nevertheless, Lionel Collier ('Shop for Your Films', *Picturegoer*, 4 June 1949, p. 16) had lamented the fact that 'Cricket as a basis for a film has been sadly neglected by our British producers.'

4. Drawing on *Criminal Statistics, England and Wales, 1958*, Montgomery cites an increase of 'indictable offences known to the police between 1946 and 1958' from 472, 489 to 626,509. John Montgomery, *The Fifties* (London: George Allen and Unwin, 1965), p. 171.

5. Arthur Marwick, *British Society Since 1945* (Harmondsworth: Penguin, 1982), p. 148.

6. Ibid., p. 146.

7. Kenneth O. Morgan, *The People's Peace: British History Since 1945* (2nd edn) (Oxford: Oxford University Press, 1999), p. 202.

8. Marwick, *British Society*, p. 149.

9. Lom in McFarlane, *Autobiography*, p. 377.

10. In *Devil Girl from Mars* (1954) there is a convict on the run who meets his match in an extraterrestrial visitant.

11. Robert Murphy, 'Maxwell Munden', in Robert Murphy (ed.), *Directors in British and Irish Cinema: A Reference Companion* (London: BFI, 2006), p. 445. Dismissing the film, in spite of a cast that included Sydney Tafler, Sandra Dorne and Peter Reynolds, as 'Tin-pot quota', *Kinematograph Weekly* (2 October 1958, p. 19) quipped that it 'is unique in one respect, it hardly has a redeeming feature'.

12. Montgomery, *The Fifties*, p. 175.

13. L[ionel] C[ollier], *Picturegoer*, 13 November 1954, p. 21.

14. Currie makes Mick-Mack a credible and touching figure and his scenes with his grandson (played by David Hannaford) evoke recollections of the memorable scenes with Magwitch and the young Pip in Lean's *Great Expectations* (1946).

15. *Kinematograph Weekly*, 7 October 1954, p. 20.

16. C. P. Snow, 'The Two Cultures', *The New Statesman*, 6 October 1956, pp. 413–14.

17. Unfortunately, we were unable to track down a viewing copy of Godfrey Grayson's *The Black Ice* (1957), in which Paul Carpenter and Gordon Jackson played trawlermen in peril in the ice floes of the North Sea. Critics found this exercise in suspense a refreshing change: 'The grim battles with the elements are realistically staged, while skilful photography [by Geoffrey Faithfull] results in the neat dovetailing of exteriors and interiors.' *Kinematograph Weekly*, 12 September 1957, p. 18.

18. There were a couple of other modern-day movie versions of Shakespeare in Britain around this time: Ken Hughes' *Joe MacBeth* (1955) and Basil Dearden's *All Night Long* (1962).

19. The *Monthly Film Bulletin* (June 1960, p. 84) grudgingly conceded that 'for a Danziger

production, this second feature has a certain novelty interest'. Meagre praise for an enterprisingly out-of-the-rut entertainment.

20. Only the New Wave films of around this decade-end – for example, *Room at the Top*, *Saturday Night and Sunday Morning* – seem to take such matters seriously.

21. *Monthly Film Bulletin*, August 1960, p. 111.

22. The BBFC's Monthly Report for March 1961 commented: '*Jungle Street*, like *The Striptease Murder* (X last month) was a story of crime with some of its background set in a striptease club, the earlier film only just gained an "X" and *Jungle Street*, from which our script letter had removed most of the unsavoury details, turned out to be an "A".' Nevertheless, this classification required the shortening of two strips, including a back view of Jill Ireland finally baring her breasts to the audience (a gender reversal of the last frames of *The Full Monty*, 1997). Steve Chibnall Collection.

23. Wolf Mankowitz, *The ABC of Show Business* (London: Oldbourne Press, 1956), p. 45.

24. Morgan, *The People's Peace*, p. 107.

25. Cate Haste, *Rules of Desire* (London: Random House, 1992), p. 152.

26. Ibid., p. 150.

27. BBFC, 'Minutes of Exceptions taken to films certified during the month of September 1954', Steve Chibnall Collection.

28. Ibid., December 1954.

29. Ibid., September 1960.

30. Paul Ferris, *Sex and the British* (London: Mandarin, 1993), p. 213.

31. Stephen Bourne, *Brief Encounters: Lesbians and Gays in British Cinema 1930–1971* (London: Cassell, 1996), p. 106.

32. As Bourne (ibid.) notes, the latter film, the first overt study of lesbian desire, was directed by the man responsible for *Roadhouse Girl*, Wolf Rilla.

33. Geoff Mayer, in Mayer and Brian McConnell (eds), *Encyclopedia of Film Noir* (Westport, CT: Greenwood Press, 2007), p. 230.

34. *To-Day's Cinema*, 4 October 1957, p. 9.

35. *To-Day's Cinema*, 8 April 1957, p. 6.

36. Earl Cameron fared better than most black actors in British films, but in a long interview with Stephen Bourne he makes no mention of *The Heart Within*. Stephen Bourne, *Black in the British Frame: Black People in British Film and Television 1896–1996* (London: Continuum, 2001), pp. 104–10.

37. As in *The End of the Road*, there are reminders of David Lean's *Great Expectations* in the boy's encounter with the man in hiding, and his subsequently kept promise to bring food.

38. *To-Day's Cinema*, 20 May 1957, p. 4. Pennington, in collaboration with the future producer of *The Italian Job* (1969) the young Michael Deeley, had just made the crime-thriller *At the Stroke of Nine* (1957). It was a pretty implausible story of a mad pianist (Stephen Murray) who kidnaps a young woman reporter (Patricia Dainton), but it was credibly handled by director Lance Comfort. Deeley moved on to set up a production company with ex-GPO Film Unit cutter Harry Booth. 'Our policy is to make films about ordinary, everyday people,' said Booth. 'We both favour the realistic approach.' *Kinematograph Weekly*, 3 January 1957, p. 21.

39. *Monthly Film Bulletin*, September 1957, p. 114.

40. *Daily Film Renter*, 31 July 1957, p. 5.

41. Text of whole speech quoted at <http://africanhistory.about.com/>

8 The Best of the Bs

1. *The Cinema Studio*, 16 June 1948, p. 7.

2. Interview with Andrew Clay, 1997.

3. *Picture Show*, 28 March 1949, p. 10.

4. Roome in McFarlane, *Autobiography*, p. 499.

5. Ibid.

6. Lionel Collier, 'Shop for Your Films', *Picturegoer*, 4 June 1949, p. 16.

7. *Picturegoer* (2 June 1951, p. 17) was concerned that she 'fluctuates considerably', but *To-Day's*

Cinema (8 February 1951, p. 7) was nearer the mark when it remarked that Fitzgerald 'plays Elizabeth with evident appreciation of the possibilities of the part'.

8. *Picture Show*, 9 June 1951, p. 10.

9. Gilb, *Variety*, 29 August 1951, p. 20.

10. Fred Hift, *Motion Picture Herald*, 1 September 1951, p. 998.

11. *Monthly Film Bulletin*, March 1951, p. 234.

12. Geoff Mayer, in Mayer and Brian McConnell (eds), *Encyclopedia of Film Noir* (Westport, CT: Greenwood Press, 2007), p. 261.

13. Valerie Hobson in *The Small Voice* (1948) and Kathleen Byron in *Prelude to Fame*.

14. *Monthly Film Bulletin*, August 1952, p. 121.

15. *Daily Film Renter*, 9 June 1952, p. 21.

16. *To-Day's Cinema*, 6 June 1952, p. 14.

17. R. H. B., *Picturegoer*, 13 September 1952. *To-Day's Cinema* (6 June 1952, p. 14) wrote that 'Jill Esmond as the gallant housewife works hard to inject some vitality into the proceedings and is, in fact, very successful.' The quality of her performance is made more vivid by contrast with Brenda De Banzie's overacting as her uppity sister-in-law.

18. Elizabetta Girelli, 'Fergus McDonell', in Murphy, *Directors*, p. 395.

19. *Monthly Film Bulletin*, November 1953, p. 164.

20. Press book, Astor Picture Corporation, 1954.

21. *Picture Show*, 3 July 1954, p. 10.

22. There is typical attention to detail in the 'fake' opening sequence when, having changed their wedding clothes, the young man flicks his fingers for the woman to pass back the 'wedding ring', its use now over.

23. *The Daily Cinema*, 29 November 1957, p. 3.

24. Compton Bennett to Ralph Bond, 9 September 1957, BFI Special Collections, ACT File.

25. S. S., *Picturegoer*, 9 November 1957, p. 19.

26. *To-Day's Cinema*, 8 October 1957, p. 6.

27. See, for example, *Kinematograph Weekly*'s (22 January 1959, p. 19) review which considered it no more than a 'so-so quota "second"'.

28. *Monthly Film Bulletin*, March 1959, p. 34.

29. *Film Index International*, British Film Institute CD-Rom, 1998.

30. Scott in McFarlane, *Autobiography*, p. 520.

31. Even so, the *Monthly Film Bulletin* (January 1960, p. 7) claimed captiously that Keen 'had his old trouble of adapting his impeccable diction to a working class character'.

32. Ibid.

33. Peter Graham Scott, *British Television: An Insider's History* (Jefferson, North Carolina and London: McFarland & Co, 2000), p. 129.

34. Mark Grantham, in his unpublished 'Life on the Cheap with the Danzigers', 1993, claims that he did an earlier draft of the film and was taken off the job as a result of refusing to do a masturbatory sex scene. 'They gave the job to another writer.' Presumably Clemens.

35. *Monthly Film Bulletin*, January 1963, p. 10.

36. Ibid.

37. *Kinematograph Weekly*, 29 November 1962, p. 10.

38. BBFC Monthly Report, December 1960. Steve Chibnall Collection.

39. BBFC Minutes of Exceptions taken to films certified during the month of March 1961. Steve Chibnall Collection.

40. *The Observer*, 12 February 1961.

41. *Sunday Times*, 8 January 1961.

42. Shaughnessy, *Both Ends of the Candle*, pp. 131–2.

43. Kim Newman, 'Opinion', *Shivers* no. 81, September 2000, p. 41.

44. Coquillon would later receive due recognition as the cinematographer of Michael Reeves' *Witchfinder General* (1968).

45. Newman, 'Opinion'.

46. Though the film was made in 1961, its release was delayed until a month before Christmas, 1963.

47. *Monthly Film Bulletin*, December 1963, p. 171.

48. *Kine Weekly*, 14 November 1963, p. 9.

49. 'Cash on Demand', *The House That Hammer Built* no. 3, June 1997, p. 155.

50. Information supplied by Allen Eyles, 1998.

51. John Krish, BECTU interview, 22 March 1994.

52. Wyer had enjoyed a distinguished career in the 1940s, during which he shot *The Seventh Veil*. His previous experience on science-fiction films included Hammer's *Four-Sided Triangle* and *Spaceways* (1953).

53. For further discussion see Peter Hutchings, 'Where're the Martians Now: British Invasion Fantasies of the 1950s and 1960s'; and Steve Chibnall, 'Alien Women', in Hunted, *British Science Fiction Cinema*.

54. Rich, *Variety*, 20 January 1965, p. 6.

55. T. M., *Monthly Film Bulletin*, February 1965, p. 19.

56. Allen Eyles, *Films and Filming*, March 1965, p. 35.

57. T. M., op cit.

58. Graham Clarke (ed.), 'Reviews', *Kinematograph Weekly*, 24 December 1964, p. 11.

59. Eyles, op. cit.

60. Daniel O'Brien, 'Bridges, Alan', in Robert Murphy (ed.), *Directors in British and Irish Cinema* (London: BFI, 2006), p. 73.

61. A decade earlier, United Artists had distributed another 'B' thriller about an insurance fraud in Brighton: *The Straw Man* (1953), starring Dermot Walsh and Clifford Evans, and produced, written and directed by Donald Taylor.

62. *Monthly Film Bulletin*, January 1965, p. 10.

Index

List of Illustrations

Whilst considerable effort has been made to correctly identify the copyright holders this has not been possible in all cases. We apologise for any apparent negligence and any omissions or corrections brought to our attention will be remedied in any future editions.

The Impersonator, © Herald Film Productions Ltd; *Sabotage at Sea*, British National Films/Shaftesbury Films; *The Seventh Survivor*, British National Films/Shaftesbury Films; *Battle for Music*, Strand Film Company; *The Man with Magnetic Eyes*, British Foundation; *Children on Trial*, Crown Film Unit; *Perchance to Sail*, Elder-Dalrymple Productions; *It's a Great Game*, Featurettes Limited; *Time Bomb*, MGM British Studios; *Face the Music*, © Exclusive Films; *Not So Dusty*, © Jaywell Productions; *Seminole Uprising*, Columbia Pictures Corporation; *The Trollenberg Terror*, Tempean Films; *Call Girls*, Rialto Film Preben Philipsen; *The Man Without a Body*, Filmplays; *It's All Over Town*, Delamore Film Productions; *The Monkey's Paw*, Kay Films; *Paul Temple Returns*, Nettlefold Productions; *Once a Sinner*, John Argyle Productions; *Cloak Without Dagger*, Balblair Productions; *To the Public Danger*, Highbury Productions/Production Facilities; *Penny and the Pownall Case*, Highbury Productions; *A Piece of Cake*, Highbury Productions; *Crime Reporter*, Knightsbridge Films; *What the Butler Saw*, Hammer Film Productions; *A Case for PC49*, Exclusive Films/Hammer Film Productions; *The Last Page*, Lippert Productions/Hammer Film Productions/Exclusive Films; *Blood Orange*, © Exclusive Films; *The Glass Cage*, © Exclusive Films; *Murder by Proxy*, Hammer Film Productions/Lippert Productions; *No Trace*, Tempean Films; *Escape by Night*, Tempean Films; *Alias John Preston*, Danziger Photoplays; *Part-Time Wife*, Danziger Productions Ltd; *Man Accused*, Danziger Productions Ltd; *Assassin for Hire*, © Merton Park; *Ghost Ship*, Anglo Amalgamated Productions; *My Death is a Mockery*, © Adelphi Films; *Stolen Assignment*, Unit; *The Diplomatic Corpse*, ACT Films; *Brandy for the Parson*, Group 3; *Behind the Headlines*, Jay Lewis Productions; *It's a Bare, Bare World*, Antler Film Productions; *The Hangman Waits*, Five Star Films; *The Adventures of Jane*, Keystone/New World Pictures; *Penny Points to Paradise*, Advance Films/PYL Productions; *One Jump Ahead*, Kenilworth Film Productions/Fortress Productions; *Date with Disaster*, Fortress Productions; *Hidden Homicide*, Luckwell Productions; *Linda*, Independent Artisits; *Colonel Bogey*, Highbury Productions/Production Facilities; *The House Across the Lake*, © Exclusive Films; *Rag Doll*, Mancunian Film Corporation; *Pit of Darkness*, © Butcher's Film Distributors; *The Man in the Back Seat*, © Independent Artists; *Strongroom*, Theatrecraft; *Wheel of Fate*, Kenilworth Film Productions; *Freedom to Die*, Bayford Films; *Cover Girl Killer*, Parroch Films; *Operation Murder*, Danziger Productions Ltd; *So Evil, So Young*, Danziger Productions Ltd; *Death Over My Shoulder*, Vicar Productions/Orb Film; *Womaneater*, Fortress Productions; *The Great Van Robbery*, Danziger Photoplays; *Danger by My Side*, Butcher's Film Service; *The White Trap*, Independent Artists; *The Large Rope*, Insignia Films; *A Woman of Mystery*, Danziger Photoplays; *Dial 999*, Merton Park; *The Crooked Sky*, Luckwin Productions Ltd; *The Man Who Was Nobody*, Merton Park; *A Lady Mislaid*, Welwyn Productions; House of Mystery, © Independent Artists; *Circumstantial Evidence*, ACT Films; *The Flanagan Boy*, Hammer Film Productions; *Barbados Quest*, Cipa Productions; *The Floating Dutchman*, Merton Park; *The Blue Parrot*, ACT Films; *Trouble in the Air*, Production Facilities/Highbury Productions; *There's Always a Thursday*, Associated Sound Film Industries; *Rock You Sinners*, Small Film Distributors; *The Fool and the Princess*, Merton Park; *The Spanish Sword*, Danziger Productions Ltd; *The Headless Ghost*, Merton Park; *Devil Girl from Mars*, Danziger Productions Ltd; *Escapement*, Merton Park; *The Javanese Dagger*, Danziger Productions Ltd; *Police Dog*, Westridge Productions; *Fabian of the Yard*, Anthony Beauchamp Productions; *The Ghost Train Murder*, © Merton Park; *Night Crossing*, Anglo-Amalgamated Productions/Merton Park; *The Silent Weapon*, Merton Park; *Face of a Stranger*, Merton Park; *Solo for Sparrow*, Merton Park; *Bang! You're Dead*, Wellington Films; *Echo of Diana*, Butcher's Film Service; *Offbeat*, Linder; *An Honourable Murder*, Danziger Productions Ltd; *Second Fiddle*, ACT Films; *Trouble with Eve*, Blakeley's Productions; *Strip Tease Murder*, Danziger Productions Ltd; *The Heart Within*, Penington-Eady Productions; *Marilyn*, Nettlefold Productions; *The Flying Scot*, © Insignia Films; *Small Hotel*, © Associated British Picture Corporation; *Devil's Bait*, Independent Artists; *The Tell-Tale Heart*, © Danziger Productions Ltd; *Tomorrow at Ten*, Blakeley's Productions; *Unearthly Stranger*, © Independent Artists; *Act of Murder*, Merton Park; *Smokescreen*, Butcher's Film Service; *Painted Boats*, © Ealing Studios; *The Late Edwina Black*, Elvey Gartside Production.